American Perceptions of the Soviet Union as a Nuclear Adversary

This book is published under the auspices of
the Center for International Affairs, Harvard University

American Perceptions of the Soviet Union as a Nuclear Adversary

From Kennedy to Bush

Erik Beukel
Associate Professor of
Odense University

Pinter Publishers, London and New York
in association with John Spiers

© Erik Beukel, 1989

First published in Great Britain in 1989 by
Pinter Publishers Limited
in association with John Spiers
25 Floral Street
London WC2E 9DS

British Library Cataloguing in Publication Data
A CIP catalogue record for this book is available from the British Library

ISBN 0–86187–033–6

Printed and bound in Great Britain by
Biddles Ltd, Guildford and King's Lynn

Contents

PREFACE

The research reported in this book has in part been financed by grants from Centre For Peace and Conflict Research, Copenhagen. and The Danish Commission on Security And Disarmament   (SNU). I have also received grants from Danish Instithte of Internatıonal (sun). I have also received grants from Danish Institute of International Studies, Knud Højgaards Fond, Provinsbankens Studielegat, and Erik and Marta Scheibels Legat. I am graceful to all for their help.

The first preparations for this study began at the Center for International Affairs (CFIA), Harvard Unıversity, where I had the privilege of spending the spring of 1983 as a Visiting Scholar. In June 1986 I collected most of the data for Chapter 2 and 3 at the Library of Congress, Washington, DC, where I received great assistance from the staff.

Parts of an early draft of this book were read by Ib Faurby, editorial writer, Politiken, who helped me with useful criticism. Of course, the inadequacies are my own. Finally I thank Inger Petersen for extensive secretarial assistance and Hanne Iversen for assistance in preparing the index.

The manuscript was finished in April 1989.

Erik Beukel
Odense University,
July 1989

1. Introduction

The Soviet Union as a nuclear armed adversary confronts American foreign policy with a critical issue. The Russian revolution and the atomic bomb represent two of the most dramatic developments in the twentieth century and it has been maintained that statesmen in the West following the Second World War were as much appalled by the specter of 'an explosive new material force, that of atomic energy', as their predecessors a generation before by the specter of 'an explosive new idea, the Bolshevik idea'.[1] Be that as it may, the existence of the Soviet Union as a nuclear power since 1949, and in particular the American continent's vulnerability to a Soviet nuclear attack since the late 1950s confronts the United States with a most intractable problem. The actual identification of the problem gives rise to very divergent diagnoses, periodically leading to heated disputes in US politics, and ideas and notions about the character of the Soviet Union as an atomic power are important variables in the making of US foreign policy. Moreover, the position of the United States in international politics with its role as a superpower together with the Soviet Union and its commitments in the Western alliance assures that America's handling of the issue will be important and controversial to the international society whatever it does.

Various conceptions of the Soviet Union as a nuclear adversary reflect different views of the combined challenge from the existence of the Soviet Union and the existence of nuclear weapons; different views of the nature of the Soviet state and its foreign policy are merged into different views of the significance of the atomic bomb. The divergent conceptions may be expounded in terms of how much the uniqueness of the Soviet state is emphasized against how much the uniqueness of nuclear weapons is emphasized, that is, either the discontinuity that the Soviet Union represents in international politics or the discontinuity of the nuclear bomb may be stressed.

Concerning the Soviet state, there has been continual disagreement in the United States since the Russian revolution about the nature of the Soviet system and the basic objectives and motivations of the Soviet leaders.[2] The dominant opinions in the debate have been constant and may be grouped around two basic views termed, respectively, the Riga axioms and the Yalta axioms which, especially since the 1940s, have vied with each other in influencing America's Soviet policy. The Riga axioms stress the particular essence of the Soviet state: the Soviet Union is a revolutionary state that denies the possibility of long-term coexistence with capitalist states, is committed to unrelenting ideological warfare and is powered by a messianic drive for world domination. Contrary to that, the Yalta axioms see the Soviet Union behaving like a traditional great power and therefore susceptible to accommodative behavior from the Western Powers; the Soviet system, according to this conception, is certainly unattractive but Soviet foreign policy has usually been cautious and motivated by traditional security concerns.[3]

Correspondingly, concerning the significance of the nuclear bomb, the positions in the debate have displayed striking similarities since the beginning of the nuclear age. Views that stress the usability of atomic weapons like other weapons in deterring, waging and winning wars have contended with views that emphasize the absolute nature of nuclear weapons.[4] According to the latter conception, nuclear weapons are qualitatively different due to their enormous destructiveness which may result in self-annihilation as well as of the opponent and are therefore useless for waging and winning wars; as atomic weapons are wholly different from traditional war-fighting means, they have irrefutable consequences for both superpowers in forcing them to the immutable fact of mutual vulnerability. Following this thinking, the challenge from the atomic bomb is a unique problem that cannot be subordinated or logically integrated in meeting the Soviet challenge because it is necessary actively to cooperate with the Soviet Union in order to meet the nuclear challenge.

Since combining two incommensurable qualities like the 'Soviet challenge' and the 'nuclear challenge' into one coherent position on the Soviet Union as a nuclear adversary is a delicate task, there is a predisposition to focus on either one or the other: as many advocates of the absolute nature of nuclear weapons adhere to the Yalta axioms, most adherents of the Riga axioms advocate the usability of nuclear weapons in waging wars. Both fighting communism and avoiding nuclear war are primary American goals, reflecting deep-seated American attitudes, and as the two goals are interpreted as leading to, respectively, confrontation and accommodation with the Soviet Union, this has often given US foreign policy an ambivalent posture resulting in frequent oscillations, and has resulted in the United States forming its Soviet policy to manifest the symptoms of a split personality.[5]

Through the oscillations, however, the most prominent feature of official American attitudes has been that the real nuclear problem originates in the basic nature of the Soviet challenge and therefore the best way to meet the nuclear challenge is by forming a clear understanding of the essence of the Soviet state and the danger it represents to the world community, and formulate one's approach to the nuclear issue accordingly. The most durable deviation from this line occurred from the early 1960s to the latter half of the 1970s: for some years after 1963 various considerations on the fundamental nature of nuclear weapons and the consequential best way to meet the nuclear challenge characterized US governments' views on how to deal with the Soviet Union as a nuclear adversary. One prominent factor behind these changing views has been the American continent's vulnerability to a Soviet nuclear attack. At some undefinable time during the late 1950s or early 1960s, the Soviet Union came to possess a nuclear capacity to destroy the United States. From about 1960 until 1983 all administrations shared the view that the United States' vulnerability to a Soviet nuclear attack was an immutable fact, however that vulnerability has actually been defined and however acceptable it has been considered; that is, the mutuality of the balance of terror predicament has been regarded as inescapable. More recently, however, that once 'immutable fact' has been challenged by the US government in that the Reagan administration from 1983 advocated, initiated and actively pursued a project aimed, more or less unambiguously, at removing America's vulnerability to a nuclear attack. That is, irrespective of whether America's vulnerability has been considered immutable or not, all American governments, since the early 1960s, have regarded it as a fact.

These views and their relations to the Soviet Union's position as a nuclear power and the domestic American setting constitute the subject of this book. I shall focus on American governments' perception of the Soviet Union as a nuclear armed opponent through six administrations, from when the Kennedy administration was installed in 1961 to the close of the Reagan administration in 1989. The starting point, 1961, thus marks an important delimitation of the perceptions to be examined: it denotes a period when the US government has considered the balance of terror predicament a reality, whether inescapable or not. By way of introduction, section 1 reviews the substance and varying manifestations of American readings of the Soviet Union as a nuclear adversary from when the Soviet Union acquired the nuclear bomb in 1949 until the point when the emerging balance of terror condition was recognized about ten years later. Section 2 reviews various studies of American images and perceptions of the Soviet Union, including the Soviet Union as nuclear power. Section 3 is an exposition of the definitions and uses of the key concept, perceptions, with a view to clarifying its use for research purposes and ending with a first delimitation of the approach and conceptual framework applied in this book. Together, this forms the basis for elaborating, in section 4, the issues and questions considered.

1.   THE SOVIET UNION AS A NUCLEAR ADVERSARY, 1949–61

1.   The Soviet bomb

When the Soviet Union exploded its first atomic bomb on 29 August 1949, it was not announced by the Soviets themselves but within days radioactive fall-out from the explosion was picked up by American aircraft and on 22 September, President Truman announced the Soviet test of a nuclear bomb. Two days later the Soviet news agency TASS confirmed the American announcement in veiled language; the Russians neither confirmed nor denied the American information but merely hinted that they had many bombs. This strengthened the American belief that something fateful had happened.[6] Compared to various American estimates on how long it would take the Russians to make their first nuclear bomb, the timing of the Soviet bomb was close to the prognoses advanced by some scientists in 1945–6 while other observers and politicians had leaned toward a much later date. As to the administration, it seems clear that the Soviet bomb was developed much sooner than expected; for instance, the Central Intelligence Agency had assured the administration that the earliest date for a Soviet nuclear bomb was well into the 1950s. On the other hand, the Finletter Report, presented in January 1948, had projected that, by 1952–3, the Soviet Union would have a substantial atomic-strike capability.[7]

One effect of what was to many Americans a shock was that Soviet nuclear capabilities loomed large in American calculations at a time when there was a widespread belief that the United States was locked in a life-and-death struggle with the Soviet Union. Thus, as soon as news of 'Joe 1' – as the first Soviet atomic explosion was called – became available, intelligence sources concluded that the Russians were now capable of detonating atomic weapons on American soil. The most direct consequence of the looming Soviet nuclear threat concerned the project for an American hydrogen (or thermonuclear) bomb since there was at that time a debate in the administration and among a narrow group of scientists on the expediency of producing a hydrogen bomb, sometimes termed the superbomb. The project was contentious. Some scientists involved in the development of the nuclear bomb were opposed to it, but their case was gravely weakened by the dramatic news that the Soviets now had the bomb; the adherents of an American superbomb were strengthened by the widespread impression of a looming Soviet nuclear capability advanced by, among others, some observers who previously had asserted that it would take the Russians much longer to acquire the bomb. Now it was argued and widely agreed that if the Soviets had already built an atomic bomb, they might well be working on the super, and it was of fundamental importance that the United States got there first. The rapid development of the hydrogen bomb was attributed a symbolic function as assuring America's superiority. On 31 January 1950, President Truman announced his decision to go ahead with the thermonuclear bomb.[8]

2.   NSC-68

At the same time President Truman requested a special State and Defense Department study group headed by Paul Nitze (who shortly before had replaced George Kennan as head of the State Department's Policy Planning Staff), to review the combined implications of the Soviet atomic bomb, the American decision to construct a hydrogen bomb, and the recent communist victory in China. The review took place in the form of the drafting of what became known as NSC-68, presented to the President and the National Security Council in April 1950. After the outbreak of the Korean War in June 1950, which appeared to confirm the validity of its analysis and conclusions, NSC-68 was endorsed by all parts of the foreign policy apparatus in the administration and on 30 September 1950, it was formally approved by President Truman as the definitive guideline for American foreign policy. An enduring legacy of NSC-68 was the view of the world it projected and as it represents the prototype of a prominent American reasoning on the Soviet Union as an atomically armed opponent, a detailed review is pertinent.

NSC-68[9] expressed the view that the Soviet Union represented a unique danger. The fundamental design of the Kremlin – a term used again and again – was the complete submission of all countries in the non-Soviet world to their absolute power and, thus, free societies unwillingly found themselves mortally challenged and there was no way the free world could make itself inoffensive to the Kremlin except by complete submission to its will. There was a basic conflict in the world between the idea of freedom and the idea of slavery represented by the Kremlin. Being a totalitarian dictatorship animated by a fanatic faith, the peace sought by the Soviet Union was the peace of total conformity to the Kremlin and the free world could expect no lasting diminution in this danger before a change occurred in the nature of the Soviet system. The Kremlin's policy was fired by a peculiarly virulent blend of hatred and fear – hatred of the free world and fear of their own people because they knew the vulnerability of their own relations with the Soviet people.

Pursuing the fundamental design for world domination, the extraordinary flexibility of Soviet tactics was emphasized. This flexibility derived from the utterly amoral character of their policy, combined with universal secrecy which engendered a formidable capacity to act with the widest tactical latitude, with stealth and with speed. The Kremlin pursued its basic design by violent or non-violent methods in accordance with the dictates of expediency, and it regarded the United States as the only threat to the achievement of its design. Concerning the tactics to use in the efforts to counter the Kremlin, NSC-68 recommended that the free world should make use of some of the current Soviet cold war techniques against the Soviet Union itself; however, free societies were vulnerable in that it was easy for people to lapse into excesses – the excess of a permanently open mind naively waiting for evidence that evil design might become noble purpose, the excess of faith becoming prejudice, the excess of tolerance degenerating into indulgence of conspiracy, and the excess of resorting to suppression when more moderate measures were not only more appropriate but more effective.

As for military power, the Soviet Union possessed armed forces far in excess of those necessary to defend Soviet territory, and the Kremlin was clearly developing its military capacity in order to support its design for world domination. These military forces were probably not yet considered sufficient by the Kremlin to wage a war which would involve the United States; however, coupled with a nuclear capability, this military strength provided the Soviet Union with a great coercive power for use in time of peace to create an overall impression in the free world of irresistible Soviet power and, at the same time, its military power would serve as a deterrent to the victims of the Kremlin's aggression from taking any action in opposition which would risk war. Therefore, it was crucial that the free world never made any dangerous underestimation of Soviet military power. In the event of war, it was important that the free world direct its military efforts against the regime in a way that the Russian people could clearly conceive as according with their own interests; otherwise, the regime and the Russian people would be united in a kind of 'last-ditch fight' in which the basic principles of the free world would be obscured.

Concerning negotiations with the Soviet Union it was essential that the free world always leave open this possibility. A diplomatic boycott of the Soviet Union might inhibit the policy pursued by the free world, but it was important to realize that in negotiating with dictatorial governments, the free world might be vulnerable because of the open and democratic process. The Soviet Union possessed a number of advantages over the free world in negotiations on any issue: its ability to enforce secrecy on all significant facts about conditions within the Soviet Union, it did not have to be responsive in any important sense to public opinion, it did not have to consult and agree with any other countries on its policy, and it could influence public opinion in other countries while insulating the peoples under its control. Hence, negotiation was not a possible separate course of action for the free world, but had to be a means for a program of building strength while helping to minimize the risks of war. A settlement would only record the progress made by the free world in frustrating the Kremlin's design for world domination – actually, the term 'frustrating the Kremlin's design for world domination' was a catchphrase in NSC-68; however, it was also stated that the efforts of the United States could not be made solely in the negative terms of resisting the Kremlin design.

NSC-68 dealt in some detail with the role of nuclear weapons after the Soviet Union had acquired the atomic bomb a few months earlier.[10] Conspicuous was the importance ascribed to taking the initiative, acting swiftly and with surprise in case of nuclear war. It was stated that when the nuclear capability of the Soviet Union grew, the possibility of a decisive initial attack from the Kremlin could not be excluded and it was estimated that within four years the Soviet Union would attain the capability of seriously damaging vital centers of the United States, provided it struck a surprise blow and no further countermeasures were programmed; hence, a further increase in American nuclear weapons was necessary in order to assure the effectiveness of a retaliatory blow. NSC-68 warned that if the Soviet Union developed a thermonuclear weapon before the United States did, there would be a greatly increased risk of Soviet pressure against the free world. On the other hand, if the United States developed a thermonuclear weapon before the Soviet Union, it should be possible for some time to bring increased pressure on the Kremlin. As to various proposals for international control of atomic energy, these were rejected because no effective plan for control could be negotiated unless and until the Kremlin's design had been frustrated to a point when a genuine and drastic change in Soviet policies had taken place. Concerning the suggestion that the United States should not use nuclear weapons except in retaliation against the prior use of such weapons by an aggressor, i.e. a 'no first-use' policy, this was rejected because such a declaration would be interpreted by the Soviet Union as an admission of weakness and by America's allies as a clear indication of an intention to abandon them.

Altogether, the reasoning of NSC-68 may be epitomized by a quote from its last pages: 'The only sure victory (for the free world) lies in the frustration of the Kremlin design by a steady development of the moral and material strength of the free world and its projection into the Soviet world in such a way as to bring about an internal change in the Soviet system' (p.441).

3. Massive retaliation

The Eisenhower administration's thinking on the Soviet Union as a nuclear adversary during its first years appeared in the so-called 'New Look'. In October 1953 a paper from the National Security Council on *Basic National Security Policy* (BNSP) described the Soviet threat as grim and any diplomatic moves of apparent peaceful intent by the Soviets were dismissed as gestures. The capability of the Soviet Union to attack the United States with atomic weapons and soon hydrogen bombs, using aircraft on one-way missions, was portrayed as growing; as the primary policy recommendation, BNSP emphasized developing a capability for inflicting massive retaliatory damage by offensive striking power as well as a secure mobilization base adequate to ensure victory in the event of all-out war. However, even if the term 'massive retaliation' was used a number of times, it was used solely in connection with the deterrence of Soviet moves toward a general war, which was expected to begin with an assault on Europe. Moreover, BNSP anticipated the major arguments of the opponents of massive retaliation in that it stated that when the United States and the Soviet Union reached 'a stage of atomic plenty and ample means of delivery' the result could be a 'stalemate, with both sides reluctant to initiate general warfare'.[11]

This reasoning was sharpened in a speech delivered by Secretary of State John Foster Dulles in January 1954.[12] Like others, Dulles underlined the uniqueness of the Soviet challenge to the free world. The critical point, according to Dulles, was that when the Soviet communists were planning for what they called 'an entire historical era', the free nations should do the same and so he stressed the 'long haul' character of the conflict between the free world and Soviet communism. However, Dulles emphasized that the Soviet Union, following Lenin, sought through many maneuvers gradually to divide and weaken the free nations by over-extending them, and for that reason it was necessary for the West not to allow the Soviet enemy to dictate the time, place and method of warfare: the way to deter aggression was for the free community to be willing and able to respond vigorously at places and with means of its own choosing. The striking power of the US strategic air force placed on a free world system of bases, the then Secretary of State declared, was fundamental because that strategy would allow the free world to frame its defense efforts without the grave budgetary, economic and social consequences leading to bankruptcy, related to a reliance on all-out local defense measures; a local defense strategy, while it might be important in some areas, for instance in Europe, would lead to that over-extending of the defense efforts of the West sought by the Soviets and being part of a communist plot to weaken the West by indirect means.

Secretary Dulles' speech represented a hard-line interpretation of massive retaliation thinking which immediately became controversial in American politics. Later in the 1950s, sensing the emerging mutual deterrence and balance of terror condition, Dulles modified his views; thus in 1957 he wrote that it might be feasible to place less reliance upon the deterrence value of 'vast retaliatory power' because nuclear weapons were becoming more tactical in character and thus more adaptable to area defense: the United States had not been content to rely upon a peace which could be preserved only by a capacity to destroy vast segments of the human race, but recent developments showed that it was possible to 'alter the character of nuclear weapons' in that their destructiveness and radiation effects could be confined substantially to predetermined targets. [13]

Comparing this reasoning to NSC-68, the similarities are obvious: the Soviet threat is represented as unique and imposing a long-term conflict on the free world, similar to the Riga axioms. On the other hand, while the Truman and the Eisenhower administrations shared some basic notions as to the essence of the Soviet threat, their conclusions as to the best American response differed in that the massive retaliation strategy was very unlike the general rearmament recommended by NSC-68.

A critical underlying issue in this dispute concerned the question of whether the United States was 'forced' to imitate the Soviets' measures. Even if America was seen as forced to follow some of the Soviets' 'rules of the game', it was, according to Secretary Dulles vital that the free world did not follow the Soviets' rules all-out – that would be tantamount to defeat and Dulles directly warned of the Soviet 'trick' to induce the United States to do just that. The same line of thinking may be found in NSC-68, but

Dulles was more cautious in following the reasoning too far that America was forced to apply some of the tactics used by the Soviets. The dilemma was evident: it seemed to be a cogent argument that since the free world was locked in a life-and-death struggle with Soviet communism, it was forced to conform to the Soviets' strategy; on the other hand, it seemed equally cogent that totally conforming would be to indulge the Russians: where was the breaking point?

The significance of this problem heightened during the Eisenhower administration's second term as the incipient balance of terror condition was realized and dealt with through a modified massive retaliation strategy, supplemented by a renewed interest in area defense which was integrated with nuclear weapons because the character of these was perceived as being altered.

4. Two gaps and a delicate balance of terror

During the second half of the 1950s until the end of 1961, American views of the Soviet–American nuclear relationship were marked by two alarms as to a 'gap' between American and Soviet nuclear capabilities which aggravated an asserted delicacy of the balance of terror.

In 1955 American assessments of Soviet nuclear forces became influenced by intelligence estimates crediting the Soviet Union with a large strategic bomber fleet and taken as indicative of a Soviet desire to concentrate resources on a further build-up of its first long-range bomber capable of reaching the United States. Air Force intelligence credited the Soviet Union with 80 strategic bombers and projected a force of 600–700 by mid-1959; the Army and Navy intelligence agencies as well as the CIA were skeptical of this estimate; nevertheless impressions of an emerging bomber gap dominated in 1955–6. However, new evidence supplemented by the U-2 reconnaissance flights over the Soviet Union during 1956 gradually established that the gap was a fiction created by, among other things, the Russians flying the same planes around the reviewing stand at the Aviation Day parade in Moscow in July 1955.[14]

From late 1957, American alarm as to a bomber gap was replaced by a more sustained agitation on a missile gap. Public debate was provoked by the Gaither Report[15] presented to the National Security Council in November 1957, three months after the Soviet Union had tested its first intercontinental ballistic missile (ICBM) and shortly after the dramatic launching of the first artificial earth satellite in October, the Soviet sputnik. The Gaither Committee had been appointed by President Eisenhower in April 1957 to consider a proposal for American civil defense in the form of an extensive fallout-shelter program. Even though the report was not declassified until 1973, many of its findings were leaked to the press in the context of a widespread impression of an important Soviet technological breakthrough that seemed to imply an immediate danger to the, hitherto safe, American continent; hence, despite the Eisenhower administration's rejection of most of its recommendations, the Gaither Report had a great impact on the US government's policy.

The report warned of an early Soviet ICBM capability much greater than the American capability. It stated that unless the United States substantially speeded up its program of intercontinental strategic forces, the Soviet Union would, as early as 1959–62, have the capacity to destroy the entire American strategic force in a surprise attack. This warning was underlined when prominent strategic analysts during the late 1950s began to question the previously held assumption that the strategic balance was inherently stable. Most telling was an article by Albert Wohlstetter in the Jannuary 1959 issue of the prestigious *Foreign Affairs*, 'The Delicate Balance of Terror', based on a speech to the equally prestigious *Council on Foreign Relations* in New York (i.e. the same influential audience as for John Foster Dulles' January 1954 speech); the speech was essentially a distillation of some studies that Wohlstetter had directed at RAND and published as RAND research papers which had been presented to the Gaither Committee in a classified version. Wohlstetter argued that by attacking American strategic forces, the Soviet Union could eventually disarm the United States without risking a counterattack; the nuclear balance was in fact precarious in that the requirements for deterrence were stringent. It was mistaken to confuse deterrence with matching or exceeding the enemy's ability to strike first; to deter meant being able to strike *in spite of* a first strike. The significant point here, besides the warning of an impending vulnerability of American strategic forces, was the importance attached to securing the survivability of second-strike forces as the basis for strategic stability. This view was not generally accepted within the defense community and it foreshadowed an essential element in the thinking on nuclear weapons in the coming years.

The warnings of American strategic forces' dangerous vulnerability became closely intertwined with domestic American politics and the mounting dissatisfaction with the Eisenhower administration's attention to national security. A coalition of Democrats and Air Force enthusiasts argued forcefully that the administration was underestimating the Soviet ICBM build-up because it wished to avoid spending the necessary money to counter the Soviet capability. In the 1960 presidential campaign the missile gap became a prominent issue when the Democratic candidate, John F. Kennedy, warned of an impending missile gap which would give the Soviet Union an ICBM force capable of destroying the American force in a coordinated first strike; the Kennedy campaign was marked by an obsession not to appear 'soft' on the Russians and it was emphasized as a critical priority to demonstrate America's 'strength of will'. The effect on the American public of this warning was reinforced by a number of speeches by the Soviet leader, Krushchev, boasting of the Soviet Union's enormous missile force.[16]

Within a month of the Kennedy administration assuming office in

January 1961, the new Secretary of Defense, Robert McNamara, concluded, after a close scrutiny of the intelligence data, that there was no missile gap but publicly he continued to maintain that there was one. In any event, it soon became clear that the United States had possessed an overwhelming lead the whole time.[17] This new finding became a headline issue in the Washington press, and proved somewhat embarrassing to the new administration that had come into office having made the necessity of meeting the impending Soviet missile threat an issue of national prestige and virility in the election campaign. Furthermore, it was hard for parts of the intelligence community and the military services to admit that their estimates over 3–4 years had been entirely wrong; it all meant that it was not before October–November 1961 that the notion of the missile gap was officially dismissed.

Both alarms about what later was acknowledged to have been fictitious gaps may be related to some conspicuous features of the American as well as the Soviet political systems. In the United States there was a tempting inclination to exaggerate the military capabilities of the communist opponent; it was a popular assumption that when faced with unreliable estimates, then better assume 'the worst' and forget the questionable, thus leaving one, if nothing else, on the safe side. This widely-held belief was reinforced in the public debate about the missile gap before the presidential election in 1960 by the needs brought about by the democratic contest for the highest political office. To a contender censuring the incumbent, it seemed obvious and necessary to criticize any ostensibly weak points in the policy pursued so far, particularly when it concerned the universally endorsed injunction of safeguarding 'national security'. The impact of these characteristics were amplified by the traditional Soviet secrecy combined with a Soviet inclination to exploit American anxieties for political purposes: parading one's strength was a tempting way to hide one's weakness, especially when the opponent seemed very credulous or needed to believe the bragging.

As to the consequences for the American strategic missile programs of the Kennedy administration's new findings, they became enmeshed in various political and bureaucratic conflicts with the result that the programmed, large-scale build-up – initiated by the Eisenhower administration and expanded by the new administration in early 1961 – continued despite the vastly changed evaluations of the Soviet ICBM capability.[18]

Altogether, the never-existing, but fraught with consequences, missile gap was the result of a symbiosis between some purposive American gullibility on the one hand and some purposive Soviet deception on the other,[19] and that particular interplay was an essential factor in the two societies' perceptions of each other.

2.   STUDIES OF AMERICAN IMAGES AND PERCEPTIONS

Writings on American images and perceptions of the Soviet Union approach the subject from various angles, apply more or less strict scholarly methods and employ different time perspectives. There is a blurred dividing line between scholarly studies of American peceptions, writings merely summing up the subject, and American studies of the Soviet Union combined with examinations of, or reflections about, the validity of different images. I shall first review, chronologically, studies of American images of the Soviet Union generally, then some studies of American images of the Soviet Union as nuclear power, and give particular attention to studies that can help in developing an analytical framework for studying American perceptions of the Soviet Union as a nuclear adversary and in locating this book, its approach and conclusions, within a broader literature.

1.   Images of the Soviet Union
The first work to be reviewed, a study by William Welch, published in 1970,[20] deals with a special kind of American image, namely appraisals from the academic community of Soviet foreign policy. Welch suggests, after a first examination, that one can speak of three distinct images types: an ultra-hard, a hard and a mixed (hard-soft). The *ultra-hard* image sees the Soviet Union as the 'great beast' whose external conduct is infinitely expansion-minded, substantially militaristic, totally amoral and relentlessly initiatory. The *hard* image sees the Soviet Union as the 'mellowing tiger' whose external conduct is highly expansion-minded, largely non-militaristic and largely initiatory. The *mixed* image sees the Soviet Union as the 'neurotic bear' whose external conduct is moderately expansion-minded, substantially non-militaristic and largely responsive to others. After having elaborated and exemplified the three image types (pp. 1–58), Welch points to their deficiencies, which he concludes are especially evident in the first type and, less so, in the third type (pp. 59–167). Welch thereafter suggests lines along which research and analysis of Soviet external conduct should proceed (pp. 171–209), and he illustrates this by analyzing the issue of 'Soviet faithlessness' which is often prominent in academic writing on the Soviet Union (pp. 210–61). He concludes that the record does not warrant the extreme charges about the faithless Soviets but he also emphasizes that a final evaluation must await a more thorough investigation.

Welch ends his book (p. 302) by a call to the American academic community that studies Soviet conduct to recognize the psychological, sociological and ethnocentric emotional commitments that are part of its make-up ('our make-up'); otherwise it is not possible to develop a 'true' image of Soviet foreign conduct. Generally, Welch's inquiry is marked by the time it was written, the later 1960s, when the (first) cold war was coming to an end and many liberal academics in the United States were demonstrating their uneasiness with parts of traditional US policy *vis-à-vis* the Soviet Union.

In a short survey, published in 1974, William Zimmerman[21] discerned three major approaches to the explanation of Soviet foreign policy among Western students of the Soviet Union: an essentialist, a mechanistic and a cybernetic (also termed an interactionist) conception. Put shortly, the *essentialist* approach describes Soviet foreign policy as flowing logically from the nature of totalitarianism. The *mechanistic* approach is concerned with Soviet behavior which it sees as opportunistic in a quest for higher security, and not as determined by some ideological essence of the Soviet system. The *cybernetic* approach is, compared to the other conceptions, voluntaristic in its explanatory orientation in that it stresses that the Soviet Union not only reacts to its environment, but learns as post-Stalin foreign policy illustrates.

A study by John Van Oudenaren[22] focuses directly on US leadership perceptions and warrants a more detailed review. It starts from the observation that as the Soviet Union has presented US political leaders with their most pressing foreign policy problems since the Second World War, there has been an ongoing debate in the United States about the 'essential' character of the Soviet state, its international behavior, and the appropriate set of policies for dealing with the Soviet Union. Early in the postwar period, US elite perceptions of the Soviet problem became polarized between two views that Oudenaren terms a 'termination by accommodation' and a 'termination by victory' group. Both views coexisted in 1945–6 within the Truman administration, with President Truman himself not yet clearly committed to one or the other. A third perception, however, challenging both 'termination' views and termed the 'management critique', emerged at the same time. As a prototype of the three perceptions, President Roosevelt and some of his advisors, NSC-68, and George Kennan are mentioned. The management approach later won general acceptance, but as a split developed between 'hard' and 'soft' camps of the management approach, with the hard managers appropriating many of the 'termination-by-victory' beliefs and the soft managers appropriating elements of the 'termination-by-accommodation' thinking, the widespread rejection of the view that there would be an early resolution of the Soviet problem did not result in an end to dissension within the US foreign policy elite.

The general characteristics of the '*termination by accommodation*' thinking are summarized (pp. 9–22): the cause of the conflict between the United States and the Soviet Union is incidental and not structural, rooted in suspicions and misunderstandings; communications and personal relationships between US and Soviet leaders are important and there are differences between hawks and doves on the Soviet as well as the American side; ideology is of declining significance in determining Soviet behavior while Soviet national interests, which are considered as legitimate and not basically a threat to the United States, are increasingly important; there is no overall struggle between the two countries which would impel each to back opposing sides in any conflict; the Soviet Union can be integrated into the international system, for example by the United States promoting functional interdependencies such as trade and scientific exchange that can help further to 'de-ideologize' the Soviets and win their trust. Oudenaren points out how such notions and ideas are linked to American political culture and the American approach to international relations. Especially important in this context is that it is incomprehensible to many Americans that a foreign power can sustain a permanent hostility toward the United States; another factor is the role that law plays in the American consciousness in that the problems of international relations have been viewed in terms of developing and enforcing a body of international law. It is also noted how competing demands of domestic US politics, especially the fear of the high costs of sustaining a permanent rivalry with the Soviet Union, have made this thinking appealing to both leaders and the general public in the United States.

The '*termination-by-victory*' perceptions are summarized (pp. 27–40): the main source of conflict is the unique characteristics of the communist adversary, namely the Soviet drive for world domination and pursuing that goal, the Soviets intend to use military power; conflicts throughout the world are largely appendages to the central conflict brought about by the Soviet drive for world domination; Soviet ideological writings can be used literally to predict future Soviet behavior; the United States has to develop 'positions of strength' before negotiating with the Soviets and personal contacts between US and Soviet leaders cannot improve relations as they are likely to be used by the Soviets to lull gullible Western publics into complacency; the Soviet leadership is monolithic without any hawk or dove factions; functional interdependencies are to be avoided and generally there are important asymmetries between the United States and the Soviet Union that favor the Soviets in political and military tests of strength. Summarizing the 'termination by victory' perception in that way, Oudenaren points out how it appealed to US political leaders and the general public for many of the same reasons as did the termination of accommodation, primarily in that both termination schools of thought betrayed an impatience with ambiguous, and difficult problems existing over longer periods of time. Moreover, Oudenaren notes how both termination schools tended to 'mirror image' when they prescribed policies for dealing with the Soviet Union: while the first-mentioned school stressed that the Soviet Union faced problems similar to the United States, the second school emphasized that the United States had to use some of the Soviets' techniques against themselves. Altogether, while the first termination school transferred American experience to the Soviet Union, the second school transferred Soviet experience to the United States and, so doing, neither termination school confronted fully the problem of the deep structural differences between the two countries or formulated policies that recognize the strengths and weaknesses inherent in the US society.

'*Management critique*' perceptions are summarized (pp. 43–62): the sources of conflict are structural and geopolitical in that ideology and national characteristics may exacerbate the conflict, but Soviet–American rivalry would persist under any Soviet or Russian regime; the Soviets remain to some extent motivated by ideology but it is necessary to maintain a distinction between what a communist wishes and expects will happen, and what in fact is possible; communicating and negotiating with the Soviet government, the emphasis is on dealing in a business-like way in that personal relations between leaders in the two countries may be useful, but it is not possible using personal communications for altering basic Soviet attitudes; negotiations with the Soviets are desirable to find out whether there exist areas of mutual interest, and not a matter of whether the Soviets can be trusted, and they must proceed from existing positions rather than be deferred until an illusory US position of strength is attained; it should be recognized that factions do exist within the Soviet leadership and US policy should be ready, if the opportunity arises, to appeal to one faction or another, but change in the effects of functional interdependencies are likely to be modest and the Soviet Union is not interested in helping the United States solve 'world-order' problems. Altogether, the Soviet challenge is composite and US policy must respond to different aspects of the Soviet challenge accordingly. Outlining these elements of the 'management critique', Oudenaren notes that it has not been particularly appealing to Americans: the idea of an open-ended conflict with another power seems to go against the grain of traditional American thinking on international relations.

In the last chapter of his highly suggestive study (pp. 65–70), Oudenaren notes briefly how both the nature of the public debate in the United States and the nature of the US–Soviet rivalry in part account for the continued influence of termination thinking in American perceptions. Thus he stresses how the very character of public strife in a democracy on how to respond to external challenges promotes the thinking that some kind of termination were a feasible option for US policy-makers. The continued influence of termination thinking may also be accounted for by the tendency, in both the US and the USSR, to ask 'who's winning', i.e. to view their relationship in zero-sum terms. The author does not attempt to assess the validity of the different perceptions, but be seems to favor some kind of 'management critique'.

A short article by Robert E. Osgood[23] surveys how shifting approaches of US governments toward implementing containment *vis-à-vis* the Soviet Union and the clashes of opinion on this have come, partly, as a result of different assessments of Soviet behavior. These appraisals have depended very little on the analyses of Sovietologists or foreign policy experts but the different analytical emphases applied by policy-makers have a distinct similarity to the findings presented by scholars and commentators. Osgood categorizes the most influential reasonings on the Soviet Union in two groups, termed Analysis A and Analysis B.

To *Analysis A*, the Soviet Union is a 'conservative, unimaginative, but expansionist state, responding ad hoc to something more than case-by-case opportunism but to something far less than a strategic grand design' (p. 8). The Soviet Union is motivated largely by insecurity, a desire for recognition of Soviet legitimacy and global parity with the United States. Out of weakness, as well as historical habit, the Soviet Union relies heavily on military power in its foreign policy, but it does so pragmatically and cautiously. The fact that the Soviet Union views peaceful coexistence as a way to improve its security interests and advance its goals does not mean that détente could not be in America's interest. A disparity between US and Soviet strategic nuclear forces within a very broad range has only a secondary political importance.

To *Analysis B*, the Soviet Union is a revolutionary state which is relentlessly expansionist and with a relentless drive for military superiority. The Soviets' ideological fixation and the Soviet regime's totalitarian nature are the basic causes of Soviet foreign policy. Détente is a Soviet grand strategy that seeks to disarm the West, morally and materially. Concerning nuclear policy, Soviet leaders reject Western notions of parity, mutual deterrence and mutual assured destruction, and they are skilled in exploiting strategic superiority for political purposes. Only the development of effective military counterpoises will contain the Soviet Union.

After having outlined the two types of perceptions, Osgood reviews their policy implications. He does not attempt to assess their validity.

Yet another scholar studying American images of the Soviet Union, Richard K. Herrmann,[24] writes that three viewpoints about Soviet motives are popular among the American elite, elite in this context meaning both scholars and politicians, namely *communist expansionism*, *realpolitik expansionism* and *realpolitik self-defense*. The first describes the Soviet Union as bent on achieving global hegemony and establishing worldwide communism, and this is seen as the unavoidable product of the Soviet political system. The second view minimizes the importance of ideology and fixed Soviet intentions; the Soviet Union is simply opportunistic in its expansionist impulse but it is also a profoundly insecure and defensive state, averse to taking risks. The third view presents the Soviet Union as a profoundly conservative state which is defensive and primarily motivated by security concerns. Outlining the three different perceptions, Herrmann emphasizes that they all apply indistinct concepts with the consequence that central claims are non falsifiable in that they cannot be subjected to empirical tests, a feature which Herrmann notes as 'disturbing'. Each remains dependent on ideological commitment but he does not elaborate this.

After having carried out an empirical study of the motives underlying

Soviet foreign policy, approached at the state level, over the past two decades, Herrmann, in the light of his evidence, evaluates the three claims about motivations into more testable propositions (pp. 166ff.) The conclusion (p. 197) is that it is 'plausible to attribute Soviet foreign policy behavior primarily to a concern for self-defense', i.e. the 'realpolitik self-defense' is the most valid perception but, at the same time, Herrmann warns against drawing too simple policy implications from this. It is especially emphasized that the study casts doubt on the perception that the Soviet Union's primary motive is to expand its domination over others, that is, the 'communist expansionism' perception seems invalid. It is also noted that as Soviet behavior has been studied at the state level, much 'internal complexity' (p. 197) has been missed wherefore it might be informative to study possible associations between various roles in the Soviet society and patterns of perception of the United States.

2. Images of the Soviet Union as nuclear power

A study by Michael Krepon[25] expounds diverging American images of the Soviet Union as a nuclear power. It presents a general review of the debate in the United States between two 'camps', or two views of the Soviet nuclear threat, termed the 'nuclear weapon strategists' (or 'the hawkish persuasion') and the 'arms control and disarmament strategists'. Both camps have internal divisions and a distinction between operationally and ideo-logically-minded wings is applied. Elaborating the 2×2 views, Krepon outlines their answers to questions about: How do they define the critical problem? What is the solution? What is the political utility of nuclear forces? What is the military utility? How important, and why, are negotiations with the Soviets and what are the requirements for useful negotiations? What ought to be nuclear war-fighting objectives?

Among 'nuclear weapon strategiss', the ideologues view the Russians as the critical problem while the operationally-minded see managing geopolitical competition as all-important. As to the solution, the first group points to superiority while the second points to strategic advantage. Concerning the political utility of nuclear arms, the ideologues see it as significant while the operationalists see it as likely with disparities in nuclear capabilities. Ideologues also view the military utility of nuclear arms as significant while the operationalists see it as possible with significant disparities in capabilities. Negotiations are seen as mainly counter-productive by the ideologues because they have a lulling effect on democratic societies and cannot lead to US superiority, and in any case the requirement is negotiating from strength; the operationalists see negotiations as having a measured utility in obtaining stability and parity. Concerning nuclear war-fighting objectives, the ideologues stress war-winning while operationalists emphasize gaining the most advantageous position.

Among '*arms control and disarmament strategists*', operationalists (or the arms control group) define the problem as managing the arms race while ideologues (or the disarmament group) see the atomic bomb as *the* problem. As to the solution, the two groups emphasize, respectively, arms control and disarmament. The political utility of nuclear weapons is, according to arms controllers, possible with significant disparities in capabilities but otherwise they serve only as a deterrent, and they are unlikely to have a military utility except to aid conflict termination. Concerning both the political and military utility, disarmers see them as counterproductive pursuing. The operationalists attach a major importance to negotiations which ought to aim at stability; ideologues see their aim as major reductions. As to nuclear war-fighting objectives, the first group sees avoidance of disadvantageous position as important while the second group sees them as counterproductive.

Krepon elaborates various aspects of the domestic debate between the divergent views and argues (p. 122) that long-term consensus would be difficult to achieve. The burden of obtaining some agreement between the two opposing camps will fall on the operationally-minded factions of both perspectives. The study also contains different, more or less distinctly defined, attempts to evaluate the 2 × 2 views, and with some variations as to the questions dealt with, and with varying distinctness, Krepon tends toward conclusions corroborating one of the two operationally-minded images.

In 1986, Daniel Frei published a study[26] which contains an examination of American perceptions of Soviet disarmament policy. By way of introduction, Frei emphasizes the obvious point that there exists no such thing as *the* American view; American views and their verbal reflections constitute an inherent part of a broad public debate and so statements about Soviet policy may have a multitude of functions. He notes that he does not aim at identifying the various positions expressed in the American debate but, rather, sets out to 'identify the common denominator shared by the various tendencies manifest in the debate' (p. 118). On the other hand, Frei's review is more a general outline of the Reagan administration's view than an identification of some 'common denominator' shared by various tendencies in the United States. As such, he emphasizes the view that Soviet nuclear strategy, as part of Soviet military strategy and overall Soviet foreign policy, is the utilization of military, including nuclear, power as a political instrument, especially by means of representing the Soviet Union as champion of peace and really aiming at dividing the West. Generally, Frei depicts the Reagan administration's image as one of the Soviet Union skillfully orchestrating public campaigns to influence the West.

Later (pp. 183ff.), Frei presents a broad survey of the Western, primarily the American, academic debate on Soviet military policy, suggesting a two-dimensional typology for grasping what in fact is an overwhelming variety of views: the first dimension distinguishes the various views according to the 'hardness' they ascribe to Soviet conduct, while the second dimension refers to the perceived consistency in this conduct over time. The review demonstrates the considerable disagreement among academic writers concerning questions as how the Soviet leadership perceives the role of nuclear war-fighting and if the Soviets accept mutual deterrence (pp. 212ff.). Toward the end of his book (pp. 254f.), Frei asks if the perceptions held by American academics, of which many have been or are actively involved in the American decision-making process, are accurate. He does not express a clear-cut evaluation as to which perceptions are more accurate but he concludes that one cannot but take due note of the scope, depth and amount of self-criticism expressed by American analysts of the Soviet Union, scholars as well as scholars-cum-politicians.

Altogether, these studies of American perceptions deal primarily with the content of predominant images while the domestic background factors and the validity of different images are considered less thoroughly. Before outlining how the suggested approaches, observations and theories form part of this study, the different definitions and methodical uses of the concept perception and the approach applied here have to be elaborated.

3. PERCEPTIONS: DEFINITIONS AND USES

1. The study of perceptions

The term 'perception' is used in a variety of ways. Generally, analyses of perceptions deal with what an actor believes to be true, i.e. his subjective knowledge or his image, and the very cognitive processes by means of which the actor forms his image.

Psychologists introduced the methodical use of the concept perception for research purposes. However, while concepts and frameworks applied by psychologists may have a heuristic value to political science by suggesting new approaches and hypotheses, many works by psychologists on human perception are characterized by some features which make their results of doubtful value from a social science point of view, especially when it comes to studying international relations. First, more attention is paid to emotional and pathological aberrations of individuals than to general cognitive factors with the effect that it is disregarded how unemotional and careful actors may draw diverging inferences from ambiguous evidence. Second, most data supporting the theories are derived from rather simple laboratory experiments and it is hard to determine whether these settings have any relevance to international politics – for the most part they seem to have none at all. Third, the structure of the international system with its lack of a legitimate sovereign is ignored and therefore there is little comprehension of why even rational actors think they have to be extremely cautious in any forthcoming interpretation of other actors. The result is that the literature on perception written by psychologists contains a great deal of over-psychologizing when directly applied to international relations with an exaggerated emphasis on how personality dispositions influence perceptions.[27]

Until the decision-making approach was introduced into the discipline International Relations in the mid-1950s,[28] scholars in the field traditionally refrained from approaching their subject in terms of perceptions. The prevalent assumption was that the actors, i.e. the decision-makers acting on behalf of the states which constitute the decisive units in the international society, perceived the environment quite accurately and those misperceptions that did occur were random accidents. That assumption was implicit in the so-called classical approach to the study of international relations with its rational actor model of states that dominated the study of international politics in earlier periods. In the later decades a more systematic use of the assumption of rational behavior has been made in game theory where it is explicitly stated that the rationality assumption may be useful for constructing models and theories even if the assumption descriptively is highly inadequate; after all, all theories and models involve simplifications and several characteristics of foreign policy decision-making suggest that the rationality model is more appropriate and fruitful for the methodical study of this area than for domestic political decision-making.[29]

Partly as a reaction to what was still considered a methodically inadequate inclination to over-rationalize the foreign policy decision-making process, partly as an offshoot of the current debate on US foreign policy, scholars have developed the decision-making approach into various more or less coherent models for the study of foreign policy. One example is the literature on 'bureaucratic politics' which experienced a boom in American political science during the 1970s, mainly brought about by scholars and journalists calling attention to the 'muddling-through' characteristics and bureaucratic constraints featuring in US foreign policy. Another is the cybernetic paradigm focusing on the uncertainty inherent in any significant decision problem and the ensuing handling of information.[30] Especially useful in the attempt to correct an over-rationalization in foreign policy studies are writings on 'image', 'perception', 'cognitive processes', 'cognitive map', 'operational code', 'belief systems' or whatever related term is used and the diverse terminology is matched by similarly diversified research techniques applied in these studies.[31]

One aspect of these social-psychological approaches, with a special relevance for this study, concerns perceived causation, i.e. what is termed 'attribution theory'.[32] Characterizing different attributions, i.e. different explanations for behavior or sources of behavior as perceived by an attributer, an important distinction is that between a perception that attributes a behavior to 'internal' dispositions of the perceived actor and a perception that attributes a behavior to aspects of the 'external' situation. That is, an attribution may be described using a centrality notion, referring to the degree to which other beliefs in the belief system are dependent on the belief in question: where the dispositional-oriented perceiver focuses on internal properties of the perceived actor (the object of perception) as abilities, traits or motives, as central, the situational-oriented perceiver focuses on environmental pressures and constraints as central.[33] Making this distinction, attribution theories have frequently identified a fundamental attribution error, namely the tendency for attributers to underestimate the impact of situational factors and to overestimate the role of dispositional factors when others' behavior is explained, and particularly so when the perceiver dislikes the other actor and his act; when one's own behavior is explained, however, there is an opposite tendency to overemphasize situational variables. This difference between self-perception and others' perception may also be expressed in the way that there are strongly self-serving biases in causal attributions.[34] As to further consequences of employing dispositional, rather than situational marked, attributions, attribution theories hold that they make perceptions harder to change. Attribution theories also deal with antecedents of perceived causation. The investigator seeks to specify factors, such as beliefs, preconceptions, stereotypes and motivation, that lead a perceiver to attribute a particular behavior, performed by the object of perception, to one cause rather than another.[35] The basic assumption is that the attributer perceives another actor's behavior with certain suppositions and expectations about its causes and effects that may lead the actual attribution to be either dispositional or situational marked.

2.   The methodical relevance of perceptions

The unifying feature of social-psychological analyses of foreign policy is that they express a deliberate attempt to construct a new approach within the overall context of the decision-making approach. The basic assumption is that an identification and elaboration of the special cognitive processes which characterize the foreign policy decision-maker may provide a useful key to understanding foreign policy and international politics.[36] By mapping out the belief structures and exploring the cognitive dynamics of the decision-makers acting on behalf of a state, the theory-building effort relies on studying the influence of broader societal and organizational contexts, i.e. unlike many studies by psychologists the influence of role variables rather than individual and idiosyncratic variables are analyzed. By focusing on a plurality of individual decision-makers operating within an institutional framework, an unfortunate tendency to reify the state as actor in international politics is corrected. In other words, it is clear that when we are talking about the United States or the US government as holding some images, it is only in a metaphorical sense.[37]

The methodical relevance of studying the decision: makers' perceptions is, generally speaking, that the way people perceive the world influences decisions and outcomes. It is assumed that the decision-makers' beliefs are major causal forces of behavior and therefore explain and predict human action; that is, the perception rather than the 'reality' of the environment is crucial to an understanding of decisions or, otherwise stated, if the decision-makers define situations as real, those situations are real in their consequences.[38] So stating, however, is only a first approximation when one attempts to determine the methodical relevance of the decision-makers' perceptions. One must be careful to avoid a methodological trap: some decision-making scholars assert that a decision-making analysis in the form of recreating the world as it is constructed by the actor is always necessary when one attempts to answer the 'why' question, and it is implied that a detailed study of the actor's goals and calculations about the interrelations between goals and means is always the most fruitful approach.[39]

However, in many cases, the decision-makers' beliefs and calculations should not be seen as cognitive elements that cause their policies and actions, but as rationalizations serving the function of permitting the decision-makers to act with clear consciences and appear as rational to observers. It is an intuitively satisfactory explanation for an action or a policy to focus on the actors' perception and cognitive process, but it cannot be presumed that a decision-maker's perception always precedes the development of his policy or action. The causation may flow in the reverse direction in that a decision-maker may first set his policy and then develop the image of the environment that supports and would have led to such a policy. This means that the relationship between, on the one hand, perception and image, and, on the other hand, action and policy, may be one of rationalization rather than rationality. Perceptions and cognitions are not autonomous in relation to policies and actions and a detailed study of images and cognitive processes may be futile if it is done as an attempt to provide the causation of behavior because it may distract from an understanding of important explanatory variables at work. In other words, an explanation that stops with perception and cognitive factors will not be satisfactory and one may have to look at the functions the perception serves.[40]

Another aspect of the methodical use of the concept perception is the fact that, logically, one may distinguish between an actor's 'psychological environment', i. e. the environment (milieu or setting) as the actor perceives it, and an 'operational environment', i.e. the environment in which a policy will be carried out.[41] That is, one may conceptualize and analyze an actor's environing factors, comprising foreign as well as domestic human beings, social patterns, and non-human objects, as it seems or appears to the actor (his perception or image) and as it is, i.e. 'is' as it may be established by a principally detached observer with total knowledge of all relevant factors. In comparing the two conceptually distinct environments, it is assumed that the psychological environment, the actor's perception, may diverge from the operational environment in ways that, in principle, can be explored and accounted for, which means that the possibility of misperception— meaning that the actor's perception diverges from the operational environment – is a relevant problem in studies of perception.

Among the hypotheses submitted by researchers,[42] one states that actors tend to establish images of others prematurely by being too wedded to the established view and too impervious to new information; another states that actors tend to see the behavior of others as more centralized, disciplined and coordinated than it really is; a third hypothesis states, as a special case of the fundamental attribution error, that actors tend toward a situational-marked perception when the others behave in accordance with the actor's desires, but toward the dispositional-marked perception when the behavior of the other is undesired; yet another hypothesis asserts that it is hard for one actor to believe that the other can see him as a menace or, more generally, that the other may perceive a situation as entirely different.

Concerning the significance of misperceptions as to the misperceiving actor's decision and the outcome of interacting actor's behavior, it is pertinent to note various conditions and implications.[43] First, misperceptions can only affect an actor's decision if it is presumed that the actor has a choice of behavior or sees that he has a choice; if the actors have no choice because of various constraints, or see themselves as having only one course of action because of their own cognitive processes, they would not have acted differently had they not misperceived others but, of course, an accurate perception might have caused them to see alternative choices and that means that the cognitive and political processes, by which an actor forms his image, are important. Second, misperceptions can only matter in relations between interdependent states, i.e. if states are independent of one another in the sense that one actor's decisions do not affect another actor's payoffs then misperception is irrelevant to outcomes. However, misperceptions need not always affect the decision of an interdependent actor who does have a choice; for example, it would not affect the behavior of an actor with a so-called dominant strategy, i.e. a course of action that maximizes its returns no matter what others do; in that case misperceptions might have affected the actor's expectations but he would not have acted differently if the perception had been accurate. Thrid, misperceptions can only matter in relations that combine elements of cooperation and conflict, i.e. if international politics is a variable-sum game, not in situations of pure conflict. Fourth, it is erroneous to presume that misperceptions necessarliy affect decisions and outcomes by increasing conflicts that would otherwise have been avoidable while accurate perceptions cause cooperation in international politics. This common presumption may, probably, be explained by the inference that misperception is 'bad' and conflict is 'bad', thus the two phenomena must be positively related. However, misperception does not necessarily cause conflict even when it does affect the actors' choices and behavior; it can also facilitate cooperation and prevent conflict and, altogether, it is fallacious to assume a one-to-one relationship between misperception, behavior and conflict.

Given such reservations on the methodical relevance of perceptions, it has to be noted that studying the subjective knowledge of political actors has a special relevance in the nuclear age which appears from reflecting on some traits marking the nuclear issue and their political manifestations.

3. Perceptions and the nuclear issue

Asserting that the 'minds of men' are critical to the war–peace issue is a widely shared commonplace.[44] That commonplace, however, implies a peculiar pertinence when it comes to assessing the danger of nuclear war as well as the political meaning of nuclear weapons in peacetime in that the special characteristics of atomic weapons lend still more plausibility to the assertion that the danger of nuclear war has its source in the minds of men who are in a position to order the use of nuclear weapons rather than in the actual multitude of atomic bombs. The very fact that the extensive use of atomic weapons in war has never occurred, and if it occurred might result in unprecedented and incomprehensible destruction approaching or tantamount to the annihilation of humankind, entails the consequence that that possibility easily becomes the object of all kinds of different conceptions, ideas and projections with different consequences besides an actual unleashing of nuclear bombs. The lack of empirical evidence regarding nuclear war and the related difficulty of establishing unambiguous data on the political meaning of nuclear weapons means that the decision-makers' subjective thinking and reasoning, their imaginations and daydreams and their public manifestations are important in a more momentous sense than concerning problems where empirical data are more ascertainable. As it has been expressed: nuclear weapons exist to be talked about, not to be used.[45]

Therefore, when people attempt to grasp the meaning of nuclear weapons and design policies to pursue, myths will often be displayed as true wisdom and hypotheses as facts and as the 'human mind' can be volatile and, at the same time, rigid and inflexible, the danger of all kinds of self-delusions and wishful thinking becomes obvious. The critical difficulty, however, is that, given the inherent characteristics of the nuclear issue, nobody is able to establish with certainty the borderline between wisdom and wishful thinking, between fact and belief, between reality and myth; when decision-makers are attempting to establish some tenable notions on the meaning of nuclear weapons, the dividing line between their subjective beliefs and facts is blurred and this is one reason why debates on nuclear issues often take on a theological tone. Therefore, one paradoxical consequence of nuclear weapons – paradoxical considering their enormous destructiveness – is that perceptions of facts create rather than mirror reality to a greater extent than was true in the past. There is no reality to be described that is independent of men's beliefs about it.[46]

A special reason for drawing attention to this arises from the relations between the scholarly and the political exchange of views on US foreign policy and various uses of the term perceptions in the American debate, a debate which often reflects the linguistic confusion as to the actual meaning of the word perception as well as the putative prestige value of that term. During the 1960s and early 1970s some scholars analyzed the cold war in terms of a spiral of (mis)perceptions;[47] these analyses implied or were accompanied by a strong criticism of American policy during the then past cold war and a guarded support for the new policy of détenté and the restrained endorsement of that policy was solely due to doubts as to whether it really represented a radical break with the traditional American cold war rhetoric. On the other hand, during the last part of the 1970s many scholarly and political writings in the United States on the significance of perceptions conveyed a very critical view of American foreign and defense policy during the years of détenté; the critique was that America's lack of resolve and will after the Vietnam débâcle, a defective defense build-up, especially concerning nuclear arms, contributed to a widely-shared perception of a steady debilitation of the United States and Soviet ascent. In the general mood of pessimism which dominated the American outlook until the Reagan administration, the word 'perceptions' often became a fashionable term that was attributed an almost mysterious explanatory force when politicians and scholars had to account for ominous developments and one-dimensional readings of world politics in terms of perceptions were predominant. A number of articles and treatises appeared on how a world-wide perception of growing Soviet military strength and declining American strength influenced non-Soviet actors all over the globe towards greater deference to Soviet interests and a turning away from American and Western interests; also a Soviet perception of America's weakness was invoked to account for many sinister trends in world politics.[48] In that pessimistic mood, invoking the expression 'this concerns perceptions' often became a clinching argument.

These uses of the term perception are important to note because they show that the word is applied in various political and interrelated analytical contexts. while it does not, of course, detract from the validity of a theory that it is put forward by political actors, this may complicate the methodical difficulties of evaluating the validity of the theory. Thus, frequent assertions from scholars-cum-politicians on the significance of 'perceptions' of military, especially nuclear, strength may contribute to their own confirmation. In other words, the old problem of a blurred dividing line between stating a theory and changing its validity has a special relevance in studies of perception that, again, adds to the difficulties of delimiting the methodical relevance of studying political actor's perceptions. The decision-makers' fundamental difficulties in establishing tenable and durable perceptions regarding the meaning of nuclear weapons enhance the methodical problems related to any attempt to construct valid theories on these perceptions, their origins, contents, significance and validity, and even if those problems are not unique compared to other areas of social research, they acquire a peculiar immediacy when we apply a perception approach to nuclear issues.

4. Approaching American perceptions

An actor's beliefs, that is, his perceptions and images, cannot be observed directly; they have to be inferred from some operational indicators. The starting point of the analysis of US governments' perceptions of the Soviet Union as a nuclear adversary will be the changing administrations' public declarations on the Soviet Union as a nuclear power, i.e. written or oral statements from leading members of the various administrations. This generally worded definition of the source material for inferring perceptions leaves problems concerning the actual delimitation of statements to be included that will be more closely considered in Chapter 2, but the crucial point so far is that the applicability of a statement for analysis is not evaluated in terms of its more or less exact reflection of some real belief, meaning a genuine and honest conviction, where the task is to 'peel off all the artificial pretenses' in order to reach the core belief. By inferring some perceptions or images from public statements and considering various readings, nothing is implied about 'true' conviction or (in)sincerity. On the contrary, the approach expresses an attempt to supplant the question of honesty vs. dishonesty as a fruitful way to understand declarations from foreign policy decision-makers and spokesmen. The underlying assumption is that the simple dichotomy between what is 'real' vs. 'just professed' in political actors' statements on a subject is based on a misunderstanding of the functions of public and private declarations and so that dichotomy is irrelevant to use for a better understanding of various pronouncements.[49]

There may, of course, be differences between statements put forward by diffferent members of the same government or between declarations in front of various audiences, but exactly such differences of social acceptability are interesting to construe and evaluate alternative readings of an actor's perception.[50] An actor's statements on a political subject and the kinds of justification for a policy that is seen as legitimate in a given context are important data not to be dismissed as 'mere words'; the linguistic categorization and featuring of an issue is a key part of reality and may influence and shape other aspects of reality; in that sense, language and perceptions are power.[51] But in any case, the theoretical value of some statement depends on its implicit or explicit interpretation; it is only by applying a conceptual framework to read an actor's words that they may be useful to reach an understanding of his perceptions and their background. Merely reproducing the spoken or written word is, by itself, of no avail; even acceptance of a statement at face value implies some kind of interpretation when used to substantiate some theoretical assumptions.[52]

While noting that the theoretical value of public statements from foreign policy actors does not depend on presuming honesty, it is worth noting that there are substantive reasons which actually support the use of public declarations as valid indicators of beliefs. Thus public declarations often act as constraints on the actors themselves by contributing to creating various expectations both within and without their country; *vis-à-vis* other countries governments may attempt to maximize their credibility and, particularly in democratic societies, government leaders are under constant scrutiny and must appear candid and steadfast if they are to exercise leadership and stay in power; sometimes political actors may actually come to believe in an assertion which they, for one reason or another, have reiterated again and again. From this it follows that after having considered the functions of public statements in different political and cognitive contexts, it is frequently possible and natural to draw some conclusions as to the question if an actor's statement reflects some more firmly held belief or is more circumstantially framed. [53]

Acknowledging the general need for an analytical framework to interpret and recover a wider meaning of a statement beyond the simple facts of time, place and text, may, however, easily lead to the pitfall of over-interpreting where one is tied up in a lot of more or less unworldly imaginations on some underlying meaning of a statement. It is tempting to forget that many statements are rather simple to interpret and it is important to note that the problems related to interpreting statements and construing perceptions may vary widely, there is no overall solution to this methodical problem — only to be generally attentive to the danger of disparate pitfalls.

Analyzing American perceptions of the Soviet Union as a nuclear adversary by studying public statements means that the focus will be on one aspect of American declaratory policy on nuclear weapons. American nuclear policy may be divided into several partially overlapping facets: first, *declaratory policy*, i.e. public pronouncements on nuclear weapons made by senior administration officials; second, *force development policy*, i.e. decisions on the size and capabilities of American nuclear forces; third, arms control negotiation policy, i.e. guidelines as to goals and tactics to be pursued in negotiations on nuclear issues with other countries; fourth, *operational policy*, i.e. guidelines for such activities as alert rates or patrol practises for various types of nuclear forces; finally, *force employment policy* , i.e. the actual war-fighting plans that the United States would adopt in a nuclear war, the so-called Single Integrated Operations Plan (SIOP). [54]

The two last-mentioned policies, and to some degree the second and third as well, are secret even in a political system as open as the American, but one may assume that there will always be some inclination toward consistency between the different facets because influence frequently rests upon a certain measure of consonance between word and deed, public statement and action and this may, again, reasonably be presumed to play a special role in a democratic society. On the other hand, the different facets may only be partially consistent with each other; sometimes there may be evident contradictions between various facets of a nuclear policy and there may be contradictions within one facet as well, at least for the reason that it is almost impossible to pursue one coherent policy in a bureaucracy as complex as an American administration. Most important in the context of this analysis, there are reasons to expect that inconsistencies are most evident between the declaratory facet and other facets of nuclear policy; however, it is a basic assumption of the approach applied here that this does not deplete the declaratory facet of its significance. On the other hand, it points to the importance of explaining and accounting for some aspects of the American nuclear policy by comparing with other aspects of American nuclear policy, thus elaborating the understanding of American perceptions of the Soviet Union as a nuclear adversary. To put it differently, the perception inferred from the declaratory policy may be compared with a perception inferred from other aspects of American nuclear policy.

4.   ISSUES AND QUESTIONS

The subject of this study has been defined as US governments' perceptions of the Soviet Union as a nuclear armed adversary since the early 1960s, with special reference to elaborating relations between these views and the Soviet Union's position as nuclear power as well as the domestic American political system. A further clarification of this definition follows from the applied operational definition of 'perceptions' as based on public statements from the six administrations incumbent during the period. This definition is stricter than the unspecified and rather vague definitions of the term mostly applied in studies of American perceptions and images of the Soviet Union (cf. section 2). It is applied to give the review and analysis of six presidencies' approaches to the combined challenge from the Soviet Union and nuclear arms a special angle which is presumed to provide the basis for elucidating new aspects of international relations in the nuclear age. By applying a definition of perceptions as based on public statements, it is possible to elaborate characteristics of the interplay between the reasonings and logics applied publicly by American political leaders through almost a generation, particularities of the American political system and the Soviet Union as nuclear superpower. As American politics is marked by frequent heated disputes about US foreign policy between politicians occupying or seeking public office, and the Soviet Union has different societal and ideological features which Americans repudiate, it can be assumed that reviewing and further examining US governments' public pronouncements about America's most prominent political adversary in the balance of terror age, will provide a fruitful basis for elaborating various propositions about dynamics of the interplay between the United Stated and the Soviet Union in the balance of terror age which is one critical aspect of current international society.[55] The specific methodical approach applied in analyzing the links between US governments' images, characteristics of the Soviet Union as a superpower and the domestic American scene is comparing psychological and operational environments. The issues and questions dealt with in the following chapters have been chosen with this in mind.

In Chapters 2 and 3 the substance of American perceptions since the early 1960s, i.e. the images of the Soviet Union as a nuclear adversary held by different administrations since the Kennedy administration took office in 1961, will be examined. Chapter 2 will review the first half of the period since 1961, the years 1961–74. Chapter 3 reviews the years 1974–89. The purpose is to capture the structure of changing administrations' images so as to give an organized representation of important features of US governments' images over 28 years. For that purpose, some of the characteristics of American perceptions of the Soviet Union suggested by studies of American images as well as the review of the perceptions approach, in particular the distinction between situational and dispositional variables suggested by attribution theories, are frutiful. Chapter 4 will synthesize the images of 1961–89 by briefly outlining fixtures, trends and relevant swings during the period.

Chapters 5 and 6 serve to provide important parts of the basis for comparing images and operational environments in Chapter 7. In Chapter 5 the American perception will be analyzed as a cognitive and domestic political process, i.e. the genesis of the images will be considered in terms of varying American cognitive and political processes. The focus will be on antecedents in the American political system which may influence the actual perception of the Soviet Union as nuclear power, aiming at elaborating whether Amercan politics, broadly conceived, tends toward a dispositional or situational-oriented perception. Chapter 6 focuses on the object of perceptions by outlining central features of the Soviet Union as a nuclear power since the early 1960s, i.e. during a time when the Soviet Union can be termed superpower.

Chapter 7 aims at evaluating American perceptions by comparing images and operational environments. It is framed as a comparison of fixtures and long-term trends of the images, 1961–89, as these have been represented in Chapter 4, to the operational environments as these can be reasoned on the basis of the findings in Chapter 6 about the Soviet Union as superpower and the findings in Chapter 5 about the domestic environment to US governments' policy-making. As the operational environment defines the setting – domestic as well as foreign – in which a foreign policy is pursued, it refers to a set of potentially relevant factors which may effect the outcomes of foreign policy decisions even if they have not been recognized by the decision-makers themselves in their images.[56] From this it follows that comparing images and operational environments contributes a basis for elaborating and understanding fundamental conditions of US government's nuclear policy in a broader perspective. While comparing operational and psychological environments (images) may provide a measure of specific decisions' rationality, it is more important, in the context of this analysis, that it elucidates the interplay between various critical factors faced by successive administrations in Washington.

The last chapter, Chapter 8, summarizes the analysis by submitting conclusions and observations concerning the domestic conditions of American foreign and nuclear policy, the American–Soviet relationship in the nuclear age and cognitive aspects of international relations. The focus will be on specific findings as to the interplay between the process of perception and the object of perception or, otherwise expressed, the interaction between the domestic scene and characteristics of the Soviet Union as nuclear power for US governments' perceptions, and generally their reactions to and ways of meeting the Soviet Union as a nuclear superpower. Lastly, I shall submit some observations and reflections that I consider important, in the light of the findings, to the policy-making process in Western states, ending with some considerations on future developments.

2.   Images, 1961–74

The exposition of US governments' images of the Soviet Union as a nuclear adversary from Kennedy to Reagan will be based on public statements from the administrations' incumbents during the period. The statements include written or oral declarations from an administration, that is, the President and his principal subordinates concerned with foreign and defense policy, primarily the Secretary of State, the Secretary of Defense, the Assistant to the President for National Security Affairs and certain of their subordinates.

The source material providing statements includes six groups: first, *The Department of State Bulletin* (DSB). DSB is published monthly (until 1978 weekly) by the Department of State and reproduces speeches, press conferences, statements in Congressional hearings and some written reports put forward by an administration or its officials. Second, *Documents on Disarmament* (Doc.), published annually by the United States Arms Control and Disarmament Agency (ACDA). Doc. also reproduces speeches, statements and press conferences by members of an administration. Third, *the Annual Report to Congress of the Secretary of Defense*. Before 1974 the corresponding report bore the name *Statement by the Secretary of Defense* to the Senate (or House) Armed Services Committee. Fourth, a large number of Congressional hearings since 1961 where administration officials have set out the government's policy. Fifth, some written reports from an administration to the public on American foreign and defense policy. Sixth, a few other sources which, until 1979, primarily include *Documents on American Foreign Relations*, published yearly by the Council on Foreign Relations, New York.

As one aim is to analyze the significance of domestic American politics, the temporal division of images 1961–89 can expediently follow the six presidencies: the Kennedy administration 1961–3, the Johnson administration 1963–9, and the Nixon administration 1969–74, all reviewed in this chapter. The Ford administration 1974–7, the Carter administration 1977–81, and the Reagan administration 1981–9, are reviewed in Chapter 3. The substance of statements from the six administrations will be analyzed in terms of two so-called ideal types of American images of the Soviet Union as a nuclear adversary.

TWO IDEAL TYPES

An ideal type is an intellectual accentuation of some aspect of reality. Being an invented construction or a logical ideal meant to educate our judgement when we are trying to recount empirical phenomena, an ideal type is a technical aid in helping us to assess reality in terms of unambiguous means of expression. An ideal type is a kind of model but has another function by offering a yardstick to which empirical phenomena can be compared and characterized as more or less approximations. Thus, it is neither a description of reality nor a political ideal or utopia but, being a logical utopia, elements of an ideal type are presumed to be present in some more or less diluted form in empirical reality.[1]

The basic argument for representing American images in terms of two ideal-type images is the observation that different conceptions of the Soviet Union as nuclear power reflect different views of the combined challenge from the Soviet Union and nuclear arms. Thus the starting point for constructing the two ideal types are different views about what is the nature or essence of, respectively, nuclear weapons and the Soviet Union wherefore they are termed 'nuclear essentialism' (ideal type A) and 'Soviet essentialism' (ideal type B). Where ideal type A is basically concerned with a perceived nature of atomic weapons and the dynamics of nuclear arms competition, ideal type B is basically concerned with a perceived political dynamics of the Soviet Union or, to put it differently, while nuclear essentialism is based on a kind of technological essentialism which tends toward technological determinism, Soviet essentialism is a kind of ideological essentialism which tends toward ideological determinism. That means that the two ideal-type images hold distinctly different notions of centrality: where nuclear essentialism emphasizes situational variables originating in the existence of nuclear weapons in the interpretation of the Soviet Union as a nuclear adversary, Soviet essentialism emphasizes dispositional variables originating in the nature of the Soviet state. The two ideal-type images thus stand for two distinct conflict orientations, or conflict strategies,[2] for the United States to apply *vis-à-vis* the Soviet Union.

Concerning the further content of the two ideal types, the review of studies of American images in Chapter 1, as well as the review of American views before 1961, provide clues, both as to the themes of the ideological and the technological factors and their relative significance. Thus, although the actual typology and labelling differ in various studies, they agree that American images of the Soviet Union can be placed along a 'hard–soft' dimension where the perceived significance of the ideological contrast between the two states is the critical variable. Concerning the weapon-technological dimension in the nuclear age, the studies indicate that American views primarily differ as to the political and military significance attached to actual disparities between the superpowers' nuclear capabilities in the way that an ideological 'hard' view of Soviet–American relations is connected with a tendency to see disparities between nuclear forces as politically and militarily very important, and vice versa.[3] The specific themes to be included in the two ideal types are suggested by recurrent ideas about the general political significance of the atomic bomb, deterrence, negotiations, and whether the Soviets share American notions about the nuclear threat.

The two ideal-type images are generalizing entities composed of several interrelated elements intended to capture the structure of existing images. Both types contain cognitive as well as affective and action components constructed around themes indicating the kinds of reasoning and argument in terms of which public declarations from American governments since 1961 will be analyzed. The themes are:

1. the importance of convergent vs. divergent interests between the United States and the Soviet Union in the nuclear age;
2. the conditions of nuclear deterrence *vis-à-vis* the Soviet Union;
3. the political significance of nuclear forces;
4. the significance of negotiations on nuclear issues;
5. the Soviet view of nuclear weapons.

A.   IDEAL TYPE A: NUCLEAR ESSENTIALISM

1.   Convergent vs. divergent interests
The mutual hostage relationship between the United States and the Soviet Union is an immutable fact, irrespective of policy. The balance of terror means that the nuclear relationship between the two superpowers is symmetrical since both the United States and the Soviet Union have an assured second-strike capability. The inevitable fact of both superpowers' physical vulnerability and hence the possibility of mutual destruction is tantamount to a common predicament of mutual interdependence which compels a convergence of Soviet and American interests in managing the nuclear issue so as to avert common holocaust. The need for détente is a result of this fundamental attribute of the nuclear age and thus the mutual concern for each other's basic interests is an obligation for the United States as well as the Soviet Union.

2.   Deterrence
Since the mutual assured destruction situation is a basic fact of life, the Soviet Union is deterred from initiating nuclear war by the United States ever maintaining an assured and invulnerable second-strike capability. Deterrence through the implied threat of retaliation is the only viable doctrine in the nuclear age while deterrence through denial is a chimera; no amount of numerical superiority as to nuclear forces can deprive the other superpower of the necessary and minimum second-strike capability. At the same time, it is important to stabilize the mutual deterrence situation by

avoiding any threat to the Soviet deterrence capability whether by a counterforce strategy, a missile defense system or an extensive civil defense program. In any case, it is self-defeating for the United States to convey the illusion that one can defend oneself against a nuclear attack or that a nuclear war can be fought and won in any meaningful way.

3.   The political significance of nuclear forces

As the basic mutual assured destruction predicament is insensitive to marginal changes in the superpowers' nuclear deployments and as nuclear forces are not transferable into usable political power, it is irrational to become obsessed with a political meaning of enlargements of Soviet nuclear forces or a political meaning of any numerical superiority. Given the abundance of American nuclear forces for any meaningful deterrence purpose, it is irrational to let speculations about malign Soviet intentions as to the political use of superiority influence American nuclear policy. The crux of the matter is that the actual state of the nuclear armaments balance between the two superpowers is politically immaterial when both have an assured second-strike capability.

4.   Negotiations

Given the common nuclear predicament, it is important and feasible to implement a close communication and negotiation process on nuclear arms control between the United States and the Soviet Union. The nuclear arms race which is initiated and continued by mutual suspiciousness and fears of the adversary may transform itself into self-fulfilling prophesies. As this action–reaction process as to both armaments and suspicious attitudes thereby involves a special danger in the nuclear age, it is vital to give the Soviet Union a stake in nuclear arms control negotiations. A close dialogue on nuclear issues will change residues in the Soviet political and military establishment about the winnability of nuclear war and nuclear superiority; moreover, this educational effort of a superpower dialogue on the nuclear issue can also have a benign impact on obsolete notions about nuclear war and nuclear superiority among some Americans. Hence, it is inopportune for the United States to establish any linkage between Soviet policy, domestic or foreign, and arms control negotiations; on the contrary, progress in nuclear arms control may smooth the way for a deepening of détente and wider accommodation between East and West.

5.   The Soviet view

The Soviet leadership shares a modernist view that fully understands the common nuclear predicament. Soviet political leaders know that the mutual assured destruction predicament is a fact of life and that it is futile and suicidal to aim for victory in a nuclear war or nuclear superiority. If some Soviet nuclear weapons deployments seem to convey another reasoning, it can be explained in the same way as similar American deployments, that is, as a result of residual military thinking or bureaucratic politics. When some Soviet writers consider nuclear arms as traditional war-fighting means and advocate victory strategies or the political usefulness of nuclear superiority, it is an historical and ideological residue conveyed for domestic political reasons and does not reflect true Soviet views. In any case, an active American arms control policy will reduce such Soviet thinking and encourage Soviet realism in the nuclear age.

B.   IDEAL TYPE B: SOVIET ESSENTIALISM

1.   Convergent vs. divergent interests

The basic divergence between Soviet and American interests originates in the fact that the Soviet Union is a totalitarian state committed by its all-encompassing Marxist-Leninist ideology to the goal of world dominance. That Soviet goal has not been changed by the appearance of nuclear weapons; on the contrary, it enhances the nuclear danger in that the Soviets attempt to abuse the danger of nuclear war in the pursuance of their aim. Consequently, it is necessary for the United States as the leader of the free world to counter the Soviet policy in all its aspects and especially Soviet nuclear policy. Putative convergent interests between the United States and the Soviet Union in the avoidance of nuclear war heighten the importance of American vigilance in pursuing the free world's political goals which are fundamentally divergent from the Soviet goal.

2.   Deterrence

Given the distinct Soviet political goal and military doctrine, deterrence has to be based upon a symmetrical American nuclear doctrine and capability. The Soviets can only be deterred from aggressive actions by a superior American nuclear force, i.e. a strategy aimed at holding and improving the capability and will to fight and win a nuclear war; military effectiveness in a nuclear war, especially a usable counterforce capability, is decisive for both deterrence and the post-war balance of forces. It is irresponsible to base deterrence on the inherently unsafe, immoral and untrustworthy threat of a retaliatory second-strike against the innocent Soviet civil population. The goal must be to build an effective and reliable shield against a Soviet nuclear attack. If that presently is impossible, it is vital that the United States deploy nuclear forces and design a strategy for their use to counter Soviet nuclear forces at all levels, geographical and weapon-technological.

3.   The political significance of nuclear forces

As Soviet long-range goals are immutable while Soviet tactics vary according to shifting correlation of forces and perceived opportunities, all changes in the nuclear balance may have important political consequences. The behavior of both the Soviets and third countries proves that the psychological impact of the perceived nuclear balance is a reality which the United States can ignore only to its own detriment; also the willingness of the American people to countenance a steadfast foreign policy *vis-à-vis* the Soviets is conditioned upon their perception of American nuclear superiority. Since superior nuclear forces are a highly usable political instrument through their usability to influence, intimidate and force other countries, it is absolutely necessary to follow the actual state of the nuclear balance in all its ramifications in order to correct any Soviet-initiated imbalances.

4.   Negotiations

Given the Soviet political goal, it is extremely difficult to obtain negotiated reductions in the nuclear arsenals or a true dialogue on the nuclear danger. The fundamental political asymmetry between the Soviet Union and the United States is prohibitive to real arms control and disarmament since any arms race is the result of the politically motivated Soviet rearmament. Negotiated arms reductions are only possible if the United States clearly and unequivocally states its resolution to carry through unilaterally the necessary arms build-up; otherwise the Soviets will not have the incentive to negotiate seriously. It is also an absolute necessity that Soviet compliance with any agreement can be verified; otherwise, the Soviets have no incentive to comply. As the political differences between the Soviet Union and the United States are decisive, linkage between negotiations on arms control and political issues is a fact of life rather than an American choice; building the American policy on just giving the Soviets a stake in arms control in order to avert nuclear war is based on self-delusion which leads to steady American concessions, and actually increases the danger of war.

5.   The Soviet view

The Soviets share a traditionalist view of nuclear war that is wholly different from the Western view. The Soviets believe that a nuclear war can be fought and won and totally reject the notion that nuclear forces ought to have only a second-strike role. This can be seen in several Soviet writings not framed for foreign propaganda and in their publications on Soviet military doctrine. Furthermore, this is corroborated by their steady nuclear build-up, especially the heavy deployment of highly capable counterforce weapons and the extensive Soviet civil defense. When some Soviet writers depict the nuclear danger in terms of mutual vulnerability requiring mutual restraint, it is just one element in a well-orchestrated campaign to seduce Western public opinion into demanding unilateral Western restraint and disarmament.

These two ideal types are, in principle, invented constructions, i.e. 'invented' on the basis of considerations outlined above, and not intended as portrayals of views actually held by somebody. The assumption is that the elaboration of two distinct types of American images of the Soviet

Union as a nuclear adversary is useful for catching trends and fixtures in US governments' declarations since the beginning of the 1960s; the two ideal types are set out with a view to being applied to expound various aspects of views actually held by American governments and follow the course of changes in those views during a period when, as noted in the Introduction, US governments for some years, in the late 1960s and early 1970s, deviated from their traditional inclination to attach more importance to a perceived essential character of the Soviet Union than a perceived essential nature of nuclear arms.

1. THE KENNEDY ADMINISTRATION, 1961–3

1. Convergent vs. divergent interests

The Kennedy administration's representation of the Soviet–American relationship was, like all US governments', worded in both adversarial terms and terms that stressed common interests. However, although the actual stressing of the cooperative vs. the conflictive aspects of the relationship varied somewhat from one occasion to another throughout the administration, the distinctive mark of the Kennedy administration's image was a pronounced shift in emphasis from Soviet essentialism in 1961–2 toward a diluted nuclear essentialism during its last year with a marked accentuation of convergent interests.

The early Kennedy administration's inclination to emphasize the adversarial aspects of the Soviet–American relationship was apparent in President Kennedy's words at the inaugural address that the 'new generation of Americans' to which 'the torch has now been passed' would 'pay any price, bear any burden, meet any hardship, support any friend, oppose any foe to assure the survival and the success of liberty.'[4] In the same speech, the President stressed that the existence of all-embracing means of destruction made special demands on all, and in general and very passionate terms he made it clear that the new administration perceived interests in common between the United States and the Soviet Union as the two prominent nuclear adversaries.[5] Thus, from the first day of its incumbency the Kennedy administration's approach to the Soviet Union was marked by heterogeneous features: on the one hand, an obsession not to appear soft on the Soviets and a distinct preoccupation with conveying a tough and virile image and, on the other hand, a penchant for stressing the common interests brought about by 'the dark powers of destruction unleashed by science'.

The general tendency to stress divergent interests *vis-à-vis* the Soviet Union was significantly hardened when the Soviet Union announced, in summer 1961, that it would resume nuclear testing and thus end the moratorium on nuclear tests in force since 1958. A White House statement declared that the Soviet government's decision was in utter disregard of the desire of mankind for a deceleration of the arms race and presented a threat to the entire world by increasing the dangers of a thermonuclear holocaust; two weeks later the White House announced that it had reluctantly been forced to resume America's underground nuclear testing, and in spring 1962 the President announced the resumption of atmospheric testing.[6] Combined with this harder attitude were carefully worded references to the existence of mutual interests between the United States and the Soviet Union in the nuclear age: either the mutuality of interests was implied in generally worded and emotive references to common interests of all mankind or qualified by the addition 'objectively considered';[7] another frequent formulation were references to opportunities for the United States to persuade the Soviet Union that, in the nuclear age, all nations had a common interest in avoiding nuclear war. A corresponding attitude was when the Soviet Union was given sole responsibility for the cold war as the direct expression of their determination to extend the 'historically inevitable' world revolution by every available means; the cold war was a Soviet program of action and it would end when those who declared it decided to abandon it.[8]

During the Kennedy administration's last year, after the Cuban missile crisis in October 1962 and most clearly demonstrated from summer 1963, the US government's image of the Soviet–American relationship in the nuclear age changed markedly. The word 'détente' came in to vogue, references to common Soviet–American interests became much more prominent and were without the former reservations; the exclusive assignment of responsibility for the cold war to the Soviet Union disappeared and the administration began to call for a re-examination of *American* attitudes toward peace, toward the Soviet Union and the cold war.

The new image was most clearly heralded in a speech given by President Kennedy in June 1963.[9] The President used what he called 'the new face of war' as a starting point: total war made no sense when great powers maintained large and invulnerable nuclear forces and could refuse to surrender without resorting to these weapons containing several times more explosive power than delivered in the Second World War; a nuclear war would be deadly to all corners of the globe and to generations yet unborn. Speaking of peace, the President portrayed it as the necessary rational end of rational men contrary to the absolute, infinite concept of universal peace and goodwill of which some fantasists and fanatics dream; as a practical and viable way to peace, he advocated not a sudden revolution in human nature but a gradual evolution in human institutions based on a series of concrete actions and agreements in the interests of all concerned. Most conspicuously, President Kennedy called upon Americans to pursue peace by looking inward and re-examining their own attitudes toward the Soviet Union and the cold war. Soviet propaganda was discouraging and as an example the President quoted some harsh anti-American sentences from a

Soviet text on military strategy and warned the American people not to fall into the same trap as the Soviets and see only a distorted and disparate view of the other side, not to see conflict as inevitable, accommodation as impossible and communication as nothing more than an exchange of threats. Both the United States and the Soviet Union, Kennedy declared, were caught up in a vicious and dangerous cycle in which suspicion on one side bred suspicion on the other, and new weapons begot counter-weapons.

President Kennedy also asserted that the Communists' drive to impose their political system on others was the primary cause of world tension, but while one ought not to be blind to differences between the United States and the Soviet Union, it was essential to direct attention to common interests and to the means by which any differences could be resolved. Among the major world powers the United States and the Soviet Union were unique in never having been at war with each other and the President stated that no nation in the history of war had ever suffered more than the Soviet Union in the Second World War. Both the Soviet and the American people had a strong abhorrence of war and today the United States as well as the Soviet Union had a mutual interest in a just and genuine peace and in halting the arms race. Above all, it was important that nuclear powers avert confrontations which could bring an adversary to a choice of either humiliating retreat or nuclear war. The United States, Kennedy stated, sought to relax tensions without relaxing its guard. Even if it was impossible to resolve differences, the United States could help make the world safe for diversity.

Later in 1963, after the Limited Test Ban Treaty (LTBT) had been signed in August, President Kennedy, as well as other prominent spokesmen for the administration, reasserted some of these views but in a more diluted version stressing, for instance, that the United States had no illusions about communist methods or communist goals, and therefore America's war readiness had to be maintained while the quest for peace continued. [10] In the same vein, Secretary Rusk stated that while the United States and the Soviet Union had a common interest, based on the nature of nuclear weapons which meant that a full-scale nuclear war could erase all that man had built over centuries, the United States had to bear in mind that the Soviet aim was still to establish a communist world. [11] Although these views were more in accordance with views put forward by the early Kennedy administration, the change in the administration's image was still conspicuous.

During the last year of the Kennedy administration, i.e. both before and after Kennedy's speech in June and the signing of the Test Ban Treaty, Secretary McNamara began, in often specific and unambiguous terms, to state that the mutual vulnerability of the United States and the Soviet Union to the other's nuclear attack was an inescapable fact. Larger American nuclear forces, McNamara stated, would have only a decreasing incremental effect in limiting the damage to the United States and its allies in a nuclear war, and he suggested that this should be accepted as one of the determinants of American nuclear policy. Thus the balance of terror reasoning, even if not always that phrase, began to emerge in the American image.[12]

2. Deterrence

The Kennedy administration's enunciations on the conditions of nuclear deterrence during the first two years of its incumbency were marked by general references to the need for assured retaliatory forces as well as more specific statements demonstrating a counterforce image of the deterrence role *vis-à-vis* the Soviet Union. During the last year of the administration, however, declarations on nuclear deterrence in the Soviet–American relationship showed an incipient manifestation of some new ideas similar to nuclear essentialism, presented in an unfinished state and an exploratory way.

In accordance with the general inclination to convey an image of virility, President Kennedy declared at his inaugural address that only when America's arms were 'sufficient beyond doubt can we be certain beyond doubt that they will never be employed'.[13] This sentiment was repeated during the following years in that the survivability of American second-strike forces was emphasized as a necessary condition for deterring a Soviet nuclear attack on the United States or its allies. Thus a typical statement pointed to the necessity of 'making clear to a potential aggressor that sufficient retaliatory forces will be able to survive a first strike and penetrate his defenses in order to inflict unacceptable losses upon him'.[14] At the same time, President Kennedy stressed the need for civil defense: because the deterrence concept assumed rational calculations by rational men and history had proved that assumption sometimes to be faulty, some civil defense measures were justifiable as an insurance for the civilian population.[15]

The early Kennedy administration's reasoning on deterrence was elaborated in a number of statements by Secretary McNamara emphasizing that the requirement for strategic retaliatory forces was to deter war by their capability to destroy the enemy's war-making capabilities. This criterion was represented as lending itself to reasonably precise calculation, in contrast to most other military requirements.[16] The distinct counterforce role attached to strategic nuclear forces was further elaborated and given a new twist in an address by McNamara in June 1962, when he stated that the United States had come to the conclusion that, as far as was feasible, basic military strategy in general nuclear war should be approached in much the same way that conventional military operations had been regarded, i.e. that the principal military objective in a nuclear war should be the destruction of the enemy's military forces, not its civilian population.[17] In this way, according to McNamara, it was possible to retain, even in the face of a massive surprise attack on the United States, sufficient reserve striking power to destroy an enemy society if driven to it, in this way the United

States would give any opponent the strongest imaginable incentive to refrain from striking its cities. McNamara stressed the importance of a centrally-controlled strategy if nuclear war should occur despite all efforts to avert it.

During the last year of the Kennedy administration after the Cuban missile crisis of October 1962, the administration began abandoning important elements of that reasoning on deterrence. In President Kennedy's address during the height of the missile crisis he had threatened a 'full retaliatory response' against the Soviet Union if any missiles sited on Cuba were fired against any nation in the Western hemisphere.[18] This turn toward a kind of 'deterrence only' thinking was restated throughout 1963 with a slowly incipient and highly cautious accentuation of the mutuality aspect as the most conspicuous new element. Thus, in January, Secretary McNamara declared that it was becoming increasingly improbable that either side could destroy a sufficiently large portion of the other's strategic nuclear forces, either by surprise or otherwise, to preclude a devastating retaliatory blow, and this might result in 'mutual deterrence ... still a grim prospect'.[19] Elaborating the conditions for deterrence, McNamara reiterated the survivability criteria for America's second-strike forces and noted that even if the United States doubled or tripled its strategic forces, it was becoming increasingly difficult to limit damage to the United States in case of nuclear war. Hence, with the growth in Soviet nuclear forces the range of contingencies in which American nuclear deterrence was credible had narrowed and since deterrence depended in large measure on the restraint, the moderation and the rationality of the potential opponent, this constituted a basic strategic dilemma for the future. The need for flexibility in retaliatory options was still stressed in the way that the expediency of a capability to destroy the enemy's war-making potential was maintained, as was the need for maintaining some deterrence forces after a nuclear war had begun; however, this was now supplemented more explicitly with the possibility of striking back at the Soviet urban and industrial complex in a 'controlled and deliberate way', presumably meaning that a counterforce strategy was downgraded as a viable option.

The late Kennedy administration's public reasoning on deterrence thus represented a retreat from the distinct counterforce and damage-limitation notions resembling a Soviet essentialism thinking on deterrence prevalent during its first years. The limited nature, however, of the retreat has to be noted and the new thinking was presented in a highly tentative manner most conspicuous in the way Secretary McNamara approached the idea of a nuclear stalemate between the United States and the Soviet Union.

3.   The political significance of nuclear forces

Several of the Kennedy administration's statements indicated an image that the common impact of both the relative size of American nuclear forces compared to Soviet forces and the actual working out of American nuclear policy was a significant asset in the overall political contest between the free world and communism, and this Soviet essentialist image did not change appreciably during Kennedy's incumbency.

The inclination to attach political significance to nuclear force levels was demonstrated in various ways. Thus the administration frequently referred to the need for keeping America's deterrent 'strong' or 'strengthening' America's strategic nuclear forces, because this would have a general psychological and political impact on the world-wide contest between the United States representing the free world and the Soviet Union representing world communism.[20] Another indication of this thinking were statements asserting as a fact that the United States possessed nuclear superiority and had a resolute will to maintain it. On some occasions Secretary McNamara seemed to define superiority as tantamount to a second-strike capability or simply as having a greater number of warheads than the 'Communist bloc'[21] but in general, the actual meaning of the term 'nuclear superiority' was vague, *apart* from the fact that all spokesmen for the administration agreed that superiority was worth having in order to maintain America's position in world affairs.

The Kennedy administration's reasoning on the political significance of nuclear forces and nuclear policy appeared most clearly when some publicly conspicuous Soviet nuclear policy action prompted the US government to issue a statement. When the Soviet Union announced its resumption of nuclear testing in August 1961 the administration portrayed it as part of the Soviet campaign of fear and as a form of atomic blackmail, designed to substitute terror for reason in the international arena: what the Soviet Union was testing were not only nuclear devices but the will and determination of the free world to defend freedom.[22] In the same way, when the Soviet Union detonated a 50 MT bomb in the autumn of 1961, the administration declared that since such a test had no military value and was unnecessary for developing nuclear weapons, it was a political act designed to frighten and panic, and chosen with an eye on Berlin and the 22nd Congress of SUKP.[23] A similar perception was presented by President Kennedy after the Cuban missile crisis: Soviet missiles in Cuba were not for use in a nuclear war but they changed the balance of power politically. As Kennedy expressed it: 'It would have appeared to, and appearances contribute to reality'.[24]

Perceiving the political significance of nuclear policy, especially nuclear tests, in that way, the administration concurrently declared that American nuclear stockpiles were wholly adequate for the defense of the United States and the free world; the Soviet attempt to use the nuclear threat for political purposes was unavailing because the United States possessed and would maintain nuclear superiority and would not, unlike the Soviet Union, undertake nuclear tests for psychological and political reasons.[25] Later, in the spring of 1962, when the administration announced its own resumption of atmospheric tests, the line of reasoning on the political impact of nuclear policy followed a slightly different path: while still disclaiming American tests for political and psychological reasons, it was stated as obvious that the United States could not *avoid* tests for these reasons. Soviet leaders were watching America's resolve on this issue and should America fail to follow the dictates of its own security, the Soviet would chalk it up, not to goodwill, but to a failure of will – not to American confidence in its own superiority, but to fear of world opinion, the very world opinion for which they had shown such contempt, and they could well be encouraged by such signs of weakness to plan new test series which might alter the balance of power.[26]

In the Kennedy administration's image of the political significance of nuclear policies, most unambiguously in its presentations of nuclear test policies, it was crucial that the aspired resolution in American nuclear policy was seen as a necessary political counter to the Soviet resolution; the Soviet leaders were perceived as cynically attempting to exploit world opinion's fear of the nuclear bomb and therefore a countering display of resolve from the United States was necessary. However, in reasoning on how to meet the challenge of resolve the administration vacillated: some deference to world opinion was legitimate but too much yielding was dangerous because it could suggest a fear of Soviet propaganda and America's friends around the world would come to insist on the United States doing what was necessary to protect their security. Where was the breaking point between fear of the bomb and fear of Soviet propaganda on the bomb? The administration's image displayed both its awareness of the problem and its uncertainty on how to meet it.

4. Negotiations

The Kennedy administration's image of negotiating and entering into agreements with the Soviet Union on nuclear issues was marked by different, partly divergent, trends of which one became predominant toward the end of the administration and was elaborated as a more comprehensive vision of the role of nuclear arms control between the United States and the Soviet Union, showing an incipient endorsement of nuclear essentialism.

Two different strains were prevalent early in the administration. On the one hand, it was stated that the mere existence of nuclear weapons was a source of distrust and discord, and therefore the United States and the Soviet Union shared common interests in negotiating and reaching agreements which could lessen the threat to all countries; the arms race generated its own tensions and if a way could be found to limit that race before broad political issues were resolved, it was worth making the effort. On the other hand, it was stressed that the key to this was not in American hands; disarmament measures could not occur if those who were prepared to act in good faith and with full public knowledge were to become what Secretary Rusk called 'dupes and victims' and since the hopes for peace and disarmament had often been frustrated by the Soviet Union, Soviet leaders really held the crucial key in their hands.[27] In the same vein, President Kennedy declared that while it was a test of America's national maturity to accept the fact that negotiations were not a contest spelling victory or defeat, no one should be under the illusion that negotiations for the sake of negotiations always advanced the cause of peace.[28]

In outlining such ideas on the potential value of negotiations, the Kennedy administration cited a number of specific dangers which the United States and the Soviet Union shared and which could form the basis for early agreements. Among these were the proliferation of nuclear weapons to new countries, a danger which was adduced as obvious to both countries as well as all others. Another was the outbreak of war by accident, miscalculation or failure of communications, and this danger was presented as growing as modern weapons became more complex and command and control difficulties increased with the result that the premium was on ever-faster reaction in crises; also the placement of vehicles carrying weapons of mass destruction in outer space was mentioned as a specific danger. In these areas the common interests were viewed as real and tangible: negotiations should build on this, aiming at the achievement of concrete agreements which could mitigate the dangers.[29]

As the obvious place to begin the entering of a treaty before summer 1961 was frequently mentioned to end nuclear tests, first by continuing the voluntary test moratorium in force since 1958, and then stopping any new series of tests. Citing the evidence of the Soviet resumption of tests, the administration, however, strongly emphasized the need for on-site inspections to assure the proper verification of a treaty banning underground tests; an open society like the United States could not undertake with a closed society like the Soviet Union an arrangement which could not be verified and, in general, the need for an active American policy to *enforce* the Soviet Union to participate positively in the arms control process was predominant in American statements on negotiations from summer 1961 until early 1963. Thus in March 1962 President Kennedy declared in a speech on nuclear testing and disarmament that the basic lesson of three years and 353 negotiating sessions at Geneva on a test ban was that the Soviets would not agree to an effective ban on nuclear tests as long as a new series of offers and prolonged negotiations, or a new uninspected moratorium would enable them once again to prevent the West from testing while they prepared their own tests in secret. Therefore, the American decision to resume tests after the Soviets had resumed theirs would actually enhance the prospects for an agreement.[30]

In the last year of the Kennedy presidency, the positive evaluation of negotiating and reaching agreements with the Soviet Union on nuclear matters became markedly more pronounced, and this attitude was noted before President Kennedy's speech in June 1963 (cf. pp. 37–8) and the signing of the Test Ban Treaty in summer 1963. Directly relating the issue of negotiating on nuclear matters to the approaching situation of mutual deterrence, Secretary McNamara referred in January to the need for creating some 'institutional arrangements' which would reduce the need for either side to resort to the use of strategic nuclear weapons in moments of acute international tension.[31] Later, in the spring of 1963, Dean Rusk elaborated some special arguments for a test ban treaty and related them to the wider effect of the contemplated institutional arrangements for verification: even if a test ban treaty would obviously not result in any substantial opening up of the Soviet society, it could have a very important impact on Soviet attitude toward secrecy in that a treaty, operating effectively and in ways which demonstrated that the inspection connected with it did not jeopardize Soviet security or result in any particular embarrassments to the Soviet Union and its people, could make the Soviet leadership more inclined to enter into similar arrangements. The first step, Secretary Rusk stated, seemed to be the most difficult and if it could be made successfully, then further steps in the same direction might be taken with less difficulty.[32]

This vision of the beneficial impact of Soviet–American arms control measures, based upon the Soviets' 'learning experience' from negotiating and carrying out Soviet–American agreements, appeared in other statements before and after the Limited Test Ban Treaty and the 'Hot Line' agreement were signed in the summer of 1963. In his address in June, President Kennedy spoke in passionate terms about assuring peace as requiring increased contact and communication and better understanding between the United States and the Soviet Union. As one step in this direction he mentioned the proposal for a direct line between Moscow and Washington to avoid the dangerous delays, misunderstandings and misreadings of the other's actions which might occur at a time of crisis. After LTBT had been signed Kennedy presented it as a 'victory for mankind' reflecting 'no concessions either to or by the Soviet Union'.[33] The President declared that the treaty could be a step toward broader areas of agreement and reduced world tensions and it could symbolize the end of one era and the beginning of another if both sides could gain confidence and experience in peaceful collaboration; thereby, the treaty might well become an historic landmark in man's age-old pursuit of peace. Kennedy also emphasized that the treaty would strengthen America's security far more than the continuation of unrestricted testing because in 'today's world', a nation's security did not always increase as its arms increased when the adversary was doing the same. He denounced the idea that unlimited competition in the testing and development of new types of destructive nuclear weapons would make the world safer for either side and looked forward to further agreements springing from the mutual interest in avoiding mutual destruction but, at the same time, the President added that these would require long and careful negotiations. Altogether, Kennedy's defense of the treaty was a mixture of both passionate rhetoric and warnings against fostering too high hopes of Soviet–American negotiations.[34]

During the autumn of 1963 some members of the Kennedy administration elaborated a vision of the long-term impact of arms control negotiations with the Soviet Union which distinctly suggested a nuclear essentialist thinking. The central reasoning was that since the balance of terror did not provide a satisfactory long-term solution to the nuclear danger, the United States had to work toward the development of an international machinery which gradually but ultimately could replace national military forces as guarantors of security. While it was necessary to maintain a strong military posture, limited arms control measures could promote stability by reducing suspicions and the dangers of stumbling into a nuclear exchange through accidents, misunderstandings, or the tensions that could develop out of an uncontrolled arms race; disarmament was a long-term goal but at the present time, according to this thinking, the major effort must be concentrated on arms control measures, including informal contacts between American and Soviet military officers which could result in some practical new suggestions for reducing the risks imposed by the new weapons technology.[35]

However, various spokesmen for the administration frequently supplemented their more visionary and, occasionally, eulogistic presentations of arms control negotiations and agreements with more prosaic evaluations. Thus, President Kennedy declared that the United States and the Soviet Union still had wholly different concepts of the world, its freedom and its future, which set limits on the possibilities of agreements. Secretary Rusk pointed to the continuous need for American vigilance and dampened down the hopes about what to accomplish through further negotiations because there could be no assured and lasting peace until communist leaders abandoned their goal of a world revolution. Secretary McNamara opined that the most serious risk of the LTBT was euphoria: the United States had to guard against a condition of mind which allowed it to become lax in its defenses; since the treaty was a product of America's military built-up, further progress in arms control agreements with the Soviet Union depended critically on the maintenance of that strength.[36] Altogether, the Kenndey administration's notable swing toward endorsing arms control negotiations with the Soviet Union, most marked in speeches by a few subordinate members of the administration but occasionally also in speeches by its superior members, was restrained by several warnings against exaggerated American visions.

5. The Soviet view

The dominating feature of the Kennedy administration's image of the Soviet view of nuclear weapons was an assertion that the Soviet leaders were slowly coming to share the view that a nuclear war would be a disaster for everybody. That assertion, however, was modified and qualified in various ways during the administration's incumbency, ending in 1963 in a composite of images which welcomed the greater realism of the new Soviet view but still cautioned against any precipitate interpretation of the Soviet change.

The early Kennedy administration only dealt with the issue of the Soviet view of nuclear weapons on a few occasions and, compared to other aspects of the Soviet Union as a nuclear adversary, that problem was not a major preoccupation of the US government during the early 1960s. The principal characteristic of its statements was that Soviet leaders 'now' were sincerely convinced that a general nuclear war would be a disaster for the Soviet Union too: Premier Krushchev's description of nuclear war as madness was cited to substantiate this. That benign interpretation of the Soviet view, however, was displaced when the Soviet Union resumed its nuclear tests in late August 1961; in commenting on that Soviet act it was emphasized that the Soviets used the nuclear threat as a means for atomic blackmail to obtain its own political ends.[37]

Statements asserting that the Soviet Union was coming to share the view that nuclear war would be a disaster for everybody were sometimes expressed in the special way that the Soviets needed active American persuasion to demonstrate that view in their actual policy. Thus in the summer of 1962, in a statement by President Kennedy on the resumption of negotiations in the Eighteen-Nation Disarmament Committee in Geneva, it was declared that the renewed sessions presented one more opportunity to persuade the Soviet Union that in a nuclear age all nations had a common interest in preserving their mutual security against the growing perils of the arms race.[38] On the other hand, that interpretation of the peculiar character of the Soviet view was on other occasions, also prior to the distinctly benign interpretations in 1963, wholly absent and replaced by a statement simply asserting that the leaders of the Soviet Union knew as well as 'we' that 'victory' in a widespread nuclear war would mean the destruction of civilization; therefore the prospect of a Soviet Union laid waste must weigh heavily on the minds of a Soviet leaders.[39]

During the last year of the Kennedy administration the benign portrayals of the Soviet approach to war, peace and nuclear weapons were clearly predominant and their weight was strengthened by references to the sufferings of the Soviet people during the Second World War. In President Kennedy's address of June 1963, cited above, a favorable interpretation of the Soviet view was clearly expressed when the President mentioned the American and the Soviet peoples' mutual abhorrence of war and explicitly stated that no nation had ever suffered more in a war than the Soviet Union in the Second World War. Similar references to the Russians' historical experience were applied when members of the administration advocated the LTBT during the summer and autumn of 1963 and sometimes the current consequences of Russian and Soviet history were drawn in unusually distinct and benign ways.[40] Another consideration demonstrating an optimistic nuclear essentialist reading of Soviet nuclear policy was offered by McNamara, who stated that the Soviets did not have anything like the number of missiles necessary to threaten the *Minuteman* missiles and nor did they appear to have any immediate plans to acquire such a capacity. On the same occasion, McNamara adduced as his interpretation of the Soviet acceptance of the American proposal for a limited test ban that it 'offers some evidence, I think, that its leadership have at last grasped an essential fact – that the sheer multiplication of a nation's destructive nuclear capability does not necessarily produce a net increase in its security'.[41] This was one of the most notable cases where a prominent member of the Kennedy administration construed the Soviet view of nuclear weapons as symmetrical to the administration's, or his own, view.

While maintaining that the Soviet leaders had begun to recognize the mutual interest with the United States in avoiding nuclear war, various prominent spokesmen for the administration still reiterated that the Soviet leadership remained committed to world domination and establishing a communist world. However, contrary to the Chinese communists, it was stressed, the Soviet communist leadership was not willing to risk a nuclear war in their pursuit of that goal and the Sino-Soviet split played a major role when some members of the Kennedy administration expounded the relationship between the Soviet view of nuclear weapons and the Soviet goal of world dominance: the incipient benign Soviet view of nuclear war was opposed to the malign Chinese view.[42] Still, although these readings of the Soviet view were emphasized by the late Kennedy presidency, it was cautious in not overdoing the change in Soviet policy: only time would tell if the changes were caused by forces less transitory than those which had brought tactical shifts in the past.

2.   THE JOHNSON ADMINISTRATION, 1963–9

1.   Convergent vs. divergent interests

The Johnson administration expressed its belief in converging American and Soviet interests in the nuclear age in generally worded and sometimes rather passionate statements stressing that the avoidance of nuclear war was a common concern of all mankind. Compared to the Kennedy administration, these statements were less mixed with assertive manifestations of Soviet–American political contrasts but, at the same time, declarations pointing to the need for a Soviet–American accommodation were less conspicuous during the Johnson presidency, especially when comparing manifestations made by the two presidents; thus there was no address by President Johnson corresponding to Kennedy's inauguration speech and no one corresponding to Kennedy's speech of June 1963. From the mid-1960s it was also characteristic that a part of the US government began endorsing the notion of a common Soviet–American nuclear predicament in more technical and detached terms, elaborating a complex set of ideas where the reasoning on converging Soviet and American interests were closely related to a specific reasoning on deterrence and the role of communications and negotiations between the two superpowers. In that way, several distinct parts of nuclear essentialism were prominent in the American government's declarations through the later half of the 1960s.

The starting point for emphasizing converging interests between the United States and the Soviet Union despite political differences was presented as, simply, survival, and the two countries had this mutuality of interest common with all humanity. As expressed by Dean Rusk, the phrase 'survival of man' had moved out of the realm of rhetoric into the realm of practical necessity for the statesmen of the world; since the appearance of nuclear weapons, man has acquired the power to obliterate himself from the face of the earth and man's survival has thus come at stake: 'for the first time in history, two nations live each with its hands on the jugular of the other – and of every other nations.'[43] Nuclear weapons were not simply bigger and more destructive than other weapons; with the existence of nuclear weapons, war had come to wear a new face in that a nuclear war would be far different, not only in degree but in kind, from any war ever fought before simply because there would be no victors and this meant that man's future has become overshadowed with the permanent possibility of thermonuclear holocaust. As stated by Secretary McNamara: 'about that fact, we are no longer free'; the freedom consisted rather in facing the matter rationally and realistically and discussing actions to minimize the danger.[44]

While all members of the Johnson administration expressed such basic notions on the conditions of the nuclear age, McNamara was clearly the most prominent and distinct advocate; moreover, he sometimes adduced further consequences and cited some considerations which were not mentioned, at least not directly, by other government spokesmen. In the speech where he most distinctly elaborated this reasoning on the nuclear dilemma, in San Francisco, on 18 September 1967, he pointed to some special psychological dangers in deciding on nuclear issues: first, a psychological lapse into an oversimplification about the adequacy of nuclear power and, second, a kind of 'mad momentum' intrinsic to the development of all new nuclear weapons in that if a weapons system worked, and worked well, there was a strong pressure from many directions to procure and deploy the weapon out of all proportion to the prudent level required. At the same occasion McNamara declared that America's nuclear forces were 'greater that we had originally planned and in fact more than we require'[45] – an unprecedented statement from an American (or any) Defense Secretary.

The crucial feature characterizing the American–Soviet nuclear relationship was, according to McNamara, that both the United States and the Soviet Union had an assured second-strike capability, and in these years McNamara and his closest associates in the Defense Department endeavored to elaborate this predicament and its political consequences in often rather technical and dispassionate terms. The United States had the physical capacity to destroy the Soviet Union, even if the Soviets tried to destroy the United States first, and the Soviet Union had the capacity to destroy the United States, even if the United States could destroy the Soviet first. Neither of the two superpowers could attack the other, even by surprise, without suffering massive damage in retaliation and, thus, the one superpower's situation was a mirror image of the other's. This fundamental trait of both superpowers' nuclear predicament was inescapable; neither the Soviet Union nor the United States could deprive the other of its second-strike capability either by providing anything approaching perfect protection for its population or by developing much larger nuclear forces to knock out the other's retaliatory forces. Given the radical destructive capability of even a small residual nuclear force, this was impossible. If one superpower attempted to deprive the other of its assured destruction capability, the extra costs incurred in such futile efforts were substantially higher than the costs necessary to maintain an assured second-strike capability for the other. The crux of the matter, it was emphasized repeatedly, was that it was precisely this mutual capability to destroy one another and, conversely, the mutual inability to prevent such destruction, that provided both the Soviet Union and the United States with the strongest possible motive to avoid a strategic nuclear war.[46]

Besides drawing a number of specific conclusions concerning both unilateral American nuclear policy and bilateral Soviet–American negotiations (cf. sections 2 and 4 below) the Johnson administration argued in general terms that since averting nuclear war hung heavily on the wisdom and judgment of the United States and the Soviet Union, the two superpowers had a special responsibility and therefore the Soviet–American relationship must be at the heart of America's concern. While differing principles and values divided the two nations, this should not divert them from acts of common endeavor to diminish the nuclear danger, it was stated. Détente could not mean that the basic issues which had given rise to the cold war were over and done with, but both the United States and the Soviet Union shared a common interest and a common responsibility to lessen tensions and build a more secure world. Détente obviously must work both ways. Discharging the mutual responsibility of the United States and the Soviet Union, the dogmas and vocabularies of the cold war were vicious, and dissociations from the policies of that period were sometimes strong in the Johnson administration's declarations *along with* stressing that the cold war had not only been caused by 'misunderstandings'; 'now', however, both superpowers had to search for every possible area of cooperation that might conceivably enhance, no matter how slightly or how slowly, the prospect for cooperation. Again, Secretary McNamara put these ideas in lucid terms suggesting a thrust toward the domestic audience: 'in a thermonuclear world, we cannot afford any political acrophobia. ... By building bridges to those who make themselves our adversaries "we can help gradually to create a community of trust, and a community of effort".'[47]

Assessing the Johnson administration's image of convergent vs. divergent interests, it is worth noting both the marked inclination to stress the significance of convergent interests and the limits to this inclination. While hailing the prospect of merging superpower interests, the American government frequently used phrases that indicated its hesitation not to overstate the mutuality of the Soviet–American nuclear predicament. Besides, there were conspicuous differences between the modes of expression applied by various leading members of the administration and current problems often influenced actual statements the one way or the other as well. Still, the general thrust toward nuclear essentialism during the latter half of the 1960s is manifest, especially when compared to the early years of the decade.

2. Deterrence

The starting point for the Johnson administration's image of nuclear deterrence *vis-à-vis* the Soviet Union was the mutual assured destruction condition perceived as an inescapable fact. Outlining this, it must be noted, however, that the US government's view of deterrence during the latter part of the 1960s was almost exclusively presented by the Secretary of Defense and his closest associates, especially in the Defense Department. Even if there is always some division of labor concerning public statements on the Soviet Union as a nuclear adversary, the detailed elaboration of this administration's reasoning on deterrence was done more overtly than usual in US governments by a special part of the administration. This is worth noting, in particular because these spokesmen obviously attached great significance to a correct reading of their nuclear essentialist approach to deterrence.

Applying this starting point, the critical priority for America's strategic nuclear deterrence policy was always phrased as maintaining an assured destruction (AD) capability, i.e. a reliable offensive nuclear force capable of destroying the Soviet Union as a viable society even after a well planned and executed surprise Soviet attack on US forces. Such a capability would, it was maintained, with a high degree of confidence, ensure that the United States could, under all foreseeable conditions, deter a calculated, deliberate nuclear attack on the United States or – it was sometimes added – on its allies.[48]

The necessary AD capability was specified in precise numbers indicating the amount of destruction the administration considered 'unacceptable' to the Soviets and thereby furnishing the United States with an adequate deterrent. The actual numbers changed from year to year but the basic thinking remained the same. In 1965 when this reasoning was first introduced in Secretary McNamara's statement on the fiscal year 1966 defense budget, it was stated that the capability to destroy one-quarter to one-third of the Soviet population and about two-thirds of its industrial capacity should serve as an effective deterrent even against the highest projected Soviet nuclear force to inflict a well-coordinated surprise attack against the United States. In the Statements in the following four years from McNamara and his successor as Secretary of Defense, Clark Clifford, the corresponding numbers changed between, respectively, one-fifth to 'more that two-fifths' and one-half to three-quarters, the higher numbers provided by Secretary Clifford in the Johnson administration's last Statement, indicating that the criteria for having an assured destruction capability were tightened.[49] Beyond these levels, it was argued, any further increments of America's offensive nuclear forces would not appreciably change the results. As a special characteristic of these numerical conditions for an AD capability and their actual fulfillment, it was stressed that a relatively small portion of America's offensive strategic forces were necessary for inflicting the 'unacceptable' levels of destruction after a Soviet attack (cf. also the above mentioned citation from a speech by McNamara on the surplus of America's nuclear forces).

It was crucial to this deterrence concept that it was America's assured second-strike capability that provided the deterrent, not America's ability to limit damage to itself in case of a Soviet attack. At the same time, however, it was stated that American strategic defensive forces, usually associated with a damage-limitation function, could also contribute to the AD capability by intercepting and destroying Soviet offensive weapons before they reached American offensive forces; analogously, strategic offensive forces, usually associated with the AD capability could also contribute to damage limitation by attacking enemy delivery vehicles on their bases or launch sites, provided they could reach those before they were launched at American cities.[50] However it was emphasized over and over again that due to a cost-exchange ratio highly favorable to offensive forces, for strategic defensive forces to contribute significantly to the AD capability in this way was impossible to accomplish but, all the same, this blurring line beween offensive and defensive forces as to their respective assured destruction and damage limitation role was noted, although downgraded, by the administration.

The downgrading of strategic defensive forces for deterrence appeared by a steady rejection of the utility of an Anti-Ballistic Missile (ABM) system to defend American cities. In arguing against ABM, the cost-exchange ratio favorable to offensive forces was closely related to an action–reaction assumption as to the deployment of defensive and offensive nuclear forces in both superpowers: any attempt to deprive the opponent of his AD capability by building, or just initiating the building of, an effective defense of one's own population against ballistic missiles would be countered by the opponent's enlargement of his offensive forces, and very easily so due to the given cost-exchange ratio. This reasoning assumed a particularly insistent character when McNamara in 1967, in the speech in San Francisco,[51] recommended a light China-oriented ABM system, the Sentinel system, and strongly emphasized that its objective was not to protect American cities against a Soviet attack. A concurrent benefit of this ABM system was, according to McNamara, that it could help defending the American missile force against a Soviet attack and thereby add greater effectiveness to the strategic offensive forces' assured destruction function. But he stressed that the danger in deploying a light Chinese-oriented ABM system was that pressures would develop to expand it into a heavy Soviet-oriented ABM shield. That temptation, McNamara declared, must be resisted firmly, not only because it would in effect be no adequate shield at all, but also because it would be a strong inducement for the Soviets vastly to increase their own strategic forces.

One distinguishing mark of the administration's reasoning on deterrence was the distinction between different levels of nuclear weapons, each with its own requirements. Thus, a theater nuclear capability was needed to deter Soviet use of tactical nuclear weapons in an attack on Western Europe, to permit NATO to respond 'in kind'; NATO theater nuclear capabilities should provide a broad, flexible range of nuclear options and the means to implement them but, it was added, it was not yet clear how theater nuclear war could actually be executed without incurring a very serious risk of escalating to general nuclear war. A closely related feature of the administration's thinking was that since strategic nuclear weapons would deter only a narrow range of threats, there was a need for the United States and its allies to maintain substantial conventional military forces fully capable of dealing with a wide spectrum of lesser forms of aggression. As McNamara stated in a telling observation in the San Francisco speech: 'one cannot fashion a credible deterrent out of an incredible action' and therefore it was necessary to possess a whole range of graduated deterrents, each of them fully credible in its own context. [52]

Elaborating the AD image of US nuclear forces' deterrent role, McNamara occasionally considered different troubling aspects of the Soviet force development but, after having discussed these developments and noted that prudence dictated the United States steadily to be in a position to strengthen its AD capability, he always concluded that America had and would continue to possess the necessary deterrent capability. Thus noting in 1968 that the most severe threat to America's AD capability was a Soviet development of a substantial hard target kill capability in the form of highly accurate small ICBMs or MIRVed large ICBMs, together with an extensive, effective ABM defense, he stated that these two Soviet actions could conceivably seriously degrade America's assured destruction capability. Both threats were, McNamara declared, quantitatively far greater than those projected in the latest intelligence estimates but, all the same, he concluded that even though the threat of accurate Soviet ICBMs was extremely unlikely, the United States had already taken account of that possibility in its longer range force planning. In January 1969, Secretary

Clifford commented on that problem that it was 'quite evident' that if the Soviets achieved greater accuracy with their ICBMs, together with a MIRV capability, the American land-based missiles would become increasingly vulnerable to a first strike. Faced with indications of a Soviet ABM deployment, the administration stressed that it had already taken the necessary steps to guarantee America's AD capability but, should the Soviets persist to expand its light and modest ABM deployment, the United States would be forced to take additional steps as to the quantity and quality of its strategic offensive forces. In the same way, intelligence information on a possible Soviet development of a fractional orbital bombardment system (FOBS) was evaluated as not threatening the American second-strike capability.[53]

The US government's image of deterring the Soviet Union during the latter half of the 1960s was thus marked by a rather abstract reasoning focusing on the threat of inflicting unacceptable destruction, clearly resembling nuclear essentialism; at the same time, other trains of thought were present too, as evidenced by the sorting out of different levels of nuclear weaponry each with its own criteria for what constituted sufficiency in terms of military hardware. Coupled with statements that America's strategic nuclear forces more than fulfilled the criteria put forward, and would continue to do so, the administration sometimes, however, showed a certain uneasiness concerning the actual durability of this situation or, rather, its own ability to persuade its audience that America's assured destruction capability was really 'assured', and assured deterrence. The administration never really decided for itself if it should stress that America's AD capability was *assured*, given technological factors, or stress the continuing need for American vigilance. The dangers of both courses were obviously realized.

3.   The political significance of nuclear forces

The Johnson presidency did not express a clear-cut view on the political significance of nuclear forces but it used phrases or referred to some aspect of the nuclear balance between the United States and the Soviet Union in a way which suggested that it perceived nuclear weapons as rendering some, not insignificant, political clout.

The case most obviously illustrating this concerns the handling of the concept 'nuclear superiority'. Sometimes the concept simply referred to superiority in numbers of atomic weapons compared to those of any other nation and it was stated that the administration intended to keep that superiority.[54] At other occasions it was far from clear what was implied by using the term, apart from the assertion that the United States had nuclear superiority and that was definitely worthwhile to preserve for the sake of America's standing in the world. Obviously, the idea of American nuclear superiority and the political impact flowing from that superiority reflected some deep-seated feelings in the Johnson presidency about America's world position. The sensitivity of this problem is illustrated by considering how it was handled by those few members of the administration who, during its last years, directly discussed it and concluded that strategic nuclear weapons had no political or diplomatic function, thus indicating an unambiguous deviation from what otherwise seemed to be a dominant sympathy in the US government for a kind of Soviet essentialism at this point.

Far and away the most distinct manifestation of this view came from Secretary McNamara. He stated[55] unambiguously that the United States had nuclear superiority over the Soviet Union; however, after having considered more closely how this superiority was measured and pointed out the 'blunt, inescapable fact' that the Soviet Union could still effectively destroy the United States, even after absorbing the full weight of an American first strike, he declared that superiority was of little significance. Strategic nuclear weaponry, McNamara stated, involved a particular irony in that, unlike any other era in military history, a substantial numerical superiority of weapons did not effectively translate into political control or diplomatic leverage; while thermonuclear power was almost inconceivably awesome and represented virtually unlimited potential destructiveness, it had proven to be a limited diplomatic instrument. The uniqueness of thermonuclear power, McNamara added, lay in the fact that it was at one and the same time an all-powerful weapon and a very inadequate weapon. This was a difficult lesson for both Americans and for their allies to accept, since there was a strong psycological tendency to regard nuclear forces as a simple and unfailing solution.

Coming primarily from America's most prominent nuclear policy-maker during the 1960s and openly directed also at the domestic American audience, McNamara's unequivocal rejection of the view that strategic nuclear power beyond the level of the assured second-strike capability had any political usability acquired an educating and exhorting quality. This was increased by the fact that the pronouncements solely appeared toward the end of McNamara's incumbency and were different from his declarations during the major part of his seven years as Secretary of Defense. By calling for a close scrutiny of the concept 'nuclear superiority' and elaborating why that notion had no political validity under the condition of mutual deterrence, McNamara and a few others in the Johnson administration evidently felt that they were up against some ingrained American feelings about American military power.[56]

McNamara's successor as Secretary of Defense during the last year of the Johnson administration, Clark Clifford, expressed a corresponding reasoning but in a vaguer fashion and without the sharp edges in McNamara's statements. Clifford maintained his intention to seek diligently to preserve America's 'margin of advantage' in the field of strategic nuclear weapons but, all the same, he reiterated the warnings against illusions that superiority alone would guarantee America's safety when neither the United States nor the Soviet Union could expect to emerge from an all-out nuclear exchange without very grave damage.[57]

4. Negotiations

The US government's public approach to Soviet–American negotiations on unclear issues during the second half of the 1960s was marked by general endorsements of both the arms control concept and concrete proposals for agreements. During the later years of the administration the broad arms control notion was elaborated by a few prominent members of the Johnson administration into some distinct reasonings on the role of communications and negotiations between the superpowers indicating a distinct nuclear essentialism which, however, were downgraded toward the end of the administration.

During the administration's first years its statements on negotiating with the Soviet Union were characterized by generally phrased emphases of the notion that the Soviet Union and the United States as the two nuclear superpowers shared a common responsibility to reach balanced and verifiable arms control and disarmament agreements to avert nuclear war to the benefit of all mankind. The American negotiations policy on nuclear issues *vis-à-vis* the Soviet Union was represented as the most important part of a broader détente policy initiated earlier in the 1960s and as the Soviet attitude to these issues, according to the administration, had undergone a considerable positive evolution – especially as to the Soviet predilection for playing the propaganda theme – American perseverance to find ways of reaching understandings and agreements with the Soviet Union for the control of nuclear weapons had proved correct. The administration emphasized that there were still major political differences between the United States and the Soviet Union but the relation between, on the one hand, unresolved political issues and, on the other hand, arms acquisitions and arms races, was a vicious cycle, as weapons became more numerous and more deadly, fear and tension grew and political differences became more difficult to resolve which, again, could escalate the arms race.[58]

These general themes were combined with concrete proposals on specific issues for negotiations. In January 1964 President Johnson proposed negotiations on a verified freeze of the number and characteristic of strategic nuclear offensive and defensive weapons. Two other proposals were, however, more important features of the administration's approach: first and foremost measures to stop proliferation of nuclear weapons. This was repeatedly emphasized as the most urgent area of possible agreement and extremely important because, as expressed at one occasion, the danger of nuclear war increased geometrically with the increase in the number of nations possessing independent nuclear forces; accordingly, the Non-proliferation Treaty in 1968 was hailed as a landmark proving that the United States and the Soviet Union could move forward. A comprehensive test ban was mentioned too as being in the mutual interest of the superpowers and providing opportunity for a formal agreement to supplement the LTBT from 1963, presented by the Johnson administration as the first vital step toward more comprehensive Soviet–American agreements on nuclear weapons. [59]

During the later years of the Johnson administration the general themes on détente and arms control were elaborated into a specific set of ideas on the role of communicating and negotiating with Soviet Union on strategic nuclear issues. The most prominent and distinct advocate of this strategic nuclear arms control reasoning was, again, Secretary McNamara. The starting point was the mutual assured destruction (MAD) situation and the consequential conditions for maintaining the necessary mutual deterrence; given the existing strategic nuclear arsenals and the continued pressure for build-ups in both countries, negotiated agreements first to limit, and later to reduce, both offensive and defensive strategic nuclear forces were obligatory. It was essential to understand, McNamara stated, [60] that the Soviet Union and the United States mutually influenced one another's strategic plans; both reacted to the other's nuclear build-up with very conservative calculations, stressing their own insufficiency and the other's surplus of nuclear forces. Whatever the Soviets' intentions, whatever America's, actions – or even potential actions – on either side relating to the build-up of nuclear forces, necessarily triggered reactions on the other side, and it was precisely this action–reaction phenomenon of both offensive and defensive nuclear forces that fuelled an arms race and had to be controlled through negotiated arms control.

McNamara illustrated the relevance of this reasoning by noting that the Soviet nuclear build-up had in part been a reaction to the American build-up since the beginning of the 1960s; Soviet strategic planners had undoubtedly reasoned that if the American build-up continued at its accelerated pace, the United States might conceivably reach, in time, a credible first-strike capability against the Soviet Union; that was not the American intention which had been to assure that the Soviets did not reach a first-strike capability but, McNamara stated, 'they could not read our intentions with any greater accuracy than we could read theirs'. The result was that both had strategic nuclear arsenals greatly in excess of a credible, assured second-strike capability and in each case for the same reason wherefore both the United States and the Soviet Union would benefit from a properly safeguarded agreement to limit offensive and defensive strategic nuclear forces. As the most urgent problem during 1967 and 1968, McNamara emphasized the mutual Soviet–American interest in limiting deployment of anti-ballistic missile defense systems; President Johnson had proposed to initiate negotiations on this issue, but both offensive and defensive nuclear weapons should be subject for negotiations.

In putting forward and elaborating this reasoning on strategic nuclear weapons and the need for Soviet–American negotiations in order to limit nuclear arsenals and increase mutual understanding and transparency, McNamara clearly endeavored to present a well-reasoned and intellectually defensible argumentation that could appeal both to the American audience and the Soviet leadership. Actually, some of the speeches where he most lucidly presented this image of the United States and the Soviet Union as mutually interdependent nuclear adversaries acquired something of the mark of a lecture. Thus the San Francisco speech, the clearest case of McNamara's attempts to reason on nuclear issues rather than appeal to emotions, concluded with some generally phrased considerations on man's wisdom in avoiding war as often having been surpassed by his folly in promoting it; however, today, McNamara declared, the consequences of human folly could be the death of hundreds of millions and the possible genetic impairment of a million generations to follow. He added: 'What the world requires in its 22nd year of the atomic age is a new race toward reasonableness'. In that way, the US government's most distinctly reasoned advocacy of nuclear essentialism through the late 1960s could combine with appealing to the emotions and pathos.

The later Johnson administration's image of communicating and negotiating with the Soviet Union on strategic nuclear arms was, however, more compounded than the views presented by the administration's most distinguished spokesman on nuclear policy indicate. Most importantly, Clark Clifford, who succeeded McNamara as Secretary of Defense during the last ten months of the Johnson administration stressed, for instance, that a 'position of substantial strength' was the best position from which the United States could negotiate agreements with the Soviet Union that made the threat of nuclear war increasingly remote. To illustrate this Clifford mentioned the Senate's decision to support construction funds for the Sentinal ABM system because, he argued, with the Soviet Union having for some time been engaged in the actual deployment of a ballistic missile defense, the decision to go ahead with America's own system would improve the chances of negotiations.[61] The conclusion is that McNamara's successor diluted his distinct approach to negotiations, even if this dilution had been heralded in part by McNamara himself.

5. The Soviet view

The Johnson presidency presented the Soviet view of nuclear weapons as a diluted version of nuclear essentialism. The issue of the Soviet view did not play a prominent role as a separate problem during these years but generally the Soviet view was portrayed – or implied – as sober. The dominating notion was that the Soviet familiarity with nuclear weapons at long last had come to have a sobering impact on Soviet thinking on war and peace: the Soviet leadership appeared to recognize a common interest with America in preventing a mutually destructive nuclear war and they genuinely shared a desire to halt the nuclear arms race and ultimately eliminate nuclear weapons. To set off the beneficial Soviet view, it was often contrasted with communist China's continued obstinacy.[62]

Presenting the Soviet view in benign terms and as promoting a positive development between the United States and the Soviet Union after the cold war, a Soviet policy shift of 1963 – which had led to the successful conclusion of the negotiations on the LTBT – was cited. During the middle of the 1960s, the US government especially advanced the interpretation that the Soviet Union was coming to share the opinion that putting a halt to the further spread of nuclear weapons was in the interests of everyone, and when the Non-proliferation Treaty was entered in 1968, it was seen as a further proof of the more realistic Soviet approach to nuclear weapons. In explaining the changing Soviet view, however, spokesmen for the administration followed diverging lines; thus when stating that there was a 'growing group in the Soviet government' who shared the American view, it was added that this group would be better off if the United States sought negotiations with the Soviet Union on strategic arms control; another interpretation of the incipient Soviet realism was that it had come about because the Soviets had no illusions about America's determination to meet force with force.[63]

The more specific Soviet view of the requirements of its nuclear forces was presented by the Johnson administration, primarily Secretary McNamara, as a mirror image of the US government's view: the Soviet goal in deploying strategic nuclear forces was, as America's, to achieve an assured second-strike capability against the other side. Elaborating the specifics of a situation where both sides could be assumed to have the same general strategic objectives, and stressing that it was a two-sided problem, McNamara used technical terms: the Soviet assured destruction problem was America's damage-limitation problem and the Soviet damage-limitation problem was America's assured destruction problem. Hence, if the United States attempted to build a damage-limitation capability for itself, even if that was illusory, the Soviets would be forced to assure their AD capability with an offsetting increase in their offensive strategic forces which, due to the cost-exchange ratio highly favorable to offensive strategic forces, would be very easy for them. Correspondingly, if the Soviets attempted to build up a defensive system against American offensive strategic nuclear forces, the United States would have to, and could easily, overwhelm the Soviet defense system. In the same way, the Soviets must always view America's strategic offensive forces as a potential first-strike threat – just as the United States must view their offensive forces – and this would further induce them to provide for their second-strike capability by reacting to an American build-up of its offensive forces beyond an assured second strike capability.[64] On the other hand, in 1965 McNamara declared there was no indication that the Soviets were seeking to develop a strategic nuclear force as large as the American and that, according to McNamara, meant that the Soviets had decided that they had lost the numbers race and were not seeking to engage the United States in that contest.[65]

On some occasions the administration supplemented this reading of the

Soviet view with references to the special Russian background. As a particular Russian reason for their build-up of defensive nuclear forces toward the end of the 1960s was mentioned their strong emotional and historical predilection to the defense of Mother Russia but, in any case, the conclusion was that maintaining an assured second-strike capability was absolutely essential to their security.[66]

Clark Clifford held similar interpretations of the Soviet view during his short incumbency but in more diluted form and with less intellectual thrust and conviction.[67] The administration's attachment to this reading clearly weakened with McNamara's departure but, altogether, the Johnson administration's image of the Soviet view was strongly marked by its view of the particularities of atomic weapons. When a special Russian angle was hinted at, it was invoked as an additional back-up to substantiate these conclusions.

3.   THE NIXON ADMINISTRATION, 1969–74

1.   Convergent vs. divergent interests

The Nixon administration stressed the significance of convergent interests between the United States and the Soviet Union as the two outstanding nuclear superpowers. Since both had a nuclear capability to destroy each other as well as the rest of the world, they shared an interest in and an obligation to settle their basic political differences without resorting to nuclear war. This view of the mutuality of the nuclear predicament was gradually elaborated into a specific philosophy on the meaning of détente which, compared to US governments' reasoning on détente during the 1960s, was more comprehensive and reflected a kind of conservative statecraft that underlines the responsibility of powerful statesmen; elaborating that conception, it is notable, however, that the early Nixon administration often seemed to avoid the word détente itself. Either way, this image of convergent interests displayed a kind of nuclear essentialism and was closely related to a nuclear essentialist image of negotiations. On the other hand, the Nixon presidency's version of an ideal type A image concerning the significance of convergent interests was not followed by a correspondingly unambiguous ideal type A image of deterrence, as the previous administration had tended to.

Early in the administration, President Nixon stated that although every instinct motivated him to provide the American people with complete protection against a major nuclear attack, it was not 'now' within America's power to do so:[68] even the heaviest defense system designed to protect America's major cities could still not prevent a catastrophic level of US fatalities from a deliberate all-out Soviet attack. Thereafter all statements from the administration on the nuclear relationship between the superpowers were based on the premise that it was unfeasible to erect an effective physical shield against the nuclear threat. The dominating notion in the Nixon administration's representations of this situation was the idea that both the United States and the Soviet Union had come into possession of power singlehandedly capable of exterminating the human race and since the survival of mankind might depend on the decisions of either the Soviet Union or the United States, this created a sort of interdependence for survival.[69]

In portraying this dilemma, the administration emphasized both the nuclear capabilities of the superpowers and their political rivalry. The postwar rivalry between the United States and the Soviet Union was not a result simply of misunderstanding or personal animosities. Bureaucratic momentum and the disillusionment created by decades of fluctuation between hopes and tensions had played a role but the conflict was also rooted in irreconcilable ideologies. Besides, irrespective of ideology, any relationship between the two countries would be highly competitive and marked by the inevitable geopolitical competition of great powers conducting global policies. Despite all this, the United States and the Soviet Union were compelled to coexist; the United States would not retreat from its principles, the Soviet Union would not sacrifice theirs, but in the nuclear age conflict and competition between them would not admit of resolution in the classical sense and it was no longer realistic to allow Soviet–American relations to be predetermined by ideology. Even if the differences between the American and the Soviet systems were sharp and fundamental and America would oppose totalitarianism, it must also keep sight of what was termed the 'hard, cold facts of life in the nuclear age' and therefore 'have the vision to seek out those things which unite us as human beings'.[70]

It followed, according to the administration, that the need for détente was based on common Soviet–American interests in averting nuclear holocaust. Elaborating its thinking on the relation between détente and convergent interests between the two superpowers in limiting the nuclear threat, the Nixon administration explicitly repudiated the idea that a gain for the one was a loss for the other and it stressed that both the United States and the Soviet Union had an obligation to define their interests with special concern for the other. If some nations defined their security in a manner that meant insecurity for others, then peace was threatened and the security of all diminished: this obligation was particularly great for the superpowers on whose decisions the survival of mankind might well depend. The nature of the common nuclear predicament required that both the Soviet Union and America were willing to practice self-restraint, or follow a code of conduct, in the pursuit of their national interests. Such a policy of restraint required reciprocity, concretely expressed in actions in the various areas of world politics.[71] In outlining this reasoning on common security in the nuclear age and defining its concrete manifestations and conditions, the leaders of the Nixon administration often displayed some uncertainty concerning America's ability to maintain such a foreign policy. For instance, when difficulties of striking a balance between accommodating and warning the Soviet Union were indicated, they were noted as originating not only in the composite character of Soviet policy but also in American politics and ideology.

During the later part of the Nixon administration, its pronouncements on converging superpower interests were more frequently supplemented with concerns as to various disturbing elements. The basic conclusions remained largely unchanged, but assumed a more assertive tone. The pace of technology was cited as introducing disturbing elements but, as aired by some members of the administration, these concerns were ill-defined and it was left open which consequences troubling technological trends actually would have as to the character of the common nuclear predicament.[72]

2.   Deterrence

The Nixon presidency's line on deterrence showed some distinct points of resemblance as well as some innovations compared to that type of nuclear essentialism prevalent through the second half of the 1960s. The innovations increasingly came to the fore during President Nixon's tenure and especially toward its end in 1974, the lines of reasoning manifested clear trends away from nuclear essentialism.

The most conspicuous similarity between the early Nixon administration's declaratory policy on deterrence and the predecessor's concerned an inclination to stress the mutuality aspect of strategic deterrence. When President Nixon a few weeks after his installation suggested the *Safeguard* ABM system to replace the Johnson administration's proposal on a *Sentinel* ABM system, he explicitly emphasized that the *Safeguard* system, unlike Sentinel, could not be misinterpreted as a first step toward the construction of a heavy city defense system which would threaten the Soviet deterrent and therefore be provocative.[73] *Safeguard* would protect the American retaliatory forces. The prevailing view was that a dense ABM system was offensive because it would deprive, or could attempt to deprive, the Soviet Union of its deterrent capability, while a defense of America's retaliatory forces, on the contrary, was defensive. In the same vein, when the administration announced other measures to ensure that the American strategic forces would not become vulnerable to a Soviet attack, it stated that it was important to avoid upgrading of America's deterrence forces such that the Soviets could misinterpret it as an attempt to threaten their deterrent. Thus, the basic reasoning was that it was America's interest, as it was Russia's, to avoid a nuclear posture which might appear threatening to the Soviet second-strike capability or a step toward an American first-strike capability, even if illusory, against the Soviet Union.

This declaratory emphasis of the mutuality aspect of American deterrence policy reappeared in various manifestations during President Nixon's tenure, especially when the SALT I agreement was entered into in

1972, but it was downgraded as other concerns increasingly preoccupied the administration. Most marked was continuous uneasiness with the expediency and acceptability of the assured destruction criterion for deterrence. In 1970 President Nixon voiced the fundamental concern by asking if a president, in the event of a nuclear attack, should be left with the single option of ordering the mass destruction of enemy civilians, in the face of the certainty that it would be followed by the mass slaughter of Americans? Corresponding wordings, slightly changed, were reiterated the following years[74] and the innovations in the administration's argumentation on deterrence may be seen as an attempt to address that question properly.

The administration named its strategic nuclear deterrence doctrine 'Sufficiency' or 'Realistic Deterrence'. President Nixon expressed his preference for the term 'sufficiency' as early as in January 1969. Later, the Secretary of Defense, Melvin Laird, outlined the criteria of sufficiency in more detail and named it Realistic Deterrence. When Secretary Laird first presented Realistic Deterrence in March 1971, he stressed that it was a new strategy and not merely a continuation of past policies in new packaging. Past policy had, according to Laird, been responsive and reactive while the new policy was positive and active, and he especially noted that the sufficiency criteria were more comprehensive than the 'retaliatory, or "assured destruction" objective followed in the past'.[75] Laird stated that the criteria for deterrence included four principal objectives: maintaining an adequate second-strike capability to deter an all-out surprise attack on American strategic forces, providing no incentive for the Soviet Union to strike the United States first in a crisis, preventing the Soviet Union from gaining the ability to cause considerably greater urban/industrial destruction than the United States could inflict on the Soviet Union in a nuclear war, and defending against damage from small attacks or accidental launches. The four criteria may adequately be summarized as, respectively, assured destruction, crisis stability, relative advantage and damage denial.

It was noted[76] that American strategic nuclear forces related primarily to the deterrence of a strategic nuclear attack, i.e. an attack on the United States, but they also served an important role, together with theater and tactical nuclear capabilities, in deterring conflict below the level of general nuclear war and especially with the rough equality between American and Soviet strategic nuclear forces the administration emphasized that reliance on strategic weapons alone was not sufficient for an effective deterrent. A more prominent consideration in the argumentation for flexibility in the application of nuclear weapons as a condition for having a credible deterrence was a reiterated concern for the survivability of the *Minuteman* force in the event of a direct Soviet attack. It was argued with increasing insistence during the early 1970s that the projected improved accuracy of the Soviet SS-9 missile force with a large, up to 25 megaton warhead, and the eventual development of a Soviet MIRV capability, could pose a serious threat to the future survivability of undefended American ICBM forces. The conclusion, however, was that the United States would continue to have sufficient strategic nuclear forces to deter general war through the 1970s provided the improvement programs, especially as to the MIRVs, wanted by the administration were approved and carried out, and provided America was not faced with a serious Soviet technological surprise.[77] In any case, it is evident that an assumed Soviet capability to attack hard targets at some unspecified future time developed as a major concern early in the Nixon administration.

During the winter and spring of 1974 the administration enunciated some new criteria for nuclear deterrence *vis-à-vis* the Soviet Union. In the yearly Report to the Congress, in hearings in congressional committees and in press conferences, Secretary of Defense James R. Schlesinger, set out what has become known as the Schlesinger strategy.[78] In these, sometimes rather detailed, reviews of the conditions for strategic nuclear deterrence two lines of reasoning were prominent. First, a strong emphasis on the need for flexibility and selectivity in order to shore up the credibility of deterrence across the entire spectrum of risk, including deterrence *in* a war, meaning that various kinds of nuclear wars were differentiated. It was reiterated several times that for deterrence to be credible, one had to have an implementable threat; the argument was that if you had a threat that was not implementable in practise, then you lost the deterrent effect of your weaponry; if your opponent, on the contrary, believed that something was possible, deterrence was improved. Second, it was stressed that the Soviet Union could not be allowed a counterforce capability and option which the United States lacked, but Secretary Schlesinger underscored that this did not mean that either side would have any possibility for obtaining a disarming first-strike capability, even against the ICBM forces of the opponent.

In some respects the Schlesinger strategy can be considerd a continuation of elements of the early Nixon administration's image of deterrence. The stress on the need for flexibility, selectivity and limited nuclear options can be seen as an offshoot of President Nixon's calling attention to the inadequacy of massive retaliation against enemy civilians, cited above. The strong emphasis on having an *implementable* nuclear deterrent threat, however, is more difficult to trace back to earlier declarations from the administration; (on the other hand, this demand for implementable deterrent threats can be seen as an offshoot of McNamara's observation that one cannot fashion a credible deterrent out of an incredible action, cf. p. 52). Furthermore, Secretary Schlesinger explicitly confirmed that he believed it was possible to have a limited nuclear war and also in other ways he presented a view of nuclear deterrence which strongly indicated a change of tack compared to the early Nixon administration.[79] The prominence given to counterforce options to bolster up deterrence was especially conspicuous and, generally, the Schlesinger strategy heralded a significant change in

American deterrence doctrine away from a kind of nuclear essentialism toward a diluted form of Soviet essentialism, also when it is noted that some aspects were present, explicitly or implicitly, in earlier manifestations from American governments.

One noticeable aspect of the Nixon administration's enunciations of its view on nuclear deterrence during this time was the different interpretations of it given by various prominent members of the administration. Most conspicuously, Secretary Kissinger publicly interpreted Schlesinger's statements as an attempt to bring about that selectivity in the targeting of American nuclear forces which clearly had been foreshadowed by earlier statements from the administration while he tended to dismiss the counterforce component or portray a counterforce strategy as tantamount to an American first-strike capability. [80]

Another manifestation of the uneasiness with deterrence based on mutual vulnerability to nuclear attack and the concomitant threat of retaliation against undefended societies were some speeches and writings by Fred C. Iklé, Director of the Arms Control and Disarmament Agency. Iklé emphasized that the whole structure of thinking about deterrence lacked empiricism; there was no trial and error, no real learning of the incontrovertible kind that buttressed the physical and even the social sciences, just simplistic abstractions which were equally convincing in their logical opposites. He noted that because the United States and the Soviet Union had achieved the necessary consensus on strategic doctrine and forces, it was a fiction to think that mutual deterrence could safely be relied on to prevent nuclear war. There were not only two nuclear powers in the world and intellectual evolution was always possible among policy-makers in the Soviet Union and the United States and, Iklé stressed, one should not always oppose the emergence of new ideas. Naked deterrence was not enough; as nuclear strategy was more like a theology than a science, there was a risk that the 'theologies' in the United States and the Soviet Union might not be in harmony and that could lead to catastrophe. [81]

Putting forward such reflections may be considered a spiritual spearhead of the tentative rethinking of what for some years had been basic to the US government's approach to strategic nuclear deterrence.

3. The political significance of nuclear forces
Declarations from the Nixon administration on the political significance of Soviet and American strategic nuclear forces were marked by some basic ambiguities, including a tendency of various members of the administration to express themselves rather differently on various occasions. Some leading members of the US government clearly advocated the nuclear essentialist view that the common Soviet–American nuclear predicament was insensitive to marginal changes in the deployment of nuclear forces and as military power in the nuclear age was not simply transferable into usable political power, they warned against overdoing the political impact of

increments in Soviet strategic forces. At the same time, all spokesmen for the administration showed uneasiness about the meaning of the Soviet nuclear build-up; this was usually followed by explicit warnings that the United States would be forced to take countermeasures if the Soviet Union did not stop its build-up because, as stated by some members of the administration, the actual American–Soviet nuclear balance had important political and diplomatic implications.

On several occasions members of the administration elaborated the theme that in the nuclear age the relation between military strength and political power was complex. With the overwhelming nuclear arsenals of the two superpowers, military and especially nuclear 'muscle' did not guarantee political influence. Marginal additions of nuclear power did not necessarily represent an increment of usable political power because of the excessive destructiveness of nuclear weapons in relation to political objectives. Therefore, the competitive accumulation of more nuclear weapons did not add to the security or political influence of either superpower. In substantiating this conclusion, a special twist of reasoning was displayed: additional increments in nuclear power were useless and dangerous because neither the United States nor the Soviet Union would passively accept a change in the overall balance; a political or military decisive advantage required a change of such magnitude that the mere effort to obtain it could produce disaster. While this reasoning presumed a kind of mechanical action–reaction process as to Soviet and American nuclear armaments, it was also used to dismiss the view that the United States ought always to act in parallel to Soviet armaments.[82]

From the beginning of the Nixon administration, however, its image of the significance of changes in superpower nuclear forces was a heterogeneous composition of elements of nuclear essentialism and Soviet essentialism: rejections of the political usability of nuclear forces were combined with consistent references to the political meaning of the actual state of the nuclear balance. Views stressing the political uselessness of nuclear forces were supplemented by underlinings that politically and diplomatically the United States could not allow the Soviet Union to be substantially ahead of the United States in overall nuclear capability, offensive or defensive forces. In 1970, President Nixon explicitly referred to the danger of 'nuclear blackmail' and stressed the importance of denying other countries (presumably the Soviet Union) the ability to impose their will on the United States and its allies under the weight of strategic military superiority. In 1971, President Nixon stated that it was of the utmost importance that the new strategic balance of the 1970s, and America's interest in strategic stability, not be misunderstood; confrontations might arise from a mistaken perception of the posture of an adversary and the President directly referred to the Middle East crisis in 1970 as an example. Secretary Laird stated in 1972 that it would be diplomatically and politically unacceptable for the United States to allow the Soviets to achieve a large numerical superiority in both land and sea-based strategic missiles.[83] Altogether, it is evident that throughout its tenure, the Nixon administration was concerned that the Soviet Union would interpret its strategic nuclear policy as a sign that America lacked the will to defend its interests in world politics. The peculiar mixture of statements that nuclear forces could not, but yet had, political impact indicated that.

References to the political significance of the strategic nuclear balance were particularly prominent during the last half-year of the Nixon administration. In statements from Secretary Schlesinger, cited above, a form of Soviet essentialism was emphasized: there was a political and diplomatic need for 'essential equivalence' between the strategic nuclear forces of the United States and the Soviet Union in order to inhibit political coercion of the United States or its allies. According to this notion, there was a close relation between *perceived* equality of American and Soviet strategic forces and political power; the importance of maintaining a *visible* strategic balance was stressed and the idea that perceptions or appearances of the nuclear balance between the superpowers, especially third countries' perceptions, were decisive for maintaining a world-wide balance of power between the United States and the Soviet Union was a significant part of the Schlesinger strategy. References to the psychological superpower balance, in the sense that the political leadership on either side must *feel* that there was no political advantage to gain from a physical, i.e. the military including the nuclear balance, came in vogue in the administration.[84]

Nevertheless, some leading members of the Nixon administration espoused a different, or much more ambiguous, attitude during this time. Most conspicuously, commenting on domestic American criticism of the administration's policy, Secretary Kissinger warned in April 1974: 'it is not helpful to us to talk ourselves into a state of mind in which we are strategically inferior.' In June, he stated that nobody should have a perception of a political advantage as a result of a Soviet–American agreement on the nuclear balance, even if in reality such an advantage did not exist, because 'the perception is more important in many respects than the reality'. Kissinger added that this was very complicated to achieve because the nuclear forces of both sides had been developed on the basis of different principles. Two days later, he declared that these principles – that neither side should perceive a political advantage – were obviously not automatic in that 'serious people' differed as to what constituted an advantage, and Kissinger stated that it was crucial that neither side fell into the trap of equating advantage simply with numbers. At a news conference in Moscow in early July, the Secretary of State said: 'What in the name of God is strategic superiority? What is the significance of it, politically, militarily, operationally, at these levels of numbers? What do you do with it?'[85]

4. Negotiations

The Nixon administration's image of negotiations with the Soviet Union on the nuclear issue was composed of divergent strains. At his inauguration, the approach to negotiations was heralded by President Nixon's pronouncement, 'After a period of confrontation, we are entering an era of negotiation.'[86] This statement was frequently reiterated by the administration and sometimes the word 'meaningful' was added to delimit the negotiations aimed at, indicating a more restrained attitude. Another prevalent feature of the administration's image was references to the need for negotiations in order to alleviate mutual suspicion and hostility and stop the arms spiral, together with other principal considerations on the long-term value of negotiations between the two nuclear superpowers. However, calling attention to the need for providing the Soviets with an incentive to negotiate seriously by initiating this or that American nuclear deployment was also a prominent feature of declarations from the Nixon administration.

President Nixon endorsed Soviet–American strategic arms limitations talks (SALT) – first proposed by the Johnson administration – in terms of the common interest of the United States and the Soviet Union in reaching agreement to limit strategic arms but warned that there was a danger of turning SALT into a tactical exercise or the kind of propaganda battle characteristic of some previous disarmament conferences. The decisive question was whether the United States and the Soviet Union jointly could pursue 'responsible, non-provocative strategic arms policies based on sufficiency as a mutually shared goal', or whether there would be another round of the arms race.[87] Generally, the administration exerted itself to portray the SALT negotiations as a positive opportunity for serious and businesslike talks where an agreement could be lasting only if it enhanced the sense of security of both sides, and it was clearly anxious not to pretend too high hopes. Most auspicious was an address by Secretary of State Rogers in the spring of 1970; he pronounced that if an agreement to limit strategic armaments could be reached, it might hasten the time when the Soviet Union would be able to abandon its view of the world as a place of 'bitter political and ideological struggle' in favor of the appeal in the United Nations Charter, which called for states 'to practice tolerance and live together in peace with one another as good neighbors'.[88]

In the period before the SALT I agreements were signed in May 1972, the Nixon administration continually expressed its hopes for an agreement to limit strategic arms but this was almost always done using circumspect wording; it was evident that the administration endeavored to phrase its endorsement for negotiations in very cautious phrases. Thus, President Nixon stated that the goal was to stabilize the strategic balance through mutual restraint and agreements which provided no unilateral advantage. Only a mutually designed balance of strategic armaments could establish a shared basis for security but, at the same time, it was warned that if the Soviet Union attempted to extend its strategic build-up beyond parity, the

United States would have no choice but to initiate compensating actions and the importance of dealing from strength was noted. Secretary of Defense, Melvin Laird, stated that Realistic Deterrence emphasized 'vigorous negotiation from a position of strength', and he noted that the foundation for the transition from an era of confrontation to an era of 'meaningful' negotiation was the American arms program. In the same vein, Laird portrayed the *Safeguard* ABM system as enhancing probabilities for SALT success by maintaining flexibility and strength of the President's negotiating position.[89]

After the SALT I agreements had been signed, they were presented in more enthusiastic phrases as the beginning of a new era in arms control. Henry Kissinger, Assistant to President Nixon for National Security Affairs, declared at a briefing for members of the Congress that the president believed that the agreements 'embedded as they are in the fabric of an emerging new relationship', could hold tremendous political and historical significance; two great powers, deeply divided by their divergent values, philosophies and social systems, had agreed to restrain the very armaments on which their national survival depended. Kissinger noted that although the final verdict must wait on events, there was at least reason to hope that the SALT accords represented a major break in the pattern of suspicion, hostility and confrontation which had dominated US–Soviet relations for a generation. Other spokesmen for the administration noted that the ABM treaty would break the action–reaction spiral between offensive and defensive strategic arms which had been a major factor in driving the strategic arms race. The agreements were presented as providing the opportunity to conduct a regular exchange of views on strategic nuclear matters, especially in the Standing Consultative Commission. In more general terms, the agreements were seen as hopefully institutionalizing habits of cooperation across a broad spectrum of creative endeavor in that the Soviet Union now would acquire a vested interest in mutual restraint. Toward the end of the Nixon presidency, Secretary Kissinger voiced the most optimistic assessment for the SALT process when he talked about a 'conceptual breakthrough' at a news conference in March 1974.[90]

Concurrent with the stressings of the bilateral and cooperative aspects of the SALT agreements, the administration exerted itself to emphasize that the positive effects hoped for depended on a continuing modernization of America's strategic nuclear forces. When President Nixon briefed members of Congress on the strategic arms limitation agreements in June 1972, he referred to statements form Soviet leaders that they were going forward with defense programs in the offensive area not limited by the agreements, wherefore for the United States not to go forward with its offensive programs or unilaterally reduce its programs would mean that any incentive that the Soviet Union had to negotiate a follow-on agreement would be removed. At a later occasion, the President noted that the only way you could get something in negotiations with a major power like the Soviet

Union, or any other major power, was if you had something to give; if the United States unilaterally cut back on its arms, the Soviets' incentive in the negotiations was destroyed because they already had what they wanted. In the same vein, Secretary of Defense Melvin Laird declared that successful negotiations were made possible by that element of America's 'strategy for peace' which was 'adequate strength' and he noted that the United States must continue to approach negotiations from a position of strength 'so that the President does not have to crawl to the bargaining table'. His successor, Elliot Richardson, stated that America's experience in the SALT negotiations and the record of other negotiations with the Sovite Union since World War II clearly showed that the Soviet leaders 'respect power' and would bargain seriously only if confronted by a position of strength. Also the next Secretary of Defense, James Schlesinger, stressed the importance of continuing American nuclear deployment decisions as well as an active research and development policy in order to provide the Soviets with an incentive to negotiate seriously and motivate them to keep the treaties and agreements already made.[91] Thus it is evident that the clear strengthening of a nuclear essentialist image after the SALT I agreement had been signed was offset by several opposite declarations.

One significant part of the Nixon adminstration's image of negotiations with the Soviet Union on nuclear issues was its view on the relation between negotiations and agreements on these issues and other problems in the American–Soviet relationship, that is, what is termed 'linkage'. When President Nixon stated that he favored strategic arms talks at his first news conference in late January 1969, he stressed that simply reducing arms through mutual agreement would not in itself assure peace; progress on outstanding political problems was important as well. In 1970 the President noted that it was essential in successful negotiations to appreciate the interrelationship of international events; the United States did not invert that interrelationship and it was not a negotiating tactic but a 'fact of life'. However, the administration qualified this generally worded expression of linkage in the way that the internal order of the Soviet Union explicitly was mentioned as not being an object of American policy. Although the administration emphasized that it rejected many features of the Soviet society, it was maintained that America's relations with the Soviet Union had to be determined by Soviet international behavior.[92] At a later stage in its tenure the administration more openly faced up to the fact that the issue of linkage presented a genuine moral dilemma which had no easy answer. Thus Secretary Kissinger declared that the Nixon administration had never had any illusions about the Soviet system; the United States would never forget that the antagonism between freedom and its enemies was part of the reality of the modern age. Kissinger added, 'we are not neutral in that struggle.' However, the Secretary of State declared: 'in the nuclear age we are obliged to recognize that the issue of war and peace also involves human lives and that the attainment of peace is a profound moral concern.'[93]

5. The Soviet view

The Nixon administration's image of the Soviet view of nuclear arms was a mixture of heterogeneous interpretations where the signficance attached to the various interpretations changed during the administration's tenure. While the issue of the Soviet view and Soviet intentions was mostly dismissed early in the administration or considered in terms of the Soviet view as a mirror image of the American view, this became increasingly supplemented with and supplanted by concerns as to the purpose of the Soviet nuclear build-up.

The early Nixon administration frequently implied or directly stated that the Soviets shared the American view of nuclear arms and reasoned on nuclear problems in a similar way. Thus in rejecting a heavy ABM system intended to protect American cities, President Nixon mentioned as an extra reason for not adopting it that, to the Soviets, it might look like a prelude to an offensive strategy threatening the Soviet deterrent but since his ABM program did not affect the Soviet retaliatory capability, it was not provocative. The President opined that the Soviet Union clearly recognized the difference between a defensive and an offensive posture and he noted that both Soviet political and military leaders had always thought in defensive terms; hence, Nixon reasoned, the new American ABM program, by avoiding the city defense element, was so clearly defensive in character that the Soviet Union could not interpret it as escalating the arms race. When Secretary Rogers referred to an American inclination to base the strategic planning on so-called 'worst-case' assumptions as to both the opponent's capabilities and intentions and one's own performance, he added that the Soviets no doubt did the same. A similar tendency to portray the Soviet Union as a nuclear power in benign terms appeared when another spokesman for the administration presented the Soviet government as 'pretty solid, sensible people who are genuinely concerned about the situation in which a massive overkill capacity has been developed on both sides'. In the same vein, President Nixon declared in the Report to Congress on US foreign policy, published in early 1970, that the Soviet goal in deploying nuclear forces was 'in all likelihood a retaliatory capability similar to ours'. On the other hand, Secretary Laird did not share that benign reading of the Soviet view and on one occasion, in March 1969, he voiced a strongly divergent perception when he declared that the Soviet Union was 'going for a first-strike capability. There is no question about it.'[94]

In considering how to handle the nuclear issue in the Soviet–American relationship, the administration stressed that the sincerity or purpose of the Soviet leadership was not at issue. When the Nixon administration exerted itself to underline that the strong differences between the United States and the Soviet Union as to their ideology and political aims could never be dismissed as insignificant, it did not draw the conclusion that the Soviet view of nuclear war was correspondingly contrary to America's. The highly diverging Soviet and American approaches to international affairs were described in terms that did not imply that some firm and malign Soviet intention was the central problem and the administration's public reflections on Soviet nuclear policy were often marked by a conspicuous balancing of contradictory considerations where the conclusions were presented in probabilistic terms. Altogether, the American government's verbal handling of the nuclear issue in the Soviet–American relationship during this period was devoid of any selfrighteousness based on polemical references to a malign Soviet view.[95]

The predominant proclivity of the early Nixon administration for applying a nuclear essentialist reasoning in portraying the Soviet approach to nuclear problems continued in a more diluted form throughout the administration's tenure when it became supplemented with more pronounced concerns suggesting another conclusion. In 1971, President Nixon rejected sharp increases in American strategic forces arguing that such might lead the Soviets to misunderstand America's intentions and force them into new strategic investments they would otherwise eschew. Commenting on the Soviet nuclear build-up in the same report, however, the President also expressed concern whether the Soviet Union had made a commitment to strategic equilibrium similar to America's and he advanced doubts whether the Soviets shared the view that small numerical advantages in nuclear forces had little military relevance; nevertheless, the question was still left open by the comment that the administration hoped that the Soviet Union would likewise recognize what the United States considered a reality. A year later, in 1972, these concerns were reiterated: the development of Soviet strategic forces raised serious questions concerning Soviet objectives; while the intentions of the Soviet leadership could not be known, it must be assumed, the President stated, that the trend reflected a calculated policy within the framework of an overall strategic rationale. Still, the President's 1972 report contained a rather detached analysis of the Soviet view of international politics. Observing that there were ambiguous tendencies in Soviet policy and that the task of American policy was to strengthen the positive tendencies, it was clearly implied that this was a matter of applying both American pressure and American restraint.[96]

Some of the early Nixon administration's optimistic interpretation of the Soviet view reappeared after the SALT I agreements had been signed in 1972, supplemented with warnings against illusions, and citing the Soviet adherence to a hostile ideology and traditional Soviet suspicions as complicating for developing contacts and mutual trust. The composite character of the interpretation of the Soviet approach appeared, for instance, from Henry Kissinger's remark at a news conference two days after the conclusion of a visit to Moscow in September 1972; commenting on his talks with Soviet leaders, Kissinger noted that it was his impression that they had the 'same intellectual problems that we have' when they entered close talks with American leaders about weapons on which the survival of both sides depended. A benign interpretation of the Soviet approach was also shown when Kissinger declared in 1973 that the American view, viz. that the principal problem was how to prevent a war and not how to conduct a war, was shared by the Soviet leaders.[97] In same vein, President Nixon stated in 1973 that Soviet policy had contradictory tendencies in that some factors pointed toward a more stable relationship with the United States while others suggested a continued probing for tactical gains, and the President declared that the United States dealt with these contradictory manifestations by responding to positive efforts and demonstrating firmness in the face of pressures. At the same time Nixon pointedly adduced that it was highly improbable that the Soviet Union would resign itself to permanent strategic inferiority.[98]

Tendencies toward imputing the Soviets a more malign view of the role of nuclear arms and a tentative acceptance of Soviet essentialism became prominent during the last months of the administration in 1974. However, it is worth noting that a predilection for a rather detached assessment of the Soviet approach was demonstrated in this period, too. Thus, as Secretary Schlesinger considered the question if the Soviets simply responded to and tried to counter American strategic initiatives or, rather, sought something more ambitious than a capability for second-strike retaliation against the United State, he concluded that it was premature to assess confidently what objectives the Soviets had set for themselves. However, Schlesinger stated, it was certainly conceivable that they foresaw both political and military advantages in the growing numerical weight of their nuclear forces and in their potential to bring major portions of America's strategic arsenal in jeopardy. The Secretary of Defense observed that the Soviets had not been reticent in stressing to a variety of audiences their superiority over the United States in numbers of ICBMs and other strategic capabilities which suggested that they saw these asymmetries as giving them diplomatic if not military leverage. But the Soviets must be under no illusion about America's determination to proceed with whatever responses their actions might require and therefore, Schlesinger emphasized, it was important to disabuse those in the Soviet Union who might hope to obtain nuclear superiority in this way and make clear to them that this was a non-productive path.[99]

3. Images, 1974–89

1. THE FORD ADMINISTRATION, 1974–7

1. Convergent vs. divergent interests

The Ford administration continued some of its predecessor's themes on the significance of convergent interests between the two nuclear superpowers. Concomitantly, the critical importance of opposite interests was increasingly stressed in the middle of the 1970s and a growing uneasiness with the tenability of maintaining the primacy of common interests was evident. When members of the administration emphasized the reality of the mutual nuclear predicament and its wider impact, such nuclear essentialist statements – unlike similar statements in the early 1970s – frequently assumed a distinctly defensive thrust, explicitly aimed at a domestic audience.

Some of the most outstanding defenses of détente and the significance of convergent interests from a US government occurred during the Ford presidency and the most articulate expositor of the issue was Secretary Henry Kissinger. At several occasions, Kissinger advocated forcefully that the destructiveness of nuclear weapons compelled a convergence of American and Soviet interests in averting nuclear war. The existence of enormously destructive weapons distinguished the present era from all previous periods and defined the necessity of the task in that peace had to be a fundamental imperative because nuclear cataclysm threatened humanity's very survival. Therefore, Kissinger stated, the highest aim of policy in the nuclear age was to create a more positive and durable relationship of peace between the superpowers; the world's fears of nuclear holocaust hinged on the American–Soviet relationship and there was no alternative to coexistence. Portraying the predicament of the nuclear age in such terms, the Secretary of State sometimes added the consideration that the fact that the Soviet Union had become a nuclear superpower was neither created by the United States, nor could it be removed by any American policy. Moreover, Kissinger frequently presented a strong criticism of traditional American attitudes to détente vs. tensions in international politics; most Americans, Kissinger declared, perceived relations between states as either friendly or hostile, both defined in nearly absolute terms, and therefore American attitudes tended to oscillate between extremes. In that context it was particularly notable that Kissinger stated that the Ford administration did not accept crises to sustain America's defense: a nation that needed artificial crises to do what was needed for survival would soon find itself in mortal danger. The issue was whether Americans had the courage to face complexity and the inner conviction to deal with ambiguity, whether Americans would look behind easy slogans and recognize that their goals could only be reached by patience and in imperfect stages. [1]

A prominent part of Kissinger's statements on common American–Soviet interests in averting nuclear war was his stressing that deep differences in philosophy and political values between the two countries impeded the necessary task of securing peace and at no time did the Secretary of State brush aside these differences as inferior when faced with the danger of nuclear holocaust. On the contrary, he emphasized that the differences did not spring from misunderstandings or transitory factors and elaborated the paradox that if peace was pursued to the exclusion of any other goal, other values would be compromised and perhaps lost, while, if unconstrained rivalry led to nuclear conflict, these values, along with everything else, would be destroyed in the resulting holocaust. The challenge of our time, according to the then American Secretary of State, was to reconcile the reality of competition with the imperative of coexistence and therefore both the United States and the Soiviet Union had to conduct themselves with restraint.

In that context Kissinger elaborated the meaning of détente. Détente was the search for a more constructive relationship between the United States and the Soviet Union reflecting the nuclear realities. It was a continuing process, not a final condition that had been or could be realized at any specific point in time, and détente could not be pursued selectively in one area or toward one group of countries only; for the Untied States, Kissinger declared, détente was indivisible. At the same time, the Secretary stressed that the whole process of détente could be jeopardized if it was taken for granted. Both American actions, as the temptation to combine détente with increasing pressure on the Soviet Union, and Soviet actions, as a Soviet use of détente to strengthen its military capacity in all fields or an attempt to undermine America's alliances, were dangerous, and the United States had to make it clear to the Soviet Union that one could not have the atmosphere of détente without the substance. In the same vein, President Ford declared in the spring of 1975 that while the United States and the Soviet Union shared an interest in reducing tensions and building a more stable relationship, this still required a combination of American firmness and flexibility; faced with American weakness and irresolution, the Soviet Union could not be expected to show restraints. [2]

As the administration emphasized the significance of convergent interests between the United States and the Soviet Union, it is worth noting how the conditions were specified. It was stated early in general terms that as both countries had an obligation to construct a new international set of relationships which reduced the risk of war, neither superpower could expect to impose its will on the other without running an intolerable risk. Later during the administration's tenure, the generally phrased conditions were replaced by specific warnings that the United States would not let this effort be used by any country to achieve unilateral advantages or to exploit local instabilities by its military forces so, as it was stated in early 1976 referring to the Soviet policy in Angola, 'the Soviet Union will have to choose.' In this situation, the administration declared that the United States would continue to pursue the dual policy that, according to Kissinger, 'we have emphasized over recent months', i.e. both resisting the expansion of Soviet political influence by military power and work for more peaceful international arrangements on the basis of strict reciprocity.[3] Thus it is evident that as time went on the administration changed its image of the relative significance of convergent vs. divergent interests.

One indicator of the changed image was the Ford administration's later abandonment in 1976 of the word détente, an abandonment which is conspicuous when related to the administration's marked endorsements of that term earlier during its tenure. As reviewed above, Secretary Kissinger was the most distinct public advocate of détente as a way to manage the nuclear threat, but also President Ford had endorsed the concept. Noting that the word itself was confusing, the President advocated détente as meaning the process of reducing tensions between the United States and the Soviet Union; by moving away from the dangerous confrontations that had characterized Soviet–American relations in the period of the cold war, it had become possible, Ford declared, to reduce the risk of nuclear war. Détente, according to the President, meant a fervent desire for peace, but not peace at any price, and he emphasized that détente had proceeded as a two-way street. It was also a mark of Ford's approach to the idea of détente that he stated at several occasions that détente had only been possible because of American strength and resolve: if America weakened its defenses, it weakened one of the foundations of détente. In January 1976, replying to a question in a television interview, the President declared: 'I think détente is in the best interest of this country. It is in the best interest of world stability, world peace.' Later in the same interview, expressing his assessment of the standing of the word détente in the American political context, he added: 'politically, I think any candidate who says "abandon détente" will be the loser in the long run.' Two months later, President Ford, as well as other members of his administration, abandoned the word détente and used instead the phrase 'peace through strength'.[4]

2. Deterrence

The Ford administration's image of nuclear deterrence *vis-à-vis* the Soviet Union was an accentuated continuation of the Schlesinger strategy's conception of deterrence. Those elements of the deterrence reasoning which had been introduced in the early 1970s became steadily more prominent during the middle of the decade and were most manifest in the yearly report by Secretary of Defense, Donald Rumsfeld, published a few days before President Carter replaced President Ford in January 1977. A common feature of these increasingly conspicuous trends toward Soviet essentialism was the significance attached to matching any Soviet nuclear capability and strategy in order to deter the Soviets.

A first significant aspect of the administration's reasoning on deterrence was a strong emphasis, reiterated again and again, on a need for maintaining and developing an American ability to respond to attacks in a controlled, selective and deliberate fashion, short of full-scale retaliation.[5] This need for flexibility was perceived as increasing with parity between American and Soviet strategic nuclear forces in that a counter-city option now was considered risking self-deterrence in a crisis; providing the President with a wide range of options would enhance the certainty of retaliation and thereby, in the end, make war less likely in the ultimate crisis. Intertwined with this was the reasoning that the condition for effective and credible deterrence was posing a threat that the Soviets could be persuaded the American government was prepared to implement. As stated by Secretary Rumsfeld in January 1977, since Soviet actions indicate that they take nuclear war seriously, the United States must, as a condition of stable deterrence, do no less, and part of taking nuclear war seriously was having options for responses short of full-scale retaliation. The crux of the matter, according to this thinking, was that maintaining a credible nuclear deterrence required, at least, the appearance of matching Soviet thinking and Soviet capabilities for various nuclear war scenarios.

A second part of the reasoning on nuclear deterrence was the prominence given to having options and capabilities to strike accurately at hardened Soviet military targets. Stating the need for counterforce options, it was underlined, however, that the United States was not interested in creating a first-strike capability which was seen as provocative and threatening strategic stability. The basic problem was observed and expected developments in Soviet nuclear capabilities in that the Soviet ICBM development could give the Soviet Union a counter-military capability which the United States lacked, with the result that the credibility of deterrence was undermined. A potential Soviet hard-target capability, unmatched by the United States, was perceived as increasingly threatening the survivability of the American *Minuteman* force and the development of an American counterforce capability would therefore depend on how far the Soviet Union would go. This close coupling of the criterion for American nuclear forces and the observed and expected Soviet force development was markedly strengthened during the middle of the 1970s and the significance attached to a developing Soviet threat against the American ICBM force was conspicuously more serious in the annual report published by the Secretary of Defense in January 1977 than in the first two annual reports from the Ford administration, even if that type of consideration was manifest in all three reports.[6]

A third feature of the administration's image of nuclear deterrence *vis-à-vis* the Soviet Union was an incipient preoccupation with an itemized list of nuclear balances, each requiring the necessities for deterrence. The reasoning was that after the Soviet Union had achieved overall parity in strategic forces with the United States, the threat of mutual annihilation limited the range of hostile Soviet actions which could be deterred by strategic forces. Hence, more emphasis had to be placed on the deterrent roles of theater nuclear forces in Europe. A need for changing NATO's theater nuclear forces into what later became known as long range Theater Nuclear Forces or Intermediate-range Nuclear Forces (INF) was suggested by Secretary Schlesinger, in 1975,[7] as he observed that the existing theater nuclear forces in Europe constituted a retaliatory capability with a perceptively lower risk of escalation than strategic nuclear forces, because they did not pose a major threat to the Soviet homeland; compared to Schlesinger's simultaneous calling attention to the declining deterrence role of strategic nuclear forces, the obvious conclusion was a need for theater nuclear forces deployed in Europe which could pose a threat to the Soviet homeland.

3.   The political significance of nuclear forces

Through the middle of the 1970s the US government increasingly attached a broad political and symbolic significance to the account of nuclear balances between the superpowers. At several occasions, however, one prominent member in particular of the Ford administration questioned the more exact political meaning of nuclear arms and so, even if the image was not homogeneous, the general tendency toward Soviet essentialism was evident.

The rationale was that strategic nuclear forces had come to be seen as important to the status and stature of a major power. That was regrettable, the administration noted, but the United States could not allow major asymmetries to develop in measures of the strategic balance, such as throw weight, accuracy or other factors that contribute to the perceptions of non-superpower nations; not only third countries saw it that way but also the Soviet Union perceived strategic nuclear forces as performing a symbolic role as shown by the high value they had placed on achieving at least parity with the United States.[8] Indeed, the word 'perception' appeared as a major catchword in the Ford presidency's enunciations on the general political role of strategic nuclear forces, and the reasoning was indicated by the the phraseology that not only had American strategic nuclear forces to be roughly equivalent to Soviet forces but they had to be 'seen as' or 'known to be' equivalent – the 'perceptions' of equivalence were all-important.

The most distinct manifestation of this image of the political significance of nuclear forces appeared in the report of Secretary of Defense, Donald H. Rumsfeld, to Congress in January 1977, a few days before the Ford administration retired.[9] It was adduced that the strength of the American strategic nuclear deterrent was the subject of many and differing perceptions which, in turn, could affect the behavior of both prospective enemies, allies, neutrals and attentive publics in the United States itself. If the nuclear balance was perceived as favoring the Soviet Union rather than the United States, America's allies would adjust their behavior and accommodate the Soviet Union, while potential enemies could make demands leading to dangerous situations; additionally, if domestic audiences saw real or imaginary imbalances, they could insist on excessive and costly crash programs to restore the equilibrium. Observing that the Soviets had 'the connoisseur's taste for the psychological and political uses of military power', American programs for offensive nuclear capabilities had to be geared to those of the Soviet Union in order to avoid American capabilities being perceived as inferior to those of the Soviet Union, because that would have damaging consequences in peacetime for America's international standing no matter if these perceptions were real or imaginary.

However, other members of the administration portrayed the political significance of nuclear forces in more circumspect phrases. The Secretary of State, Henry Kissinger, emphasized that in the nuclear age the relation between military strength and political power was highly complex. On a number of occasions[10] Kissinger declared that with the existing nuclear arsenals and when the characteristics of the nuclear weapons of the two sides were so incommensurable, it was very difficult to determine what constituted a political useful superiority. Nevertheless, while a decisive advantage was hard to calculate, the appearance, Kissinger stressed, of superiority and inferiority – whatever its actual significance – could have serious political consequences. With weapons that were unlikely to be used and for which there was no operational experience, the psychological impact could be crucial and therefore each side had a notable incentive to achieve not only the reality but also the appearance of equality. On the one hand, Kissinger maintained that additional increments of strategic weaponry did not automatically lead to political gains, on the other hand, he stated the importance of 'perceived equality'; neither the United States nor the Soviet Union would, or could, permit a perceived inequality to arise even if its precise significance was difficult to define.

Thus the Secretary of State displayed a distinctly two-sided approach to the problem but the outcome of his reflections was clearly that nuclear arms played an important political role. The Secretary of Defense, especially the second Secretary of Defense in the Ford administration, approached the issue in a more straightforward way and, overall, it is evident that the administration attached a major political role to nuclear forces.

4. Negotiations

Pronouncements from the US government on the role of negotiations with the Soviet Union on nuclear matters were heterogeneous during the middle of the 1970s. Declarations stressing the importance of negotiating and reaching agreements with the Soviets alternated with statements displaying a rather skeptical view of the whole idea of cooperating with the Soviet adversary in order to cope with the nuclear threat, and the skeptical views became increasingly prominent toward the end of the Ford administration.

Like the preceding administration, this administration's rationale for endorsing negotiations originated in the notion that in the nuclear age the United States had an obligation to engage the Soviet Union in settlements of concrete problems in order to push back the shadow of nuclear catastrophe. Negotiations would develop a Soviet self-interest in fostering a process of relaxation of tensions; by acquiring a stake in a wide network of relationships with the West, the Soviet Union might become conscious of what it would lose by a return to confrontation. A salient point in this reasoning was a special form of linkage: progress in one area would add momentum to progress in other areas of negotiation and by moving forward across a wide spectrum of negotiations on concrete problems, a new standard of international conduct appropriate to controlling and reducing the dangers of nuclear war might grow up. Thus the signing of an agreement on underground nuclear explosions for peaceful purposes in the spring of 1976 was portrayed by President Ford as an historic milestone in the history of arms control agreements and the ultimate purpose of the network of such agreements as bringing about a more peaceful world and pushing back the shadow of nuclear war.[11] Conversely, it was stressed that if negotiations, primarily SALT, should fail, both sides would not only be forced to keep on building nuclear forces but since that would be justified by references to increased dangers, the rhetoric of both sides would become more confrontational leading to a substantial chilling in the Soviet–American relationship and, possibly, a return of the cold war.[12]

Concerning SALT, negotiations on strategic arms limitations were presented as one means by which the United States and the Soviet Union could enhance stability in the nuclear age by setting mutual constraints on their respective nuclear forces and gradually reaching an understanding of the doctrinal considerations that underlay the deployment by nuclear arms. Through SALT the two sides could reduce the suspicions and fears which fuelled the arms race. Only by showing restraint as to their own nuclear developments could they expect to prevent proliferation of nuclear arms to other nations. Another important aspect of SALT, one spokesman for the administration noted,[13] was that the very fact that such negotiations were going on, forced the Soviet political leadership to pay attention to the purposes of their strategic armaments and to weigh arms control objectives against other political and military objectives; in the long run, this indirect impact of arms control through changing attitudes could be more beneficial than specific arms limitations, according to this spokesman.

While sometimes suggesting that the long-term impact of arms control agreements could be more important than the specific content of some agreement, the administration also emphasized the significance of both sides' compliance with the terms of the SALT I agreement. This appeared in a special form in that the Ford administration strongly repudiated charges that the Soviet Union violated parts of the 1972 agreement and, particularly, that the US government colluded with the Soviet Union in masking Soviet violations. While noting that there were ambiguities in certain activities underway in the Soviet Union which needed clarification, the administration maintained several times that the Soviet Union had been in compliance with SALT I. Secretary Kissinger reviewed the charges detailed, also noting the Soviet willingness to close any loophole in SALT I. [14]

Other enunciations demonstrated, however, a more skeptical view of negotiating and reaching agreements with the Soviet Union on nuclear issues. The annual reports from the Secretary of Defense to Congress were devoid of views stressing the long-term benefits on negotiating with the Soviets. The expediency of negotiated arms control was clearly downgraded compared to unilateral American measures as, at most, the necessity of demonstrating an American competence and will to continue developing nuclear arms to motivate the Soviets to negotiate seriously was stated; indeed, this divergence between the approaches applied by leading members of the administration was conspicuous during the mid-1970s. The skeptical view of negotiations was especially prominent in the last report from Secretary Rumsfeld in January 1977. Rumsfeld noted that the Interim Offensive Agreement from 1972 had reduced one element of uncertainty by placing a ceiling on the number of American and Soviet ICBMs and SLBMs, but it had not lessened the Soviet determination to acquire new strategic offensive systems. Self-restraint by the Soviets in the expectation that the United States would follow, Rumsfeld observed, had not been a part of Soviet behavior and neither had the Soviets reciprocated American restraint with restraint on their part. Western weakness and irresolution were not examples the Soviets were likely to emulate but an opportunity to seize. [15]

One notable feature of the Ford administration's image of negotiating with the Soviet Union was that the statements were often framed as an overt rejection of divergent American views criticizing the administration's policy; however, the kind of criticism repudiated varied widely from one prominent member of the administration to another. Secretary Kissinger frequently stressed that since limiting the growth of nuclear arsenals was an overriding global problem which must be dealt with for America's own sake and for the sake of world peace, negotiating with the Soviet Union for that purpose was not a favor which the United States granted to the Soviet Union to be turned off and on according to the ebb and flow of American–Soviet relations. Still, while repudiating that kind of linkage, Secretary Kissinger also observed that no negotiations could proceed in isolation from the general foreign policy stance of the two superpowers and he especially stressed the damage of the negotiations by the Soviet policy in Angola. [16]

However, when other members of the administration parried off domestic criticism of American negotiating policy, they argued against a wholly divergent objection. Secretary Rumsfeld, for example, countered the allegation that the United States, primarily the Defense Department, exploited every loophole in arms control agreements to develop exotic and unnecessary weapons by stating that such charges might better be directed at the Soviet Union. As to the assertion that arms control negotiations and agreements were counterproductive when they created demands for bargaining chips subsequently converted into legitimized weapons programs, the Defense Secretary noted that, for instance, President Johnson's use of the ABM defense system as a negotiating counter 'did not serve the United States badly' in that the ABM treaty could hardly have been signed without it; none the less, Secretary Rumsfeld stressed that a weapons program could only be effective as a bargaining chip if there was a serious military need for the weapon – what were seen merely as bargaining chips would not be effective.[17]

5.   The Soviet view

The Ford presidency's image of the Soviet view of nuclear weapons was marked by two divergent features: on the one hand, more or less distinct declarations suggested that the Soviets shared the American view of the nuclear predicament while, on the other hand, other statements, prominent toward the end of the administration, manifested serious doubt that the Soviet leadership actually shared the American view.

When the administration indicated that the Soviet Union shared the American conception of a mutual nuclear predicament, it usually implied so in a roundabout way by stating that both the United States and the Soviet Union must conduct their foreign policies within the framework of the imperatives of the nuclear age. The relevance and tenability of applying that reasoning was substantiated by, for instance, the observation that as a consequence of nuclear parity both the United States and the Soviet Union had 'objectively' acquired essentially reciprocal incentives to avoid a nuclear war. In one case, replying to a question at a news conference after the United States and the Soviet Union had entered the Vladivostok agreement which established equal ceilings on the number of missiles for both, Secretary Kissinger hinted at that type of reading by declaring that he supposed that General Secretary Brezhnev had come to the same conclusion as the US government, namely that in a situation where both superpowers could destroy humanity several times over, the actual level of the ceiling on missiles was not as decisive as the fact that a ceiling had been put on at all.[18]

These more or less veiled suggestions that the Soviets shared the American view of the nuclear age were repeatedly replaced by, or supplemented with, statements to the effect that the issue of the Soviet purpose of intention was immaterial since the United States did not base its policy solely on the Soviets' good intentions. Such declarations did not directly refer to the Soviet view of nuclear weapons but as they were put forward in a context of debate and strife about Soviet policy, that kind of consideration often intimated some notion about the Soviet view of nuclear arms and its significance. Thus Secretary Kissinger observed that the Soviet view of peaceful coexistence was different from the American view of détente: where many Americans regarded international tensions and enmity as anomalies caused by either deliberate malice or misunderstandings, the Soviet Union as a communist state regarded tensions as inevitable byproducts of the struggle between opposing social systems, and where many Americans perceived relations between states as either friendly or hostile, for the Soviet Union East–West contracts were in part designed to promote Soviet influence abroad. However, having accounted the Soviet view as different from the American in that way, Kissinger strongly emphasized that the issue was not whether peace and stability served Soviet purposes but whether it served the American goal: 'constructive actions in Soviet policy are desirable whatever the Soviet motives.' To the extent, the Secretary noted, that America's attention focused largely on Soviet intentions, the United States created a latent vulnerability for itself, but the United States relied on a balance of mutual interests, rather than Soviet intentions. In addition, Kissinger observed that contradictory tendencies contested for pre-eminence in Soviet policy and the American policy seemed, together with other factors, to have encouraged Soviet leaders to adopt the more cooperative policy.[19]

Toward the end of the Ford administration some statements displayed a deep concern about the actual Soviet view of nuclear weapons. This was most evidently displayed in Defense Secretary Rumsfeld's annual report to Congress in January 1977, published three days before President Ford was replaced by President Carter. The Secretary of Defense stated that Soviet nuclear capabilities indicated a tendency toward war-fighting and damage limitation rather than for the more modish Western models of deterrence through mutual vulnerability. But the Soviets had never really agreed to the assumption that the mutual vulnerability of the superpowers' populations and industries was a condition of stability; when the Soviets had signed the ABM treaty in 1972, some analysts, Rumsfeld observed, saw it as an acceptance of the theory that mutual vulnerability was a condition of stability but it had now become equally plausible that they had entered the treaty either because of severe resource constraints or because they feared that, without an agreement, American technology over the near term would give America a continuing and growing advantage. Moreover, as shown by the deployment of the newest Soviet generation of ICBMs, the SS-17, SS-18 and SS-19, the Soviets were acquiring a comprehensive hard target capability and creating the prospect of developing a first-strike capability. Also the Soviet negotiating policy, for example their rejection of American proposals for reductions in throw-weight, indicated that they were not interested in mutual assured destruction and, Secretary Rumsfeld stressed, the Soviets must be accepted for what they were, not for what Americans wanted them to be. [20]

Although this appraisal showed an inclination for stating conclusions in terms of plausibilities rather than certainties, its thrust demonstrated the increasing concern of the American government for the actual Soviet view of nuclear arms and its significance and, altogether, the Ford presidency manifested a cautious but clear move from nuclear to Soviet essentialism concerning this factor too.

2.   THE CARTER ADMINISTRATION, 1977–81

1.   Convergent vs. divergent interests

While the Carter administration always called attention to the reality of both cooperative and competitive interests in the Soviet–American relationship, the relative significance assigned to the two aspects changed markedly during the Carter presidency. Even if different members of the administration expressed themselves somewhat differently throughout the period from January 1977 to January 1981, and although the direction of the change was not constant, the overall trend was clearly toward giving greater weight to Soviet–American conflicts.

When the early Carter administration emphasized the cooperative aspects, the conceptual starting point of that nuclear essentialism was different from that adopted by previous US governments. Where East–West issues and bipolar Soviet-American relations conceived in power-political terms had been elaborated as the basis for stressing convergent interests between the two superpowers in the nuclear age by the preceding two administrations, the Carter administration presented an image of an increasingly complex and interdependent international society perceived in a multilateral and global context. Notions of a global community with human rights and economic progress for all besides arms control and peace marked this approach; traditional issues of war and peace, it was adduced, could no longer be separated from the new global questions of justice, equity and human rights. In the global community power to solve the world's problems no longer lay solely in the hands of a few nations but was widely shared among many nations with different cultures, different histories, and different aspirations. Both the United States and the Soviet Union had learned, President Carter declared, that they were not all-powerful and the United States wanted the Soviet Union further engaged in the growing pattern of international activities designed to deal with human problems; both countries should accept the new responsibilities imposed by the changing nature of international relations, whereby they would acquire a greater stake in the creation of a constructive and peaceful world order. [21]

This conceptual approach to international problems was presented as new and it was associated with a certain – occasionally a distinct – repudiation of a traditional American approach to international politics and the communist adversary. President Carter thus decried that 'inordinate fear of communism which once led us to embrace any dictator who joined us in that fear', and he added: 'I am glad that that is being changed.' Other spokesmen for the Carter administration spoke of simplified and polarized stereotypes about the nature of the Soviet Union which had caused American public opinion to fluctuate widely in its moods about the Soviet Union.[22]

Combined with downgrading Soviet–American relations and traditional security issues, the Carter administration stressed both the profound differences between the two countries as well as their common interests and shared obligations. The differences and the competition were likely to remain because they were real and deeply rooted in the values and the history of their respective societies. However, as expressed by President Carter, 'our two countries' also shared many overlapping interests; Americans and Russians belonged to the same civilization whose origins stretched back hundreds of years and today the leaders of both countries had the capacity to destroy human society in a nuclear war. But in the nuclear era, the President averred, war could no longer be thought of as merely a continuation of diplomacy by other means. Nuclear war could not be measured by the archaic standards of 'victory' or 'defeat' and this imposed an awesome and special responsibility on the United States and the Soviet Union. In his inauguration address in January 1977, President Carter had declared that the elimination of nuclear weapons from the earth was the ultimate goal and later that year he stated that the security of the global community could not forever rest on a balance of terror; peace would not be assured until the weapons of war were finally put away, he noted. While working toward the final goal of abolishing the nuclear threat, the imperative of the nuclear age laid a special obligation on both superpowers to pursue cooperation and détente. The direct endeavor to reduce the nuclear threat would not only make the world a safer place but would also free the two countries to concentrate on broader constructive actions to secure peace and improve upon the global community. The administration endorsed détente as one way to lessen the nuclear danger but with varying emphasis in that some spokesmen stressed that détente must be more comprehensive and reciprocal. In any case, it was a salient characteristic of the Carter administration's approach that détente and bilateral Soviet–American cooperation to reduce the nuclear threat was portrayed as closely related to both countries' participation in broader multilateral efforts to secure peace and development in the global community.[23]

While this image of the role of convergent American–Soviet interests in managing the common nuclear predicament was predominant during the first year of the administration, it slowly abated later in the 1970s and was replaced by growing attention paid to divergent interests; otherwise expressed, the seeds of a critical attitude to the actual course of détente and American–Soviet cooperation, present from the beginning of the administration, gradually prevailed. The change appeared in different ways. Most notably, the administration continued stating that both the United States and the Soviet Union had to make continuous choices between emphasizing either the conflicting or the cooperative elements in their relationship but where the early Carter administration then added the observation that if the Soviet leaders chose the cooperative course of restraint and responsibility, they would find the United States responsive because it was America's interest to enlarge the areas of cooperation, the later Carter administration added the observation that if the Soviet Union chose the confrontational policy, the United States was fully prepared to counter that even if it continued to be America's interest to have meaningful cooperation. A significant indication of the changing attitude appeared when President Carter, in a speech in June 1978, declared that, to the Soviet Union, détente seemed to mean a continuing aggressive struggle for political advantage and increased influence through military power and military assistance, and he explicitly mentioned the Soviet use of proxy forces in Angola and Ethiopia.[24] Altogether, it is evident that the enunciation of the changing American approach was marked by its close combination with the perception of the Soviet behavior in the Third World.

Still, however, it is worth noting that both statements which displayed the new pessimistic attitude to the actual significance of convergent interests and statements which maintained the early Carter administration's optimistic assessments contained references to the existence of convergent as well as divergent interests between the United States and the Soviet Union. None the less, the conversion was evident, not least in that the declarations insisting on the reality of common interests took on a conspicuously defensive form of manifestation when they considered Soviet interventions in Third World conflicts.

In 1979, particularly after the SALT II agreements had been signed in June, the manifestations emphasizing convergent interests assumed a more concrete and frequently exhorting character, void of references to the need for new world order which had been prominent early in the administration. President Carter now declared that in America's relations with the Soviet Union, the possibility of mutual annihilation made a strategy of peace the only rational choice for both sides and as the administration defended SALT II, the reality of a simple common interest in survival was reiterated over and over again. For example, when the President addressed a joint session of the Congress, just after having returned from the signing ceremony with President Brezhnev in Vienna, he began: 'The truth of the nuclear age is that the United States and the Soviet Union must live in peace, or we may not live at all'; in the age of the hydrogen bomb, Carter said, there is no longer any meaningful distinction between global war and global suicide.[25] At several occasions through the rest of 1979 when they advocated ratification of SALT II, leading members of the administration phrased the convergent interests of the superpowers and the rest of humanity in simple terms stressing the origin in the common nuclear predicament; the continuing existence of competition and political conflict between the United States and the Soviet Union was noted but the arguments on the essential importance of recognizing the vital common interest were emphasized repeatedly and often assumed an urgent tone.

During the last year of the administration after the Soviet invasion of Afghanistan, the continuing existence of converging interests and the superpowers' responsibility to mankind was maintained, even if the Soviet behavior was strongly censured as aggression. This was sometimes observed with resignation, or it was hinted that just at a time of increased tensions, the significance of common interest became all the more important. The most distinct advocate of this reasoning was Secretary Vance and, after his withdrawal, the new Secretary of State, Edmund Muskie. Muskie's declarations were stamped both by his strong censure of the invasion and his taking sharp issue with domestic opponents. At the same time, however, other members of the administration clearly downgraded the theme of common interests or posed the possibility of a strongly escalated arms race in unambiguous terms. Thus in an address in August, President Carter declared that if an unlimited nuclear arms race should be forced upon the United States, it would compete and compete successfully – 'Let no one doubt that for a moment.' On the other hand, Carter also declared at this occasion that for the United States to initiate such a dangerous and costly race and abandon the efforts for nuclear weapons control would be totally irresponsible; the destructive power of the world's nuclear arsenals was already adequate for total devastation and it did no good to increase the destructive power in search of a temporary edge or in pursuit of an illusion of absolute nuclear superiority.[26]

2. Deterrence

The Carter administration's image of nuclear deterrence vis-à-vis the Soviet Union was marked by an appreciable change during its tenure and, to some degree, different spokesmen displayed different images, especially during the early years. Toward the end of the administration, in 1980, the ever-advancing tightening of the conditions for deterrence acquired a pronounced amplification toward distinct similarities to Soviet essentialism.

The very first declarations from the Carter administration on deterrence in February 1977 indicated a move away from the Ford administration's pronouncements, particularly the latest pronouncement in January 1977 (cf. p. 77 above). In a statement to Congress on the defense budget by the new Secretary of Defense, Harold Brown, he gave expression to a profound skepticism toward the expediency of selective nuclear options by emphasizing that any use of nuclear weapons would run the risk of rapid escalation to a full-scale thermonuclear exchange that could only result in a catastrophic outcome for both the Soviet Union and the United States: while not outrightly rejecting selective options for deterrence purposes, Brown underlined the importance of a kind of assured second-strike capability. In the same vein, Secretary Brown declared later in spring 1977 that if either side approached a first-strike capability, relations between the superpowers would become extremely volatile and hazardous. The Defense Secretary noted that if the American deterrent was to be stable and secure, the Soviet deterrent must be secure as well, and he added that the United States had forgone the quest for a first-strike superiority over the Soviet Union. Brown observed that the necessary strategic stability between 'essential' or 'rough' equivalent deterrent forces was then existing and, noting that the strategic relationship was not self-stabilizing, he portrayed a future vulnerability of both sides' ICBM forces as a mutual Soviet–American problem. Altogether, the thrust of the Defense Secretary's statements was a kind of MAD reasoning, even though he also displayed some clear deviations from that thinking. [27]

Other manifestations from the administration showed a more pronounced adherence to a nuclear essentialist type of reasoning. In speeches and articles, the head of the Arms Control and Disarmament Agency and chief SALT negotiator, Paul Warnke, presented that view. Warnke maintained that the decisive mark of the strategic nuclear balance was that both the United States and the Soviet Union had a capability to deliver a devastating retaliatory strike and eliminate the other country as an industrialized society; this was a grim picture, Warnke added, but mutual deterrence was the best to hope for in the way of stability in the nuclear age. Later, in an address two months before his departure from the administration in October 1978, Warnke singled out former Defense Secretary McNamara's San Francisco speech of 1967 (cf. Chapter 2, section 2.1) as the seminal statement for understanding how the realities of deterrence originated in the mutual vulnerability of the United States and the Soviet Union to the nuclear missiles of the other side, and he followed McNamara in elaborating how the problem with anti-ballistic missile defense was that any system could be overcome by the other part adding offensive nuclear warheads. Warnke played down a *Minuteman* vulnerability problem as 'theoretical' and he dismissed the notion that a Russian civil defense program could deprive the United States of its assured destruction capability. In the same vein, but a little more cautiously, a pamphlet from the Arms Control and Disarmament Agency in November 1978 stressed that the vulnerability of the *Minuteman* missiles must be viewed in perspective in that it was not synonymous with the vulnerability of the United States, even if nothing was done about it. Assessing the Soviet civil defense program, it was concluded that there was no possibility for the Soviets in an all-out nuclear war of avoiding the deaths of millions of their citizens and the destruction of most of their industrial resources and urban areas.[28]

However, the incipient doubts of a part of the early Carter administration as to the conditions of nuclear deterrence increasingly appeared, especially in statements from Secretary Brown that assessed deterrence problems in elaborate and circumspect, often detached, terms. In his first annual Report, published in early February 1978, Brown stated that as deterrence of nuclear war was the most fundamental American defense objective, what counted was what Soviet civilian and military leaders believed and on that score America faced uncertainty in that what Americans saw as sufficient might appear as quite inadequate to the Soviets: 'What would deter us might not deter them.'[29] Later in the report, however, the condition of mutual deterrence was maintained as existing and it was declared to be in everyone's interest to accept it, just as it was stated that the United States had no current desire or plan for a disarming first-strike capability against the Soviet Union. In the same way, the early Carter administration's openly expressed doubts as to the possibility of keeping an initial use of nuclear weapons from escalating to a full-scale nuclear war were repeated and the Defense Secretary stated that he was 'not persuaded' that the right way to deal with a major Soviet damage-limiting program would be by imitating it because that would 'almost certainly' be self-defeating.

All the same, such manifestations by the Defense Secretary indicating adherence to a kind of assured destruction thinking, although a diluted one, were supplemented with several statements suggesting clear deviations from that reasoning. For example, the capability to respond effectively to an attack at a variety of levels was maintained as necessary to a credible deterrent and a complete distinction between deterrent forces and, as Secretary Brown put it, 'what are so awkwardly called war-fighting forces' was rejected. The potential vulnerability of the American silo-based ICBM forces was singled out as a major issue of concern but it was also stated that the issue had to be approached in perspective which included all the uncertainty associated with any Soviet attempt to execute a coordinated and successful attack against all US *Minuteman* silos. A more evident indicator of the move away from assured destruction toward war-fighting reasoning was a short remark stating that the requirement for strategic warheads was also a function of the need for some residual postwar capability. The conditions of nuclear deterrence were presented as having become increasingly demanding with the years as nuclear forces had grown more sophisticated in both the Soviet Union and the United States and, everything considered, it is evident that Defense Secretary Brown's first annual report, published one year after the Carter administration was installed, indicated a cautious but unmistakable change in the US government's image of deterrence.

The Carter administration's reasoning on deterrence during its last years, until the summer 1980, maintained several of the early similarities to an assured destruction type of thinking, but in a still more mitigated form as the inclination to nuclear war-fighting and counterforce arguments became more prominent. In his next two annual reports, as well as in other statements, Secretary Brown maintained that an assured destruction capability was the bedrock of nuclear deterrence, but it was not sufficient in that a fully effective deterrence required forces of sufficient size and flexibility to attack selectively a range of military and other targets and holding back a significant reserve, and Brown stressed that deterrence was not maintained automatically; among the necessary other options in this countervailing strategy, as Secretary Brown named it, he mentioned attacking the Soviet political power structure.[30] At the same time, Brown stated that the necessary American counter-military capability was not a first-strike force, so the Soviet Union would retain a survivable deterrent and the mutual deterrence situation would continue. Strategic nuclear forces, according to the Defense Secretary, could deter only a relatively narrow range of contingencies, and he reiterated that it was difficult to visualize any nuclear war that could be kept from escalating to all-out attacks on cities but nevertheless it was important to retain the capability to respond to a limited nuclear attack in a controlled and deliberate way. As to the ICBM vulnerability problem, it was characterized as having the utmost seriousness, and a calculated balance between the two nuclear forces in the early 1980s after a Soviet first strike and an American retaliation was invoked to substantiate that. Another indication of the administration's changing reasoning was the still stronger emphasis on strategic defense as an integral part of deterrence, combined with a declared recognition that attempting to construct a complete defense against a massive Soviet nuclear attack would be prohibitively costly and destabilizing and, as it was put, in the end almost certain to fail.

A special indication of the changing image of deterrence was the increasing significance attached to the state of nuclear sub-balances. In Brown's first annual reports, in early 1978 and 1979, the theater nuclear balance in Europe was shortly reviewed; it was noted that theater nuclear capabilities had critical deterrent functions of their own which required attention wherefore the size and mix of NATO's nuclear stockpile was under review in the Alliance. Particularly after NATO's double-track decision in December 1979, it was emphasized that parity between central strategic nuclear systems gave rise for concern about the continuing credibility of the Alliance's deterrent and the Soviet SS-20 missile was singled out as causing a potentially dangerous weakness in the deterrence.[31] The deployment of land-based Pershing II missiles and GLCM in Europe was presented as a visible demonstration of America's resolve to respond with an in theater system to Soviet nuclear threats against Western Europe, thereby reducing even further any Soviet misperception that it might be possible to fight a theater limited nuclear war from a sanctuary. However, assessing the role played by the TNF issue in the Carter administration's overall image of nuclear deterrence, it seems clear that restoring the sub-strategic deterrence balance was subordinate compared to the growing preoccupation with problems of strategic nuclear deterrence.

This growing preoccupation culminated through the last half-year of the administration from the summer of 1980 as distinct endorsements of some kind of nuclear war-fighting reasoning became manifest in several statements mixed, however, with a few remarks suggesting residual uncertainty about the validity and tenability of that deterrence view. The crux of the matter, according to this strengthened countervailing strategy, was that America's strategy, as a strategy of deterrence, necessarily had to be designed with the Soviet thinking on nuclear war in mind. As strongly emphasized, particularly by Secretary Brown when he explained Presidential Directive No. 59 (PD-59) in August and elaborated in the last annual report to Congress in January 1981,[32] deterring the Soviet Union, by definition, required taking account of Soviet perspectives on and assessments of the risk of nuclear war, not American. The reality of deterrence simply drove the United States to consider Soviet models, even if Americans thought American models of nuclear war were more accurate. Since the Soviet perspective on nuclear war included fighting a relatively prolonged nuclear war, it was necessary for deterrence purposes to adapt American strategy to this reality. To achieve effective deterrence, i.e. to insure that the ability to retaliate was fully credible, it was indispensable to give greater attention to how a nuclear war would actually be fought if deterrence failed. Special weight was assigned to American options to target organs of Soviet political and military control; such centers were highly valued by the Soviets and, the argument ran, a clear US capability to destroy them posed a marked challenge to the essence of the Soviet system and thus contributed to deterrence. However, it was added as a qualification that, of course, the administration recognized the role that a surviving Soviet supreme command could play in the termination of a nuclear war, and one could envisage many scenarios in which destruction of the Soviet leadership would be inadvisable and contrary to America's best interests. Possession of a capability was obviously not tantamount to exercising it, Brown noted. It is also noticeable that Secretary Brown emphasized that PD-59 was not a new strategic doctrine and not a radical departure from American strategic policy over the past decade or so.

It characterized this image of nuclear deterrence that the conditions were presented in extremely demanding terms. For example, the essence of the countervailing strategy was worded as 'convince the Soviets that they will be successfully opposed at any level of aggression they choose, and that no plausible outcome at any level of conflict could represent "success" for them by any reasonable definition of success.'[33] Hence, flexibility, escalation control, survivability and endurance, targeting objectives including Soviet strategic nuclear forces and other military forces as well as leadership and control organs and the industrial and economic base, and providing for adequate American reserve forces during and after a protracted conflict were all enumerated as basic elements to achieve the objectives of the countervailing strategy. Again, however, as they elaborated the countervailing strategy, both Secretary Brown and Secretary Muskie adduced various qualifying comments: the countervailing strategy was not a new strategic doctrine and it was not a radical departure from American strategic policy over the last decade, it did not assume that a nuclear war could remain limited, it did not assume that a nuclear war would in fact be protracted over many weeks, neither was it a first-strike strategy nor, according to Muskie, did it signify a shift to a war-fighting strategy.[34]

3.   The political significance of nuclear forces

The Carter administration's image of the Soviet Union as a nuclear adversary comprised the view that the state of the Soviet–American nuclear balance had a wider significance for the standing of the two superpowers in world politics, However, this Soviet essentialism appeared in a somewhat diluted form in that some members of the administration omitted any commitment on the issue while others who advocated this image also made various softening comments on the complexities of the issue.

The notion that the superpowers' relative nuclear strength had significance for everyday international politics was present in the early Carter administration's statements on nuclear policy but these statements lacked the urgency which later manifestations from the administration on the issue came to acquire. The thinking was manifest in steady declarations that 'essential equivalence' between American and Soviet strategic forces was an important objective, reflecting, according to this reasoning, the reality that nuclear forces like other military forces had a broader political role which was not entirely determined by either static criteria (counting technical characteristics of nuclear forces as war-heads, throw-weights, and so on), or dynamic criteria (war-gaming calculations of military capabilities). Nuclear capabilities, the administration declared, were part of the backdrop against which nations assess one another and conduct international politics. The basic notion was that America's allies, third countries, or America itself could be influenced, threatened, coerced, intimidated or blackmailed – words frequently used – into behaving contrary to American interests because of the state of a nuclear balance and therefore it was important to correct any lopsided balance so the Soviet Union was never able to use an edge in nuclear arms as an instrument of political or diplomatic leverage, or gain any other advantage from an imbalance between the superpowers. Stating this correlation between nuclear strength and political strength, the administration attached great importance to the idea that not only needed there be essential equivalence between American and Soviet nuclear forces, but American forces had to be *seen* on a par with Soviet forces; whether an imbalance was real or perceived, the *appearance* or *perception* of greater numbers or stronger nuclear forces could be a powerful diplomatic currency. On one occasion, at least, the significance of this was substantiated by referring to what theorists of international politics had long held, namely that perceptions could be as important as realities in the international arena. Indeed, it was added, in some sense the political advantages of being seen as the superior strategic power were more real and more usable than the military advantages of in fact being superior in one measure or another.[35]

The political significance of essential equivalence between American and Soviet nuclear forces was sometimes maintained, or substantiated, by invoking the Soviet approach: since the Soviets had insisted on equality as the basis for arms control agreements, the United States had to insist on equal aggregated and common ceilings as the principal ways of measuring and symbolizing that equality. In particular, the argument ran, any disparity would be reflected in a more confident Soviet leadership increasingly inclined toward more adventurous behavior in areas where American and Soviet interests clashed and where America's ability to respond by conventional military means could be circumscribed. At the same time, however, it was stated that to be driven in American force planning by perceptions of the military balance based on static indicators, and to seek or grant equality in every measure across the board, was to ensure the misuse of US and allied resources.[36] It was also noted that America itself did not find its numerical nuclear superiority particularly useful as it had it before the early 1960s but, as it was phrased, 'the Soviets, of course, are different' and should they somehow obtain a perceived nuclear superiority, they might mistakenly try to use it for political advantage.[37] In any event, the assumption or assertion that the Soviet Union attached supreme political and symbolic significance to nuclear arms, forcing the United States to imitate the Soviets to counter their proclivity, was predominant in the Carter administration.

The anxiety about the political impact of perceptions of any disparity between American and Soviet nuclear forces was elaborated by considering three problems. First, and most important, the prospective vulnerability of the *Minuteman* silo-based missiles was dangerous because it might contribute to a perception, in the Soviet Union as well as in other parts of the world or in the United States itself, of Soviet nuclear superiority, however illusory that superiority was and even if the vulnerability did not seriously impair America's retaliatory capability. Therefore, the decision to modernize the American ICBM force would demonstrate to the Soviets that their threat to American land-based missiles was not an avenue to Soviet nuclear superiority and American inferiority; it would be evidence that the United States was competitive in a major area of strategic power or, as expressed by Secretary Brown in 1979, 'what the Soviets have chosen as *the* major' area.[38] Second, although the United States did not need to match Soviet nuclear capabilities in all respects, the United States must insure that the Soviet Union did not have a monopoly of any major capability and therefore some long-range theater nuclear forces in Europe were needed to insure that the Soviets were left under no illusion that they would have a political leverage on NATO even if US central strategic systems remained the ultimate deterrent. Third, enlarging the small American civil defense program, in the light of the extensive Soviet civil defense program, should contribute to removing perceptions of any Soviet advantage in the strategic balance and reduce the possibility that the Soviets could coerce the United States in time of crisis.[39]

However, the continued stressing of the need for essential equivalence for political purposes and its specification frequently combined with reflections which suggested serious doubts as to the handling of the issue. On the one hand, the steady Soviet military build-up was emphasized and the intensity of Soviet programs compared to American restraint was noted; on the other hand, it was stated as paramount that the United States did not exaggerate what the Soviet build-up had meant for the worldwide balance of military power; it was best to avoid expressing the balance in tendentious terms, whether this was done in order to excite alarm or calm fears.[40] Particularly during the last year of the administration, this doubt was sharpened to strictures on what Secretary Muskie called 'the evangelists of American weakness': false declarations of American weakness only intensified the dangers because they could cause America's friends to doubt and America's enemies to discount the United States. In the same way, but in more discreet language, when Secretary Brown stated in his last annual report to Congress that the political advantages of being seen as the superior strategic power was more real than the military advantage, that observation was followed by the observation that those who emphasized one specific index of strategic power, out of the many that legitimately could be used, often did a disservice in helping to create a misperception of the actual state of the overall balance – a misperception that could have serious political consequences.[41]

4. Negotiations

Expounding the Carter administration's very composite image of negotiating with the Soviet Union on nuclear issues can be divided in four interrelated points: first, the need for arms control measures for stabilizing the Soviet–American nuclear relationship; second, the relation between arms control negotiations and agreement and broader political issues; third, the significance of unilateral American measures in connection with bilateral Soviet–American agreements; fourth, domestic American impediments to successful negotiations. Although the concrete presentation varied somewhat from one spokesman to another and was affected by the actual context as well – especially in that the SALT II agreement was withdrawn from the Senate in January 1980 after the Soviet invasion of Afghanistan – the administration's principal representation of the benefits of nuclear arms control negotiations and agreements with the Soviet Union did not change markedly over the years 1977-81. Elements of nuclear essentialism above all but mixed with Soviet essentialism were present throughout the Carter presidency.

Concerning the first point, the predominant argument for arms control measures was the need to stabilize the competition in nuclear arms between the United States and the Soviet Union. Uncertainty in both superpowers about the adversary's weapon development was singled out as a major factor propelling the arms race and thus SALT was essential because without an agreement there was the possibility of an escalating arms race with a greater risk of nuclear war. A SALT agreement placed definite bounds on the nuclear arms competition in that force structures ·of the future would be more predictable and the need to design against a wider range of uncertainties in strategic force planning was reduced. The SALT I interim agreement on strategic offensive forces had contributed somewhat to easing the uncertainties which faced defense planners, and in particular the ABM treaty had removed one major concern, it was argued; moreover, through 8-10 years of negotiations on SALT the United States and the Soviet Union had gradually become accustomed to talking with each other about the sensitive subject of strategic arms and had had the opportunity of developing a better understanding of each other's premises and concerns. At the same time the administration noted that, of course, no SALT agreement could solve all America's defense problems as to strategic arms or end the strategic nuclear competition with the Soviet Union, and neither would a SALT agreement be ideal from the standpoint of the United States or the Soviet Union; the important benefit was that it would reduce uncertainty about the nature of Soviet strategic forces in the 1980s, and thus make it easier to plan America's. In accordance with this reasoning, the administration announced in September 1977 that in order to maintain the status quo while SALT II negotiations were being completed, and provided that the Soviet Union exercised similar restraint, it would take no action inconsistent with the provisions of the interim agreement which was going to expire in October.[42]

The administration sometimes adduced that the conclusion of a new SALT agreement would enhance the prospects for other arms control problems, especially obtaining a comprehensive ban on nuclear tests and avoiding nuclear proliferation. President Carter and Paul Warnke, in particular, stressed that the major nuclear powers had to demonstrate to all the world that they took seriously their obligation to reduce the nuclear threat; Warnke argued that concerning nuclear proliferation the United States and the Soviet Union shared the same objectives and the same problems and an effective SALT agreement would meet the commitment made by the superpowers, as well as other nuclear weapon states that had signed the Non-proliferation Treaty in 1968, to restrain their nuclear arsenals; otherwise it could not rightly be expected that other nations would feel compelled to eschew nuclear weapons indefinitely.[43]

Such principal considerations on the value of a SALT agreement were reiterated after the SALT II agreement had been signed in June 1979 but in more urgent terms; on many occasions through autumn 1979 the administration argued strongly that if the Senate rejected the treaty, it would have pernicious effects on strategic stability.[44] Also after the administration had asked the Senate to delay consideration of the new SALT treaty in January 1980, the arguments for ratification were restated and often in strong terms. Throughout 1980, the administration declared that it remained firmly committed to ratification even if that in the present circumstances had become impossible because of the Soviet invasion of Afghanistan. Occasionally, a spokesman observed that precisely at times of increased tensions between the superpowers, effective mutual restraints on the strategic arms race became all the more important; in the same vein, outlining the ongoing modernization of America's strategic nuclear forces, Secretary Muskie once referred to a 'secret weapon' – the SALT II treaty.[45] It is also noteworthy that the last two annual reports from Defense Secretary Brown, published after the Senate had been asked to delay ratification, maintained that ratification remained an American interest and various reasons were given: reducing Soviet strategic forces, imposing some important qualitative constraints on the strategic arms competition, bringing greater predictability and stability to the nuclear relationship between the superpowers, and so on. Brown also emphasized that continued observation of the SALT II limits on strategic forces was important.[46]

As to the second point – the relation between bilateral Soviet–American arms control and broader political issues – the Carter administration frequently argued that the merits of the SALT process had to be judged in a broader political context as well. SALT was an element of stability in a turbulent world, establishing the foundations for an enduring political relationship between the superpowers that would reduce tensions and set important visible boundaries to their political and military competition. A new SALT agreement and a continuing SALT process would contribute to creating a climate in which the United States and the Soviet Union could resolve many other differences between them which were adding to the troubles of the world, and thus they could free themselves to concentrate on constructive action to give the world a better life. Indeed, it was argued, if the Soviet Union, like the United States, would emphasize negotiation and cooperation rather than competition, it would further enhance the prospect of a healthier state in US–Soviet relations.[47]

On the other hand, the administration also showed its circumspection in not overdoing this presumed link between a SALT agreement and its wider political benefits. A more beneficial political climate in international politics was predicted as consequence of a SALT agreement in vague and hedged terms but at the same time it was maintained time after time that the SALT process must stand on its own and the SALT II treaty should be judged on its own merits, based upon the enlightened self-interest of the United States and the Soviet Union. The general argument was that limitations on strategic arms were desirable in themselves and should not be held hostage to other American and Soviet policies or the general competition between the two countries. The United States could not insist that the Soviet Union accommodate American concerns, for instance as to human rights in the Soviet Union, as a condition for an agreement and neither could SALT be used to constrain Soviet expansionism or as a bribe to make the Soviets behave in a fashion which America could approve. In the same way, the administration dismissed objections that its human rights policy damaged the prospects for SALT because it caused the Soviets to hesitate in the negotiations. Overall, the Carter administration argued that one should avoid too close a linkage between reducing the nuclear danger and Soviet–American differences.[48]

However, the administration also followed a different line of reasoning on this veiled issue. While rejecting linkage as an American preference and a premediated American policy, the later Carter administration stressed that SALT did not and could not exist in total isolation, and two arguments were used.

First, since public opinion in a democratic society sets limits on what a government can do in foreign policy, some sort of linkage was a simple fact of life. As stated by President Carter in 1978: unless the Soviets did honor some basic human rights and showed some constraints on their involvement in Africa, it would be much more difficult to conclude a SALT agreement and have it ratified in the American Senate. After the Soviet invasion of Afghanistan, this form of linkage as a simple 'fact of life' was emphasized particularly by the administration's most outspoken advocate of SALT, Secretary Muskie, as he declared on several occasions that it would be impossible to rally the necessary support of the Senate to achieve ratification of SALT II unless there was a significant change in Soviet behavior. A quite different invocation of a kind of linkage-reasoning, but leading to the same conclusion, was made by Muskie when he declared that for the United States to be seen as the opponent of arms control would be a propaganda *coup* of enormous value to America's adversaries, the United States' credibility – its standing in the world as a nation of peace – also rested on the fate of SALT II.[49]

Second, combined with repudiating the view that the Soviets had to accommodate American concerns as a precondition for SALT, the administration stressed that the continuing SALT process could not be allowed to divert America's attention from or undermine America's will to meet challenges of Soviet military power, especially in the Third World. While it was America's interest to control the nuclear arms race by negotiating and entering agreements with the Soviets, a SALT agreement in no way limited the importance of promoting other American interests or answering Soviet threats to those interests. Thus, as the United States would not impose linkage between Soviet behavior and SALT, it would not accept any Soviet attempts to link SALT with aspects of American foreign policy of which the Soviets might disapprove; in that way the administration stressed that its rejection of linkage worked two ways: the essentiality of SALT did not detract from the significance of other political issues.[50]

Regarding the third point – the connection between unilateral American and bilateral Soviet–American measures – the Carter administration generally emphasized that maintaining appropriate US force levels was a necessary condition for useful arms control agreements, and this was stressed during the last years of the administration's tenure. The basic reasoning – frequently observed as a matter of course – was that no SALT agreement would obviate the need for unilateral American arms acquisitions or continued research and development efforts. Moreover, a sustained American arms modernization was useful precisely in negotiations because it increased the Soviets' motivation to negotiate seriously and it encouraged their compliance with agreements. This argument was applied, for instance, as the administration advocated its MX-program in the summer of 1979 and, in particular, when it was noted that the pursuit of the modernization of the long-range theater nuclear forces in Europe was the best way of providing incentives for the Soviets to negotiate in good faith.[51] On the other hand, this one-way relation between arms acquisitions and SALT was turned upside down, so to speak, when Secretary Vance noted, in October 1979, that it would have an adverse effect on the ability to go forward with the TNF modernization if SALT was not passed.

Another notable deviation from the dominant line of reasoning occurred when Secretary Muskie declared, in October 1980, that the American deployment of MIRV had done more to complicate negotiations over arms control than any other single technological advance; Muskie pointed out that when MIRV had first been deployed in the late 1960s, he had urged, in a speech from the Senate floor, that the United States should not proceed with the deployment on the grounds that once America had deployed MIRV, it would never be able to persuade the Russians to do without it and therefore, Muskie stressed, if the United States now suspended the SALT process, each side was going to go full speed at developing more sophisticated and more advanced nuclear weapons – hence controlling the nuclear technology would be even more difficult.[52]

As the administration elaborated the significance of American armaments and their relation to the negotiating process, the statements on the prospective vulnerability of the *Minuteman* force occupied a special place. It was claimed, over and over again, that with or without a SALT agreement the *Minuteman* missiles would increasingly become vulnerable; that problem was not created by SALT and it would not be solved with a SALT II agreement.[53] It was evident that the Carter administration exerted itself to detach this hotly debated issue from the debate on SALT and the judgment of the new SALT agreement. The vulnerability of American land-based ICBMs was, according to the administration, a primary example of how no arms control agreement with the Soviet Union could solve all America's defense problems.

The importance of unilateral American measures was also brought into relief in connection with monitoring Soviet compliance with arms control agreements. The administration emphasized that verification of a SALT agreement did not depend on trusting the Soviets: assuring Soviet compliance was based on American means of verification, including extremely sophisticated satellites, powerful electronic systems, and a vast intelligence network. To substantiate this, it published extensive reviews of the actual verification of SALT I and the adequate verifiability of SALT II. Still, the administration observed, the possibility of some undetected cheating in certain areas existed, but such cheating would not alter the strategic balance since any cheating on a scale large enough to change the balance would be discovered in time by unilateral American means to make appropriate response; furthermore, the American research and development program as well as the substantial capabilities of American strategic forces provided a hedge. Altogether, it was a prominent mark of the Carter administration's presentation of the benefits of Soviet–American arms control agreements that it was stressed repeatedly that in assuring Soviet compliance, the United States did not rely on trusting Soviet intentions or on political incentives for the Soviets to comply.[54]

The fourth point concerns some reflections to the effect that there were various American impediments to successful arms control negotiations between the United States and the Soviet Union. President Carter hinted at the problem when he noted, in a speech in June 1978, that Americans must avoid excessive swings in public mood about the Soviet Union – from euphoria when things were going well to despair when they were not, from an exaggerated sense of compatibility with the Soviet Union to open expressions of hostility. In the same vein, the President stated in January 1979, in an address before a joint session of the Congress, that it was important that the American people understood the nature of the SALT process as not based on sentiment but on the self-interest of both the United States and the Soviet Union.[55]

Such reflections were upgraded to distinct criticism of American attitudes by the administration's most outspoken advocates of Soviet–American negotiations and agreements on nuclear arms control. Most unambiguously, Paul Warnke commented on what he termed ingrained American attitudes about arms control. At the conclusion of any arms control negotiation, Warnke said, there was a natural disposition to ask, 'Who won?' Americans as a sports-minded nation saw everything in terms of competition: there had to be a winner and there had to be a loser. But, Warnke continued, that was not the way arms control worked. Arms control was not a sporting contest or a zero-sum game in which one side had to win and the other must lose; the net result of a successful arms control agreement had to be fair to both sides. It had to be a draw, and the parties did not have to be friends in order to reach agreement in the interests of both sides. Warnke observed that the American public had to be educated on and think through the benefits of arms control negotiations and learn that it was not a favor America did the Soviet Union or a reward for good Soviet behavior. Nor did SALT mean that the United States approved of the Soviet form of government or Soviet foreign or domestic policies.[56]

That kind of reflection – in its most overt manifestation from a prominent official in the American government – came to an end when Warnke left the Carter administration in October 1978. It was unrivalled, even if it is plain that other members of the administration shared similar views. It is evident, though, that also the later Carter administration harbored doubts, corresponding to some of Warnke's, concerning the expediency of many American attitudes toward negotiating with the Soviet Union.

5.   The Soviet view

The Carter administration's representation of the Soviet view of nuclear weapons changed somewhat during its tenure in the way that statements maintaining that the Soviets shared the American view were gradually replaced by statements pointing to the basic uncertainty of any conclusion, with the late Carter administration tending toward the interpretation that the Soviets actually held a view which was distinct from the American. Again, however, different members of the administration presented slightly different readings but the general trend from nuclear essentialism toward Soviet essentialism was unmistakable.

Directly questioned if he saw the Soviet Union as a defensive or an aggressive power, President Carter answered in November 1978 that the Soviets first of all wanted peace and security for their own people, and they undoubtedly exaggerated any perceived threat to themselves and wanted to be sure that they were able to protect themselves. The Soviets would like, the President declared, to expand their influence among other people in the world, believing that their system of government, their philosophy, was the best; however, his basically benign reading of the Soviet approach was demonstrated by the comment that in doing so, the Soviets were behaving like America. Directly concerning nuclear weapons, Carter stated that both the Soviet Union and the United States realized that no one could attack the other with impunity and neither did either of them intend to evolve a first strike capability; the United States and the Soviet Union shared a common recognition that their survival depended in a real sense on each other. In the spring of 1979, shortly before SALT II was signed, the President displayed another aspect of this type of interpretation of the Soviet perspective when he argued that the actual effect of an American rejection of a SALT agreement (i.e. a rejection by the Senate) would certainly be to encourage and strengthen the most intransigent and hostile elements of the Soviet political power structure.[57] Altogether, it is obvious that during the first 2–3 years of his tenure, President Carter portrayed the Soviet view of nuclear arms in very accommodating terms.

Secretary Vance presented the Soviet view in similar terms. Both the Soviet Union and the United States, Vance declared in June 1977, recognized that a nuclear war could result in the destruction of the world, and therefore it was something that both countries obviously would do everything within their power to avoid. Commenting on whether the two nations agreed on, quoting the Secretary of State's words, 'such refinements as strategic deterrence as opposed to counterforce', those were much more difficult questions, Vance noted. However, he added that the important point was that both recognized that they must do everything within their power to avoid nuclear war, and therefore they must take the necessary steps to stop the arms spiral and begin to move along the road toward real nuclear arms disarmament. Questioned, also in June 1977, to what extent he believed the human rights issue had clouded or inhibited the SALT talks, Vance answered that he still believed that the Soviets would make their decision in the SALT talks on the basis of what they considered to be their national interests in military and strategic terms. Later in 1977, Secretary Vance declared that his reading of Soviet objectives was that they were seeking strategic parity, like the United States.[58]

In the same vein, but applying more straightforward terms, Paul Warnke, answering a question in the spring of 1978 about whether he thought the Soviets shared American views on mutual assured destruction, declared that he found the logic of that position to be so compelling that he could not believe that any rational person would think otherwise. But Warnke also noted that you cannot be sure of anything in the strategic arms field. Commenting on how to be sure that the Soviets really understood that there was no defense against nuclear weapons, Warnke stated that the United States should continue to emphasize that there was no way in which the Soviet Union could spare itself millions and millions of casualties and the destruction of its society, if they were to launch a nuclear attack and America were to respond. He specifically deplored the reports that the Soviets had an effective civil defense; the real problem was not that they would have an effective defense but that they might fool themselves and, as a consequence, feel a greater freedom to brandish the nuclear threat. Later in 1978, two months before he resigned from the administration, Paul Warnke stated that the Soviets could not have been expected to allow the American lead in strategic nuclear capability to persist as long as they possessed the resources to close the gap; even if America's nuclear edge could not be used to thwart Soviet foreign policy objectives, a combination of historic Russian sensitivity to the activities of the West and Soviet ideology had, according to Warnke, driven the Soviet Union to catch up with the United States in strategic nuclear forces.[59]

Other members of the administration presented the Soviet approach to nuclear arms in less clear-cut terms. In July 1977, Defense Secretary Brown stated that whether the United States liked it or not, the Soviet leadership seemed intent on challenging it to a major military competition; the principal factor driving the nuclear arms race now, Brown observed, was the Soviet build-up, and whatever the motives behind it, the challenge was serious, even if the United States should recognize that the resulting competition was not an all-out contest or a purely military competition. Asked in September whether the Russians were preparing to fight a nuclear war rather than simply deter it, Secretary Brown stated that he could not say whether that was the Soviet doctrine and plan and he was not sure that the Soviet leaders knew themselves. Brown also said that the level of the Soviet civil defense effort was of some concern because it suggested that they might arrive at the conclusion that they could survive an all-out thermonuclear exchange. In both cases Brown recommended that the best answer was to disabuse the Soviets of such mistaken notions by some modifications of America's own strategy but the United States should not imitate and outmatch the Soviets in their efforts. Commenting on the Soviet nuclear build-up later in the autumn 1977, Brown noted that the United States could certainly not ignore their efforts or assume that the Soviets were motivated by considerations of defense or even altruism; as deterrence of nuclear war was America's most fundamental objective, what counted was the Soviet view and what Americans considered a credible deterrent, Soviet leaders might dismiss as bluff.[60]

In his first annual report, published in early February 1978, Secretary Brown mentioned that a number of hypotheses had been advanced to explain the objectives and motives of the current Soviet leadership. However, the Defense Secretary stated, owing to the traditional secrecy of the Kremlin – and because its collective leadership did not think with a single mind, as in Stalin's day – America faced great uncertainty as to the intentions of the Soviet leadership; Brown quoted Winston Churchill's famous words in 1939 which characterized Russia as 'a riddle wrapped in a mystery inside an enigma' and added: 'As far as can be judged, we are not much more enlightened today.' Later in the report, Brown noted that in the 1950s and 1960s much of the impulse for an interaction between American and Soviet strategic postures might have come, however unwittingly, from the United States; now, however, it was the Soviets who were driving the interaction and exactly what the Soviets were trying to accomplish with their large and growing strategic capabilities was uncertain. The Defense Secretary considered various explanations: if it was pure deterrence, their definition of pure deterrence appeared quite different from the American. Conceivably, Brown observed, the Soviets were as interested as the United States in the concepts of options and controlled nuclear campaigns. Much of what they were doing coincided with the actions that would support a damage-limiting strategy and it was within the realm of possibility that they were attempting to acquire what had been called 'war-winning' capabilities.[61]

Secretary Brown's predilection for a cautious and detached assessment of the Soviet approach to nuclear arms was also seen in the next annual report, published in January 1979. After having reviewed Soviet strategic nuclear capabilities, Brown observed that these programs made it clear that the Soviets were concerned about the failure of deterrence as well as its maintenance, 'just as we need to be and are'. Furthermore, the Soviet programs made it clear that they rejected the concept of minimum deterrence and assured destruction only, 'just as we should and do. That much is understandable.' However, according to the Defense Secretary, much more troublesome was the degree of emphasis in Soviet military doctrine on a war-winning nuclear capability, and the extent to which current Soviet programs were related to the doctrine which, Brown added, sounded like World War II refought with nuclear weapons. Commenting on the Soviet approach to negotiations, Brown noted that the Soviets had proved willing to engage constructively in a range of negotiations with the United States to constrain the military competition on the basis of detailed and verifiable arms control agreements; undoubtedly, Brown stated they had done so 'principally or at least largely to constrain the United States' and he followed this assessment with the statement: 'Our motive with respect to them is similar.'[62] The Defense Secretary's prudent assessment of the Soviet view also showed when he, together with Secretary Vance, was interviewed on television in May 1979; questioned whether the Soviets were actually preparing to fight and win a nuclear war and if the assumption that they believed in the American sort of deterrence was wrong-headed – which, as the questioner noted, was maintained by some opponents of SALT – Brown answered that there was probably a spectrum of views in the Soviet Union, 'as there is in the United States', on what deterred a nuclear war and on whether a nuclear war was winnable. Elaborating this answer, he mentioned the difficulties for military people, including students of military matters, to learn that with nuclear weapons and ballistic missiles the previous capabilities for defense had been wiped out, thereby obviously characterizing the mode of thinking among some people in both superpowers.[63]

The Carter administration's inclination to a benign interpretation of Soviet nuclear policy was especially demonstrated by Marshall Shulman, Special Advisor to the Secretary of State on Soviet Affairs. Noting that the Soviet military build-up seemed, to the United States, to have gone beyond a reasonable, prudent concern with legitimate Soviet defense requirements, Shulman stated that from the Soviet perspective they might no doubt see themselves as still seeking to catch up with the United States, to come out from under the burden of the strategic inferiority under which they had labored for so many years. It might be, Shulman added, that one of the problems was that the Soviet Union and the United States assessed differently the different attributes of the strategic nuclear balance and were inclined to give different weight to those fields in which the other side had an advantage. Outlining how the Soviet interest in reducing the danger of nuclear war overlapped with America's interest, he said that the Soviet leadership had committed itself to a political strategy of reduced international tension as the most prudent course for the advancement of its interest, and the Soviets saw SALT as a testament to the efficacy of this policy as well as a symbol of equal status with the United States. Concerning the Soviet view of the United States, Shulman observed that the multiple political viewpoints in the American society did not always present a unified face to the Soviets, and this had been a source of uncertainty to them; the Soviets mistrusted the volatility that sometimes resulted from the projection of America's pluralism onto the foreign policy plane.[64]

The administration's incipient doubt concerning the Soviet view reappeared in Secretary Brown's third annual report, published in late January 1980. In view of the fact that the report appeared four weeks after the Soviet invasion of Afghanistan, the persistent circumspection is, none the less, notable and it is one of the most searching on this issue from the Carter administration. Thus, the basic precariousness of any assessment of Soviet policy was emphasized: exactly what grievances and ambitions, what fears and nightmares were harbored by the Soviets we do not know; indeed, he added, the closed and authoritarian nature of the Soviet system and the secrecy with which they surrounded most of their decisions was one reason why they aroused so much suspicion about their motives. In these circumstances, the Defense Secretary continued, it was easy to equate them with the more demonic dictatorships of the past and, because of their ideological assumptions, to attribute the most soaring ambitions to them. In the same way, when the uncertainty of reaching any clear-cut understanding of Soviet concepts of the role and possible results of nuclear war was mentioned, one of the causes for the ambiguity was that 'even in the totalitarian Soviet state different leaders address these inherently uncertain issues from different perspectives.'[65]

An equally telling example of Defense Secretary Brown's cautious approach in interpreting the Soviet view was an insertion when Brown expressed his concern that some declarations by Soviet spokesmen and some Soviet military preparations suggested that they took the possibility that a nuclear war might actually be fought more seriously than the United States had done: '*at least in our public discourse*' (emphasis added). The pronounced inclination to maintain a reasonable interpretation of the Soviet view can also be seen in the observation that to recognize that strong war-winning views were held in some Soviet circles, and that Soviet advocates of such concepts as minimum deterrence or assured destruction were rare or absent, was not necessarily to make any accusation of special malevolence, for these were traditional military perspectives by no means unreflected in Western discussions of these matters. Despite all reservations, however, this report, like the previous ones, from the American Secretary of

Defense (1977–81) stressed that if the United States did not take the necessary countermeasures, the Soviets might succumb to the illusion that a nuclear war could actually be won at acceptable, if heavy, cost.[66]

From the summer of 1980, the administration emphasized more clearly the distinctive attributes of the Soviet view and, in particular, the necessity of taking into account the divergent Soviet perspective on nuclear arms when the American government shaped its nuclear policy. When Defense Secretary Brown announced PD-59 in August, he noted that the Soviet leadership appeared to contemplate at least the possibility of a relatively prolonged exchange in a nuclear war and in some circles they seemed to take seriously the theoretical possibility of victory in nuclear war; therefore, for the United States it was very important to ensure that the Soviet leadership could have no illusions about what a nuclear war would mean for Soviet state power and for Soviet society. A similar reading of the Soviet perspective and its significance for American policy was presented in the Defense Secretary's last annual report in January 1981.[67]

A special feature, as some members of the late Carter administration portrayed the Soviet view of nuclear arms, was an increasing propensity to counter Soviet polemics against new trends in American nuclear policy with their own polemizing against Soviet nuclear policy, combined, however, with endeavors to reassure the Soviets. As pointed out by Secretary Muskie – the most distinct advocate of a diluted kind of nuclear essentialism among the leading members of the administration – the Soviet public reaction to PD-59 (charging, according to Muskie, that PD-59 was a war-fighting strategy and an effort to achieve a first-strike capability that would undermine strategic stability) rang hollow in view of the Soviets' own doctrine, their attention to nuclear war-fighting, and the size and character of their strategic nuclear forces. Moreover, Muskie declared, the Soviets had never been particularly comfortable with what they regarded as America's 'city-killing' philosophy of nuclear deterrence. Secretary Muskie stated that he did not believe that the Soviets genuinely regarded the evolution in America's nuclear strategy as a move to a first-strike, war-fighting doctrine, and he reiterated that the United States wanted to make sure the Soviets got the right message, i.e. that it both underscored the consequences for the Soviets if they should ever initiate the use of nuclear weapons and that the United States remained fully alert to the risk of misperception and miscalculation in that the Soviets might see provocation where America intended none.[68]

3. THE REAGAN ADMINISTRATION, 1981–9

1. Convergent vs. divergent interests

During its first years the Reagan administration expressed the most distinct Soviet essentialist image presented by an American government since the early Kennedy administration twenty years earlier. A pronounced proclivity for letting the reading of the essence of the Soviet state determine the image of various aspects of the Soviet Union as a nuclear adversary was evident in the early Reagan presidency. After the first years the administration put more emphasis on convergent interests and occasionally hinted at a rather different interpretation, most markedly in connection with the December 1987 summit in Washington and the summit in Moscow in late May 1988.

The most prominent declarations stressing the moral and political contrast between the United States and the Soviet Union were put forward by President Reagan during the first 2–3 years of his presidency. The starting point, according to the President, was a recognition of what the Soviet empire was about; the Soviet Union was a totalitarian power committed by its all-encompassing Marxist-Leninist ideology to the goal of dominating the world and establishing a communist world state. Depicting Soviet goals in unambiguous terms as offensive and bent on world domination, the President attributed paramount importance to Marxism-Leninism as the ideology of Soviet leaders and having a direct and sinister significance for day-to-day Soviet policy in that it did not permit 'any western weakness unprobed, any vacuum of power unfilled'. In stark contrast, the United States was a democratic country pursuing democratic goals and as a country's foreign policy originated in the essence of its domestic political system, the world was torn by a great moral struggle between democracy and its enemies, between the spirit of freedom and those who fear freedom. Portraying Soviet–American antagonism in such simple terms, President Reagan also invoked the Scriptures and the conflict became even more a struggle between right and wrong, good and evil, with the Soviet Union 'the focus of evil in the modern world', or 'an evil empire'.[69] President Reagan at times supplemented this distinct ideological and moralizing depiction of the Soviet–American conflict with strong polemical observations on the Soviet Union. Thus on the occasion of his very first press conference, in January 1981, he declared that all Soviet leaders since the revolution had repeated their goal as the promotion of world revolution and had openly and publicly declared that the only morality they recognized was what would further their cause, meaning that they reserved unto themselves 'the right to commit any crime, to lie, to cheat, in order to attain that'. When President Reagan was later confronted with the opinion that he might have overdone the rhetoric a little by his accusations, he defended himself by saying that he had actually quoted the Soviets themselves concerning their rights to practise any morality that furthered their goal.[70]

Concurrently with presenting a distinct Soviet essentialist image, President Reagan at some occasions also talked about the American–Soviet relationship and proposed measures to deal with the nuclear danger which implied a different thinking, and this became more manifest after the turn of 1982–3. In late November 1982, the President spoke in a broadcast from the

White House about a letter sent to the Soviet leaders in which he had proposed various provisions to reduce the risk of nuclear war by accident or misunderstanding, and he presented the proposals as 'in order to clear away some of the mutual ignorance and suspicion between our two countries'. A few weeks later Reagan spoke appreciatively about 'encouraging' words and proposals from the Soviets laying a 'serious foundation' for progress.[71]

In the same vein – but more outspoken in its hint of a nuclear essentialist thinking – as President Reagan in a speech in January 1984 noted the differences between the American and the Soviet societies and philosophies which could not be wished away, he added: 'but we should always remember that we do have common interests. And the foremost among them is to avoid war.' The President also stated that a nuclear conflict could 'well be mankind's last'. Toward the end of the address Reagan observed that the people of the United States and the Soviet Union shared with all mankind the dream of eliminating the risks of nuclear war; our two countries, President Reagan declared, had never fought each other and there was no reason why they ever should. He recalled World War II when the United States and the Soviet Union fought common enemies and added: 'Today our common enemies are poverty, disease, and, above all, war', after which Reagan quoted President Kennedy's speech of June 1963: 'So let us not be blind to our differences, but let us also direct attention to our common interests and to the means by which those differences can be resolved' (cf. pp. 37–8, above).[72] After 1984, President Reagan, from time to time, called attention to areas of mutual interests between the United States and the Soviet Union: the two countries had a special responsibility to bring greater stability to their competition and to show the world a constructive example of the possibility of peaceful solutions to political problems.[73] Such declarations demonstrate the change compared to the early 1980s, but at the same time, Reagan always stressed that the two countries were adversaries and this two-sided approach was especially conspicuous in the President's speeches and comments at the December 1987 summit in Washington: when he mentioned that 'we have fundamental disagreements', he added some considerations about common interests in the nuclear era, for instance by noting that 'there is a great bond that draws the American and Soviet peoples together ... the common dream of peace.' On that occasion President Reagan also opined that the new Soviet leadership was not bent on world revolution and world dominance.[74]

The theme of common as well as divergent interests between the United States and the Soviet Union was elaborated in several other statements made by the administration, notably in speeches given by the first Secretary of State, Alexander Haig, and his successor from July 1982, George Shultz. Secretary Haig stated that the competition between Soviet totalitarianism and the forces of democracy, which dominated politics of the late twentieth century, would continue but the rivalry between the two philosophies was constrained by another central factor, nuclear weapons, because total victory by military means had become a formula for mutual catastrophe. Haig said that in developing and sustaining a relationship with the Soviet Union which recognized both competition and constrained force, the extremes that had distorted American foreign policy over the postwar period should be avoided.[75] Shultz further elaborated this theme of mixed American–Soviet interests in the nuclear age by noting that the United States needed to defend its interests and values against a powerful Soviet adversary but at the same time the two countries had a fundamental common interest in the avoidance of nuclear war, impelling them to work toward a relationship that would lead to a safer world for all, and the Secretary emphasized that there was no escape from this dual responsibility. Shultz noted too that the Marxist-Leninist ideology gives Soviet leaders a perspective on history and a vision of the future fundamentally different from the American, but he rejected the notion that the contention between the United States and the Soviet Union is inevitable and necessarily dominates and distorts international politics. The Secretary of State warned against being misled by 'atmospherics', whether sunny or stormy, and called on Americans to come to grips with the complex reality instead of swinging from one extreme to the other.[76]

As the Reagen administration stressed the reality of some common interests between the United States and the Soviet Union, one theme was frequently singled out, namely nuclear non-proliferation. Compared to other US governments, the actual significance of convergent Soviet and American interests was, though, clearly minimized, especially in that the importance of having the United States as a reliable alliance partner for third countries was strongly emphasized as a condition for non-proliferation. Nevertheless, when spokesmen quoted the several areas of divergent interests, they often observed that as far as non-proliferation of nuclear weapons was concerned the United States and the Soviet Union had a common stake with considerable potential for greater cooperation.[77]

Through the later years the Reagan administration's image of convergent vs. divergent interests was marked by a theme which can be epitomized as follows: America is once again a strong and vigorous leader of the free world. As American power is the indispensable element for securing both peace and freedom, renewed American strength and unity are an invaluable gain for all in a world where there are also common interests between the United States as the democratic and open society and the Soviet Union as the totalitarian and closed dictatorship. The reasoning that American military strength is the critical prerequisite for peace played a predominant role in the administration's manifestations: when the United States can deal from strength rather than weakness, the American–Soviet relationship is redefined so that American can manage the complex of divergent and convergent interests to the benefit of both peace and democracy. The important thing, it has been stressed time and again, is to persuade the

Soviets that the American commitment to strength is not short-term and transient but sustained and persistent.[78]

2. Deterrence

The distinctive feature of the Reagan administration's image of nuclear deterrence *vis-à-vis* the Soviet Union was a strong emphasis that deterrence turns on influencing a set of beliefs in the minds of Soviet leaders about American capabilities and will, given *Soviet* values and attitudes. According to this reasoning it is critical to deterrence to influence specific Soviet views, decisions and capabilities and pay careful attention to how the Soviets perceive the role of nuclear weapons. Singling out Soviet measures of effectiveness and criteria of success as decisive, it was often stated that there are many reasons to believe that Soviet assessments of nuclear war and deterrence are different from those usually made in the United States and it was implied that previous US governments had ignored that criterion.[79] Outlining this distinct Soviet essentialist image of deterrence it has to be pointed out, however, that the administration at no time expressed an all-out ideal type B image of deterrence in that it frequently declared that there would be no winners in a nuclear war; on the other hand, it declared that the United States must 'prevail' in a nuclear conflict.[80]

Emphasizing that the Soviet view of nuclear war was critical to the design of an effective American deterrence, the administration stated that it is characteristic of Soviet assessments of nuclear war that they focus on outcomes of large-scale global war. Hence, to deter the Soviet Union effectively it is necessary to forge an American capability and will to prevent the Soviets from prevailing in and after a nuclear conflict and assure that this is recognized by the Soviet leaders. This being so, the United States has to generate a flexible military capability in order to answer decisively and effectively Soviet aggression at any level and demonstrate its resolve to use that capability. In particular, this basic need for flexibility includes a survivable and powerful ICBM force to redress the asymmetry in prompt counterforce capability that has developed to the point where the Soviet ICBM force is becoming a sanctuary; it is also necessary that American nuclear forces are able to destroy those political, military and economic assets which the Soviet leadership values most highly, namely itself, its military power and political control capabilities, and its industrial ability to wage war. Indeed, the two criteria – 'prompt counterforce capability' and 'targeting what the Soviets value most highly' – have been catchwords for the Reagan administration's reasoning on deterrence. Pointing to these requirements for American deterrence policy, the administration reiterated that it is not simply a matter of military hardware where American nuclear systems have to mirror image Soviet systems by trying to match them in a symmetrical fashion. It is primarily a question of having flexible nuclear forces and shaping a perceived (i.e. 'perceived' by the Soviets) American *will* to counter the manifestly strong Soviet will, and this need for flexibility and 'perceived will' is related to a frequently stressed requirement for credibility: a deterrence solely based on nuclear weapons designed to destroy cities is neither moral nor prudent but will tend to defeat the goal of deterring the Soviet Union, and so it is necessary to be able to use nuclear forces responsively, discriminately and in good conscience.[81]

An essential feature of this reasoning on the conditions of deterrence is that it implies a detailed plan of what to do and which goals to pursue if deterrence fails. While the United States has to work to preserve deterrence, it would be irresponsible and immoral to reject the possibility that the terrible consequences of a nuclear war might be limited. The need for flexibility if deterrence breaks down actually bolsters up deterrence according to this reasoning, and it includes the planning of nuclear options so that the conflict might terminate on terms favorable to the United States and its allies or, as it has been put, the 'forces of freedom'; in that way deterrence can be re-established at the lowest possible level of violence and further destruction avoided. The most important requirement for this was improving the American command and control system so it can endure for an extended period after a nuclear attack.[82]

During the Reagan presidency's first term the presumed vulnerability of the American land-based missiles, the so-called 'window of vulnerability', was mentioned with fluctuating emphasis as the most immediate problem for an effective deterrent posture. The early Reagan administration strongly emphasized the urgency of the 'window of vulnerability' and used it to substantiate its claim that the Soviets had acquired a margin of nuclear superiority which the United States was forced to counter with, among other measures, MX. However, when President Carter's proposal for MX basing, the multiple protective shelter (MPS) basing scheme, was cancelled in October 1981 and replaced with a two-phase ICBM modernization program, beginning with a deployment of 40 MX missiles in the existing (and presumably vulnerable) *Minuteman* silos, the significance of the *Minuteman* vulnerability problem was not that urgent.[83] After that proposal had been rejected by Congress and President Reagan announced a new basing mode in November 1982, the so-called 'closely spaced basing' or 'dense pack' and renamed it 'Peacekeeper', the vulnerability problem of the existing land-based *Minuteman* missiles was, on the other hand, given a new supreme significance.[84] Again, however, after this proposal had been rejected by Congress and the strategic modernization program had been reviewed by the Scowcroft Commission, appointed by the President, and the Commission's report in April 1983 – endorsed by the administration – virtually disposed of the vulnerability problem, the administration was cautious not to stress the urgency of the problem; nevertheless, as the administration supported the recommendation from the Commission to deploy 100 MX missiles in *Minuteman* silos, the significance of the 'window of vulnerability' was recalled in guarded terms and Secretary Weinberger declared that the report could not be read as an elimination of the whole concept.[85]

Elaborating the requirements for deterrence, the administration singled out a separate intermediate-range level in Europe and claimed the need for a kind of equality on that level, too. The Soviet SS-20, SS-4 and SS-5 missiles represented a major threat against Western Europe and the only deterrent preventing Soviet use of these weapons was a counter-threat of a like response against Soviet territory, i.e. American land-based intermediate-range nuclear forces in Europe. Comparing what an administration spokesman termed 'truly comparable systems' no balance or approximate equality existed or – as expressed by Richard Perle, Assistant Secretary of Defense for International Security Affairs in early 1982 – the Soviets possessed the ultimate superiority; in the autumn of 1982 President Reagan declared that against the 945 warheads in Soviet medium-range missiles aimed at targets in Europe, 'we' had no deterrent whatsoever.[86] Consequently, it was argued in particular before late 1983 (when the American deployment in Europe had begun), in the event of a decoupling of the deployment component of NATO's double-track decision the Soviet Union would be left with an undeterred capability to wage nuclear war in Europe and they would not be dissuaded from believing that they might be able to conduct a nuclear war in Europe from a sanctuary in the Soviet Union. Moreover, it seems that President Reagan more than anyone considered the Pershing II missile a more effective deterrent against SS-20 than the slower cruise missile.[87]

Until spring 1983, the Reagan administration's considerations concerning deterrence were mostly presented in terms of the need to maintain and restore some kind of retaliatory capability, shading off into a capability to fight a protracted nuclear war, but also during the first two years of Reagan's presidency the possibilities of some kind of strategic defense were observed in positive terms. Thus the gap between several strategic defense measures adopted by the Soviet Union, for example in the area of civil defense, and the lack of American defense measures was noted with concern.[88] In his television address of March 1983, however, President Reagan mentioned toward the end of the speech, largely made as a strong appeal to the American people to support his rearmament program then facing opposition in Congress, that in recent months he had become convinced that there was an alternative to the awful situation of only threatening the existence of the adversary. The United States should be able to intercept and destroy ballistic missiles before they reached their goals; the President recognized that defensive systems against nuclear weapons had their limitations and raised problems and gray areas, but he called upon the scientific community in the United States to 'turn their great talents now to the cause of mankind and world peace, to give us the means of rendering these nuclear weapons impotent and obsolete.' A few days later Reagan said in an interview that if the United States at some future date were able to develop a comprehensive defense against nuclear missiles, he could foresee an American President offering to share it with the Soviet Union to encourage the elimination of *all* nuclear missiles; as to the idea of some sort of joint venture between the United States and the Soviet Union toward providing a defensive system, the President declared that he had not given it any thought – that was something to think about and consider.[89]

President Reagan's March 1983 speech foreshadowed a much stronger advocacy of deterrence by denial than ever before in American nuclear policy. The administration initiated an extensive program, the Strategic Defense Initiative (SDI), to develop a shield against ballistic nuclear missiles which was presented as an intensive research program focusing on advanced defensive technologies and distinct from an actual weapons deployment program. SDI is fully consistent with the ABM treaty and is pursued to provide the means for a more stable and credible deterrence, the administration declared. The purpose of SDI was presented as a way to 'strengthen deterrence' or 'secure a thoroughly reliable defense against all incoming Soviet missiles, either intermediate or long-range, and to destroy, by non-nuclear means, those missiles before they get near any target'.[90] Later, in the early 1990s, the research program would give a future President and Congress the knowledge necessary to support a decision whether to develop and deploy an advanced defensive system against nuclear missiles. Members of the administration elaborated key criteria by which the results of SDI research would be judged that, in principle, were as demanding as the above-mentioned goal; most important, any defensive system to be developed and deployed must be cost-effective relative to offensive forces, meaning that it must be able to maintain its effectiveness and survivability against offensive countermeasures.[91]

The value of a defense against nuclear missiles has, however, frequently been presented in terms that suggest a profound doubt as to the actual feasibility of a genuine deterrence by denial. As stated in general terms, the aim of SDI was making nuclear weapons impotent, but put in more concrete terms the aim converged into providing a defense for America's retaliatory capability. Thus it was said that deploying defensive systems has potential for enhancing deterrence because 'they could significantly increase an aggressor's uncertainty regarding whether his weapons would penetrate the defenses and destroy our *missiles and other military targets*'[92] (emphasis added). When spokesmen for the administration – in particular prominent members other than the President – argued for the value of defensive systems, they presented it as a supplement to the traditional nuclear deterrence through retaliation by providing the prospect of being able to block or blunt an attack and it was stated that progress toward an effective defense against nuclear missiles would have to proceed hand in hand with securing and regaining an effective offensive deterrent – the continuous need for modernization of offensive forces was claimed in unambiguous terms when the vision of an effective defense was presented. Besides, as the justification given for SDI changed somewhat from one member of the administration to another, and from one time to another, all suggested a profound uncertainty among most parts of the administration as to the most stable – or rather, least unstable – basis for deterrence. In any case, the Reagan administration showed a distinct preference for deterrence by denial as a supplement to, occasionally as a replacement for, the so far predominant deterrence by the threat of retaliation: effective defenses to confront an adversary with the likelihood that his attack will not succeed was presented as a more reassuring deterrence.[93]

The ambiguity as to the actual goal of SDI was related to a claimed need to build an American strategic defense to counter a Soviet technology. As frequently stated, the Soviet Union is the only country maintaining an operational ballistic missile defense system and the threat was invoked that the Soviet Union would unilaterally deploy a defense against ballistic missiles which, together with their impressive air and civil defense and massive offensive nuclear forces, would weaken the American deterrence. As put by Defense Secretary Weinberger: 'A vigorous American strategic defense research program is thus essential to ensure that we do not awake some day to find the Soviets rushing to full-scale ABM deployment.' Not only was SDI presented as a hedge against a Soviet breakthrough as to defensive technologies and a Soviet breakout from the ABM treaty, but it seems that a firm belief that Soviet military planners are confident that strategic missile defense will be effective worked as an essential argument for SDI, and both the Soviets' extensive effort to acquire such defenses and their major effort to stop the United States from proceeding with its defense initiative was invoked.[94]

3.   The political significance of nuclear forces

The Reagan administration saw the political significance of nuclear arms in unambiguously Soviet essentialist terms and contrary to the predecessor there were few openly declared doubts as to some 'complexities' of the issue. Nuclear weapons are current coinage in the global political conflict between the United States and the Soviet Union and have a supreme symbolic and political meaning in that the international political environment in which the United States pursues its foreign policy objectives to an important degree is shaped by the American–Soviet military balance, and in this nuclear arms are the ultimate arbiter. In statements expressing this view it was an important argument that the Soviet leaders perceive political conflicts that way so that the United States cannot ignore this reality.

According to the administration it was not the balance, however, as an objectively determinable quantity that is critical but rather all the subjectively accumulated impressions of the state of the balance or, as it was usually put, perceptions of the nuclear balance are politically decisive. The basic consideration was that all nations, in particular the Soviet Union but also America's friends and allies around the world who rely on the United States, make their foreign policy decisions profoundly affected by their perception of the relative strength and will of the United States and the Soviet Union. The nuclear balance was taken as a key indicator of the two superpowers' general strength and willpower and, hence, it is necessary for the United States to adapt its nuclear policy to negate any Soviet influence originating in that country's nuclear forces.[95]

This image has appeared by continual references to America's resolve and reliability as being at stake in any American decision on nuclear arms acquisitions. For example, discussing building up an American counterforce capability it has been argued that when the Soviet Union has a counterforce capability, without the United States having a comparable capability, that imbalance is dangerous because it will undermine the confidence of America's friends that the United States will support them when faced with Soviet challenges and Soviet attempts to blackmail in some acute crisis, and the further result of any Soviet nuclear counterforce superiority would be a steady loss in cohesion in America's alliances around the world. Likewise, the critical danger related to the 'window of vulnerability' has been presented as the perception of America's lack of resolve quite apart from the question of whether the Soviets would actually be prepared to launch a nuclear first strike, and considered in that context it has been advanced as vital for the United States' standing in world politics to deploy the *Peacekeeper* MX and be firm in its resolve; for America to back down on MX, the administration invoked, will deliver a blow to the allies' confidence in the United States as MX is seen by the world as a key test of America's resolve. Also in relation to SDI it has been stated that with the Soviet Union having a defense against ballistic missiles and the United States having none, America's position in global politics would be prejudiced and the United States and its friends could be vulnerable to nuclear blackmail.[96] Thus ever outlining the significance of America's resolve and reliability, the Reagan administration emphasized over and over again that this or that imbalance is dangerous because, if uncorrected, the Soviet leadership could come to *believe*, however mistakenly, that its nuclear forces could be used to gain political and diplomatic ends. A continuing stress on the need to elaborate American nuclear policy in order to demonstrate to the Soviet Union that it cannot achieve its political objectives through political coercion based on any nuclear advantage was supreme in the Reagan presidency's image of the political role of nuclear forces, and in that way the administration's notion of deterrence slid into a general idea on how to influence the whole complex of determining forces in world politics.

However, inherent in the administration's considerations on 'perceptions' of nuclear strength as critical was often some vacillation as to what is actually decisive when it concerns this issue. On the one hand, it often emphasized that the principal danger facing the world was not nuclear war but political intimidation based on the credible threat of nuclear war or, as vividly expressed by Eugene Rostow who was the Reagan administration's first Director of ACDA: 'the political radiation of nuclear arsenals' applied as an 'aggressive instrument of political coercion'. Rostow used the phrase 'equal deterrence' to indicate the necessary condition to deter any form of nuclear predominance and blackmail. On the other hand, the administration sometimes hesitated to overstate the dangers from 'the political radiation of nuclear arsenals' and Rostow repudiated the apocalyptic gloom of those who believe that resisting Soviet expansionism would be suicidal.[97] Other members of the administration emphasized a second danger – that of exaggerating Soviet military power – and Secretary Haig warned against a tendency to paint Soviet military capabilities in '10-foot tall proportions'.[98] Accordingly, the Reagan administration expressed a two-pronged view of the political significance of the nuclear balance: the situation (in the early 1980s) was gloomy but not *that* gloomy; the crux of the matter was always expressed as the American willpower to redress lopsided balances and meet any Soviet challenges.

The image of nuclear arms as the 'coinage' of international politics assumed a special topicality during the Reagan administration's first term with respect to the balance on intermediate-range nuclear forces in Europe. As in other instances concerning the political significance of nuclear forces, the administration argued that a Soviet monopoly of INF could lead the Soviet Union to believe that the United States might not respond to Soviet nuclear intimidation. Accepting Soviet freeze proposals as to these nuclear forces would legitimate Soviet superiority and secure for the Soviet Union unchallenged hegemony in Europe which would give the Soviets meaningful coercive power whether in peace or in a crisis. The critical importance of this Soviet belief would be amplified if NATO did not fully stick to the deployment component of the two-track decision in face of the Soviet propaganda campaign. If that happened, it would be a confirmation of the ominous political significance of the Soviet superiority as to TNF and a portent of further sinister political consequences.[99]

4. Negotiations

In particular during its first years, the Reagan administration was negative about Soviet–American negotiations and agreements on nuclear issues. But its criticism of arms control was never all-embracing and it was often directed at traditional *American* approaches rather than Soviet. Toward the end of the period, in 1987–8, the administration's statements on the issue were marked by a reformulation of long-standing Soviet essentialist themes as well as by a greater weight attached to a few nuclear essentialist reasonings.

President Reagan and other prominent members of his administration mentioned early some American–Soviet arms control agreements, for instance the 'Hot Line' agreement from 1963 with later improvements, as a good example of how the two nations can work together to reduce the risk of nuclear war and occasionally the importance of engaging the Soviets in a dialogue on reducing the nuclear threat was stressed. Concerning the SALT

II treaty, the administration stated early in 1981 that as it was fatally flawed it would not seek ratification, but neither would it take any action that would undercut the agreement so long as the Soviet Union exercised the same restraint. It also declared that there were no American preconditions for the resumption of the SALT negotiations – now renamed START – or for the opening of TNF negotiations – later renamed INF. In more general terms it has been stated, especially since about 1984, that there is no sane alternative to negotiations on arms control between the two nations which have the capacity to destroy civilization.[100]

Nevertheless, it has been a prominent theme throughout the years 1981–9 that negotiations in themselves are not the solution: the belief that merely sitting down with the Soviets and negotiating across the table will enhance the prospects for arms control is self-delusionary and pernicious. Negotiations, the administration stated repeatedly, do not exist in a vacuum. First, since negotiated arms control is not sought for its own sake – which previous administrations had often done – the United States cannot turn a blind eye to Soviet actions that undermine the very foundations of stable American–Soviet relations and thus Soviet behavior in other areas can and will at times impact on negotiations and that is inevitable in a democracy. Claiming this kind of 'linkage' as fact of life, some spokesmen, however, also stated that the US government does not aim at linking arms control negotiations to other areas of Soviet behavior because arms control efforts should not be overburdened with the task of resolving the major political conflicts between the United States and the Soviet Union.[101]

While presenting the linkage issue in somewhat divergent terms, the administration stressed more distinctly other conditions for arms control negotiations to be productive. The first prerequisite to any succesful arms control negotiations is that the United States clearly and unequivocally states its resolution to carry through unilaterally the necessary build-up to maintain an adequate balance. The notion that the United States actively, by maintaining a steady military build-up, has to provide some incentives to the Soviets to initiate serious negotiations and keep them moving in negotiations was by far the most dominant theme in the administration's statements on any negotiations. The idea of negotiating from a 'position of strength' was universally endorsed. Without a visibly demonstrated American will to take unilateral actions to rebuild and later maintain its military strength, the Soviets have no incentive to agree at negotiations to significant, equitable and mutual nuclear arms reductions; substantiating this image the administration cited Soviet conduct before the ABM treaty in 1972 and NATO's dual-track decision in 1979 as proving that Western willingness and willpower unilaterally to initiate its own nuclear build-up is a condition for serious negotiations.[102] The Reagan administration dismissed as naive the idea that the necessary incentive to the Soviets can be some kind of American restraint in its build-up. Stating this it often strongly censured previous US governments' approach to negotiations. The 'lessons' of arms control negotiations since the late 1960s have been construed as unambiguously supporting this conclusion. One member of the administration, Assistant Secretary of Defense for International Security Policy, Richard Perle, directly cited the negotiations in Munich in 1938 as a warning.[103]

This interpretation of Soviet negotiating behaviour was invoked when the administration had to defend any contentious nuclear arms acquisition. All members of the Reagan administration repeatedly warned against the dire consequences of abandoning this or that program, arguing that that would be sending the Soviets the wrong signals and would remove the basis for concluding successfully current or future negotiations. Thus when the strategic modernization program was presented in late 1981, it was stated that the program would increase the incentives to the Soviets to seek meaningful arms reductions through negotiations. However, it is notable that that argument for the early Reagan administration seemed to be subordinated to more prominent considerations concerning deterrence and the political significance of strategic modernizations.[104] Later, references to the importance of strengthening America's negotiating position *vis-à-vis* the Soviet Union increasingly became prominent but mostly still as an additional back-up to the decisive arguments; for example, as the administration strongly recommended the *Peacekeeper* MX in 1982–3, the importance of providing the United States with a negotiating leverage in START was usually advanced as an additional argument. On the other hand, the importance of initiating some nuclear deployments, especially the MX missile, in order to have a negotiating leverage was increasingly invoked as actual negotiations began.[105] Prominent references to the negotiation requirements were also evident when the Soviet Union left the INF negotiations in late 1983 and the administration argued that only the actual initiation of deployment of nuclear missiles in Europe could induce the Soviets to return to the negotiation table.[106] In a similar way the administration opposed domestic proposals for a freeze: it would either remove an incentive for the Soviets to negotiate seriously or, after the Soviets left START in late 1983, it would be a reward to them for not negotiating.[107] In any case, whether in relation to some prospective arms deployment, the actual initiation of deployments or the continuation of deployments in progress, the notion that an obviously visible American nuclear arms deployment is imperative as a major incentive for the Soviets to negotiate seriously, and thus a key to successful negotiations, was paramount throughout the Reagan presidency, and the shift in argumentation from the former to the latter type of reasoning was geared to the progress in American nuclear arms deployment policy.

The idea that an active and persistent American arms and arms research program is a necessary means by which the United States can agree with the Soviet Union on deep nuclear arms reductions – eventually the elimination of ballistic missiles – has also been present in a somewhat vaguer form in the presentation of SDI. It has been argued that SDI, combined with the demonstrated resolve to modernize America's offensive strategic deterrent, brought the Soviet Union back to the negotiating table. It has also been advanced that, faced with effective defenses against nuclear missiles at some future time, the Soviets would have strong incentives for agreeing to offensive arms reductions and different more or less vague notions have been conveyed that a cooperative Soviet–America arms control endeavor pursuant to the terms of the ABM treaty (interpreted broadly[108]) can help manage the transition period to advanced and effective defensive systems.[109] The ambiguity of the administration's approach to this issue, though, was amplified by several statements to the effect that SDI is not a bargaining chip. Considered in the light of the fact that the concept 'bargaining chip' universally has a bad reputation and assuming the durability of the administration's declarations that it would not give up SDI for Soviet reductions in offensive missiles, there does not need to be any ambiguity at all; however, considering hints from the administration that a *negotiated* transition from 'mutual assured destruction' to 'mutually assured survival'[110] was both desirable and necessary, the many declarations that SDI was not a bargaining chip add to the profound ambiguity of the perceived role of SDI in relation to negotiating with the Soviets. However that may be, the administration's equivocal approach to some future implementation of fully effective defensive systems evidently indicates its profound predilection for American self-reliance, compared to negotiations, in whatever form in managing nuclear threats.

The Reagan administration's approach to negotiating agreements on nuclear issues with the Soviet Union was more direct when it concerns another problem, namely Soviet compliance with agreements. The administration often claimed that the Soviet Union had violated several Soviet–American arms control agreements and it produced extensive reports to substantiate Soviet violations.[111] The violations comprised, for example, the ABM Treaty, the Limited Test Ban Treaty, the SALT I Interim Agreement and the SALT II Treaty. Some violations were presented as more evident than others and some were claimed to have more military significance than others, but politically all violations were equally important because they suggested, it was stated, that the Soviets would violate agreements whenever they find it in their interest to do so even for modest improvements from their own point of view, and in any case the Soviet violations raised serious questions about the integrity of the whole arms control process. To the administration, it all pointed to the importance of insuring that any arms control agreement should be verifiable by national technical means; indeed, maintaining this requirement as an absolute need for meaningful arms control has been a predominant mark of the Reagan presidency's approach to negotiations. Despite the many Soviet violations of the unratified SALT II document, the administration stated over more than five years that it would not violate that agreement. However, in late

May 1986, it declared that the United States must base its strategic force structure on the 'nature and magnitude of the threat posed by Soviet strategic forces' and not on standards contained in the flawed SALT II treaty wherefore it would deploy cruise missiles on the B-52 bomber beyond the terms of that treaty from the end of 1986. [112]

Presenting these various elements of its image of negotiating with the Soviet Union and in particular outlining the Soviet behavior as to negotiations and compliance with agreements, the Reagan administration attached a special significance to the differences between traditional Soviet and American approaches to negotiations. The Russians, it stated on several occasions, always display an extraordinary degree of patience and take the long view in negotiations; they just react to American proposals, rather than initiate some themselves, and are bent on outlasting the United States, while the Americans, by contrast, are problem-solvers who want quick results. The traditional Soviet approach to arms control negotiations has been to combine tough bargaining at the negotiating table with a hard-headed public propaganda campaign designed to undercut support for the adversary's positions and force unilateral concessions. As the administration outlined its own approach to negotiations, it often underscored the differences to earlier American governments' negotiating policy and stressed some obvious lessons of earlier negotiations: if the United States wants to negotiate arms reductions with the Soviets, it must not appear to be too eager for an agreement but must be patient and demonstrate steadfastness and resolve because the Soviets always try to divide the United States from its allies and attempt to exploit divisions in the United States which are openly observable. Otherwise expressed, if America wants to reach productive arms control agreements with the Soviets, it is necessary to imitate and emulate the Soviets' negotiation tactics which always attempt to test the American resolve and strength of purpose, and some members of the administration clearly displayed a certain envy of what was seen as the strong Soviet purposefulness and ruthlessness – if America wanted to stand up to the Soviets in the arms control negotiations, it must learn from the Soviets. [113]

The Reagan administration's reading of divergent Soviet and American approaches to negotiations assumed another – partly similar, partly dissimilar – form when the domestic American context has been used as a starting point. On the one hand, Secretary Shultz stressed that unity in the United States is critical for progress in negotiations; if America appears divided, the Soviets will conclude that domestic political pressure will undercut America's negotiation position and they will dig in their heels even deeper. On the other hand, President Reagan stated that this Soviet belief is illusory; even if the Soviets block American proposals and apparently believe that their uncompromising attitude in negotiations will ultimately win out, the diversity of democracies is a source of strength, not weakness, and from free discussions among free people come unity and commitment;

the sooner this is understood by the Soviets, according to the President, the sooner an agreement in the interests of both sides will be reached in the negotiations.[114] This shows that the Reagan administration's conception of the American democracy's ability to stand up to the Soviet dictatorship in negotiations was composite: some nagging doubts were mixed with strong statements on democracies' strength, tending towards exhortations.

In 1987–8, the administration's Soviet essentialist dominated reasoning on the Soviet Union as a negotiating adversary was recast and some nuclear essentialist themes appeared in a more distinct version. Thus when an agreement to establish 'Nuclear Risk Reduction Centers' was signed in September, President Reagan presented it as a practical step in the two countries' effort to reduce the risks of conflict that could result from 'accident, miscalculation, or misunderstanding'.[115] More important were the presentations as to INF. The Soviet statement of late February 1987 that it would no longer insist on linking agreement on reductions in INF to agreement in other negotiations was welcomed and it was emphasized that allied firmness and unity in carrying out NATO's 1979 decision had helped to bring about the new opportunity for arms reductions.[116] When the December 1987 treaty was signed at the summit between Reagan and Gorbachev, this was reiterated but often in guarded terms. President Reagan emphasized that the verification procedures aopted by the treaty were new and could have far-reaching implications; on-site and short-notice inspections to be permitted within the Soviet Union was a breakthrough and the treaty and 'all that we have achieved during this summit' signalled a broader understanding between the United States and the Soviet Union, according to the President.[117] On the whole, though, the administration endeavored not to overdo the new situation and the prospects, and it stressed (in particular when the two leaders did not address the public together) how the treaty was a result of NATO's steadfastness. The theme that the INF Treaty proved the importance of NATO's resolve and tough-mindedness in going forward with deployments despite protests was especially stressed when the administration defended the treaty in the Senate in early 1988; as expressed by Secretary Shultz: 'we succeeded because we and our allies stayed the course – on both tracks.'[118]

5.   The Soviet view

The preceding outline of various aspects of the Reagan administration's image of the Soviet Union as a nuclear adversary shows the significance attached to the *Soviet* view of nuclear arms. In fact, the specific substance of the Soviet approach to the role of nuclear weapons in the superior political conflict in the world was the dominating starting point and other aspects were presented as corollaries of its peculiarities. In that sense, the Reagan presidency's reading of the Soviet Union as a nuclear power represented the most distinct type of Soviet essentialism set out by a US government.

The principal point characterizing the Soviet view of nuclear arms was, according to the administration, that Soviet nuclear weapons as part of overall Soviet military power constitute the critical backdrop for pursuing their long-term goal which is attaining pre-eminent influence in world affairs. In peacetime this means that the mission of Soviet nuclear forces is intimidation and coercion, to induce paralysis and create disarray in free societies by capitalizing on the coercive leverage inherent in powerful nuclear forces. Indeed, the notion of nuclear blackmail holds a critical place as the Soviet view is interpreted and therefore, the administration stated, the principal danger facing the world was not nuclear war but political coercion based on the credible threat of nuclear war.[119] In wartime it means that the employment of nuclear forces is viewed by the Soviets as the key to survival and winning. The Soviets, declared President Reagan in 1981, believe that a nuclear war is winnable and that makes them constitute a threat, and he referred to 'everything in their manuals' as indicating that. Secretary Weinberger presented the Soviet view in similar terms, and as a special point it has been adduced that the Soviet command, control and communication system looks like one that proceeds from the belief that nuclear war could be fought and won. In the same way, various features of the Soviet military posture – particularly their hard-target nuclear capability, their civil defense and their military doctrine – have been advanced to substantiate this interpretation of the Soviet view: the Soviet Union has built nuclear forces clearly designed to strike first and disarm their adversary.[120]

Presenting this Soviet view of nuclear arms has often included a sharp censure of previous US governments' – and many existing American – naive interpretations. As spokesmen for the Reagan administration stressed that the priority accorded nuclear war-fighting by the Soviets was in sharp contrast to the American policy of deterrence, it has been emphasized that Americans should discard the illusion that the Soviets share the American view. That illusion, it was declared, has for many years haunted American nuclear arms policy but as Soviet doctrine and forces emphasize the ability to fight and win a nuclear war, it was now obvious that the Soviet Union 'marches to a different drummer'.[121] Put in more general terms, some members of the administration stressed that the Soviets clearly understand the relationship between military power and foreign policy and again the difference from naive Western opinions was emphasized: contrary to many observers in the West who have spoken of the 'impotence of power', the Soviets understand that military power at all levels – and better, military superiority – is a critical backdrop for conducting a successful foreign policy and is an essential precondition for a coherent strategic approach to international relations; the Soviets have grasped that military force, including nuclear forces, alter political perceptions which many Americans prefer to ignore.[122] Altogether, presenting this reading of the Soviet view members of the Reagan administration often displayed admiration for the Soviet hard-headedness and disdain for American softness.

Some members of the administration have given their presentation of the

Soviet view the twist that while the Soviets would like to achieve their foreign policy objectives by threatening the use of nuclear weapons, they recognize that attempting to make good that threat carries with it the seeds of their own destruction: many examples abound where the Soviets have fuelled and exploited crises, but they have only done so when they believe the risk of nuclear war was small.[123] The Soviets, according to this interpretation, realize that nuclear war is not a viable option; the Soviet view of nuclear weapons is therefore highly malign, but that potentiality only becomes an actual danger if the West – particularly the United States – appears hesitant and afraid of posing a comparable counter-threat, and as to that imperative the American policy was at fault until the Reagan administration took office. In the late 1980s this primarily means that the United States has to carry on steadfastly with SDI since this will cancel the potential malign consequences of the Soviet view – just as the resolute deployment of intermediate-range missiles in Europe has cancelled the Soviet intentions with SS-20.

At the same time that the Reagan administration presented this interpretation of the Soviet view, it has occasionally, in defending SDI, invoked the traditional Soviet preference for strategic defense. Thus President Reagan referred to former Premier Kosygin's statement in 1967 that an anti-missile system is designed to preserve human lives and not to kill people, and defensive systems are not the cause of the arms race but constitute a factor preventing attack and the death of people. In the same vein, Secretary Shultz called attention to Gromyko's speech to the United Nations General Assembly in 1962 where he stated that anti-missile defenses could be the key to a successful agreement reducing offensive missiles. [124] To the administration, this too confirmed the reading of the Soviet view of nuclear arms, namely that in peacetime they are means of intimidating political adversaries and, in any case, countering the Soviet view is a matter of Western willpower to stand up to massive Soviet propaganda campaigns.

However, the Reagan administration sometimes supplemented that reading of the Soviet view by more conciliatory remarks, a tendency that was most marked during the administration's second term. But even in 1982 President Reagan noted that over the years Soviet leaders have expressed a sober view of nuclear war and both the Soviet people and their leaders understood the importance of preventing war. Calling attention to the Soviet war experience, the President stated that the Soviet Union, within the memory of its leaders, had known the devastation of total conventional war and they knew that nuclear war would be even more calamitous. In the same vein, the President declared in 1985 and 1986 that he was pleased that the Soviet Union appeared to agree in principle with America's ultimate goal of moving to the total elimination of nuclear weapons when this becomes possible. [125] A benign reading of the Soviet view was also implied in several of President Reagan's statements at the summits in Washington in December 1987 and in Moscow in late May 1988. At the same time, however, it is evident that the administration endeavored not to seem too optimistic in its more benign readings of the Soviet view of nuclear arms. It was still emphasized that the Soviets continue to place great stress on nuclear war-fighting capabilities at all levels of the conflict spectrum and that this reflected a belief that a nuclear war 'may under certain conditions, be fought and won'.[126] Moreover, President Reagan noted, in January 1988, that this strategic outlook was very different from 'our own'.[127] In the same way, when it was noted, in spring 1988, that recent Soviet statements appear to reject their previously held positions on nuclear war-fighting and war-winning, it was added that such statements cannot be accepted 'solely at face value',[128] particularly in light of their unflagging efforts to develop command, control, and communication facilities, necessary to support a nuclear war winning strategy. Such Soviet declarations seemed to be a part of their new 'peace offensive'.[129]

4. Synthesis: fixtures, trends and swings, 1961–89

As the further purpose of this study is to elaborate long-term constancies and changes, the review of US governments' images of the Soviet Union as a nuclear adversary through more than 25 years in terms of the nuclear essentialism vs. Soviet essentialism distinction will be synthesized by identifying fixtures, trends and prevalent swings during the period. What is termed a 'fixture' is an invariable constituent part of public statements on the Soviet Union and nuclear arms, i.e. some reasoning persisting as an integral part of six administrations' presentations through the period from the early 1960s to the late 1980s. A 'trend' is a general course or direction, that is, a prevailing tendency demonstrable for a number of years and through more than one administration. A 'swing' is a change followed by a return to a position similar to the dominating fixture or trend and occurring inside one administration or between two successive administrations. In this sense, which fixtures, trends and prevalent swings characterize US governments' portrayals of the Soviet Union as a nuclear armed political antagonist, 1961–89?

Applying these concepts in synthesizing the images of 1961–89, one problem to be examined concerns the relations between fixtures, trends and swings of the five conceptually different but interrelated themes. Can relations between themes be identified that suggest that some aspects of American governments' manifestations are more 'primeval' than others? This is first of all a matter of identifying some fixture(s) but it is also a problem of elaborating the content and temporal course of trends and swings.

1. FIXTURES

Throughout the period 1961–89 all administrations have endorsed the idea that in the nuclear age there are both convergent and divergent interests between the United States and the Soviet Union. Some administrations have, at least for a time, strongly emphasized divergent interests while others have assigned more importance to mutual interests, but none has portrayed the Soviet–American relationship exclusively in terms of cooperation or conflict. It has been a fixture too that the deterrence notion has universally been adopted at least just as an abstract preference for negotiating with the Soviets on the nuclear issue has been voiced through all the years. Again, we have seen obvious differences from one presidency or period to another but, put in general terms, all administrations have endorsed 'deterrence' and 'negotiations'. That much is unproblematic and, in the context of this analysis, less interesting. None the less, it is worth noting these fixtures. Another notable common trait is the widespread use of what can be called high-flown rhetoric when many prominent members of US governments have portrayed the Soviet–American relationship in the nuclear age. Whatever the actual content of this or that declaration, it is evident that several American leaders throughout the period 1961–89 have employed a pretentiously lofty usage on the issue.

Having noted such characteristics, the pertinent question is whether US governments' images of the Soviet Union as a nuclear adversary through almost a generation have displayed some continuity that can be expressed in terms of the nuclear essentialism vs. Soviet essentialism dichotomy. The most evident common feature through more than 25 years is *a sustained manifestation of some kind of Soviet essentialism as to the political significance of nuclear forces*. All administrations have tended toward presenting the actual state of the Soviet–American nuclear balance as an essential symbol of the course of the political conflict between the totalitarian Soviet Union and the democratic United States. Adherence to the political symbolism of nuclear weapons has been a fixture. Through the 1960s, this adoption of one kind of Soviet essentialism appeared in the notion 'nuclear superiority' perceived as an essential asset for the United States in the Soviet–American political conflict while, in the 1970s and 1980s, frequent accentuations of 'perceptions' of nuclear strength appeared as a functional equivalent. The salience of this fixture can be elucidated by noting the few deviations that actually have occurred, namely the declarations from a few – although prominent – members of the administrations in the late 1960s and first half of the 1970s indicating an exceptional deviation toward nuclear essentialism. Through the late 1970s a similar doubt appeared when some officials underscored the complexities of the issue.

Related to the established dominance of a Soviet essentialism as to the political benefit of nuclear strength is *the continuous stressing of a need for steady American nuclear deployments to induce the Soviets to negotiate seriously*. The idea that the Soviet government ever needs a foreign, actively generated incentive to negotiate 'seriously' has been attractive to all administrations. While it has to be noted that some administrations have emphasized this more than others, the overall conclusion is that all presidencies have tended toward this type of Soviet essentialism. This common trait has, of course, been most prevalent when negotiations have actually been in progress or forthcoming but considering the general adherence to negotiations, it is notable that the notion of negotiating 'from strength' has been endorsed by all presidencies. Noting the general prominence of this idea, it is an interesting point too that it was particularly stressed by the Carter administration and then in combination with that administration's general emphasis on the need (i.e. the need for the United States too) for Soviet–American arms control agreements. On the other hand, the one administration that most distinctly rejected the idea that the United States needs Soviet–American arms control agreements – the early Reagan administration – downgraded this argument and only later, concurrent with the Reagan administration's increasing adherence to negotiations, did that argument get a prominent role. In that way one type of nuclear essentialism (stressing the importance of Soviet–American arms control agreements) has promoted one type of Soviet essentialism (stressing the requirement for more nuclear arms to induce the Soviets to negotiate), while the corresponding type of Soviet essentialism (arguing that the United States has no need for arms control agreements) has obviated another kind of Soviet essentialism (stating that the United States needs more nuclear weapons to press the Soviets to negotiate).

Identifying these Soviet essentialist fixtures of American governments' images through the years when the balance of terror has been viewed as an immutable fact, it is worth noting that they accord with the most prominent official document from the first post-war – and nuclear age – period, NSC-68, published by the Truman administration in spring 1950. From the review of the images 1961–89 in Chapters 2 and 3 (especially Chapter 2) it is evident that salient features of some US governments' approach to the Soviet Union as a nuclear armed opponent have diverged markedly from NSC-68 and so one may easily overdo the intellectual impact of the views in NSC-68. None the less, it is remarkable that the fixed aspects of all administrations' images since the balance of terror predicament was first recognized accord with that most important official document, published after the Soviet Union acquired the nuclear bomb but before the balance of terror came to be seen as a fact. Moreover, it is notable that the first administration that openly has declared that abolishing America's vulnerability to atomic weapons is American policy – the Reagan administration, since March 1983 – is the administration that most distinctly shares the reading of the Soviet Union as a nuclear power contained in NSC-68 and Soviet essentialism.

It all points to the observation that the Soviet essentialist fixtures represent an enduring continuity of America's meeting with a political adversary in the nuclear age.

2.   TRENDS

Two long-term trends have been evident since the early 1960s. First, a trend toward nuclear essentialism through the 1960s and into the early 1970s, initiated by the Kennedy administration from 1963 and most evident during the later 1960s while it assumed a more diluted form in the early 1970s. Second, a trend toward Soviet essentialism since the mid-1970s, passing its peak in the early 1980s and continuing in a different form in the mid to late 1980s. As for both trends, particularly the first, it applies that they were combined with opposite tendencies but the general picture is unmistakable.

The nuclear essentialist trend was initiated by the Kennedy administration in 1963 and was first reflected in the weight attached to convergent interests and the role of negotiations while the deterrence doctrine and the interpretation of the Soviet view was more ambiguous. Later in the 1960s, the reasoning on deterrence too began to follow a kind of nuclear essentialism and related to what was an often implicit assumption that the Soviet view of the balance of terror predicament was a mirror image of the American. It was furthermore distinctive that the most pronounced cases of this nuclear essentialism were manifested in a few conspicuous speeches by the former Secretary of Defense, Robert McNamara.

Toward the end of the 1960s, and particularly in the first years of the 1970s, the dominating nuclear essentialist thinking was toned down. The deterrence reasoning lost its most distinctive nuclear essentialist qualities after only a short time while both the image of convergent interests and negotiations were frequently restated in unambiguously nuclear essentialist terms which, however, were changed compared to the late 1960s. Concurrent with this, doubts appeared as to the actual content of the Soviet view and its significance. Still, the mainly nuclear essentialist conclusions were maintained.

On the other hand, the different administrations' image of the political significance of nuclear arms (cf. above) only sporadically followed a nuclear essentialist reasoning during these years when that trend was prevalent. Of course, this discrepancy is not necessarily self-contradictory – it is only so from a clear-cut nuclear essentialist or Soviet essentialist point of view (as are all other 'deviations') – but it is still worth noting because it suggests a salient feature of US governments' perception when this perception in some respects demonstrates a nuclear essentialist mark. Another noticeable 'discrepancy' is that this trend was combined with a clearly displayed differentiation between different levels of nuclear arms, each with its own requirements: as to the theater nuclear level in Europe, the requirements for deterrence always included some kind of limited nuclear options.

The Soviet essentialist trend became evident in the mid-1970s and has concerned the image of deterrence and the Soviet view. *As to deterrence*, the promulgation of the Schlesinger strategy in 1974 marked a turning point even if traces of that type of reasoning on deterrence have existed in all administrations' statements throughout the period since 1961 – only excepting a few notable statements in the late 1960s – and even if one can now, with the benefit of hindsight, identify the intellectual origins of the Schlesinger strategy in earlier statements from the US government through the first years of the 1970s. Outlining the characteristics of this trend, it is noticeable, however, that it has not been unswerving in that the first years of the Carter administration broke with what otherwise seems to be a linear evolution in American governments' reasoning on deterrence but after that 'interruption' the long-term trend continued and was amplified. Moreover, concurrent with the resumed Soviet essentialist trend on deterrence in the late 1970s, the ever-present differentiation between different levels of nuclear balance with divergent requirements for deterrence and the concomitant need for coupling became much more pronounced; otherwise expressed, this aspect of the Soviet essentialist trend appeared with a time-lag even if its basically general occurrence can be considered a fixture.

The promulgation of the Schlesinger strategy in 1974 can be considered a crucial turning point. However, considered from another angle, the year 1983 is a turning point. The much greater weight attached to deterrence by denial since then may herald a change in US governments' thinking on deterrence that is even more crucial. Whether this will be the case depends on the criteria for what is considered a 'satisfying' deterrence by denial, as defined in peacetime, and considered that way there has been no marked change in the Reagan administration's fundamentally Soviet essentialist approach to deterrence.

Closely related to this Soviet essentialist trend on deterrence has been a Soviet essentialist trend *concerning the Soviet view*. Contrary to the 1960s, when there was no publicly displayed interest for the Soviet view of nuclear arms as an independent problem, the US government has, since the mid-1970s, displayed a mounting interest for the actual substance of the Soviet view. The focus has been on a specific content of Soviet nuclear doctrine and its close relation to Soviet nuclear deployments, with the assumed vulnerability of American ICBMs, and the dominant conclusion has been that the peculiar nature of the Soviet view forced a revision of American nuclear policy, in particular the deterrence posture. Yet neither this part of the Soviet essentialist trend has been constant, primarily in that the increasing interest for the Soviet view in the late 1970s was combined with a notable readiness, in particular demonstrated by Secretary Brown, to approach the issue in highly circumspect terms. Contrary to that, the Reagan administration's Defense Secretaries, in particular Secretary Weinberger, presented their reflections and conclusions in much more straightforward terms. Still, it is evident that a Soviet essentialist trend on deterrence since the mid-1970s has been combined with a similar change in US governments' reading of the Soviet view of the role of nuclear weapons.

Concurrent with the Soviet essentialist trend concerning deterrence and the Soviet view has been a change as to the fixed element concerning the political significance of nuclear arms: while the reasoning on this issue in the 1960s was characterized by its espousal as a matter of course and stated in rather loose terms, the manifestation of that thinking has, since the mid-1970s, been marked by a steadily increasing attention paid to the immediate criticality of the issue – an attention that occasionally has become an obsession. However, in the mid-1980s that evolution slightly abated as the Reagan administration downgraded the ICBM vulnerability issue and proclaimed America's reborn strength.

Another feature of the Soviet essentialist trend has been its more restrained and mixed character when the image of negotiations and convergent vs. divergent interests is considered. Thus it is noteworthy that the Carter administration continued to display nuclear essentialist notions on the centrality of arms control negotiations and the significance of convergent interests throughout its incumbency, i.e. parallel with its changed reasoning on deterrence and the Soviet view toward Soviet essentialism and only with the first years of the Reagan administration did a distinct Soviet essentialist image become evident in these fields too, particularly concerning the role of negotiations. At the same time it is noticeable that that image has become somewhat tempered by the mid-1980s as it combined with more or less clarified ideas on deterrence through denial. It all points to the observation that a Soviet essentialist image of negotiations and convergent vs. divergent interests has been less consistent and more mixed than other aspects of US governments' predominating Soviet essentialist images since the mid-1970s.

Considering the prominence of some Soviet essentialist fixtures throughout the period since the early 1960s and in view of the Soviet essentialist trend predominant since the mid-1970s, the nuclear essentialist trend in the 1960s and early 1970s may seem an aberration, while the later dominant Soviet essentialism becomes a return to normality. This proposition is strengthened by the fact that the seeming normalcy accords with the views in NSC-68 and the observation that the nuclear essentialist trend prevalent for some ten years was particularly mixed with opposing tendencies. On the other hand, the Soviet essentialist trend too has been mixed with countervailing tendencies, although less pronounced. More important, the actual occurrence of more or less distinct nuclear essentialist statements for a large part of the balance of terror period shows that that 'normalcy' has been far from 'normal'; the empirical reality of a counter-trend for about ten years cannot be dismissed as a mere aberration. Still, it must be concluded that as the Soviet essentialist trend has been more distinct and prevalent – especially viewed in its combination with the fixed Soviet essentialist aspects throughout the years 1961–89 – that trend is a more 'primeval' part of different US governments' perception of the Soviet Union as a nuclear superpower. This means that US governments, in perceiving the Soviet Union as a nuclear armed political adversary, have tended more toward attributing inherent dispositions of the Soviet Union central importance than constraints inherent in the balance of terror situation. However, situational oriented perceptions have always, in more or less distinct form, been present.

3. SWINGS

Talking about a 'swing' as a change in image followed by a return to the
original position, expressed in terms of a predominant fixture or trend, one
type is related to a common trait of US governments' perceptions in that
parts of Soviet essentialism as well as a few elements of nuclear essentialism
never have been totally absent from any administration's reasoning. In all
administrations there have been differences between the image presented by
different members; an administration where a reasoning close to one of the
two ideal types has been stated by some member has often been
supplemented by another – or the same – presenting traces of the alternative
type. In some administrations and through some periods, the differences
have been conspicuous, while in others they have been minor; but in no case
has an administration been a monolithic unit, universally 'speaking with one
voice' on all aspects of the issue. Thus, through fixtures and long-term
trends over 28 years, it has been a general trait of all US governments'
portrayals of the Soviet Union as a nuclear superpower and political
antagonist that doubts as to the tenability of some aspect of the approach
applied have recurred in one form or another. However that may be
explained and whatever its further significance, it is evident that in this sense
all administrations have displayed swings – or, otherwise expressed, a
certain ambiguity has been a fixture of all presidencies' presentations of the
Soviet–American nuclear relationship.

Noting the general occurrence of fluctuations in US governments' public
representations of the Soviet–American nuclear relationship, four cases can
be singled out as particularly conspicuous. They include:

1. The hardening of the early Kennedy administration's Soviet essentialist
    marked image after the Soviet announcement in the summer of 1961
    that it would resume nuclear testing in the atmosphere.
2. Secretary McNamara's presentation of a more distinct nuclear
    essentialist image of deterrence 1965–8, especially during his last year in
    office, 1967–8.
3. The most systematic swing away from and back to what now appears as
    a long-term trend occurred during the Carter administration. While the
    early Carter administration's moderate nuclear essentialism 1977–8
    clearly differed from the Soviet essentialist trend initiated by its two
    predecessors, the later Carter presidency's stand manifested a return to
    the trend dominating since the mid-1970s.
4. Compared to the early Reagan administration's general Soviet essen-
    tialist image, its approach to convergent vs. divergent interests and
    negotiations 1981–4 does not stand out. However, compared to both the
    predecessor's image and the later Reagan administration's, the early
    Reagan presidency's stand represents a swing.

Two types of fluctuations toward **nuclear** essentialism have also been conspicuous: First, after a Soviet–American agreement on nuclear arms has been entered into, it has been represented in distinct nuclear essentialist terms by the incumbent administration, supplemented, however, by the stressing of a few opposite themes. This happened with LTBT in 1963, SALT I in 1972 and SALT II in 1979. After the December 1987 agreement, a few indications of a similar swing have appeared. Second, marked nuclear essentialist representations by a member of a heterogeneous administration and explicitly aimed at the domestic audience. The most obvious cases are Secretary Kissinger's stressing of a nuclear essentialist marked inter-pretation of convergent Soviet–American interests in the nuclear age in 1974 and corresponding statements from members of the Carter administration.

This review of fixtures, trends and prevalent swings from 1961 to 1989 points to the relevance of examining antecedents of the perceptions. Which beliefs, preconceptions and motivations have led US governments to these images through almost a generation? Chapter 5 focuses on the domestic setting for the genesis and evolution of US governments' perception of the Soviet Union as a nuclear adversary.

5. The process of perception: the domestic setting

Examining the genesis of images is a risky business. It will frequently, of course, be evident what caused some spokesman for an administration to expound the Soviet Union as a nuclear adversary in this or that way – the stated motivation or the actual context often makes further speculations superfluous. However, when the problem concerns accounting for fixtures, trends or typical swings in US governments' presentations through almost a generation and six administrations, any conclusion will necessarily be tentative and that means that in explaining constancies and changes in images, one must first focus on the methodical problems involved with analyzing the process of perception.

1. ANALYZING PROCESSES OF PERCEPTION

Analyzing a process of perception means examining the cognitive and political process which influences the way an actor's image about an object is formed. The basic assumption in analyzing antecedents of perceptions is that all observation is an activity occurring in a context of expectations and interests; since the process of perception is not autonomous but guided by anticipations and with an aim, the needs of the observer, 'needs' broadly conceived, affects the genesis of an image. That is, images have certain functions and examining those functions and their impact may provide a clue to understanding the process of perception and antecedents of perceived causation. [1]

Another way of expressing this is that the actors' attempts to form their images, their psychological environment, are marked by 'bounded rationality'. [2] Because of various limits to man's capacity as information processor – political, organizational, psychological or physical – any observer applies simplified notions and models that extract the main features of an object without capturing and dealing with all its complexity which is impossible. It is essential to what may be called the logic of inquiry, including a political actor's logic of inquiry, that any explanation and interpretation of some object, event or information must contain at least one so-called universal law or theory developed from previous cases, i.e.

from 'experience', as well as a suitable number of initial conditions, and therefore one cannot dismiss simplified models of cognition and attribution, in general, as irrational or regrettable 'political and red-tape interfering' with the process of perception.[3] All cognition applies simplified models and different cognitive processes may be more or less rational; one can be too open-minded as well as too closed to new information and an observer who lacks a theoretical framework will succumb to any fashionable interpretation. For that reason, examining the features of 'bounded rationality' of a process of perception is not, by itself, a demonstration of sources of misperception.

In understanding how cognitive and political processes may have an impact on perceptions, it is useful to distinguish between an expressive and an instrumental function of images.[4] As for the expressive function, the language applied is seen as an expression of certain values, attitudes, beliefs, stereotypes or anticipations. As to the instrumental function, the language applied is seen as an instrument calculated to influence various audiences and stimulate to certain desired actions. The distinction denotes two different perspectives analytically fruitful in understanding the process of perception while it, of course, does not indicate a way to separate political manifestations in two groups.

Analyses of the *expressive* function of images resemble a genetic (some say causal) analysis and explanation of ideas.[5] This mode of analysis sees the formation of images as a rather unconscious process and focuses on the tendency for people to see what they expect and are conditioned to see by their experience, their general notions and ideas, their values and interests – the images are, so to speak, rooted in a political culture. The assumption is that political actors tend toward consistency and balance in their belief structures and therefore fit incoming information into their pre-existing ideas to keep them 'balanced and consistent'.[6] One may also say that actors tend toward 'grooved thinking'[7] because too complex and multidimensional cognitive and value structures are uncomfortable and socially disadvantageous in that they are difficult to communicate.

Analyses of the *instrumental* functions of images resemble a teleological explanations of ideas. The process of perception is seen as a more conscious process where the actors select their statements after having considered the probable effects of various pronouncements. The focus is on the interaction between images and goals actively pursued by the image-holder and the image is explained by referring to some aims, intentions or motivations stated by or imputed to the perceiving actor. Applying a term from game theory, this mode of analysis assumes that political actors form their images as a 'game against other players' rather than a 'game against nature', showing what is termed 'strategic behavior'.[8]

The analysis of the processes leading to US governments' images of the Soviet Union as a nuclear adversary applies this distinction as a starting point and it proceeds as an attempt to assess the significance of selected factors in American society in accounting for the fixtures, trends and swings in the images through 1961 to 1989. In the next section some expressive functions are considered; then some instrumental functions; and in the final section the conclusions of the analyses are compared and summarized with a view to suggesting some propositions concerning the significance of various domestic American factors as to the inclination to perceive the Soviet Union as nuclear power in terms of either dispositional or situational oriented attributions.

2.   THE EXPRESSIVE FUNCTION

The images, as defined and reviewed in Chapters 2 and 3 and synthesized in Chapter 4, amount to a broad set of ideas and notions held by US governments from 1961 to 1989. Trying to explain fixtures, trends and swings of these ideas, I shall first review the historically-formed American attitudes toward the world and America's place in the world, i.e. what is termed the American tradition. How is America's historical, conceptual and ideological legacy as it has been formed over many years long before the appearance of the balance of terror, the Soviet bomb, the nuclear age or the Soviet state? After having outlined that legacy, I shall attempt to assess its impact on US governments' portrayals of the Soviet Union as a nuclear adversary through almost a generation and most of the nuclear age. How and to which extent can a traditional American outlook account for constancies and changes in US governments' perceptions? Can the American tradition of apprehending the world and America's role be said to have 'expressed' itself in US governments' statements on the Soviet–American nuclear relationship? Has America's historical predispositions made it a prisoner of the past in its meeting with the Soviet Union as a nuclear superpower?[9]

A.   The American tradition
The American tradition in approaching foreign relations comprises a plurality of ideas and values that defies synthesis into some harmonious and logically consistent set of national attitudes. The principal elements of the traditional American style, character or outlook form congeries of disparate notions which sometimes are rather antithetical. All generalizations about the 'American tradition' are hypothetical in nature and so the term must be utilized with due regard for its contradictory and paradoxical nature and its limitations in simplifying and distorting a rich reality of ideas. A review of the American tradition will be an exposition of the interplay among rival intellectual traditions and conflicting cultural and ideological sub-values neither of which has ever achieved a monopoly or been accepted without qualification even if some trains of thought definitely have been predominant at various times. Diversity rather than uniformity of

viewpoints among public discussants has often been a conspicuous feature of American political culture; tensions and conflicts not only among but *in* what Americans believe about themselves and their nation have always been apparent or just below the surface.

With these reservations, what is summarized under the head 'the American tradition' represents an essential continuity of more than 200 years of ideas about the United States and its proper role in the world that have enjoyed broad acceptance in America. The review will focus on the following aspects of the American tradition: the idea of an American mission, the religious bias of the American outlook, the uneasiness towards cooperation with an antagonist, the belief in America's omnipotence, the approach to war and peace between nations, the significance attached to legal procedures in international relations and the related Idealism–Realism contradiction. The basis for reviewing these aspects is several writings by historians, political scientists, journalists, philosophers, and others who have presented their observations and reflections in a more or less methodical way and with varying empathy. [10]

The idea of an American mission

The most prominent characteristic of the American tradition is the idea of America's mission. The theme that America occupies a unique place and has a special destiny, a mission, among the nations of the earth has dominated the minds of Americans throughout most of America's history. While many other nations have acquired a sense of mission at some time in their history, America was born with it. The United States was declared into existence by a group of men having some definite ideas about the nature of the state they were creating and its proper mission in the world. The Declaration of Independence and the Constitution defined that mission and in drawing up those documents, the Founding Fathers' philosophy was based on the ideas of the eighteenth-century Enlightenment which were held to be self-evident truths and representing values all mankind embraced. [11]

The idea of an American mission was based on the notion that the United States was *different*, an exceptional society representing a *common* cause: America was a young country, a new and free society, a 'New World' which was innocent and born to exemplify the virtues of democracy and extend the principles of democracy throughout the corrupt 'Old World', that is, all the rest of the world that is not America. It was America's destiny – its Manifest Destiny – to lead the world toward a higher and better life, by which was meant the realization of the virtues on which America was founded. Americans believed that their novel political system in time would have a profound and revolutionary impact upon world politics; the United States has been conceived as a school for the world in that the American example would fire the imaginations of foreign peoples, it would be a spur and an inspiration to the victims of tyranny in other parts of the world so they would free themselves from sluggishness and from enslavement to outworn habits and institutions. Americans have regarded America's institutions as purer exemplifications of the common democratic cause setting a pattern which the rest of the world aspired to and would come to follow, and it was America's mission to serve as a shining example to mankind of the potential of freedom, liberty and self-government and thereby bring the blessings of these universally embraced and enduring values to oppressed people of the rest of the world. The conception of America's special mission was thus closely related to America's self-image: America's mission was to redeem the Old World by high example. [12]

In that way the idea of America's mission reflects a desire to educate, liberate and improve the world. Since America had discovered self-evident truths that can set men free all over the world and as the United States has created and set into practice a way of life that far surpasses all others in its possibilities for justice and happiness, the American example would be contagious. Thus America's role has been presented by Americans as the moral one of spearheading the inevitable trend toward democracy in the world, and idealism, moralism and ideological usage have been a marked feature of the American tradition. There has been a persistent affinity for universalizing America's foreign policy goals and a pronounced tendency to invoke abstract and ideal standards to justify specific actions. It was America's duty to promote and defend a just world order, not to pursue what has been termed *Realpolitik*.

The religious bias

The distinct Messianic strain prevalent from the beginning in America's self-conception was intimately related to religious themes dominant, in particular New England Puritanism. One characteristic of the Puritan ethic was a fundamentalist absolutism: 'right is right and wrong is wrong' and 'somehow, some way, right will prevail over might'. [13] Puritans were God's chosen people and America was an Old Testament people divinely appointed to fulfill a great mission in the history of this planet. Since victory of the righteous is assured, compromise is capitulation retaining the connotation of appeasement and duplicity. Diplomacy and bargaining become associated with 'secret deals' and 'sell-outs'. The Puritan ethic is optimistic and confident and its espousal of fundamentalist principles as unconditional surrender, total victory, no appeasement and universal democracy testifies to that. As it has been phrased, the essence of the Puritan character is a mixture of practicality and faith in the power of God expressed by Oliver Cromwell when he stated: 'Trust in God, my boys, and keep your powder dry'. [14]

The strong religious elements in American patriotism reassure many Americans of an inner rightness of purpose in the nation's conduct; it strengthens an evangelical and missionary quality and a distinct moralism of the American approach to the outside world. The nation's involvement in foreign affairs is presented in terms of a simple and sweeping moral crusade where extension of America's value system to other nations is seen as the crux of the matter. The pious tradition, the inclination to secularize a religiously-derived view of the world and deal with political issues in Christian imagery and the concomitant tendency to think in terms of an ethic of intentions, of absolutes and abstract standards, engenders a willingness to make ready judgements of the 'good' and 'bad' and perceive foreign affairs in crude alternatives. In that Manichean world-view politics is understood in terms of universal conflicts of values – between freedom and unfreedom, reason and force, orderly progress and despotism. America is morally superior and beyond the reach of the wicked; despotism and evil are easily identified, are fightable and eradicable, and triumph is possible if only the righteous has the conviction of his cause. Sometimes this religiously-derived view of the world as a battle between Good and Evil develops into a paranoid style where history is envisaged as a conspiracy and all ills are traced to a single center which can be eliminated by some kind of final act of victory which extinguishes the enemy. A peculiar paradox of this style is an inclination to imitate that final enemy, to outdo him in dedication, discipline and ingenuity.[15]

Cooperation with the antagonist?
Related to these features is a profound uneasiness with the idea of an adversarial relationship in international politics within which limited cooperation is both possible and necessary. The very notion of mixed interests between equal antagonists has been alien to the American tradition. Since America was the first democratic country in the world representing the wave of the future and its involvement in world affairs a moral fight for a just order, the idea of cooperating with an adversary is both immoral and unnecessary. America has perceived itself as morally superior to the Old World and this fosters a basic difficulty as well as impatience in cooperating with other nations as equals. Despite strong support for the notion of equality between nations, America's encounter with the world has not been egalitarian but marked by unilateral actions.[16]

A sustained participation in world affairs as an absorbing, routine requirement to pursue bargaining with other nations has not held much appeal for Americans. Foreign affairs has rather been considered a matter of dealing with contingencies; based on the sense of having a mission and being morally superior, dealing with other nations has been seen as a problem of dispelling others' prejudice and ignorance so they would come to see things the way they were. It is an ingrained part of the American tradition that America is unadjusted and unaccustomed to basic conflicts of ends where both parts can be right. America's historical and ideological genesis and experience has fostered an impatience with and intolerance of such protracted conflicts.

The belief in America's omnipotence
The idea of America's moral superiority encourages a belief that the world is responsive to America's will. Problems have solutions, usually meaning technological solutions, and any problem is approached with the expectation that it can be brought to a swift conclusion. The belief in American omnipotence is intimately related to the nation's experience in that the ability to control nature and eliminate obstacles has been an essential part of the American nation-building process. That experience fosters an optimistic and activistic 'can-do' attitude in approaching foreign affairs which mostly appears in the form of a technological ethos, i.e. the thinking that technology is the solution to political problems and an 'engineering' approach according to which America's superior technology combined with a little ingenuity and goodwill can solve the problems. The preference for mechanical solutions engenders a tendency to forget or ignore the political and psychological problems and instead concentrate on the seemingly tractable 'hardware' aspects of the dealings with other nations.[17]

A corollary to the ingrained belief in America's omnipotence is the thinking that foreign trends or events detrimental to America have simply been 'permitted' by some American inaction, mistake or stupidity. The very idea that an American policy does not succeed when it has openly and honestly been announced and pursued becomes unfamiliar. Situations that distress or endanger the United States are understood as a result of some poor American policy, that is, originating in some Americans having been fools or knaves or, at least, that the actual policy has not been carried out with the support of the American people. This approach fosters a self-centered conception of foreign affairs with its search for scapegoats when a policy fails. The notion that America is omnipotent easily brings about an alternation between a spontaneous optimism and a spontaneous pessimism or defeatism, it enhances the rhythm in American moods between activism and quietism and shapes cyclical patterns between outbursts of evangelism and offended withdrawals.[18]

War and peace between nations
The traditional American approach to war and peace between nations is based on the conception that the world is divided between inherently peaceful democratic societies and inherently aggressive totalitarian regimes. Wars are caused by, i.e. instigated by, the aggressors' insatiable lust for power and aggrandisement, and, therefore, it is the moral duty of democratic and peaceful nations to chastise the breachers of peace in order to restore a safe peace. Since the war–peace dichotomy is simple, political aims are something to be pursued in normal peacetime while it is just a matter of securing victory in abnormal wartime. As war is an abnormal contingency *forced* upon the peaceful and to be dealt with as a problem of rebuking the guilty, peace-making is a matter of identifying and punishing the actual war instigator – not a question of mediating between equal

opponents – after which one may return to peaceful normality. The anti-militarism in this thinking appears in its dislike of military preparedness in peacetime; a paradoxical concomitant of that anti-militarism, however, is a marked combativeness and belligerency *in* war in that the quickest feasible strategy for victory is advocated regardless of political aims and, the moment victory is assured and hostilities are over, instant demobilization is recommended.[19]

The peculiar characteristics of this approach are related to the tendency to a certain periodicity in national moods where periods of activism alternate with periods of quietism. There is a basic unwillingness to live with and conceive of permanent conflicts of ends between nations as legitimate in the American tradition, and the other side of this yearning for harmony is an inclination to portray an enemy as the epitome of evil while America is elevated to a position of moral superiority combined with a posture of self-righteousness. In that way, the traditional American approach to war and peace is characterized by a basic anti-militarist dislike of force as well as a crusading propensity to resort to force.[20]

The belief in legal procedures and the Idealism–Realism contradiction

Another prominent component of the American tradition is the belief in legal procedures in international relations. Again, this exemplifies how a domestic experience is transferred to foreign affairs: successful American principles as to the building of governmental institutions must be transferable to the otherwise chaotic international society. Hence, legal provisions and the sanctity of law have supreme importance as regulators of the international political process.[21] This legalism relates to an inclination to equate international standards not only with idealized American standards but with personal ones: as 'trust', 'goodwill' and 'friendship' are major criteria for good pesonal relationships, they are the clue to good relations between nations.

The legalist tradition is accentuated and elaborated in the intellectual and political philosophy termed *Idealism* which has often been salient in the American tradition. Idealism presumes an underlying harmony of interests among states and peoples and has a profound distaste for power politics. It reasons more in terms of human beings than state interests and emphasizes ideas at the expense of interests, and Idealist usage is the language of community and harmony. Grounded in an optimistic faith that the ideas of the Enlightenment which inspired the founding of America have universal validity, Idealism asserts that conflicts are not inherent in a world of formally sovereign states or any other structural features of societies. On the contrary, adherents of the Idealist tradition see conflicts in the international society as resolvable by intellectual give-and-take and they dislike the Clausewitzian doctrine that war is a continuation of politics by other means. Therefore it is stressed that America has a commitment to reform the international system through a progressive replacement of power relations with legal principles. It is America's duty steadily to promote the codification of international law, to negotiate arbitration and mediation treaties, and to organize cooperation in the international society institutionally: a persevering search for mutually profitable agreements among nations can and ought to discipline international politics in a civilized manner.[22]

Advocates of Idealism as a starting point for American foreign policy have almost always been adherents of a kind of liberalism in domestic American politics. However, as Idealism is a rather broad and long-winded school of thought, it has developed into very divergent directions. Since it contains a certain moralism as well as self-righteousness and overtones of millenarianism, Idealist thinking has sometimes evolved into Utopianism with notions like 'brotherhood of man', and 'moral uplifting of the world' as central.[23] On the other hand, it has also developed into very pragmatic versions where the Idealist elements have been less prominent or subordinate. In any case, the actual version of Idealism has constantly been marked by the interplay with its intellectual counterpart in the American tradition, termed Realism.

Realism conveys a dour attitude toward human nature and has limited expectation of a common betterment. It is skeptical regarding the applicability of legal and liberal principles beyond America's borders and emphasizes the role of power and force in the relations among sovereign states. As a persistent struggle for power is inherent in an international system composed by sovereign political collectivities – the states – there is always a latent risk of war in international politics, and the pertinence of the Clausewitzian doctrine that war and diplomacy are merely modalities of a lasting condition is stressed. Realist thinkers conceive international politics as dominated by divergent national interests where conflicts are resolvable primarily through the application of power and so the primacy of national security, national interests, power and force are realities that a nation can ignore only to its detriment. In continuation of this reasoning, many Realists assume that America's authority in the international community is always enhanced by the overt display of American military power.[24]

Like Idealism, Realism has developed into different directions. Some advocates of a Realist way of thinking have represented the pervasiveness of physical and military force in international politics in a deterministic way: as war is the final arbiter, a nation is always faced with the possibility of victory or defeat and therefore one's own willingness to foster military virtues is decisive for survival. Others advocating a Realist thinking, and so also skeptical to the general applicability of legal principles to world affairs, stress, however, the limits of America's national interests and warn against illusions of American omnipotence: whether such illusions originate in a Realist version of national security or Idealist versions of America's duty, they easily become self-defeating – America's power is always limited.[25]

B. Impact

Assessing the impact of the American tradition on US governments' perceptions of the Soviet Union as a nuclear adversary means examining how the images relate to various constituent parts of that tradition and in so doing, it is assumed that the image-holders identify with traditional American outlooks. Taking fixtures and trends in 1961–89 as a point of departure one can assess the explanatory value of this aspect of the domestic American setting by pointing out how different reasonings applied by six administrations through more than 25 years accord or are at variance with some part of the American tradition.

Applying the term 'explanation' in this context, it is, however, important to note its broad meaning and the hypothetical character of any conclusion. Even if some relation between US governments' pronouncements and the American tradition may appear obvious, this mode of analysis cannot form the basis of any conclusion as to the 'cause' of images and their evolution. Analyzing the significance of the American tradition in this way can only lead to propositions that some relations are more or less natural. The question is can that tradition of apprehending America's role in the world – i.e. if an assumption that US government leaders in 1961–89 have shared that thinking – improve our understanding of the process through which the administrations have interpreted the Soviet Union as a nuclear superpower and political antagonist?

Fixtures

First of all, the widespread use of high-flown rhetoric by many US government leaders is comprehensible in view of the outlines of the American tradition. Presupposing that US leaders have acquired salient parts of that tradition through their political socialization, it is natural to see their rhetorical style as an offshoot of traditional American outlooks.

Concerning the content of the images, the commonly held notion that the state of the nuclear balance between the United States and the Soviet Union is critical to the world-wide political conflict between the American democracy and the Soviet dictatorship can be understood as originating in salient parts of the American tradition. Considering that the idea of an American mission in the world forms an essential part of the American tradition it is natural that US governments have seen the shaping of their nuclear policy as a vital part of the pursuance of American goals in world politics. Since the United States is not merely one 'superpower,' American nuclear policy – combined with other aspects of American foreign policy – has to be formed as an integral component of democracies' pursuing of the common democratic cause *vis-à-vis* the Soviet dictatorship. America's position as an exceptional society representing a common cause involves as a matter of course that the world expects and presumes that the United States is ever superior or, at least, leading. In fact, accepting that America has a mission in leading the world, it is a simple duty for the United States as part of its world leadership ever to assure its military superiority.

The relevance of this part of the American tradition can be further elaborated when it is seen in combination with the traditional belief in American omnipotence. That belief fosters a persuasion that technological superiority is always crucial and a reasoning that the world is ever responsive to a display of America's – or anybody's – will to sustain its dominance of the nuclear balance or its nuclear superiority. Any moral doubt as to the tenability of that posture is dismissed when the political and moral superiority of America as the leader of the world in its progressive march toward freedom and democracy is considered and particularly when the moral and political inferiority of its opponent, the Soviet Union, is included. America as the 'Number 1' nuclear power is not just one casual leader among many. On the contrary, it is the true world leader that confirms its duty toward mankind and exactly because America has the technological ability to sustain this role, it has the duty to perform it. The American technological omnipotence enhances its moral duty to serve its mission in the world by proclaiming the political significance of American nuclear weapons as a counter to Soviet nuclear weapons, and in that way the perception of the Soviet Union a a nuclear armed political opponent is closely related to an historical American self-image.

The constant stressing of the political value of American nuclear forces can also be related to the Realist tradition in American history with its emphasis on the role of power and force in international politics. As Realism holds that a persistent struggle for power is inherent in an international system composed of sovereign states, it is natural to draw the conclusion that in the nuclear age this struggle is translated into a political struggle where the physical use of force has been replaced by the psychological display of nuclear strength for political purposes. Thus throughout the 1960s, members of the US government – but, as reviewed, with a few exceptions – stated their belief in nuclear superiority and later, especially since the middle of the 1970s, all administrations have stressed the significance of 'perceptions' of nuclear strength. In both periods this belief in political and psychological significance of 'strong' nuclear forces accords with the Realist tradition.

The impact of the American tradition on US governments' images of the political significance of nuclear arms can be elucidated in a circuitous way, namely by examining those few cases when some member of an administration suggested a reasoning different ·from the prevailing one. Thus, during the later 1960s Defense Secretary McNamara's vacillating attitude to and cautious handling of the concept 'nuclear superiority' becomes more understandable when it is seen in the light of an ingrained American faith that the United States is and ought ever be superior to a political adversary. Particularly McNamara's tentative, publicly displayed, scrutinizing of the concept (cf. especially McNamara's San Francisco speech in September 1967, p. 54 above) becomes politically reasonable when it is assumed that the speaker wanted to question the political appropriateness of that concept in a balance of terror age *and* it is assumed that in so doing, McNamara realized he was shaking a fundamental belief about America's world role. Later, during the first half of the 1970s, Henry Kissinger's two-pronged approach to the concepts 'nuclear superiority' and 'perceived superiority' becomes more understandable when the audience's attachment for the American tradition is considered. In the same way, as members of the Carter administration advanced various notions on the 'complexities' of the political significance of 'perceptions' of nuclear strength, it is useful to understand this in the light of ingrained American attitudes.

Another fixture of US governments' images has been a continuous stressing of the need for American nuclear deployments in order to negotiate from a position of strength and force the Soviets to negotiate seriously. The wellsprings of this thinking too can be traced back to traditional American beliefs. The American tradition harbors a profound uneasiness toward the idea of a limited adversarial relationship where it is necessary to cooperate with the political enemy, besides opposing him, in order to pursue some common interest. As the notion that the United States has to engage itself in a continuing negotiation process with a political and ideological opponent is at variance with a prominent part of the American tradition, the frequent emphasizing of the requirement for steady American nuclear deployments in order to press the ideological enemy to negotiate seriously can be seen as a kind of compensation for the, in some ways, un-American idea of negotiating with the enemy. Otherwise expressed, since the fact that all administrations have endorsed the negotiation concept can be seen in the light of that part of the American tradition which shows a belief in legal procedures in international relations, emphases of the importance of *negotiating* from *strength* become a way of simultaneously 'doing homage' to different components of the American tradition. In that way the interplay between divergent parts of the American tradition is reflected: the disparate elements of US governments' more stable images of negotiations can be traced back to disparate parts of that tradition. Given the composite character of that tradition – and the approach applied here – it is not possible to state the relations in clear-cut terms but, anyway, it is important to point up such relations.

Expounding the intricate relations between US governments' approach to negotiations with the Soviets on nuclear issues and America's historical and ideological legacy, it is useful to note how members of different administrations have commented on that problem in different ways: while officials in the 1960s and 1970s advocating negotiations deplored the continuing impact of one part of traditional American modes of thinking, officials in the 1980s expressing a more skeptical view of negotiations deplored the impact of other parts of these thought tracks. Thus in the 1960s both President Kennedy and Secretary McNamara, as well as some other officials, showed traces of 'lecturing' their audiences on the obsolescence of traditional American ways of thinking in the nuclear age. More conspicuously, faced with increasing domestic criticism of American negotiation policy in SALT Secretary Kissinger stated in strong terms in the mid-1970s that traditional American attitudes in a situation with détente and negotiations with a political adversary could be a danger to America itself: the usual American impatience when faced with protracted negotiations and complex problems was pernicious in the nuclear age. Later in the 1970s, President Carter and particularly Paul Warnke voiced similar concerns as they countered widespread domestic criticism. On the other hand, as some members of the Reagan administration have made observations on how traditional American approaches to negotiations differ from traditional Soviet ones, they have warned against placing too much emphasis on negotiations. Altogether, while the divergent conclusions from government officials as to the impact of different parts of the American tradition have to be noted, it is evident that especially spokesmen advocating a positive attitude to negotiations have felt the uncomfortable weight of that tradition.

This leads to an examination of relations between trends in images and the American tradition.

Trends
Assessing the impact of the American tradition on the two long-term trends in American governments' perceptions since the early 1960s, some general relations can, to begin with, be stated as obvious in that the Soviet essentialist trend since the mid-1970s accords with prominent parts of the American tradition while the preceding nuclear essentialist trend contradicts salient parts of that tradition. However, some aspects of the nuclear essentialist tendency also fit with a part of the American tradition and, analogously, a few aspects of Soviet essentialist trend contradicts with parts of that tradition. In any case, the more detailed character of these composite relations has to be examined and elucidated to give an adequate presentation of the relevance of traditional American conceptions for the evolution of American governments' perceptions through almost a generation.

The trend toward nuclear essentialism can, to some degree, be understood as originating in the American tradition. This primarily applies to those versions of a nuclear essentialist thinking which include the notion that extensive Soviet–American negotiations and agreements can stabilize the balance of terror in that they reflect a traditional American belief in legal principles and legal procedures in international relations. The similarities between, on the one hand, nuclear essentialist images that assume that the negotiation process with its human contacts and presumed give-and-take between negotiators sharing a common concern will contribute to a beneficial growth of trust and goodwill, and, on the other hand, Idealist notions presuming an underlying harmony of interests among states and peoples, are evident. When some members of the US government have declared, in more or less distinct terms, that by engaging the Soviets in a continuing dialogue, it would be possible to 'educate' the Russians in the virtues of recognizing the mutual balance of terror predicament as an immutable fact which the superpowers can dismiss only to their own detriment, this clearly reflects a traditional American belief that in dealing with other nations it is America's duty to dispel others' prejudices and ignorance so they will come to see things as they are. Considered that way, a nuclear essentialist approach to negotiations reflects an urge to educate the ignorant and improve the world, and when the goal of American negotiation policy has been presented in abstract terms as exemplifying self-evident truths on the conditions of the nuclear age, it fully accords with Idealist beliefs.

These relations are most apparent when some administrations' advocacy of SALT are examined. The general idea behind SALT was often presented as aiming at mutually profitable Soviet–American agreements to 'manage' the common nuclear age predicament and occasionally this was presented in terms of an intellectual give-and-take between the United States and the Soviet Union. Acknowledging these similarities between American SALT images and the Idealist tradition, it is also notable, however, that nuclear essentialist images of negotiations accord with those versions of the Realist tradition which stress the limits of American power and warn against the illusion of American omnipotence. Thus one can demonstrate roots of the nuclear essentialist trend in both this version of the Realist tradition and in the Idealist tradition. Indeed, the varying interplay between *different* parts of the American tradition and *similar* conclusions as to American nuclear policy has often appeared in the way that some SALT advocates have endeavored to argue for SALT solely in terms of a Realist tradition, combined with what was considered the most 'realist' part of an Idealist tradition and an explicit dismissal of the relevance of 'naive' Idealist notions, while others, also advocating SALT, have argued in terms of an Idealist tradition.

However, the nuclear essentialist trend clashed with salient parts of the American tradition and a closer review of these relations can indicate one aspect of the domestic background to *the decline of that trend and the rise of the Soviet essentialist trend*. First of all, a nuclear essentialist-like reasoning, contrary to a Soviet essentialist one, conceives the nuclear relationship between the superpowers in symmetrical terms: the United Sates and the Soviet Union are equally vulnerable to the nuclear threat and therefore share symmetrical predicaments and duties. But that thinking strongly contradicts the self-image inherent in the idea of America's special mission. When it is held as basic that the United States represents a common cause that all mankind aspires to, it becomes extremely uncomfortable to acknowledge that the society incarnating righteousness is put on a par with a dictatorship, even if it is argued that that 'on a par with' is in relation to a common threat. The very balance of terror notion is ideologically unacceptable, quite apart from any dislike of the nuclear threat inherent in the concept, and for strong believers in America's special mission it is ideologically anathema to countenance the view that it places some restraints on American foreign policy. The religious bias and the Messianic strain in the American tradition amplifies that uneasiness in that any version of nuclear essentialism seems to imply that 'right' and 'wrong' has become all 'grey'. Any nuclear essentialist reasoning seemingly leads to accepting that because of nuclear weapons, the difference between 'good' and 'bad' societies has disappeared.

Moreover, as hinted above, the American tradition's profound dislike of the notion of a mixed relationship in international politics where both limited cooperation and limited conflict is possible and necessary is violated in the nuclear essentialist trend's version of negotiating extensive arms control agreements with the Soviet Union. Images of negotiations advocating a continuing close dialogue with the Soviet dictatorship in order to control a common nuclear threat conflict with a traditional American aversion to being involved in a routine bargaining process with another country as an equal. In the same way, accepting the balance of terror predicament as immutable contradicts the persuasion that America is omnipotent. Also that part of the nuclear essentialist trend which held that the primary danger of nuclear war is the interplay between the superpowers contradicts the belief that wars are instigated by inherently aggressive and totalitarian against inherently peaceful and democratic nations. As nuclear essentialist versions of the best way to avert nuclear war reject the notion that the peaceful must ever be 'stronger' than the aggressive and instead advocate some kind of 'managing' one's own, as well as the opponent's, inevitable vulnerability to the atomic bomb, they differ essentially from traditional American thinking on war and peace. In fact, the classical arms control conceptual edifice – endorsed by the most distinct official advocates of the nuclear essentialist trend in the later 1960s – is profound anathema to salient parts of the American tradition.

On all these points it is evident that the nuclear essentialist trend conflicts with the American tradition or, conversely, that the Soviet essentialist trend is consistent with that tradition. Most important, the basic proclivity toward focusing on the peculiarities of the Soviet state fits in perfectly with the idea that America as a different and exceptional society has a special mission to promote values like freedom and democracy which the Soviet society obviously does not represent. The inclination to reason on the Soviet Union as a nuclear power by starting from some consideration on what the Soviet state *is* and, therefore, how it must *act* – nuclear weapons or no nuclear weapons – accords with basic trains of thought in the American tradition. The urge to reason on the Soviet Union as a nuclear adversary in terms of Soviet dispositions becomes natural when the American tradition is applied as a frame of reference. In the same way, the occasional outburst of bombastic ideological rhetoric characteristic for advocates of a Soviet essentialist trend becomes more comprehensible when considered in the light of that tradition, especially its religious bias, rather than as a manifestation of some suspicious oddity related to some individuals.

The relation between the Soviet essentialist trend and the American tradition can be elaborated by focusing on some aspects of the deterrence reasoning in that trend. Thus the emphasis on building effective nuclear forces capable of performing a variety of military tasks presumes a strong belief in American technological potency. The steady pointing to this or that military-technological deficiency of America's nuclear forces, which merely requires some feasible reconditioning to make the deterrence effective, accords with a traditional American belief that political problems can be corrected by American technological ingenuity. In the same way, the frequent critique from an administration against the preceding administration's 'neglect' of America's nuclear forces reflects a thinking similar to a traditional American belief that some development detrimental to the United States really is due to American inaction. One special aspect of this evolution of the Soviet essentialist trend in deterrence doctrine concerns the reasoning that to counter a Soviet counterforce and damage limitation strategy, it is necessary to forge a corresponding American strategy. That thinking may be seen in the light of that peculiar part of the American tradition which holds that to counter the enemy you have to imitate and outdo him on his own ground.

The trend toward deterrence by denial apparent in the Reagan administration fits in several ways with salient parts of the American tradition. First, it shows a strong belief in American technological power as capable of altering the balance of terror condition. This applies especially to the version of SDI that advances the goal as building an impenetrable shield against nuclear missiles but also more cautious versions of SDI presume that a highly embarrassing and irksome problem can be solved by American technological ingenuity. As the ultimate goal of SDI is presented in highly visionary – even metaphysical – terms, it expresses essential parts of the American tradition.[26] The evolution toward deterrence by denial furthermore accords well with that component of the American tradition which sees wars as instigated by aggressors wherefore a peaceful nation has to be able to defend itself physically against assault. A deterrence by denial reasoning can also be related to that part of the American tradition which emphasizes that there is always a latent risk of war in international politics wherefore a nation has to be capable of surviving that contingency. Moreover, in the light of the American tradition it is natural that Soviet objections to SDI are dismissed as sincere – America's benign intentions are obvious to all people of goodwill.

Concerning relations between swings in US governments' images and the American tradition, one can point out that the usual occurrence of a few elements of nuclear essentialism as well as parts of Soviet essentialism throughout most of the period since 1961 fits in with the composite character of the American tradition. A more detailed elaboration of these relations, however, has to await a review of the instrumental use of American governments' manifestations in a domestic context.

3.   THE INSTRUMENTAL FUNCTION

US governments, like most governments, are multi-goal institutions which means that their statements may be formed with the intention of reaching a variety of domestic and foreign audiences. The basic assumption in this section is that the domestic political context may have an impact on an administration's declarations and writings on foreign policy in that a statement may be worked out or framed with a domestic audience in mind, primarily or as a subsidiary consideration, i.e. to affect other parts of the American political system and obtain their support for a variety of reasons. Analyzing the process of perception from that angle means focusing on the interplay between the US government and different institutions in the American society and is an attempt to assess how and to what extent an administration's role in the domestic political structure influences its interpretation of a specific foreign policy problem.

The analysis will consider the significance of the administration's relations to two institutions in American politics: Congress and the public. Initially, some distinctive features of the Executive's position in relation to Congress and the American public are outlined with a view to identifying main factors and critical problems. Then I shall assess the impact of these relations on US governments' representations of the Soviet Union as a nuclear adversary by reviewing the interplay between the Executive, Congress and the public as it evolved in various issues related to the making of American nuclear policy through 1961–74 and 1974–89. Can the Executive's roles and aims *vis-à-vis* Congress and the American public help us understand constancies and prominent changes in six administrations' images?

A.   The executive in American politics
A starting point for describing the position of the Executive branch in the American political system is that the President as leader of the Executive is the sole nationally elected government official (together with the Vice-President) in the American polity. Being the only holder of a national mandate endows the President as chief executive with a unique stature in American politics and makes him the focus of multifarious expectations and demands. The President brings to the Executive a weighty psychological influence and whatever the incumbent's personal style or views, the office of President and chief executive symbolizes a personal leadership of the nation.[27]

It is a distinctive mark of the Executive's role in American politics that the Constitution and the political process as it has worked distributes and balances power. The Constitution has created a government of separated institutions meaning that powers in the American polity are shared rather than consolidated among mutually dependent institutions. Considered in that perspective the President as chief executive is just one actor in a system of separation of powers and checks-and-balances where the sharing of authority among separate institutions prescribes the terms on which the Executive acts. The checks-and-balances system means that the Executive and the chief executive's powers *vis-à-vis* other institutions is a power to persuade,[28] that is, a power to bargain in order to convince others that what the President wants of them is what they ought to do for their own sake. In that sense the adversarial character of the American governmental process is already a result of constitutional stipulations: an administration must always consider any need to persuade other institutions in the American governmental system. Tension and struggle between the Executive and the legislature over foreign policy – as concerning domestic policy – is intrinsic to the American political system and was consciously created by the Constitution with the result that conflict is a built-in part of the American governmental system.

As for lawmaking power, the Constitution lays down that all legislative powers shall be vested in Congress but a Bill which has passed Congress shall be signed by the President before it becomes law. If the President disapproves the Bill, it may still become law if it is approved after a reconsideration by two-thirds of both the House of Representatives and the Senate (article 1, section 7).[29] In the field of foreign policy, it applies that the division of power between the Executive and the legislative branches is vaguer than in the domestic area. Thus the Constitution mentions no general foreign policy power. Instead, it assigns certain specific powers to the President and some to Congress, while others are designated to be shared by the Executive and the Senate. The only power given to the President in this field is that he 'shall be Commander in Chief of the Army and Navy' and 'he shall receive Ambassadors and other public Ministers' (article 2, sections 2 and 3). By contrast, Congress is allotted several explicit powers in the foreign affairs field. Especially important is that Congress shall 'provide for the Common Defence', 'declare war', 'raise and support Armies', 'provide and maintain a Navy' and 'make Rules for Government and Regulation of the land and naval forces' (article 1, section 8). The power to make treaties is assigned to the President 'by and with the Advice and Consent of the Senate ... provided two-thirds of the Senators present concur' (article 2, section 2).

Despite the vagueness of the constitutional allocation of foreign policy powers between the Executive and the legislature, the pre-eminence of the President as chief executive has, by and large, been unambiguous and taken for granted, in particular after the Second World War. Before the late

1960s, members of Congress showed little interest in or knowledge of foreign affairs. Congress fulfilled its constitutional duty to 'provide for the Common Defense' but it had largely relinquished oversight responsibility for American security policy to the Executive branch. It contented itself with sometimes increasing the administration's request for appropriations for a particular weapon system while, on a few occasions, it cut marginally in the request. Subsequent to the mid–to late 1960s, however, Congressional cuts in the defense budget became deeper.

Another indicator of the Executive's pre-eminence in foreign affairs is the wide use of so-called Executive agreements, not mentioned in the Constitution. The number of executive agreements has been far greater than the number of treaties, especially in the twentieth century, and this has not changed since the 1960s.[30] Since they are not subject to the Senate's approval by a two-thirds majority but only to Congress's approval by simple majority, it seems ever-tempting for a President to apply this form in concluding a contentious agreement. A special problem concerns Congress's exclusive war-making power according to the Constitution that has become diluted by the President's use of his power as Commander-in-Chief. Congress attempted in 1973, after the Vietnam War, to resurrect its constitutional power when it passed the War Powers Resolution over President Nixon's veto, requiring the President to cease any deployment of American forces abroad or any military action he had undertaken within 60 days unless specifically authorized by Congress within that period. This Resolution, however, has never really been tested and there is doubt as to its actual significance. The strife on War Powers Resolution points to the importance of examining any attempt by Congress to control the Executive's nuclear arms policy making and assess the further impact of such attempts.

Potentially increasing Congress's influence on foreign policy is the vastly increased Congressional staffs during the later decades. The term staff denotes different categories of Congressional employees, each performing different funtions and operating under different rules in Congress's policy-making activities. Some belong to the members' personal staff, some to permanent or temporary committees, and there are research staffs attached to a number of Congressional support agencies too. The enormous growth of various kinds of staffing has meant that Congress has given itself a counter-bureaucracy to the Executive with additional sources of information to break the (near) monopoly formerly held by the Executive. Of course, the staffs are still heavily dependent upon the Executive branch for information, but they have cultivated other sources as well, such as the press and independent research institutions from where experts often testify at Congressional hearings or make their own studies under contract with Congressional committees. Altogether, the Congress's possibilities for checking and balancing the Executive have become markedly greater and the immediate result of this has frequently been to enhance the adversarial nature of the US governmental process.[31] In any case, the significance of Congress may appear as anticipated reactions when the Executive frames its policy.

Concerning the position of the Executive in relation to the public, the citizens who constitute the public may show its views in multifarious ways: through voting, through public opinion polls, through organizd groups or through political parties, and as to all these channels of influence the role of the media is important. This indicates that when we are talking about the 'public' it is not that useful to view it as a monolith wherefore some distinctions and clarifications are expedient and as a first rough distinction the following operates with the 'mass public' and 'opinion leaders'.[32]

The mass public consists partly of people who are unaware of or only slightly informed about all but the most major events in foreign affairs, partly of people who show a higher level of information about and interest in foreign policy. In the latter case one can talk about part of the public as the 'attentive' public. The mass public, particularly the 'non-attentive' part, has generally weakly held opinions which lack intensity and internal consistency. Studies have shown that a great number of Americans are profoundly ignorant of the specifics of international politics, even at the most elementary level. In the same way, the mass public is only partly aware of even the most obvious in the statements and documents which form the basis for talking about US governments' perceptions. This does not mean, however, that citizens such as these are incapable of holding opinions. Considered from one angle the mass public's opinions and beliefs are consistent. Thus studies show that the mass public has continuously shared the core values of peace and strength from a basically non-internationalist point of view, meaning that they react to what they consider to be too much American involvement in foreign affairs. On the other hand, the non-internationalist-minded mass public is very unstable in that it often fluctuates markedly, and unpredictably, in response to (dramatic) reports of (dramatic) international events, its current fears and concerns, or public officials' declared positions.[33]

The potential significance of this is enhanced by the fact that while presidential elections take place every fourth year, elections for the House of Representatives and one third of the Senate come up every second year and this means that the United states is close to a permanent election situation. Hence, if an administration must present its policy to a largely ignorant mass public, threats will readily be overstated and dangers magnified in order to mobilize popular support. The reverse may also occur if efforts to improve relations with a normally adversarial foreign power are oversold. Similarly. the easiest way for opposition groups or a party out of office trying to score points against an incumbent administration is, in preparation for a forthcoming election, to accuse it of being insufficiently attentive to some threat. As political issues are primarily handled as media events in American politics, and politicians (have to) compete for public attention, this may all have a dramatizing effect on a much-debated political issue. In the American political process there is a built-in need to stir the imagination of the public and 'sell' it a policy by solely stresssing its advantages and ignoring its disadvantages; there is a tendency to exaggerate as a means of building and maintaining public support and consensus. This is substantiated by data showing that public opinion polls are primarily used by officials when they present the public rationale for administration policies; public opinion influences administrations' declaratory policies more than other aspects of their policies.[34] The actual effect of this depends not only on the characteristics of the mass public but also on the attitudes held by people who are termed 'opinion leaders'.

Opinion leaders are people who communicate their opinions to others using various channels of influence. They consist of that segment of the public who actively (i.e. besides through voting or opinion polls) attempt to influence Congress, the public or the incumbent administration. One segment of this category belongs to organized foreign policy groups who directly strive to influence the public's or policy-makers' opinions on foreign affairs. Another, partly overlapping group of opinions leaders are people who in their professional capacity give exclusive attention to foreign policy problems, either by belonging to staffs on newspapers, magazines, radio or television, or by being foreign policy experts in universities or research institutes. In both these groups some people may be actively involved with an incumbent administration, or with Congressional groups criticizing and opposing the incumbent administration. It all means that features of the public debate between opinion leaders, together with members of Congress and spokesmen for the Exectutive, may be significant in that the level of conflict encompassing a political issue – in the public debate as well as among the mass public as shown in opinion polls and elections – constrains official decision-makers. An administration is much freer to design its public statements disregarding domestic opinion when an issue is a non-issue in American politics.

B.   Issues

a.   1961–74

Assessing the impact of the Executive's relations to Congress and the public during the first half of the period since 1961 when a moderate nuclear essentialist trend was apparent after 1963 will be based on a review of the interplay between the three institutions as to: the accelerated American nuclear build-up in the early 1960s and Secretary McNamara's enunciation of a counterforce strategy in 1962; the Limited Test Ban Treaty in 1963; McNamara's 'assured destruction' doctrine later in the 1960s; the strife on ABM during the late 1960s and early 1970s; the MIRV issue during the same years; and the first SALT talks 1969–72 with the 1972 SALT I agreement.

Nuclear build-up and counterforce

As the Kennedy administration presented a strongly accelerated nuclear build-up immediately after its coming to office in January 1961, considerations on dominant Congressional attitudes played a prominent role. The new administration felt that it could not face Congress and gain support for its programs and political commitments without a heavy increase in the Eisenhower administration's nuclear missile program and it realized that Congressional pressures would be all the more difficult to dismiss because the Joint Chiefs would support them. Thus in justifying his preference of 950 *Minuteman* missiles – a number that has to be compared to the predecessor's 450 and the Air Force's recommendation of 3000 – Secretary McNamara is reported to have told President Kennedy that that was the smallest number he could imagine asking Congress for and 'not get murdered'.[35] Congressmen all but universally shared as a general principle that the best way for the United States to pursue security in the nuclear age was by accumulating nuclear hardware. Then, it was felt, the embarrassing fact that America itself was becoming vulnerable to Soviet nuclear missiles did not have to be faced. Not only did the need for American strategic nuclear superiority go unquestioned within Congress but many Congressmen advocated that the United States had to adopt a first-strike policy.[36] There were some confrontations between Congress and the administration during these years as Congress allocated money for weapons systems that the administration did not want and, altogether, many Congressional pressures – for instance, a vociferous B-70 bomber lobby, strongly supported by the Air Force – were exerted to expand the Kennedy administration's acceleration of the Eisenhower administration's missile program.

Opinion polls did not restrain these pressures. Thus a July 1961 poll – that is, before the Soviet Union resumed its nuclear testing in September – indicated that the respondents, especially the non-attentive mass public, favored unilateral American resumption of nuclear tests by a majority of more than two to one, and other polls showed that the mass public supported the early Kennedy administration's rearmament measures, including the strong nuclear build-up.[37] In addition, the Kennedy administration was concerned to contrast itself with its predecessor wherefore a vigorous military build-up was expedient. While it would definitely be erroneous to explain the Kennedy administration's arms policy solely in terms of domestic pressures *on* a wholly reluctant administration, it is evident that the domestic context favored the strong nuclear build-up.

The short–term impact of these domestic political factors was to strengthen the Kennedy administration's Soviet essentialist marked presentations of the Soviet adversary. However, in the long term these factors tended to have the opposite effect. Regarding the reactions to McNamara's announcement of a counterforce strategy in 1962 – and particularly Secretary McNamara's further reaction to these reactions –

some action–reaction processes in American politics surfaced which contributed to the opposite nuclear essentialist trend later in the 1960s. The point is that McNamara's conspicuous Ann Arbor speech of June 1962 (cf. pp. 39–40) with its notion of damage limitation through counterforce strikes strongly tended to perpetuate and amplify existing Congressional thinking on the role of nuclear weapons.[38] As the reaction in Congress and the military (in particular the Air Force who saw McNamara's counterforce, or 'no-cities', option as a first-strike strategy to fight and win a nuclear war) was to rationalize wishes for what McNamara considered excessive nuclear weapons in terms of the Defense Secretary's own reasoning in the Ann Arbor speech, the long-term impact of that speech as well as the Kennedy administration's accelerated nuclear build-up was to push McNamara toward adopting an 'assured destruction' criterion. As McNamara realized in the months after June 1962 when he began to retreat from the 'no-cities' strategy, his announcement of that reasoning had become an invitation to Congressmen as well as the American military to press for decisive counterforce capabilities sufficient to disarm Soviet strategic forces by attacking them first. In that way Secretary McNamara's attempt to devise a credible nuclear strategy at a time when all agreed on the necessity of American nuclear superiority became, via the interplay with other American political institutions, a factor which later caused the administration openly to stress a nuclear essentialist thinking. Before that appeared publicly, however, the domestic environment to another important departure in American nuclear policy has to be considered.

LTBT

Even if the support for a limited test ban was increasing in the Senate during the spring of 1963, the Kennnedy administration was under no domestic pressure to reach an agreement with the Soviet Union on a moratorium on nuclear tests before the Limited Test Ban Treaty (LTBT) was signed in early August 1963. Strong groups in Congress and the military, as well as among the public, were opposed to a test ban agreement and, considered in the American context, the administration's initiative in May–June was clearly the decisive factor.

After the treaty was signed the Senate's approval was, in the President's judgement, far from assured. Kennedy was very sensitive to the strong anti-communist sentiments prevalent among the public and a large part of Congress, and he was anxious not to appear too soft on the Soviets. After all, he had earlier made a similar accusation and was intensely aware of its domestic strength. The President initiated a large-scale campaign on behalf of ratification; for example, he oversaw the creation of and collaborated closely with a number of citizen groups that actively supported the treaty by attempting to influence the public and the Senate. Opinion leaders strongly endorsed the treaty: ratification was welcomed by a large majority of newspaper editorials and many leaders of organizations in the American society. As to the mass public, several opinion polls showed a substantial majority approving the treaty with the attentive segment showing the strongest support. A few days before the Senate vote in September, a Harris Poll reported 81 per cent in favour of ratification and only 8 per cent opposed, a clear increase compared to the 67 per cent who in early July registered approval, qualified or unqualified, for negotiations with the Soviets on a test ban and 17 per cent who opposed. Thus the public's attitudes had shifted markedly over a few months and both the US government's actual entering into a treaty and President Kennedy's seminal address in June (cf. pp. 37–8) seems to have been important. When the Senate approved the treaty in late September, it was carried with a margin safely above the two-thirds majority needed, 80 against 19. It was an essential part of the process of seeking the Senate's approval, however, that President Kennedy was careful to get the consent of those departments of the Executive branch whose endorsement would carry significant weight in Congress and among the public, namely the Joint Chiefs. In order to obtain their support the administration pledged that the United States would maintain an active program of underground nuclear testing, and as if to underscore this point, a few underground explosions were carried out during the Senate's deliberations.[39]

Hence, while the Kennedy administration's policy departure on the test ban issue is one of the first overt manifestations of a nuclear essentialist reasoning and can be considered as the initiation of the nuclear essentialist trend, the process of obtaining domestic support for this policy was double-edged. On the one hand, the administration initiated a large-scale public campaign applying nuclear essentialist-like slogans that was intended to impress skeptics among the public, in Congress and the Executive branch (particularly the military); on the other hand, it pledged its continuing support for some Soviet essentialist-like measures and so doing, it publicly struck a few corresponding themes. That is, it was a significant part of that domestic American process whereby the nuclear essentialist trend in the 1960s was launched that it combined a vociferous advocating of nuclear essentialist themes with a stressing of parts of the opposite view.

From this two conclusions follow: if President Kennedy's outspoken advocacy of détente and a kind of nuclear essentialism in 1963 can be termed 'overselling' because it heightened public expectactions far too much, that overselling can be accounted for in terms of the peculiarities of the American political process. However, another conclusion can also be drawn: the American political process seems to assure that a nuclear essentialist-like policy departure will be balanced by contrary manifestations and measures.

Assured destruction
Explaining the Johnson administration's moderate nuclear essentialist

image during 1965–8, in particular Secretary McNamara's distinct advocacy of an 'assured destruction' criterion for strategic nuclear forces, it is useful to consider the administration's position *vis-à-vis* Congress. Tensions between McNamara and Congress mounted in the second half of the 1960s as a number of influential Congressmen increasingly feared that the administration was not doing enough to maintain the American nuclear superiority they considered necessary.[40] In that situation McNamara's assured destruction notion was adopted as a tool for beating back what the Defense Secretary considered excessive demands for ever more strategic nuclear weapons. Those demands came primarily from the military and the Joint Chiefs but they were backed by powerful members of Congress and by proclaiming the seemingly simple assured destruction concept the administration could turn down demands it did not support. As noted, McNamara's strong espousal of this concept must also be seen as a reaction against the domestic repercussions to his own announcement of a 'no-cities', counterforce strategy earlier in the 1960s and considered in that context, it is evident that the most distinct swing toward a nuclear essentialist reasoning from an US government official through all the years 1961–89 was an instrument to counter Soviet essentialist-like views in the American political system – views which were partly prompted by the Defense Secretary's own earlier policy statements.

Examining the domestic sources of assured destruction, it is worth noting that when that notion was introduced in the administration's vocabulary, the state of public opinion played no role. Only later, when groups in American society began to oppose America's involvement in Vietnam and with the ABM issue from 1968, did public opinion become significant to the administration's shaping of American nuclear policy. Explaining the assured destruction concept's adoption by the administration, one can, however, point to the intellectual influence of those opinion leaders who in a number of papers and books issued from universities and research institutes had advocated a similar nuclear arms policy for some years. That thinking later became popular among wider groups in American society as many began to oppose an ABM deployment. Initially, however, the pressure on the administration as to ABM went in the other direction.

ABM
Congress as ever was concerned that the administration was too reluctant in its nuclear build-up and from 1966 this became more apparent as key Congressmen pressed strongly for an American ABM deployment. By late 1966, the pressure received a boost with reports that the Soviet Union was installing an ABM defense around Moscow. For President Johnson this created a special problem in that the mounting demands from influential members of Congress for an American ABM to offset the now 'visible' Soviet ABM system received strong support from the Joint Chiefs. No President could ignore pressures form senior military officers, supported by

Congressional leaders, since it was commonly accepted in American politics that the maintenance of America's strategic superiority over the Soviet Union required the Americans to match any Soviet military deployment. The Republicans were beginning to use the ABM issue in their campaign against the administration and could charge President Johnson with allowing a 'missile defense gap' at the forthcoming presidential election. Remembering the significance of the 'missile gap' of 1959–60, the President fully realized the political danger of the issue and he therefore sought to persuade McNamara that some sort of ABM was necessary for domestic reasons. Secretary McNamara, on the other hand, supported by other civilian leaders in the Defense Department, viewed an American ABM system as technically useless and politically pernicious since it would fuel a defensive–offensive arms race (cf. chapter 2, p. 56).[41]

In the light of that domestic background, the special make-up of the late Johnson administration's ABM policy becomes more understandable, particulary McNamara's San Francisco speech in September 1967. The marked advocacy of an assured destruction notion with the strong rejection of the expediency of a heavy ABM directed aganist the other superpower, combined with a China-directed light ABM deployment which could be seen as a first step toward a heavy Soviet-directed system, could be – and was – described by the various groups in Congress, the White House, the civilian leadership in Pentagon, and the Joint Chiefs in the way they preferred. Also the administration's public approach to Soviet–American negotiations on the limitation of offensive and defensive nuclear weapons can be interpreted against the background of these domestic pressures and focusing on the later Johnson administration's handling of the ABM issue, particularly the Defense Secretary's approach, it is thus obvious that when a composite – but still relatively distinct – nuclear essentialist image was presented, both the most pronounced nuclear essentialist elements as well as the deviations from that reasoning can be understood as vital parts of the administration's strategy *vis-à-vis* different domestic groups.

Elaborating domestic sources of different parts of the administration's presentations of the Soviet–American nuclear relationship, it is, again, worth noting that public opinion played no role. The mass public showed no interest in and was largely ignorant about these matters. Surveys showed, for examply, that more than 70 per cent of American citizens believed that the United States *did* have an ABM system and almost 60 per cent thought that the Soviets had one too.[42] In the same way, when McNamara announced a light China-directed ABM system in September 1967, the American mass opinion showed no immediate reaction. In the space of two years, however, that changed completely.

During 1968, mainly in Senate deliberations on the Johnson administration's *Sentinel* ABM proposal, a growing number of Congressmen became doubtful about the wisdom of an ABM deployment. As a psychological by-product of the Vietnam War, in particular, a critical review of and potential opposition to major weapon programs emerged in Congress and in 15 Senate votes on the ABM issue, during 1968–70, the divisions mainly followed ideological positions, with conservatives favouring ABM and liberals opposing it.[43] The institutional development of Congressional staffs was significant in that active staff works enabled members opposed to ABM to elaborate extensive reasonings for their opposition. This Congressional opposition to an important arms acquisition proposal, presented by an administration (from early 1969, the Nixon administration's *Safeguard* ABM proposal), was a new phenomenon in the American political process. The Congressional opposition was strengthened as it enlisted a number of scientific and technical professionals who had worked on ABM programs for some years. Moreover, this development coincided with, and followed, a lot of arms control literature from research institutes, universities and experts-cum-politically engaged persons in American society, mainly based on a kind of nuclear essentialism. Much of this thinking had been presented in books, pamphlets and articles earlier in the 1960s but the ABM debate now made it useful to many members of Congress. Several of these experts some of whom had been active in the Kennedy and Johnson administrations, appeared in Congressional hearings on ABM, opposing an American deployment.[44]

The opposition from Congress was strengthened as many public groups at grass-roots level sprang up across the country. Contrary to expectations, these groups emerged particularly in areas scheduled to be defended by the first ABM sites in that the sites were seen by the opponents as targets for a nuclear attack. The Nixon administration's *Safeguard* system was partly designed to accommodate such fears but, all the same, the public anti-ABM forces had acquired a certain momentum with the result that the coalition of opposition did not dissolve in the wake of the *Safeguard* announcement redirecting the ABM deployment and changing its strategic rationale. Public opinion, both as concerns the mass public and opinion leaders, was, however, more divided than experts' and grass-roots activities could indicate. While opinion polls on the attitude to defence spending in 1969 showed more skepticism than for many years, polls focusing specifically on ABM showed both that many respondents did not understand the issue and that opinions were sometimes closely divided; some polls even found a considerable margin approving ABM. Similarly, newspaper editorials on ABM in the spring of 1969 were evenly divided between supporters and opponents.[45] At the elite level, this strongly divided state of opinion reflects the breakdown of the consensus on American foreign policy after 1968, splitting the traditionally internationalist minded elite – that had dominated the shaping of American foreign policy since, roughly, 1948 – between conservative and liberal internationalists.[46] This seminal division among opinion leaders became significant to American nuclear policy from 1969.

The immediate outcome was a narrow defeat for the opposition to ABM in the Senate vote in August 1969, of 49 against 51. The razor-thin majority supporting ABM encouraged the opponents in Congress to continue their attempts to modify the administration's ABM proposals and during the following years they succeeded in cutting the program.[47] It seems probable that without the Congressional opposition to *Sentinel* and *Safeguard*, by 1972 the United States would have been well on the way to building an infrastructure across the country for an extensive ABM system and the 1972 SALT treaty limiting ABM as a significant part of a nuclear essentialist reasoning would have been impossible. Altogether, one can conclude that the vocal opposition to an important part of the administration's nuclear policy induced the Nixon administration to emphasize and continue nuclear essentialist elements of its policy for a few years. Thus, while Congress or the public did definitely not press the administration in the early to mid-1960s to initiate the nuclear essentialist trend, and in fact restrained it for some years, toward the end of the 1960s and the early 1970s Congress impelled the administration to continue the nuclear essentialist trend. Ironically, this pressure from parts of Congress and the public began just about the time the most distinct spokesman for this reasoning left the Johnson administration, namely Secretary McNamara in spring 1968.

But was ABM the most important weapons acquisition bearing on the nuclear essentialist vs. Soviet essentialist distinction during these years?

MIRV

While Congress was preoccupied with the ABM issue, it neglected the administration's efforts to develop multiple independently targetable re-entry vehicles (MIRV) with their potential counterforce capability and its further impact. (The first public use of the acronym MIRV apparently occurred in 1964 in technical periodicals but the MIRV concept and the development of MIRV has its genesis early in the Kennedy administration when it was related to the then dominating counterforce doctrine.) Major operational decisions involving MIRV had been taken currently in the defense bureaucracy and toward the middle of the 1960s, reports on Soviet ABM deployments boosted the MIRV program. Secretary McNamara strongly supported MIRV throughout his time in office and in 1965 he finally authorized its development, i.e. just at a time when he began propagating the assured destruction concept. One reason was that he saw MIRV as a means of reducing Congressional and Air Force opposition to his holding down the number of strategic missiles. Uncertainties concerning Soviet ABM deployments also acted as a stimulus to MIRV, and flight tests of MIRV began in August 1968 while the installation of MIRV on *Minuteman* III and *Poseidon* missiles began in 1970–1. Although Congress through the years had appropriated sizeable sums for the MIRV program, Congressmen were generally ignorant of MIRV and its potential consequences, however. MIRV was hardly mentioned in the extensive debates on ABM during 1968, despite the fact that MIRV considered from those types of reasonings applied against ABM would have more pernicious strategic implications than ABM and despite the fact that MIRV was already closer to deployment than anti-ballistic missiles defenses.[48]

From late 1968, however, there was mounting awareness among some members of Congress that MIRV might be an even graver problem than ABM. These doubts first appeared in informal meetings among a small number of members of Senators' staffs where some voiced the view that the heavy focus on ABM was misplaced and that Congress ought instead to examine the MIRV issue. Others, however, argued that too much attention to MIRV would dilute efforts to beat the ABM deployment. The most prominent MIRV opponent in the Senate, Senator Edward Brooke (R. Mass.), initiated in early 1969 a process with the goal of restraining the American MIRV development and securing a mutual Soviet–American ban on MIRV.[49] Brooke's activities included private conferences with President Nixon and other administration officials as well as letters to administration members and some public addresses to opinion leaders. In June 1969, Senator Brooke, together with forty other Senators, sponsored a Senate resolution calling for a mutual suspension of MIRV flight tests by the Soviet Union and the United States; in April 1970, the Senate passed the resolution by the overwhelming majority of 72 to 6. During 1969–72, Congress also cancelled a few MIRV programs and the Defense Department omitted requesting some MIRV-related funds it had planned. Other MIRV programs, however, continued. One reason for this was the Nixon administration's endeavor to develop a more discriminating strategy for nuclear war (cf. p. 62) which the Joint Chiefs, together with influential members of Congress, strongly endorsed because, according to Henry Kissinger, they understood that the assured destruction doctrine could lead to decisions halting or neglecting and in time reducing strategic nuclear forces.[50]

Throughout his activities Senator Brooke endeavored to present his proposal for a MIRV ban as a call for a *mutual* Soviet–American moratorium. He fully realized the widespread attachment in the United States to the view that one should never bind oneself to exercise restraint unless the Soviet Union displayed a similar restraint – a view which was predominant even at a time of an otherwise defense-critical mood in Congress and the public. The Senators leading the opposition to MIRV knew it was almost impossible to gain acceptance for the view that whatever the Soviets did with regard to their own counterforce capacity, it was America's interest to avoid a hard-target capability, and Senator Brooke therefore emphasized that it was America's objective to render American strategic forces invulnerable, not to render Soviet forces vulnerable.[51]

Concurrent with this development in Congress, parts of public opinion were coming around to endorsing a MIRV moratorium and especially among liberal internationalist opinion leaders, concern over MIRV was mounting rapidly.[52] However, it was evident that the opposition to MIRV was far less viable than the opposition to ABM. One obvious reason was that while ABM could be denounced as technically unworkable and the immediate 'visibility' of scheduled ABM deployments around the country aroused public opposition by engaging widespread grass-roots organizations, the critique of MIRV had to rest upon strategic reasonings which could easily seem esoteric. Moreover, MIRV was not an expensive program. As some members of Congress opposed to both ABM and MIRV recognized, the popular basis for beating ABM was simply far greater than the popular basis for beating MIRV.

The impact of the Senate's, and especially Senator Brooke's, endeavors to restrain the development of MIRV was to reinforce the early Nixon administration's firm declaratory policy against a hard-target MIRV capability. With Senator Brooke's persistent calling attention to the dissonance between the President's declared policy of not threatening the Soviets' retaliatory capability and the actual character of the evolving MIRV program, the administration was forced or induced to explicate its policy in a way that stressed nuclear essentialist aspects.[53] As the administration wanted Congress's endorsement for its policies, it was necessary to comply with those, seemingly strong, groups that opposed the development of a hard-target counterforce capability. The existence of divergent views occurred, however, not only in Congress but also in the administration, meaning that the Senate's support for the administration's attitude against threatening Soviet retaliatory forces can be seen as a support for one part of the administration against another part which preferred a more Soviet essentialist-like policy. The wider effect of this was the emergence of a heightened awareness among a greater number of Congressmen and opinion leaders in the country of the need for refining American nuclear policy: the intense, partly public, debate on MIRV – and ABM – provided a benchmark both for administration officials, members of Congress, opinion leaders as well as broader segments of the public to use in gauging trends in American nuclear policy. The emergence of an extensive public debate and disagreement on American nuclear policy where the dividing lines can be represented, roughly, as following a nuclear essentialist vs. Soviet essentialist distinction can to a great part be traced to the dispute over ABM and MIRV during the later 1960s and early 1970s. The initiation of Strategic Arms Limitation Talks (SALT) in November 1969 completely altered the domestic setting, however, in that considerations for the United States' diplomatic position from that time onward played an essential role in Executive–Congressional deliberations on American nuclear policy.

SALT I

Congress was not directly involved in the administration's SALT policy-making and even if the chief SALT negotiator briefed Congressional committees several times, it received little detailed information on the negotiations before the SALT I agreements were entered in 1972. SALT was considered a matter better left to the Executive, especially by those members who were most positive to the negotiations. Only a few Senate members endeavored to follow SALT closely and they were mainly the skeptical ones. Besides, while the administration was somewhat impervious to any guidance from Congress, it paid greater heed to those members of the Senate whose restrained support for the negotiations left their votes in a future ratification process in doubt and since these were the same who had salvaged the administration's *Safeguard* ABM proposal from Congressional defeat in August 1969, the Nixon administration had an evident interest in repaying SALT skeptics the debt it had accrued.[54]

In addition to this was the impact of 'bargaining chip' considerations. While the initiation of SALT in November 1969 was promoted by concerns in the administration that Congress, in the absence of Soviet–American agreements, would go for unilateral nuclear arms limitation, the actual existence of negotiations could have the opposite effect: Congressmen who questioned the expediency of some weapons acquisitions requested by the administration came to modify their views by the persuasiveness of the argument that the American bargaining power *vis-à-vis* the Soviet Union needed to be strengthened by one weapon or another. Congress increasingly came under pressure to approve the administration's nuclear arms requests as a means of supporting America's bargaining position in SALT and hedging against a failure of the negotiations. Thus it was felt (by Congressmen opposed to MIRV and ABM also), that a unilateral American restraint on these weapon systems would tie the hands of American negotiators and impede the possibilities for a SALT agreement. Still, however, there were strong domestic pressures during the early 1970s to curtail American weapon programs. In 1971, for example, parts of Congress and the public wanted to end the ABM program or, at least, accept a Soviet proposal for a separate treaty banning or restraining ABM which the administration opposed.[55]

Hence, while some distinct Congressional attitudes supporting the nuclear essentialist trend ebbed away after the boom of 1968–9, the mere initiation of the SALT process – that is, both the negotiations between the two governments and the domestic American deliberations on these negotiations – shifted the political leverage from members of Congress favorable to a kind of nuclear essentialism to members skeptical about that reasoning. Ironically, an administration pursuing a kind of nuclear essentialist policy as to negotiations became vulnerable to Senators who harbored a skeptical attitude to that policy: the domestic position of the executive branch *vis-à-vis* the legislative branch enhanced the Nixon administration's tendency to adopt Soviet essentialist-like policies concerning other aspects of American nuclear policy.

The changed domestic context appeared most clearly after the SALT I agreement had been signed in May 1972 and the administration had to secure the Senate's approval of the agreement. Public opinion strongly favored the agreement. Polls in May–June 1972 found some 80 per cent approving the SALT agreement while only about 12 per cent voiced disapproval. In the same way, opinion leaders strongly favored the agreement; for instance a great majority of newspapers advocated prompt ratification of the ABM treaty and Congressional approval of the agreement limiting offensive weapons. The Joint Chiefs, on the other hand, had at one point come close to openly refusing support but, in the end, that did not materialize. [56] The focal point of the administration's concern, however, was the position of those Senators who were skeptical about arms control negotiations with the Soviets or voiced criticism of the administration's procedures in the final negotiations leading up to the agreement. The central figure was Senator Henry Jackson (D. Wash.) who in early August proposed an amendment to the Interim Agreement which called for numerical equality as to intercontinental strategic forces in future strategic arms agreements between the United States and the Soviet Union. In late September the Senate passed Jackson's amendment by a vote of 56 to 35. The administration supported the amendment after the original wording had been modified but several of the most SALT-positive Senators opposed it. [57]

The impact of the Jackson amendment was clearly to restrain the administration's diluted version of nuclear essentialism. Moreover, a mini-purge, reportedly conducted at Senator Jackson's urging, of the pro-SALT staff of the Arms Control and Disarmament Agency was carried out after President Nixon's re-election in November and with the exception of one, Paul Nitze, the entire membership of the SALT delegation was replaced. [58] Altogether, it is evident that both the process of negotiating the SALT I agreement and the process of securing the Senate's approval of the concluded agreement pushed the Nixon administration toward Soviet essentialism. Differently expressed: the domestic American political process related to carrying through one nuclear essentialist measure – the SALT I negotiations with the 1972 agreement – prompted contrary Soviet essentialist tendencies.

Concluding observations
One conclusion as to the significance of the domestic political context 1961–74 is that, considered in relation to the long-term nuclear essentialist trend from 1963, the impact of US governments' position *vis-à-vis* Congress and the public has generally been incremental. The initiation of the nuclear essentialist trend cannot be accounted for in such terms and it is not possible to conclude that the continuation of that trend always has been either promoted or impeded by Congress and the public. On the other hand, even if there is no overall unidirectional impact, the significance of Congress and the public to different administrations' portrayals of the Soviet Union as a nuclear adversary was noticeable on several occasions in that various swings can be accounted for by including an administration's actual

position in American politics, and these swings have been in divergent directions. For most of the period, the effect of an administration's relations to Congress and the public has been a strengthening of inclinations displayed by the incumbent administration while only during the late 1960s and early 1970s, did Congress restrain contrary tendencies in the administration. However, the actual form and direction of these factors has assumed divergent shapes which indicate the often paradoxical nature of the relation between the declaratory aspect of American nuclear policy and domestic American politics.

In the early 1960s, the Kennedy administration's basically Soviet essentialist image was shared by Congress and the public and in that sense one can conclude that the more pronounced Soviet essentialist image after the Soviet resumption of nuclear tests in the summer of 1961 was prompted by an (almost) universal consensus in the American society. Considering the background to later swings, it is worth noting that that reaction in 1961 was not conditioned by any current domestic dispute on American nuclear policy. Generally, nuclear issues did not become highly contentious among a greater part of the public before the dispute over ABM from 1968. The administration's relations with Congress, however, early acquired a specific significance: through 1965–8, when Congress still shared more Soviet essentialist attitudes, they were seen in the roundabout way that distinct nuclear essentialist notions – particularly Secretary McNamara's pronounced swing to a nuclear essentialist-like reasoning on deterrence – was proclaimed partly in order to beat off Congressional demands for ever more nuclear weapons which were supported by an important part of the administration itself, namely the Joint Chiefs. Public opinion played no role during that time. Later, as the administration's attachment to nuclear essentialist notions obviously had weakened and parts of Congress had come to share such ideas, the Nixon administration still displayed some of these reasonings because (among other reasons) it assessed that that was the most expedient way to obtain Congress' support for its policies, including, paradoxically, some weapons acquisitions. As to the public, both the mass public and opinion leaders showed divergent views from 1968 that did not offer any clear-cut guidance for an administration anxious to please majority opinion. In any case, it was only during these years, at the end of the 1960s and into the early 1970s, that an administration's position in US politics provided a motive for emphasizing the nuclear essentialist trend in order to accommodate groups in the American society sharing these views rather than to counter opposite views. At the same time, the existence of the SALT negotiations after 1969 was used by the administration to weaken some nuclear essentialist elements in the American policy.

b.   1974–89

With the exception in particular of the first part of the Carter administration and a change in the Reagan administration's stance on negotiations, the years 1974–89 have been dominated by a Soviet essentialist trend. Assessing the impact of the interplay between Congress, the public and the administration through this period will be based on a review of various issues during the period and related developments: the strife on counterforce between the administration and parts of Congress in the mid-1970s; the 1976 presidential election campaign; the SALT II negotiations and the 1979 SALT agreement; the American rearmament during the late 1970s, accelerated after the Reagan administration's accession to office in 1981; the nuclear freeze issue in the early 1980s. The last three issues partly overlap in time through the late 1970s and early 1980s and a closer examination and analysis can elucidate how changing public moods affect US governments' public representations of the Soviet–American nuclear relationship. Lastly, the Strategic Defense Initiative (SDI) as a part of American politics after 1983 will be considered.

Counterforce questioned and reaffirmed

Following the enunciation of the Schlesinger strategy in early 1974, some members of the Senate voiced apprehensions about the changes in American strategic nuclear policy. While the tenets of the Schlesinger strategy were supported by one group of Senators, primarily Senator Henry Jackson and some of his colleagues on the Armed Services Committee, others – who included Senators who had opposed the administration's ABM and MIRV policy in the late 1960s – were apprehensive that the development of the more effective counterforce capability with its weight on improved missile accuracy was unwise.[59] They agreed to Secretary Schlesinger's proposal that US command and control systems should be improved but through letters to the Defense Secretary, in meetings in Senate committees, through amendments on the Senate floor to restrain counterforce programs, and through a request to a Congressional support agency for conducting a critical review of the issue, the opponents questioned and challenged the administration's policy. These activities were, in a way, a residue of some Senators' endeavors 5–7 years earlier which had also been directed at restraining Soviet essentialist tendencies in the administration's nuclear policy.[60]

In the end, the Senate skeptics enjoyed only little success. The administration's requests for monies to finance counterforce programs were approved by Congress after a few fruitless efforts to block the accounts. None the less, Senate involvement in the making of the counterforce strategy represented a new departure compared to Congress's usual non-involvement in that type of issue and it contributed to, and was prompted by, opinion leaders' focus on the issue. As the divisions in the Senate, by and large, coincided with divisions in the executive branch, it is – apart from a probable sharpening of the disagreements in the administration – difficult, however, to point to any effect on the government's policy. The Senators' querying counterforce neither restrained nor strengthened the Soviet essentialist trend apparent from the mid-1970's.

One reason that the Senators' attempt, unlike a few years earlier, was futile was the trend in opinion, both among the mass public and opinion leaders. From 1974, the public's support for higher defense spending increased markedly. Similarly, the public's attitude toward the Soviet Union chilled sharply from 1975–6.[61] The mass public were evidently disappointed with the results of détente and were beginning to feel insecure about growing Soviet military strength and adventurism, particularly in Africa (notably Angola). In the media, and especially on television, the generally disinterested public could 'see for itself', so to say, the manifestations of Soviet expansionism and it had a marked impact on its attitudes in that it began to show more sympathy for notions like 'strength' and 'toughness' in American foreign policy. As the general public in the United States are non-internationalistically inclined and show a strong and persistent commitment to two basic values – peace and strength – the relative salience attached to these values varies over time.[62] From 1963 to 1974, roughly, and particularly around 1970, peace was the overriding public concern but from 1974 strength – meaning military strength – became the dominant concern. That meant that from the mid-1970s the non-internationalistic mass public increasingly supported what can be termed an elite conservative internationalist view with its demands for military strength and suspicion of the Soviets and détente.

Also the dominant themes and conclusions among opinion leaders shifted markedly during the mid-1970s. While the writings from politically engaged experts had been dominated by various kinds of nuclear essentialism a few years earlier (cf. above), articles, pamphlets and books on foreign policy and strategic problems increasingly focused on the dangers of America not matching Soviet counterforce capabilities; the political significance of 'perceptions' of asymmetrical nuclear strengths and a tendency to underestimate the Soviet nuclear build-up was stressed by several foreign policy observers.[63] Generally, traditional arms control thinking was under assault when strategic experts-cum-politicians pointed to its deficiencies or emphasized the fact that Soviet writings on nuclear arms did not share its reasonings. These writings were read by only a small, but often influential, segment and since they coincided with the changing mood among the mass public, it all reduced any possibility that attempts by Senators to restrain the Ford administration's slide toward counterforce could succeed. The broader societal background in the mid-1970s impeded such attempts even more than usually in the United States.

It follows that the administration's turn toward a more pronounced Soviet essentialism during the mid-1970s can be seen as a means to engender and maintain the necessary support for its policies from various groups in American society. More specifically, one can reason that the strengthening of the ever-present elements of Soviet essentialism in US governments' statements was an instrument to get public and Congressional support for a renewed military build-up after the decline in the US defense budget since the late 1960s and secure support for a stronger political and military stand against the Soviets. The Ford administration had to realize that by maintaining nuclear essentialist residuals of its policy, it would make itself dangerously vulnerable to those Congressional and opinion leaders who demanded or endorsed a 'tougher' American policy to counter the Soviets around the globe. Thus, main currents in American politics strongly encouraged Soviet essentialist proclivities in the US government in the mid-1970s.

The 1976 presidential campaign
The 1976 presidential election campaign evidenced the changing domestic context as American foreign policy was a central issue in Ronald Reagan's nearly successful challenge to President Ford in the primaries and at the Republican Party's convention. It was not normal for an incumbent President to be strongly challenged in an election year by a prominent faction of his own party. The Reagan forces assailed the Ford administration from a distinctly conservative internationalist point of view for being soft on the Russians and having ignored the necessity of a strong and superior American military and they portrayed SALT and détente as an American sell-out. On the other hand, President Ford's Democratic challenger, Jimmy Carter, voiced a widespread popular unease in the United States over the Nixon and Ford administrations' Realpolitik and through his stress on human rights he pledged a stronger moral commitment in American foreign policy. In a way, the Ford administration was assailed from opposite points of view, both containing strong moralistic strains. However, as Jimmy Carter was no pacifist and felt uneasy with the strong anti-militarism shared by sections in the Democratic Party, the two presidential contenders were, in fact, quite close to each other on foreign policy but, given the election contest, Carter focused on the disagreements with the incumbent administration.[64] The long-drawn-out election campaign in 1976 manifested the deep-rooted aversion among a great part of the non-internationalistic mass public to any Soviet-American cooperation and as these widespread public attitudes were elaborated and channeled into a strong challenge to significant parts of several years of American foreign policy by a conservative internationalist-minded elite, the year 1976 was a watershed in that for some years marginal views in the American political spectrum returned as a part of the main current. While the Ford administration, until the spring of 1976, vacillated between accommodating and countering the right-wing challenge head-on, its choice during its last ten months in office was clearly to accommodate and appease that challenge and the impact of this was to strengthen the Soviet essentialist trend, directly and indirectly.

Two events after Carter's election but before he succeeded Ford as President prepared the ground for Soviet essentialist views among the

American public. First, the announcement just one week after the election in November of the formation of 'Committee on the President Danger' (CPD), a bipartisan group of several well-known people (including Paul Nitze who had resigned from the American SALT delegation in June 1974) many of whom had served in former administrations. CPD strongly advocated American rearmament and warned against a SALT II agreement as this was then taking shape. Second, very pessimistic findings on the Soviet–American military balance by a so-called 'Team B' appeared in the American press during the very last days of 1976. Team B was a panel of experts on Soviet military, set up in June by the Director of Central Intelligence, George Bush, to check whether official intelligence estimates of Soviet strategic capabilities and intentions were too optimistic, and leaks from its report contributed strongly to a general popular impression that the US government had underestimated the Soviet military build-up and misjudged Soviet intentions during the détente years.[65] It all contributed heavily to an increasingly pessimistic mood in the American public concerning the Soviet Union as a nuclear power, and especially as to SALT.

SALT II

When the Vladivostok agreement was entered into in late November 1974, a great majority of the mass public endorsed it but many with the reservation that the missile ceilings were too high and the Russians were unlikely to keep their side of the bargain. Opinion leaders too supported the agreement; newspaper editorials, for instance, considered the agreement worthwhile but the ceilings were deplored as too high.[66] Organizations traditionally advocating arms control from a kind of nuclear essentialist reasoning were split, however, between supporters giving qualified approval and opponents arguing that the agreement would stimulate the arms race because it gave a green light for weapons programs that might otherwise never have been approved. In Congress, the sharpest criticism was voiced by Senators–primarily Senator Henry Jackson, who demanded a more Soviet essentialist-like policy, and he too assailed the ceilings as too high. Traditionally arms control-minded senators, on the other hand, expressed only muted support and it was obvious that the agreement could not generate much enthusiasm among the different attitudes to the nuclear issue in the United States. The domestic reactions to the Vladivostok agreement thus signaled a significant feature of opinion leaders' and Congressional attitudes to SALT through the rest of the 1970s: strong and often vociferous opposition mixed with others' cautious and disappointed approval.

As developments in 1976 too had increased the American public's skepticism, it was evident that when the Carter administration came into office in January 1977, the domestic context of the evolving debate on SALT was markedly different from the highly favorable context of 1969–72. Not only were the avowed opponents now much stronger but many supporters, both among opinion leaders and in Congress, had lost their enthusiasm. On the other hand, the Carter administration, unlike both the Nixon and Ford administrations, was eager to have Congress involved in the SALT policy-making process and in the spring of 1977 several members of the Senate and the House were designated, by the President of the Senate and the Speaker of the House, as advisers to the SALT delegation in Geneva. Generally, the relations between the Executive and the legislative branches concerning SALT were characterized by an unprecedented sharing of information throughout the Carter administration.[67] The administration's efforts were obviously intended to allay Congressional opposition to a new SALT agreement that was expected to be controversial. However, as the negotiations dragged on for more than two years – during which the final breakthrough was expected more than once – the administration's endeavors to broaden the governmental decision-making process in order to secure the necessary consensus turned out to harden the opposition. Contributing to this was a lingering suspicion in the Senate, among foes and friends of SALT alike, that the administration would submit a SALT II agreement as an Executive agreement, requiring a simple majority of both Houses only, rather than as a treaty which required a two-thirds majority in the Senate. The suspicion was real in the sense that a number of 'trial balloons' from the administration to test that possibility had been angrily rejected by Senate leaders, and the end-result was a less favorable Congressional environment to a new SALT agreement.[68]

A first indicator of the Senate's attitudes had already appeared in February–March 1977 when it confirmed Paul Warnke as Director of ACDA and chief SALT negotiator. Warnke was known as a classical 'arms controller' in the nuclear essentialist mold and his confirmation as chief SALT negotiator was carried with a margin of only 58 to 40, that is, well below the necessary two-thirds majority required for approval of a new SALT treaty.[69] Thus both Warnke's appointment as a distinct arms control advocate in a heterogeneous administration, the strong Senate opposition, and the increased Senate involvement in the SALT negotiations indicated main lines of the mounting dispute on SALT: an administration internally split but initially inclining toward a diluted nuclear essentialism faced a Senate which had become more heavily involved in SALT and with several influential members increasingly favoring Soviet essentialist views. The end-result was that when the SALT II agreement was finally concluded in the summer of 1979 and the ratification process initiated, the SALT process had become a highly contentious issue in Congressional politics and the Senate's approval very doubtful.

Concurrent with this trend in Congressional attitudes was a notable development in public opinion. Polls through 1978–9 showed that the mass public remained strongly favorable to the idea of a new Soviet–American agreement to limit nuclear weapons: about three-quarters approved such an agreement while less than one-fifth voiced opposition even if this group tended to increase.[70] However, while the general idea of a Soviet–American arms control agreement remained very popular among the mass public, questions focusing specifically on a SALT II agreement showed a much more limited support. Actually, after the agreements had been signed in the summer of 1979, polls showed that a plurality of the mass public opposed the agreements. Even if different polls showed somewhat varying margins, all polls agreed that the prevailing trend of public opinion toward the SALT II agreement was negative. Besides, several polls indicated that the mass public's level of information was quite low. Polls in 1977, for instance, showed that 33 per cent of those interviewed had never heard of SALT. In early 1979 a poll indicated that a substantial majority of Americans did not know which countries were involved in SALT, and later polls in 1979 showed a widespread lack of knowledge about the actual provisions of the SALT II agreement.[71] Whatever the level of information among mass public (and that was not markedly different from usual), it was in any case evident that the new SALT agreement, quite unlike the first SALT agreement of 1972, was opposed by many Americans, and it was characteristic that as SALT II became the object of a heated controversy among political elites in the media, the divisions reappeared at the level of the mass public.

The conclusion from this review of public and Congressional attitudes toward the SALT negotiations and the 1979 agreement is that the domestic American context clearly influenced the Carter administration's representations of the Soviet–American nuclear relationship but, considered in terms of the nuclear essentialism vs. Soviet essentialism distinction, the impact went in diverse directions and varied over time. On the one hand, it is obvious that deliberations in the administration on how to accommodate and reassure the Senate in order to obtain the necessary two-thirds majority for a SALT II treaty led the administration to emphasize Soviet essentialist marked views, particularly as to deterrence (cf. MX), which were shared by several influential Senators (as well as by a prominent part of the administration itself) and appealed to a great part of the public. Unlike 1969 –72, Senators speaking in favor of these views evoked a response among the mass public: public opinion was now disposed toward accepting such views. On the other hand, after the new SALT agreement had been entered in 1979, the administration reasoned that in order to ensure Senate approval it had to mount an offensive and apply clear-cut nuclear essentialist views on negotiations. That, it was assessed, would beat back the Congressional opposition and raise public opinion's support for the SALT II agreement.

Thus, the Carter administration applied a two-pronged strategy in its attempt to cope with the domestic opposition to the SALT II agreement but, in the end, this proved unsuccessful. The Soviet invasion of Afghanistan gave it the final deathblow but also before the turn of the year 1979–80 it was highly doubtful if the administration would succeed. One reason was that there was obviously no reserve among the mass public which the administration could raise through a strong public appeal. While the mass public ever harbored strong support for arms control as an abstract idea, it was apparently very difficult for the Carter administration to convert this into support for SALT II. A highly troublesome domestic environment could not be managed through elaborating a two-sided public strategy. As the administration's approach evidently was too heterogeneous to be successful in the American political process, it can be concluded that the overall impact of American politics during the late 1970s was a strengthening of the Soviet essentialist trend.

Rearmament and assertive moods
Closely related to the opposition against the SALT II agreement was a strong feeling of frustration combined with assertiveness in the public and Congress, particularly of 1979–81. Toward the end of the 1970s, American politics was dominated by a mounting sense that America's military weakness was decisive to that declining position in world politics the United States, according to the great majority of Americans, was experiencing. Both the public and most Congressmen felt strongly that many years' Soviet military build-up and foreign activism now really presented a serious threat to America's security. The Soviet invasion of Afghanistan contributed to that feeling but especially the Iranian hostage crisis beginning in November 1979 vastly strengthened a widespread sense that America was letting itself be 'pushed around'. In particular, the fact that the public night after night were reminded on television that 52 fellow Americans were held hostage in Teheran had a vast effect and that at a time when the Soviet Union had brutally invaded a foreign country. The humiliation and outrage over America's 'loss of control' was profound and the public mood became one of deep frustration. [72]

The reaction was a strong trend in favor of a much more assertive, or 'tough', foreign policy and a consensus grew that the first condition for this was a significant strengthening of the American military. In the early 1970s there had, as noted, been a majority against increased defense spending and, as late as December 1978, a majority of the mass public still opposed higher defense spending. In 1979, however, this changed profoundly and from the middle of the year, i.e. months before the hostage crisis and the Soviet invasion of Afghanistan, a plurality favored higher military spending. A Gallup Poll conducted in late September showed that an absolute majority, namely 60 per cent, supported increased defense expenditures while only 9 per cent favored reduction. After the hostage crisis had begun and the Soviet Union had invaded Afghanistan the support reached a peak in early 1980 of more than 70 per cent. [73] Among Congressmen and opinion leaders too the overwhelming majority advocated a strong increase in the defense budget.

Considered against this background, it is evident that the later Carter administration's more pronounced Soviet essentialism was in accordance with highly dominant trends in both Congress and among the public. The Carter administration undoubtedly felt itself even more vulnerable to the challenge from Republican presidential candidate Ronald Reagan if it did not present a much 'tougher' foreign policy to the American people and in that situation Soviet essentialist declarations can be considered an instrument in American politics. Explaining the later Carter presidency's image in that context, it is, however, important to note the limits of this explanation since it is evident that the Carter administration maintained and even stressed a moderate nuclear essentialist perception of negotiations and Soviet–American agreements on the nuclear issue also after it had withdrawn the treaty from the Senate and it was obvious to everybody that the treaty had no chance of getting the Senate's approval, i.e. during a time (1980) when the public and Congressional mood clearly indicated the domestic political drawback of that view. Of course, one could reason that the Carter administration continued presenting a two-sided image through 1980 because it expected – albeit erroneously – that it would be beneficial in terms of the mass public's traditional endorsement of 'peace and strength'. However, given the clear evidence that a great majority of the American public in 1980 preferred a 'strength' policy more than a 'peace' policy, that explanation seems less valid. From this it follows that even if domestic politics during that critical time influenced the American government's representation of the Soviet–American nuclear relationship, it is not possible to account for all its distinctive marks in that context. That conclusion may seem a matter of course but is still worth noting because it suggests some limits to how the US government is sensitive to the American people's volatile moods.

The early Reagan administration's pronounced Soviet essentialism can be explained as a reflection of deeply held beliefs about the Soviet Union. President Reagan's strong rhetorical style can be regarded as a gut response of the representative of the American right.[74] However, an explanation in terms of current American politics seems valid as well in that the early Reagan presidency's general representation of the Soviet–American relationship in distinct Soviet essentialist terms can be considered as a means to sensitizing and arousing the American public and Congress to the Soviet danger and support the administration's acceleration of the American military build-up. Again, however, one could also reason the opposite: precisely the fact that the state of public opinion and Congress already unambiguously favored a strong rearmament obviated a need to stir up American opinion to that end. Nevertheless, particularly considering the vacillating nature of American opinion and indications that prominent members of the Reagan administration were aware of this, an instrumental explanation of the early Reagan administration's distinct Soviet essentialist image in terms of American politics is also tenable. In addition, data suggest that Ronald Reagan won the 1980 presidential election in spite of his foreign policy stance, not because of it, and that notwithstanding that a majority of Americans shared his preference for a 'tougher' American foreign policy.[75]

Changing moods: a nuclear freeze?
Predictions that the public's and Congressional support for increased defense spending would not last proved correct. Within the first half of the Reagan administration's first term, opinion polls demonstrated a sharp decline in support for increases in defense spending: according to a Harris poll,[76] while 71 per cent favored increasing the defense budget in 1980, only 17 per cent supported this in late 1982 and, apart from a surge during the autumn of 1983 (after the Soviet Union shot down a Korean passenger airliner flying in Soviet airspace), support remained at that level. Generally, polls showed that after the Reagan administration had been in office for less than two years, there were important disparities between public opinion and administration policies in areas as defense spending and nuclear arms control. The November 1982 Congressional elections similarly indicated public opposition to the administration's defense policy. In 1982 and particularly in 1983, Congress cut the administration's proposals for the defense budget and various, now controversial, defense programs (especially MX; cf. p. 110) were rejected.[77] On the other hand, it was evident that both the public and Congress still shared other aspects of the Reagan administration's security policy as its distrust of the Soviet Union and its focus on American–Soviet relations and concern with military security.

Related to the declining public and Congressional support for defense spending was a sharp increase in the support for freezing the development of nuclear weapons. At the end of 1981, a mass popular movement in support of a bilateral American–Soviet nuclear freeze suddenly emerged as a great number of grass-roots organizations, including some traditionally conservative groups, began to agitate for a freeze throughout the country. One indicator of their initial success was a rally of 800,000 people in New York City, on 12 June 1982, to protest against the nuclear arms race, the largest demonstration of its kind in American history.[78] Polls taken during 1982 and 1983 showed big majorities in favor of a joint superpower agreement to ban the testing, production and development of nuclear weapons. Thus more than 70 per cent, particularly among the more aware of the public, favoured a freeze while only about 20 per cent opposed it and these polls were confirmed in the November 1982 Congressional elections when nuclear freeze proposals were passed on almost every ballot on which they appeared.

However, while there was widespread support for the idea of a freeze, the American public definitely did not favor an unconditional freeze. The freeze had to be *mutual* and the great majority opposed anything that hinted at unilateral American disarmament or put the United States at a military disadvantage. More notable, support for a freeze appeared to have little to do with opinions on how to deal with the Soviet Union: those who wanted to get 'tougher' with the Soviets and those who wanted to be more conciliatory both almost equally supported a freeze. Strong support for a freeze had more to do with a growing feeling that the United States did not need more nuclear weapons; building up the stock of nuclear weapons, the majority of the mass public felt, did not mean greater security, but greater risk, and a nuclear arms race was dangerous and pointless. In the House of Representatives, a freeze resolution was lost by only two votes in August 1982, while a much-amended and diluted version (compared to the original proposal) was adopted by an almost two-thirds majority in May 1983. In both cases, the resolution had little chance of passage in the Senate with its Republican majority and since a freeze resolution in any case faced strong opposition from the administration, and probably a presidential veto, it was primarily seen by its supporters as a symbolic rather than a substantive measure. [79]

Related to the special features of public support for a nuclear freeze was a basic ambivalence in attitudes on how to deal with the Soviet Union and nuclear arms in that contradictory conclusions can be drawn from responses to different questions put in opinion surveys as well as from the American electorate's choices. While a great majority of Americans (73 per cent vs. 15 per cent at the end of 1981) believed that a nuclear war could not be won (that is, they agreed with the administration's declarations), only about 15 per cent shared the opinion that, once nuclear weapons were used, a conflict could be limited to something less than a full-scale nuclear war (that is, only a small minority agreed with the administration on this point). Even more notable, a majority of the mass public were concerned that the Reagan administration did not share its view on the unwinnability of a nuclear war; for instance, while a majority of 46 per cent to 32 per cent in April 1982 felt that the United States could not win a nuclear war with the Soviet Union, an even bigger majority – 50 per cent to 29 per cent – said that President Reagan believed that the United States could win a nuclear war. [80] In the same month, another poll showed that a similar majority felt that President Reagan had not done enough to reach an agreement with the Soviet Union to reduce nuclear weapons. All polls, as well as the presidential election in November 1984 when President Reagan was re-elected by a landslide, showed, however, that a substantial majority of the American people supported President Reagan as President. It was obvious that Ronald Reagan received the electorate's ovewhelming support in 1984 *despite* his administration's nuclear policy, not because of it, even if it is also worth noting that opinion polls on the eve of President Reagan's election victory showed that a majority preferred him to the Democratic candidate, Walter Mondale, on arms control negotiations. [81]

These highly complex and anomalous characteristics of the American public's attitudes to President Reagan, his administration and its policy stress that conclusions as to the relation between changing public and Congressional moods and the administration's portrayals of the Soviet–

American nuclear relationship have to be uncertain. The softening of the administration's early espousal of a most distinct Soviet essentialist view of negotiations can be explained in terms of the need to placate Congress and public opinion and secure their support for administration policies, especially a continuing strong defense build-up. However, considering the fact that, until late 1986, President Reagan always had a strong standing in public opinion polls in particular, and in Congress, and in view of evidence that his outspoken denunciations of the Soviet Union were shared by most Americans, it is easy to exaggerate the impact of these domestic restraints. Besides a probable diluting effect on the administration's Soviet essentialist approach to negotiations, it is difficult to ascertain any impact. The attitudes of the American public and Congress to the administration's nuclear policy are usually complex and ambiguous, and cracks in a seeming consensus have always been apparent. These features of American politics will be even more obvious when it comes to the last issue, the Strategic Defense Initiative.

SDI

SDI has given rise to a storm of controversies in Congress and among opinion leaders with many of those traditionally advocating Soviet essentialist views supporting SDI while advocates of nuclear essentialist views mostly opposing it. However, one prominent characteristic of the dispute is that SDI supporters diverge as to its basic aim. While a few opinion leaders endorse President Reagan's vision of a world where nuclear weapons have become 'impotent and obsolete' as realistic, others favor some reduced version of SDI as a necessary counter to the Soviet strategic defense program, for instance as a bargaining chip to induce the Soviets to restrain their offensive missile build-up and achieve a breakthrough in arms control negotiations, or as a means to build an effective defense of American land-based missile forces. But these supporters signify that there is no realistic hope that it will ever be possible to erect an effective shield to protect the American population against a nuclear attack. Opponents also diverge somewhat in their approach but almost all recognize that the United States as a hedge has to continue some research in strategic defense programs along the lines followed before 1983. Altogether, the lines of division in the dispute on SDI are even greater than usual in American debates on nuclear issues, blurred as they are by hazy conceptions about what are immutable physical facts compared to psychological and political variables, and how all these factors interact.

Public opinion polls have shown ambivalent attitudes to SDI. In April 1983, 67 per cent thought the United States should try to develop a defensive system that would destroy incoming Russian missiles while only 25 per cent opposed it, and a corresponding majority thought such a system could work. Later polls too have shown that a majority favors SDI, but this depends on the way the question is put. However, when a general question on the desirability of defensive systems is combined with references to costs – for instance, 'billions of dollars' – a majority opposes defensive systems. At the same time, the mass public have tended to agree that SDI will make it more likely that the Soviet Union will agree to a treaty halting the nuclear arms race; besides, a clear majority (64 per cent to 26 per cent) agreed with the statement: 'The Soviet leaders are extremely concerned about Star Wars, which means we must be on the right track with this idea.' Another notable feature of the mass attitude is that while a clear majority, in principle, favors the development of a defensive system to protect the American population, only about one-fifth supports a system to protect American missiles. Thus a poll in September 1985 showed that only 21 per cent would support a system designed to protect missile sites, key military bases and Washington, DC, but not other areas, while 73 per cent would oppose such a system.[82] Altogether, it is evident that the very notion of erecting a shield against nuclear missiles appeals to the security consciousness of the American public in the same way the nuclear freeze idea appealed to the public's desire for stronger arms reduction efforts.

These polls indicate that there are important disparities between, on the one hand, the mass public's support for defensive systems designed to protect the American population and its belief that such a system is technically feasible and, on the other hand, several opinion leaders, probably a clear majority, who believe that such a system is not feasible, and these include many who support SDI. Similarly, while the majority of opinion leaders endorse a defense of American missiles, the large majority of the public do not. Assessing the impact of these differences of opinion it is worth noting that President Reagan (and probably others in his administration) sided with the mass opinion against the majority of opinion leaders – opponents and supporters of SDI alike – provided the question in polls was put without reference to costs. This suggests that the mass public's attitude to SDI may be volatile.

Concerning relations between the administration and Congress on SDI, one important issue relates to the administration's new interpretation of the ABM Treaty, announced in October 1985. Congress insists on the strict interpretation of the ABM Treaty; in December 1987, for instance, it insisted that any testing of strategic defense in the fiscal year to 30 September 1988 should be in conformity with the strict interpretation. The administration's position has been heavily censured by Senators, among which Senator Sam Nunn's critique is particularly noteworthy. Senator Nunn has solid pro-defense credentials. More than most Democrats, he has supported the Reagan administration's arms policy, and he is not generally opposed to strategic defense. Thus he has suggested the possibility of a limited defense against unauthorized ballistic missile launches, an option that, in his view, might be possible within the terms of the ABM Treaty. Moreover, a reinterpretation of the ABM Treaty has been opposed by six of the last seven Secretaries of Defense, among whom are strong supporters of

SDI, and it all means that opposition to SDI in this respect receives an unusual respectability.[83] On the other hand, it is evident that actual or expected American–Soviet negotiations weaken Congressional opposition to an American arms program. Congress is ever sensitive to the charge that it is 'fighting the Soviets' battles for them' and some kind of strategic defense clearly appeals to influential members of Congress.

On this basis, it is difficult to reach any clear-cut conclusion concerning the impact on the Reagan administration. Congress has cut heavily into the administration's SDI funding request but, after all, the appropriations for strategic defense research and development have increased markedly since 1983. The administration has not faced any need to clarify the aim of SDI and its commitment to SDI had not been weakened as a result of many opinion leaders' strong criticism. Evaluating the future impact of the interplay between the Executive, the public and Congress, it is especially important to note the cleavage as to the purpose of SDI which marks SDI adherents. That cleavage could be seminal but not necessarily in the sense that it will enforce a clarification of SDI's purpose and a 'final' decision on the issue. American nuclear policy has always contained ambiguities and in a democracy like the United States any 'firm' decision on the nuclear issue is disputable and therefore, after some years, proves to be provisional.

Concluding observations
The general impact of American politics on the Executive's representation of the Soviet Union as a nuclear adversary through 1974 to 1989 has been a strengthening of the Soviet essentialist trend. When the period is considered as a whole, it must be concluded that the administration's position *vis-à-vis* Congress and the public has enhanced this tendency. The deviations from the dominant trend — the two prominent swings – namely, the Carter administration's swing toward moderate nuclear essentialism in 1977–8 and the Reagan administration's softening of its pronounced Soviet essentialism as to negotiations after a couple of years in tenure, can, however, be accounted for in terms of American politics. Concerning a third swing – Secretary Kissinger's strong defense of some nuclear essentialist notions in September 1974 – this was directly addressed to domestic audience.

The early Carter presidency's turn toward a diluted kind of nuclear essentialism can be seen as a corollary of the Democrats' taking office in January 1977. As a newly installed administration, representing the other party, endeavors to emphasize the innovation compared to its predecessor, this may naturally reflect itself in the new administration's representations of the Soviet–American nuclear relationship as different from the preceding administration's representations. During 1977–8 this coincided with the Carter administration's general liberal internationalist-inclined policy. The fact that the long-term Soviet essentialist trend reappeared, by and large, after 1–2 years confirms the validity of this explanation and, at the same time, points to the limited explanatory value of shifts between parties in administration when we try to account for long-term trends in US governments' images: other factors, domestic and non-domestic, have to be included too. As to the early Reagan administration's distinct Soviet essentialism concerning negotiations which, compared to the Carter administration, represents a swing and the Reagan presidency's later softening of its stand on negotiations, it can be explained in corresponding terms: the new administration in 1981 endeavored to stress its innovative character and, given the later Carter administration's stand on negotiations, a conspicuous tightening of the US government's public statements on Soviet–American negotiations was a natural measure, especially since this fitted the new administration's conservative internationalist bias. When the Reagan administration later changed to a moderate Soviet essentialist image of convergent vs. divergent interests and negotiations, this can be seen as an expedient means to placate critics in the public and the Congress – as both now manifested uneasiness with the state of the Soviet–American nuclear relationship – and secure support for the administration's policies.

4.   CONCLUSIONS

It appears that internal differences in administrations must often be included in the elaboration of the actual substance and composite character of US governments' statements on the Soviet–American nuclear relationship. All administrations have, in effect, been constellations of loosely allied and separated institutions where different parts have manifested divergent perceptions. Of course, it has sometimes been obvious that the divergent perceptions expressed by sub-units in an administration have been aimed at by the chief executive. Given the many divergent institutional and intellectual pressures on a president, this is natural. All things considered, however, it is unfruitful to see the general occurrence of different perceptions manifested by the same administration as centrally directed by a superior unitary actor; at most, they can be considered as not unwelcome by the chief of the administration. Anyway it is evident that no US government functions as a monolithic unit (cf. the writings on bureaucratic politics),[84] and in some cases it has been apparent that the various government institutions' interests *vis-à-vis* each other have influenced their statements on the Soviet Union as a nuclear adversary.

However, while the bureaucratic politics perspective is fruitful for descriptive purposes, it has only limited explanatory value when it concerns explaining fixtures, long-term trends and typical swings. Neither enduring parts of the images, the nuclear essentialist trend after 1963 nor the Soviet essentialist trend after 1974 can be accounted for in terms of necessities flowing from the internal politicking in the US government. On the other hand, some prominent swings can be explained as a move by one part of the governmental bureaucracy to counter another part of the administration.

For example, Secretary McNamara's pronounced nuclear essentialist reasoning on deterrence around 1967 can be explained as a move to counter demands from the Joint Chiefs. Adopting this perspective on a governmental statement is only fruitful, however, when the interplay with non-governmental parts of US politics is included. Thus McNamara's statements cannot solely be accounted for in bureaucratic politics terms but must be seen as directed at other domestic audiences too. They are comprehensible in terms of domestic politics only when expectations as to the effect on institutions outside the administration are included and considered that way, the conclusion concerning the significance of the internal politicking in the various administrations points to the deficiency of viewing an administration as a self-contained unit in US politics rather than the relevance of a strict bureaucratic politics analysis. Thus institutionally and conceptually, discords in administrations have to be explained in terms of the interplay with other institutions in American society. Furthermore, it is essential to this interplay that it frequently occurs by voicing appeals to some part of the American tradition.

Concerning the importance of changes in government between the two dominant parties in the United States, the analysis of the changes in 1977 and 1981 indicated its significance in that both the Carter and the Reagan administrations endeavored to emphasize the difference between their own and the predecessor's approach to the American–Soviet nuclear relationship. As to the third shift during the examined period, in 1969, there was no corresponding change. This indicates that one cannot generally maintain that all shifts between parties in the administration mean a change in the public approach to the Soviet Union as a nuclear adversary. All newly installed parties and presidents in the United States may wish to stress that something has changed in Washington but the record shows that this need not appear in its public representations of the nuclear relationship between the superpowers.

The most important conclusion as to the significance of the domestic setting is that prominent parts of US governments' portrayals of the Soviet–American nuclear relationship through more than 25 years can be understood in terms of ingrained habits of traditional American ways of seeing America's role in the world. Soviet essentialist colored fixtures of US governments' perceptions, and Soviet essentialist trends in the second half of the period since the early 1960s as well as swings toward Soviet essentialism become natural when considered in relation to the American tradition. Moreover, this basic predilection for portraying the Soviet Union as a nuclear superpower in such terms is enhanced by features of the current political process in the United States. The point is that American politicians – members of an administration and outside critiques alike – still face a domestic political need to explain and justify their policies in exalted idealistic and rhetorical styles which appeal to broader constituencies and in that situation appealing to some ingredient in the American tradition becomes tempting. Politically unaware sectors of the public seem reachable only through dramatic statements that express traditional American modes of thinking, but also those Soviet essentialist marked statements which are addressed to more limited constituencies among opinion leaders and in Congress can be understood in terms of a combination of historically prominent trains of thought in the United States and the democratic features of US politics. As Americans perceive the Soviet nuclear opponent in terms of their own experience and frame of reference, a certain kind of ethnocentric[85] bias follows from constituent parts of the American tradition which is enhanced by 'needs' brought about by the adversarial character of the everyday political process in the United States. In view of this it can be concluded that salient aspects of the domestic setting encourage Soviet essentialist images: *the American political system induces US governments to represent the Soviet Union as a nuclear adversary in dispositional oriented terms.*

But it is important to note that there have been exceptions to this general conclusion about the impact of the American setting. An opposite nuclear essentialist trend, based on situational-oriented interpretations, was apparent for some years after 1963 and there have been different swings towards nuclear essentialism through the years. It was noted that these too can be seen as expressing some parts of the American tradition which have been supported by current domestic political needs and distinct nuclear essentialist interpretations may too reflect some ethocentric bias as American observers project their values onto Soviet society and approach to nuclear arms as a mirror image of the (preferred) American approach.[86] In any case there is no one-to-one relation between the domestic setting and US governments' images.[87] Moreover, concluding that prominent parts of American images from Kennedy to Reagan fit in with salient trains of thought in the American tradition, or have been prompted by current domestic needs, is not tantamount to saying that these perceptions have been misperceptions. Whatever the features of the domestic setting, it is relevant to ask if the substantive conclusions of any perception are tenable and valid. Hence, what really characterizes the Soviet Union as the United States' nuclear adversary?

6. The object of perception. The Soviet Union as a superpower

Expressed in terms of the distinction between a psychological and operational environment (cf. p. 22), outlining features of the object of perception – the Soviet Union as the United States' nuclear adversary during a time when the Soviet Union has been superpower – constitutes a step in delimiting and analyzing the operational environment US governments have faced. As the purpose of this is to provide important aspects of the basis for comparing, in Chapter 7, fixtures and trends of US governments' psychological environments (their images) to their operational environments, the synthesis in Chapter 4 has to be used as a starting point for deciding which policies, conditions and developments concerning the Soviet Union as a superpower are relevant to examine. Two Soviet essentialism-marked fixtures of US governments' images from Kennedy to Reagan were identified: one according to which the Soviet–American nuclear balance and the two countries' nuclear policies have broad political significance for the course of the basic conflict between the two countries (F1), another according to which the United States needs an active nuclear deployment policy to induce the Soviets to negotiate seriously (F2). Two trends were identified: a diluted nuclear essentialist trend for some years in the late 1960s into the early 1970s, and a more distinct Soviet essentialist trend since the mid-1970s, both concerning the Soviet view (T1) and deterrence (T2). (F1) thus focuses on changes in the Soviet–American nuclear balance, particularly in relation to the Soviet willingness to take risks in its use of armed forces to pursue political goals and interests, and third countries' views of and responses to the nuclear balance. (F2) deals with Soviet negotiating behavior and its relations to the nuclear balance. (T1) focuses on the Soviet approach to nuclear issues as manifested in Soviet nuclear deployments, the Soviet military doctrine as well as other Soviet writings and speeches. (T2) deals with the putative Soviet willingness to risk nuclear war in different situations, Soviet nuclear deployments and Soviet views of the role of its nuclear forces, including the Soviet military doctrine.

Together, this broad range of subjects indicates the problems which have to be taken up as a first step in evaluating US governments' images; other issues may be relevant as well but these are certainly the most important. In order to avoid making the preliminary review and examination of these problems and issues unnecessarily extensive and multifarious, this chapter focuses on one crucial factor, namely the relevant aspects of Soviet behavior as a superpower. The basic argument for dealing separately with problems directly related to Soviet behavior is, moreover, the criticality attached to different aspects of the Soviet Union's behavior and policy in both fixtures and trends. A few other problems relevant for evaluating the images will be taken up in connection with the direct comparison in the following chapter, as will specific problems related to the reasonings applied by various images. Dealing with different aspects of the Soviet Union as a superpower and Soviet policy raises some methodical and practical problems which, by way of introduction, have to be elaborated.

1.   ANALYZING THE SOVIET UNION AS A SUPERPOWER

As noted, analyzing the Soviet Union as a superpower is one part of examining US governments' operational environments. While the psychological environment (the image) is defined as the environment as an actor sees it, the operational environment is defined as the environment in which an actor's policy will be carried out as established by an outside observer or scholar. This distinction can be expressed as a distinction between two kinds of image in that the methods applied by an outside, principally detached, observer in working out an empirical theory on the operational environment does not differ essentially as to the nature of the learning process from the methods used by political actors working out *their* image. The difference is a matter of degree: outside analysts preparing empirical theories apply, in principle, well-defined concepts, a methodical accumulation of data and coherent models; some political actors endeavor to use similar methods while other attempts by actors forming their psychological environment approach what can be termed the process of 'folk learning in everyday life',[1] Thus one difference between the two kinds of image concerns the complexity of the elements involved, i.e. the refinements of perceptions, but, strictly speaking, an outside observer's or scholar's empirical theory on some operational environment may still be termed that observer's psychological environment in the same sense that many social science theories and descriptions may be termed some scholars' 'psychological environment'. Hence, while the distinction between psychological and operational environments – or political actor vs. observer/ scholar – does certainly not imply a dichotomy between 'subjective imagination' and 'objective reality', it denotes some important differences.

When assessing an operational environment includes identifying Soviet nuclear policy, the problems assume a special character which is due to particularities of both the nuclear issue and the Soviet society. In the Introduction (pp. 24–5) the peculiarities of the nuclear issue were mentioned with a view to drawing some conclusions as to the situation faced by decision-makers, and it is a premise underlying the following attempt to analyze the Soviet Union as a nuclear superpower that an outside observer faces corresponding problems wherefore an attempt, based on a methodical analysis, to reach a clear-cut and indisputable overall conclusion is presumed futile. Concerning the second, and in this context closely-related, problem – the particularities of the Soviet Union – the issue of how to approach the Soviet Union as an object for scholarly analysis has given rise to widespread debate among Western scholars. The contentious methodical issue concerns the appropriate conceptual framework to apply: do the particular characteristics of the Soviet Union require a particular approach and research method, different from all those usually applied in social sciences?

In one sense it is a commonplace to state that the Soviet society has particular, even unique, characteristics. Strictly speaking, all societies have. From the recognition that the Soviet society represents a *sui generis* phenomenon – which, at the risk of being trite, cannot be questioned – does not, of course, follow that analyzing Soviet foreign policy requires a unique conceptual framework.[2] Being an ordered series of questions to be asked about the object under observation, a conceptual framework assumes, by itself, nothing as to the specifics of the answers that various data will return and a framework fruitfully applicable for analyzing pluralistic societies and their foreign policies may be fruitful also for analyzing the Soviet Union and its foreign policy. While a study of Soviet policy and Soviet politics gives rise to special problems of identification (as well as special problems of application), these problems are not necessarily unique and entirely unlike 'normal' problems in international studies.[3] The central methodical problem is always which framework for empirical analysis and which research method are the most expedient to apply to the given subject matter.

Focusing on problems related to identifying Soviet nuclear policy, it is obvious, though, that many methods applied in studies of Western countries' foreign policy cannot be applied in the Soviet case, particularly when it concerns Soviet defense and military policy. The most important reason for this is the secretiveness that encompasses significant aspects of the Soviet decision process and Soviet military forces as well as the absence of freedom of expression in the Soviet society for publicly and directly challenging the incumbent leadership of CPSU and the Soviet government. With a few exceptions, Soviet writings on Soviet military forces omit more detailed reviews where specific force and weapons characteristics or numbers are stated; the Soviet government publishes nothing commensurate with the detailed information provided in US governments' yearly posture statements and it only publishes one number indicating its total defense expenditure. Generally, as there is no public debate in Soviet society where current Soviet foreign policy is openly queried, a number of methods normally used by scholars in preparing reports on a country's military policy are obviously not applicable to identify Soviet policy.

However, in some respects the Soviet Union produces a great deal of evidence concerning its military policy which can be used for empirically-based attempts to identify Soviet nuclear policy. The fact that many Soviet writings on military matters are heavily loaded with long ideological expositions, have been subject to censorship and are more or less polemical against Western countries does not, of course, invalidate them as useful data in an empirical study, Any use of evidence implies an evaluation of its validity in relation to a conceptual or theoretical framework and here it may be relevant to take into account the specific societal context in which some statement or writing has been presented. This means, in turn, that it may be important in an outline of Soviet nuclear policy to include a description of particular aspects of the Soviet society. As to the basic methodical issue – the appropriateness of empirical methods in studies of Soviet nuclear policy – the conclusion is, therefore, that the particularities of the Soviet society pose several special problems for empirical studies rather than make them devoid of sense.

Noting that the amount and sort of information on military issues in Soviet publications pose special – but not unique – problems, it is important to note that changes *have* occurred during later years. Soviet publications have increased the substantive information provided on military matters. For example, the simple fact of the number of ballistic missile launchers on submarines agreed on in the SALT I agreement in 1972 was included in a part of the agreement which was not published in the Soviet Union. Beginning in April 1977, however, a Soviet newspaper provided its readers with some simple information about the numbers for nuclear weapons launchers and MIRVed missiles that had been agreed by the United States and the Soviet Union two-and-a-half years earlier at the Vladivostok summit. Some unprecedented specific data on Soviet military forces have also been contained in speeches by Soviet leaders and in official Soviet statements since the last years of the 1970s. More important, since the early 1980s the Soviet Union has issued a number of publications containing unusually detailed information on Soviet and, in particular, Western military forces, of which the first were *The Threat to Europe*, published in late 1981, and *Whence the Threat to Peace*? published in early 1982 by the Soviet Ministry of Defense. In nearly all cases, data on military forces have been derived from Western sources and are sparse compared to those actually available in Western publications;[4] yet, the small amount of data on the Soviet military now published in the Soviet Union evidently represents a departure compared to the Soviet tradition which is important to note in a review of the Soviet Union as superpower.

Reflecting these considerations on principal as well as practical problems related to analyzing the object of US governments' perception the following review and examination of the relevant aspects of Soviet behavior as superpower (cf. above) aims both at submitting substantive observations and conclusions and at pointing out methodical problems connected with the conclusions. Section 2 focuses on Soviet and American nuclear deployments and provides various measures of Soviet nuclear capabilities and trends therein. Section 3 considers Soviet behavior in bilateral Soviet–American negotiations on nuclear issues. Section 4 reviews the Soviet military doctrine. In close continuation of this, section 5 reviews Soviet leadership statements on nuclear issues while section 6 considers various other Soviet manifestations on the nuclear issue.[5] Section 7 focuses on the Soviet use of armed forces with a special view to establishing patterns of Soviet risk-taking.

The review of Soviet military doctrine, Soviet leaders' statements on nuclear issues and various other Soviet authors and writers aims at outlining different Soviet statements on nuclear issues as part of the basis for identifying the Soviet view. For this, a number of Soviet publications (in English) as well as several Western translations from Russian into English of Soviet writings and statements are used as source material. However, as the intention is only to present an outline, the review is not based on a systematic examination of all (or a widely-defined group of) available Soviet sources. Besides, some Soviet statements and manifestations are included as they have been reproduced by Western analysts. Such a use of Western writings as a source of Soviet manifestations is, of course, problematic so it has to be done carefully with a view to noting any doubt about the truth-value and validity of a quotation. Given the contentiousness of the Soviet approach to nuclear arms among Western scholars, prudence is advisable.

2. NUCLEAR DEPLOYMENTS

Soviet nuclear forces deployed since the early 1960s consist of many different deployments with various characteristics. As a first classification I shall differentiate between weapons aimed at an adversary's homeland – *offensive weapons*; and weapons designed to defend the Soviet homeland against an adversary's nuclear arms – *defensive weapons*.

1. Offensive weapons
Soviet strategic, or intercontinental, delivery vehicles can reach the American continent and, given the basic approach in this study, the following will primarily focus on these nuclear systems. They can be land-based intercontinental ballistic missiles (ICBM) with a range of over

6400 km (4000 miles) or submarine-based (SLBM). Also long-range Soviet bombers with a range of over 9000 km (5600 miles) can reach the United States (and return to the Soviet Union). No one measurement can give an accurate impression of Soviet strategic nuclear forces and their evolution since the early 1960s. The different counts of nuclear weapons characteristics include: numbers of delivery vehicles, numbers of warheads, total megatonnage (explosive power yields), total equivalent megatonnage (EMT), missile throw weight and bomber payload, and missile accuracy.[6] The following review focuses on these *static measures* for selected years since 1960 and to put the various counts of Soviet deployments in a first perspective, the corresponding counts of American deployments are given in parentheses.

The most commonly used indicator of strategic nuclear forces is the number of delivery vehicles, i.e. missiles and bombers:

Table 1   Soviet strategic nuclear delivery vehicles. Selected years 1960–88 (American figures in parentheses)[7]

	1960	1966	1971	1976	1982	1988
ICBM	50	300	1510	1527	1398	1386
	(12)	(904)	(1054)	(1054)	(1052)	(1000)
SLBM	48	125	440	845	989	942
	(48)	(592)	(656)	(656)	(520)	(640)
Bombers	190	200	140	135	150	175
	(540)	(630)	(560)	(437)	(316)	(362)
Total	298	625	2090	2507	2537	2503
	(600)	(2126)	(2270)	(2147)	(1888)	(2002)

Table 1 shows a heavy increase in the number of Soviet strategic nuclear missiles since 1960; by contrast the number of bombers has decreased slightly. The most pronounced increase in Soviet nuclear forces, measured in the number of intercontinental missiles, occurred during the second half of the 1960s while the American increase took place a few years earlier, during the first half of the 1960s. In the early 1970s, the Soviet Union reached a gross parity with the United States and since then it has surpassed the United States in the number of strategic nuclear missiles, while the United States has had a plurality of bombers, although a decreasing plurality, throughout the period. Since the mid-1970s, the number of Soviet strategic missiles has remained almost unchanged with a slight change from ICBM to SLBM.

Another measure of strategic nuclear forces is the number of warheads:

Table 2   Warheads on Soviet strategic nuclear delivery vehicles. Selected years 1960–88 (American figures in parentheses)[8]

	1960	1966	1971	1976	1982	1988
ICBM	50	475	1530	2061	5230	6412
	(12)	(1054)	(1454)	(2154)	(2152)	(2373)
SLBM	48	120	560	909	1809	3662
	(48)	(656)	(2832)	(5440)	(4768)	(6656)
Bombers	380	310	280	270	300	1620
	(2160)	(2169)	(1828)	(1476)	(2348)	(5608)
Total	478	905	2370	3240	7309	11694
	(2220)	(3870)	(6114)	(9070)	(9268)	(14637)

Table 2 shows that one characteristic of the Soviet strategic nuclear force, compared to the American, is the weight attached to land-based missiles and the lesser role played by submarine-based missiles and bombers. A similar trend appears from the comparison of delivery vehicles but it is much more pronounced when the number of warheads is included. The table shows too that the strongest increase in Soviet warheads occurred in the late 1970s and early 1980s after the Soviet Union had begun deploying MIRV on its missiles from 1975, while the heaviest American increase also took place earlier. Measured in the number of warheads deployed on strategic vehicles, the Soviet Union has a smaller nuclear force than the United States, contrary to the situation displayed in Table 1.

A third measure of strategic nuclear power is 'equivalent megatons' (EMT) which reflects the fact that the destructiveness of a warhead does not increase proportionally with increasing explosive power.

Table 3   Aggregate EMT on Soviet strategic nuclear delivery vehicles. Selected years 1960–85 (American figures in parentheses)[9]

1960	1966	1972	1978	1982	1985
600	1200	4000	5400	7100	5837
(7200)	(5600)	(4100)	(3800)	(4100)	(3625)

The increase in aggregate explosive power, measured in EMT, deployed on Soviet strategic nuclear delivery vehicles was especially prominent during the late 1960s. Measured in terms of aggregate EMT, in particular, the strategic balance in the mid-1980s is completely reversed compared to the early 1960s when the vast American superiority was mainly due to the big American bomber force.

A fourth measure of strategic nuclear capability is missile throw-weight and bomber payload. Missile throw-weight is the weight of the missile delivery package after the boost phase of flight and it includes the weight of the warheads, guidance systems, penetration aids and (if the missiles are MIRVed) the weight of the MIRV dispenser and its fuel. Bomber payload is the weight of the full weapons load that a long-range bomber can deliver. [10] Also considered that way, it is evident that the Soviet Union has concentrated an overwhelming part of its strategic power on land-based missiles, contrary to the United States whose bomber force is even more overwhelming. As an illustration, the missile throw-weights and bomber payloads in 1976 are stated in Table 4.

Table 4   Soviet missile throw-weight and bomber payload in millions of pounds in 1976 (American figures in parentheses) [11]

Missile throw-weight		
ICBM	7.0	(2.4)
SLBM	1.2	(0.9)
Total missiles	8.2	(3.3)
Bomber payload	4.7	(22.8)

A fifth measure of strategic nuclear capability is missile accuracy, measured in terms of Circular Error Probability (CEP), that is, the radius of a circle around the target point within which half of the warheads launched at the target are expected to land. Assessments of missile accuracy are particularly uncertain, one reason being that the missiles have never been tested under realistic conditions. However, there seems no doubt that missile accuracy has improved markedly since the early 1960s and this improvement has been most pronounced as to Soviet missiles so they now approach a putative CEP comparable to the putative accuracy of American missiles. Thus the Soviet SS-18 and SS-19, first deployed in 1975, are assessed to have a CEP of 300–450 m while the most accurate American missiles, *Minuteman* III, are assessed to have a CEP of 220–80 m. The new Soviet SS-25 missile, first deployed in 1985-6, is estimated to have a CEP of 200 m. [12]

Missile accuracy and missile destructiveness, measured in EMT, can be combined into yet another measure of strategic nuclear capability, counter-military potential (CMP) or 'lethality'. As CMP is defined, [13] it is far more sensitive to improvements in accuracy than to increases in explosive power. While the United States has emphasized accuracy in her missile forces, the Soviet Union has traditionally deployed missiles with highter yields (explosive power) and in 1980, for instance, the total CMP of American strategic nuclear forces was estimated to be almost three times greater than that of Soviet forces with the trend toward equality in CMP. More potentially significant, the CMP of the Soviet land-based missile force surpasses that of American ICBM. Especially the increased accuracy of SS-18 must be seen in combination with its big throw-weight (16,000 1b while *Minuteman* III has a throw-weight of 2400 1b) and the deployment of ten independently targetable re-entry vehicles (MIRV) on some of these missiles, each with an explosive power of 500 KT where *Minuteman* III missiles (each with three independently targetable vehicles) have an explosive power of either 170 or 350 KT.[14]

In addition to all these static measures of Soviet strategic capabilities, one can elaborate *dynamic* measures which indicate how Soviet and American nuclear forces would interact in time of war, eventually trying to depict the two countries' relative positions after a nuclear exchange. The results of such calculations are highly sensitive to various assumptions, not only about weapon characteristics (and already that is highly speculative, cf. above,) but also about the even more insecure reactions of human decision-makers.[15] In any case, a vast number of static as well as dynamic measures of relative Soviet and American strategic nuclear capabilities can be combined into several models which can be used to prove many, highly divergent, assertions about Soviet or American strategic capabilities.

Soviet offensive nuclear forces with a range shorter than intercontinental range can reach countries allied to the United States, primarily in Western Europe. They include several types of missiles and bombers with different characteristics, and only a few features of these deployments will be outlined, in particular those with a longer range.

As to Soviet intermediate-/medium-range ballistic missiles (I/MRBM), i.e. missiles with a range between 800 and 6400 km (of which the land-based will be dismantled, according to the agreement of December 1987), and bombers with a corresponding regional range, the number of delivery systems since 1960 is shown in Table 5. Since the two superpowers' I/MRBM forces and bombers are not directly comparable, American figures are not shown.

Table 5   Soviet regional-range delivery vehicles. Selected years 1960–86[16]

	1960	1965	1970	1975	1980	1986
Land-based missiles	248	733	681	670	652	683
Sea-based missiles	36	105	365	569	445	343
Bombers	1296	880	724	660	655	905
Total	1580	1718	1770	1899	1752	1931

Table 5 shows that there has been no considerable increase in the number of Soviet regional-range delivery vehicles since the early 1960s. There has been a marked change from bombers to missiles, but the difference between the trends in Table 1 and Table 5 is still striking. The development in Soviet intermediate- and medium-range nuclear forces appears when more specific characteristics are considered.

Until the late 1970s, the great majority of Soviet IRBM was SS-4 and SS-5 missiles, first deployed in 1959 and 1961. They were aimed at Western Europe and had a range between 2000 and 4000 km. Each SS-4 and SS-5 had one warhead with an explosive power between 500 KT and 3 MT and the CEP of these missiles was estimated from 1 to 3 km. That is, SS-4 and SS-5 were characterized by a relatively high yield and low accuracy. From 1977, they were gradually replaced by SS-20 with a range of 5000 km. Each SS-20 has three independently targetable vehicles with an explosive power of 150 KT and a CEP estimated to 400 m which means that while the total explosive power of Soviet I/MRBM has decreased, the total number of warheads has increased. Of 441 SS-20 missiles deployed in 1986, about two-thirds were aimed at Western Europe while the rest were aimed at China. The remaining land-based I/MRBM in 1986 were 130 SS-22 (first deployed in 1979), a modernized version of SS-12 which had first been deployed in 1969, and 112 SS-4 missiles. SS-22 has a range of 900 km and a single warhead with an explosive power of 500 KT or 1 MT, and an estimated CEP of 300 m; SS-12, also with a single warhead, had almost the same range but a lower accuracy (a CEP of 750 m) and a lower yield (200 KT). Altogether, it means that the CMP of Soviet I/MRBM aimed at Western Europe increased considerably from the late 1970s; about 300 SS-20 missiles are especially important at this point.

Since the late 1960s, the great majority of Soviet sea-based intermediate-range missiles have been SS-N-6 *Sawfly* missiles with a range of 3000 km and a CEP estimated to be 1300 m; SS-N-6 missiles are armed with either a single, 500 KT-1 MT warhead or 2 MRV-ed (i.e. not independently targetable) warheads with a yield of 500 KT. In addition, there are some SS-N-5 *Serb* sea-based missiles; they have a range of 1400 km and a single warhead with an explosive power of 1 MT and a CEP estimated to 2800 m. Concerning the putative CMP of these sea-based missiles, their low accuracy means that it is negligible. The intermediate-range bombers include Tu-16 *Badger* (first deployed in 1955 and in 1986 numbering 480), Tu-22 *Blinder* (first deployed in 1962 and in 1986 numbering 165), and Tu-22M *Backfire* (first deployed in 1974 and in 1986 numbering 260). All these aircraft are armed with one or a few cruise missiles or bombs.[17]

Soviet short-range ballistic missiles (SRBM) capable of delivering nuclear warheads at a range up to 800 km have been deployed throughout the period since the early 1960s and include a variety of land-based and sea-based types as well as aircraft. Among the most important SRBM are SS-23, first deployed in 1979, with a range of 500 km and a single warhead with an explosive power of 100 KT; they have an estimated CEP of 350 m. Besides, SS-21 missiles, first deployed in 1978, have a range of 120 km and a single warhead with an explosive power of 100-200 KT and a CEP estimated to be 300 m. In 1986, SS-23 and SS-21 each numbered 250-300 and these missiles can be assumed to have a significant CMP. In addition, the Soviet Union has deployed about 3500 battlefield, nuclear capable artillery delivery vehicles with a range of about 20 km.[18] After the December 1987 agreement, Soviet SRBM forces with a range of more than 500 km (i.e. SS-23) will be dismantled.

Concerning Soviet short-range cruise missiles with nuclear warheads, they too have been deployed throughout the period. Early Soviet cruise missiles were primarily designed for tactical applications against surface ships with a range of maximum 550 km. Toward the late 1970s and during the early 1980s, however, indications appeared that the Soviet Union was developing and deploying various types of cruise missiles with a longer range, up to 3000 km, and a higher accuracy.[19] Altogether, the significance of cruise missiles in Soviet nuclear forces is difficult to assess but there is no doubt that the Soviet development and deployment of cruise missiles, short-range as well as long-range, is considerably less than the American.

2. Defensive weapons

Defensive weapons include active and passive defense (civil defense). Active defense includes defense against nuclear missiles (ballistic missile defense (BMD)), anti-submarine warfare (ASW) and air-defense systems against bombers.

Soviet *BMD* efforts have been oriented toward protecting the civil population and especially political and economic centers against a nuclear attack rather than the retaliatory capability of its land-based strategic forces. In the first part of the period considered, through the 1960s, the Soviets seemingly made extensive preparations for building BMD systems and they publicly stressed the significance attached to these efforts, for instance by displaying hardware components of ABM systems at the 7 November parades in Red Square, Moscow. In 1962, deployment of an ABM system around Leningrad had begun but it was stopped the year after and dismantled by 1964. At about the same time, constructions around the north-western city of Talinn (the capital of Estonia) seemed to be part of an ABM system but a few years later it became clear that the Talinn system had been an advanced air defense system rather than an BMD deployment.[20] Around Moscow, construction of a BMD system had also begun in the early 1960s and continued until late 1968 when part of the work stopped, leaving only a minor ABM system operational by 1971. Since the 1972 ABM treaty, the Soviet Union has kept an ABM system around Moscow with 100 launchers which is the maximum permitted in the 1974 amendment to the ABM treaty and this system has continued to be upgraded through the mid-1980s.[21]

The Soviet ASW capability seems to be limited but the issue is shrouded in some uncertainty. Contrary to that, there is no doubt that the Soviet *air-defense* system is extensive and has been so throughout the period. It includes a vast number of both surface-to-air missiles and interceptors that have been modernized repeatedly. However, the technological shortcomings of the Soviet air defense system means that it is almost impossible to counter an American bomber force attack effectively, even with a very liberal criteria for 'effectiveness'. The existence of air-launched cruise missiles degrades the efficiency of the extensive Soviet air defense effort even more. [22]

Soviet *civil defense* measures are widespread. They include organizational plans for population and leadership dispersal and physical preparations (shelters, for example) for protecting various parts of the Soviet society in case of nuclear war, especially the political and military leadership as well as vital parts of Soviet industry (the defense industry). Even if the actual scale of the Soviet civil defense program – quite apart from its actual effectiveness in a nuclear war – cannot be ascertained with certainty, there is no doubt that the Soviet efforts in this field are more extensive than the American. Civil defense is clearly a high priority in the Soviet Union; about 70,000 government officials and several senior generals seem to be engaged in overseeing Soviet civil defense efforts and the organizational responsibility for the program has been ranked high in the Soviet defense bureaucracy. [23]

3.   NEGOTIATING BEHAVIOR

The Soviet Union has conducted extensive negotiations on nuclear issues with foreign countries and entered a number of international agreements since the early 1960s. A review of Soviet behavior as to the most prominent Soviet–American negotiations and agreements through 25 years – LTBT 1962–3, SALT I up to 1972, SALT II up to 1979, START since 1982, and INF negotiations after 1981 – can elucidate what types of accord the Soviet Union has aimed at and by relating the Soviet negotiating behavior to Soviet force deployments, further aspects of Soviet nuclear policy can be elaborated. What has characterized the Soviet Union as the United States' partner/adversary in negotiations on nuclear issues and what role and importance has the Soviet Union attached to the very existence of negotiations as well as the actual conclusion of formal accords?

1.   LTBT

In the months following the Cuban missile crisis in October 1962, the Soviet Union began to show its interest for a separate agreement between the Soviet Union, the United States and Great Britain, banning nuclear tests. Until then, it had maintained its traditional position pointing to a solution of the testing issue conjointly with an agreement on General and Complete Disarmament (GCD) which had been negotiated in various multilateral negotiating fora, since March 1962 at the Eighteen-Nation Committee on Disarmament (ENDC), which convened at Geneva. The new Soviet interest first found expression in a letter from Krushchev to President Kennedy in December 1962 and as the Soviet Union, at about the same time, abandoned its traditional refusal to consider any inspection at all in the absence of GCD, claiming that all inspection then would equal espionage. However, that concession to an old American demand was temporarily withdrawn when the United States considered the Soviet proposal of two or three yearly inspections as a starting point for new negotiations on the number of inspections but, after all, the new direction in Soviet policy continued as it began to show its willingness to settle for a partial test ban, thereby overcoming the control problem and signalling a major shift of position.[24]

A decisive Soviet move came in an address by Krushchev in East Berlin on 2 July 1963, formed as an answer to Kennedy's speech at the American University three weeks earlier (cf. pp. 37–8 above) and undoubtedly also aimed at countering the favorable affects of Kennedy's visit to West Berlin a few days earlier ('*Ich bin ein Berliner*'). President Kennedy's American University address had been given widespread circulation in the Soviet Union (aided by the decision to end jamming of Western radio broadcasts) and until then got a mixed but predominantly – and unusually – favorable reception by commentators in the Soviet press. Krushchev now gave a definitive positive answer to Kennedy's overture. He declared that the Soviet Union was willing to conclude an agreement banning nuclear tests in the atmosphere, outer space and underwater – i.e. areas which did not post inspection problems – while awaiting an agreement on the more difficult matter of underground tests.[25] As direct talks on a partial test ban had been prepared in a correspondence between the American, the British and the Soviet government during April–June 1963, negotiations on a treaty began swiftly after Krushchev's seminal speech two weeks later in Moscow. The Moscow talks were conducted in a favorable atmosphere, helped by the signing of the 'Hot Line' agreement in June, and after only ten days agreement on a LTBT was reached. LTBT was formally signed in Moscow by the Soviet, the American and the British Foreign Secretaries on 5 August and the ratification procedure was concluded in late September.

Examining the Soviet negotiating behavior in the test ban case, it is evident that it changed significantly over time: there was no invariable policy line, patiently and scrupulously pursued. When LTBT was signed in early August 1963, Krushchev declared that it constituted a 'document of great international significance' signifying an 'important success for all people of good will, who in the course of many years have conducted an active struggle for the cessation of nuclear tests.' However, until a few months before, the Soviet government had pursued a different policy; thus as late as November 1962 (i.e. *after* the Cuban missile crisis), a Soviet negotiator in ENDC had declared that the Western co-negotiations were 'very mistaken if they think that the Soviet Union can be satisfied with an agreement which would permit the continuance of nuclear weapon tests underground'.[26] Explaining the Soviet policy shift, the aftermath of the Cuban missile crisis is obviously one important factor, but the actual course of the Soviet negotiating policy from October 1962 to August 1963 indicates the interplay between various factors. Both Kennedy's general tone in the American University speech and Krushchev's in the speech in East Berlin evidently helped to prepare the adversary's political homefront for the two governments' policy departures – together with the fact that the Soviet Union, together with other nations, had stood face to face with the immediate threat of nuclear war in October 1962.

2.   SALT I

One origin of SALT was President Johnson's message of January 1964 to ENDC, at its first session after the conclusion of LTBT five months before, that the United States and the Soviet Union as a follow-on should explore a freeze on strategic offensive and defensive weapons. The proposal called for freezing strategic nuclear weapons at then-current levels and for verification by on-site inspection of production facilities. The Soviets immediately rejected the American proposal, one reason being the inspection provisions, but more important seems to have been that a freeze at that time would have frozen the Soviet Union into a clear position of inferiority as to the number of strategic nuclear delivery vehicles (cf. Table 1). Later, in January 1967, the Soviet government responded more positively but still cautiously to the Johnson administration's confidential proposal of December 1966 (prompted by a mounting domestic pressure for an American ABM-system; cf. pp. 156 ff. above) to begin talks on strategic arms limitations, especially on limiting anti-ballistic missile systems. In their principally positive reply, the Soviets proposed that discussions should cover offensive missile systems as well as defensive but they still seemed concerned that the Americans would exploit their numerical superiority in negotiations, for instance, to repeat their freeze proposal.[27] In any case, the actual opening of SALT was delayed for more than two years and one reason for the Soviet reticence to initiate negotiations seemed clearly to be that the Soviet Union still had fewer strategic nuclear missiles than the United States. Only as it really caught up with the United States was it ready to begin SALT.

When SALT finally opened in Helsinki in November 1969, the head of the Soviet delegation, Deputy Foreign Minister Semenov, issued a statement – not made public at that time but later reported by American negotiators[28] – expressing the view that a situation of mutual deterrence existed. Even if one side was first subjected to attack, it would undoubtedly retain the ability to inflict a retaliatory blow of destructive force, the Soviet chief negotiator is reported to have stated, and it would therefore be tantamount to suicide for the one who decided to start war. Semenov declared that the subject matter of the negotiations was so complex in itself that linkage to other international problems would mean directing it into a blind alley; on the other hand, a vague kind of 'reverse' linkage was implied in Semenov's statement that concrete results would contribute to the improvement of relations between the two countries. Semenov had begun by stating that both sides recognized the importance of curbing the strategic arms race and in one of the first formal meetings ABM deployments were singled out: it was argued that they could stimulate the arms race and be destabilizing by casting doubts on the inevitability of effective retaliation. On the whole, it was clear early in SALT and throughout SALT I (1969–72) that the Soviet negotiation line was to seek a maximum ABM limitation, maybe apart from securing a minimum protection of Moscow against third-country nuclear attacks, and this Soviet policy on limiting strategic arms represented a sharp reversal compared to pre-1968 Soviet policy – a fact that was acknowledged indirectly by the Soviet chief negotiator in SALT.[29]

When the SALT I agreements were concluded in 1972, the ABM treaty was evidently the most important arms limitations measure to the Soviet Union. Considering the state of the two superpowers' weapons technology, the Soviet anxiety for limiting primarily ABM deployments seems to have been related to a recognition by Soviet leaders that the United States had a superior ABM technology wherefore non-restrained ABM deployments were seen as a unilateral American advantage. While it is quite improbable that the Soviet leadership preferred the ABM treaty in the expectation of an American anti-ballistic missile system to defend the American population as the alternative (which, in turn, could severely limit the Soviet retaliatory capability), it is more plausible that the Soviet government wanted to avert an American ABM deployment to defend US ICBM sites. In the final resort, a Soviet ability to limit damage to the Soviet homeland depended on its capability to attack and destroy pre-emptively American ICBM sites and Soviet leaders may have considered that worst case option worth having, even if they recognized its hypothetical and highly dangerous character.[30] The tenability of such a proposition – which is in any case highly conjectural – can be assessed by relating it to other aspects of Soviet nuclear policy as force deployments and verbal manifestations but, considered so far, some Soviet nuclear deployments seem to corroborate it.

Another factor behind the Soviet negotiation policy on ABM seems to have been the notion that a ban on extensive ballistic missile defense would contribute to Soviet control over a defense-offense interaction between American and Soviet strategic nuclear arms. That reasoning obviously did not play a role for Soviet policy until the late 1960s and early 1970s but the Soviet negotiation record during these years points to the conclusion that Soviet leaders were beginning to share the notion that there was a need to limit an action–reaction induced arms race if the Soviet–American political rivalry should not develop into recurrent crises with an immediate danger of nuclear war. That this Soviet desire for some kind of 'arms race stability' was far from being the exclusive Soviet consideration behind their eagerness for an ABM ban is shown by the fact that they did not maintain their stress on offensive limitations as well from January 1967 (cf. above). Both the US and the Soviet governments changed their positions on these issues during the last years of the 1960s, and one reason – maybe the primary reason – for the Soviet acceptance of an agreement on offensive weapons too as part of SALT I can have been obtaining American acceptance of the ABM treaty; besides, regarding strategic offensive arms the Soviets may have seen themselves at a competitive disadvantage with the United States, even at a time when there was a strong anti-weapons mood in the United States. Despite ambiguous indicators, however, it must be concluded that notions of 'arms race stability' played a role for the Soviet behaviour in SALT I.[31] Assessing that proposition, it has to be considered that different reasonings may have been important to different parts of Soviet decision-making bureaucracy, without those divergencies needing to be settled by the top leadership. As Soviet policy may change over time, it may be ambiguous at any one time as well – unpleasant trade-offs are not a monopoly of Western governments.

If the Soviet negotiation behavior showed some interest in arms race stability, the interest in other aspects of strategic stability was more difficult to ascertain. Thus Soviet behavior in the negotiations showed that they were not concerned about what is called 'mutual crisis stability', especially in regard to the two superpowers' land-based missile forces' putative vulnerability. Throughout the negotiations, the Americans focused frequently on their *Minuteman* missiles' vulnerability to a Soviet attack in a crisis situation and argued that this (American) nervousness was a *Soviet* problem too since it could enhance the mutual danger of nuclear war in a high-tension situation. The Soviets did not seemed especially concerned about this danger and argued that both sides had more than one type of retaliatory force; generally, Soviet negotiators were very reluctant to discuss what they saw as 'details' of the two countries' strategic nuclear forces.[32] It is impossible to determine if the Soviet negotiators actually considered the American concern paranoid (as some argued it was in the American public debate) or, on the contrary, they reasoned that the American worries actually proved that the characteristics of the Soviet strategic build-up was a good deterrent – 'when the Americans are worried, they are deterred'. Several Soviet writings could indicate the tenability of the last-mentioned reasoning; others, however, point to the first (cf. section 6 below). At the same time, the Soviet Union actually entered a number of bilateral agreements with the United States during the early 1970s which showed their interest in crisis stability. In 1972, the Soviet policy in this field assumed a special turn when they proposed a bilateral 'understanding' between the United States and the Soviet Union not to use nuclear weapons against each other in case of nuclear war.[33]

Noting the Soviet focus on ABM limitations and the varying roles played by different strategic stability considerations, it was an important characteristic of all these Soviet negotiations policies that they were subordinate to the primary Soviet goal in pursuing SALT and concluding the 1972 I agreements, namely obtaining the US government's recognition of the Soviet Union's position as the United States' equal. American acknowledgement of the Soviet Union as the United States' political peer was clearly all-important to the soviet Union in SALT I. 'Basic Principles of Relations Between the United States of America and the Union of Soviet Socialist Republics' was evidently the most important part of the SALT I agreement to the Soviet Union, It declared, for instance, that there was 'no alternative to conducting their mutual relations on the basis of peaceful coexistence' and emphasized the principles of 'sovereignty, equality, non-interference in internal affairs and mutual advantage'.[34] The general Soviet aim in pursuing SALT I can also be seen from the numerous cases throughout the negotiations when Soviet negotiators underlined phrases like 'equality' and 'equal security'. To the Soviet Union, obtaining specific arms limitation agreements were important both to prevent the political rivalry between the Soviet Union and the United States from leading to nuclear war and to prevent the rivalry from being dominated by arms races, particularly in areas where the Soviet Union was in a competitive disadvantage. However, the superior goal seems to have been a politically meaningful accord, that is, an accord which the Soviet government saw as expedient in the context of the dominant Soviet foreign policy goals during these years, namely through controlled détente and peaceful coexistence at government-to-government level between the leading capitalist country and the leading socialist country to gain an official and unchangeable American recognition of the Soviet Union's inherent right to be America's equal in world politics.

3.   SALT II

In the SALT II negotiations, which began in September 1972 and ended in June 1979 with the signing of a new agreement, the Soviet behavior indicated, on the whole, similar interests. Thus the Soviet interest in joint Soviet–American crisis management to prevent nuclear war reached a peak with the signing of the Prevention of Nuclear War agreement in June 1973 which they clearly regarded as profoundly important. The Soviet interest in some minimal arms race stability was indicated by the Vladivostok agreement in November 1974 and they now showed a stronger interest in concluding agreements limiting offensive strategic arms, maybe because they now felt themselves in a better competitive position with the United States.

During the continuing negotiations, various incidents elucidated both the relation between Soviet negotiation policy and other aspects of Soviet nuclear policy and special features of the Soviet negotiating style. Most important, the strong Soviet refusal even to discuss the Carter administration's new SALT proposals in March 1977 indicated a profound interest in preserving and continuing . The deployment of their land-based missile forces, particularly the SS-17, SS-18 and SS-19 which had begun being deployed and MIRV-equipped merely 1–2 years earlier. The Soviet Union was not prepared to cut back on its plans for replacing the land-based forces and modernize the sea-based forces instead in order to reach a new SALT agreement; the new Soviet ICBM forces increased the American nervousness (cf. above) but the Soviets undoubtedly saw them as a means to catch up with the United States, similar to the situation in the late 1960s. Besides, the strong Soviet reaction against the new American proposals – underlined by Foreign Minister Gromyko's quite unprecedented press conference on 31 March 1977[35] – showed the Soviets' preference for dealing with a predictable and stable administration in Washington that would not lightly dismiss the predecessor's policy. Neither did the Soviet government like the Carter administration's public announcement of its SALT proposals before it was notified through usual diplomatic channels. The Soviet Union preferred continuity in SALT and was clearly unprepared to cope with sudden departures.

The difficulties in the spring of 1977 were overcome and SALT channeled back onto more traditional tracks, resulting in the 1979 SALT II agreement. Assessing the Soviet interest in that accord, it is clear that they appreciated its political symbolism and saw a need for some arms race stability as well as various high-level dialogues with the United States on the strategic nuclear development. The elaborate stipulations of the new SALT agreement and the preceding 6–7 years' intricate and difficult negotiations on its numerous details indicate too, however, that the Soviet Union saw political–military significance in the actual substance and details of an agreement. The increasing American preoccupation with the military significance of the many 'details' – as different from the overall political value of just obtaining some sort of (even weak) joint superpower control with the strategic arms development – was met by a corresponding Soviet persistence in pursuing *its* military interests. Both countries agreed, so to say, that divergent interests were more important than convergent interests in the negotiations. If the primary Soviet interests in SALT II had been the broad political value of an accord, the Soviet government would have accepted, for instance, the Carter administration's proposals of March 1977. Again, however, this reasoning on Soviet negotiation policy is conditioned upon the validity of interpreting the Soviet behavior in terms of a unitary actor model, an assumption which may be inexact as a description even if it is methodically fruitful in various analytical contexts.

Examining Soviet behavior in START and in negotiations on INF can elaborate these observations and elucidate new aspects of Soviet negotiating behavior.

4. START

Soviet negotiating behavior in START has included more prominent elements of public posturing than Soviet SALT policy, especially compared to Soviet behavior in SALT I. As negotiations between the superpowers in the 1980s generally have been marked by close relation between diplomatic exchanges and public exchanges, Soviet and American moves have often had a dual function or, otherwise expressed, frequent public statements have aimed at influencing the broader context of diplomatic interlocutions.

Negotiations on strategic arms opened in Geneva in late June 1982. The basic Soviet position in START has been that the strategic nuclear balance is one of parity which has to be preserved and especially through the first years this contradicted strongly the US government's view. Thus the Soviets have often objected that American proposals were one-sided and aimed at obtaining unilateral advantages for the United States. That argument was used, for instance, against the first American proposals for START, unveiled in President Reagan's speech on 9 May 1982, a few weeks before the negotiations were initiated. At the same time it characterized the Soviet behavior that while the American proposals were not rejected out-of-hand, it included strong warnings that American deployments of INF to Europe might interfere with, or even disrupt, further negotiations. The Soviet Union also stressed that long-range cruise missiles (which the American proposals had only suggested could be considered in a second phase of the negotiations) would have to be banned as part of any agreement on strategic arms.[36] Through the first part of START 1982–3, the Soviet Union began altering its stance on various points toward a slightly more accommodating position *vis-à-vis* American proposals. However, the first round of START came to nothing as the Soviet Union suspended the talks in early December 1983 after the American deployment of intermediate-range nuclear forces in Europe had been initiated in November.[37]

Negotiations on strategic arms were resumed in March 1985 as part of 'nuclear and space talks' as the negotiations had been christened at a meeting between the Soviet and the American Foreign Ministers in early January 1985. Under a single umbrella there should be three sets of negotiations about strategic nuclear weapons, intermediate-range nuclear forces, and defense and space weapons. In the negotiations that have followed, it has been a basic feature of the Soviet position that it is impossible to consider deep reductions in strategic offensive forces as long as the United States pursues SDI research but it had not always been evident what the Soviets included in the term 'research' and what should actually be allowed and not allowed. Sometimes the Soviet Union has demanded abandonment of even such strategic defense research that is permitted under the 1972 ABM treaty and which both superpowers have carried out also before the SDI programme was initiated; at least on one occasion (at a press conference after the summit in Geneva in November 1985), Gorbachev emphasized the demand that all American SDI research should be stopped by offering to open all Soviet laboratories to demonstrate that no similar research was taking place in the Soviet Union.[38] A few months later, however, the Soviet Union relaxed the strict demand for a ban on research when a Soviet initiative in January 1986 proposed to allow research, development and testing of SDI components, as long as these activities were confined to the laboratory and provided that the United States would agree not to withdraw from the ABM treaty for 15–20 years. That position clearly represented a change in Soviet negotiating policy on SDI but a change which is most conspicuous compared to the Soviet position 1983–5; in important respects this 'new' position seems close to what had been the Soviet position since the ABM treaty was concluded.

Concerning the Soviet negotiating line on offensive arms reductions, it has always been maintained that a START agreement has to be linked to a curb on strategic defense weapons but this principal position has been combined with some mobility as to the actual content of an agreement on offensive arms. Thus, in mid-1985 Soviet negotiators hinted that they would not only be willing to see a reduction of 50 per cent in the number of missiles and bombers but perhaps even in missile and bomber warheads – a clearly accommodating move even if no details were provided. Later in 1985, these proposals were elaborated in the negotiations in Geneva and formally presented by Foreign Minister Shevardnadze to President Reagan in September. In January 1986, General Secretary Gorbachev introduced a proposal to eliminate all offensive nuclear weapons, in three phases, up to the year 2000. The Soviet proposals were refined in various ways through 1986, including as for verification measures where they clearly went beyond the traditional national technical means, but they were ever conditioned upon curbing strategic defensive systems. Another feature of Soviet proposals on limiting strategic nuclear arms was that the Soviet definition of 'strategic' applied to all delivery vehicles that could reach the territory of either the United States or the Soviet Union, that is, it included all American nuclear forces deployed in Europe and Asia and capable of reaching the Soviet Union but excluded both SS-20 missiles and *Backfire* bombers. During the SALT negotiations, the Soviet Union had initially argued for a similar definition of strategic but, in the end, it had abandoned the demand that American forward-based systems should be included. Indications of a similar change in Soviet policy have appeared in the mid-1980s but, anyhow, the demand for an effective limitation on the development of strategic defense systems seemed to be a far more important part of Soviet policy in START, at least until 1987 when a more flexible line was hinted, step by step, also in this field.[39]

5.   INF

Soviet negotiating policy as to INF has been marked by two traits. First, elements of public posturing have been prominent since NATO's double-track decision in late 1979; thus the Soviet Union has frequently appealed to the opinion in Western Europe that its interests in this field are opposed to the United States'. Second, the Soviet negotiating position – manifested either by negotiators in Geneva or in public Soviet declarations – has changed markedly since 1979.

After NATO's double-track decision, which included an invitation to the Soviet Union to enter negotiations on a mutual limitation of the Soviet Union's deployed intermediate-range forces and NATO's planned deployments, the Soviet position was that it could enter no negotiations before NATO abandoned its future deployments. In July 1980, however, the Soviets accepted in talks with the West German Chancellor, Helmut Schmidt, that negotiations on INF were not conditioned upon NATO's abandonment of its deployment plans and more than one year later, in September 1981, Foreign Minister Gromyko and Secretary Haig agreed that negotiations would begin in November. As INF negotiations were initiated, it was basic to the Soviet position that it strongly opposed any deployments of American INF systems in Europe. This Soviet policy was combined, first, with strong appeals to public opinion in Western Europe to oppose the new American missiles and, second, with several proposals to freeze intermediate-range nuclear systems where the freeze on Soviet forces was conditional upon inclusion of British and French nuclear forces in an agreement. The actual substance of Soviet proposals varied as to the number of missiles, reduction phases, and so on, but the principal elements of Soviet negotiating policy were maintained and it stated that there was an approximate East–West balance as to these nuclear systems. In a private meeting in July 1982 between the American INF negotiator, Paul Nitze, and his Soviet counterpart, Yuli Kvitsinsky, it seems that the Soviet Union back-tracked on its principal opposition to any American INF systems in Europe but this attempt to reach an 'interim' solution – later known as the 'walk in the wood' agreement – was disavowed by both the Soviet Union and the United States and the actual meaning of the incident (which was not publicly known at the time, nor did the United States consult its allies) as to Soviet negotiating policy is difficult to determine.[40] Also at various points during the sixteen months following the 'walk in the wood' incident did the Soviet Union modify its INF position. However, at no time did the Soviet Union deviate from what seemed to be the bedrock of its INF policy: not to sanction the deployment of any new American missiles in Europe. In late November, after the West German *Bundestag* had given its final yes to accepting the new missiles on West Germen territory, the Soviet Union left the INF negotiations.[41]

When negotiations on intermediate-range nuclear forces were resumed in March 1985 as one part of the 'nuclear and space' umbrella talks, the initial Soviet position was similar to that of November 1983, namely that American INF missiles should be eliminated and the Soviet Union should be permitted to maintain a level of SS-20 deployments to compensate for British and French nuclear forces. Later in 1985, however, the Soviet position changed in that it suggested proposals which would imply that it had abandoned its principal opposition to any American INF deployments in Europe. In early 1986, the Soviet Union also appeared to have changed its position on British and French systems in that it no longer required formal compensation for these forces in the INF arena; at the same time, it proposed that both the United States and the Soviet Union should eliminate their INF forces in Europe after five to eight years, that is, the 'zero option'. During autumn 1986, the Soviet Union continued to show flexibility in its INF policy in that it now expressed interest in an interim agreement and more openly confirmed that the issues of British and French nuclear forces would not be an obstacle in the attempt to reach such an agreement. On the other hand, at the summit in Reykjavik in October it reiterated that a solution of the INF issue was conditional upon settling the SDI strife. In February 1987, the Soviet line changed anew as Gorbachev called for the elimination of INF missiles in Europe without first resolving differences over SDI and shortly later the Soviet Union expressed its willingness to completely eliminate its short-range missiles in Europe with a range of more than 500 km. Accordingly, the Soviet Union entered an agreement with the United States in December 1987.[42] One noteworthy aspect of this agreement is that it signifies a marked change in Soviet verification policy toward a much greater willingness to adopting strict verification measures.

On the whole, the Soviet negotiating position on INF had changed markedly since INF became an issue for negotiations 7–8 years earlier and, apart from accepting the initiation of formal negotiations at all as the Soviet Union did already in 1980 without NATO having cancelled the then forthcoming American INF deployments, all main changes occurred during the last 2–3 years of the period. Elements of public posturing did not vanish during those years but what the Soviet Union earlier stated it could 'obviously' not accept, has since been included in its negotiating position.

4.   MILITARY DOCTRINE

In Soviet terms the Soviet military doctrine (*voyennaya doktrina*) expresses the Soviet Union's official policy concerning military matters. It is defined by CPSU's leadership and not openly subject to public debate. The military doctrine is presented as constituting a total set of ideas and reflections on the purpose and character of war and as providing the correct basis for the structuring and build-up of the Soviet Union's armed forces, its war preparedness and the methods for fighting a war. It is, in principle, *a single officially sanctioned set of military policy guidelines*. This means that military doctrine, in the Soviet definition, has two closely connected – and in practice overlapping – aspects, the political and the military–technical, and while a key element of the political aspect is a stressing of both the possibility and the importance of preventing a world war between capitalism and socialism (first expressed by Krushchev at the 20th Party Congress in 1956), the military-technical aspect attends to questions of fighting a war 'if the imperialists should unleash it' (to use a standard Soviet phrase). The military-technical aspects may change over time while the political aspect is more constant. [43]

The starting point of the political aspect of Soviet military doctrine is *the Marxist-Leninist conception of war as a socio-political (or socio-historical) phenomenon*, i.e. war as a method for settling conflicts between antagonistic social classes or states representing antagonistic social classes. [44] Soviet writers often use the expression 'war is a continuation of politics by other [i.e. violent] means', a sentence first formulated by the Prussian philosopher –soldier Carl von Clausewitz (1780–1831) whose famous work *Vom Kriege*, published after his death, is frequently cited by Soviet interpreters of military doctrine. However, as Clausewitz was a bourgeois, he had only grasped a part of the essentials about war: Lenin supplemented Clausewitz by giving the scientifically correct conception of politics as an expression of the class struggle. Combining these insights, it means that wars do not occur merely as 'accidents' or at random but with objective necessity, i.e. independent of human consciousness and will. Wars are a continuation by violent means of the conflicts which exist in and between states in peacetime, meaning that wars are a continuation of the class struggle.

It is often emphasized by Soviet writings on military doctrine that the socio-political origin of wars does not mean that war is always a reasonable political means for suppressed classes or states representing the objective interests of suppressed classes. Neither does it mean that wars' devastations or human sufferings are ignored. It means, however, that if a war is imminent or in progress, then it applies that the actual war danger or the ongoing war is a result of the same political conflicts which determine the contradictions between classes and states in peacetime. The substance, or essence, of war – a term often used in Soviet writings – is that its origin is always to be found in one cause: wars originate with logically necessity in the class struggle. Certain states, representing certain classes, prepare and initiate wars to defend their class interests.

Which consequences does the appearance of nuclear arms have according to this conception of the origin and character of war? How do Soviet writings on military doctrine incorporate the existence of nuclear weapons in their interpretations?

The important point is that the basic relation between the class struggle, politics and war has not changed; however, it has assumed a more 'complex' character, as Soviet writers often state. While the Marxist-Leninist proposition on war as a continuation of politics by violent means is immutable, it does not mean that the essence of war remains immutable. The scientific correctness of Lenin's dictum that wars are a continuation of the class struggle also applies to a possible nuclear war – indeed, the scientific truth value of Lenin's insight *cannot* be changed – but the development of nuclear missiles still means that there will be radical differences between the essence of a nuclear missile war and that of all past wars, an idea which is often expressed by the term the 'revolution in military affairs'.[45] The differences will be determined both by the concrete political content of a nuclear war and by the actual methods of fighting a nuclear war in that the development of nuclear weapons has caused qualitative changes on combat operations. The political essence of any war means that a moral assessment of a nuclear war must concern the political aims pursued rather than the kind of weapons used. No weapon by itself determines the substance of war. The substance of war, including a nuclear war, is determined by the political character of the war and as to this, there is no difference between nuclear war and conventional war. It is something else that, given the existence of nuclear arms and the possibility of an all-devastating nuclear war, no capitalist state can use a nuclear war successfully for political purposes. The important point is that also concerning a nuclear war it applies that the Leninist principle of dividing wars into, on the one hand, just and progressive wars which pursue liberational ends and, on the other hand, unjust and reactionary wars based on imperalist goals, fully retains its significance.[46] In all cases it is possible to give a scientifically and morally correct assessment of a war before it occurs and for that purpose it is necessary to apply a dialectical analysis of the social and class factors which cause the war and whereby one can determine the actual war's role in the liberation of suppressed classes. So doing, one cannot let formal characteristics decide the matter as, for example, who started the war or where armed forces are actually fighting.[47] It is a duty of Marxist-Leninists always to assess a situation to see if a war will advance the course of history and, thereby, save human lives in the long term.

Until recent years, many Soviet expositions on military doctrine maintained the notion of victory in nuclear war. Thus Marshal Sokolovskiy's *Soviet Military Strategy* stated, in more or less direct terms, that Soviet victory over the aggressor in a world nuclear war could be achieved by a combined effort of all Soviet armed forces. In its political and social essence a new world war, Sokolovskiy asserted, will be a 'decisive armed clash between two opposed world social systems. This war will naturally end in victory for the progressive Communist social-economic system over the reactionary capitalist social-economic system, which is historically doomed to destruction.'[48] Victory must be prepared for and assured not only by the Soviet Union's military superiority and the advantages of its socio-economic and political system, but also by its ability to organize the defeat of the enemy and to use effectively the available means of combat as well as the Soviet people's high morale. Later, seemingly official Soviet expositions on military doctrine have expressed a similar view of victory in nuclear war.[49] On the other hand, since the early 1970s most accounts of military doctrine have not included corresponding assurances of Soviet victory; thus Marshal Grechko's book of the mid-1970s did not include such explicit declarations. In the same way, callings for Soviet military superiority have disappeared. A more enduring notion has been the idea that even if nuclear missiles constitute decisive means of warfare, waging war requires the combined use of all Soviet armed forces.

Soviet expositions of military doctrine frequently stress the importance of all Soviet armed forces' constant readiness to repel a sudden attack of the enemy in any form. Mass nuclear strikes, it has been stated, at the armed forces of the opponent and at his key economic and political objectives at the very beginning of the war can largely predetermine the subsequent course of the war or 'determine the victory of one side and defeat of the other'.[50] As vigilance in peace is stressed, surprise and pre-emption in war has been emphasized. Examining the development of the Soviet military doctrine in more detail and focusing particularly on such notions of pre-emption, it seems, however, that some significant shifts took place in the late 1960s. While the Soviets until the late 1960s seemed to assume that a world nuclear war would inevitably escalate to include nuclear attacks on the Soviet Union, wherefore the role of Soviet intercontinental nuclear systems was that of pre-empting an American attack as the lesser evil, Soviet military doctrine has since changed from pre-emption (if war seemed/ was inevitable) to deterring an intercontinental nuclear exchange.[51] A major reason for that change seems to have been the conclusion that, given the size and diversity of the American nuclear forces, strategic nuclear pre-emption could no longer yield any meaningful military advantage.

If that interpretation of a changed Soviet military doctrine since the late 1960s is correct – and the evidence presented by Michael MccGwire seems cogent even if his more detailed timing can be questioned – it signifies a special Soviet adaptation to the situation of mutual deterrence between the United States and the Soviet Union. In addition, it detracts from the interpretation given above (p. 195) of the Soviet interest in averting an American ABM defense of its ICBM sites and enhances the importance of other Soviet interests during the SALT I negotiations, especially as to 'arms race stability'. In the end, the evidence is not definitive – no evidence is – but as to the special point of pre-emption, it clearly indicates a significant change in Soviet military doctrine since the early 1960s. At the same time, it has to be noted that some Soviet, seemingly official, works (re)published in the early 1970s still held paragraphs which clearly suggested notions of pre-emption (cf. note 50). During the most recent years, further changes in Soviet military doctrine, both as to its political and its military–technical aspects, have occurred, primarily in that some of the ideological doctrinaire elements have been downgraded together with a stronger accentuation of preventing war as a fundamental goal.[52] These changes mark a further adaptation to mutual deterrence as a reality in the nuclear age.

In the elaborate Soviet scheme of conceptions on military matters, several other concepts are included with a nominally fixed meaning.

Military science (*voyennaya nauka*) is chiefly a prerogative of the General Staff and the military academies and subordinate to military doctrine. It covers a wider range of military questions and may be called a science of war as it is presented as revealing the 'laws inherent in armed combat and in all military affairs' and investigating the 'objective conditions and possibilities of waging armed combat'.[53] The difference between military doctrine and military science is stressed by Soviet authors in that military doctrine as determined by CPSU and the Soviet government is held to be a unified system of views and guide to action; military science, on the other hand, is characterized by controversy as there may be several different points of view and scientific concepts or hypotheses. The basic component of military science is military art (*voyennoye iskusstvo*) which is defined as the theory and practice of engaging in combat operations, and armed conflict with the use of all the resources of the services of the armed forces. Military art, in turn, is divided into three parts of which the most important is military strategy (*voyennaya strategiya*), a 'system of scientific knowledge concerning the phenomena and laws of armed conflict'. The other parts are tactics (*taktika*) and operational art (*operativnoye iskusstvo*), dealing with various aspects of the preparation for and conducting of the armed forces in war. All these definitions may seem scholastic and the actual substance of the different concepts a matter of conceptual hairsplitting. Nevertheless, in order to comprehend different aspects of the Soviet approach to nuclear issues it is important to note the most prominent concepts and terms frequently used by Soviet authors and speakers.

The further meaning of the Soviet military doctrine is elucidated by examining how Soviet leaders have commented on the role of nuclear weapons during the period.

5.   LEADERSHIP STATEMENTS

Soviet leaders, that is, members of the Politburo and top members of the government, including primarily the Chairman of the Council of Ministers (the Soviet Premier), the Foreign Minister and the Minister of Defense (who often has presented elaborate accounts of Soviet military doctrine, cf. above) frequently expound on nuclear issues. In order to get a comprehensive view of the multitude of statements by different leaders of the Soviet Union through the years since the early 1960s, it is necessary to impose a certain structure and coherence, and as the purpose of reviewing Soviet leaders' expositions is to evaluate US governments' images, the starting point can expediently be the two principally different views, modernism and traditionalism,[54] which constituted a part of the two ideal types of American images (cf. pp. 33–5). The basic question in these views is how the role of nuclear weapons is conceptualized in a broader political framework. How revolutionary are the consequences of nuclear arms and how are they to be handled? As reviewed, Soviet military doctrine has answered such questions in a way which can be identified on the basis of various sources and the aim in this section is to elaborate on the military doctrine and examine how Soviet leaders have approached these problems in their public statements, 1961–89. Applied directly to identify Soviet declarations, the two ideal types have to be further elaborated.

Modernism denotes the view that traditional concepts like victory and defeat in war are obsolete and senseless when it comes to nuclear war. There are no military-technical means of defense against nuclear missiles and it makes no sense to destroy the opponent when the inevitable consequence is the simultaneous destruction of one's own society. Hence, the primary element in Soviet military policy ought to be deterrence of nuclear war through the retaliatory capability of Soviet strategic nuclear missiles. Bilateral Soviet–American agreements are important to control the nuclear arms race and generally to manage the reality of mutual deterrence so as to avert nuclear war. Indeed, such agreements with the United States are becoming possible because realistic forces who favor détente are growing stronger than traditional cold war groups in the capitalist world.

Traditionalism, on the other hand, denotes the view that the existence of nuclear arms has not altered the fundamental relation between war and politics. Nuclear weapons are particularly powerful weapons but they are still weapons to be used in war and also defensive systems against nuclear attacks are therefore meaningful. Hence, for the Soviet Union, the purpose of nuclear weapons is in combination with all other Soviet defense means to be used victoriously in a war instigated by the imperialists. Victory and defeat in war have their traditional meanings and connotations and the Soviet Union must therefore always make sure of its ability to get through a nuclear war victoriously. Soviet–American agreements may sometimes be useful but the imperialists are only willing to enter agreements if they are forced by the Soviet Union's military superiority and the changed force relations in the world.

As noted, modernism and traditionalism are ideal types, that is, they are not assumed to correspond exactly to actual views. Rather, they may be visualized as poles on a spectrum in which all professed views can be placed and in which the positions in proportion to the two extremes can be characterized in that the two ideal-type views in various forms and to varying extents may be recognized in expressed views. The review of Soviet military doctrine indicated that it has moved from distinctly traditionalist to more modernist marked notions; however the actual identification of what is termed 'Soviet military doctrine' at various times through the years – and that identification is hard, one reason being the difficulty of fixing an operational definition of the concept – the overall trend from the 1960s to the late 1980s seems indubitable. To elaborate the Soviet approach to the nuclear issue and show how that trend in military doctrine has not been straight and how it has been related to, or manifested in, various political leaders' speeches and writings since the early 1960s, the review of leadership statements can expediently be divided into three periods: the 1960s, the 1970s, and the 1980s. The first period covers the time up to the initiation of SALT in November 1969 and includes some notable shifts in the Soviet leadership's presentations of nuclear issues. In the second period, the 1970s, Soviet leaders presented a more steady, or slowly evolving, view, especially up to the end of the decade. Through the 1980s, Soviet leaders have again manifested some pronounced changes, even if the modernist mark has been maintained and, during recent years, strengthened.

1. 1960s

Apart from a few remarks in speeches by Premier Malenkov and his Politburo colleague Mikoyan on 12 March 1954, indicating a kind of modernist thinking, Soviet leaders had used to endorse traditionalist notions on nuclear arms.[55] In early 1960, however, Party Secretary and Premier Krushchev announced some seminal departures in Soviet nuclear policy as he embraced what amounted to a 'deterrence only' policy. In a speech delivered before the Supreme Soviet in January 1960, Krushchev voiced a nuclear policy that relied very heavily on the retaliatory capability of Soviet nuclear-armed strategic missiles. He stated that the Soviet Union had a powerful rocket technology and the significance of bombers was downplayed compared to land-based missiles and submarines; in addition, a reduction of Soviet armed forces by one-third, from 3.6 million men to 2.4 million, was proposed in order to stress the new policy. Krushchev advanced the view that a country like the Soviet Union, even if struck first by nuclear weapons, would always be able to retaliate and in the face of that possibility, also an imperialist country was deterred by Soviet military might. So far as its military posture was concerned, the Soviet Union would therefore continue to have all the means necessary for its defense. In fact, the then Soviet leader came very near to openly accepting the reality of mutual deterrence based on Soviet and American nuclear armaments.[56]

But it soon became apparent that the Soviet leadership harbored divergent attitudes towards Krushchev's modernist marked position. In a speech to the same session of the Supreme Soviet, Defense Minister Marshal Malinovski, while concurring in principle with Kruschev's position, cautioned against over-reliance on nuclear missiles and stressed that victory in war required the combined use of all types of military forces. In accordance with that view, the troop reduction envisioned by Krushchev was halted by the summer of 1961. At the 22nd Congress of CPSU in October 1961, Malinovski delivered a speech that – though still reflecting many of the points made by Krushchev in January 1960 – again included some notable amendments, for instance that large, multi-million-man armies continued to be necessary for securing victory in any future war; on that occasion, Malinovski also made the remarkable claim that 'the problem of destroying missiles in flight ... has been successfully solved.' In his concluding speech to the 22nd Party Congress, Krushchev stated that the Soviet Union had 'achieved indisputable superiority in rocketry and nuclear arms' and he frequently bragged about the Soviet Union's nuclear might. Thus, in July 1962, he declared that the Soviet Union had developed an ABM missile that could 'hit a fly in outer space'.[57] However, at other occasions before his removal in October 1964, Krushchev repeated his most distinct modernist representations of nuclear issues and this was often combined with heavy polemics against Maoist China. Particularly after the Cuban missile crisis in October 1962, the irrationality of nuclear war was a persistent theme in Krushchev's public speeches and even if that kind of consideration was present in other Soviet leaders' statements too, Krushchev was clearly the most outspoken on this matter; likewise, when he publicly advocated the limited test ban treaty after it had been concluded in the summer of 1963, Krushchev stressed modernist themes. On the other hand, divergent views among Soviet leaders on that treaty were indicated when Defense Minister Malinovski, in his order of the day on Soviet Navy Day just two days after LTBT had been initialed in late July, did not refer to it.[58]

Altogether, several of Krushchev's speeches during the early 1960s – with the January 1960 speech as the most exceptional case – stand out as clearly modernist marked even if some traditionalist notions and several boastings of the Soviet Union's rocket power were interspersed. But it is also obvious from other statements by Soviet leaders that a part of the Soviet leadership was reluctant to endorse the Soviet Party leader's and Premier's enthusiam for what came close to a 'minimum, deterrence-only' nuclear policy. Sharing a traditionalist outlook, this group in the Soviet leadership held the view that while providing for an effective nuclear retaliatory force was important, it was still necessary to think about how to fight a war, including a nuclear war, successfully if imperialist countries attacked the Soviet Union.

Shortly after Krushchev had been removed from office by his Politburo colleagues, the new Party Secretary (from 1966 General Secretary), Brezhnev, and the new Premier, Kosygin, expressed modernist themes but definitely more cautiously than Krushchev had done and it soon became obvious that the post-Krushchev leadership generally represented the nuclear issue in a more traditionalist way.[59] During the second half of the 1960s it was characteristic that Soviet leaders' speeches were a peculiar heterogeneous mixture where some political leaders on occasion presented unusually distinct traditionalist claims while the Minister of Defense moderated his own earlier pronounced traditionalist assertion and the Foreign Minister, from 1968, announced a new modernist marked approach. Thus Defense Minister Malinovski toned down his claim at the 22nd Party Congress in 1961 that the problem of destroying enemy missiles in flight had been successfully solved when he stated at the 23rd Party Congress, in April 1966, that Soviet defense 'ensure the reliable destruction of any aircraft and many of the enemy's rockets' – the word 'many' denoting an important qualification compared to his claim in 1961.[60] At the other hand, Premier Kosygin presented a significant part of traditionalist thinking when he, in a press conference in London in February 1967, totally dismissed the idea of restraining defensive systems against nuclear weapons; defensive systems, Kosygin declared, were not a cause of the arms race but designed to prevent the death of people. Later in 1967, at the summit in Glassboro in June, Kosygin reiterated a similar view as Secretary McNamara tried to persuade him on the urgency of restraining the development of ABM systems. Another essential part of traditionalism appeared when Brezhnev, in November that year, declared that the Soviet Union would emerge victorious from any war with an aggressor; that particular statement from the Soviet Party leader is worth noting because it was among the last where a top Soviet political leader called for victory in nuclear war.[61]

From about the summer 1968, statements from Soviet leaders began changing course in that a cautious endorsement of modernist themes became more dominant. Thus Foreign Minister Gromyko proclaimed, in a speech to the Supreme Soviet in June, that the Soviet government was prepared for an 'exchange of views' with the United States aiming at an 'understanding on the mutual limitation and subsequent reduction' of strategic offensive and defensive missiles, including anti-ballistic missiles, and that announcement was confirmed by Brezhnev in a speech a few days later.[62] Combined with the evident change away from more or less traditionalist marked statements was a clear toning down of the prominent elements of polemic against American imperialism which had marked many speeches by Soviet leaders.

2. 1970s
During the early 1970s, it became increasingly clear that Brezhnev was pre-eminent in the Soviet leadership, and in 1977 he also became Chairman of the Praesidium of the Supreme Soviet, a post referred to as President of the Soviet Union. Reviewing Brezhnev's statements on nuclear issues through the 1970s, his expositions can, on the whole, be termed diluted modernism. It can be epitomized in these points:[63]

1. Brezhnev frequently, and especially from 1973–4, underlined the destructive consequences for mankind of a nuclear war and at no point did he profess the opinion that the Soviet Union, or anybody, could win a nuclear war. On some occasions he did express himself in terms which directly suggested a deterrence reasoning. The most obvious case occurred in a speech in Tula in January 1977, a speech which in other respects indicated a quite distinct modernist view.[64] But, a modernist reality of mutual deterrence was not directly stated.
2. Brezhnev used unambiguous modernist language when he commented

on SALT and military détente, i.e. a reduction in the danger of military confrontation, a term coined by Soviet speakers and writers in the 1970s and apparently first used by Brezhnev in his speech to the 24th Party Congress in 1971.[65] The need for a new SALT agreement (before 1979) was stressed by referring to the danger that its absence would mean a further spiralling of the arms race which would not simply be a repetition of what had already taken place. The technological development of nuclear arms was attributed an independent role which, however, could be controlled by the entering of a new Soviet–American agreement and the further growth of trust between the two countries. Brezhnev often stated that the Soviet Union did not try to obtain military superiority but, so doing, he stressed the peaceful Soviet intentions, omitting any closer consideration if some aspects of the Soviet military build-up could convey another view. In the same way, Brezhnev omitted an explicit statement that SALT symbolized genuine mutual interests between the United States and the Soviet Union; one was normally left to infer such a view indirectly.

3. SALT showed that the general trend in international politics was from cold war to détente, or peaceful coexistence. The strengthening of peaceful coexistence and military détente was primarily due to the changed correlation of forces in the world in that the socialist countries' influence in world affairs was becoming ever stronger, according to Brezhnev. However, the positive development with the increasing possibility for averting nuclear war and controlling the arms race was also due to a 'certain realism' displayed by some political leaders in a number of capitalist countries, including in the United States. While the impact of 'objective factors' (the changed correlation of forces) was basic to the whole process, Brezhnev often attributed a more independent role to American supporters of détente. In any case, he differentiated between various groups in the United States and often reiterated that influential American forces (still) opposed the President's détente policy.

4. Through all Brezhnev's positive comments on SALT, it was a dominating theme that it was an absolute condition for success that the United States recognized the Soviet Union's rightful demand for 'equality and equal security'. It is apparent from Brezhnev's statements that particularly the political distinction of being recognized as the United States' peer was a vital benefit of SALT.

Foreign Minister Gromyko, who was member of the Politburo from 1973, appeared as a diluted modernist when he commented on nuclear matters in the 1970s but modernist features were often more pronounced. Generally, the Soviet Foreign Minister stated on numerous occasions that in the nuclear age there was no reasonable alternative to peaceful coexistence. Within that overall view, Gromyko's statements mainly dealt with SALT and he displayed a strong attachment to the SALT process. This showed up, among other things, in the fact that when problems arose in the negotiations, Gromyko preferred to consider them as questions of how to achieve goals rather than a matter of different goals. The SALT negotiations, Gromyko often stressed, dealt with problems of exceptional complexity wherefore early success could not be anticipated; that special way of 'containing' problems in SALT was most apparent at the Soviet Foreign Minister's rare press conference in March 1977 when a flat rejection of the Carter administration's new proposals was combined with an outspoken emphasis of the Soviet willingness to continue the SALT process.[66] More than other Soviet top leaders, Gromyko emphasized the special responsibility of the Soviet Union and the United States for controlling the nuclear arms race; that responsibility was in the interests of the world as a whole and not just the two countries actually negotiating SALT; indeed, to Gromyko – as to other Soviet leaders – it was obviously essential to repudiate any assertion about superpower hegemony, and neither Gromyko nor any other Soviet leader used the term 'superpower'. On the whole, though, while some terms used by the Soviet Foreign Minister suggested a stronger modernist reasoning than typical for Brezhnev, Gromyko omitted the most distinct modernist conceptions on, for instance, the reality of mutual deterrence. Like Brezhnev, Gromyko showed himself a forceful public advocate of the Soviet Union's right to be an equal to the United States in nuclear issues; occasionally, he appeared the stronger defender of this stand.

The Soviet Defense Minister presented nuclear problems in more traditionalist terms, also apart from his elaborate expositions of Soviet military doctrine. Marshal Grechko had replaced Marshal Malinovski as Minister of Defense in 1967, and in 1973 he became a member of the Politburo; in 1976, he was replaced by Ustinov who had become a member of the Politburo shortly before; a few months after his appointment as Defense Minister, Ustinov – not a professional military officer – was promoted to Marshal. Grechko, in particular, and Ustinov basically treated nuclear weapons as a new means of warfare which had profoundly changed the roles of time and space in war. The idea that nuclear missiles were a kind of ultimate weapon which had changed the role of war – not just the rules of warfare – was rejected, and the importance of a combined arms strategy in nuclear war was frequently stressed; on the other hand, neither Grechko nor Ustinov directly called for Soviet victory in nuclear war, even if Grechko occasionally came close to proclaiming that notion in his writings. A more conspicuous difference compared to other Soviet leaders was that Grechko displayed a strong skepticism toward détente and the SALT I agreements, during their heyday in the early 1970s; it was emphasized that despite the ongoing process of détente, brought about by the peace-loving policy of the Soviet Union, imperialist countries had not yet given up their aggressive designs. Talking about problems of détente and hinting at the possibility of fruitful arms limiting agreements, the need to coerce capitalist countries played a prominent role in Grechko's speeches and writings. This was related to the fact that Grechko seldom differentiated between factions in capitalist countries, and then mostly by referring to 'reactionary circles' rather than, like Brezhnev and Gromyko, by talking in positive terms about a 'certain realism' displayed by some political leaders in capitalist countries. Altogether, the notion of Soviet–American cooperation to manage or solve nuclear problems was scarcely present in Grechko's presentations.[67]

His successor, Ustinov, presented nuclear issues in less traditionalist terms and this was closer to Brezhnev. Generally, as Defense Minister, Ustinov delivered speeches and wrote pamphlets and articles on these matters toward the end of the 1970s at a time when all Soviet leaders were displaying a less optimistic pro-SALT and pro-détente view, and the differences between the Soviet Minister of Defense and other Soviet leaders became less marked.[68]

3.   1980s

The modernist marked positions enunciated by most Soviet leaders since the late 1960s have been maintained, and occasionally even strengthened, in the 1980s but during the first half of the 1980s they were frequently combined with a much stronger criticism of the West, particularly the United States, than usual for Soviet leaders in their modernist manifestations. Since the mid-1980s, marked modernist views have been put together with some distinctly new general conceptions of international relations and a clear downgrading of criticism of capitalist countries.

Brezhnev presented a clear-cut modernist attitude when he specifically repudiated the notion of winning a nuclear war in his report to the 26th Party Congress in February 1981; to count on victory in a nuclear war, Brezhnev declared, is 'dangerous madness'. This view was reiterated several times through 1980–2 as he stated that the future of all mankind would be at stake in a nuclear war. Other modernist ideas, some direct, some oblique, were supported by Brezhnev, for instance concerning the arms race and the need for 'dialogue at all levels' between the United States and the Soviet Union; Brezhnev also expressed the notable view that the military-strategic balance between the two countries, and between the Warsaw Treaty and NATO, 'objectively' served the maintenance of world peace.[69] Another, even more direct challenge to the traditionalist position was revealed in a speech by Chernenko, a member of the Politburo and considered a protégé of Brezhnev, which was delivered on the anniversary of Lenin's death on 22 April 1981. Given that authoritative context of his address, it is noteworthy that Chernenko stated that it was 'criminal' to consider nuclear war as a rational continuation of policy; any nuclear war, he stressed, was a threat to civilization and 'even to life in our world'. Related to such pronounced modernist views was Brezhnev's declaration, in June 1982, that the Soviet

Union would not use nuclear weapons first in a conflict. This unilateral no first-use statement was supported by Defense Minister Ustinov but he added a number of points which clearly indicated his own reservations. Likewise, his speeches and writings on nuclear issues did not include the kind of more distinct modernist ideas expressed by other Soviet leaders. All the same, Ustinov expressed views clearly different from traditionalist ones presented by his predecessors. And in a pamphlet published in May 1982, he stated that to count on victory in nuclear war was madness.[70]

One specific characteristic of Soviet leaders' modernist-type statements during the early 1980s was that they were combined with unusually harsh criticisms of the United States' nuclear policy. This was unusual because earlier modernist-inclined statements by Soviet leaders had been associated with a more veiled criticism of the United States while the more forceful censure of American policy was expressed by leaders expressing a traditionalist view. The declaratory war-fighting between the Soviet Union and Western governments, primarily the United States, evidently influenced the Soviet leaders' declarations on nuclear issues in the early 1980s in a more persistent and direct way than at any other time since the early 1960s, and both the Reagan administration's policy on strategic nuclear arms, especially its notions of limited nuclear war, and NATO's double-track decision were singled out for condemnation. As a specific censure of NATO's plan to deploy intermediate-range missiles in Europe it was stated that the Pershing II missile would be targeted primarily at government and military command centers in the Soviet Union as well as at Soviet strategic missiles and that would be a 'qualitative change in the strategic situation in favor of the United States' because it would be difficult to take counter measures against missiles with a flight-time of only about six minutes.[71]

In addition, three features characterized Soviet leaders' statements: first, the Soviet Union would be forced to counter-arm faced with the strong American arms build-up; second, the Reagan administration's 'zero-option' proposal concerning INF from the autumn of 1981 was heavily censured for being an attempt to disarm the Soviet Union unilaterally and a clear violation of the principles of 'equality and equal security'; third, the aggressive American policy was in opposition to the strong support for peace in Europe. Altogether, it was apparent that Soviet leaders had become more sensitive to the impact on Western public opinion of its statements on nuclear issues and in the early 1980s opinion in Western Europe no doubt played a significant role as Soviet leaders framed their declarations.[72]

Soviet leaders' warnings against the dangers of nuclear war reached a peak during Andropov's tenure as General Secretary and President (1982–4) when the initiation of the deployment component of NATO's double-track decision was imminent and began to be implemented. An apocalyptic assessment of the world situation assumed an unprecedented dominant place in the Soviet General Secretary's statements. Thus

Andropov directly accused the United States of preparing a first strike against the Soviet Union and he, as well as other Soviet leaders, suggested that the world was on the verge of nuclear catastrophe; at the same time, the portrayal of an aggressive US government was mixed with strong appeals to the reasonable and peaceful public opinion in Western Europe to oppose the deployment of American missiles in Europe. One specific characteristic of this was that the continuous stressing of modernist themes was mixed with direct allusions to traditionalist-like themes, for example, that Soviet Union would be forced to initiate a counter-arming or that talks in Geneva would be impossible. Defense Minister Ustinov in particular, but also General Secretary Andropov, stated that the new American missiles were first-strike weapons; the doctrine of a first nuclear strike, Ustinov declared in *Pravda* in late July 1983, has become dominant in US stategy.[73]

In the mid-1980s Soviet leaders' public statements changed toward a quite distinct kind of modernism. As a new feature, it was combined with a 'new political thinking' in foreign policy, meaning that ensuring security was increasingly becoming a political task which had to be solved by political means and not simply by military power. General Secretary Gorbachev was a forceful advocate of this reasoning and on CPSU's 27th Party Congress, in February 1986, he first outlined how a comprehensive system of international security had to include various measures in the military, the political, the economic and the humanitarian fields. Gorbachev did not use the long-standing phrase 'equality and equal security' but in stating that military potential ought to confined within the bounds of 'reasonable sufficiency', he coined a new phrase which has since been used regularly in Soviet writings and speeches.[74] Compared to earlier Soviet leaders' diluted versions of modernism, one noteworthy characteristic of Gorbachev's and Foreign Minister Shevardnadze's declarations has been that the war-preventing role of *Soviet* military power is downplayed; nuclear war, especially inadvertent nuclear war, has been portrayed as a threat in its own right, the prevention of which is not primarily a question of maintaining adequate Soviet military power. In December 1988, these statements were given a new weight when Gorbachev announced a unilateral Soviet cut in conventional forces. Harsh attacks on imperialist countries continue but the more strident allegations, advanced in the preceding years, disappeared. On the whole, statements during 1986–8 showed clear departures in the Soviet leadership's public reasoning on how to approach the nuclear issue.

6. VARIOUS MANIFESTATIONS

Articles in Soviet periodicals and the Soviet press as well as Soviet books, even if they are not presented as official Soviet policy, may often be seen as a manifestation of some aspect of that policy. The actual borderline between 'official' and 'non-official' policy may also be blurred in the way that writings purportedly being expressions of the official policy instead may express what the author(s) wished were Soviet policy; thus some writings cited as expressions of Soviet military doctrine above might better be placed in this section. The significant point is that many Soviet writings, in addition to those reviewed in sections 4 and 5, may be relevant to an attempt to identify aspects of Soviet nuclear policy and evaluate American images.

The general societal context of Soviet writings must be noted in order to assess their significance, both as to their actual appearance and their substance. Most importantly, all Soviet writings, particularly those on military policy, are under strict censorship. Only authors who are members of an organization or institution subordinate to CPSU or the Soviet government are permitted to publish anything substantive about military issues and at no time during the period considered has an organization approaching independent status been allowed to operate publicly. While the censorship institution does not mean that all Soviet writings can be presumed to be a manifestation of a superior and unified political actor, it means that no standpoint appearing regularly in Soviet writings can reasonably be assumed to be without support in the Soviet leadership, hence a review of different viewpoints over the years may indicate the parameters of Soviet policy. Moreover, Soviet writings never openly criticize a policy officially pursued by the incumbent leadership or primary Party institutions, and Soviet writers never directly propose that Soviet authorities should adopt a different policy, either as to force deployments, negotiations or otherwise. Another general feature is that no Soviet writer carries out a detailed and searching analysis of the Soviet policy and only in a very few cases has a Soviet writer dealt in any detail with the substance of Soviet nuclear policy.[75] The actual Soviet decision-making process seems even more sacrosanct for a critical Soviet analyst and all Soviet writings state, or presume as a matter of course, that the Soviet Union follows the correct Marxist-Leninist policy devoted to peace, disarmament and peaceful coexistence which has the full support of the Soviet people.

Western military forces are reviewed in much more detail in Soviet writings and when substantive information is given, a Western source is usually cited explicitly; yet, compared to the information on Western countries' military forces available from open Western sources – especially IISS in London and SIPRI in Stockholm (whose publications are not publicly available in the Soviet Union) – information on the Western military in Soviet writings is quite limited. For instance, even if publications from IISS and SIPRI are available to a number of Soviet journalists and scholars, they have not normally used them for rigorously substantiating general assertions about inimical developments of Western military policies. When Western writers have published that kind of elaborate criticism, it has usually been selectively reproduced in articles in the Soviet press with the censuring conclusions emphasized.

Within such common features of Soviet writings, the actual substance of the views presented on nuclear matters has, none the less, been quite divergent and the course of the differences through the years 1961–89 may be outlined in terms of the traditionalism–modernism distinction. While the use of that distinction is a Western device, a traditionalist/modernist-inclined Soviet writer has at times openly stated his disagreement with a modernist/traditionalist-inclined Soviet author, in particular since the mid-1980s. More significant, many reflections on nuclear weapons are undertaken in a way that clearly suggests an extensive public exchange between different opinions. There is a variety of debating techniques in this masked Soviet debate and one typical form has been the attribution of certain reprehensible views to the Americans, or 'bourgeois ideologists' in general. The actual ascription of views may be right or wrong – since it is never difficult to find some Americans advocating almost any view, it is often correct – but the significant point in this context is that the rejected views frequently resemble opinions presented by Soviet writers too.[76] In that way, an extensive debate by stooges has been prominent when Soviet writers have commented on fundamental nuclear problems. It is therefore important to take note of these characteristics when attempting to outline matters of substance in various Soviet manifestations since the early 1960s.

1. 1960s

In the early 1960s, many writers, for the most part leading officers in the armed services, selectively endorsed portions of Krushchev's defense policy as it had been announced in his January 1960 speech and some of these endorsements were put forward in a way that clearly suggested that Krushchev's policy was meeting substantial resistance in the Soviet armed forces. Indeed, some publications came very close to publicly disputing parts of the Party leader's views even if some military officers evidently supported Krushchev's new doctrine. Another indicator of divergent views on Krushchev's modernist marked nuclear policy was *Krasnaya zvezda's* late and cautious endorsement of the limited test ban treaty, an endorsement which stressed the opposition to the treaty in NATO countries and China. However, it has to be noted that other military writers during the early and mid-1960s expressed modernist marked ideas on nuclear weapons and so spokesmen associated with Soviet armed forces were far from unanimous.[77] On the other hand, all Soviet writers harshly attacked McNamara's counterforce strategy after it was announced in 1962.

The Soviet domestic dispute on the tenability of modernist notions often surfaced in disagreement on whether nuclear war was a continuation of policy: some writers stated that war could no longer be regarded as a continuation of policy, and one writer in *Izvestia* declared in September 1963 that 'war can only be the continuation of madness'. More traditionalist-inclined writers reaffirmed, however, that war was a continuation of policy but agreed that nuclear war was not a viable policy option for the Soviet Union.[78] The most outspoken advocate of modernist ideas was Major General Talenskiy who – although he had included some traditionalist equivocations in an article published in 1964 – emerged as the strongest spokesman for the modernist line. Thus in an article in May 1965 (i.e. after Krushchev had been ousted and the new leaders had begun to tone down more distinct modernist themes), he wrote that 'in our days' there was no more dangerous illusion than the idea that thermonuclear war could serve as an instrument of politics, 'that it is possible to achieve political aims by using nuclear weapons and at the same time survive'.[79]

After Krushchev was ousted in autumn 1964, several articles in the press and periodicals strongly asserted traditionalist notions such as the value of strategic superiority and the winnability of nuclear war. Altogether, the mid-1960s was a heyday for traditionalist writings. While some military writers still charged others for having underestimated the complexity of achieving victory in nuclear war, they all now seemed to agree that one could not deny any possibility of victory in 'world rocket-nuclear war'.[80] In 1967, this wave of strongly traditionalist articles in military periodicals came to an end. An important signal seems to have been an unsigned *Krasnaya zvezda* editorial in January 1967 which had the appearance of an authoritative Party-directed rejoinder: it criticized directly some of the more distinct traditionalist writings and stated that 'all peace-loving and anti-imperialist forces oppose a world nuclear war as a means of the continuation of politics'.[81] After this, no significant debate on modernist vs. traditionalist issues appeared for 6–7 years.

In the closing years of the 1960s, a number of articles in the Soviet press pointed to the continuing significance of a kind of modernist vs. traditionalist controversy. Thus as some Soviet leaders began to show interest in Soviet–American talks on strategic arms limitations, they were supported by various arguments advanced by certain civilian writers on, for example, imperialist governments who were displaying more realistic attitudes to foreign policy problems. The military press, however, took another line; most notably, it reported selections of speeches by Foreign Minister Gromyko in that Gromyko's favorable statements on missile talks were omitted.[82] Another indicator was that some military spokesmen continued to present strong cases for a Soviet ABM system and even if a few military officers were voicing a more negative attitude toward the effectiveness of anti-ballistic missile systems, the overall impression of the 'disguised' debate in the Soviet press certainly was a continuing disagreement between advocates of a modernist-like nuclear policy and advocates of a traditionalist-like policy, with modernists slowly getting the upper hand toward the end of the 1960s.[83]

2.   1970s
Through the 1970s, modernist marked descriptions and analyses of nuclear issues became much more prominent in Soviet periodicals and in the Soviet

press. While rather crude descriptions of imperialist countries', particularly America's preparations for a nuclear surprise attack on the Soviet Union still appeared from time to time, it is evident that much more sophisticated analyses of both US foreign and nuclear policy as well as different aspects of the danger of nuclear war now assumed an assured position in various verbal expressions in the Soviet media.[84]

An early sign of the new prominence of modernist analyses was the appearance in the Soviet academic press in 1970 of analyses that showed both an unusual (i.e. 'unusual' in the Soviet public context) knowledge of the American debate on strategic issues and applied unusually distinct modernist, or 'sophisticated', arguments concerning the requirements for strategic nuclear stability. Modernist writers in the early 1970s elaborated the reasoning for SALT and Soviet détente policy and explained why 'sober-minded' politicians in the United States now recognized the nuclear stalemate as a fact and had come to favor a limitation of the arms race without many of the usual harsh attacks on the United States.[85] On the other hand, several traditionalist writers, mainly military analysts, offered analyses of American nuclear policy which differed sharply from the modernists' and the Soviet military press mostly kept silent on the subject of strategic arms limitation talks or indicated its opposition in valid terms during the SALT I period (1969–72). After the SALT I agreements had been signed, the military press too endorsed the agreements but these endorsements were usually accompanied by warnings that the imperialists were as aggressive as ever; besides, contrary to modernist commentators, traditionalists emphasized heavily that any positive change in American policy had been enforced by the military power of the Soviet Union.[86] On the whole, the signing of SALT I clearly meant that modernist positions gained ground in the Soviet press and in Soviet periodicals. Several writings elaborating modernist views appeared through the years immediately following, and some of these modernist writers are reported to have been close to political leaders.[87]

Through 1973–5, however, a new surge of traditionalist articles were appearing in the Soviet press. They restated main traditionalist themes, for instance, that with nuclear arms war was still an extension of politics. Views that there would be no victors in a nuclear war were based on oversimplified mathematical calculations but, it was stated, in order to understand such a complex socio-historical phenomenon as war, its nature, course and results, it was essential to take into consideration the actual correlation of political class forces both in the international arena and within countries; if the imperialists unleashed a war, the weapons in the hands of the Soviet Union would be a means of routing the aggressor and defending civilization. A frequently recurring theme in traditionalist writings was a strong criticism of Western 'ideologues' that the concept of heroism in a nuclear war was obsolete and that there would be no victors, only victims. That type of argument had often been advanced by traditionalist writers but it evidently received a more prominent place during these years. The refutation of fallacious views was mostly directed at 'false' Western views but on a number of occasions Soviet traditionalists directly criticized similar views expressed in the Soviet press.[88] Traditionalist writers both attacked notions that the importance of military force in international relations was declining and repeatedly insisted that militarism and aggressiveness were still strong forces influencing US foreign policy, thereby taking issue with such Soviet writers who openly advocated that there was a change in US policy.

One specific point worth noting during these years was Soviet writers' reactions to the Schlesinger strategy of early 1974. While several Soviet commentators were describing it as an attempt to undermine SALT and détente and generally criticized it, it was also characteristic, however, that many Soviet commentators were relatively restrained in their criticism and tended to display some analytical detachment. It was evident that they did not like the Schlesinger strategy's departures but, at the same time, Soviet commentators seemed to avoid being too outspoken in their criticism, seeking, for instance, to stress that the Pentagon was the culprit while the then incumbent administration in Washington was still committed to détente. This moderate reaction was especially conspicuous compared to the militant reaction against Secretary McNamara's counterforce strategy in 1962.[89]

During the latter half of the 1970s, the modernism–traditionalism division continued but its concrete manifestations changed, primarily because pessimistic tones came to assume a more predominant role in modernist writings as the Soviet American relationship chilled and SALT negotiation met increasing difficulties; the modernist tone generally became more defensive. However, it was also in these years that some of the most pronounced modernist assessments of the role of strategic nuclear weapons appeared in Soviet periodicals combined, though, with a stronger criticism of US nuclear policy than used to be presented by modernist writers. Another, more remarkable, trait of Soviet writings during the second half of the 1970s was that writers, who usually had advocated distinctly traditionalist positions, began endorsing modernist notions on the strategic nuclear balance, the possibility of peaceful coexistence and the prevention of war. Arguing that way, these writers now cited some modernist marked statements by Brezhnev while they previously had ignored such statements.[90] Thus, while some traditionalist writers openly began to adopt modernist arguments, modernist writers maintained, and occasionally strengthened, their arguments but became evidently less assured of the political tenability of their positions.

Toward the end of the 1970s, various verbal manifestations indicated that traditionalist positions had been strengthened. The signing of the SALT II agreement in the summer of 1979 stimulated the appearance of modernist comments in the Soviet media[91] but only for a short time and the established expression of opposite views was conspicuous all the time. One specific pointer to a strengthening of the traditionalist view was Marshal Ogarkov, Chief of the General Staff, who in an article on military strategy in Volume 7 of the *Soviet Military Encyclopedia*, published in 1979, defended the feasibility of victory in a nuclear war.[92] That case of a pronounced traditionalist statement by a top military officer seems, however, to have been unique, and the general impression at the end of the 1970s was a certain convergence between modernist- and traditionalist-inclined writers toward a diluted modernism that was hardened in the sense that the current influence of reactionary forces in the United States was stressed. Still, evidence of divergent views among Soviet commentators frequently appeared as traditionalist-minded writers pointed to some new development as further evidence of the inherent American belligerence, while modernist-minded civilian analysts presented more optimistic reviews.

3. 1980s

Through 1980–9, Soviet manifestations on nuclear issues have displayed both continuities as well as conspicuous departures compared to the 1960s and 1970s. The heterogeneity of Soviet writings has still been appreciable but some characteristics of traditionalist writings have changed in interesting ways. In addition, in the mid-1980s modernist views began to be combined with a new set of ideas about international relations.

Traditionalist marked books and articles have appeared continuously with the familiar descriptions of Soviet military policy in heavily ideological and eulogistic terms while Western countries are harshly censured. It has been stated, for example, that the imperialists are planning a surprise nuclear attack against the Soviet Union and other socialist countries.[93] Moreover, these writings stress, as a matter of course, that only the imperialists will be responsible for unleashing a nuclear war. Concerning points like these, traditionalist-inclined writings have not changed. However, when such views are put forward they used to be combined with clear-cut traditionalism – or, at least, non-modernist admixtures – but now it is notable that the threat of nuclear war is a threat to the whole of civilization. The future of all mankind, it is said, will be at stake in a nuclear war and thus one mark of traditionalist writings has disappeared: a nuclear war is not solely depicted as destruction of capitalism.

Concerning the development of traditionalist views, one notable example appeared in the writings of Marshal Ogarkov, until the autumn of 1984 Chief of the Soviet General Staff. In 1979, he had written about the possibility of attaining victory in nuclear war, (cf. above) and in the early 1980s he published articles and pamphlets which, on the one hand, did not include references to victory in nuclear war and declared that the fate of all mankind would be a stake in a nuclear war but, on the other hand, maintained some distinct traditionalist conceptions.[94] Much more conspicuous, however, in an interview with *Krasnaya Zvezda*, in May 1984, he stated that a further nuclear build-up was becoming senseless and as a result a paradox arose: on the one hand, the nuclear powers steadily increased their potential for destroying the enemy while, on the other hand, there was a steep reduction in the potential for an aggressor to inflict a so-called 'disarming strike' on his enemy. With the quantity and diversity of nuclear missiles already achieved, Ogarkov stated, it has become impossible to destroy the enemy's nuclear systems with a single strike; a 'crushing retaliatory strike against the aggressor ... inflicting unacceptable damage' has become inevitable and in elaborating this reasoning, Ogarkov on one occasion referred to former Defense Secretary McNamara.[95] Marshall Akhromeyev, who succeeded Ogarkov as Chief of the General Staff in the autumn of 1984, was less outspoken and more cautious but he also has expressed modernist-type views.[96] The significant point in these statements is that top Soviet military leaders present distinctly modernist views and not only as to substance but also as to the symmetrical reasoning applied; moreover, the views have often been put forward without the usual traditionalist additions about the imperialists' or the United States' guilt. Thus, whatever their actual meaning and further significance, these views stated by top military officers represent, by themselves, an innovation.

Soviet writers who used to write modernist articles have continued to express their views, often more forcefully. Thus some scholars' analyses in the early 1980s foreshadowed Gorbachev's innovative statements on security issues in the nuclear age and the 'new political thinking'.[97] During the early 1980s, it was also characteristic, however, that many of these manifestations were closely combined with hard-line attacks on imperialist 'circles' in capitalistic countries and some governments in NATO countries, especially the US government, and their aim of obtaining military superiority over the Soviet Union. It seemed clear that Soviet manifestations of unusually distinct modernist views were linked with vigorous peace campaigns, aimed at public opinion in Western Europe, where the Reagan administration was singled out for heavy censure; some writers, though, continued warning against exaggerating the importance of military factors and suggested that cooperation should still be possible as American policy was not immutable.[98] While earlier modernist manifestations seemingly had also been directed at traditionalist views in the Soviet Union, through the early 1980s they appeared more openly in combination with a campaign against Western governments. As Soviet verbal manifestations have had a preference for presenting the problem in terms of a simple fight between the peace-loving Soviet Union and reactionary circles in imperialist countries, this feature of modernist views was not totally new. The point is, rather, that this enduring feature of Soviet manifestations has varied in conspicuousness from time to time and during the first half of the 1980s, the increasing dominance of modernist views and abuse of some Western governments – with the Reagan administration the principal culprit – merged into each other.[99]

In the mid-1980s, modernist writings changed. The harsh censure of

Western governments and reactionary circles was toned down and new themes and types of consideration appeared. General Secretary Gorbachev's new policies received enthusiastic support from modernist writers and now the criticism was aimed more directly at groups in the Soviet society. Modernist writings have stressed that in the nuclear age security cannot merely be a matter of military measures directed against the adversary but has to include considerations for the interests of the other side as well. Collaboration and negotiation with an adversary is emphasized, compared to unilateral measures, and ideas similar to the notion of 'common security' have been expressed by writers and speakers elaborating the 'new political thinking'.[100] Again, whatever the actual meaning and further significance of these manifestations, they clearly represent a new departure in Soviet reasonings on nuclear weapons. A 'modernist' version of modernism, so to say. Also writers, primarily professional military officers, not advocating distinctly modernist notions have presented some of the new ideas but have tended to give them another interpretation. They often link the new phrases to old doctrines on military forces and adduce veiled counter-arguments to aspects of the new political thinking on the role of military forces in the nuclear age. Generally, it seems that the new notions have no 'true meaning' which is concealed from observers. Their meaning is simply undetermined and open for divergent interpretations in Soviet writings.[101]

As distinctly modernist manifestations have increasingly become prominent, they have, since the mid-1980s, occasionally been combined with other distinctive traits. Thus a report, published in 1984, provided an unprecedented detailed analysis of technical and strategic problems of the American SDI. As in other cases of Soviet openness (cf. p. 184), most data were based on American sources but, still, it represented a clear departure in Soviet writings on nuclear issues and military issues have generally received a more candid coverage in Soviet media during recent years.[102] Another innovation in modernist writings has been, in at least one case, a cautious call for *glasnost* in the military sphere; today, it has been argued, strategic armaments have in large measure ceased to be a secret for the other side and the absence of 'reliable' information has often been used by 'unscrupulous propaganda agencies for the systematic exaggeration of data and the fabrication of non-existent "threats"'. Soviet secrecy is not mentioned but a reader cannot fail to draw his own conclusions, even if the charge can also be directed at Western 'exaggeration of data'. The years 1987–8 also saw other, more or less veiled, criticisms of Soviet policy in some writings in the Soviet Union and among these a few were unprecedented in that *Soviet* nuclear deployments were questioned.[103] However, one dominant feature of modernist writings in the late 1980s has, as always, been support for all Soviet modernist marked policy departures *after* they have been announced by the current political leadership, combined with complaints that the former Soviet policy was too rigid. Also, modernist writers who earlier defended Soviet positions, which are now abandoned and deplored, embrace the new positions.[104] But it is evident that the most marked public advocates of modernist views in the late 1980s are writers who have not earlier committed themselves.

7. RISK-TAKING AND THE USE OF ARMED FORCES

The Soviet Union can use conventional armed forces to help achieve foreign policy objectives in various ways. As a rough and simple classification, solely put forward as expedient for indicating the focus of this review, Soviet foreign policy objectives in using armed forces can be of three types: to secure the Soviet homeland against external threats, to preserve interests outside Soviet state territory, and to advance Soviet interests by changing some international status quo. The methods can vary from using armed forces as a general 'background' for the political process amongst nations for example, various geographical deployments in peacetime, to the more direct use of military force as support for countries or groups outside Soviet territory, e.g. sea- and air-lifts of military advisers or troops, to the use of armed forces as a deterrent or a coercive means ('compellence'), to the actual combat involvement of armed forces in warfare.[105] The concept 'risk-taking' refers, in this context, to that subjective assessment of the risk for escalation and eventually confrontation with the United States which Soviet leaders can be assumed to include in a decision about the use of armed forces, particularly when it concerns a crisis or an actual war; this means that the concept 'Soviet risk-taking' refers to an outside observer's assumptions about the Soviet decision-making process, primarily inferred on the basis of Soviet and other countries' behavior.[106] The distinction between different types of objectives and methods may often be difficult to apply in that some actual Soviet use of military forces cannot be classified as exemplifying just one objective and method, but because the aim of this section is to assess trends in the Soviet use of armed forces beyond Soviet borders and the level and pattern of Soviet willingness to take risks in so doing, the focus is on the last-mentioned types of objective, i.e. the Soviet use of armed forces to preserve its interests outside Soviet territory or further advance them. As to methods, the focus will be on Soviet use of armed forces as a direct or indirect coercive instrument (for example, through marked changes in peacetime deployments) or in actual war beyond Soviet borders.[107]

The early part of the period 1961–89 saw two cases where Soviet leaders engaged in what seem to have been high-risk undertakings, one in Central Europe, the other in an area close to the United States. In the Berlin crisis, Krushchev announced, in June 1961, that the Soviet Union would sign a separate peace treaty with East Germany by the end of the year if the West refused to accept an all-German treaty. The Soviet leader stated that if Russia signed a treaty with East Germany alone, Western rights of access to

Berlin would cease. During the following months the Soviet Union took a number of military as well as non-military measures to signal its determination, but in the autumn, as Krushchev lifted the deadline for a peace treaty, the crisis gradually petered out.[108] As to the Soviets' goals, they seem to have been fluid but their primary objective probably was to consolidate the East German regime's vulnerable position while the more wide-ranging, but ill-defined, goal was to demonstrate their ability to prevail in regulating significant international relations in Central Europe.[109] Altogether, some of Krushchev's early speeches during the 1961 Berlin crisis indicated a marked willingness to run risks in pursuing these goals, but actual Soviet behavior, particularly the fact that the Soviet Union backed down in the end, indicated a greater reluctance to take risks. In the second case, the Cuban missile crisis in October 1962, the Soviet Union attempted secretly to deploy a number of IRBMs, MRBMs and bombers on Cuba, in addition to other weapon systems and about 20,000 military personnel. However, after Kennedy had announced the Soviet move in a dramatic speech on television where he warned of the consequences if the missiles were not removed, the Soviet Union, after a few days of intense fear of a military conflict between the superpowers, announced that the missiles would be withdrawn. The Soviet motive for initiating what, from a Soviet point of view, clearly must have been a high-risk move, is difficult to determine. Different hypotheses can be offered but they all seem inadequate at some point. Among the more plausible – or least implausible – one Soviet goal can have been to redress the strategic balance after it had been publicly revealed that there was no, and had never been, a missile gap; another motive can have been generally to strengthen the Soviet position *vis-à-vis* the United States and the West, in particular to force the United States to comply with Soviet demands in Central Europe.[110] Whatever the Soviet objective, the affair showed that the Soviet Union was willing to initiate high-risk moves but not willing to follow up and stand firm.

After the Cuban missile crisis, the Soviet Union did not resort to the use of armed forces in any significant way until the Middle East crisis and the June war of 1967. A few days before the war broke out, the Soviet Union reinforced its naval units in the Mediterranean and together with other actions carried out during and immediately after the war, it was apparently done to demonstrate Soviet support for Egypt. At the same time, as the actual composition of the Soviet navy in the Mediterranean seemed to signal that the Soviets would not escalate the local crisis and war into a superpower confrontation and the Soviet Union took measures to restrain Egypt, it all points to the conclusion that the Soviet Union deliberately pursued a low-risk policy.[111] The next year – 1968 – the Soviet Union invaded Czechoslovakia and, as a measure to restore the Soviet version of socialism in power in a Warsaw Pact country, that military action must have been assessed by Soviet leaders as quite low-risk. The most important development after the June 1967 war was, however, that various types of

Soviet military activity in the Third World, particularly the Middle East, intensified in the late 1960s and early 1970s. One conspicuous engagement was that the Soviet Union, from 1970 to 1972, placed about 20,000 military personnel, including missile crews and pilots to man its suface-to-air missiles and fighter aircrafts, in Egypt to provide air defense against Israel.[112] The level and character of that involvement was unprecedented in the Soviet use of armed forces. Other engagements during these years were: air support missions in civil wars in North Yemen (1967) and Sudan (1970-1); in Iraq, it supported the government with air-strikes in 1974 against the Kurdish minority, despite the Iraqi government's repression of the country's Communist Party; but the most important indicator of Soviet willingness to take risks in the early 1970s was its stance during the 1973 Middle East war. Thus the Soviet Union initiated various military measures, notably a major increase in the Soviet Mediterranean navy, a large-scale airlift of military supplies to Egypt and Syria, and putting three airborne divisions on alert at some point, thereby apparently seeking to preserve its credibility as the Arab countries' sponsor against Israel. While these measures clearly went beyond those undertaken during the 1967 war, and at one time prompted a worldwide American military alert which probably involved the greatest risk of superpower confrontation since the Cuban missile crisis, there was also clear evidence of Soviet restraint and willingness to cooperate with the United States in controlling escalation. On the whole, Soviet behavior suggested an increased willingness to run risks but a quite deliberate risk-taking policy.[113]

A notable aspect of Soviet military activities during this period was the forward deployment of the Soviet navy. It had begun earlier in the 1960s: the first significant Soviet naval activity in the Norwegian Sea took place in 1961, extensive naval exercises in the north-east Atlantic were initiated in 1963 and Soviet warships came into the Mediterranean in 1964. From 1967, there was a strong rise in the continuous presence of Soviet naval units in the Mediterranean where, among other things, they shadowed the American Sixth Fleet, visited foreign ports and displayed a special activity in connection with local crises and wars, for example the 1970 Jordanian crisis when they presumably sought to deter any US intervention and the 1973 Middle East war (cf. above). From 1968, Soviet warships went into the Indian Ocean where they were used for some covert Soviet 'naval diplomacy' in the 1971 Indo-Pakistani war, seemingly to discourage an American intervention. From 1969, Soviet naval units went into the Caribbean; and from 1970, a Soviet naval presence was established in West African waters.[114] The Soviet naval presence in the North Atlantic and the Pacific increased in these years too. Thus Soviet naval units were on the 'scene' during the 1973 'cod war' between Great Britain and Iceland but their purpose is difficult to determine, other than an indistinct 'increasing Soviet influence on West European affairs'. One part of the new Soviet naval activity during these years was some conspicuous exercises: the first worldwide Soviet naval exercise, *Okean*, was held in 1970 and was reported extensively in the Soviet press, the second, *Vesna*, took place in 1975, and their aim appears to have been to demonstrate the Soviet ability to coordinate its navy's activity worldwide.[115]

On the whole, the late 1960s and early 1970s were distinguished by an evidently increased and widespread Soviet military involvement in the Third World, especially in the Middle East. One feature of this new Soviet military activity outside Europe was that while it endeavored to display its support for right causes, often at the invitation of Third World countries, its behavior indicated as well that it persuaded its friends in the Third World to restraint, even if the 'right' cause was a Third World country's resistance to a European colonial power's raids on its capital.[116] It was also evident that the Soviet Union was very cautious about using its armed forces in a Third World country when US military units were already engaged, even if the target for the American forces was a Soviet ally. But noting the *changed* pattern and level of these involvements, they still suggest Soviet leaders' increased willingness to take risks on behalf of their new allies far from Soviet borders, in particular as at least some crises indicated the possibility for actual confrontation between the superpowers, with the Middle East war in October 1973 as the most distinct case.[117] An original motive for some of the forward deployments of the Soviet navy seems to have been to counter the deployment of US submarines with nuclear missiles capable of reaching the Soviet Union (*Polaris*) on oceans around the world, rather than pursuing foreign policy interests through practicing 'naval diplomacy',[118] a fact that shows how measures to defend the homeland in the long-range missile age may require military activity far from own borders. Neither did the slowly enhanced navy deployments on oceans far from Soviet borders necessarily indicate a markedly more risk-willing policy. But whatever the original motive for the Soviet navy's forward deployment, several aspects of the actual use of Soviet armed forces, including the navy, in the Third World in the late 1960s and early 1970s suggest basic changes in the Soviet leadership's approach to risk-taking. While Soviet risk-taking ten years earlier was abrupt and marked by a seeming willingness to take high risks in pursuing its interests in areas where the United States had clear interests, namely Europe and the Caribbean, the Soviet Union was, for some years after 1967, much more incremental and cautious in its use of armed forces and averse to high-risk adventures in Third World countries where the United States did not have similar interests. The Soviet involvements were often an opportunistic response to local intervention requests and thus it may be concluded that an increased Soviet willingness to run risks was very dissimilar to the Soviet high-risk adventures in the early 1960s.

In the mid-1970s, Soviet military involvements in the Third World diminished, compared to the years before, but the actual Soviet performance and its context changed. The most noteworthy case was the Soviet airlift of about 20,000 Cuban troops to Angola in 1975–6, after

Portugal had announced the country's independence and a civil war had broken out between contending liberation movements. Different attributes of the Angola situation facilitated a successful Cuban–Soviet intervention which Soviet leaders probably considered low-risk, first of all that it was precipitated by a request for assistance from one of the liberation movements, the Popular Movement for the Liberation of Angola (MPLA). Besides, even small amounts of external intervention seemed to produce victory for the Soviet-supported side in the civil war in a country which, in some respects, could be seen as a political and military vacuum in 1975. Another factor was that the United States was extremely reluctant to become involved in another war in the Third World after Vietnam, even if the CIA, until the appropriations were cut off by the Senate in late 1975, had assisted other liberation movements in Angola against the Soviet-supported MPLA. Also Soviet rivalry with China seemed to have had some relevance to the Soviet decision to intervene.[119] Two years later, in 1977–8, the Soviet Union intervened on behalf of Ethiopia in the Ogaden war between Ethiopia and Somalia in the Horn of Africa, primarily by airlifting about 16,000 Cuban troops to Ethiopia. In this case too, different factors, similar to the Angola case and including an invitation from the ruling military committee in Ethiopia, the *Dergue*, contributed to what Soviet decision-makers must have considered a low-risk action.[120] It follows that both involvements were largely reactive and opportunistic in that they came in response to indigenous developments not of Soviet making.

At the end of the 1970s and the beginning of the 1980s, there was a new increase in the Soviet use of armed forces. While the Soviet military pressure against Poland, in 1980–1, as a coercive means against a member of the Warsaw Pact did not signify a new Soviet policy or changed willingness to run risks, the Soviet invasion of Afghanistan in December 1979 suggested a wholly new pattern of Soviet use of military forces, and possibly an increased willingness to take risks. By early December 1979, the Soviet military personnel in Afghanistan seem to have numbered about 4000 at every level in the Afghan army, and the Soviet invasion, in late December, probably included about 80,000 combat troops. It was the first direct involvement of Soviet armed forces on a mass scale in the Third World and unprecedented in that it involved a direct use of Soviet armed forces to overthrow an existing government. It also signified a departure from previous Soviet action by ignoring sensitivities in Third World countries. Moreover, while it could be said that the Soviet Union had been ruthless in its use of military force *vis-à-vis* its allies in Eastern Europe (Hungary in 1956, Czechoslovakia in 1968), but cautious beyond that, the tenability of that generalization was called in question after December 1979. However, the question is whether these new features indicate a markedly increased willingness to take risks.[121] Assessing that, it must be noted that Afghanistan has a common border with the Soviet Union, a fact which can be assumed to have decreased the risk seen from the Soviet point of view. Furthermore, the political development in Afghanistan up to December 1979 was clearly seen as dangerous for Soviet interests in controlling a Marxist, but highly unreliable, regime in a neighboring country, and Soviet leaders apparently believed that a 'limited' Soviet military engagement *could* be successful in controlling Afghanistan. Neither did the invasion, in itself, carry a risk of a military confrontation with the United States, irrespective of the different expressions of 'deep concern' about the growing Soviet involvement from the United States before the invasion, and one reason could be that the United States was preoccupied with the hostage crisis in Teheran. A Soviet interest in continuing détente with the United States can have been seen as subordinate as Soviet–American relations had already deteriorated in late 1979, and so Soviet leaders may have thought there was little to lose from worsening these relations.

Some of these Soviet calculations proved wrong, but the central point is that they all, besides explaining why the Soviet invasion was actually launched, make it doubtful to take it as a indicator of a markedly increased Soviet willingness to expose itself to a risk for Soviet–American military confrontation. The Soviet invasion of Afghanistan was a reaction to a rapidly deteriorating situation in a neighboring country which faced Soviet leaders with highly unpleasant options.[122] Therefore, while the Soviet invasion, to Soviet leaders, must have been more risky than other Soviet military actions in the late 1960s and 1970s, apart from some of the measures during the 1973 war in the Middle East, and it in many respects deviates from the typical Soviet low-profile use of its armed forces in a Third World country, it can be concluded that it definitely was considered less risky by the Soviet leadership than the two Soviet adventures at the beginning of the 1960s.

What these various Soviet uses of armed forces since the early 1960s, and the inclination to risk-taking they suggest, mean for evaluating different aspects of US governments' images of the Soviet Union as superpower is considered in the following chapter.

7. Comparing images and operational environments

1. ON EVALUATING IMAGES

Proceeding from Chapters 2–4 through Chapter 7, the analyses in this study of American perceptions of the Soviet Union as a nuclear adversary from the Kennedy presidency in the early 1960s to the end of the Reagan presidency in the late 1980s illustrate the increasing range of uncertainty associated with analyzing different nuclear problems, and evaluating US governments' images is the most precarious part. It involves comparing psychological and operational environments, that is, asking whether and how there is any similarity or discrepancy between the Soviet Union as a nuclear adversary as observed, reasoned/imagined and presented by changing US governments (i.e. their images as reviewed in Chapters 2–3 and summarized in 4) and as it is, i.e. 'is' as observed, reasoned/imagined and outlined by a detached observer with total knowledge of all relevant factors. Obviously, these conditions of an observer are ideals which cannot be realized in practice, but only aspired to. A 'detached observer with total knowledge of all relevant factors' does not exist and, as touched on in the introduction to Chapter 6, comparing images and operational environments does not mean that changing American 'subjective imaginations' are contrasted with some 'objective reality'. Of course not. What it means is that enduring aspects, i.e. fixtures and trends, of the ways changing administrations in Washington have publicly presented the Soviet Union as a nuclear adversary are analyzed in terms of various assumptions and observations that are deemed tenable, primarily on the basis of the review in the two preceding chapters of the object of perception, the Soviet Union as a superpower, and the process of perception, the domestic American setting. As comparing images to operational environments in any case is a hazardous enterprise, it is expedient as a first step to record some common fallacies.

Most important, evaluating an image and attempting to separate misperceptions is not dependent on whether and how it is logically structured. There is no one-to-one correspondence between, on the one hand, the logical structure of an image (argument or explanation), i.e. its internal validity, and, on the other hand, the factual truth of the image (argument/explanation), i.e. its external relationship with the facts.[1]

Examining the internal validity of an image may be useful when we try to assess its external validity but its structure cannot, by itself, determine its validity. Neither can the genesis of an image be decisive for its external validity, nor whether it can be demonstrated that the process of perception has involved some 'extraneous' concerns. One may certainly be right for 'wrong' reasons and wrong for 'right' reasons.

This has a special pertinence in the context of this analysis because US governments' public statements on the Soviet Union and nuclear arms frequently have an instrumental function as they are made to influence various domestic or foreign audiences and stimulate certain actions. But it can never serve as a refutation of the empirical validity of an assertion or assumption to demonstrate that it goes well with this or that US government's political aims, as these may be declared by the government itself or imputed to it, or that it inheres in some deplorable part of the American tradition. One should avoid the pitfall that an observation about the Soviet Union as a nuclear power has to be empirically wrong because one happens to disagree with the political goals professed by or attributed to the observer, be it a politician from the United States, the Soviet Union or a third country. Conversely, neither has an assertion to be empirically valid because it supports a valuable recommendation. Likewise, it is not a confirmation of the validity of a statement to point out that it originates in a commendable political process (for instance, a democratic structure), and neither can it serve as a refutation to demonstrate that an image did not originate in a democratic process. In any event, the conceptual distinction between evaluating an image's factual truth value and its political expediency and valuableness is crucial to remember.

All that is fairly obvious, but as it is often disregarded in heated debates about the Soviet Union and nuclear issues, it is still worth emphasizing in connection with an attempt to evaluate perceptions. Moreover, its relevance applies not only to statements from professional politicians. 'Outside' or professed non-political and non-partisan scholars and observers too may try to influence political decisions and this is particularly noteworthy when writings of American as well as other Western – or Soviet – scholars are examined and assessed. In any case, it is important to note that it can never serve as a confirmation or refutation of the empirical validity of an analysis to demonstrate that a theory about the Soviet Union as a nuclear power fits in with a declared or imputed political aim, be it Western or Soviet. The assessment of the empirical validity of some specific analysis or perception always depends on the content of the theory/image.

Applying the examination of the Soviet Union as a superpower and the domestic American setting in an attempt to identify and delimit important parts of the operational environment approximates what is called an environmental possibilism approach, that is, the focus is on factors in the environment which limit the operational results of some policy associated with an image irrespective of whether or not such factors have been recognized by the decision-makers in question and included in their image.[2] The analysis aims at evaluating opportunities and limitations in some part of the environment: how features of the environment may affect the operational results or outcome of some policy, actual or hypothetical, evaluated in a given historical context, currently or in some future situation. As concerning all attempts to delimit and evaluate the operational impact of some environmental factors, it applies in this case that the most one can do is frame hypotheses concerning which factors have been or are relevant and in what ways. Analyzing and reaching conclusions about the operational environment will always be based on assumptions about principally indeterminable factors and therefore, in the end, be hypothetical even if a conclusion may seem either probable, only possible, rather improbable, or the issue is plainly doubtful. Still, as delimited aspects of images are evaluated by being compared to delimited aspects of operational environments, it should thereby be possible to make a little headway in replacing 'bounded rationality' with a more 'comprehensive rationality' through a kind of 'learning and reality-testing process'[3] even if it must be underlined that no 'reality-testing' of images can provide all premises for a judgement of their political value.

In the context of this analysis, these general problems connected with identifying operational environments mean that no empirical evaluation of US governments' images can reach the conclusion that the one ideal-type image is valid while the other, *per contra*, is invalid. Among the specific reasons for this is that the two ideal-types, nuclear essentialism and Soviet essentialism as defined (pp. 32–5), in many respects are incommensurable quantities. The divergent starting points and reasonings applied result in disparate analytical and political paradigms where explanations and assertions advanced by one ideal-type image often are irrelevant and absurd to the other more than factually wrong, a condition most evidently illustrated by strongly divergent views of deterrence. Considered that way, the transition from one form of essentialism to another resembles the structure of scientific revolutions as expounded by Thomas Kuhn.[4] Moreover, particularly evaluating the fixture concerning the political significance of nuclear arms implies examining that many extensive and complex empirical questions that it is only feasible, in this study, to try to answer some of the questions, viz. those directly related to Soviet policies and positions, while others must be answered (even more) preliminarily, particularly emphasizing critical methodical problems. Thus, no evaluation can reach a clear-cut and general characterization of the relative empirical validity of the two ideal-type images. But this does not mean, of course, that a political preference for one ideal type's guidelines cannot be backed up by references to cogent empirical examinations.

In comparing psychological and operational environments, it can be useful to distinguish between different aspects of an image. The content of an actor's image may be described as consisting of three analytically distinct aspects.[5] A set of *cognitive* attributes by which the pronouncer expounds the object, that is, the actor's view of the object's 'inherent' characteristices. An *affective* component representing a liking or disliking for the object. And an *action*, or policy, component consisting of a set of responses to the object that is deemed appropriate in the light of its perceived attributes, other aspects of the environment and the actor's goals. As the three conceptually distinct aspects of an image usually are closely connected and intertwined, it may only be by scrutinizing the image that the different aspects can be distinguished and those which can be evaluated by empirical methods can be separated and compared with an operational environment. On the other hand, political actors will often endeavor to present their image with consistent relationships between different parts in the way that, for example, the presented analyses and declared goals strongly suggest a particular measure, and that may facilitate an evaluation.

Evaluating US governments' perceptions of the Soviet Union as a nuclear adversary looks at cognitive and action aspects. Chapter 5 outlined aspects of the domestic American setting, Chapter 6 various attributes of the Soviet Union as superpower, and the aim in sections 2 and 3 is to recast and elaborate the findings so as to facilitate a direct comparison of fixtures and trends of the images with the operational environments. Section 2 focuses on fixtures, section 3 on trends. It is not fruitful generally to separate the analysis of cognitive aspects from the analysis of action aspects, but since cognitive aspects ascribe different attributes to the object of perception, it follows that comparing this aspect of images to operational environment will apply the outline in Chapter 6 as a starting point. (Whether *explaining* cognitive aspects may include domestic factors is a different problem.) Comparing action aspects of the images to operational environments, on the other hand, must include an examination of how the domestic political system influences the appropriateness of this or that response, and the analysis of action aspects may thereby suggest various explanations. Section 4 approaches the comparing of images and operational environments from another angle as the starting point is that both fixtures and trends dominating since the mid-1970s tend toward emphasizing dispositional factors, while situational factors are belittled. As this perception may reflect the fundamental attribution error (cf. p. 21), the analysis is framed as an elaboration of how dispositional, respectively situational, variables have influenced Soviet nuclear policies and positions since the early 1960s, with a view to testing the fundamental attribution error as US governments have interpreted and presented the Soviet Union as a nuclear adversary.

2. FIXTURES

The analysis of US governments' images of the Soviet Union as a nuclear adversary since the early 1960s in Chapters 2–3, synthesized in Chapter 4, showed that two fixtures have been apparent: a kind of Soviet essentialism concerning the political impact of nuclear strength and the notion that the United States ever needs to negotiate with the Soviet Union from a position of strength.

1.   The political impact of nuclear strength

The core reasoning in this version of what is termed 'Soviet essentialism' is that the actual state of the Soviet–American nuclear balance and the two countries' nuclear policies are essential symbols of the course of the basic political conflict between the totalitarian Soviet Union and the democratic United States, and this ought always to be an important guideline for American policy. Through the period since the early 1960s, the notion that the superpowers' nuclear strengths and policies have political impact has been expressed in varying ways by changing US administrations and with somewhat changing weight by different spokesmen. The idea, which has been termed 'perceptual arguments',[6] has often been presented in an elusive form, implying its self-evident truth, and to some observers it has seemed not only abstruse but artificial and fanciful. But noting that cannot, of course, serve as a basis for simply dismissing the question if these images have empirical validity. That question still stands back as significant, in particular for observers and political actors who share a skeptical view combined with the view that rational examination and discussion ought to have some place, at least, when nuclear issues are debated.

An image holding the political impact of nuclear strength needs clarification in various ways in order to be subject to empirical evaluation. If the relative sizes of the two superpowers' nuclear forces are held to have political significance, what are then *the relevant criteria for measuring these forces*? Is it number of delivery vehicles or warheads or only missiles? Is it missile accuracy, yield, throw-weight or any other specific weapons characteristics, eventually combined in various ways? The review in Chapter 6 (pp. 185–9) showed that the actual selection of indicator could be important even if all measures of Soviet strategic nuclear forces compared to the American point to a relative strengthening of the Soviet position since the early 1960s. But the question whether the strategic balance has political significance cannot be meaningfully answered simply by pointing to changes in some indicators of the balance, of course, and that is not only because focusing on different indicators may support somewhat different conclusions. Whatever indicator, or combination of indicators, is used, it implies an assertion as to the impact on political actors' views and behavior, and one characteristic mark of this image is that there is a close connection between the specific Soviet view which sees great political utility in nuclear strength and actual Soviet behavior in the way that greater Soviet nuclear strength induced the Soviets to more extensive and risky use of its armed forces.

The following evaluation of an image claiming that nuclear strength has political impact first deals with the *cognitive aspects* by considering two questions: first, what has been the Soviet view of the political significance of nuclear arms; secondly, what has been the impact of the Soviet view on Soviet behavior? Another set of questions concerns *the action component* of an image holding that nuclear forces have political significance, i.e. whether the recommended set of responses are appropriate in the light of characteristics of the operational environment, external as well as internal, and the image-holder's goals. Typically, this concerns whether a recommended arms program and/or the applied American declaratory policy will affect Soviet views and behavior as well as the attitudes among different political actors in the American political system in the direction aimed at. This obviously includes questions dealt with in the cognitive aspects of an image but the starting point here is directly the appropriateness of the image-holder's set of responses.

Concerning *Soviet views of the political significance of nuclear strength*, the examination of different aspects of the Soviet Union as superpower offered several pointers that Soviet leaders during the period have shared a view that the Soviet Union's general nuclear strength is a valuable political asset. First of all, both the rate of the Soviet nuclear build-up since the early 1960s and essential characteristics of Soviet negotiating behavior support that conclusion. Several statements by Soviet leaders as well as other Soviet spokesmen also point to the conclusion that the leaders of the Soviet Union value its nuclear superpower status highly. Moreover, it is interesting that concerning this specific point there is not much difference between modernist and traditionalist inclined leaders and spokesmen, and when Soviet leaders, in the late 1960s and early 1970s, clearly changed toward modernist positions (cf. pp. 210f.), it was not followed by a change as to this issue. Thus all Soviet spokesmen and writers have noted that the changing correlation of forces, which include the nuclear balance as one factor, favor the socialist countries and force the American leadership to adopt a more restrained foreign policy. Although there have been differences between the weight attached to this among Soviet manifestations, with traditionalist-minded commentators and Soviet military doctrine tending toward emphasizing it most, the predominant tendency has been to present the changing strategic balance as an important symbol of the Soviet Union's, as well as all other peace-loving forces', strengthened position in world politics. Assessing the further meaning of this generally shared view, it is worth noting, though, that no Soviet writings have developed and elaborated such refined and subtle theories about the use of strategic nuclear power in coercive diplomacy that are so popular in American images and scholars' writings. Another indicator of the peculiar symbolic mark of this view is the strong reaction against American politicians who want to deny them an 'equal' status. As the widespread underlinings of the necessity for 'equality and equal security', it shows the supreme importance attached to some general idea about the Soviet Union's international distinction and the nuclear strength deemed requisite for that status. However, toward the very end of the period 1961–89, several speeches and writings from Soviet leaders and spokesmen, as well as some of the recent changes in Soviet negotiating positions, indicate a notable modifying of the general inclination to attach supreme political significance to the Soviet Union's nuclear strength and status.

Thus, to the extent that the fixture concerning the political significance of nuclear arms focuses on the general Soviet view, the examination of Soviet manifestations and positions confirms its validity.

Concerning *the impact of the general Soviet appreciation of the political value of nuclear forces on Soviet behavior*, one way of approaching the problem is examining the relation between changes in the nuclear balance and patterns of the Soviet use of armed forces to promote its foreign policy interests, especially the Soviet willingness to accept risks. The basic methodical problem in examining that relation is the difficulties related to an attempt to abstract the impact of the nuclear balance from other factors influencing Soviet behavior. Parts of this problem are general to studies of foreign policy decisions as any isolation of one particular variable contains the seeds of distortion and over-simplification. It has a special character in this case, however, which originates in the opaque character of the Soviet decision-making process. Since the actual deliberations in the Soviet leadership are unknown, conclusions about the weight of the nuclear factor have to be inferred on the basis of a combination of Soviet behavior, Soviet verbal manifestations and different environmental factors which an observer reasons have been influential when Soviet leaders made their decisions. Hence, it has to be stressed beforehand that any conclusions necessarily contain a good deal of speculation. The following attempt to assess the significance of the nuclear factor in Soviet uses of armed forces and risk-taking therefore only pretends to elucidate the problem by delimiting critical factors and suggesting some preliminary answers. Two complementary angles are applied: what has characterized the most risky Soviet use of armed forces in the period 1961–89, and what has distinguished the Soviet use of armed forces after it obtained nuclear parity with the United States?

The two most high-risk Soviet undertakings, the initiatives that gave rise to the 1962 Cuban missile crisis and the 1961 Berlin crisis, occurred in years when the Soviet Union clearly was in a position of nuclear inferiority, whether that 'inferiority' is measured in the numbers of delivery vehicles, warheads or aggregate explosive power (cf. Tables 1–3, pp. 186–7) While this does not prove, of course, that the risky Soviet undertakings were prompted by the Soviet strategic inferiority, it does show, at least, that there is no simple overall correlation between Soviets nuclear strength and Soviet risk-taking in the way that inferiority necessarily induces or forces the Soviet to caution. Examining the relation between the nuclear balance and

Soviet proneness to risk-taking in the two cases more closely, various features of the Soviet attempt to deploy missiles in Cuba – the most evident example of Soviet nuclear brinkmanship during 1961–89 – suggest that one reason for sending missiles to Cuba was, indeed, the Soviet weakness in intercontinental nuclear forces. However, since it also can be reasoned that the Soviet move did not succeed because the Soviets realized their nuclear inferiority, it can be concluded that *both* the Soviet high-risk move and its failure can be related to the then state of the nuclear balance – even if it is evident that the Kennedy administration's fear of escalation outweighed any advantage it might have felt because of its numerical superiority in nuclear arms.[7] Thus, even if the methodical difficulty of isolating the impact of the strategic nuclear balance from other factors (especially the local balance of conventional military forces) is noted, the course of the Cuban missile crisis seems to point to a conclusion that it may have had some impact but this was far from unidirectional in relation to Soviet proneness to risk-taking. In any case, the conditional nature of this conclusion must be emphasized. As to the 1961 Berlin crisis, one can say that, viewed as a Soviet attempt to compel the three Western Powers to leave Berlin, it failed, and that may have been due to a Soviet realization of its nuclear inferiority. At the same time, neither did the West attempt to force the Soviet Union to undo the new *fait accompli* in the Berlin situation, the Berlin Wall, and also that can have been due to a feature of the nuclear balance, namely the Western realization that the Soviet Union had a kind of second-strike capability against the United States.[8] Therefore, while the 1961 Berlin crisis, like the Cuban missile crisis, shows that the Soviet nuclear inferiority did not restrain Soviet leaders from a high-risk undertaking, or from creating a local *fait accompli* which the Soviets must have realized the West would strongly deplore, it also points to an observation that already then some kind of mutual deterrence seemed to influence both the Soviet Union and the United States from further pursuing their putative political goals.

The Soviet Union obtained a kind of nuclear parity with the United States in the early 1970s when the SALT I agreement was taken as a symbol of strategic nuclear parity between the two superpowers. One indicator of the impact of nuclear parity on the Soviet use of armed forces to pursue political goals is a comparison of Soviet behavior in the Middle East crisis in 1973 with its behavior during the 1967 crisis. While the various Soviet measures in 1967 were quite low-risk, its military activities in connection with the 1973 war indicated a higher willingness to run risks. That difference may be related to a number of contextual factors of which the changed nuclear balance is one, and especially given the fact that Soviet leaders clearly attached great value to their new status as the United States' 'equal', it may be a natural – but still a highly conditional – conclusion that there was some positive relation between the changed strategic balance and the increased Soviet willingness to risk-taking in 1973. However, the record of two high-risk Soviet ventures in the early 1960s shows the deficiency of a plain assertion that the increased proneness to risk-taking simply reflected the Soviet Union's increased nuclear strength. The changed local possibilities for Soviet engagement must obviously be included.

A more significant indicator of the actual impact of strategic parity on Soviet behavior is the special organization and implementation of the many new Soviet military involvements in the Middle East and the Third World during these years. The point is that the changing characteristics of several Soviet engagements and interventions in the 1970s – particularly Egypt 1970–2 and 1973, Angola 1975–6 and Ethiopia 1977–8 – showed an unprecedented willingness to make use of various opportune circumstances, including local requests for assistance, for military interventions in regional conflicts in the Third World. In some cases the engagement occurred in the form of direct employment of Soviet military forces, in others by sea- and air-lifting of Soviet-allied (primarily Cuban) forces. As this new pattern of Soviet military engagements developed parallel with Soviet leaders' and several Soviet writings' giving more than usual weight to the Soviet Union's internationalistic duty to help progressive forces in the Third World, and noting the direct and indirect criticism in Soviet media of Krushchev's hare-brained adventures, it is natural to reason that at least some of the background for the clearly increased Soviet willingness to become involved in what were low-risk engagements far from Soviet borders has to be found in the Soviet Union's changed nuclear position. Soviet leaders may have seen the general international, including the United States', recognition of the Soviet Union as the United States (nuclear) 'equal' as providing better opportunity for performing its rightful role as midwife for progressive developments in the Third World. One interesting characteristic of this development is that its beginning coincided with the years when Soviet leaders changed toward more modernist positions (cf. p. 210f.). Another notable characteristic of the new Soviet military engagements is that the Soviet Union clearly endeavored to avoid high-risk involvements and in crises actively sought Soviet–American cooperation to control any escalation risks.

Altogether, the various new features of Soviet uses of armed forces through the 1970s lead to the conclusion that the general Soviet appreciation of the political utility of nuclear forces had some impact on Soviet behavior in the first decade after it obtained nuclear parity. The record does not provide a basis for wording the conclusion in more definite terms, and it must be emphasized that any explanation has to consider the significance of many different regional developments. However, considering the low-risk features of almost all new Soviet military engagements during this period, it is plausible to conclude that the Soviet leadership had learned to adapt its use of armed forces to the changing international context, where this includes both the new relationship between the superpowers and a variety of developments in the Third World. Thus Soviet interventions were a reaction to non-Soviet events, that is, an opportunistic exploitaion of new possibilities which were not of Soviet making. Concerning another notable development in Soviet military policy during this period, the forward deployment of Soviet naval units through the 1960s and early 1970s, its initiation can be related to the nuclear balance in the roundabout way that it seems to have aimed at countering the *Polaris* submarines, from which follows that it is difficult to include the actual initiation of the Soviet navy's forward deployment as an example of a beforehand calculated Soviet decision to conduct naval deplomacy under the umbrella of Soviet nuclear strength. But the actual Soviet willingness to use its navy on different occasions during the 1970s for an indistinct 'naval diplomacy' may be related to the Soviet Union's new nuclear 'equality' with the United States for reasons similar to the above referred. Hence, also in this respect it may be said that the Soviet decision-makers 'learned' to adapt the use of Soviet armed forces to both the umbrella of mutual nuclear deterrence and different regional developments which were not of Soviet making. As to the most conspicuous and massive Soviet use of armed forces since the early 1960s, the invasion of Afghanistan in December 1979, it is difficult to relate to some aspect of the developments in the nuclear field, even in the same conditional way as applies to Soviet engagements far from Soviet borders. The Soviet invasion signified a departure from traditional Soviet behavior but considering the many special features of the Afghanistan situation in December 1979 (cf. pp. 228–9), it cannot be related to any nuclear factor. (Neither can an even more conspicuous departure from traditional Soviet behavior: the withdrawal from Afghanistan, 1988–9.)

The conclusions from this rough examination of the impact of the Soviet view of the political utility of nuclear weapons on Soviet behavior, from 1961 to 1989, can be summarized in four points:

1. The Soviet Union did not show an increased propensity to high-risk use of its armed forces after it obtained nuclear parity with the United States in the early 1970s. On the contrary – and whatever the reason – the two most high-risk Soviet moves occurred in the early 1960s during a time of Soviet nuclear inferiority, and their general policy points to the conclusion that they were more conscious of controlling nuclear risks after having reached parity.

2. The Soviets became more inclined to a low-risk use of armed forces to pursue political interests far from their borders for some years after they had obtained nuclear parity, and, it is worth noting, this coincided with a widespread dominance of modernism in Soviet writings and speeches. Any conclusion, however, as to whether the increased disposition to use military forces was caused by their new nuclear status has to be conditional but the examination of various features of Soviet policies and manifestations suggests that that explanation is plausible. At least, it cannot generally be dismissed that a specific Soviet interpretation of the meaning of strategic parity probably was important for Soviet

behavior in parts of the Third World during the 1970s.

3. As to the most massive, but still quite low-risk, Soviet use of armed forces during the period (i.e. Afghanistan), it is clear that what may be termed the 'mutually perceived balance of interests' in the local area was far more important than any actual characteristic of the strategic balance.[9] Concerning the Soviet withdrawal from Afghanistan, it is evidently an unprecedented example of Soviet adaptation to the limited expediency of using armed forces, but this has no relation to some nuclear reality.

4. Considering the fact that any reasoning includes a good deal of speculation where different factors have to be singled out as decisive among a vast and complicated pattern of events, various indicators point to the conclusion that it has more been a general Soviet inclination for utilizing low-risk opportunities to promote political interests than a conscious reading of the 'correlation of nuclear forces' that determined the heightened Soviet use of armed forces through the 1970s.[10] There is obviously no one-to-one relation between the Soviet view of the utility of nuclear forces, the Soviet–American strategic balance and the Soviet use of armed forces.

It is therefore important that any attempt to evaluate this fixture of US governments' images distinguishes between a general conclusion about Soviet *views* (or 'perceptions') and a claim about Soviet *behavior*. While Soviet leaders' and commentators' views undoubtedly included, at least until the mid-1980s, a high appreciation of the political value of Soviet nuclear forces, a conclusion about a definite impact on Soviet behavior is more doubtful.[11]

Evaluating *action aspects* of this fixture of US government's images means assessing how attributes of the American political system as well as the Soviet Union as superpower and their interplay influence the appropriateness of responses suggested by the image's advocates. The distinctive mark of the action (or policy) component of this Soviet essentialist-marked image is the notion that the United States can counter deleterious political effects of the Soviet view of the political utility of nuclear arms by adopting a policy clearly marked by a steadfast and ever credible readiness to meet any Soviet challenge by posing an American counter-challenge – and that primarily means that any Soviet attempt to gain what is seen as a politically usable nuclear superiority has to be met by the United States increasing *its* nuclear stockpile.

The domestic American conditions for successfully pursuing that policy put special requirements on American political leaders. Given the democratic features of the American political system, it is necessary for American politicians to stir the electorate's imagination about the impending dangers arising from some new Soviet nuclear system. It is necessary to beat the drum loudly about the growing Soviet threat and stress how the Soviets are within an ace of obtaining a politically highly dangerous nuclear superiority if this or that American arms program is not adopted as a 'visible' counter. Prominent features of the American tradition make it natural to conduct a vociferous and extensive campaign to draw support for a wider arms program that will show how America, as the free world's leader, has 'resolve' and 'will' to 'stand up to' the Soviets. The record shows that, indeed, this has been an appropriate strategy as the American electorate has responded positively to such campaigns. Even if there have always been politicians in the United States who approach nuclear issues in such terms, the significant point is that it *has* been possible for a clearly dedicated US government to bring about the required domestic support for a strong rearmanent in this way – note in particular the Kennedy administration in the early 1960s and the Reagan administration twenty years later. While US governments' endeavors to drum up support for a marked arms build-up usually have given rise to at least some domestic opposition – and here the opposition to the Reagan administration is a better example than the almost non-existent opposition to the Kennedy administration's arms build-up – the critical point in this is that a campaign that strongly advertises the growing Soviet threat has appeared successful *in terms of the American political process*.

However, it is important to note that a part of the reason for the domestic appropriateness of this policy originates in a peculiar feature of such campaigns stressing the political utility of the opponent's nuclear weapons: when American political leaders have domestic success as they proclaim the political dangers of giving up some arms program, it is not only because their campaign may reflect widespread beliefs in the American society but *the campaign may actually shape, influence and strengthen such beliefs*. That means that any conclusion about the appropriateness – assessed in terms of American politics – of this policy must consider the problem if political leaders' statements about how the paramount significance of 'perceptions' of the nuclear balance may become self-fulfilling prophecies.[12] Especially considering the inept Carter administration's and the apt Reagan administration's different handlings of the political dangers related to the 'window of vulnerability' – where the greater aptitude of the Reagan administration was due far more to its rhetorical success in changing domestic perceptions of the issue than to any marked change in a 'hardware' nuclear balance (cf. Tables 1–3 above, which indicate that the strategic balance since 1981 has not markedly changed)–it is a natural conclusion that the question about the policy validity of this image is closely related to any incumbent administration's ability to handle the dominating views in the domestic political process, rather than its ability actually to change any military balance. It follows that this primarily is a matter of restoring America's self-confidence, and not that much of changing the nuclear balance – it turns on an administration's aptitude to cope with delicate symbolic issues. Moreover, both the Kennedy administration's coming to power in 1961 and the Reagan administration in 1981 point to the observation that the key to rebuilding America's self-confidence is the very replacement of a highly censured administration by some of the censurers who, for some time, talk forcefully about how they are *now* restoring the nuclear balance. Whether they are actually doing so is not that critical. In a democratic political system this side of the issue is extremely important *and* may pose insurmountable obstacles for an incumbent government.

As to the validity of the action aspect of this image in relation to Soviet views and behavior, it is first of all clear that one cannot account for the Soviet view that nuclear arms have political value as a simple result of a reversed 'learning process' – reversed compared to nuclear essentialist notions about who should teach whom about what (cf. p. 34) – where Soviet leaders and writers have merely imitated and copied American ideas, implying that that Soviet view would never have been present if only the United States had not 'taught' them the idea. As demonstrated by the review of different Soviet manifestations, in particular Soviet military doctrine, the Soviet Union has had no need for teaching on this point. From this it follows that this American image of the Soviet view cannot merely be dismissed as inappropriate because it has worked as a self-fulfilling prophecy. However, the issue has another and more difficult aspect. The problem is that this fixture in American policy has probably strengthened the Soviet view and any political effects it might have: when Soviet leaders are predisposed to perceive nuclear forces in a politically competitive light, it can easily be politically self-destructive for American leaders to draw attention to, and occasionally appear obsessive about, the coercive potential of nuclear weapons[13] and that irrespective of domestic, short-term benefits of that behavior. The possiblity of self-fulfilling prophecies then becomes yet more natural wherefore the policy appropriateness of such declarations is highly doubtful.

But these relations appear even more precarious when some special aspects of the development between the two superpowers since the early 1960s are examined. When the early Kennedy administration pursued a quite Soviet essentialist policy, it was followed by the two most risky Soviet uses of armed forces through the whole of 1961–89, the Berlin crisis in 1961 and the Cuban missile crisis in 1962, thereby seemingly indicating that this American policy induces the Soviets to risky behavior. However, after the Johnson administration, and in particular Secretary McNamara, had hinted at deviations from the traditional American appreciation of the political utility of nuclear arms, it was followed, during the 1970s, by several new Soviet military engagements in the Third World, and this could indicate that even weak suggestions that the United States intended to pursue a different policy will be used by the Soviets to strongly extend their military interventions far from Soviet borders. In the 1980s, when the Reagan administration pursued a distinctly Soviet essentialist policy, it was followed, after a few years, by some marked restraints in Soviet military engagements, indicating that that policy actually induced the Soviet Union to restrain their use of armed forces. The conclusion to be drawn on the basis of this is not that there actually was this or that positive relation between American nuclear policy and Soviet military policy. In fact, as in all cases there clearly were other influential factors, it is artificial to conclude anything in positive terms about the overall relation between American nuclear policy and the Soviet use of armed forces. Thus it is more tenable to word a conclusion about the period 1961–89 in negative terms: there is no simple correlation between the action aspect of a Soviet essentialist-marked American policy and the Soviet propensity to use armed forces.

On the whole, the picture is highly ambiguous when policy aspects of this fixture of US governments' images is compared to the operational environments. It appears that the domestic American environment facilitates Soviet essentialist manifestations in the peculiar sense that some administrations actually have had success in changing domestic perceptions of the nuclear balance without this having depended on any actual change in some hardware balance. But the delicacy of this observation becomes even more intricate when Soviet behavior is included in comparing image and operational environment, and no empirical examination of Soviet policy and the interplay between Soviet and American policies can result in definite conclusions concerning the policy validity of this image. The findings are simply not that unambiguous. Both the domestic American and in particular the Soviet aspect of the operational environment suggest that the operational environment is highly ambiguous.[14]

2. Negotiating from strength

Another fixture of US governments' images has been the notion that the United States still needs an active nuclear arms deployment policy in order to induce the Soviets to negotiate seriously (cf. pp. 125–6). Successive administrations have adhered to the idea that a continuous and vigilant American nuclear arms acquisition process is necessary to enter fruitful negotiations with the Soviet Union and obtain meaningful arms control agreements. The findings of the review of the Soviet Union as superpower in Chapter 6, as well as various aspects of the domestic American setting in Chapter 5, can elucidate the cognitive and policy validity of this idea about 'negotiating from strength'.

Focusing on the interplay between the two superpowers' negotiating behavior and nuclear deployments since the early 1980s, the first important case concerns the Kennedy administration's departure on the test ban issue in 1963 which led to the Limited Test Ban Treaty later that year. Krushchev's positive response to Kennedy's move represents a distinct case of that kind of interplay between the two superpowers' negotiating policies where a forthcoming American action is answered by a forthcoming Soviet reaction. As the American president's initiative was the initiation of the nuclear essentialist trend in the 1960s and the Soviet leader's response was clearly modernist marked, the test ban case seems to represent that type of interplay envisioned by a nuclear essentialist image, and clearly rejected by the 'negotiating from strength' image as possible. However, examining other aspects of the issue shows the record to be more ambiguous. Most important, the Kennedy administration had continued and enhanced a strong nuclear build-up and while this does not prove that the American arms program was necessary to engender the forthcoming Soviet response, it demonstrates that a restraint in the US arms build-up is not a *conditio sine qua non* for a forthcoming Soviet response to an American departure marked by a kind of nuclear essentialist thinking. Moreover, various features of the American political system – besides the administration's own proclivities – caused the Kennedy administration's successful nuclear essentialist-like departure to be combined with different Soviet essentialist-marked manifestations and measures, meaning that those measures were one condition, at least considered in domestic terms, for the administration's policy.

Later in the 1960s, American proposals about initiating Soviet–American talks on limiting strategic nuclear arms were initially met by Soviet rejection or cautiousness and, from 1967–8, by Soviet acceptance. That acceptance followed not only the American proposal which was combined with a distinct arms control reasoning, but also a strong American nuclear expansion that was inconsistent with that reasoning. Thus the 1960s saw a marked build-up of American intercontinental nuclear missiles (cf. Tables 1 and 2, pp. 186–7) and although the aggregate explosive power (or 'overkill'), measured in EMT, fell after the early 1960s (cf. Table 3, p. 187), Soviet leaders undoubtedly perceived the trend as one of strongly increasing American nuclear strength. Moreover, the Soviet acceptance of negotiations occurred when the United States adopted an ABM program (*Safeguard*) in 1969. As the Soviet government accepted the proposal for talks on limiting strategic nuclear arms exactly during those years, one can use this fact, separately considered, as a confirmation of an assertion about the need for 'strong' American nuclear forces in order to induce the Soviets to enter negotiations on limiting nuclear arms and conclude a fruitful agreement. Considering the issue in a broader perspective, it becomes evident, however, that this is a too rigid and partial reasoning. The examination of Soviet negotiating behavior during the latter half of the 1960s showed that the Soviet Union was not willing to initiate negotiations before it had reached a position close to numerical parity with the United States: the Soviet acceptance of bilateral talks did not appear before but after a strong expansion in Soviet offensive nuclear missiles (cf., Chapter 6, sections 2.1 and 3.2). That is, the Soviet willingness to enter SALT followed both an American (nuclear essentialist-like) offer, a strong American (Soviet essentialist-like) nuclear build-up *and* a strong Soviet build-up – which means that it is not possible from this to draw an unambiguous conclusion as to the validity of the 'negotiating from strength' image.

During the SALT I negotiations (1969–72), the Soviet negotiating behavior was in some respects markedly accommodating without it being possible always to explain that Soviet behavior as a reaction to an American action. Among such Soviet moves, seemingly intended as bargaining signals, was an unannounced unilateral moratorium on the construction of additional Soviet ICBM which, during 1970, was followed by the curtailment of some constructions already underway.[15] In early 1971, as the talks reached stalemate, the Soviets resumed the construction of new strategic launchers, hereby presumably also sending a signal, but a different one, to the United States. Following the agreement of May 1971, the Soviet Union again seemed to place a moratorium on new ICBM constructions. However, the American reaction to what could have been Soviet bargaining signals was cautious and their significance downplayed by the Nixon administration when they became known publicly. Perhaps changes in Soviet deployments were never intended to be perceived as a part of Soviet negotiating policy but as the actual deployment patterns during the SALT I negotiations showed unusual features, that interpretation cannot be excluded. As some of these Soviet moves can be invoked as evidence that an American 'negotiating from strength' policy paid off while others are more ambiguous, neither can this serve as the basis for an unambiguous conclusion concerning the validity of the 'negotiating from strength' notion. At most, it can be concluded from this broad overview of the SALT I negotiations that *both* American and Soviet nuclear 'strength' were a prerequisite for successful negotiations. Further scrutinizing the record through the late 1960s and early 1970s shows that the relation between American weapon programs and Soviet negotiating behavior varied, but one overall observation is that *while an American arms program sometimes seems to have been a necessary conditon for inducing the Soviet Union to accept limits on their own military capabilities, it was far from a sufficient condition.* Thus, while the *Safeguard* ABM program, adopted by the Senate in 1969, was followed by a clear Soviet interest in limiting both superpowers' strategic defenses – which the Soviet Union had strongly repudiated before the late 1960s – the American MIRV program was not followed by a corresponding Soviet line. One reason for the limited, and incalculable, American ability to influence Soviet negotiating behavior by pursuing an impressive nuclear deployment policy is that the Soviet Union mostly placed a higher priority on protecting their own military programs than on limiting American.[16]

Later in the 1970s, in 1977, the Soviet negotiating position did not respond forthcomingly to the Carter administration's cancellation of the B-1 bomber program, or other restraints in the American arms program. That 'missing' Soviet response may, of course, be explained by the simultaneous acceleration of other American arms programs, for example, cruise missiles. But in any case, the Carter administration's nuclear arms deployment policy – including that policy during its first years with the swing toward nuclear essentialism – was simply too heterogeneous to indicate any conclusion as to the validity of the 'negotiating from strength' notion. Hence, the record during those years does not substantiate a proposition that the Soviet Union did not reciprocate a unilateral and unambiguous American arms restraint with a forthcoming position in negotiations.

The apparent tightening of the Soviet negotiating line on strategic weapons in the late 1970s and early 1980s can be seen as a reaction to the evident changes in American nuclear policy during those years, including both a more distinct counterforce and war-fighting policy, a hardened negotiating position and an accelerated nuclear build-up. That is, that tightening of Soviet negotiation behavior could be a response to an American policy generally marked by 'negotiation from strength' features. On the other hand, it is worth noting that the Soviet Union in the 1980s (for example, in May 1982; cf. above) also has presented proposals surprisingly close to those proposals from the Carter administration which it strongly rejected in March 1977 and these Soviet proposals have been presented at a time when American nuclear policy in all respects was even more marked by distinct 'negotiation from strength' traits than a few years earlier. As to the Soviet reaction to SDI, an arms program which is also characterized by traditional 'negotiation from strength' ideas, it has been marked by a strong rejection and what seems to be a conspicuous hardening of Soviet START policy. However, as other aspects of Soviet negotiating policy have changed toward a more accommodating position and it generally applies that several aspects of Soviet policy were in a state of flux in the mid–to late 1980s, it is even more difficult than usual to single out specific actions as causing specific reactions. In any event the Soviet negotiating policy as to strategic arms has not, until 1987, displayed a similar flexibility as other aspects of Soviet policy during these years and this could be accounted for as a reaction to SDI.[17]

Concerning Soviet INF policy, the strong Soviet refusal in 1979 to enter negotiations if NATO's double-track decision was adopted suggests an action–reaction pattern where a proclaimed American nuclear deployment gets the Soviet Union to reject negotiations. The actual Soviet breaking off of the INF negotiations, as well as START, in late 1983 points in the same direction: American deployments stiffen Soviet negotiating behavior. However, the mere fact that negotiations on INF had been initiated in late 1981 represented a change in the Soviet position compared to two years earlier and the first conclusion one can draw from this is that a NATO/American decision to proceed with deployments has not, in itself, excluded a later Soviet willingness to enter negotiations. Several changes in the Soviet negotiating stance since the deployment of American intermediate-range nuclear missiles in Europe began in late 1983, particularly the agreement in December 1987, indicate a similar Soviet flexibility compared to what once seemed an immutable reaction to

American nuclear deployments. Whether the Soviet flexibility actually has been caused by the Western deployments is a moot question which cannot be completely settled on the basis of empirical observations. So far, it can only be concluded that if NATO's INF deployment has had this effect, the mere temporal distance between 'action' and 'reaction' suggests that other factors have been working as well. One should also note that the Soviet willingness to eliminate their short-range nuclear forces in Europe, where there have been no equivalent American forces deployed, shows the inadequacy of the 'negotiation from strength' idea if this applies to a general need for matching Soviet nuclear forces in all respects in order to have successful negotiations. Another noteworthy aspect of the changed Soviet line as to the two superpowers' INF deployments is that it indicates a possibly seminal alteration in a traditional Soviet preference (cf. above) for protecting their own deployments rather than limiting American. Generally, while empirical data on Soviet behavior can reasonably be interpreted as indicating that the Soviet Union would not have accepted the dismantling of its SS-20 missiles without at least some Western INF deployments (or expected deployments), the record also shows that Western deployments are not a sufficient cause for change in Soviet policy.

The conclusion from this examination of Soviet and American behavior since the early 1960s is the incentives for Soviet negotiating concessions have varied considerably during the years, the possibility for an efficient use of American arms programs as a negotiating leverage *vis-à-vis* the Soviet Union is highly incalculable beforehand. As a *cognitive* description of Soviet negotiating behavior, the notion that the United States has to 'negotiate from strength' cannot be maintained generally and in unqualified form.[18] It is something else that the record shows that an American arms program sometimes may have been one necessary conditions, among others, for fruitful negotiations. Another important conclusion is negative in that the record shows that what at one time has been presented as an unalterable negotiating position, or refusal to negotiate, by the Soviet government sometimes has proved alterable after a couple of years. That record does not prove the universal validity of an action–reaction pattern according to which any Soviet negotiating policy can be changed by American or Western standing firm. It only shows that a once 'unalterable' Soviet position *may* later be changed, for one reason or another.

Concluding that *the cognitive aspects of the 'negotiating from strength' image cannot be dismissed as baseless but also noting the inadequacy of that notion when Soviet behavior is examined*, it is evident that the interplay between the domestic American and the Soviet conditions for an American government's pursuing of the *action* aspect of that image pose peculiar problems. As it appeared from the review in Chapter 5, section 3, one reason for different administrations' difficulties in carrying out a coherent and steadfast policy *vis-à-vis* the Soviet Union originates in the very character of the American constitutional system with its checks-and-balances mechanisms. These make it extremely difficult for an administration to coordinate, control and orchestrate all aspects of its foreign policy, and persist in such a policy over some years. As shown in the review of several nuclear and Soviet-related issues since the early 1960s, the American political system's pluralism has often posed insurmountable obstacles for an efficient and expedient 'negotiating from strength' policy. At the same time, the review of the American tradition showed the close relation between that policy and historically dominant ideas about America's role in the world. That is, the domestic setting in the United States promotes both *needs* for that policy and *difficulties* for its implementation which means that *the domestic aspect of the operational environment is highly troublesome*. As one of the conditions for meaningful and successful Soviet–American negotiations on nuclear issues is a measure of American self-confidence, one can conclude that some American 'strength' is a necessity solely for this reason. Expressed with a nuance that is important: it is necessary that Americans *believe* in their own nuclear strength – and as shown in the section above, this is far from only a matter of the actual state of the nuclear balance. But as the analysis also demonstrated, the whole issue is not solely a matter of American beliefs. Also Soviet behavior indicates that an American 'negotiating from strength' policy has at least some relevance for obtaining successful negotiations between the superpowers without it being possible to determine its more exact conditions. In noting this clash between American ideas and policies and their indeterminable and changeable conditions – domestic as well as foreign – lies a critical conclusion of comparing image and operational environments as to the 'negotiating from strength' fixture.

3.   TRENDS

The analysis in Chapters 2–4 showed that two long-term trends are apparent in US governments' images since the early 1960s, namely a nuclear essentialist trend initiated in 1963 and a Soviet essentialist trend which became prominent after the early to mid-1970s. The two trends have been manifested in most aspects of US governments' images but with highly varying strengths (cf. pp. 126–9) and two features stand out: the changes concerning deterrence and US governments' interpretation of the Soviet view of nuclear arms. Comparing the two trends to operational environments will therefore concentrate on these two problems. First, the Soviet view of nuclear weapons and the changed American reading thereof, and while the Soviet view of the broad political impact of nuclear strength in peacetime was considered above, the following will focus on the Soviet view of the role of nuclear arms as outlined in item 5 of the two ideal types, i.e. the question of which role nuclear weapons should have as to war-prevention and war-fighting, with a view to evaluating the Soviet essentialist trend toward ascribing the Soviets a traditionalist, war-fighting view. Second, deterrence *vis-à-vis* the Soviet Union and the changed American image of it toward Soviet essentialism. While the first primarily considers cognitive aspects and therefore concentrates on drawing conclusions on the basis of elaborating the review of the object of American perceptions in Chapter 6, an examination of the validity of different deterrence images has to deal more closely with action and policy components and therefore includes findings of the examination of the domestic setting in Chapter 5. But the two aspects are closely related, primarily in that an analysis of deterrence concepts has to involve an examination of the significance of the Soviet view of deterrence.

1. The Soviet view

Synthesizing the examination of aspects of the Soviet Union as superpower with special reference to determining the Soviet view of nuclear arms, a first point concerns a basic methodical reservation. As an overall methodical procedure in attempts to understand the Soviet view of the role of nuclear weapons, the review in Chapter 6 showed that it is not fruitful generally to presume that the Soviet view is determined by some immutable technological features of nuclear weapons and the nuclear threat. This means that the Soviet view cannot be comprehended as a simple mirror image of those Western views which perceive the nuclear issue in such terms, cf. some nuclear essentialist marked views. However, this does not mean that the Soviets cannot possibly share Western approaches and attitudes to nuclear issues, including nuclear essentialist attitudes. While presuming that the Soviets' view of nuclear issues generally must be a mirror image of Western views becomes a conceptual straitjacket which prevents a deeper understanding, it is also fallacious to apply what has been termed a Reverse Mirror Image:[19] that because the Soviets 'are what they are' (and they are 'different'), they approach the nuclear issue in a wholly different way. Both such deductive methods are inadequate, and we are left to apply inductive methods.

Proceeding from this starting point, a first important observation is that there is no overall, constant, unambiguous and distinct 'Soviet view' of the role of nuclear arms. While all Soviet manifestations have embraced the opinion that the general recognition of the Soviet Union's 'equality' with the United States, including its nuclear equality, is a support for all peace-loving forces in the world (cf. above), the review of different aspects of the Soviet Union as superpower cannot wind up with one simple conclusion epitomizing *the* Soviet view of nuclear issues. However, while it is evident that Soviet society harbors divergent approaches to nuclear weapons which are publicly advanced, any adequate exposition of Soviet views must pay regard to three features which form the manifestation of Soviet views: the range of different views is clearly more circumscribed than in Western countries, open disputes between dissimilar views are very few, even if they recently have become more prominent, and it is impossible to point to just one case where a Soviet citizen has directly and publicly criticized the incumbent leadership's nuclear policy. (While former leaderships' policies are often denounced, current nuclear policies are not.) Still, these traits do not detract from the tenability of the conclusion that it is unfeasible to discern one specific view that can be presented as the Soviet view wherefore the term has to be applied cautiously and recognizing its defectiveness.

Attempting to identify the Soviet view(s) by going beyond this negative but useful point, it is expedient to apply the concept 'Soviet strategic culture'. A strategic culture means the 'sum total of ideas, conditioned emotional responses, and patterns of habitual behavior that members of a national strategic community have acquired through instruction or imitation and share with each other with regard to nuclear strategy'.[20] Applying this concept in an attempt to fathom the way the Soviets approach nuclear issues underlines that it is not merely a matter of discerning some more or less casual and volatile opinions but much more a problem of understanding how attitudes and positions may originate in a specific set of historical, structural and ideological background factors. As the Soviet view of deterrence plays a prominent role in the Soviet essentialist trend, it is highly relevant to consider the approach to deterrence in Soviet strategic culture – an issue that is frequently dealt with and contested in Western scholars' writings on the Soviet view of nuclear arms.[21]

A first point to stress in an outline of the Soviet view of deterrence is that Soviet writers and speakers generally dissociate themselves from the concept 'deterrence' which is represented as a highly pernicious Western idea. The second point is that sheer linguistic problems matter. There is no precise equivalent in the Russian language for the term 'deterrence' with all its connotations. The Russian language provides two corresponding terms: *sderzhivanie* which means 'checking', 'holding back', 'keeping out' or 'restraining', and *ustrashenie* which means 'frightening', 'intimidation' or 'terrorization', and while the term *yadernoye* (nuclear) *sderzhivanie* is sometimes used by Soviet writers to describe Soviet policy, *ustrashenie* is applied to Western policy.[22] Going a little further into the approach to deterrence in the Soviet strategic culture, three points have to be stressed: first, as a policy posture in peacetime deterrence is conceived of more broadly in the Soviet Union than in the United States, where both advocates of a nuclear essentialist and a Soviet essentialist-like policy tend to see deterrence solely in terms of a balance of armaments (but, of course, with highly divergent end results). Second, to the Soviet it is deterrence of *war*, rather than some kind of intra-war deterrence, that is crucial; it is essential to understanding the Soviet approach that they are not preoccupied with distinctions among various levels of (nuclear) war, contrary to many American strategic theories and government images.[23]

Third, it has been a basic trait of the Soviet view of the Soviet deterrence, at least until recently, that its starting point is deterrence by 'denial' rather than deterrence by 'punishment' – to apply a Western term[24] (cf. also the Soviet use of the term *yadernoye sderzhivanie*). To understand the Soviet view of or approach to deterrence, its dualism and composite character must be emphasized, however, and for that purpose the concept 'strategic subculture' is useful.

A strategic subculture is defined as a subsection of a broader strategic community with reasonably distinct beliefs and attitudes to strategic issues, with a distinct and historically traceable analytical tradition, with characteristic institutional associations, and with more or less distinct patterns of socialization to the norms of the subculture.[25] Focusing on the existence of divergent views in Soviet verbal manifestations throughout the period, both among leaders and other more or less official Soviet spokesmen, and asking about their relevance for an attempt to identify the Soviet view(s), it is useful to consider modernism and traditionalism as two strategic subcultures. The point is that the modernist and traditionalist spokesmen generally have been associated with different institutional structures in the Soviet society. While most modernist writers, *on the one hand*, have been either affiliated to civilian research institutions or commentators/journalists employed by Soviet media, primarily the most important Soviet newspapers, most traditionalist writers and writers expounding Soviet military doctrine, *on the other hand*, have been either so-called political officers, i.e. affiliated to the political administration of the Soviet armed forces, termed the Main Political Administration of the Soviet Army and Navy (MPA), or professional military officers in the armed forces. Even if this institutional distribution of different manifestations is not universal (cf., for example, Major General Talenskiy), a review of these Soviet strategic subcultures, the purposes and working methods of the different institutions provides an important contribution to evaluating the American image in that it explains how divergent Soviet manifestations throughout the years since the early 1960s may originate in tasks assigned to various institutions and in varying approaches predominant in these institutions.

Civilian research institutions devoting their time to international problems have been strongly expanded in the Soviet Union since the late 1960s.[26] The development of the institutes is related to different changes in Soviet foreign policy and international politics. One is the growth in international disarmament negotiations and the changed line pursued by the Soviet Union in these negotiations. Up to the early 1960s, Soviet negotiation policy was often merely made up of putting forward declarations on the need for complete and general disarmament and the preparatory work needed for such a policy is not that exacting. On the other hand, if you begin to participate actively in negotiations about specific and limited agreements, then the preparations needed become much more extensive and include, for example, a closer knowledge about those countries you negotiate with and their foreign and security policy. That type of of information cannot be provided through the usual channels of information, i.e. the diplomacy, which is primarily directed at providing day-to-day information about foreign countries, and the military research. Preparing Soviet policy in SALT during the 1970s and START and INF in the 1980s can necessitate more thorough analyses than the diplomacy is able to provide in addition to their routine work. It means, for example, that Soviet negotiators have a need to know something about the debate on security policy going on in the countries the Soviet Union negotiates with, especially the vast American literature and debate on strategic nuclear issues. Western, primarily American, writings that otherwise have been considered subtle trivialities – and/or Soviet negotiators and writers did not know at firsthand – got a new political relevance due to international trends and a changed Soviet policy. *Amerikanisti* (Americanologists) became a prestigious profession in the Soviet Union.[27] In some ways, the development of Soviet research institutes has been part of a professionalization and specialization of the foreign policy decision-making apparatus, 'apparatus' conceived in a broad sense, which is a process that has occurred in many countries.

A related development is the strong extension of contacts with Western research institutes and political organizations which creates a need for Soviet institutions that can take care of the contacts without formally being part of CPSU. The staffs of Soviet civilian research institutes are expedient to convey a more reasonable and academically marked version of Soviet peace and détente policy as they are rather sophisticated – particularly compared to traditional Soviet spokesmen – and 'understand' Western objections to aspects of Soviet foreign policy, especially when these are combined with strong dissociations from Western policies. Members of the civilian research institutes are thus much better fitted to propagate Soviet détente and peace policy in its various versions than other institutions in the Soviet political structure. Altogether, it follows from this review of the civilian research institutes' origins, focus of interest and working methods that they naturally incline toward a modernist persuasion. Their professional and political approach to international relations and nuclear issues predispose the institutes' staffs, as well as prominent modernist commentators in Soviet media some of which are affiliated with the institutes, to pay attention to a number of problems and issue areas – especially as to Soviet–American relations – that are not comprehensible in terms of rigid Marxism-Leninism. Whatever the actual motives for the vast growth in institutes since the late 1960s, it is indisputable that the professional and political needs flowing from new directions in Soviet foreign policy since then have created conspicuous built-in elements of modernist thinking in the upper Soviet political structure. Moreover, it is evident that some of this thinking, in embryo for two decades in the institutes, in a new and strengthened version recently has become much more prominent in Soviet policy.

As to the *Main Political Administration of the Soviet Army and Navy* (MPA), from which many traditionalist writings originate, it is an institution peculiar to the Soviet political system. MPA is the Party's 'watchdog' in the military as it has the responsibility of faithfully and vigilantly ensuring that the armed forces comply with the Party's policy. It shall monitor and report upon the state of morale within all parts of the Soviet military and supervise the activities of the many Party and Komsomol (CPSU's youth organization) organizations in the Soviet armed forces. MPA designs and administers an extensive program of political education in the military and it shall assure inculcation of the correct attitudes and values among military personnel; likewise, it is responsible for evaluating that persons who are being promoted have the correct 'party spirit'. It steers a comprehensive publication activity, including books, pamphlets, periodicals and newspapers, which have elaborated the Soviet military doctrine and mostly expressed traditionalist views.[28] As the official task of MPA is to supervise political education and maintain pure Marxism-Leninism in the Soviet military, it may be difficult to authorize assertions that a nuclear war might result in the annihilation of (also) the Soviet Union as the first socialist country and the vanguard in mankind's progressive development toward socialism. Putting the Soviet Union on a par with capitalist countries – even when the nuclear threat is considered – is ideologically damaging and puts a question mark on that historical determinism which forms the legitimization of the Soviet rule. Thus when prominent political officers stress traditionalist views and repudiate modernist thoughts (mostly by censuring similar views in the United States), they have at a few occasions directly stated that modernist views in Soviet writings were *ideologically* dangerous.[29] Noting this institutional and ideological background does not prove the actual meaning of a traditionalist statement from a political officer, but it indicates an important factor that has to be considered in any conclusive reasoning based on these Soviet statements.

Having outlined these diverging strategic subcultures in the Soviet Union, and proceeding to ask which subculture underlines the Soviet, leadership's overall approach to nuclear arms, it is first worth emphasizing that modernism and traditionalism only to a limited degree can be comprehended as different contending and struggling views, groups or 'wings' among which one – via the specific Soviet political process – prevails or gets the upper hand in the Soviet leadership. The issue is not so much separating 'hawks' (traditionalists) from 'doves' (modernists) in the Soviet society and leadership. Rather, the different strategic subcultures must be seen as varying approaches that, seen from a Soviet point of view, supplement each other and constantly influence Soviet decision-makers' approach to nuclear issues. Modernist-minded leaders may definitely be more sympathetic to one strategic subculture with its stress on diplomatic means than traditionalist minded leaders with their emphasis on unilateral military means. But all Soviet leaders share some basic objectives and they do not necessarily feel a contradiction between different subcultures/ approaches/views/methods in the same way as Western leaders do. In this context it means that all Soviet leaders can easily recognize mutual deterrence as a reality even if they all share a basic predisposition for deterrence by denial, and even if some in the Soviet leadership may experience more political and intellectual discomfort in recognizing that reality than others. In any case, it follows from Chapter 6 as well as these elaborations that *Soviet leaders since some time around the later 1960s have seen mutual deterrence as a reality*, therefore a plain assertion that they consider a nuclear war as 'winnable' cannot be upheld. At the same time, it is also evident that they do not see that situation as ideal and, within some limits that are not determinable in detail, seek to assure that the Soviet Union can survive a nuclear war.

Understanding the existence of this dualism in the Soviet approach to deterrence and nuclear war and grasping why and how Soviet political and military leaders can paper over what seems a double attitude, it is important to remember that no incumbent Soviet leader has ever been challenged, in a public debate or an election campaign, to explain the Soviet Union's nuclear policy. These issues are simply not subject to public debate. Where many inherent contradictions in Western approaches to deterrence are openly displayed in public discussions about Western nuclear policies, and sometimes recognized directly by government officials, corresponding inconsistencies in Soviet approaches are papered over in a dualistic and composite deterrence doctrine that nobody in the Soviet Union queries in public.[30] This is crucial to note because it helps us understand why divergent trends can be present in the Soviet approach without necessarily jumping to the explanation that they consciously are produced and manipulated by a leadership which has carefully prepared and reasoned out all implications. To be sure, Soviet duplicity may sometimes be a valid explanation and it must also be noticed that the Soviet political system gives better possibilities for getting away with that behavior than democratic systems do. Still, when we try to comprehend the Soviet approach to the, after all, self-contradictory concept 'nuclear deterrence', it is important to pay regard to other explanations too.

Assessing the validity and more precise nature of an overall conclusion that Soviet leaders have accepted some kind of mutual deterrence and adopted a more modernist marked view since the late 1960s, one specific problem concerns the weight of Soviet leaders' and other Soviet spokesmen's statements pointing in that direction. Can these declarations and writings be used as evidence? Answering that question, it is important to stress that modernist statements from Soviet spokesmen frequently have an external function in that they are aimed at appealing to Western publics. However, that obviously correct observation does not, by itself, rule out that modernist declarations reflect Soviet views (or 'real views'). As one cannot presume that the Soviets 'always mean what they say', neither can one presume that the Soviets 'never mean what they say'.[31] Such commonplaces are simply deceptive when one considers the Soviet view on the basis of their public statements. This appears, first, when Soviet essentialist interpretations of the Soviet view are supported by references to the Soviet military doctrine and traditionalist statements ('the Soviets mean what they say and say what they mean'), while Soviet modernist expositions are simply dismissed as propaganda. On the other hand, some nuclear essentialist readings of the Soviet view turn this deficient reasoning on its head: modernist statements are used to 'prove' the real Soviet view while traditionalist statements are dismissed by referring to their domestic homiletic function. But in no case is the relation between Soviet verbal manifestations and a/the Soviet view straightforward and it therefore has to be emphasized that the evidently increasing prominence of modernist statements can only be a conditional corroboration of the overall conclusion.

Another specific problem in assessing the tenability of this conclusion is the meaning of Soviet manifestations stressing the political nature of nuclear war. Do such traditionalist statements prove that the Soviets think they can fight and win a nuclear war?[32] As reviewed above (pp. 203f.), the Clausewitz–Lenin dictum that 'war is a continuaton of politics by other means' plays an essential role in the general Marxist-Leninist conception of the relation between war and politics. The notion inherent in the dictum is that notwithstanding how military means (including nuclear arms) are used, political purpose must ultimately be in control – and that is something quite different from a plain war-winning notion. This reading of Soviet uses of the dictum can certainly be subject to querying in various ways but the central point is that statements about the political nature of nuclear war cannot meaningfully be used to prove that the Soviets share a distinct war-fighting and war-winning view of nuclear arms. One could rather reason that precisely the fact that Soviet leaders do see nuclear war as an extension of politics strengthens a hope of avoiding it, through deterrence, arms control, or some combination of these. Soviet manifestations about the political essence of nuclear war seem cynical to Western, in particular nuclear essentialist-minded, observers and that may be one reason why they have become less prominent and recently directly repudiated by Soviet writers. It is therefore important not to draw simplistic conclusions about the Soviet view of nuclear weapons from the presence or absence of Soviet reiterations of the Clausewitz–Lenin dictum. In particular, the fact that Soviet commentators since the mid-1980s have openly rejected Clausewitz's dictum (it is no longer attributed to Lenin) cannot be used to prove that the Soviets *now* repudiate that a nuclear war can be won.

Concluding that the Soviet leadership has moved toward modernist views since the late 1960s, it must be noted that different indicators of the Soviet view are ambiguous, primarily because aspects of Soviet nuclear deployments may indicate another conclusion. The problem with using characteristics of a country's military hardware as an indicator of the decision-makers' views/intentions/policy is that any reasoning on the basis of force deploymennts has to include some additional assumptions concerning the decision-makers' subjective interpretations that, in principle, are unverifiable and irrespective of all differences between the Soviet Union and Western countries, it therefore has to be maintained that in the Soviet case, as among other countries, the relation between force development and what is termed 'view' is not straightforward.[33] Still, even when this methodical reservation is observed, it has to be noted that parts of the evidence on the Soviet view of nuclear arms may weaken the conclusion that the Soviets have moved towards modernism.

One could adduce that the conclusion that Soviet leaders have moved toward a modernist view since the late 1960s is shored up by a simple examination of some basic common-sense Soviet self-interests in the nuclear age which has nothing to do with ascribing Soviet leaders an altruistic do-gooder point of view. While not dismissing the tenability of this argument completely, it has to be noted, though, that uses of that reasoning easily become a mere display of one's own ethnocentrism. It is a basic assumption underlying this study that an assertion as to this or that country's 'obvious self-interest' is a shaky ground for explaining or predicting somebody's whole thinking about and approach to the nuclear issue (as distinct from predicting the behavior in a situation with immediate danger of nuclear war); thus, applying a similar 'common-sense' reasoning in an attempt to explain the development in US governments' views of nuclear issues since the early to mid-1970s shows its inadequacy. It is more relevant to point out that as Soviet modernist statements/propaganda about the 'common nuclear threat' increasingly have supplanted traditionalist expositions Soviet speakers and writers may become hostages to their own rhetoric. Even leaders in a country with many authoritarian and totalitarian characteristics cannot anticipate and determine the outcome of their own actions and public declarations/propaganda.

Altogether, the conclusion that the Soviets have moved toward some diluted, and more recently marked, modernist views since the late 1960s must be put forward with due reservations, 'but's and 'on the other hand's. It is particularly worth stressing that the Soviet approach has had a dichotomous mark in that more or less distinct modernist opinions have been advanced side by side with traditionalist opinions during most of the time, and this has been closely related to salient political structures of the Soviet state. Recently, however, this has become less prominent as more traditionalist views have disappeared. Still, that conclusion means that the cognitive aspect of this part of the Soviet essentialist trend of US governments' image cannot be validated. The further meaning of this will be set out in the next section.

2. Deterrence

Assessing the validity of US governments' images of nuclear deterrence *vis-à-vis* the Soviet Union, a first observation concerns the elusive and slippery meaning of the term 'deterrence'. Deterrence is a buzz-word in debates on nuclear policy and the phrase 'deterring the Soviets' is often a slogan invoked to explain and justify many kinds of policy without it being evident what is meant. Like other catchwords in political debates, uses of the term often hide, intentionally or unintentionally, the nature of contested issues. But in this case, of course, simply noting the ambiguous use of a term does not dispose of a fruitful analytical use of the term. What it means, though, is that an essential part of evaluating deterrence images and associated measures must focus on unravelling and clarifying conceptual ambiguities.

As a first rough delimitation of the concept is that deterrence denotes the manifestation of some physical or verbal activities designed to influence somebody not to do something.[34] Under this broad definition deterrence has to do with the relationship between adversaries and involves the use of a *threat* in order to prevent an adversary *action*. The adversaries in this context are the Soviet Union as the one to be 'deterred' and the United States as the 'deterrer'. The 'threat' manifested may consist of many different nuclear or non-nuclear measures and as a basic differentiation one may distinguish between deterrence resulting from an American capacity to *deny* some gains (territorial or other) to the Soviet Union (deterrence through denial), i.e. physically impeding an unwanted Soviet action, and deterrence resulting from an American capacity to *retaliate* against the Soviet Union (deterrence through punishment) in the extent of that unwanted action. As to the Soviet action that the deterrence is designed to prevent, it may range from all kinds of *military actions* (from a Soviet-initiated nuclear war to a lesser conventional attack, against the Unites States or its allies, the last termed extended deterrence) to many kinds of unwanted *political and non-military actions* of which some come close to the situations considered in section 2.1 above. One problem which is central to evaluating any deterrence posture concerns its *credibility* in the eyes of the deterred (the Soviet Union) and that has to be assessed in relation to the action the deterrence threat is designed to prevent as well as the character of the threat invoked, where the last has to make allowance for both the capability and the will to implement it, either by denying the Soviet Union some gain or retaliating against the Soviet Union in the event of some Soviet action. As to credibility, it is important to note whether the action a deterrent threat is designed to prevent concerns the adversary's employment of nuclear arms in some context – for example, in a direct nuclear attack – or whether it concerns the deterrer's threat to employ nuclear arms if the adversary initates war with or without employing nuclear arms, i.e. a deterrence that includes a possible first-use of nuclear weapons.

Applying this rough conceptual scheme as a starting point for evaluating US governments' images of deterrence *vis-à-vis* the Soviet Union, a first problem concerns the criteria to be applied when a nuclear deterrence doctrine is evaluated, that is, what is a relevant concept of truth when we assess the validity of a certain deterrent threat in relation to some action that is to be prevented?[35] A deterrence image cannot be tested in the same strict sense as many empirical theories because usual concepts of truth (for example, factual verification) cannot be adequately applied. It is also a logical fallacy to infer that since there has not been a Soviet military attack on Western Europe or the United States (or any other specific unwanted Soviet action), this proves the effectiveness of the American deterrence; at most, one can conclude on this basis that the effectiveness of the American deterrent has not been *dis*proved. The central problem in any attempt to evaluate a deterrence doctrine or policy is that one has to allow for the cumulative effect of a number of uncertainties and unknowns that are critical for reaching any final, and even approximately final, conclusion.[36] Stating this, it is important to note that the uncertainty as to the actual substance of the Soviet leadership's view of the role of nuclear arms and other aspects of Soviet nuclear policy is only one factor underlying this uncertainty. Also if the Soviet policy were much more distinctive, *in whatever direction*, than concluded in this study, then many factors which are critical for evaluating a deterrence policy would be indeterminate. The essential point is that the validity of a deterrence posture can only be reasoned on the basis of a long chain of assumptions about Soviet as well as American behavior in various imagined situations, and the tenability of these assumptions can only hypothesized or postulated, never known for certain, and that irrespective of the substance of Soviet policy. The actual reasoning applied can seem, of course, more or less reasonable in the light of different conclusions as to the character of Soviet policy, but the crux of the matter is that there will always be a critical remnant of uncertainty when any deterrence doctrine is evaluated.

One conclusion from this short introduction to the validity question concerning deterrence images is that a persistent quest for the correct answer to the question 'what deters the Soviet Union?' is futile. There can be no perfect solution to the problem of nuclear deterrence.[37] Moreover, it has to be emphasized that the lack of adequate empirical theory by which to determine the validity of a deterrence policy cannot be made good through the development of more extensive empirical theory, for example, following a greater opening of Soviet society.[38] More adequate empirical theory may elucidate various subsidiary questions when a deterrence policy is shaped, but it cannot form the basis of *the* valid image or policy, and that is due to some fundamental problems linked to the very idea and logic of nuclear deterrence.

The validity question can be approached from another angle as well – the credibility issue. Focusing on the credibility of a deterrence posture, and again simplifying a problem that is complex in the sense that it can and has been elaborated into a vast number of subproblems which can be considered from many imaginable angles, the central problem is that any deterrence policy based on whatever type of nuclear retaliation carries with it salient elements of self-deterrence, therefore it will appear defective when the credibility criterion is stressed. Otherwise expressed: since all deterrence doctrines which include some employment of nuclear weapons are bound to be based on a mixture of inherent and calculated considerations – 'inherent' in the sense that a deterrence effect arises from the very existence of nuclear arms ('existential deterrence'), 'calculated' in the sense that a deterrence effect is designed and manipulated by the deterrer – any nuclear deterrence posture will include a certain measure of inherent self-deterrence that cannot be removed by the deterrer by any technological or intellectual 'fix'.[39] Deterrence and self-deterrence are inextricably intertwined, therefore all deterrence policies will appear defective when credibility is focused and it can reasonably be assumed that, given the very existence of nuclear arms, some self-deterrence is inherent in a deterrence policy which include some kind of retaliation. That applies especially to a first-use of nuclear arms but also in other cases may the possibility of self-deterrence work; while credibility of a threat to apply nuclear arms may be less unattainable if it concerns a situation where the opponent initiates the use of nuclear weapons, any type of deterrence in the nuclear age – or a situation where the deterrer believes his own society is vulnerable to nuclear attack – may be defective when credibility is focused, primarily due to the self-deterrence contingency.

This can be illustrated considering one specific problem often raised in this context, namely the consequences for credibility of the evidently massive increase in Soviet nuclear forces since the early 1960s, in particular when American ICBM's increasing vulnerability is included. Assessing the censure of a nuclear essentialist-like deterrence policy from various angles – which cannot all be dismissed as merely fanciful in the light of different characteristics of Soviet nuclear policy – there seems no doubt that nuclear essentialist deterrence images and policies *are* defective, and increasingly so when the credibility criterion is emphasized in the light of the self-deterrence contingency. However, the ever-present, outstanding problem is that suggested Soviet essentialist remedies also cause critical self-deterrence problems and therefore are faulty as well when credibility is stressed. The contingency of self-deterrence cannot be removed unilaterally. As no Soviet essentialist suggestion can point out a procedure whereby the United States unilaterally could remove or reduce Soviet nuclear forces to an insignificant level, the actual size and composition of Soviet nuclear forces has – at least since some point in the late 1960s – been inessential when it comes to evaluating various ways to abolishing or seriously reducing the credibility problem. Especially concerning the ICBM vulnerability issue, it is worth keeping in mind that any conclusion about its meaning, politically and militarily, is substantially determined by the framework of assumptions applied. The problem is far more a state of mind than a technical or physical fact and by continually paying attention to it in their public manifestations, American policy-makers and opinion leaders may enhance the self-deterrence and encourage adversaries' inclinations to risky actions.[40] Noting that does not solve the problem but directs attention toward a more basic, and even more intractable, predicament, particularly in that it shows how the problem is closely related to the character of the domestic American political system. No government in a democratic society can fully control public manifestations on such an issue (or any issue), and so that aspect of the problem cannot be removed. The point is, however, that in its attempts to deal with the issue and correct it, US governments may have aggravated it.

The conclusion that there are critical self-deterrence problems related to any deterrence policy which is based on some kind of nuclear retaliation has been one of the basic arguments adduced by advocates of a Soviet essentialist deterrence policy and has lead to a greater interest for deterrence by denial strategies. The American SDI program was presented by the Reagan administration in somewhat changing and diverging terms (of. pp. 111–13) but one aim has been that it should demonstrate whether a fully effective shield against nuclear arms is possible, thereby elucidating the feasibility of fully credible deterrence by denial policy. Now (in the spring of 1989) it seems that the Bush administration has abandoned that idea, primarily because it thinks the Soviet Union can easily implement countermeasures which can assure a Soviet retaliatory capability against the American continent. That is, the Bush administration has concluded that deterrence by denial is defective for technological reasons.

However, in particular in the light of the findings in this study another consideration is much more significant when the validity of deterrence by denial images has to be evaluated. The problem is that even if various technological problems are overcome in ways that cannot be imagined today, a fundamental and disquieting uncertainty will remain concerning the 'fully effective shield's' actual effectiveness in a nuclear war, limited or unlimited. In the absence of an actual test – that is, 'test' in a war, not a peacetime test – this can never be known.[41] That means that not even the deployment of an all-embracing shield against all kinds of nuclear attack can remove what is ultimately the crux of the matter in this field in the nuclear age, namely the fear of nuclear obliteration. Furthermore, the very democratic characteristics of the American political system, especially the freedom of expression for challenging the incumbent administration in Washington, assures that any residual doubt concerning the actual operation of a deployed defensive system against nuclear missiles and bombers can play a political role. The review of the American political process (cf. Chapter 5, pp. 148ff.) clearly demonstrated the political vulnerability of any administration to criticism of the 'credibility' of its nuclear policy. A deterrence policy based on deterrence by denial will, if anything, be even more vulnerable in the American political process than a deterrence policy based on some type of retaliation and can therefore easily give rise to claims for some 'assured' retaliation capability to back up the deterrence effect of a defensive shield – and then the defective credibility of deterrence by the threat of retaliation is back as a political issue. Thus even if there may be more or less valid arguments for a greater role for strategic defense as a component in US nuclear policy, the conclusion is that no deterrence through denial policy, or combination of deterrence through denial and deterrence through retaliation, can remove the credibility problem. For evaluating that argument, it is all-important to note that this is not an assertion on the technical unfeasibility of a 'fully effective shield'. The central point is that the 'effectiveness' and further meaning of such a shield, will be assessed by actors *in the American political system* – and then it easily breaks down, quite irrespective of technological 'facts'. From this it follows that if the Strategic Defense Initiative can be seen as a prominent expression of the Reagan administration's regeneration of America's self-confidence, the analysis of the domestic American setting in Chapter 5 leads to the observation that any aspiration to self-reliant, and supposedly (i.e. by an incumbent administration) fully credible, deterrence policy also contains the seeds of several future discords in American politics.

One specific aspect of the Soviet essentialist trend has been the idea that an efficient and credible American deterrence policy must be based on and be symmetrical with the Soviet view of deterrence, and as the Soviets, according to this interpretation, clearly share a counterforce and war-fighting approach (eventually including a war-winning notion), the United States has to adopt a similar nuclear deterrence policy. Considered in a broader · social science context, this idea of the necessity of a symmetrical deterrence doctrine is a special case of *Duprée's theorem*[42] which states that in a protracted conflict, the opponents must employ the same means and if they do not, that side which fails to modernize these particular means to match the other side, is doomed – that is, if the United States does not imitate the Soviets' nuclear doctrine, it will be defeated, politically and militarily. As a first step in evaluating this special convergence idea, it can be noticed that it has often been supported by a highly selective and inconsistent reading of the Soviet view where some Soviet verbal manifestations (for instance, writings on nuclear war-fighting) have been picked out as highly representative of the Soviet view and significant to the shaping of American deterrence policy, while other Soviet expositions (for instance, the repudiations of limited nuclear war and intra-war deterrence) have been ignored or rejected as irrelevant.[43] However, while such fluctuating lines of argument are important to note in an examination of American perceptions, merely calling attention to logical inconsistencies in Soviet essentialist arguments does not constitute a refutation of the conclusion: that the United States has to imitate and emulate Soviet deterrence policy in order to deter the Soviet Union. Evaluating that image must be based on an independent assessment of both action and cognitive aspects, i.e. is the Soviet view relevant as guideline when American deterrence policy is shaped and, if so, what is the Soviet view?

Strictly speaking, a claim that the Soviet view will determine the efficiency and credibility of a deterrence posture *vis-à-vis* the Soviet Union is obviously correct. That is implied in the very notion of deterrence where the aim is to influence 'somebody's' mind or decisional calculation of net gain or loss connected with some behavioral choice in a given situation. From that it follows logically that one must focus on how this or that deterrence policy conceivably may influence that 'somebody's' choice of behavior in different future situations.[44] However, stating that logical and linguistic *definition* of the problem does not, by itself, tell which factors will enter into the adversary's calculations in some future situation. That is a much more cumbersome problem than it seems when the term the 'Soviet view' is presented as an unambiguous clue to determine the way Soviet leaders will reason in a given situation and the outcome of that reasoning. It therefore has to be emphasized that neither does the conclusion in this study – that Soviet leaders have moved toward a more, and lately a distinct, modernist view – provide the key to answering the question 'what deters the Soviets'.

For the 'deterrer' (here the United States) trying to figure out the 'deterred''s (here the Soviet Union's) decision calculus in some future contingency, it is always a natural mistake that he unrealistically projects his own perception onto Soviet decision-makers. That objection may sometimes be raised meaningfully against nuclear essentialist images of the Soviet decision calculus. However, advocates of a Soviet essentialist image may too unrealistically 'project' their own thinking on the role of nuclear weapons onto Soviet leaders, for example, when they stress the danger of a limited Soviet counterforce strike against American ICBM.[45] Another common inference among advocates of a Soviet essentialist reading of the Soviet calculus in some future situation is the reasoning, based on a kind of reversed mirror-image, that Soviet leaders will be deterred only if their won leadership bunkers are targeted in a nuclear war. Quite apart from the impact such American statements may have on Soviet perceptions – and imagining that, it may be fruitful to infer from the impact corresponding Soviet writings have had on American observers – it is a question whether or not that way of figuring out Soviet leaders' choice of behavior in a given situation represents a fundamental error about the Soviet leadership's level of callousness about Soviet sufferings in a nuclear war.[46] Moreover, as the number of Soviet deaths in the event of a nuclear 'exchange' would probably be counted in millions over a few hours or days, rather than years as in the Second World War, it is highly superficial to refer to Soviet behavior in that war as a basis for imagining the Soviet view of nuclear war and its consequences for deterrence,[47] and that quite apart from the fact that the Soviet losses during those years cannot be seen as a result of any prepared decision calculus.

From the preceding section it appeared that an interpretation of the Soviet view that concludes that the Soviet Union has adopted a clear-cut counterforce and war-fighting – eventually including a war-winning – approach is far too simplistic. The Soviet view of nuclear arms and deterrence undoubtedly includes elements of counterforce and war-fighting but it is clearly much broader and composite. Also if it is presumed that the Soviet approach is distinctly oriented toward war-fighting and war-winning, though, a claim that American deterrence *vis-à-vis* the Soviet Union has to 'mirror-image' that doctrine in order to make the deterrence effective and credible is difficult to validate. First, one must be deeply skeptical about the feasibility of any over-complex nuclear war-fighting notion; there are good reasons to conclude that nuclear weapons are simply too powerful and have too many disparate and unpredictable effects, therefore the very idea that a nuclear 'exchange' can be limited and controlled is far-fetched. Besides, no single country can assure that a nuclear war can be controlled and limited for that requires that all or both participants are able and willing to exercise various restraints, and so it may be pertinent to note that it is much easier for the United States to persuade the Soviet Union to keep the peace, by deterrence or otherwise, than to persuade the Soviet Union to fight a certain kind of war by showing targeting restraint in intercontinental nuclear warfare.[48] All that is important to keep in mind and stress as a first step in assessing the validity of this special type of 'reverse mirror-image' deterrence doctrine. But the question whether such American 'war-fighting in order to deter the Soviets' images are valid is even more complicated and abstruse: it depends on determining whether Soviet political and military leaders *believe* that American leaders *believe* in a war-fighting strategy because the Soviets *believe* in ... In any case, that elaborate psychology of nuclear deterrence is immune to validation as any testing (i.e. 'testing' in peacetime) will be lost in abstract and imaginary reasonings about Soviet reasonings about American reasonings, and so on (and vice versa). However, it must be emphasized that neither is there any empirical method which unambiguously can disprove the validity of this aspect of a Soviet essentialist image of deterrence. No empirical or scientific procedure can settle the issue of whether the cognitive aspect of this special convergence-in-reverse image is valid.[49] But such examinations can help clarify the problem, primarily by showing the numerous fallacies arising from any absolute conclusion about how to 'deter the Soviets'.

But the Soviet choice of behavior in a situation with immediate danger of nuclear war cannot be figured out merely by examining the Soviet view of nuclear deterrence in abstract and its interplay with American nuclear policy. Soviet behavior in such a situation will be highly influenced by Soviet leaders' assessment of the political interests at stake, and when that factor is included a hypothetical situation becomes even more complex to survey. Yet, some guidelines seem clear. Soviet leaders' primary political priority is undoubtedly the continuing existence of the Soviet state, therefore a danger, or a perceived (i.e. 'perceived' by the Soviets) danger, to it can be assumed to induce them to run much higher risks of nuclear war. Next in Soviet leaders' putative list of priorities is preserving the socialist one-party system in Eastern Europe and their membership of the Warsaw Pact. Then, the interplay between Soviet and Western interests in the Persian Gulf and the Middle East can conceivably escalate into war and nuclear war, but Soviet interests in these areas are clearly less vital than the first two.[50] Next, the preservation of Soviet-supported Marxist-Leninist governments in countries in the Third World can be assumed to be important to Soviet behavior in a given situation. Other factors too may well be significant. For example, it can reasonably be argued that Soviet leaders in some situations will run higher risks of nuclear war if they see the societal fabric of Western countries is breaking down, because in such a situation they may perceive Western leaders as less inclined and less able to behave rationally.

Altogether, it follows from this short overview of the conjectured Soviet willingness to risk nuclear war in order to protect and pursue political interests that it cannot provide one general and unambiguous answer to a question about what it requires to deter the Soviets from nuclear war. But it indicates that Soviet behavior in a high-tension crisis is not a given quality that can be grasped and understood by locating a hidden, but 'real', Soviet view or doctrine in abstract which will be influenced only by the actual American or Western deterrence posture. That is why when assessing the (in)appropriateness of the action aspect of a Soviet essentialist image of deterrence it is not especially important to discover how far the Soviet leadership has moved from a traditionalist to a modernist view. Other factors are more important. Thus there is little doubt that the effectiveness of a deterrence policy would decrease if Western countries ignore the fact that any war-averting policy vis-à-vis the Soviet Union must include elements of both deterrence and reassurance, the last primarily in relation to high-priority Soviet goals as indicated above. Rejecting the relevance of that problem may be the most critical defect of the more explicit versions of Soviet essentialism reasoning on deterrence. But two problems should be noted when the significance of 'reassuring' Soviet interests is stressed as an inherent part of any deterrence. First, calling a Soviet goal or interest 'high-priority' does not mean that it is immutable; thus it is obvious that Gorbachev perceives the actual meaning of the two top priorities – the continued existence of the Soviet state and the preservation of socialist one-party systems in Eastern Europe – somewhat differently from Brezhnev, for instance. Second, as challenges to such Soviet goals may arise *inside* the Soviet-dominated sphere, particularly in Eastern Europe, one important conclusion is that no American deterrence policy can obviate the need for some embarrassing trade-offs between essential political values in various future situations where the actual criticality of the stakes are unknown, apart from the fact that they are all high. On the whole, this examination indicates that the action aspects of different Soviet essentialist images of deterrence are at least as flawed in their attempt to narrow down or eliminate awkward choice situations as the nuclear essentialist images whose defectiveness they aim to put right. Otherwise expressed, any nuclear deterrence policy, including all distinct types of 'minimum' or 'existential' deterrence, will include the presence of multiple, competing values and interests – i.e. value-complexity[51]–and uncertainty. From this it is only a small step to conclude that the very *contingency* of such awkward choice situations is an inherent part of the nuclear age.

Another conclusion concerns the relation between the credibility of a nuclear deterrence posture and the character of the American political system. While the credibility of a deterrence policy logically turns on the actual substance of the Soviet view in a particular situation (as distinct from the general Soviet view of nuclear arms), both the review in this section and the review of the process of perception in Chapter 5 clearly point to the conclusion that any deterrence policy which may have 'enough' credibility in Soviet eyes will be vulnerable viewed from an incumbent administration in Washington. The very logic of nuclear deterrence may be defective but the democratic and open character of the domestic political system in the United States assures that *no matter how credible any deterrence posture is in Soviet eyes, it will easily become defective viewed from an incumbent administration in Washington.*

4. AMERICAN PERCEPTIONS AND THE FUNDAMENTAL ATTRIBUTION ERROR

Dealing with how ordinary people perceive and explain the actions of their fellow human beings, social psychologists have developed attribution theories (cf. pp. 20–1) and identified a *fundamental attribution error*, by which they mean a tendency for human beings to overemphasize dispositional variables when observing and interpreting the behavior of others. Focusing on actors in the international system, students of international affairs have elaborated these theories and demonstrated their relevance, in particular for adversaries' perception of each other.[52] The central notion in the fundamental attribution error is that an adversary's 'bad' behavior is seen in dispositional terms, while his 'good' behavior is seen in situational terms.[53] There is, however, some confusion in the literature on attribution theories about whether the term 'error' denotes the existence of a *bias* in the *process* of attribution or a *distortion* in the *content* of the attribution, which presupposes laying down some criteria for estimating accuracy and validity. [54] As concluded at the end of Chapter 5 (p. 180), salient chacteristics of the domestic political process in the United States induce US governments to represent the Soviet Union as a nuclear adversary in dispositional terms, which means that the fundamental attribution error can be confirmed as to the process of perception in this case. However, as elaborated in the introduction to this chapter, it is important to distinguish between the process of perception and the content of images – i.e. between the attributional process and the content of attributions.

Focusing on the contents of attributions/perceptions, the fundamental attribution error has a special relevance for comparing US governments' images with operational environments in that both the two fixtures and the two trends dominating since the mid-1970s tend toward interpreting Soviet nuclear policies and positions as a manifestation of the Soviet state's basic traits – Soviet nuclear policies and positions have been seen as manifestations of the inherent nature of the Soviet state. As fundamental characteristics of Soviet behavior as a nuclear superpower, directly or indirectly, are attributed to and explained by referring to underlying internal dispositions of the Soviet Union, rather than to aspects of the Soviet Union's external situation, it may be asked if the cognitive aspects of these constancies and long-term trends of American perceptions reflect the fundamental attribution error – 'error' denoting inaccurate attributions. That is, have US governments overestimated the impact of dispositional factors and underestimated the role of situational factors in their images of the Soviet Union as nuclear superpower? framed as a hypothesis about American perceptions of the Soviet Union as nuclear adversary, the fundamental attribution error states: *US governments have overestimated the significance of dispositional factors in interpreting the Soviet Union as a superpower and underestimated the degree to which undesired Soviet behavior has been a response to situational factors.* [55]

Given the predominant characteristics of US governments' perceptions through almost a generation, this hypothesis can serve as a framework for a complementary procedure for comparing images with operational environments. An examination aimed at delimiting and assessing the validity of the fundamental attribution error in different respects can add perspectives which will elucidate critical traits of American (mis) perceptions of the Soviet Union in a new way. Applying this perspective means that the political and intellectual problems for US governments' public interpretations and representations of the Soviet Union as the United States' political opponent in the nuclear age is approached more abstractly than when the actual content of fixtures and trends are directly compared with operational environments. Thus, the aim in this section is – given US governments' predisposition for dispositional attributions – to elaborate if and how basic internal and external characteristics of the Soviet superpower lead to dispositional – (respectively situational) oriented interpretations of Soviet behavior.

In order to establish a basis for that it is first necessary to consider and elaborate such aspects of the Soviet Union as a superpower which may offer alternative explanations of Soviet nuclear policies and positions in terms of the distinction between dispositional and situational variables. The first part therefore focuses on two dispositional variables: first, some historical characteristics of Russian and Soviet relations with the outside world with a special view to assessing how they have engendered a legacy that may have consequences for the Soviet position as a superpower; secondly, Marxism-Leninism as the official Soviet ideology with a special view to assessing how its doctrine on international relations influences the Soviet Union's position as superpower. The criterion for focusing on these tow factors and their impact is that Soviet essentialist fixtures and trends held by US governments have assumed and asserted, although in varying compositions and with varying weight, that fundamental historical and ideological traits of the Soviet state ultimately underlie essential characteristics of Soviet nuclear policy. The second part focuses on two situational variables which have largely been dismissed as insignificant by US governments, viz. American nuclear policy and behavior and changing patterns of East–West tension and détente during the period.[56] The elaboration of these internal and external properties of the Soviet Union as the United States' nuclear adversary can therefore form the basis for assessing the tenability of central characteristics attributed the Soviet superpower by US governments, and thereby the fundamental attribution error as this refers to the content of the attribution.

1. Dispositional variables

Both the legacy of Russia's and the Soviet Union's relations with the outside world and Marxism-Leninism are considered constant – as distinct from their actual interpretations by Soviet writers and speakers – in this examination. Thus the idea is, as a first part of the basis for evaluating the fundamental attribution error applied to the content of American perceptions, to examine how entrenched characteristics of the Soviet state predispose – possibly predetermine – the Soviet approach to nuclear issues and Soviet nuclear policy.

1. *Russian and Soviet history*

In the history of the Russian state since its founding as a Grand Duchy around Moscow in the fourteenth century, wars with neighboring countries have played a prominent role. These wars have, time after time, resulted in geographical expansion of the territory of the Russian state, and this has often happened after Russia itself had been invaded. In wars with the Tartars and Mongols, Poles, Swedes and Germans, Russia was almost defeated, but after mobilizing all its resources in an all-out war, the Russian state survived and expanded. The idea that the survival of the Russian state depends on its military power being stronger than all its adversaries' is deeply ingrained in Russian experience and, in a sense, suffering from foreign invasions and expansion of the state are two sides of the same coin in Russian history. At the same time, it is an essential characteristic of the progressive expansion of the Russian state since its founding that it has not brought any sense of stability and security to Russia. Rather, the expansions have incurred increased commitments with an exacerbation of foreign 'threats' and revelations of its own military weakness as corollaries. [57]

Russia's history engenders a sense of geographical vulnerability and encirclement, a siege mentality, and an awareness of the possibility of invasion. It breeds a basic mistrust of the outside world, growing into xenophobia; defense of the homeland and risk-aversion become supreme. Such attitudes are combined with an inferiority complex *vis-à-vis* the 'advanced' Western world, which are compensated by arrogant self-assertion. Russia's relations with the outside world have also been marked by a moralizing tone and a self-appointed missionary role toward foreigners. The idea that Russia institutions and values, as symbolized in the Russian Orthodox Church for example, represent the culmination of world history has been prominent in Russian history long before the Soviet Union displayed a similar view through Marxism-Leninism. [58]

Soviet experience enhances many of these attitudes. The very founding of the Soviet state was closely related to wars with foreign countries, but the Second World War, which the Soviets call the Great Patriotic War, is clearly an essential Soviet experience. Russia lost some 20 million people in that war and it has left an indelible impact. However, it is important to understanding the distinctive character of that experience that it is not a fixed history, given once and for all. Strongly biased interpretations of the Great Patriotic War play a key role in Soviet life today, in schools, in the armed forces, in the media, in periodicals and in fiction, and new books and films about the war often receive wide publicity in the press. Endless references to the Great Patriotic War foster a patriotism and nationalism which is shared by the Soviet people to a degree that far exceeds any comparable phenomenon in Western countries. Moreover, a dominant element of these manifestations is that Russia won the war because it is led by CPSU. The victory over Nazi Germany, it is stated again and again, proves the superiority of socialism, and patriotism and Marxism-Leninism are combined in a way that enhances CPSU's authority.

The lesson is the need for vigilance, ideological steadfastness, self-sacrifice and patriotism; it is a lesson, never to be forgotten, that Russia/ the Soviet Union must always be on a war-footing in order to repel a surprise attack, and only Russia's own strength – not trust in the adversary/ enemy – is decisive. The fact that other countries also had a cruel fight against Nazi Germany and that Russia received a good deal of help from the United States among others is largely neglected. Also, the fact that Russia's immeasurable suffering during the war was massively increased by Stalin's crimes in the 1930s has mostly been ignored; it is a fundamental feature of Soviet society that nobody openly poses the question how a socialist society could allow its leader to commit such crimes for so long. On the other hand, Stalin's lack of preparedness and tactical mistakes immediately before and after the German attack are sometimes mentioned and considered in more detail but mostly by reference to unspecified errors. Apart from a few occasions during Krushchev's era and in recent years, the issue of Stalin's personal responsibility for Russia's suffering has not been dealt with in detail and publicly in the Soviet Union. Therefore, strictly speaking, it is immaterial to a determination of the substance of the Soviet experience. Both as to this issue and the broader problem of CPSU's, compared to foreigners', responsibility for various human afflictions borne by the Soviet people during the first thirty years of the Soviet Union's existence, the problem is not that history's record is self-evident and fixed and wholly contrary to the official version; many horrible depictions by Soviet authors of the Germans' atrocities in Russia are very graphic and accurate. The crux of the matter, in this context, is rather that official interpretations of the broader political context of the course of the war and preceding events and trends have been basically unchallenged in the Soviet public and *that* shapes an important part of the manifestation of the Soviet experience. However, some developments in the mid-1980s may augur significant departures.

Bearing in mind that the Russian and Soviet experience is not a fixed quantity, what is the impact of these experiences for Soviet nuclear policy and the Soviet Union's general approach to nuclear issues? The consequences can expediently be outlined in three related points:

First, Russian experience means that the Soviets will be skeptically predisposed toward an assertion that war-prevention in the nuclear age must necessarily be based on both superpowers' vulnerability to the adversary's nuclear attack. Given its history, the Soviets are very uncomfortable with the idea of having their security dependent on the rival's rationality and they are naturally reluctant to accept that the Soviet homeland's vulnerability is not only an unalterable fact but even a fact to be used for war-preventing purposes (see N. Talenskiy's observation in 1964; cf. Chapter 6, note 79). The Soviets' experience of war makes them predisposed to dismiss the idea that the maintenance of the superpowers' mutual vulnerability should be pursued as irresponsible and dangerous; that notion is alien to the Russian tradition and reflects, according to that reasoning, an otherworldly sophistry which only naive intellectuals in a country that has never itself experienced a war caused by foreign invasion can waste their time on.

Second, the Russian tradition means that considerations concerning military efficiency and how to defend the Soviet Union *in* a war – rather than an abstract and ahistorical notion of deterrence – will have a prominent place when Soviet nuclear policy is worked out. Given that Russian history, defense needs and the primacy of defending Mother Russia enjoy broad support in the Soviet population and as the armed forces stand as a symbol of national power and integrity, they are a prestigious institution in Soviet society. While the principle of Party supremacy is not challenged, there has been widespread consensus that the professional military expertise is best fitted to assess what is necessary for defending Russia in terms of military, including nuclear, hardware.[59] Unlike the United States, until recently the Soviet Union has not had a group of civilian 'strategists' who can exert any impact on the intellectual foundation of the country's nuclear policy.

A third consequence is that any Soviet weapons acquisition is seen as a contribution to the Soviet Union's defense capability and the prevention of war. The evolution of more and better (nuclear) weapons enhances the Soviet ability to defend itself and survive if the enemy launches an attack. The specific experience of 22 June 1941, may have the consequence that the Russians are predisposed to pre-empt an anticipated pre-emptive strike by the enemy. In peacetime, a strengthened Russian defense capacity influences enemies to greater caution, according to this reasoning. There is an historically-determined inclination to over-insure by a steady accumulation of military hardware, and the defense tradition has the effect that the Russians are predisposed to dismiss the claim that a Soviet military build-up can appear threatening and offensive to other countries.

Summing up, the specific Russian historical experience means that the advent of nuclear weapons and long-range delivery vehicles did not represent a similar clear break with the past as it did to other countries, particularly the United States. As great parts of western Russia had been destroyed by a war which had caused extensive human suffering before the atomic bomb was ever used, the nuclear threat did not mark a sudden appearance of a threat; the Russian people *had* experienced wars and foreign threats. That experience also inclines the Soviets to see a strong military defense as valuable in itself, without it necessarily meaning that their defense forces are built up with the intention of being used offensively against other countries. In that sense, the Soviet Union can be termed defensive. On the other hand, this does not mean that the Soviet Union will only use its military forces to defend itself after an outside attack: on the contrary, Soviet experience can have the effect that they are predisposed to pre-empt an attack when war seems imminent. Neither does it follow that the Soviet Union will not use military force to pursue broader foreign policy interests; rather, Russian and Soviet history shapes an inclination to see a strong and usable military force as an absolute requirement for surviving and sustaining its goals in a hostile world.

2.   Marxism-Leninism

As the aim is to evaluate the significance of Marxism-Leninism as a dispositional variable explaining Soviet nuclear policy since the early 1960s, the following broad outline disregards the fact that the present Soviet leadership has dissociated itself from parts of Marxism-Leninism as it, until recently, has been construed in Soviet writings. It is precisely the significance of 'orthodox' Marxism-Leninism as a dispositional variable that is at issue. According to the official Soviet interpretation, Marxism-Leninism is both a cognitive method and a guide to action, and the prevailing Soviet interpretation of Marxism-Leninism, until the late 1980s, can be summarized in six points. [60]

1. World affairs are only seemingly a chaotic agglomeration of events, conditions and developments. Applying *the dialectical method* one reaches *the* scientifically correct understanding of the complex multiplicity in international society. The social relations ('general laws') uncovered by the Marxist dialectical method are basically independent of human consciousness, i.e. they are objectively necessary.

2. *The objectively true general laws* mean that the world moves with inexorable logic toward socialism. Countries belonging to the socialist system today simply represent a qualitatively higher stage in mankind's progressive development. Being historically and morally preordained, the development toward socialism is not direct, however, but the ultimate victory of socialism is always assured.

3. A country's *foreign policy is determined by* its domestic structure, i.e. its class structure. Hence, the foreign policy of any state has to be assessed in the light of who dominates its domestic class structure. Scientifically and morally, it is decisive who determines a country's foreign policy rather than what is done, that is, whether it is in accordance with the objectively necessary historical development.

4. The world today has three constituent parts: *capitalist states, socialist states* and *progressive revolutionary states* (these include the Third World). The first two are offsprings of the basic antagonistic classes whose objective interests they represent. Between the capitalist and the socialist systems conflict is inevitable but in the present epoch it assumes a special form.

5. The conflict between capitalist and socialist states today takes place as *peaceful coexistence* (*mirnoe sosusjtjestvovanie*) between states with different social systems; sometimes the terms relaxation of tensions or détente (*razrjadka*) are used by Soviet authors. Peaceful coexistence means that all problems between the opposing systems must be settled without war but the ideological conflict (the class struggle) both within capitalist countries and between the two camps continues and deepens. In that conflict the decisive question is who dominates *whom* (*kto – kogo*) and peaceful coexistence makes it possible to wage the ideological conflict in a way which is best for all humankind and will lead to the ultimate victory for socialism without too much human suffering.

Thus peaceful coexistence is not a particular platform adopted by somebody. Neither does it mean reconciliation between socialism and capitalism or the preservation of the status quo. Peaceful coexistence between states with different social systems is rather a specific form of class struggle, or social law, which the objectively necessary development toward socialism has forced upon capitalist countries.

6. The capitalist world is forced to accept peaceful coexistence because of the changing *correlation of forces* (*sootsheniye sil*) between capitalist countries and the socialist system which means a strengthening of socialism.[61]

The concept 'correlation of forces' is multidimensional and denotes a complex of material and spiritual forces which are not measurable in any strict sense. The assessment of the present state of the correlation of forces is a matter of intuition as it includes a broad spectrum of political, economic, techno-scientific, military as well as spiritual components. The changing correlation of forces in favor of socialism cannot be invalidated by any actual event or development and they are only marginally susceptible to policies actively pursued by countries, socialist or capitalist. In consequence of the changing correlation of forces, the aggressive capitalist countries are checked while the peaceful socialist countries, supported by progressive and peace-loving forces in the other camps, acquire better working conditions for 'pushing' and helping the historically and morally correct development toward socialism.

How does Marxism-Leninism bear on Soviet nuclear policy and the Soviet Union as the United States' atomically armed adversary? As a starting point for answering that question, one can distinguish between three connected functions of the official Soviet ideology: an authenticating function, i.e. promulgated policies are justified by citing their accordance with Marxism-Leninism; a cognitive function, i.e. Marxism-Leninism provides an epistemological framework for the perception of reality; and a directive function, i.e. Marxism-Leninism serves as a guide to action when a policy is framed.[62]

Concerning the *authenticating* function, the first important point to note is that Marxism-Leninism constitutes the basic legitimization of the Soviet state. It is by accepting the scientific correctness of Marxism-Leninism that the leaders of CPSU are conferred the right to govern the Soviet Union; it justifies Soviet leaders' authority. As the legitimization of the Soviet leadership is based on accepting Marxism-Leninism as the scientific truth about history's development, the authenticating function of Marxism-Leninism cannot be understood in terms of a corresponding role of Western ideologies: because of this specific role of their ideology, Soviet leaders and spokesmen have to claim its validity and truth-value whether or not they 'really' believe it. On the other hand, it is very important to note the limit of this reasoning when it concerns the further role of Soviet ideology: thus it does not follow that Soviet spokesmen do not 'really' believe in their ideological statements and justifications ('they only talk that way because they have to'). Undoubtedly, they believe in their ideological justification. The all-important point, however, is that when it concerns Marxism-Leninism's authenticating function, it is not a matter of answering the question: 'But do they actually believe in that ideology?'

These considerations have an immediate relevance as to the most obvious relationship between the official ideology and Soviet nuclear policy, namely the relation between Marxism-Leninism and the political aspect of Soviet military doctrine. In fact, that relation approaches an identity, given as per definition. As to other aspects of Soviet nuclear policy, the authenticating function has frequently shown in that different concrete measures have been publicly defended and justified as 'objectively necessary' and fully in accordance with Marxism-Leninism. Indeed, the official ideology has served as an arsenal for arguments where Soviet spokesmen have picked up support for any foreign policy actually pursued by the Soviet government.[63] In terms of Marxism-Leninism, both a heavy nuclear build-up combined with a confrontational declaratory and negotiating policy, a highly accommodative policy with arms restraint or arms cuts, or any combination of the two extremes can be presented as authenticating and justifiable.

As to Marxism-Leninism's *cognitive* function and its relation to Soviet nuclear policy, it is first worth noting that the general Marxist thinking predisposes Soviet leaders to downgrade the importance of military factors compared to the socio-economic. While Marxism-Leninism teaches that military force may have an auxiliary role to play in that the Soviet Union's military strength restrains capitalist countries' temptation to unleash another world war, its central theoretical theme is that socio-economic factors – not military – assure socialism's final victory. In a concrete situation military force may help promote that victory (which, in any case, is predetermined) but military power is not *the* essential means.

An important point concerning Marxism-Leninism's cognitive function originates in its emphasis on the ultimate zero-sum character of the relation between socialist and capitalist countries and the built-in assumption about Western countries' hostility to the Soviet Union. Marxism-Leninism predisposes Soviet decision-makers and observers to stress the basic hostility behind any Western arms build-up or opposition to the Soviet Union; on the other hand, they will tend to interpret accommodative policies pursued by capitalist countries as having been forced on these countries by objective factors and a concept like 'good will' has no place in a rigid Marxist-Leninist conceptual framework. Concerning Soviet military and nuclear policy, Marxism-Leninism enhances any tendency to see Soviet measures in self-righteous terms. For instance, from a strict Marxist-Leninist point of view, no Soviet nuclear deployment can increase the danger to peace as this will solely be a result of capitalistic countries' arms build-up. At this point, however, one sees how Marxism-Leninism's cognitive role varies: while some Soviet spokesmen stress that view, others describe the effects of different nuclear deployments in less rigid ideological terms, even though no Soviet spokesmen ever openly criticize Soviet nuclear policy. Still, it must be concluded that Marxism-Leninism's cognitive function increases the conflictual elements of the Soviet cognition of the nuclear issue.

A specific problem concerns Marxist-Leninist conceptions of the consequences of the existence of nuclear arms for the course and outcome of the basic political conflict between capitalism and socialism. As Marxism-Leninism states that socialism;s worldwide extension is predetermined by historical-economic factors, it is difficult to acknowledge that a nuclear war may make this historical determinism irrelevant. The epistemological framework acquired tends to ignore or shirk that issue and Soviet ideological literature is marked by references to the inevitable victory of socialism even if the possibility of civilization's destruction in nuclear war is also recognized. [64] This, however, cannot be used to prove that the Soviets are 'forced' by ideological reasons to believe that they can win a nuclear war, and hence their explicit statements on the destruction of civilization in a nuclear war have to be insincere. It only shows that, from a strict Marxism-Leninist point of view, there are certain limits to how radical implications can be drawn in public from the existence of nuclear weapons. Moreover, the fact that some Soviet leaders as well as a number of Soviet writers and spokesmen publicly dismiss the concept of victory in nuclear war – without drawing negative conclusions concerning the validity of scientific socialism, of course – shows that Marxist-Leninism's impact on the Soviet attitude to the nuclear issue is somewhat complex, and also if it is included that these public statements may have an instrumental role in Soviet foreign policy. However, the problem is more intricate than that: the fact that it is ideologically difficult for a Marxist-Leninist to accept the view that the nuclear threat has made historical determinism and scientific socialism obsolete is neither, in itself, a proof that the Soviets 'really' agree that an all-out nuclear war means the end of civilization (including socialism) – 'their ideology merely prevents them saying so.' Strictly, that reasoning is fallacious and no ratiocination on the logic of Marxism-Leninism's determinism vs. the determinism of nuclear war can settle and dispose of the problem.

On the whole, Marxism-Leninism certainly entails consequences for Soviet cognition of the nuclear issue but the whole character of that ideology, especially its dialectic, means that the relation is basically indeterminate. Besides, it must be noted that there is a close relation between the cognitive and the authenticating function of Marxism-Leninism in all this.

As to Marxism-Leninism's *directive* function in relation to Soviet nuclear policy, the most evident relation concerns some aspects of declaratory policy, especially Soviet military doctrine (cf. above). Concerning force deployment and negotiating posture, however, the relationship is ambiguous: as a long-range historical vision, legitimizing the existence of the Soviet government and its measures, including Soviet help to 'push' the historically predetermined development toward socialism, Marxism-Leninism is flexible when it comes to actual policies.

Thus the heavy Soviet nuclear build-up since the early 1960s is not inconsistent with Marxism-Leninism (or peaceful coexistence and Soviet peace policy); on the contrary, it is precisely the Soviet military build-up that is an important factor contributing to détente (or the changed correlation of forces), especially because it has forced capitalist countries, primarily the United States, to adopt a more realistic policy as exemplified in SALT. However, at this point it is important to note that neither is an ever-increasing Soviet military build-up a logical corollary of Marxism-Leninism. Applying Marxism-Leninism as a starting point, the Soviet level of aspiration as to military, including nuclear, forces is not fixed. Nuclear forces are one factor in the broad concept 'correlation of forces' and even if the Soviet Union always has a duty to strengthen the socialist side, it is not thereby given a definite guide to action.

A similar indeterminism applies to Soviet negotiating policy. Marxism-Leninism sets some vague limits on the possibility for extensive arms control agreements with capitalist countries but these ideologically determined limits are not fixed beforehand. In the long term, Marxism-Leninism is uncompromising (socialism will prevail in the world) and that certainty has often given Soviet negotiators a fair degree of patience compared to many Western negotiators; in the short term, however, the official ideology legitimizes compromises with the capitalists (capitalist governments are forced to be 'realistic'). Hence, neither in this respect is the Soviet level of aspiration fixed once and for all with Marxism-Leninism. The point is that almost irrespective of the actual content of an agreement, it is possible to maintain the long-term vision.[65] From this it also follows that the mere fact that the Soviet Union enters a given arms control agreement with a capitalist state does not indicate that Soviet leaders are beginning to abandon their Marxism-Leninism; that reasoning is based on a simple misunderstanding of the content and function of official Soviet ideology.

Does Marxism-Leninism direct Soviet policy to plan for Soviet victory in nuclear war? This is one of the most vexed questions among Western scholars and observers. Basically, it is fallacious to reach any clear-cut conclusion about Soviet military planning solely on the basis of Marxism-Leninism, however. In the same way, one cannot state with certainty how the Soviet ideology will influence Soviet military actions in a given situation with immediate danger of nuclear war. Marxism-Leninism simply includes that many part-reasonings that it is highly hazardous to present *one* conclusion as final: the ideology's long-term patience could lead to one conclusion, its built-in suspicion of capitalist countries to another (for instance, that Soviet military planners plan for pre-emption). In any case, it is impossible to maintain how the ideological guide to action *is*, contrary to how it *may* be.

Assessing the impact of Marxism-Leninism on Soviet nuclear policy, it is important to note that Soviet leaders' general assertion that they always follow Marxism-Leninism in their day-to-day policy is never publicly gainsaid in the Soviet Union. As the basic Marxist-Leninist framework is never directly disputed in Soviet writings, the issue of what actually is the true Marxist-Leninist policy is not subject to public dispute in the way that the incumbent leaders' statements are openly questioned. The officially correct policy has changed over time, the ideological justification for some policies has shifted from one occasion to another and former leaders' policies have been denounced as not reflecting true Marxism-Leninism, but incumbent leaders are never gainsaid in public when they state that some arms control agreement, or the absence of such an agreement, some force deployment (as far as these are cited publicly, at all), or other Soviet nuclear policy measures, are fully in accordance with Marxism-Leninism. All this means that even if Soviet leaders are not totally free – i.e. 'free' ideologically – nor are they narrowly constrained by their allegiance to Marxism-Leninism. As reviewed above, the official ideology may influence Soviet nuclear policy in various ways but that influence never shows in the way that incumbent leaders of CPSU are censured publicly for having betrayed true Marxism-Leninism. That salient feature of the Soviet political structure is one reason that one has to be cautious in drawing absolute conclusions about the relation between Marxism-Leninism and Soviet nuclear policy.

2. Situational variables

1. American nuclear policies

Examining the significance of American nuclear policies as a situational variable, two problems are particularly relevant to consider: first, the interplay between the two superpowers' development of nuclear weapons viewed in the light of action–reaction theories about arms developments;[66] and second, the significance of the relation between American force development policy and American declaratory policy as to nuclear weapons.

Concerning *the relation between Soviet and American nuclear force deployments*, reference to Table 1 (p. 186), which indicates the development in the number of Soviet and American strategic nuclear delivery vehicles in the period 1960–88, shows that the expansion of Soviet nuclear forces in the late 1960s and early 1970s followed a corresponding expansion by America in the early 1960s. Considering the lead-times involved in the production of nuclear weaponry – which means that one cannot take the first appearance and deployment of a system as proof of a reaction to an immediately preceding deployment by the adversary – the strong increase in the number of Soviet strategic missiles from the mid-1960s to the mid-1970s can be explained as an imitative and emulative reaction to the increase in American missiles during the early 1960s which, moreover, had become publicly known in the late 1950s and expanded in the first year of the Kennedy administration. This explanation seems to be confirmed by a reference to Table 2 (p. 187) which shows the number of warheads on Soviet and American strategic nuclear forces since the early 1960s; this action–reaction pattern as to the total number of warheads on strategic missiles seems to have continued after the mid-1970s and in that way one may also explain the Soviet MIRV-ing from 1975. On the other hand, Table 3 (p. 187), which shows aggregate EMT on Soviet and American strategic nuclear delivery vehicles, reveals another picture: a strong Soviet increase until the early 1980s – and thereafter a decrease – has followed a halving of American EMT since 1960.

The conclusion from this gross examination of action–reaction processes, assessed in aggregate terms, is that the build-up of Soviet strategic nuclear arms for a large part may be explained as a reaction to an American action, i.e. a preceding American nuclear build-up. However, this general and overall review shows that the interaction between American and Soviet strategic programs is not mechanical: the Soviet nuclear build-up has not been symmetrical to the American and the primary difference concerns the high yield of Soviet land-based missiles. [67]

Examining characteristics of Soviet nuclear deployments in a little more detail, some evidence appears of another type of Soviet reaction to American nuclear build-up, besides the above-mentioned imitative and emulative reaction, namely an offsetting variety in the manner of the classical competition between offense and defense. That was especially apparent in the 1960s when the initial deployments of ABM systems around Leningrad and Moscow can be seen as a response to the American *Polaris* and *Minuteman* deployments in the early 1960s. [68] Also the extensive Soviet air defense system and civil defense measures seem to fit in with this explanation. On the other hand, the seemingly limited Soviet ASW capability indicates the limited tenability of the explanation. Altogether, it is evident that a Soviet reaction in the form of a strong build-up of defensive systems to offset an American build-up of offensive nuclear systems primarily applies to the 1960s.

Assessing the tenability of an action–reaction theory in explaining Soviet force deployments, the centrality of the unknown Soviet decision to initiate the production of nuclear systems – both as to the exact time of a decision and the closer character of it – is obvious. That means, in turn, that the general secrecy which surrounds the Soviet decision-making and weapons acquisition process increases the methodical difficulties of testing the theory. Therefore, it is difficult to go beyond the general conclusion that it evidently is not without meaning. Focusing on the contrast between Soviet secrecy and American openness – even if the contrast is not total – one can, however, point to the possibility that precisely that difference can enhance a

Soviet tendency to react against American arms deployment by increasing own deployments: because of the adversarial character of the American political process, an administration will often trumpet its weapons deployments and stress how they are a guarantee against the Soviet 'threat'. A democratic system may also give rise to a contrary trend, but in the American case there has been a tendency that the government exaggerates the effectiveness and criticality of new weapons and that may incite the Soviet Union to insure itself even more, especially as the Soviet Union, at least until the late 1980s, has been predisposed toward military over-insurance.

The second problem concerns *the Soviet reaction to the relation between American force development policy and American declaratory policy*. Even if it is unknown precisely how much nuclear hardware is needed for 'assured destruction' of the Soviet Union, it is obvious that American nuclear deployments during the years when the US government proclaimed a doctrine close to 'assured destruction' vastly exceeded any reasonable requirement as assessed in those terms; the American nuclear build-up through the 1960s clearly went beyond what can be identified with any deterrence through punishment.[69] In particular, the decision to go ahead with MIRV-ing American missiles, made in the years when 'assured destruction' was most distinctly presented, is difficult to reconcile with that doctrine and must have raised doubts among Soviet political and military leaders about the genuineness of the American commitment to a stable mutual deterrence. Considered from that angle, one can say that Soviet leaders, paradoxically, can have been more reassured by the proclamation of the Schlesinger strategy in 1974, as well as some later developments in American deterrence doctrine, for the simple reason that these changes closed the gap between declaratory and force development policy. But one has to be wary, of course, to resort to this observation as *the* explanation for the cautious Soviet reaction to the Schlesinger strategy (cf. above, p. 220).

Various other factors too are relevant for depicting the Soviet reaction to the discrepancy between American declaratory nuclear policy and other aspects of its nuclear policy for some years after the mid-1960s. First, Soviet leaders could never harbor any doubt that American nuclear force employment plans included many elements of counterforce; that could be seen from open sources and if the Soviets did not trust open sources – which they have sometimes indicated – they could surely get the information from secret channels. It can also be adduced that the Soviets, given their ideological lenses, could not have been too upset by a gap between a capitalist country's declarations and that country's actual plans for fighting a war and, besides, one can say that Soviet leaders must have been well acquainted with grasping differences between various aspects of a country's foreign policy, even considering that many wordings and phrases have a different meaning to Soviet and Western politicians. Something else is how much of the gap Soviet leaders really noted and it is also highly questionable whether they actually understood those features of the American political system which contributed to the dissonance between different aspects of American nuclear policy, quite apart from the question if Soviet leaders realized how their own policy might have influenced American nuclear policy. Yet, the conclusion of all this is that the discrepancy between American force development policy and declaratory policy did not moderate a Soviet tendency to react to American nuclear build-ups by increasing own nuclear forces. If anything, it may have increased Soviet nuclear deployments.

2.   East–West tension and détente

Concerning the significance of changing patterns of tension and détente as a situational variable, a first problem relates to the fact that the concepts of tension and détente are ambiguous. Different definitions of the concepts, often fixed implicitly, merge into different political attitudes as to the value of particular policies, trends and events. This shows up, for example, in disputes about whether one international agreement or trend or another represents 'real' détente or only the appearance of détente. Generally, the two concepts refer to mutual expectations of conflict between actors in the international system: détente implies low or decreasing expectations of conflict while tension implies high or increasing expectations. The question of how to obtain a reliable measure of such expectations with theoretical and political relevance involves a number of methodical problems, and one thorough study of variations in tension and détente in Europe has been based on a quantitative content analysis of public statements by governments in NATO and the Warsaw Treaty.[70] One reason for this operational measurement of tension is that governments' public expectations of conflict (for instance, war) can be assumed to be a good indicator of the probability of conflict (war). The following short examination of relations between tension/détente and Soviet nuclear policy will apply a similar broad definition of the concepts and focus on the early 1970s as representing a peak of détente and the late 1970s and early 1980s as representing a peak of tension.[71]

Détente in the early 1970s was manifested at the superpower level by the concluding of a number of Soviet–American arms control agreements and in several other extensions of contacts between the two states. At the European level, it was related to the West German *Ostpolitik* (Eastern policy) and in various agreements on the German question (1970–2). Preparatory talks on the Conference on Security and Cooperation in Europe (CSCE) began in late 1972, and in 1975 the CSCE negotiations resulted in the Final Act (the Helsinki Agreement), adopted by 33 European states as well as the United States and Canada. Asking if and how this détente process influenced various aspects of Soviet nuclear policy, one can demonstrate that it occurred concurrently with a number of changes in

Soviet nuclear policy. As reviewed in Chapter 6, section 5, Soviet leaders' statements showed a cautious endorsement of modernist themes from about 1968, and this tendency became more prominent in the early 1970s; various statements by other Soviet writers and speakers showed a similar or even stronger trend. The development of Soviet negotiating behavior, in particular, and Soviet military doctrine during these years also showed a trend that can be related to the détente process in the early 1970s. Pointing to these relations, one reservation must be noted, however: on the basis of this short overview one cannot draw any conclusions as to what is cause and what is effect. For instance, both détente and the observed changes in Soviet nuclear policy may have been caused by an underlying factor.

Concerning the relation between détente and Soviet nuclear deployments, it is difficult to point to any discernible change in the Soviet behavior after détente reached its peak in the early 1970s. The momentum of the Soviet nuclear build-up does not seem to have been influenced by détente, either in upward or downward direction. Particularly at this point, however, a reverse relation can have been actual in that both superpowers' vulnerability to the adversary's strategic nuclear forces seems to have been the main reason why tension remained relatively low after the mid-1960s,[72] the 'underlying' factor referred to above. In that sense, the first part of the Soviet nuclear build-up since the early 1960s was one significant cause of détente. Further scrutinizing the relation between détente and Soviet nuclear deployments, it is also worth noting that the deployment of the intermediate-range SS-20 from 1977 seems to have been decided around the time when the European détente process reached a peak a few years before. Whether that decision was reached with definite foreign policy aims in mind or as a simple, and long overdue, modernization of Soviet I/MRBM forces, one can conclude that the prominent European détente in the early 1970s, centered on the new West German *Ostpolitik*, did not cause the Soviet leadership to cancel its modernization plans in this field.

As to the rising tension in the late 1970s and early 1980s, it was manifested by the intensification of the verbal warfare between the superpowers, the Soviet invasion of Afghanistan, the breakdown of arms control negotiations and the conflict over NATO's dual-track decision. Examining the specific content of Soviet nuclear policy during these years, it is noteworthy that the decline of détente was not combined with distinct weakening of Soviet leaders' tendency to present the nuclear issue in modernist terms. A few allusions to traditionalist themes were heard but it was a notable during the tense East–West climate that Soviet leaders did not adopt the same traditionalist views that some Soviet writers presented. On the contrary, modernist themes were sometimes atypically emphasized in combination with tension-typical Soviet statements (cf. above pp. 221f.). Concerning Soviet force deployments, neither is it possible to discern any impact of the breakdown of détente; Soviet leaders occasionally hinted that they might be forced to counter-arm but no actual escalation of Soviet nuclear armaments seems to have followed. The rising tension between East and West in the late 1970s and early 1980s had an impact on Soviet negotiation policy but otherwise it is difficult to discern a substantial impact on Soviet nuclear policy.

The conclusion from this short overview of the relation between détente tension and Soviet nuclear policy is that a theory that détente will *cause* a deceleration of Soviet nuclear deployments combined with a more marked tendency to adopt modernist views – while rising tensions will cause the opposite tendency – is difficult to maintain in pure form. Soviet negotiation policy has changed concurrently with détente and tension and as Soviet leaders' statements have tended to change parallel with tension and détente, one cannot fully disprove the theory, either. A methodical problem is that the concepts of tension and détente have to be defined in more distinct terms for an answer not merely to be begging the question, and if that is done the relation between tension/détente and Soviet nuclear policy appears ambiguous. Moreover, one has to include the time dimension; for example, it cannot flatly be repudiated that the détente period examined has been too short and fragile to have had an impact on Soviet deployment policy. At the same time, neither can the opposite general theory be substantiated – viz. that the Soviets abuse any East–West détente to escalate their nuclear deployments – but the SS-20 is the most obvious case pointing to that conclusion. Altogether, the overview of the relation between East–West détente and Soviet nuclear policy points to the validity of another conclusion, however: that both superpowers' mutual vulnerability was one main cause behind détente and in that reverse sense one can say that there is a clear relation between Soviet nuclear policy and détente tension between East and West.

3. Concluding observations

Summarizing with a view to evaluating the fundamental attribution error as applied to US governments' perceptions, the first general conclusion to be drawn is that it is only to a very limited degree that the two dispositional characteristics of the Soviet state unambiguously have determined Soviet nuclear policy. The review of the impact of Russia's and the Soviet Union's historical relations with the outside world and Marxism-Leninism as the official Soviet ideology shows that while several general Soviet approaches to the nuclear issue can be accounted for by referring to basic traits of the Soviet state, it is much harder to point out distinct causal relations between historical and ideological peculiarities of the Soviet state and its nuclear policy. It follows that it is highly inadequate to assert that what the Soviet Union 'is', historically and ideologically, has determined what it has 'done' in the nuclear field. Moreover, it is worth noting that the inadequacy of applying inherent Soviet dispositions as an overall basis for explaining Soviet nuclear policy applies to 'orthodox' Marxism-Leninism, that is, this reasoning was inadequate well before the 'new political thinking' and the changes in Soviet nuclear policy in the mid-1980s. In that general meaning, the Soviet essentialist marked fixtures and trends of US governments' perceptions have overestimated the significance of dispositional factors and thus exemplify the fundamental attribution error. However, as it is not always clear which Soviet propensities dispositional attributions (among US governments' images) attach superior weight – which means that they are difficult to evaluate in distinct terms – the overall and quite abstract nature of this conclusion should be stressed. Furthermore, since the review considered the impact of dispositional variables primarily in terms of logical possibilities and tendencies, it must be followed by an attempt to reach more substantive and empirically-based conclusions about the actual significance and relevance of dispositional and situational variables and their interplay as to Soviet positions and policies on nuclear issues, thereby providing a basis for answering the question about to which degree the fundamental attribution bias in US governments' perceptions has been followed by actually erroneous attributions.

The most obvious relations between dispositional variables and Soviet nuclear policy concern, first, the political aspect of Soviet military doctrine, second, some characteristics of Soviet nuclear forces. As to Soviet military doctrine, it was pointed out that its political aspect can be clearly accounted for in terms of the Marxist-Leninist conception of war as a socio-historical phenomenon – indeed, as this relation is given as per definition, it is doubtful if it can be attached an independent significance. The actual impact of Marxism-Leninism on other aspects of Soviet nuclear policy was more questionable and must be assessed in relation to historical dispositions influencing Soviet policy. Thus a more interesting and potentially significant impact of dispositional variables concerns some of the consequences of Russian and Soviet history which meant that the Soviets would be predisposed toward rejecting the 'mutual assured destruction' doctrine as otherworldly sophistry and attaching a high value to Soviet military, including Soviet nuclear, forces' ability to defend the country and fight a war, as distinct from an ahistorical notion of deterrence. In the light of some of the characteristics of the Soviet nuclear arms developments (cf. pp. 185–92), particularly the weight of defensive as well as nuclear counterforce and war-fighting weapons (to apply Western terms), it is natural to conclude that Russian and Soviet history actually has had an impact in this respect in the way that it provided the general conceptual backdrop for planning Soviet arms developments, a backdrop which has been strengthened by the Soviets' ideological mindset. This conclusion is corroborated by the observation that the rise and fall of détente does not seem to have had a marked influence on the momentum of the Soviet nuclear build-up. For assessing the tenability of that conclusion it is important to note that it applies to the Soviet historical and ideological experience – in particular the historical factor – as dispositional variables influencing the development of Soviet nuclear arms, not to the issue of whether this force actually has had some additional military and foreign policy impact in the international society. Moreover, the tenability of this conclusion is not critically diminished by the observation that the Soviet nuclear build-up for a large part followed, and therefore can be seen as a reaction to, a preceding American build-up. The point is that the historical disposition increases the likelihood of a strong Soviet reaction to an adversary's arms build-up. Altogether, this underlines that the actual impact of inherent Soviet dispositions on Soviet policy is conditioned by different situational variables – the Soviet bias for one or another action does not operate in an international vacuum and so the other superpower's nuclear policy in some ways enhanced the Soviets' predilection for building a 'strong' nuclear force.

In connection with evaluating the interplay between dispositional and situational variables, one particularly important problem concerns the impact of the incongruity between the American 'assured destruction' doctrine in the late 1960s and the marked American nuclear build-up during the same period. As reviewed (cf. pp. 50–3), when Secretary McNamara, in particular, pronounced his ideas on 'assured destruction', strategic stability and the like, he endeavored in unusually distinct terms to elaborate what he had in mind. McNamara was the first US Secretary of Defense who carefully and with great intellectual energy sought to prescribe a nuclear doctrine for America's adversary in the hope that that adversary would adopt it for its own sake, a Soviet self-interest which, according to the then US Secretary of Defense, would coincide with the United States' interests.[73] However, these American expositions were flawed in two respects at least, pointing to central conclusions concerning the relative significance of dispositional and situational variables behind Soviet nuclear attitudes and policies. First, even if McNamara and other outspoken advocates of these ideas apparently recognized the Soviets' ingrained aversion to their reasoning on the common nuclear predicament – that is, they realized that dispositional factors draw the Russians in another direction – they clearly underrated the difficulties of communicating with the Soviets on this. (The fact that they also underrated the problems connected with 'educating' *Americans* on this does not subtract the relevance of this observation.) The second fault in this nuclear essentialist reasoning presented by US government officials in the late 1960s was that they overrated, at least in the public pronouncements, the degree to which the various aspects of American nuclear policy projected an unambiguous image to the Soviets. Only on a few occasions – for instance, in the notable San Francisco speech, cf. p. 56 above – did McNamara publicly recognize Soviet difficulties with reading American policy in unambiguous terms. Apart from the fact that McNamara's way of arguing exemplifies typical misperceptions,[74] the important point in all this is that the Soviet Union has never, as a situational variable, faced a distinct American 'mutual assured destruction' policy which it has then rejected. What the Soviet Union encountered was a US Secretary of Defense who, for a short time, endeavored to 'educate' them in the common predicament in the nuclear age but this occurred concurrently with an American nuclear build-up which suggested a different thinking. Thus, while the review of Russian and Soviet history in particular but also the official Soviet ideology provides a solid basis for concluding that the Soviets were predisposed toward rejecting that kind of reasoning, it has to be stressed that they have never actually faced this thinking, encapsulated in an overall distinct policy from the other superpower, as a situational variable which could have influenced their nuclear policy.

The conclusions can be epitomized in four points:

1. Expressed in general terms, the fundamental attribution error is confirmed by prominent aspects of US governments' perceptions through the period 1961–89.
2. There are important exceptions to this, primarily in that a closer scutiny of characteristics of the Soviet nuclear build-up suggest the significance of dispositional factors, with Russian historical experience the most significant.
3. One must distinguish between general Soviet attitudes to nuclear issues and Soviet nuclear policy. While the first have been markedly influenced by Soviet dispositions, situational factors have been more influential as to different policies.
4. There is no deterministic relation between basic historical and ideological essentials of the Soviet state and its nuclear policy. The link between the two outstanding dispositional variables, Soviet history and Marxism-Leninism, and Soviet attitudes and policies in the nuclear field has to be phrased in possibilistic and probabilistic terms.

8.   Conclusions

In dealing with American perceptions of the Soviet Union as a nuclear armed political adversary from the beginning of the 1960s to the late 1980s, the aim has been to describe and elaborate how the nuclear issue has been related to and manifested itself in different political relations and issues. The criterion for applying various approaches has been elucidating dynamics of the interplay between, on the one hand, the ways changing political leaderships in the United States publicly have construed the Soviet American nuclear relationship and, on the other hand, the domestic American political process and Soviet policies and positions.

Chapters 2–4 reviewed how six administrations in Washington, since the early 1960s, have represented the Soviet Union as a nuclear power and the consequences for American policy. In reviewing US government public statements through the period, the approach applied was a variety of that used by 'lumpers', as distinct from 'splitters'.[1] That is, the aim with 'mining' a number of sources (enumerated on p. 30) of American Statements was to impose some sort of order on innumerable speeches, statements and writings, put forward by incumbent administrations and dealing with various aspects of the American–Soviet relationship in the nuclear age. The basic methodical means were two idealtype images – nuclear essentialism and Soviet essentialism – which primarily stand for two distinct conflict strategies, for the United States to apply *vis-à-vis* the Soviet Union and while nuclear essentialism fastens upon the inherent nature of nuclear weapons, Soviet essentialism fastens upon the inherent nature of the Soviet state. The conclusions of the analysis in Chapters 2 and 3 of US government images from 1961 to 1989 were synthesized in Chapter 4 in terms of fixtures, trends and swings. The two main conclusions were, first, that there have been two Soviet essentialist-like fixtures, one concerning the political significance of nuclear arms and one concerning negotiating from strength; and second, two long-term trends, namely a diluted nuclear essentialist trend for some years after 1963 and the mid-1960s and a more marked Soviet essentialist-like trend since the early 1970s, both trends primarily manifested in the reading of the Soviet view of nuclear arms and the interpretation of deterrence.

In order to elucidate the perceptions from different angles and provide some of the foundation for assessing the validity of American images, the following chapters focused on aspects of what is termed 'operational environments' of US governments. Chapter 5 analyzed the process whereby administrations in Washington have portrayed the Soviet Union as a nuclear power and political adversary as a process taking place within the ideological and political framework of the American society and political system. The main finding was that, altogether, the domestic American setting encourages Soviet essentialist-like images. Chapter 6 focused on the object of American perceptions and aimed at describing and elaborating characteristics of the Soviet Union as a superpower. The main finding was emphasizing the composite and, in some ways, ambiguous character of Soviet policies and positions as superpower since the early 1960s.

Chapter 7 attempted the precarious problem of evaluating perceptions by comparing fixtures and trends of the images to operational environments, primarily on the basis of the exposition in the preceding chapters. The main finding was to stress the peculiar uncertainty associated with reaching any clear-cut conclusion, an uncertainty that was due to both the lack of adequate empirical data and the very logical nature of the images. Still, it was tentatively concluded that the fixture concerning the political significance of nuclear arms can be confirmed as to the broad Soviet view of nuclear arms and its impact on Soviet willingness to use military forces in the Third World in the 1970s; but as to other respects, including the action aspect, it has a much more doubtful validity. Concerning the 'negotiating from strength' fixture, it appeared valid considered in domestic American terms; evaluated in relation to Soviet behavior, the conclusion was that an American arms program on some occasions has probably been a necessary condition for getting the Soviet Union to enter arms limitations, but far from sufficient in that Soviet nuclear 'strength' was necessary to obtain arms control agreements between the superpowers. As to the two trends since the mid-1970s, the analysis of the Soviet view of the specific role of nuclear arms in relation to war-fighting (stressed by Soviet traditionalists) and war-prevention (stressed by Soviet modernists) indicated the doubtful validity of US governments' images in that the Soviet approach has been marked by its dichotomous nature throughout the period, with a move toward modernism since the late 1960s which has recently become quite distinct. Concerning the image of deterrence, it was demonstrated that the doubtful validity of the Soviet essentialist trend inhered in the logical character of images of deterrence rather than in specific of empirical data. As the dominating fixtures and trends express a tendency toward emphasizing dispositional (i.e. Soviet-specific), rather than situational, factors, American images were also analyzed in terms of evaluating the fundamental attribution error, and the conclusion was – with important exceptions – that US governments' perceptions confirm this attribution theory. To the degree that Soviet-specific factors have been important, Russian and Soviet history was found to be more significant than Marxism-Leninism.

Comparing these conclusions with the studies of American perceptions reviewed in the Introduction (pp. 12–19), it should be noted, first, that even if the classifications of American images applied in those studies generally correspond to that used here, none directly applied a time-dimension, therefore they are difficult to compare as it concerns the trends of US governments' images. But in other respects a comparison is fruitful. Thus focusing particularly on Oudenaren's outline of how the domestic American scene favors one of the two 'termination' schools (cf. p. 14) while the 'management critique' has not appealed to the Americans (cf. p. 15) – and noting that conclusions reached in Chapter 7 on comparing images and operational environments correspond with some of the observations presented by the 'management critique' (cf. the summary p. 15) – this further elucidates the inherent difficulties of the United States' meeting with the Soviet superpower. It underlines the fundamental domestic problems for any US government preparing its policy *vis-à-vis* the Soviet Union. Another point worth noting is that while Krepon reviews the central ideas held by operationally-inclined nuclear weapon strategists and arms controllers – which together have dominated much of the thinking in US governments – this study has demonstrated why these 'moderate' groups face critical problems, not only *vis-à-vis* the Soviet adversary but also in relation to the American political system. On the whole, while none of the findings in this study is clearly at variance with the studies reviewed , it can be seen as an elaboration of how images that roughly correspond to these have worked as to a particular field. In particular the comparison of US governments' images of the Soviet superpower to internal and external aspects of the operational environments should serve as an important clarification and elaboration of general studies of American perceptions of the Soviet Union.

The further theoretical meaning and political significance of the findings in Chapters 2–7 can be considered in different contexts. First, I shall elaborate the interplay between the American process of perception and the object of perception by submitting six tentative conclusions about the political dynamics of the nuclear issue. Thereafter, I venture some political reflections I think should be taken into consideration in the light of the findings. Lastly, I briefly consider future developments.

1.   POLITICAL DYNAMICS OF THE NUCLEAR ISSUE

1.   The domestic American process of perception is a peculiar mixture of rigidity, volatility and incisiveness. Put crudely, the conflict between nuclear essentialist and Soviet essentialist-like positions sometimes resembles a strife between the 'infantile will of confident liberalism' and the 'paranoiac obsessions of ultra-patriotic alarmism.'[2] That strife, however, exists concurrently with a unique high-quality and enlightened public debate in

parts of the American media and periodicals and occasionally among politicians holding or seeking public office. The domestic context is therefore heterogeneous and complex in a way that is extremely difficult to calculate beforehand for any observer or purposeful political actor. As the mood of not only the public, the media and Congress, but also the US government, is often volatile, it follows that for any consistent and enduring American policy in this field to succeed, in terms of American politics, it must be based on firm principles which are articulated as forcefully and as clearly as possible before the different parts of the American political system. To do so successfully, there is need for education in complexity and modesty which goes against the American grain,[3] and that task is exceedingly arduous for any purposeful leadership or other political group in the United States, given both the composite and contradictory character of traditional American trains of thought and the pluralism of American politics. Thus it is apparent that the American political system is going round in circles with the problem and this is also related to the existence of cyclical patterns in American foreign policy moods without it being possible to determine the more specific character of the relation on the basis of the findings in this study. Altogether, it must be concluded that however great the inherent difficulties of assessing the Soviet Union as a nuclear superpower, the character of the American tradition and political process – including such democratic features that it shares with other Western countries – enhances the problem.

From this it follows that *long-term stability in and domestic political quietness about American nuclear policies is unlikely, one reason being the pluralism and democratic features of the American political process as well as salient characteristics of traditional American conceptions of its role in the world.*

2. The review in Chapters 2 and 3 demonstrated how changing administrations' perceptions have been influenced by varying Soviet-related developments as well as by more general international trends and trends related to the evolution of nuclear hardware. The analysis in Chapter 5 showed how fixtures and trends accord with salient parts of the American tradition and how the administrations' image-manifestation often played a crucial role in American politics. Thus it has been shown how a multitude of international and domestic American developments have to be included in an explanation. Still, for any deeper understanding of the origin and strength of various Soviet essentialist-like features since the early 1970s, it is fruitful to consider the relevance of factors not directly mentioned in Chapters 2–7. As the Kennedy administration's initiatives in 1963 can be seen as an expression of a strong American self-confidence in the early 1960s, many conspicuous Soviet essentialist-like themes since the early 1970s can be seen as an expression of a widely shared self-doubt in American society. This self-doubt must primarily be related to the defeat in Vietnam, the first war the United States had lost, and the Watergate affair,

the first resignation in such circumstances of an American President. It was occasionally directly hinted by administration spokesmen that there was a danger that the Soviets would mistake America's retreat from Vietnam as a sign that the United States lacked resolve and steadfastness to defend its interests and its allies around the globe; therefore it was necessary to adopt a more assertive nuclear policy. Also the increasing adherence of elite opinion and the mass public to such a nuclear policy has to be viewed against the background of the Vietnam experience. Considered in that light, the Soviet essentialist trend had been related to two 'non-nuclear' and 'non - Soviet' events, Vietnam and Watergate, and has been a means to counter wider pernicious effects of these shocks, in the United States as well as the rest of the world. Other factors have been shown as important too in a broader attempt to account for all the phenomena expressed in the term the 'Soviet essentialist trend' but it must be concluded that a crucial part of the background for that development had been the Vietnam and Watergate traumas. [4]

From this it follows that *developments not directly related to nuclear arms or the Soviet Union are important to how US governments' perceive and react to the Soviet Union as a nuclear adversary.*

3. The third conclusion originates in the observation that a prominent part of the American tradition naturally leads to Soviet essentialist marked perceptions with their basic aversion to nuclear arms control agreements with the communist adversary. As these attitudes are widely shared in the American society, and because of the different check-and-balance mechanisms in the US political system, it is very difficult for nuclear essentialist-inclined administrations to enter and implement extensive American–Soviet arms control agreements. As Soviet essentialist-inclined administrations are above suspicion for being 'soft' on the Soviets, they are in a much better position to meet the recurrent challenges from such prominent and strong groups in the American society who are averse to any nuclear essentialist-like arms control arrangement with the Soviet Union. It therefore follows that *nuclear essentialist-like arms control agreements with the Soviet Union can only be entered by administrations that advocate parts of a Soviet essentialist attitude.*

4. The fourth conclusion concerns problems of communication between the two nuclear superpowers and the establishment of a US–Soviet nuclear security regime, i.e. a mutually agreed 'range of principles, norms, rules, and procedures which constrain' both superpowers' behavior in the nuclear field. [5] Different national experiences, ideological assumptions and political systems have made the problem of communication and mutual understanding between the United States and the Soviet Union extraordinarily difficult. [6] Both superpowers find it difficult to predict the other's behavior, but for different reasons. The United States cannot predict Soviet behavior and that is often because it has too little information, and is therefore tempted to an uncritical use of preconceived interpretations in

order to understand Soviet policy. The Soviet Union, on the other hand, cannot predict American behavior and that is frequently because it has too much information which can lead to highly divergent conclusions; in turn, the result is that it easily resorts to all the over-simplified Marxist-Leninist notions about the United States. There are other facets of the communication problem between the superpowers than these but, in any case, it must be stressed that the consequences of the *dissimilarities* between the two societies in this respect may be in *parallel*. That is important because it illustrates how one cannot expound the problems between the two superpowers on the basis of a superficial and general 'equality' assertion. West Europeans dissociating themselves 'equally' from both superpowers have indulged an inclination to do so but this exemplifies the logical fallacy of reasoning from one's political antipathies to empirical conclusions. However, it must be added that one similarity between the United States and the Soviet Union in particular as exacerbates problems of mutual understanding: both countries define their identity primarily in political and ideological terms and this often develops into attributing to their own political and moral code a potential universal value which they therefore have the right to make sure will prevail. [7]

While societal differences as well as the peculiar similarity between the United States and the Soviet Union do not mean that they cannot come to agree on more significant and weighty disarmament and nuclear arms control agreements in the future, these features can form the basis for the fourth tentative conclusion: *the establishment of a long-term and mutually agreed nuclear security regime between the United States and the Soviet Union is unlikely because of their basic societal and political traits.*

5. The last two conclusions more specifically concern cognitive problems as to American perceptions. First, advocating the validity of some image of the Soviet Union as a nuclear adversary, US governments display a propensity to maintain that their beliefs are unambiguously supported by reasons that are not logically linked. These beliefs may or may not all be valid but the noteworthy feature is that the validity of one belief is stated on the basis of the validity of another without their being logically connected, a tendency that accords with a general hypothesis that political actors seek consistency between different parts of a perception. [8] This appears most clearly in positions held by images close to the two ideal types: an adherent of views similar to nuclear essentialism combines a special technological 'pessimism' with a special ideological 'optimism' while some adherents of positions close to Soviet essentialism combine a special kind of technological 'optimism' with a special kind of ideological 'pessimism', and both have tended to present their ideological/technological versions of optimism, respectively, as self-evident, given their respective technological/ ideological unalterable facts. When some US government spokesmen have stated that a mutual assured destruction situation is an immutable fact of the nuclear age, they have often taken it as given that Soviet leaders actually shared, or could be persuaded or 'educated' to share, that view of the

common nuclear predicament. On the other hand, when many supporters of Soviet essentialism strongly emphasize that the Soviets do not share that view, they tend automatically and instinctively to endorse different counterforce and war-fighting or strategic defense doctrines as feasible. The point here is not that both conclusions are 'equally' wrong as this study has concluded that the Soviet Union clearly has moved toward a kind of modernist position and thereby a kind of 'mutual assured destruction' view.

Instead, the point is that *it has been a common characteristic of US governments' images that beliefs about the ideological essence of the Soviet Union are presented as logically leading to what is, or should be, technologically feasible. In the same way, beliefs about the technological essence of nuclear arms are presented as logically leading to what Soviet leaders will think.*

6. The last conclusion concerns tendencies of centralization and rationalization in the images. Perception theorists[9] have advanced the hypothesis that as actors perceive and interpret the behavior of others, too many complex events are squeezed into a single pattern. Others are seen as more internally united and their behavior as more centrally directed than they in fact are. The degree to which the other side's policies are the product of internal bargaining, misunderstandings or subordinates not following instructions is underestimated, partly because actors tend to be unfamiliar with the details of the other's policy-making process. The result is that an actor assumes that the adversary has all the information and rationally prepares his behavior.

Evaluating this hypothesis on the basis of the findings in this study, some of the conclusions reached in comparing images and operational environments (cf. Chapter 7) bear it out. More important as a characteristic of US governments' images, however, is the point that it is a basic feature of one of the central notions in American perceptions – the notion of deterrence – that it has a built-in tendency to conceive the Soviet Union as a nuclear adversary in terms of concepts that strongly emphasize centralization and rationalization, without it being possible to test the validity of such ideas. Whether it is Soviet essentialist or nuclear essentialist marked images of deterrence, they assume some kind of rationality, that is, a centralized, reasoned and coordinated decision-making process in the Soviet leadership in some imagined situation. Quite apart from the political expediency of such assumptions and quite apart from the fact that some presumptions always are necessary in political decision-making, this leads to the sixth conclusion: *it is an integral part of central elements of US governments' images that they rely on and operate with assumptions about centralization and rationalization that are extraordinarily open to dispute.*

2. REFLECTIONS ON WESTERN POLICIES

What is the political signification of the findings in this study? Before I embark upon answering that question, it should be emphasized that the relation between political theory and political action is never self-evident.[10] Thus the following attempt to point out what I consider as important political conclusions from this study does not pretend to be the 'conclusive and final' political consequences of the preceding 290 pages. What I intend to outline are various tentative suggestions and political reflections that I deem essential in a policy-making context in democratic societies faced with the Soviet Union as a nuclear superpower. Whether the reader agrees or disagrees with the political views expressed, the considerations put forward deal with critical political issues in the Western debate. Moreover, some of the points focus in particular on what European countries allied to the United States in NATO should take into consideration as they frame their policies in relation to United States, the two superpowers and the nuclear 'reality'.

The first point most directly involves Europe and concerns the credibility of extended deterrence, the American nuclear 'umbrella' over Western Europe. The analysis indicated that all strategic deterrence postures, based on whatever type of retaliation or deterrence by denial, are inherently open to doubt, both given the logic of nuclear deterrence, the character of Soviet policy and the fact that government measures in democratic societies are open to querying from the citizens. But the credibility of all types of extended deterrence are, at least marginally, even more open to doubt. While this does not mean that any extended deterrence policy is without credibility, or that various measures cannot marginally increase the credibility, it means that the recurrent search for some provision to *ensure* the credibility of the American nuclear guarantee to Western Europe is entering a deadend. By always calling for new manifestations of the United States' willingness to 'sacrifice Chicago for Hamburg', as it is sometimes simplified, West Europeans are asking for something that can neither be fully credible nor totally without credibility, given both an obvious American interest in survival and an obvious American interest in a Western Europe not occupied by the Soviet Union.[11] Thus, by being obsessed with a principally insoluble problem – how to 'strengthen and ensure the credibility' of extended deterrence – Western Europe and the United States may be politically highly self-destructive.

The second point, closely related to this, concerns the prominence and further consequences of Soviet essentialistlike images of the political significance of nuclear weapons. That perception was shown being shared by the Soviet leadership (see p. 235–6); actually, this has been a main argument for the political expediency and necessity of a corresponding American perception. But talking about the political meaning of military means, and in particular stressing the actuality of various kinds of nuclear 'coercion' and 'intimidation', observers and politicians are entering a jungle of blurred facts, perceptions, perceptions of perceptions, distortions, fantasies and imaginations where one should be very cautious with insisting on any clear-cut conclusion. If anything, examinations point to an observation that if political actors become obsessed with such problems, they can easily contribute to the realization of their own fear. The crucial problem is therefore whether or not the US and other Western governments are digging a big hole for themselves when they argue that in order to counter this Soviet position, the United States and NATO must adopt a corresponding policy.

The United States and its NATO allies may, I think, be politically self-deceiving and self-destructive if it is allowed – or, rather, if one allows oneself to be persuaded – that these weapons of mass destruction are political symbols, besides the military usefulness in more strict deterrence terms they may have.[12] Any nuclear deterrence policy, including one based on 'existential deterrence', is intrinsically problematic but by being infatuated with the political meaning of all kinds of 'number balances', one may not only remove any basis of rational discourse about nuclear arms decisions, but one risks that one's own obsession with nuclear hardware's 'reputation and commitment' meaning develops into a partly self-inflicted militarization and nuclearization of East–West relations, combined with wildly exaggerated claims from strongly diverging political groups in Western countries. The last-mentioned risk is non-existent in authoritarian and totalitarian political systems, but in democratic societies it can be *politically* shattering. One specific point that the United States' allies in Europe should note in this context is that by calling for strengthening the credibility of the extended deterrence and America's political–military commitment to Western Europe, Europeans may contribute to this. The crux of the matter is whether Americans and other Western observers and politicians are not simply indulging in political self-torture when they assert, as a matter of course, that the United States and NATO must imitate and emulate the Soviets in this field. For assessing the political relevance of these considerations, it is important to note that I do not argue that since the Soviets have recently shown that they are abandoning their traditional view of the political significance of nuclear arms balances, the United States and NATO could *now*, without risk, abandon that view. That may be a politically expedient argument in the Western debate, but my reasoning goes beyond this. The critical issue is whether this 'emulation' of the Soviets has not always been politically fallacious *from a Western point of view and irrespective of the Soviet view* – and will be so again if the Soviets return to their traditional thinking.

This leads to the third point which is related to the elaboration of Soviet policies and positions as a superpower. One main conclusion of this study has been the inadequacy of searching for any Soviet leader's or leadership's 'real intentions' as a way to catch some essence of Soviet policy. It follows that a good deal of the debate on, for example, whether Gorbachev unlike previous Soviet leaders, is 'really peace-minded' and not entertaining ominous designs, is dealing with the issue in immaterial terms. What is summarized by the form 'the Soviet Union as a superpower' is a composite, heterogeneous and changeable quality that is conditioned both by specific Russian and Soviet background factors as well as the Soviet Union's international environment. That, mainly negative, conclusion may be of little help when Western observers and countries (nuclear and non-nuclear) attempt to perceive the issues and lay down their policies, but in this field it is important to clear away a vast undercover of distorting Western preconceptions *and* still realize that some preconceptions may not only be an intellectual and political necessity but may cognitively be fruitful as well. The meaning of this can be illustrated by quoting Stanley Hoffmann's note that Western clichés about an enemy may 'tell us a great deal about ourselves; but sometimes they contain half-truths about the enemy and not just revelations about us.'[13]

One evident example of the complex and changeable character of Soviet nuclear policy is the change in Soviet INF policy between 1979 and 1987. Compared to what the Soviets once said they could 'obviously never countenance', their adherence to the zero-zero solution in 1987 is really staggering, even if one assumes that the primary Soviet goal throughout the period has been averting the deployment of American land-based missiles in Western Europe capable of reaching the Soviet Union. This switch in Soviet policy shows, first of all, that Western governments and publics should be cautious about attaching an overly independent weight to Soviet statements about what it 'obviously' can or cannot accept. But the word 'independent' indicates its double-edged nature. One side of the problem arises from many Western (primarily West European) observers' and politicians' predilection for taking Soviet declarations as indicating an immovable and, it is often implied or openly stated from an oddly 'reversed' nuclear essentialist point of view, reasonable and justifiable Soviet position. But the problem has another side too: when the Soviet Union strongly opposes a particular Western position, that fact may, after some time, be transformed into *the* predominating argument for a Western position, particularly when the issue is highly contested in the Western debate. The result easily turns into the Western policy-making process developing into a simple matter of performing the one correct move in a Western vs. Soviet zero-sum game, accompanied by the argument that the *Soviets* see it that way. (And, again, that may be correct but not necessarily conclusive for Western policy.) Noting this trap does not solve a Western policy-making problem, but it illustrates that the political process in democratic countries risks becoming a hostage of Soviet manifestations in more than one way – and that point is essential.

This touches on the fourth point: American and Western negotiating policy in relations with the Soviet Union where the 'negotiating from strength' idea is dominant. Evaluating that idea in a broader political perspective, the most important observation concerns the problem that a persistent trumpeting of the idea risks a pernicious distortion of the image-holder's goals and values. This is obviously a natural danger considered from a nuclear essentialist point of view but also from other perspectives – including different, more cautious, versions of Soviet essentialism. Not only can the idea cause a greater nuclear arms stockpile than otherwise would have been 'necessary' and whether or not this has further damaging consequences (for example, by causing a 'needless' arms race) it means drawing resources away from other goals. More important is the possibility that this fixture in American images may appear self-confirming in that all indicators pointing to its political and cognitive dubious validity simply may be dismissed in favor of an interpretation which focuses solely on those cases that indicate its validity. Thereby it is assured a continuing prominence in American and Western policy, but one based on a doubtful record. This self-serving function of images can be observed among many highly divergent readings of the Soviet Union as a nuclear power – but noting this general trait of images does not obviate this case, of course – and it has to be emphasized that any pernicious effect specifically originating in the 'negotiating from strength' notion increases strongly the more nuclear essentialist goals and values are adopted. Still, the crux of the matter is that comparing the 'negotiating from strength' idea with the record of Soviet negotiating behavior shows that a general fixed adherence to this idea may blur the issue of shaping a policy *vis-à-vis* the Soviet Union as a nuclear superpower, and that also considered from goals and values held is some versions of Soviet essentialism. A democratic policy-making process will often mitigate that risk, but this is far from always the case, especially considering the character of the American tradition.

As the last point in these reflections, one may ask specifically about the possibilities of shifting American and Western nuclear policies toward a more nuclear essentialist marked policy. The inquiry in this study showed several features of Soviet policies and positions – which recently have become particularly prominent – that could be used as a starting point and for backing up a much more nuclear essentialist policy. One of the remarkable features of the new Soviet policies and positions is the degree to which the reasonings on nuclear arms presented by Soviet observers and leaders in the late 1980s resemble the reasonings presented by the most distinct American advocates of nuclear arms control in the 1960s. (Compare the visions reviewed on pp. 37–8, 43–5 and 48–50, 55–7 with Gorbachev's statements.) However this Soviet 'nuclear learning'[14] may be explained, the hopes of the classical Western arms controllers as to the possibility for 'educating' the Soviets seem really close to becoming fulfilled – after 20–25 years. However, as the Soviet policy is not solely a reaction to the outside world's, in particular the American, policy, it is important to note that a meaningful nuclear essentialist policy cannot simply be a matter of initiating a straight nuclear disarmament process combined with issuing some faithful nuclear essentialist proclamations. Of course, no one ever knows with certainly in this field but the findings in this study cannot be used as an unequivocal argument for that line – even if the remarkable changes in Soviet policy since 1986–7 are included.

What this examination suggests, however, in that the operational environment to American and NATO's nuclear policy is highly ambiguous, that is, Soviet nuclear policy and its sources are ultimately indeterminate when it comes to evaluating the feasibility of a distinctly more nuclear essentialist policy. An observer can pick out those aspects of the Soviet policy which point to its impossibility while others can emphasize opposite traits, and the last group can stress those traits' prominence during recent years. Thus, as no empirical examination can result in definite conclusions because the findings are simply not that unambiguous, that leaves a critical scope for broader political reflections. Noting that point, it is natural to conclude that the recent Soviet changes really open a possibility for nuclear essentialist marked agreements between the superpowers – even if some 'final' settlement on the nuclear issue is illusory.

One principal difficulty in adopting a more nuclear essentialist policy is that prominent parts of the American tradition press in the opposite direction. However, both aspects of Realist and Idealist thinking can fruitfully be used as a basis for an alternative perception and policy. In particular, that type of Realism which warns against illusions about America's omnipotence – and which occasionally has appeared in parts of the US governments in the 1960s and 1970s – seems highly pertinent when it concerns evaluating the tenability and political value of American nuclear policies. Equally important is a need to ask – as a shrewd American scholar and observer has put it[15] – if the more straightforward versions of what here is termed 'Soviet essentialist policies', will be constrained by American considerations about what kind of people Americans suppose themselves to be. In the end, an effective, well-functioning and persistent Soviet essentialist policy may be impossible for a democratic nation to pursue, in particular when this nation is allied to other democratic nations. That discrepancy between image and operational environment could be the most insoluble problem for this aspect of American nuclear policy.

Altogether, while there is an evident need for better communication and understanding between the two superpowers – in the sense of 'empathy' as distinct from sympathy, i.e. what is needed is better cognition rather than affection[16] – it is a main conclusion of these reflections that it is far too easy to underestimate and, in particular, misjudge the character of the problems and present the two countries in facile terms, be they simply similarity or dissimilarity terms. Observers – in particular many West Europeans – should also avoid exhortations about the need for mutual goodwill as an unambiguous requirement and be cautious of asserting that a shared interest in averting nuclear war is or ought to be an overall key to establish a positive superpower cooperation. Simply stating the reality of common security is a poor guideline for action.

3. LOOKING TO THE FUTURE

A final attempt to assess future developments in the American–Soviet nuclear relationship in continuation of the findings in this book will apply three starting points: the situation prevailing after the Bush administration took over from the Reagan administration in January 1989, new departures in Soviet policy, and the prospects after the agreement on the elimination of land-based intermediate- and short-range nuclear missiles in December 1987.

Compared to the situation when President Reagan took over from President Carter in January 1981, one of the most notable changes is the new American self-confidence. Indeed, the regeneration of that undefinable and elusive quality–America's self-confidence – during the Reagan administration's tenure is remarkable. As it has often appeared that factor is important for the development of the relationship between the superpowers, the situation in the spring of 1989 is clearly promising for the near future, whether détente, nuclear arms control and disarmament agreements or strategic stability is seen as desirable. In addition, if the third conclusion (p. 289) holds, the prospect for a strategic arms reduction agreement between the superpowers, that is an agreement which can be implemented in the American political system, was enhanced by President Bush's victory over Governor Dukakis in the election in November 1988, primarily because Dukakis would have been more vulnerable to domestic opposition in this field. The problems arise if the time-horizon is extended. If the first conclusion (p. 288) holds, the American political structure will cause several 'disturbances' in the future. Moreover, considered in the light of traditionally dominating American perceptions of the Soviet Union, the changes in Soviet policy initiated by the Gorbachev leadership constitute a real and unprecedented challenge.[17] The United States and Western Europe may be faced with problems and policy choices where appeals to familiar trains of thought and solutions could appear highly contentious and futile.

It is evident that several aspects of Soviet military policy have changed markedly since 1986–7. Particularly in view of the putative consequences of Russian and Soviet history for attaching military efficiency and defensive strength supreme importance (cf. p. 269–70), the new features of Soviet policy seem seminal. Even if the review of traditional Soviet dispositions can point out several natural possibilities for 'relapses' in Soviet policy, both these changes and corresponding innovations in the years to come can reasonably be seen as reducing the danger of military confrontations, and especially so if the United States and other Western countries adopt, or go on adopting, complementary policies. Thus, the specific developments of Soviet military doctrine, its force structures (nuclear and conventional), as well as Soviet negotiating polices are critical to future developments and always in their interplay with Western initiatives and reactions.

But even if these directly military-related aspects of Soviet policy are important for a lasting and significant reduction of the danger of military confrontations and war, there is one specific aspect of general Soviet foreign policy whose development is critical for any long-term decrease of the danger of war, conventional and nuclear, in particular in Europe. If the Soviet Union continuously considers it a fundamental interest to maintain the Soviet version of socialism and one-party systems in East European countries and is prepared to intervene militarily to ensure that (the Brezhnev doctrine), one substantial source of tension and war in Europe will endure. As the Soviet Union could come to see its interest in allowing some diluted – and markedly more diluted than today – version of one-party socialism in some East European countries, the issue is far from being a Soviet choice between two simple alternatives. However, one specific problem could be that while the Soviet Union's willingness to acquiesce in such a development may increase in the future, it may also vary from one country to another – especially considering the geographic location of different East European countries – and it is far from certain that a greater Soviet compliance with political pluralism and freedom of expression in Eastern Europe will be greatest *vis-à-vis* those countries that most markedly incline to liberate themselves from the Soviet version of socialism. Poland might become a test case, given the combination of its geographical location and urge to independence. In addition, it will be important that Western countries see the crucial difference between recognizing, on the one hand, the evident *relation* between this political factor (Soviet policy *vis-à-vis* Eastern Europe) and the risk of military confrontations and, on the other hand, adopting that relation as a *linkage* in their policies *vis-à-vis* the Soviet Union in arms control and disarmament negotiations.

But in any case it follows that the development concerning this aspect of the Soviet policy is critical for the long-term development and the danger of war in Europe. Assessing the prospects in the spring of 1989, there are clear indicators that the present Soviet leadership inclines toward approving much more independent developments in Eastern Europe than ever since the Second World War. [18] Western policies are important for this, but while it is relatively easy to argue how Western policies could destroy a positive development in this field, it is more difficult to reason how some Western policy could markedly promote such a Soviet policy. In the end, the internal development in the Soviet Union is the crucial factor.

One aspect of this problem which must be noted is the relation between a continuation and strengthening of *perestroika* and *glasnost* and possible repercussions in Eastern Europe. [19] One effect could be a strong increase in demands for similar policies in East European countries, directed at the incumbent Soviet-allied leaderships in these countries, and combined with extensive demands for more independence in relation to the Soviet Union. That situation could escalate into a critical test of the tenability and steadfastness of all aspects of the new Soviet policy, foreign and domestic, that could be followed by a serious backlash in Soviet policies. If that happens, many Western observers and politicians will surely take it as proof that the Soviet policy departures were not 'sincere' and not even Gorbachev could be 'trusted'. But as a foundation for assessing current or future developments in Soviet politics and policy, it is far too narrow to search for any Soviet leader's 'sincerity'. Further, if Gorbachev's innovations in Soviet Eastern Europe policy are *not* 'honestly' meant, they could, in some future situation, seriously restrain this or a future Soviet leadership's possibilities for military intervention against a country in Eastern Europe. It is therefore much more important to assess the significance of a broad and only vaguely observed, set of societal factors in the Soviet state and its foreign policy. Moreover, it cannot be presumed that there is always a positive one-to-one relationship between liberalization in domestic Soviet politics and a more liberal Soviet policy *vis-à-vis* Eastern Europe.

Concerning the significance and long-term impact of the December 1987 disarmament agreement between the United States and the Soviet Union, one can start by noting that the agreement is indeed unique and unprecedented, primarily in that the two superpowers have agreed to *abolish* some of their nuclear weapons. Even if the arms to be dismantled only constitute a small percentage of all nuclear stockpiles in the world, and even if a quantitive cutback does not necessarily mean less war danger, the agreement may have a significant political-psychological impact. If the agreement is followed, within a couple of years, by an agreement to cut strategic nuclear weapons by 50 per cent and that agreement is endorsed by the US Senate, then a truly new and seminal departure will seem in prospect. If these conditions are realized within a few years, it will surely be hailed by political leaders in East and West and many others as indicating the initiation of a true and lasting period of détente (or whatever equivalent term will be used) and limitation of the nuclear threat.

If these conditions are fulfilled – and there are several critical if's – a wise and prudent observer should reduce his or her expectations as to the long term. The fulfillment of all such unprecedented events cannot be used as a basis for further 'unprecedented' developments, of course. A study of history or current history can result in calling attention to various factors that seem significant. It has been shown in this book that both American approaches to the nuclear issues and foreign affairs as well as Soviet approaches to the nuclear issue and foreign affairs are closely related to ingrained historical and ideological attitudes, and so it leads to a clear caution against not only exaggerating the durability of conspicuous and marked swings in nuclear policies and superpower relations but also against taking 'seminal' and 'epoch-making' developments as indicating an enduring trend.

At a time of cooperative relations between the United States and the Soviet Union aimed at controlling and cutting nuclear arms with lasting benefits for the rest of the world (and the last condition is not an obvious corollary of the first), that conclusion may seem overly pessimistic. At a time of antagonistic relations between the two nuclear superpowers, it gives new reason for optimism, however. But it may appear a prudent and correct observation in both cases.

Notes

CHAPTER 1 INTRODUCTION

1. William T.R. Fox, 'International control of atomic weapons', Bernard Brodie (ed.), *The Absolute Weapon: Atomic Power and World Order*, New York, 1946, p. 169.
2. Eugene Anschel (ed.), *American Appraisals of Soviet Russia, 1917–1977*, Metuchen, N.J. & London, 1978, pp. 329–52; Peter G. Filene (ed.), *American Views of Soviet Russia 1917–1965*, Homewood, Illinois, 1968, pp. 233–51 and 360–401; John Lewis Gaddis, *Russia, the Soviet Union, and the United States. An Interpretative History*, New York, 1978, pp. 57–279; John Van Oudenaren, *U.S. Leadership Perceptions of the Soviet Problem Since 1945*, R-2843-NA, Rand, California, March 1982, p. 1.
3. Daniel Yergin, *Shattered Peace. The Origins of the Cold War and the National Security State*, Pelican Books, 1980, p. 11.
4. Cf. The review of 'schools of thought' in the debate on nuclear weapons: William R. Van Cleave, 'The nuclear weapons debate', Richard G. Head and Ervin J. Rokke (eds), *American Defense Policy*, third edition, Baltimore and London, 1973, pp. 87–98 (reprinted from *U.S. Naval Institute Proceedings*, May 1966, pp. 26–38); see also Charles-Philippe David, *Debating Counterforce. A Conventional Approach in a Nuclear Age*, Boulder, Colorado and London, 1987, pp. 12–28.

    The view of nuclear weapons as 'absolute' weapons was first manifested in Brodie (ed.), *op. cit.* A part of the early debate on this view is reprinted in *Arms Control. Readings From Scientific American*, San Francisco, 1973, pp. 24–9. The usability of nuclear arms was stressed in William Liscum Borden, *There Will Be No Time*, New York, 1946.
5. William Hyland, 'The Soviet Union in the American perspective: perceptions and realities, America's security in the 1980's', *Adelphi Papers*, No. 174, The International Institute for Strategic Studies (IISS), London, Spring 1982, p. 52. A general exposition of these problems is: Joseph S. Nye, Jr (ed.), *The Making of America's Soviet Policy*, New Haven and London, 1984.
6. See, for instance, the two vivid articles 'The thunder-clap' and 'A little something', *Time*, Vol. LIV (3 October 1949), pp. 7–8 and 55, reprinted in Filene (ed.), *op. cit.*, pp. 237–42. See also Gabriel A. Almond, *The American People and Foreign Policy*, seventh printing, New York, 1967, p. 110.
7. Brodie, (ed.), *op. cit.*, p. 63; Norman Moss, *Men Who Play God. The Story of the Hydrogen Bomb*, Penguin Books, 1972, p. 22; Herbert York, *The Advisors. Oppenheimer, Teller & The Superbomb*, San Francisco, 1976, pp. 35–6. On the Finletter Report, see John Prados, *The Soviet Estimate. U.S. Intelligence Analysis & Russian Military Strength*, New York, 1982, p. 39; George H. Quester, *Nuclear Diplomacy. The First Twenty-Five Years*, New York, 1970,

p. 36; Robert C. Williams and Philip L. Cantenon (eds), *The American Atom. A Documentary History of Nuclear Politics from the Discovery of Fission to the Present. 1939–1984*, Philadelphia, 1984, pp. 114f; and Survival In The Air Age. Finletter Commission (excerpts), Carroll W. Pursell, Jr (ed.), *The Military–Industrial Complex*, New York, 1972, pp. 178–97, especially p. 181.

8. Lawrence Freedman, *The Evolution of Nuclear Strategy*, New York, 1981, pp. 65ff.

9. A Report to the National Security Council by the Executive Secretary on United States Objectives and Programs for National Security, reprinted in Thomas H. Etzold and John Lewis Gaddis (eds), *Containment: Documents on American Policy and Strategy, 1945–1950*, New York, 1978, pp. 385–442, especially pp. 387–95, 398, 402–4, 422–6, 430, and 435. NSC-68 was declassified in 1975.

See also Samuel F. Wells, Jr, 'Sounding the tocsin: NSC-68 and The Soviet Threat', *International Security*, Vol. 4, No. 2, Fall 1979, pp. 116–58; two articles by, respectively, John Lewis Gaddis and Paul Nitze, 'NSC-68 and the Soviet threat reconsidered', *International Security*, Vol. 4, No. 4, Spring 1980, pp. 164–76.

A thorough review of NSC-68 is in Paul Y. Hammond, 'NSC-68; prologue to rearmament', Warner R. Schilling, Paul Y. Hammond and Glenn II. Snyder, *Strategy, Politics, and Defense Budgets*, New York and London, 1962, pp. 271–378.

10. Etzold and Gaddis (eds), *op. cit.*, pp. 415–21.

11. Freedman, *op. cit.*, p. 83. On the New Look, see Samuel P. Huntington, *The Common Defense. Strategic Programs in National Politics*, New York and London 1961, pp. 64–88, and Glenn H. Snyder, 'The "New Look" of 1953', Schilling, Hammond and Snyder, *op. cit.*, pp. 383–524.

12. Secretary Dulles delivered the speech on massive retaliation to the Council on Foreign Relations in New York on 12 January; cf. *The Department of State Bulletin*, 25 January 1954. See also John Foster Dulles, 'Policy for security and peace', *Foreign Affairs*, Vol. 32, No. 3, April 1954, pp. 353–64.

13. John Foster Dulles, 'Challenge and response In US policy', *Foreign Affairs*, Vol. 36, No. 1, October 1957, pp. 25–43. Besides, see Huntington *op. cit.*, pp. 88ff., on 'The New New Look'.

14. Lawrence Freedman, *U.S. Intelligence And The Soviet Strategic Threat*, London, 1977, pp. 65–7.

15. The report was entitled 'Deterrence and Survival in the Nuclear Age' and declassified in 1973, subject to the deletion of three lines which continue to be classified 'Top Secret', cf. Desmond Ball, *Politics and Force Levels. The Strategic Missile Program of the Kennedy Administration*, Los Angeles and London, 1980, p. 27. Morton H. Halperin, 'The Gaither Committee and the policy process', *World Politics*, xiii: 3, April 1961, pp. 360–84; Fred Kaplan, *The Wizards of Armageddon*, New York, 1983, pp. 125–43.

16. Prados, *op. cit.*, pp. 77ff.

17. Cf. McNamara's statement, *Hearings Before The Subcommittee Of The Committee On Appropriations. House of Representatives*, 7 April 1961, p. 58.

See also Ball, *op. cit.*, pp. 5–25 and 88–104; Edgar Bottome, *The Missile Gap: A Study Of The Formation Of Military And Political Policy*, Cranbury, New Jersey, 1971 (see especially the appendix, pp. 224ff. about the quantitative changes in the estimations of the Soviet missile force); Roy Licklider, 'The missile gap controversy', *Political Science Quarterly*, Vol. LXXXV, No. 4, December 1970. pp. 600–15; Prados, *op. cit.*, pp. 86–95; Quester, *op. cit.*, pp. 145–203.

18. Ball, *op. cit.*, pp. 41ff., 170ff. and 234–52.
19. Freedman, 'U.S. intelligence and the Soviet strategic threat', *op. cit.*, p. 78.
20. *American Images of Soviet Foreign Policy. An Inquiry into Recent Appraisals from the Academic Community*, New Haven and London, 1970.
21. 'Choices in the postwar world (1): containment and the Soviet Union', Charles Gati (ed.), *Caging The Bear: Containment And The Cold War*, New York, 1974, pp. 85–108.
22. *U.S. Leadership Perceptions of the Soviet Problem Since 1945*, R-2843-NA, Rand, California, March 1982. (Cf. note 2.)
23. *Containment, Soviet Behavior, and Grand Strategy*, Policy Papers in International Affairs, Number 16, Institute of International Studies, University of California, Berkeley, 1981 (Osgood's introduction to a publication edited by him).
24. *Perception and Behavior in Soviet Foreign Policy*, University of Pittsburgh Press, 1985.
25. *Strategic Stalemate: Nuclear Weapons and Arms Control in American Politics*, London, 1984.
26. *Perceived Images. U.S. and Soviet Assumptions and Perceptions in Disarmament*, New Jersey, 1986.
27. Robert Jervis, *Perception and Misperception in International Politics*, Princeton, 1976, pp. 3ff; Herbert C. Kelman, 'Social-psychological approaches to the study of international relations: definitions and scope', Kelman (ed.), *International Behavior. A Social-Psychological Analysis*, New York, 1965, pp. 3–39, and Kelman,'Social-psychological approaches to the study of international relations: the question of relevance', *ibid.*, pp. 565–607.

   Also see: Ole H. Holsti, 'Foreign policy formations viewed cognitively', Robert Axelrod (ed.), *Structure of Decision*, Princeton, 1976, pp.18–54, especially pp. 22ff. (a reprint of Ole R. Holsti, 'Foreign policy decision-makers viewed psychologically: cognitive processes approaches', G. Matthew Bonham and Michael J. Shapiro (eds), *Thought and Action in Foreign Policy*, Proceedings of the London Conference on Cognitive Process Models of Foreign Policy, March 1973, Basle and Stuttgart, 1977, pp. 10–74).
28. Cf. Richard C. Snyder, H.W. Bruck and Burton Sapin, 'Decision-making as an approach to the study of international politics', Snyder, Bruck and Sapin (eds), *Foreign Policy Decision-Making. An Approach to the Study of International Politics*, New York, 1963 (the article was first published in 1954.)

   See also Richard Little and Steve Smith, *Belief Systems and International Relations*, Oxford, 1988, pp. 1–7.
29. Sidney Verba, 'Assumptions of rationality and non-rationality in models of the international system', Klaus Knorr and Sidney Verba (eds), *The International System. Theoretical Essays*, Princeton, 1961, pp. 93–117, especially pp. 113ff.
30. Cf. respectively Graham T. Allison, *Essence of Decision. Explaining the Cuban Missile Crisis*, Boston, 1971, and John D. Steinbruner, *The Cybernetic Theory of Decision*, Princeton University Press, 1974.
31. One of the first expositions is Kenneth E. Boulding, *The Image. Knowledge in Life and Society*, The University of Michigan Press, 1966 (first edition 1956). See also John C. Farrell and Asa P. Smith (eds), *Image and Reality in World Politics*, New York and London, 1968. (First published in *Journal of International Affairs*, Vol. XXI, No. 1, 1967.)

   Various aspects of this approach are reviewed in Kenneth E. Boulding, 'National Images and International Systems', James N. Rosenau (ed.), *International Politics and Foreign Policy*, New York, 1969, pp. 422–31 (first published in *The Journal of Conflict Resolution*, III (1959); in the same volume:

Robert Jervis, 'Hypotheses on misperception', *ibid.*, pp. 239–54 (reprint from *World Politics*, Vol. XX. 1968, pp. 454–79); Michael J. Shapiro and G. Matthew Bonham, 'Cognitive Process and Foreign Policy Decision-Making', *International Studies Quarterly*, Vol. 17, No. 2, June 1973, pp. 147–74; Alexander L. George, *Presidential Decsion-Making in Foreign Policy: The Effective Use of Information and Advice*, Westview Press, Boulder, Colorado, 1980, especially chapters 2 and 3 on 'Psychological Aspects of Decision-Making: Adapting to Constraints on Rational Decision-Making' and 'The Importance of Beliefs and Images'; Christer Jönsson (ed.), *Cognitive Dynamics and International Politics*, London, 1982.

Two other important publications are: Robert Jervis, *The Logic of Images in International Relations*, Princeton University Press, 1970, and Joseph de Rivera, *The Psychological Dimension of Foreign Policy*, Columbus, Ohio, 1968. Also see the publications cited in note 27.

The theory on cognitive maps has developed notable approaches, cf. in particular Edward C. Tolman, 'Cognitive maps in rats and men', Roger M. Downs and David Stea (eds), *Image and Environment. Cognitive Mapping And Spatial Behavior*, Chicago, 1973, pp. 27–50.

32. Harold H. Kelley, 'The process of causal attribution', *The American Psychologist*, February 1973, pp. 107 28; Harold H. Kelley and John L. Michela, 'Attribution theory and research', *Annual Review of Psychology 1980*, 31, pp. 457–501.

33. Leo Ross, 'The intuitive psychologist and his shortcomings: distortions in the attribution process', Leonard Berkowitz (ed.), *Advances In Experimental Social Psychology*, Volume 10, London, 1977, pp. 175ff.; Daniel Heradsveit, *The Arab –Israeli Conflict. Psychological Obstacles to Peace*, Oslo, 1979, pp. 17–23.

34. Richard Nishett and Lee Ross, *Human Inference: strategies and shortcomings of social judgment*, New Jersey, 1980. pp. 231f.

35. Harold H. Kelley, 'The two major facets of attribution research: an overview of the field', Hans Hiebsch (ed.), *Social Psychology*, New York, 1982, pp. 11f.; Kelley and Michela, *op. cit.*, pp. 468f.

36. Cf. especially the two articles by Herbert C. Kelman in Kelman (ed.), *op. cit.*, and Katarina Brodin, 'Belief systems, doctrines, and foreign policy', *Cooperation and Conflict*, VII, 1972, pp. 97–112; see also Philip M. Burgess, *Elite Images and Foreign Policy Outcomes. A Study of Norway*, Ohio State University Press, 1967, pp. 4–11.

37. J. David Singer, 'The level-of-analysis problem in international relations', Klaus Knorr and Sidney Verba (eds), *op. cit*, pp. 86–9.

38. Lawrence S. Falkowski, 'Predicting flexibility with memory profiles', Falkowski (ed.), *Psychological Models in International Politics*, Westview Press, Boulder, Colorado, 1979, p. 50; David J. Finlay, Ole R. Holsti and Richard R. Fagen, *Enemies in Politics*, Chicago, Illinois, 1967, p. vi; Alexander L. George, 'The causal nexus between cognitive beliefs and decision-making behavior: the "operational code" belief system', Falkowski (ed.), *op. cit.*, p. 98; Jerel A. Rosati, 'The impact of beliefs on behavior: the foreign policy of the Carter administration', Donald A. Sylvan and Steve Chan (eds), *Foreign Policy Decision Making. Perception, Cognition, and Artificial Intelligence*, New York, 1984, p. 158ff.

39. Snyder, Bruck and Sapin, *op. cit.*, approaches this view (for instance p. 33); James N. Rosenau, 'The premises and promises of decision-making analysis', in James C. Charlesworth, *Contemporary Political Analysis*, New York, 1967, pp. 200f.

40. See especially George, Falkowski (ed.), *op. cit.*, pp. 107ff., Robert Jervis,

'Political decision-making: recent contributions', *Political Psychology*/Summer 1980, pp. 86–101; and Philip E. Tetlock, 'Policymakers' images of international conflict', *Journal of Social Issues*, Vol. 39, No. 1, Spring 1983 (special issue on 'Images of nuclear war'), pp. 67–86, especially p. 70.

41. Harold and Margaret Sprout, 'Environmental Factors in the Study of International Politics', *The Journal of Conflict Resolution*, Vol. I, No. 4, 1957, pp. 309–28, and *The Ecological Perspective on Human Affairs*, Princeton, 1965. Due to the physical connotations of the word environment, the two authors prefer the word milieu (but the adjective environmental); this is not considered necessary here, but the broad meaning of the term environment has to be noted. Harold and Margaret Sprout have elaborated this approach in: *An Ecological Paradigm for the Study of International Politics*, Research Monograph No. 30, Center of International Studies, Princeton University 1968, and *Toward A Politics of the Planet Earth*, New York, 1971.

   Also Michael Brecher, *The Foreign Policy System of Israel. Setting, Images, Process*, London, 1972, p. 5 on the external (foreign) and internal (domestic) segments of the operational environment; and Michael Brecher, Blema Steinberg and Janice Stein, 'A framework for research on foreign policy behavior', *Journal of Conflict Resolution*, No. 13, March 1972, pp. 75ff.

42. Cf. Robert Jervis, 'Hypotheses on misperception', Rosenau (ed.), *op. cit.*, pp. 239–54.

43. Arthur A. Stein, 'When misperception matter', *World Politics*, Vol. XXXIV, No. 4, July 1982, pp. 505–26 and Jervis, 'Hypotheses on misperception', *op. cit.* Also see Jack S. Levy, 'Misperception and the causes of war: theoretical linkages and analytical problems', *World Politics*, Vol. XXXVI, No. 1, October 1983, pp. 76–99.

44. In the introduction to the Charter of United Nations' Educational, Scientific and Cultural Organization (UNESCO), it reads: 'since wars begin in the minds of men, it is in the minds of men that the defences of peace must be constructed'.

45. Cf. Strobe Talbott, *Deadly Gambit. The Vivid Inside Story Of Arms Control Negotiations*. Vintage Books Edition, New York, 1985, p. 5.

   Seweryn Bialer, 'Soviet–American conflict: from the past to the future', Seweryn Bialer, Lee Hamilton, Jerry Hough and John Steinbruner, *U.S.–Soviet Relations: Perspectives for the Future*, Center for National Policy, Washington, DC, September 1984, pp. 11ff; also see especially Max Beloff, *Foreign Policy and the Democratic Process*, Johns Hopkins Paperbacks edition, Baltimore, 1965, p. 131.

   At a conference in Brussels in January 1984, Henry Kissinger stated: 'The danger of war after all, resides less in the existence of the weapons of mass destruction than in the minds of men who are in a position to order their use', cf. *The Washington Quarterly*, Vol. 7, No. 3, Summer 1984, p. 142.

46. A good introduction to this vexing problem is Richard Betts, 'Nuclear peace: mythology and futurology', *The Journal of Strategic Studies*, Vol. 2, No. 1, 1979, pp. 83–101 (review of David C. Gompert, Michael Mandelbaum, Richard L. Garwin and John H. Barton, *Nuclear Weapons and World Politics: Alternatives for the Future*, New York, 1971).

   See also, for example, Lawrence Freedman, *The Price of Peace. Living with the Nuclear Dilemma*, London, 1986, pp. 1–26; Robert Jervis, *The Illogic of American Nuclear Strategy*, Ithaca and London, 1984, especially pp. 22 and 38, and 'The Nuclear Revolution and the Common Defense', *Political Science Quarterly*, Vol. 101, No. 5, 1986, pp. 698–9.

47. See Richard J. Barnet, *The Giants. Russia and America*, New York, 1977. On

p. 95 Barnet writes: 'The cold war is a history of mutually reinforcing misconceptions'.

Also C. E. Osgood, *An Alternative to War and Surrender*, Urbana, 1962, and Anatol Rapoport, *The Big Two. Soviet–American Perceptions of Foreign Policy*, New York, 1971.

48. Cf. especially Ray S. Cline, *World Power Trends and U.S. Foreign Policy for the 1980's*, Westview Press, Boulder, Colorado, 1980 (revision of *World Power Assessment. A Calculus of Strategic Drift*, The Center for Strategic and International Studies (CSIS), Georgetown University, Washington, DC, 1975); Edward Luttwak, 'Perceptions of military force and US defense policy', *Survival*, January–February 1977, pp. 2–8, and Luttwak, 'The missing dimension of U.S. defense policy: force, perceptions, and power', Donald C. Daniel (ed.), *International Perceptions Of The Superpower Military Balance*, New York, 1978, pp. 21–39.

A thorough analysis of this type of writings is Earl C. Ravenal, 'Perceptions of American power', Franklin D. Margiotta (ed.), *Evolving Strategic Realities: Implications for U.S. Policy-Makers*, National Defense University Press, Washington, DC, 1980, pp. 145–70.

49. This is extensively considered in: Gunnar Frederikson, *Det Politiska Språket* (The Political Language), Uddevala, 1969 (first published in 1962), and: Arne Næss, *Empirisk Semantik* (Empirical Semantic), Oslo, 1970.

50. Kjell Goldmann, *International Norms And War Between States*, Stockholm, 1971. pp. 12–13 and 33–4.

51. Murray Edelman, *Political Language. Words That Succeed and Policies That Fail*, New York, 1977, pp. 23f.; Thomas M. Franck and Edward Weisband. *Word Politics. Verbal Strategy Among the Superpowers*, New York, pp. 114ff.; J.G.A. Pocock, 'Verbalizing a political act: toward a politics of speech', Michael J. Shapiro (ed.), *Language and Politics*, Oxford, 1984, pp. 25ff.; Michael J. Shapiro, 'Interpretation and political understanding', *NUPI notat*, Nr. 186, July 1980, norsk utenrikspolitisk institut, Oslo.

52. Cf., for instance, Richard K. Herrmann, *op. cit.*, pp. 30–1. It has to be noted that the concrete definition of the terms 'images' and 'perceptions' differs from one scholar to another.

53. Brodin, *op. cit.*, passim, and Rosati, *op. cit.*, p. 163.

54. Desmond Ball, 'U.S. strategic forces: how would they be used?', *International Security*, Vol. 7, No. 3, Winter 1982/3, pp. 32–3; Desmond Ball, 'Targeting for strategic deterrence', *Adelphi Papers*, No. 185, IISS, London, Summer 1983, p. 37.

55. Cf. Roman Kolkowicz, 'Strategic elites and politics of superpower', *Journal of International Affairs*, Vol. 26, No. 1, 1972, pp. 40–59; and J. David Singer, 'Threat perception and national decision makers', Dean G. Pruitt and Richard C. Snyder (eds), *Theory & Research On The Causes Of War*, Englewood Cliffs, N.J., 1969, pp. 39–42 (excerpt from 'Threat perception and the armament-tension dilemma', *Journal of Conflict Resolution*, Vol. 2 (1958), pp. 90–105). Also Stanley Hoffmann, *Janus and Minerva. Essays in the Theory and Practice of International Politics*, Boulder and London, 1987, p. 434.

56. Brecher, *op. cit.*, pp. 2–4.

CHAPTER 2   IMAGES 1961–74

1. Max Weber, *Gesammelte Aufsätze zur Wissenschaftslehre*, Johannes

Winckelmann (ed.), Tübingen, 1968, pp. 190ff; besides, see Carl J. Friedrich, *Man and His Government. An Empirical Theory of Politics*, New York, 1963, pp. 28ff; and H.H. Bruun, *Science, Values and Politics in Max Weber's Methodology*, Copenhagen, 1972, pp. 201–39.

2. Noel Kaplowitz, 'Psychopolitical dimensions of international relations: the reciprocal effects of conflict strategies', *International Studies Quarterly*, Vol. 28, No. 4, December 1984, pp. 373–406, especially pp. 375–86.

3. Cf. Robert A. Levine, *The Arms Debate*, Cambridge, Mass., 1963.

4. *Department of State Bulletin* (DSB), 6 February 1961, p. 175. See also Secretary McNamara on 'our major adversary in the world struggle', *Military Procurement Authorization Fiscal Year 1962*, Hearings Before the Committee On Armed Services. United States Senate, 4 April 1961, p. 4.

5. Kennedy declared: 'To those nations who would make themselves our adversary, we offer not a pledge but a request: that both sides begin anew the quest for peace, before the dark powers of destruction unleashed by science engulf all humanity in planned or accidental self-destruction'; he referred to 'that uncertain balance of terror that stays the hand of mankind's final war' and stated 'Let both sides explore what problems unite us instead of belaboring those problems which divide us', *DSB, op. cit.*, p. 176.

6. White House statement on the resumption of Soviet tests, 30 August 1961, *Documents on Disarmament 1961* (Doc.), United States Arms Control And Disarmament Agency (ACDA), Washington, DC. 1962, pp. 348f.; Radio Television Address by President Kennedy on Nuclear Testing and Disarmament, 2 March 1962, *Doc. 1962*, pp. 66–75.

7. In his address to the UN General Assembly 'Let us call a truce to terror', on 25 September 1961, Kennedy stated: 'Today, every inhabitant of this planet must contemplate the day when this planet may no longer be habitable. Every man, woman, and child lives under a nuclear sword of Damocles, hanging by the slenderest of threads, capable of being cut at any moment by accident or miscalculation or by madness. The weapons of war must be abolished before they abolish us', *DSB*, 16 October 1961, p. 620.

    Secretary Rusk mentioned 'basic areas of mutual interest, objectively considered', cf. statement to the Preparedness Investigating Subcommittee of the Senate Committee on Armed Services, 19 September, 1962, *Doc. 1962*, p. 888.

8. Secretary Rusk, 'The current danger', Address on 8 September 1961, *DSB*, 25 September 1961, p. 509f.

9. 'Toward a strategy of peace', address at the American University, Washington, DC, on 10 June 1963, *DSB*, 1 July 1963, pp. 2–6; In a speech 'New opportunities in the search for peace' to the UN General Assembly on 20 September, some of the same themes were reiterated, *DSB*, 7 October 1963, pp. 530–5.

10. 'Strength for peace and strength for war', speech by Kennedy on 19 October *DSB*, 4 November 1963, pp. 694–7; see also McGeorge Bundy, Special Assistant to the President, 'The next steps toward peace: some notes on the two-legged process', *DSB*, 21 October 1963, pp. 625–30.

11. Interview on a national broadcasting company television program on 28 July 1963, *DSB*, 12 August 1963, p. 244; *Nuclear Test Ban Treaty*. Hearings before the Committee On Foreign Relations. United States Senate, 12 August 1963, pp. 66 and 73.

12. Statement of Secretary of Defense McNamara before the House Committee on Armed Services, 30 January 1963, *Doc. 1963*, pp. 17ff.; also McNamara in *Military Procurement Authorization Fiscal Year 1964*, Hearings before the

Committee on Armed Services. United States Senate, 19 February 1963, pp. 36ff. and the exchange with senator Smith, pp. 88–90.

A distinct presentation of the new reasoning on a balance of terror was made by McNamara in a speech on 18 November 1963, cf. *Doc. 1963*, pp. 587–8; see also several speeches by William C. Foster, Director of US Arms Control and Disarmament Agency (ACDA), for instance, *DSB*, 7 January 1963, pp. 3ff. and, *ibid.*, 28 January 1963, p. 116.

13. *DSB, op. cit.*, p. 176.

14. Defense message from President Kennedy to the Congress, 28 March 1961, *Doc. 1961*, p. 67; State of the Union Address by President Kennedy to the Congress, 30 January 1961, *Doc. 1961*, p. 18; see also Secretary McNamara's statements on 23 February 1961, *Military Posture Briefings*, Hearings before the Committee on Armed Services. House of Representatives, 1961, p. 634, and on 4 April, *Military Procurement Authorization Fiscal Year 1962, op. cit.*, pp. 4ff.

In Kennedy's radio television address on 2 March 1962, mentioned in note 6, the criteria for deterrence was tightened: 'deterrent strength, if it is to be effective and credible when *compared with that of any other nation*, must embody the most modern, the most reliable and the most versatile nuclear weapons' (my emphasis).

15. Address by President Kennedy to the Congress: Urgent National Needs, 25 May 1961, *Doc. 1961*, pp. 156–7; in January 1962 McNamara declared on civil defense: 'If we believe what we say about being able to fight an all-out war if one should be forced upon us, then we must take whatever reasonable measures are available to us to protect our population', *Military Procurement Authorization Fiscal Year 1963*, Hearings Before the Committee on Armed Services. United States Senate. 19 January 1962, p. 11.

16. *Ibid.*, p. 14; *Hearings on Military Posture And H.R. 9751*. Committee On Armed Services. House of Representatives, 24 January 1962, p. 3171; *Department of Defense Appropriations For 1963*. Hearings before a Subcommittee of the Committee on Appropriations. House of Representatives, 29 January 1962, p. 13.

17. McNamara's address at the University of Michigan, Ann Arbor, 'Defense arrangements of the North Atlantic Community', 16 June 1962, *DSB*, 9 July 1962, pp. 67–8.

18. *DSB*, 12 November 1962, p. 718.

19. Cf. the statement cited in note 12.

20. Cf. note 14.

21. *Military Procurement Authorization Fiscal Year 1964, op. cit.*, p. 88, and Nuclear Test Ban Treaty. Hearings before the Committee on Foreign Relations. United States Senate, *op. cit.*, p. 98; see also Dean Rusk, *ibid.*, p. 45.

22. White House statement on the resumption of Soviet tests, 31 August 1961, *Doc. 1961*, p. 350.

23. White House statements, 17 and 30 October 1961, Preparations for Atmospheric Tests: Statement by President Kennedy, 2 November 1961, Richard B. Stebbins (ed.), *Documents on American Foreign Relations 1961* (DAFR), Council on Foreign Relations, New York, 1962, pp. 208–11; address by Deputy Secretary of Defense Gilpatric, 21 October 1961, *Doc. 1961*, p. 545.

24. Review of the world scene: television interview with the President, 17 December 1962, *DAFR 1962*, p. 52.

25. Cf. the statements cited in note 23.

26. Radio Television address by President Kennedy on nuclear testing and disarmament, 2 March 1962, *Doc. 1962*, pp. 66–75.

27. Secretary Rusk's address on 8 September 1961, cited in note 8.
28. 'Diplomacy and defense: a test of national maturity', address on 16 November 1961, *DSB*, 4 December 1961, p. 917.
29. 'Disarmament and arms control', address by Secretary Rusk on 16 June 1962, *DSB*, 2 July 1962, pp. 3–7.
30. *Doc. 1962*, p. 72; as Kennedy put it: 'it is my hope that the prospects for peace may actually be strengthened by this decision'.
31. Statement before the House Committee on Armed Services, 30 January 1963, *Doc. 1963*, p. 17.
32. Statement before the Senate Foreign Relations Committee: Negotiations for a Test-ban Treaty, 11 March 1963, *Doc. 1963*, p. 108.
33. 'The Nuclear Test Ban Treaty: a step toward peace', address by President Kennedy, delivered from the White House by television and radio on 26 July 1963, *DSB*, 12 August 1963, pp. 234–8, especially p. 235.
34. See especially Message From President Kennedy to the Senate: Transmittal of Test-Ban Treaty, 8 August 1963, *Doc. 1963*, pp. 299–302 and Kennedy's address to the UN General Assembly, cited in note 9.
35. One of the most thoroughgoing presentations of this arms control reasoning was given by ACDA Director Foster in an address 'National strategy, security, and arms control' on 31 October; he ended the speech thus: 'Over the long run we hope that the development of international inspection and peacekeeping machinery will contribute toward the development of an international climate in which the rule of law could gradually displace the rule of force. We do not expect such a change to take place quickly. The achievement of such a goal will require a major change in the traditions of diplomacy and in the minds of men. But over the long run, it is the only real hope of avoiding disaster. It is a goal toward which we must work. We must not be misled into accepting the balance of terror as a satisfactory substitute for the rule of law', *Doc. 1963*, pp. 566–74.
36. 'Strength for peace and strength for war', address by President Kennedy on 19 October 1963, *DSB*, 4 November 1963, pp. 694–7; statement of Secretary Rusk, Nuclear Test Ban Treaty, Hearings before the Committee on Foreign Relations, United States Senate, 12 August 1963, *op. cit.*, p. 18; Testimony of Secretary McNamara, *ibid.*, pp. 97–203. Address by Dean Rusk 'Unfinished business', 10 September 1963, *DSB*, 30 September 1963, pp. 490–6.
37. Cf., for example, *DSB*, 1 May 1961, p. 638. As to the interpretation of the Soviet tests in August 1961, see note 22.
38. *Doc. 1962*, p. 657.
39. Dean Rusk, 19 September 1962, *Doc. 1962*, p. 888, cf. note 7.
40. Under-Secretary Averell Harriman declared: 'Of all the people in the world, there are no peoples that are more conscious of war than the Soviet Union, the people of Russia, because they have suffered so much and because the problems are always held before them by what they get from the press' and: 'Mr. Krushchev is becoming more and more a political leader than the dictator that Stalin was. Even though there is only one party, it is necessary for him to keep a certain popularity with the Russian people in order to maintain his leadership within the party.... you have got to think in terms of what is useful for the Kremlin leaders in connection with controlling their own people'; cf. *DSB*, 19 August 1963, p. 280 and 12 August 1963, p. 244.
41. Nuclear Test Ban Treaty. Hearings before the Committee on Foreign Relations. United States Senate, *op. cit.*, pp. 102 and 109.
42. Secretary Rusk, *DSB*, 30 September 1963, pp. 492–3.
43. Statement by Secretary of State Rusk to the Joint Committee on Atomic Energy: Non-proliferation of Nuclear Weapons, 23 February 1966, *Doc. 1966*,

p. 49, *Non-proliferation Treaty*, Hearings before the Committee on Foreign Relations. United States Senate, 10 July 1968, p. 7, and Under-Secretary Katzenbach, *DSB*, 15 May 1967, p. 753; see also address by President Johnson, 'Direction and control of nuclear power', 16 September 1964, *Doc. 1964*, pp. 429f., and: The State of the Union: message delivered by President Lyndon B. Johnson to a Joint Session of the Congress, 10 January 1967, *DAFR 1967*, p. 5.

44. 'The dynamics of nuclear strategy', address at San Francisco, 18 September 1967, *DSB*, 9 October 1967, p. 443.

45. *Ibid.*, pp. 450 and 445.

46. *Ibid.*, pp. 443–51; statement by McNamara to the House of Armed Services Committee, 18 February 1965, *Survival*, May–June 1965, pp. 98ff.; statement before the Senate Subcommittee, 23 February 1966, *Survival*, May 1966, pp. 138ff.; *Statement Of Secretary of Defense Robert S. McNamara Before The House Armed Services Committee On the Fiscal Year 1968–72 Defense Program And 1968 Defense Budget*, 23 January 1967, pp. 38ff.; *Statement by Secretary of Defense Robert S. McNamara on The Fiscal Year 1969–73 Defense Program And 1969 Defense Budget*, 30 April 1968, pp. 41ff. Also military posture statement by Secretary of Defense Clifford to the House Committee on Armed Services: Strategic Forces, 15 January 1969, *Doc. 1969*, especially p. 5, referred to this.

47. 'The limitations of military power', speech in Montreal, 18 May 1966, cf. *Survival*, July 1966, p. 216; address by President Johnson, 26 August 1966, *DSB*, 19 September 1966; President Johnson's State of the Union address to Congress, 10 January 1967, *DSB*, 30 January 1967.

48. Cf. note 46. Also McNamara in *Hearings On Military Posture*, Before The Committee On Armed Services. House of Representatives, 2 March 1967, p. 389, and *Authorization for Military Procurement, Research And Development, Fiscal Year 1969, And Reserve Strength*, Hearings Before The Committee On Armed Services. United States Senate, 2 February 1968, p. 108f.

49. Cf. comparing the statements referred in note 46.

50. Cf. the four first statements in note 46, pp. 99, 138, 38 and 47, respectively.

51. See note 44, pp. 449f.; President Johnson expressed the same view, but less distinctly, cf. State of our Defenses, Message to the Congress, 18 January 1965, *DSB*, 15 February 1965, p. 214.

52. *Op. cit.*, p. 446; *Survival*, May 1966, *op. cit.*, p. 142.

53. See the last-mentioned reference in note 48, p. 119; *Doc. 1967*, 559–60, and Clifford's posture statement in January 1969, *op. cit.*, p. 17.

54. President Johnson, 'National security and world responsibilities', address on 3 June 1964, *DSB*, 22 June 1964, p. 951; 'State of our defenses', Message of the President to Congress, 18 January 1965, *DSB*, 15 February 1965, p. 213; and: The budget for fiscal year 1968: Message of President Johnson to the Congress, 24 January 1967, *DAFR 1967*, p. 33. On one occasion Secretary McNamara expounded strategic nuclear superiority as 'the absolute foundation of our deterrent power', cf. interview with *U.S. News & World Report*, 12 April 1965, pp. 53 and 56.

55. The San Francisco speech, *op. cit.*, pp. 445–6; see also the last-mentioned reference in note 48, p. 115, and McNamara's Statement, 30 April 1968 (note 46).

56. Cf. also: 'More weapons – less security', address by ACDA Director William C. Foster, *DSB*, 18 November 1968, p. 527. A clear indicator that the rejection of the political significance of strategic nuclear superiority touched some delicate political conceptions appears from some comments made by McGeorge Bundy,

Special Assistant to the President for National Security Affairs from 1961 to 1966: in 1964, occupying a prominent job in the administration, he stated that American presidents had aimed at strategic superiority and added 'that superiority has had different meanings at different stages, but seen from the White House its value for Peace has never been small', 'The Presidency and the Peace', *Foreign Affairs*, Vol. 42, No. 3, April 1964, p. 355.

After having left his job in the administration, Bundy wrote: 'It follows that in political, as distinct from technical, terms we have all been wrong to talk of nuclear superiority', 'To cap the volcano', *Foreign Affairs*, Vol. 48, No. 1, October 1969, p. 11.

57. Address by Secretary of Defense Clifford on 5 September 1968, *Doc. 1968*, pp. 615f. and Military Posture Statement by Secretary of Defense Clifford to the House Committee on Armed Services: Strategic Forces, 15 January 1969, *op. cit.*, p. 5.

58. 'Peace on earth', address by Vice-President Humphrey on 17 February 1965, *DSB*, 8 March 1965, pp. 326f.; 'Roadblock to arms control and disarmament negotiations', address by Director William C. Foster, Arms Control and Disarmament Agency, 4 June 1965, *DSB*, 12 July 1965, pp. 77–84, and Foster 'Arms control – a serious business', address on 20 June 1966, *DSB*, 11 July 1966, pp. 50ff.; 'The political future of the family of man', address by Secretary Rusk on 14 November 1967, *DSB*, 4 December 1967, p. 738, and Remarks by President Johnson at Signing of Arms Control and Disarmament Act, 27 May 1965, *Doc. 1965*, p. 204.

59. The term 'geometrically' was used by McNamara, cf. *DSB*, 29 August 1966, p. 304. See also, Message from President Johnson to the Conference of the Eighteen-Nation Committee on Disarmament, 21 January 1964, *DAFR 1964*, pp. 161–3, and Message from President Johnson to the Eighteen-Nation Disarmament Committee, 27 January 1966, *Doc. 1966*, pp. 5–8; Statement by President Johnson, *DSB*, 5 February 1968, p. 164; Remarks by President Johnson to the United Nations General Assembly on its approval of the Nuclear Non-Proliferation Treaty, 12 June 1968, *DAFR 1968–69*, pp. 56–9; and: Message from President Johnson to the Eighteen Nation Disarmament Committee, 16 July 1968, *Doc. 1968*, p. 531.

60. Cf. note 44, pp. 446f.

61. *Doc. 1968*, p. 616, cf. note 57.

62. 'The pursuit of peace', address by Secretary Rusk on 2 August 1964, *DSB*, 17 August 1964, p. 216; 'The search for agreements in the cause of peace', address by President Johnson on 26 August 1966, *DSB*, 19 September 1966, p. 412; 'The challenges to freedom and peace', address by W. Averell Harriman, Ambassador at Large, 31 October 1965, *DSB*, 29 November 1965, p. 865.

63. See, respectively, 'More weapons – less security', address by ACDA Director William C. Foster, *DSB*, 18 November 1968, p. 528, and 'East–West Relations: Shaping a stable world', speech on 22 December 1967 by Deputy Under Secretary for Political Affairs, Foy D. Kohler, *DSB*, 2 January 1967, p. 8.

64. Cf. the statements mentioned in note 46, passim; Secretary Rusk, *DSB*, 6 March 1967, p. 361, and news conference remarks, 19 July 1967, *Doc. 1967*, p. 305.

In an interview with the BBC on 15 February 1967, McNamara stated that it would increase the risk to both the United States and the Soviet Union to deploy ABM systems and stressed that both countries needed a deterrent against a potential strike by the other; he added: 'We have that deterrent capability today; in a very real sense the Soviets have it as well. We feel we must keep it. I don't know of any reason why they should think differently than we in this point', *DSB*, 20 March 1967, p. 442.

65. *U.S. News & World Report*, 12 April 1965, p. 52.
66. See McNamara's interview with the BBC, cf. note 64, pp. 443–4.
67. *Doc. 1969*, p. 12, cf. note 46.
68. *DSB*, 31 March 1969, p. 273.
69. See, for example, Henry Kissinger's briefing of members of Congress on Strategic Arms Limitation Agreements, 15 June 1972, *DSB*, 10 July 1972, pp. 40 ff.
70. 'Pragmatism and moral force in American foreign policy', address on 5 June 1974, by President Nixon, *DSB*, 1 July 1974, p. 2; *U.S. Foreign Policy for the 1970's. Shaping a Durable Peace*, A Report to the Congress by President Nixon, 3 May 1973, *DSB*, 4 June 1973, pp. 716–834, especially pp. 730 and 735 (this report is referred to as 'Report 1973' in the following).
71. *U.S. Foreign Policy For The 1970's. Building For Peace*, A report to the Congress by President Nixon, 25 February 1971, *DSB*, 22 March 1971, pp. 340–432, especially pp. 403–4, stating: 'the natural expansion of Soviet influence in the world must not distort itself into ambitions for exclusive or predominant positions. For such a course ignores the interests of others, including ourselves. It must and will be resisted. it can, therefore, lead only to confrontation' (referred to as 'Report 1971'). Concerning the necessary restraint on both sides, Secretary Kissinger observed at a news conference in Moscow in early July 1974 that 'both sides have to convince their military establishments of the benefits of restraint, and that is not a thought that comes naturally to military people on either side', *DSB*, 29 July 1974, p. 210.
72. For instance, Secretary Kissinger at a news conference on 27 December 1973 (Kissinger had been appointed Secretary of State on 22 September), *DSB*, 21 January 1974, pp. 52 and 55.
73. Cf. note 68; see also statements by Secretary Laird to Congressional Committees, 19 and 21 March 1969, on the difference between *Sentinel* and *Safeguard*, cf. *Doc. 1969*, pp. 121–31.
74. *U.S. Foreign Policy For The 1970's. A New Strategy for Peace*, A Report to the Congress by President Nixon, 18 February 1970, *DSB*, 9 March 1970, pp. 272–332, especially p. 319 ('Report 1970'); *Report 1971*, p. 408; *U.S. Foreign Policy For The 1980's. The Emerging Structure of Peace*, A report to the Congress by President Nixon, 2 February 1972, *DSB*, 13 March 1972, pp. 312–418, especially p. 391 ('Report 1972'); *Report 1973*, p. 809.
75. President Nixon's news conference of 27 January 1969, *DSB*, 17 February 1969, p. 143; see also *Report 1970*, p. 319. *Statement Of Secretary Of Defense Melvin R. Laird Before The House Armed Services Committee On The FY 1972–1976 Defense Program And The 1972 Defense Budget*, 9 March 1971, pp. 1 and 61–2; *Statement Of Secretary Of Defense Melvin R. Laird Before The Senate Armed Services Committee On The FY 1973 Defense Budget and FY 1973–1977 Program*, 15 February 1972, p. 65.
    See also *Statement Of Secretary Of Defense Elliot L. Richardson Before The House Armed Services Committee On The FY 1974 Defense Budget And FY 1974–1978 Program*, 10 April 1973, passim.
76. Melvin Laird, Statement, 1971, *op. cit.*, pp. 23 and 75, and Statement 1972. *op. cit.*, p. 79.
77. Secretary Laird, *Strategic And Foreign Policy Implications Of ABM Systems*, Hearings before the Subcommittee on International Organization And Disarmament Affairs Of The Committee On Foreign Relations, United States Senate, 6 March 1969, p. 173; see also Laird's Statement, 1971, *op. cit.*, p. 46, and Statement, 1972, *op. cit.*, pp. 30, 41 and 44; Elliot Richardson's Statement,

1973, *op. cit.*, p. 58; *Report 1971*, p. 407.

Also Melvin Laird, *Authorization For Military Procurement, Research And Development, Fiscal Year 1971, And Reserve Strength*, Hearings before the Committee on Armed Services, United States Senate, 20 February 1970, p. 36; *Hearings On Military Posture*, Committee on Armed Services, House of Representatives, 27 February 1970, p. 6848, and statement to the Senate Armed Services Committee, 12 May 1970, *Doc. 1970*, pp. 204ff.

78. *Report Of The Secretary Of Defense James R. Schlesinger To The Congress On The FY 1975 Defense Budget And FY 1975–1979 Defense Program*, 4 March 1974 (Schlesinger Report 1974); *U.S.–U.S.S.R. Strategic Policies*, Hearing before the Subcommittee on Arms Control, International Law and Organization of the Committee on Foreign Relations, United States Senate, 4 March 1974, top secret hearing, sanitized and made public on 4 April; *Nuclear Weapons And Foreign Policy*, Hearings Before The Subcommittee On U.S. Security Agreements and Commitments Abroad and the Subcommittee on Arms Control, International Law and Organization Of The Committee On Foreign Relations, United States Senate, 7 March 1974.

The Schlesinger strategy was presented publicly at Secretary Schlesinger's two press conferences in January; cf. *Survival*, March–April 1974, pp. 86ff.; the reasoning behind the Schlesinger stategy was foreshadowed at news conferences by Schlesinger during the autumn 1973, cf. *Doc. 1973*, pp. 511–19, and *ibid.*, pp. 833–40.

79. Hearings, 4 March 1974, *op. cit.*, p. 11.

80. See Kissinger's news conference of 21 March 1974, *DSB*, 8 April 1974, p. 360; at this occasion, Kissinger stated that he understood Schlesinger's objective as seeking 'an ability to bring about discriminating targeting of the American nuclear forces. This in itself is a problem separate from counterforce strategy, which implies the ability to wipe out the Soviet retaliatory force in a first strike'; see also Kissinger's remarks at a news conference, 26 June 1974, *Doc. 1974*, p. 202.

81. 'The prevention of nuclear war in a world of uncertainty', address by Fred. C. Iklé before the Joint Harvard–MIT Arms Control Seminar at Cambridge, Mass., 20 February 1974, *DSB*, 25 March 1974, pp. 314–18; see also Iklé's notable article from before he entered the administration, 'Can nuclear deterrence last out the century?', *Foreign Affairs*, Vol. LI, No. 2, January 1973, pp. 267–85.

82. *Report 1973*, pp. 814–15; Assistant to the President for National Security Affairs, Henry Kissinger, *DSB*, 3 July 1972, p. 41, and Secretary of State, Henry Kissinger, 'Moral purposes and policy choices', address made at Washington, DC, on 8 October 1973, before the Third *Pacem in Terris* Conference Sponsored by the Center for the Study of Democratic Institutions, *DSB*, 29 October 1973, p. 529.

83. *Report 1970*, p. 319; *Report 1971*, p. 404; at a briefing for media executives in Portland, Oregon, 15 September 1971, Nixon stated: 'neither power at this time could if it wanted to, gain that superiority which would enable it to ... blackmail the other one', *DAFR 1971*, pp. 107–8.

Melvin Laird, Statement, 1972, *op. cit.*, p. 69. In early 1973, when he left the administration, Melvin Laird stated: 'we have sufficiency at the strategic nuclear level because Congress agreed with us that the American people may perhaps be willing to accept strategic nuclear parity, but would never accept inferiority', *Final Report To The Congress Of Secretary Of Defense Melvin R. Laird Before The House Armed Services Committee*, 8 January 1973, p. 5.

84. *Schlesinger Report 1974*, pp. 3 and 28; *Survival*, March–April 1974, *op. cit.*,

p. 88, and the first-mentioned hearing in note 78, p. 45.

85. Kissinger's news conference of 26 April, *DSB*, 20 May 1974, p. 543; news conference of 24 June 1974, *DSB*, 22 July 1974, p. 133; news conference at Moscow, 3 July 1974, *DSB*, 29 July 1974, pp. 207 and 215, see also his statement on a news conference at Brussels, 26 June, *ibid.*, p. 196.

86. *DSB*, 10 February 1969, p. 122.

87. *Report 1970*, pp. 327, 320 and 331–2.

88. 'Two aspects of the search for peace', address on 18 April 1970, *DSB*, 11 May 1970, p. 606; also 'Strategic arms limitation talks', address made on 13 November 1969, *DSB*, 1 December 1969, pp. 465ff., and United States Foreign Policy, 1969–1970: A Report of the Secretary of State, March 1971, cf. *Doc. 1971*, pp. 171ff.

89. President Nixon's two-sided approach to the strength theme appeared in a radio address when he transmitted 'Report 1971' to Congress: 'The United States will deal, as it must, from strength ... America's strength will be, as it must second to none; but the strength that this nation is proudest of is the strength of our determination to create a peaceful world', *DAFR 1971*, pp. 10–11. President Nixon, *Report 1972*, p. 390.

Laird, Statement, 1971, *op. cit.*, p. 2, and Statement, 1972, *op. cit.*, p. 77.

In March 1969, Secretary Laird argued to a Senate Committee that *Safeguard* gave the Soviet Union 'an added incentive to negotiate a meaningful agreement on limitation of both offensive and defensive weapons', cf. *Doc. 1969*, p. 130; see also Laird's statement to the Senate Armed Services Committee in May 1970, *Doc. 1970*, p. 208.

90. Henry Kissinger, *DSB*, 10 July 1972, pp. 40–9, especially pp. 47–8, cf. note 69; and Kissinger's news conference of 21 March 1974, *DSB*, 8 April 1974, p. 353.

Secretary Rogers before the Senate Committee on Foreign Relations on 19 June 1972, cf. *DSB*, 10 July 1972, pp. 50 ff.; *United States Foreign Policy 1972. A Report of the Secretary of State*, 19 April 1973, p. I. Statement before the Senate Committee on Armed Services, 28 July 1972, by Gerard Smith, Director of the Arms Control and Disarmament Agency, *DSB*, 31 July 1972, pp. 147–52.

91. President Nixon, briefing of members of Congress (together with Kissinger) on Strategic Arms Limitation Agreements, 15 June 1972, *DSB*, 10 July 1972, p. 39, and 'The role of national defense in our efforts for peace', address by Nixon on 24 August 1972, *DSB*, 25 September 1972, p. 347; and President Nixon's two radio addresses on 29 October and 4 November 1972, *DAFR 1972*, pp. 49 and 53.

Melvin Laird, Final Report, 1973, *op. cit.*, p. 22, and statement to the Senate Armed Services Committee, 6 and 20 June 1972, *Doc. 1972*, pp. 259ff. and 368–71; Elliot Richardson, Statement, 1973, *op. cit.*, p. 31; *Schlesinger Report 1974*, p. 71.

The administration's continuing two-sided approach to SALT was also demonstrated by Kissinger in his nomination hearings as Secretary of State before the Senate Foreign Relations Committee in September 1973 when he noted that in the absence of a permanent agreement on the limitation of strategic arms, 'a spiralling of the arms race is inevitable' because the United States would 'be driven to reply to the new Soviet developments in MIRVs with some modifications in our own strategic programs', cf. *Doc. 1973*, p. 635.

92. *DSB*, 17 February 1969, p. 142, and the President's remarks at a news conference, 4 March 1969, *Doc. 1969*, p. 67; *Report 1970*, p. 324; *Report 1972*, p. 403.

93. *DSB*, 29 October 1973, p. 529, cf, note 82.

94. President Nixon, *DSB*, 31 March 1969, pp. 273–4 and 278; Secretary Rogers, *DSB*, 1 December 1969, p. 465, cf, note 88; Under-Secretary Elliot Richardson, *DSB*, 19 May 1969, p. 418; *Report 1970*, p. 318; Secretary Laird, *Strategic And Foreign Policy Implications Of ABM Systems*, Hearings before the Subcommittee on International Organization and Disarmament Affairs of the Committee on Foreign Relations. United States Senate, March 1969, p. 196.
95. See, for example, *Report 1970*, p. 325.
96. *Report 1971*, pp. 408–9 and 417; *Report 1972*, pp. 392 and 321.
97. A Report of the Secretary of State, *op cit.*, pp. 308–10, and Secretary Rogers' address, 'From containment to engagement', on 28 September 1972, *ibid.*, pp. 534–7; Henry Kissinger, *DSB*, 9 October 1972, p. 397, and *DSB*, 23 July 1973, p. 141.
98. *Report 1973*, pp. 731 and 734.
99. *Schlesinger Report 1974*, pp. 3, 29f. and 42f; Nuclear Weapons And Foreign Policy, Hearings, 7 March 1974, *op. cit.*, p. 173.

CHAPTER 3   IMAGES 1974–87

1. See especially 'Détente with the Soviet Union: the reality of competition and the imperative of cooperation', statement by Secretary Kissinger to the Senate Committee on Foreign Relations on 19 September 1974, *DSB*, 14 October 1974, pp. 505–19; it was telling that Kissinger ended his statement by quoting from President Kennedy's address at American University in June 1963: ' For in the final analysis our basic common link is that we all inhabit this small planet. We all breathe the same air. We all cherish our children's future. And we are all mortal.'
    Also Lester A. Sobel (ed.), *Kissinger & Detente*, New York, 1975 (extract from Kissinger's speech on 12 May 1975); 'The moral foundations of foreign policy', address 15 July 1975, *DSB*, 4 August 1975, pp. 161–8, especially p. 167; 'The permanent challenge of peace: U.S. policy toward the Soviet Union', address 3 February 1976, *DSB*, 23 February 1976, pp. 201–12; 'Moral promise and practical needs', address 19 October 1976, *DSB*, 15 November 1976, pp. 597–605; remarks at a press conference, 2 October 1976, *Doc. 1976*, p. 660.
    While Secretary Kissinger noted that the fact that the Soviet Union had become a nuclear superpower was neither created by the United States nor could be removed by any American policy, Fred C. Iklé, Director of the Arms Control and Disarmament Agency, mentioned in a speech on 23 April 1975, that the United States in the mid-1960s had taken the initiative of restraining the expansion of its strategic offensive and defensive nuclear forces and this American self-restraint had found formal expression in the 1969 decision to discard 'strategic superiority' as official; Iklé then added: 'The Soviet Union would thus be *allowed* to achieve equality where the United States had held an advantage for 25 years' (my emphasis); cf. 'The second nuclear era', *DSB*, 19 May 1975, p. 642.
2. Statement to the Senate Committee on Foreign Relations, 19 September 1974, *op. cit.*, especially p. 519; United States Foreign Policy: Address by President Ford before a Joint Session of the Congress, 10 April 1975, *DAFR 1975*, pp. 93ff., especially p. 103.
3 Questions and answers following Kissinger's address on 3 February 1976, cf. *DSB*, 23 February 1976, p. 213, and news conference of 22 April 1976, *DSB*,

17 May 1976, p. 617.
4. President Ford interviewed for NBC television, 5 January 1976, *DSB*, 26 January 1976, p. 102; Ford's approach to détente before the change appears from 'The national interests and national strength', address on 15 April 1975, *DSB*, 5 May 1975, pp. 572–6, and 'America's strength and progress toward freedom and peace', speech on 25 August 1975, *DSB*, 15 September 1975, pp. 410–14; see also remarks in a television interview with President Ford, 25 August 1975, cf. *Doc. 1975*, p. 388.

Replying to a question on why the word détente had been dropped from his vocabulary, Kissinger declared on 22 March 1976: 'Because the President ordered it', cf. *DSB*, 12 April 1976, p. 470. See also *DAFR 1976*, p. 19.
5. Henry Kissinger, statement to the Senate Committee on Foreign Relations, 19 September 1974, *op. cit.*, p. 513; James R. Schlesinger, *Briefing On Counterforce Attacks*, Hearing before the Subcommittee on Arms Control, International Law And Organization of the Committee on Foreign Relations, United States Senate, Secret Hearing held on 11 September 1974; sanitized and made public on 10 January 1975, pp. 3ff.

Report Of Secretary Of Defense James R. Schlesinger To The Congress On The FY 1976 And Transition Budgets, FY 1976 Authorization Request And FY 1976–1980 Defense Programs, 5 February 1975 (Schlesinger Report 1975), p. 1–16; Secretary of Defense Donald H. Rumsfeld, *Annual Defense Department Report. FY 1977*, 27 January 1976 (Rumsfeld Report 1976), p. 13; *Report Of Secretary Of Defense Donald R. Rumsfeld To The Congress On The FY 1978 Budget, FY 1979 Authorization Request And FY 1978–1982 Defense Programs*, 17 January 1977 (Rumsfeld Report 1977), pp. 68–70.
6. See the three reports referred to in note 5, respectively, pp. 3ff., pp. I–13ff. and II–9ff.; pp. 13, 46f. and 53; pp. 71ff., 78 and 106.
7. James R. Schlesinger, 'The theater nuclear force posture in Europe'. A report to the United States Congress, April 1975, extracts in Robert J. Pranger and Roger P. Labrie (eds), *Nuclear Strategy And National Security. Points of View*, American Enterprise Institute for Public Policy Research, Washington, DC, pp. 167–88, especially p. 168.
8. *Schlesinger Report 1975*, pp. I–13 and II–7; *Rumsfeld Report 1976*, pp. 12–13 and 51.
9. *Rumsfeld Report 1977*, pp. 71–4, 116 and 122.
10. Statement to the Senate Committee on Foreign Relations, 19 September 1974, *op. cit.*, pp. 506 and 512; statement at a news conference in Copenhagen, 20 January 1976, *DSB*, 16 February 1976, p. 163; address, 3 February 1976 (cited in note 1), *DSB*, 23 February 1976, p. 206; 'Foreign policy and national security', address on 22 March 1976, *DSB*, 12 April 1976, p. 461; 'The Western Alliance: peace and moral purpose', address made in London on 25 June before the International Institute for Strategic Studies, inaugurating the Alastair Buchan Memorial Lecture series, *DSB*, 26 July 1976, pp. 105–15, especially p. 108.
11. Remarks at the signing of the Treaty and Protocol on Underground Nuclear Explosions for Peaceful Purposes, 28 May 1976, *Doc. 1976*, pp. 348–9.
12. Cf. television interview with President Ford, 25 August 1975, *Doc. 1975*, p. 388; interview of Secretary of State Kissinger by *Time Magazine*, 'Strategic arms limitations', 27 October 1975, *Doc. 1975*, pp. 498–9; remarks of President Ford at a question-and-answer session with the World Affairs Council of Oregon: 'Strategic arms limitation talks and mutual and balanced force reductions', 22 May 1976, *Doc. 1976*, p. 326.
13. Statement by ACDA Director İklé to the Subcommittee on International

Security and Scientific Affairs of the House Committee on International Relations: The Vladivostok Accord, 8 July 1975, *Doc. 1975*, pp. 236f.

On the relation between Soviet–American negotiations and nuclear non-proliferation, see 'An age of interdependence – common disaster or community', address to the United Nations General Assembly by Secretary Kissinger on 23 September 1974, *DAFR 1974*, p. 351: and statement by Fred C. Iklé to the Review Conference of the Parties to the Treaty on the Non-Proliferation of Nuclear Weapons, Geneva, 5–30 May 1975, *DAFR 1975*, pp. 155–6. See also President Ford on the Vladivostok agreement at a news conference in Washington, DC, 2 December 1974, *DAFR 1974*, pp. 512–13.

14. News conference remarks by Secretary of State Kissinger: 'Compliance with the strategic arms limitation agreements', 9 December 1975, *Doc. 1975*, pp. 746–61; testimony of Defense Secretary James R. Schlesinger, *Soviet Compliance With Certain Provisions Of The 1972 SALT I Agreements*, Hearings before the Subcommittee on Arms Control of the Committee On Armed Services, United States Senate, 6 March 1975, pp. 3–22.

See also press conference with President Ford, 25 June 1975, *Doc. 1975*, p. 202.

15. *Rumsfeld Report 1977*, pp. 49 and 116.
16. 'Implications of Angola for future U.S. foreign policy', statement by Secretary Kissinger before the Subcommittee on African Affairs of the Senate Committee on Foreign Relations on 29 January 1976, *DSB*, 16 February 1976, pp. 174–82; Kissinger's address on 3 February 1976, cited in note 1, *DSB*, 23 February 1976, pp. 209–11, and remarks at a news conference, 14 January 1976, *DSB*, 2 February 1976, pp. 125ff.
17. *Rumsfeld Report 1977*, pp. 75–6.
18. Kissinger at a news conference, Vladivostok, 24 November 1974, *DSB*, 23 December 1974, p. 900.

Also see 'U.S.–Soviet relations in the nuclear age', address by Helmut Sonnenfeldt, Counselor of the Department of State, 6 April 1976, *DSB*, 3 May 1976, pp. 576–83.

19. Statement to the Senate Committee on Foreign Relations, 19 September 1974, *op. cit.*, pp. 507f.; address on 15 July 1975, cited in note 1, *DSB*, 4 August 1975, p. 165.
20. *Rumsfeld Report 1977*, pp. 28, 59, 64, 70, 72 and 76.
21. See especially three speeches by President Carter: 'Peace, arms control', 'World economic progress', 'Human rights: basic priorities of U.S. foreign policy', made to the United Nations, New York, 17 March 1977, *DSB*, 11 April 1977, pp. 329–33; 'President Carter outlines the U.S.–Soviet relationship', address made 21 July 1977, *DSB*, 15 August 1977 pp. 193–7; 'U.S. role in a peaceful global community', address made before the United Nations General Assembly on 4 October 1977, *DSB*, 24 October 1977, pp. 547–50.
22. President Carter, 'A foreign policy based on America's essential character', address made at Notre Dame University, Ind., on 22 May 1977, *DSB*, 13 June 1977, p. 622; Marshall Shulman, Special Advisor to the Secretary of State on Soviet Affairs, 'U.S.S.R.: an overview of U.S.–Soviet relations', *DSB*, January 1978, pp. 1f.
23. 'The Inaugural Address of President Carter', *DSB*, 14 February 1977, pp. 121–2; see also the four speeches by Carter, cited in notes 21 and 22.
24. 'The United States and the Soviet Union', address by President Carter, Annapolis, 7 June 1978, *DSB*, July 1978, pp. 14–16; the President's State of

the Union address before a joint session of the Congress, 23 January 1979, *DSB*, February 1979, pp. 1–2; report of 31 December 1978, on US policy toward the Soviet Union, approved by President Carter and transmitted to Congress by Secretary Vance, *ibid.*, pp. 38f.

The notion that the Soviet Union was approaching some fundamental choices between allowing the elements of conflict in the Soviet–American relationship to deepen or follow the course of restraint and responsibility was presented in slightly more accommodating terms by Marshall Shulman, cf. statement before the Subcommittee on Europe and the Middle East of the House Committee on International Relations on 26 September 1978, *DSB*, November 1978, pp. 28–33, especially p. 33.

25. *DSB*, July 1979, p. 1; see also President Carter, 'SALT II – The Path of Security and Peace', address on 25 April 1979, *DSB*, June 1979, pp. 11–14; Secretary Vance, Testimony on SALT II before the Senate Committee on Foreign Relations on 9 and 10 July 1979, *DSB*, August 1979, 30–7.

Also testimony by different administration officials before the Senate Committee on Foreign Relations, 9, 10 and 11 July 1979, *DSB*, September 1979, pp. 13ff.

26. President Carter, 'National security policy', address before the annual convention of the American Legion in Boston on 21 August 1980, *DSB*, October 1980, p. 9; the President's State of the Union address before a joint session of the Congress on 23 January 1980, *DSB*, February 1980, pp. A–D.

Secretary Vance, 'U.S. foreign policy: our broader strategy', Statement before the Senate Foreign Relations Committee on 27 March 1980, *DSB*, May 1980, pp. 16ff; Secretary Muskie: 'Essentials of security: arms and more', address before the World Affairs Council in Pittsburgh on 18 September 1980, *DSB*, November 1980, pp. 27f.; 'U.S. nuclear strategy', Statement before the Senate Foreign Relations Committee on 16 September 1980, *ibid.*, pp. 33–5; and 'The challenge of peace', address at Notre Dame University, Ind., on 11 October 1980, *ibid.*, p. 35.

27. Statement by Secretary of Defense Harold Brown, 22 February 1977, to Congress, *Survival*, May–June 1977, pp. 121f.; 'Defense planning and arms control', address by Secretary Brown at the University of Rochester, 13 April 1977, *Doc. 1977*, pp. 224ff. Also Zbingniew Brzezinski, Assistant to the President for National Security Affairs, presented a similar reasoning; cf. *DSB*, 25 April 1977, p. 415; on the other hand, some comments by Brzezinski on that occasion suggested a reasoning much closer to a kind of Soviet essentialism.

28. Paul C. Warnke, 'Arms control: SALT and the test ban – cause for optimism', address on 10 November 1977, DSB, January 1978, pp. 20–4; Warnke singled out McNamara's reasoning on deterrence in 'Arms control: SALT II–the home stretch', address before the Foreign Policy Association in New York on 23 August 1978, *DSB*, October 1978, pp. 17–23.

'SALT and American security', pamphlet by the Arms Control and Disarmament Agency, released in November 1978, *DSB*, December 1978, pp. 1ff.

29. Harold Brown, *Department of Defense. Annual Report. Fiscal Year 1979*, 2 February 1978 (Brown 1978), p. 5 and pp. 45, 53–4, 59–60, 62f. and 116.

See also Harold Brown, 'Arms control: a balanced and effective defense', address before the annual national convention of the American Legion in New Orleans on 22 August 1978, *DSB*, November 1978, pp. 14–17.

30. Harold Brown, *Department of Defense. Annual Report. Fiscal Year 1980*, 25 January 1979 (Brown 1979), pp. 18, 61, 74ff., 116 and 125; *Department of*

Defense. Annual Report. Fiscal Year 1981, 29 January 1980 (Brown 1980), pp. 65f., 85 and 136.

See also 'Arms control: SALT II and the national defense', address by Secretary Brown before the Council on Foreign Relations and the Foreign Policy Association in New York on 5 April 1979, *DSB*, May 1979, pp. 51ff., and Brown's statement before the Senate Committee on Foreign Relations on 9 and 11 July 1979, *DSB*, September 1979, pp. 13–18.

31. *Brown 1978*, pp. 134–5; *Brown 1979*, pp. 82–6; *Brown 1980*, pp. 145–9, and *Report of Secretary of Defense Harold Brown To The Congress On The FY 1982 Budget, FY 1983 Authorization Request And FY 1982–1986 Defense Programs*, 19 January 1981 (*Brown 1981*), pp. 125–9.

For a similar comment from President Carter, see his remarks on 'U.S. defense policy', *DSB*, February 1980, p. 59.

32. 'Countervailing strategy', address by Secretary of Defense Brown, on 20 August 1980, *Doc. 1980*, pp. 374–7, and *Brown 1981*, pp. 38f.

33. *Ibid.*, p. 40. (However, the word 'reasonable' indicates a critical reservation.)

34. *Ibid.*, pp. 37 and 42–3, and Muskie's statement before the Senate Foreign Relations Committee on 16 September, cf. note 26. Se also Secretary Brown's more detailed review of PD-59 in *Nuclear War Strategy*, Hearing before the Committee on Foreign Relations, United States Senate, 16 September 1980, pp. 6ff. (Top Secret Hearings; Sanitized and Printed On 18 February 1981).

35. Cf. *Brown 1981*, p. 44. See also the three sources cited in note 27, Secretary Brown's statement on 2 August 1977, *Hearings on H.R. 8390 and Review Of The State of U.S. Strategic Forces*, Committee On Armed Services, House of Representatives, 1977, pp. 161f.; Brown's address on 5 April 1979, cited in note 30; and Brown 1980, p. 68.

President Carter presented a similar image in his address 'National security interests', at Wake Forest University, N.C., on 17 March 1978, *DSB*, April 1978, p. 18; a somewhat divergent view was implied by Paul Warnke before a National Foreign Policy Conference for Editors and Broadcasters held at the Department of State on 19 January 1978, cf. *DSB*, April 1978, pp. 1–9; a view more in accordance with the administration's general one was presented by Warnke's successor as ACDA Director, George M. Seignious II, in a statement before the Senate Committee on Foreign Relations on 10 July 1979, cf. *DSB*, September 1979, p. 19.

36. *Brown 1979*, p. 11.

37. *Ibid.*, p. 36.

38. *Ibid.*, p. 118 (Brown's emphasis); *Brown 1978*, p. 64 and Brown's address 5 April 1979, cited in note 30.

39. *Brown 1980*, pp. 69 and 94; on civil defense, *Brown 1979*, p. 130.

40. *Ibid.*, pp. 35 and 64.

41. Muskie's address on 18 September 1980, cited in note 26 – on this occasion Muskie also rejected 'the chimera of nuclear superiority'. *Brown 1981*, p. 44.

42. Statement by Secretary of State Vance: United States Intent Regarding the SALT I Interim Agreement, 23 September 1977, *Doc. 1977*, pp. 577–8; President Carter's address on 21 July 1977, cited in note 21; Defense Secretary Brown's on 13 April 1977, cited in note 27; Secretary Vance, 'Arms control and national security', address before the American Society of Newspaper Editors in Washington, DC, on 10 April 1978, *DSB*, May 1978, pp. 20–2.

Also ACDA's pamphlet, cited in note 28; the report on US policy toward the Soviet Union, cited in note 24; 'Arms control: preserving freedom and peace in a nuclear age', address by Vice President Mondale on 22 February 1979, *DSB*, April 1979, pp. 14–16; *Brown 1979*, pp. 8–9 and 38–43.

43. President Carter's addresses on 22 May 1977, 4 October 1977 and on 25 April 1979, cited in, respectively, notes 22, 21 and 25.

Speech by Paul Warnke on 3 April 1978, *Survival*, July–August 1978, pp. 179–82, and 'Progress and problems in arms control negotiations', an address by Warnke before the United Nations Association–United States Annual Symposium at New York on 19 September 1977, *DSB*, 28 November 1977, pp. 772ff.

44. See *DSB*, September 1979, passim.

45. Muskie's address on 18 September 1980, cited in note 26. News conference remarks by President Carter: 'Compliance with strategic arms limitation agreements', 14 March 1980, *Doc. 1980*, pp. 148–9; remarks by Carter on strategic arms limitation, 5 May 1980, *ibid.*, p. 215; address by Carter on strategic arms limitation on 9 May 1980, *ibid.*, pp. 216–17, and remarks by the President on SALT II , 20 June 1980, *ibid.*, pp. 255–6.

See also news conference remarks by Secretary Muskie on 13 May 1980, *ibid.*, pp. 217ff., and interview with Secretary of Defense Brown by *U.S. News & World Report*: 'Soviet–American relations and SALT II', 4 August 1980, *ibid.*, pp. 323–5.

46. *Brown 1980*, pp. 39f. and *Brown 1981*, pp. 60–1.

47. President Carter's address on 21 July 1977, cited in note 21. 'America's role in a turbulent world', address by Carter on 20 February 1979, *DSB*, March 1979, pp. 21–3.

Marshall Shulman, cited in note 22; Paul Warnke's address on 10 November 1977, cite in noted 28; Brzezinski's address before the Chicago committee of the Council on Foreign Relations on 4 April 1979, *DSB*, May 1979, pp. 48–51, and Brown's speech on 5 April 1979, *ibid.*, pp. 51–5.

48. Cf. President Carter's news conference of 8 February 1977, *DSB*, 28 February 1977, pp. 157–60, and Carter's press conference on 30 March 1977, *Survival*, May–June 1977, pp. 129–31, and statements by President Carter during an interview: 'Linkage of strategic arms limitation treaty with Soviet activities', 7 September 1979, *Doc. 1979*, pp. 567–8.

Secretary Vance interviewed by AP and UPI correspondents on 3 February 1977, *DSB*, 21 February 1977, pp. 147ff.; Vance's news conference, Moscow, 27 March 1977, *DSB*, 25 April 1977, pp. 389–95.

Secretary Brown's statement before the Senate Committee on Foreign Relations on 9 July 1979, *DSB*, September 1979, pp. 13–18, especially p. 17, and *Brown 1980*, p. 42.

Brzezinski's address on 4 April 1979, cited in note 47.

Speech by ACDA Director Warnke to the Women's National Democratic Club: 'Strategic arms limitation talks and comprehensive test ban', 10 November 1977, *Doc. 1977*, pp. 704–12, and Warnke's address on 23 August 1978, cited in note 28.

Statement by Marshall Shulman before the Subcommittee on Europe and the Middle East of the House Foreign Affairs Committee on 16 October 1979, *DSB*, December 1979, pp. 40–5.

49. Secretary Muskie's address before the Women's National Democratic Club, 'SALT and the future of arms control', Washington, DC, on 16 October 1980, *DSB*, December 1980, pp. 6–7; see also Muskie's news conference of 20 May, *DSB*, June 1980, pp. A–B; and question-and-answer session following Foreign Policy Association address by Muskie on 7 July, *DSB*, August 1980, p. 30.

President Carter, news conference, 2 March 1978, *DSB*, April 1978, pp. 20–1, and the President's address on 7 June 1978, cited in note 24.

50. See the President's address on 20 February 1979, cited in note 47; on 25 April 1979, cited in note 25; and 'Soviet troops in Cuba and SALT', address to the nation on 1 October 1979, *DSB*, November 1979, pp. 7f.
    See also Brzezinski's address on 4 April 1979, cited in note 47.
51. President Carter's address on 17 March 1978, cited in note 35, and Statement by President Carter on the MX missile, 7 September 1979, *Doc. 1979*, pp. 565–7. (However, in this statement the President also noted that MX was not a bargaining chip.)
    See also Secretary Brown's statement before the Senate Committee on Foreign Relations on 9 July 1979, *DSB*, September 1979, p. 15, *Brown 1978*, p. 124, *Brown 1980*, p. 136; and *Brown 81*, p. 68 (on TNF) and p. 116.
52. Secretary Vance at a news conference in Gainesville, Florida, on 26 October 1979, *DSB*, December 1979, p. 24; Secretary Muskie, question-and-answer session following address in Memphis on 6 October 1980, *DSB*, November 1980, p. G.
53. For instance, *Brown 1978*, pp. 63 and 106, and ACDA's pamphlet from November 1978, cited in note 28.
54. President Carter's address before a joint session of the Congress on 18 June 1979, *DSB*, July 1979, p. 2; Secretary Brown's address on 5 April 1979, cited in note 30.
    Administration Report on Compliance with the SALT I Agreements, 21 February 1978, *Doc. 1978*, pp. 79–90; and Administration Report on Verification of the Proposed SALT II Agreement, 23 February 1978, *ibid.*, pp. 91–5.
55. President Carter's address on 7 June 1978, *op. cit.*, p. 1, cited in note 24; and *DSB*, February 1979, p. 2.
56. Warnke's address on 19 September 1977, *op. cit.*, p. 775, cited in note 43; address by Warnke on 10 November 1977, cited in note 28; and his address on 3 April 1978, cited in note 43. See also Warnke's reply to a question after an address on 19 January 1978 (cf. note 35) *op. cit.*, p. 5, and ACDA's pamphlet from November 1978, *op. cit.* (cf. note 28), p. 5.
57. President Carter, interview for 'Bill Moyers' Journal', 13 November 1978, *DSB*, December 1978, pp. 14–16; the President stated, for instance; 'We don't intend to evolve, and neither do the Soviets intend to evolve, a capacity to destroy the other nation without ourselves being destroyed by nuclear forces.'
    See also Carter's address on 25 April 1979, cited in note 25.
58. Secretary Vance interviewed by *Il Tempo* correspondent, 18 June 1977, *DSB*, 18 July 1977, p. 88; Vance's remarks to questions at State Department's National Foreign Policy Conference for Editors and Broadcasters on 28–29 June, *DSB*, 25 July 1977, p. 124; and Secretary Vance Interviewed for *U.S. News and World Report*, 7 November 1977, *DSB*, 21 November 1977, p. 733.
59. Question-and-answer session with ACDA Director Warnke: 'Strategic arms limitation talks', following a lecture at Columbia University, 3 April 1978, *Doc. 1978*, pp. 222–30; Warnke's address on 19 January 1978, *op. cit.*, p. 4, cited in note 35; Warnke's address on 23 August 1978, *op. cit.*, p. 1, cited in note 28.
60. Remarks by Secretary of Defense Harold Brown before the World Affairs Council of Northern California at San Francisco on 19 July 1977, *DSB*, 5 September 1977, p. 298; interview with Secretary of Defense Brown, *U.S. News & World Report*, 5 September 1977, *Doc. 1977*, pp. 549–57; address by Secretary Brown: 'Strategic nuclear forces', 15 September 1977, *Doc. 1977*, pp. 574–6.
61. *Brown 1978*, pp. 33f. and 62.

62. *Brown 1979*, pp. 80 and 38.
63. *DSB*, July 1979, pp. 67–8.
64. Shulman's statement on 16 October 1979, cf. note 48, and 'Identifying U.S. security interests in U.S.–Soviet relations', address on 4 October 1979, before the International Studies Association at the University of Pittsburgh, *DSB*, January 1980, pp. 17–20.
65. *Brown 1980*, pp. 31 and 82–3.
66. *Ibid.*
67. Secretary Brown's address on 20 August, cited in note 32; *Brown 1981*, p. 38.
    A good demonstration of Brown's reading of the Soviet view of nuclear arms is his statement before the Committee on Foreign Relations, United States Senate, on 16 September, cited in note 34.
68. Secretary Muskie's statement, *ibid.*
69. See especially 'Reducing the danger of nuclear weapons', address by President Reagan before the Los Angeles World Affairs Council on 31 March 1983, *DSB*, May 1983, pp. 1–5; cf. also my review of the Presidnet's views in 'The Reagan administration, the Soviet Union and nuclear arms: hopes and fears', *Cooperation and Conflict*, Vol. XIX, No. 1, March 1984, pp. 17ff.
70. *DSB*, March 1981, p. 12, and *DSB*, April 1981, p. 9.
71. 'Paths toward peace: deterrence and arms control', address to the nation, broadcast from the White House, 22 November 1982, *DSB*, December 1982, pp. 1–6, particularly p. 6; 'U.S. relations with the Soviet Union', radio broadcast to the nation from Camp David, 8 January 1983, *DSB*, February 1983, pp. 1–2 (see also the references in note 120).
72. 'The U.S.–Soviet relationship', address in the White House on 16 January 1984, *DSB*, February 1984, pp. 1–4; and 'Relations with the U.S.S.R', radio address by the President on 11 February 1984, *DSB*, 22 April 1984, pp. 1–2.
73. *DSB*, November 1987, pp. 2–4.
74. *DSB*, February 1988, passim, for instance pp. 5, 6 and 8.
75. Cf., for example, 'American power and American purpose', address before the annual meeting of the U.S. Chamber of Commerce, Washington, DC, on 27 April 1982, *DSB*, June 1982, pp. 42–4.
76. 'U.S.–Soviet relations in the context of U.S. foreign policy', Statement before the Senate Foreign Relations Committee on 15 June 1983, *DSB*, July 1983, pp. 65–72.
    See also 'Realism and responsibility: the U.S. approach to arms control', address by Secretary Shultz before the League of Women Voters in Detroit on 14 May 1984, *DSB*, June 1984, pp. 28–32; 'Managing the U.S.–Soviet relationship over the long term', address by Shultz before the Rand/UCLA Center for the Study of Soviet International Behavior in Los Angeles on 18 October 1984, *DSB*, December 1984, pp. 1–5 (especially this address applies a detached approach); and 'The Charter's goals and today's realities', address by Schultz before the UN General Assembly in New York on 23 September 1985, *DSB*, November 1985, p. 11.
77. Cf. statement by President Reagan on American non-proliferation policy, 16 July 1981, *Doc. 1981*, pp. 278–80; and statement by Reagan on the fifteenth anniversary of the Treaty on the Non-Proliferation of Nuclear Weapons, 1 July 1983, *Doc. 1983*, pp. 511–13. (In both these cases, though, references to common Soviet–American interests are rather indirect.)
    In the speeches by Secretary Shultz, cited in note 76, common Soviet–American interests in this field are stated openly; besides, see 'Science and American foreign policy: the spirit of progress', address by Schultz before a symposium on science and foreign policy sponsored by the National Academy

322   NOTES TO PAGES 109 TO 109

of Sciences, 6 March 1985, *DSB*, May 1985, p. 31.

See also statement by the first ACDA Director Eugene Rostow, before the First Committee of the UN General Assembly, 21 October 1981, *Doc. 1981*, p. 485; report to the Congress by Secretary of Defense Weinberger: 'Direct communications links and other measures to enhance stability', 12 April 1983, *Doc. 1983*, pp. 309–24, especially p. 313; statement by Kenneth Adelman (ACDA Director after April 1983) *Review of Arms Control And Disarmament Activities*, Hearings before the Special Panel on Arms Control And Disarmament of the Procurement and Military Nuclear Systems Subcommittee of the Committee On Armed Services, House of Representatives, 10 September 1985, where Adelman said: 'The NPT is one area where the interests of the US and the Soviet Union coincide' (p. 45).

78. 'Military strength and peace', address by President Reagan at the US Naval Academy commencement exercises in Annapolis, Maryland, 22 May 1985, *DSB*, August 1985, p. 11. 'U.S.–Soviet relations', President Reagan's radio address to the nation broadcast, 23 November 1985, *DSB*, February 1986, p. 23; 'Strengthening American security', President Reagan's televised address to the nation, 26 February 1986, *DSB*, April 1986, pp. 18–21; 'America's agenda for the future', excerpts from President Reagan's message to the Congress of 6 February 1986, *ibid.*, pp. 26–9; President Reagan's address 'Keeping America strong', 23 September 1986, *DSB*, November 1986, pp. 8–9; Reagan's address to the nation after the summit with Gorbachev in Iceland in October 1986, *DSB*, December 1986, pp. 17–20; and *DSB*, March 1988, pp. 25–6.

Caspar Weinberger, *Annual Report to the Congress. Fiscal Year* 1987, 5 February 1986 (Weinberger 1986), pp. 3ff. and 43ff.; and Caspar Weinberger, 'US defense strategy', *Foreign Affairs*, Vol. 64, No. 4 Spring 1986, pp. 675–97, especially the end.

79. For example, *ibid.*, pp. 677–8; Caspar W. Weinberger, *Annual Report To The Congress On The FY 1983 Budget, FY 1984 Authorization Request And FY 1983–1987 Defense Programs*, 8 February 1982 (Weinberger 1982), pp. II–10f; and *Report of the Secretary of Defense Caspar W. Weinberger to the Congress on the FY 1985 Budget, FY 1986 Authorization Request and FY 1985–89 Defense Programs*, 1 February 1984 (Weinberger 1984), p. 27.

Weinberger 1984, p. 27, epitomizes the Reagan administration's thinking on deterrence by quoting from the Scowcroft Commission's report: 'Deterrence is not an abstract notion amenable to simple quantification. Still less is it a mirror image of what would deter ourselves. Deterrence is the set of beliefs in the minds of Soviet leaders, given their own values and attitudes, about our capabilities and our will. It requires us to determine, as best we can, what would deter them from considering aggression, even in a crisis – not to determine what would deter us'.

Report of the Secretary of Defense Caspar W. Weinberger to the Congress on the FY 1986 Budget, FY 1987 Authorization Request and FY 1986–90 Defense Programs, 4 February 1985 (Weinberger 1985), p. 45, quotes the same words; see also *Report of the Secretary of Defense Caspar W. Weinberger to the Congress on the FY 1988/FY 1989 Budget and FY 1988–92 Defense Programs*, 12 January 1987 (Weinberger 1987), pp. 42f; *Report of the Secretary of Defense Frank C. Carlucci to the Congress on the Amended FY 1988/FY 1989 Biennial Budget*, 18 February 1988 (Carlucci 1988), pp. 25, 28 and 53–4; and *DSB*, April 1988, pp. 11ff.

80. Cf. news conference remarks by President Reagan: 'Nuclear war and strategic arms', 1 October 1981, *Doc. 1981*, p. 460; news conference remarks by

President Reagan: 'Nuclear arms reductions and the U.S.–Soviet nuclear equation', 31 March 1982, *Doc. 1982*, p. 187; address by President Reagan: 'Nuclear war and strategic arms reduction', 17 April 1982, *ibid.*, p. 218.

Letter From Secretary of Defense Weinberger to the *Los Angeles Times*: 'Nuclear war', 25 August 1982, *ibid.*, p. 563; statement of Weinberger, *U.S. Strategic Doctrine*, Hearing before the Committee on Foreign Relations, United States Senate, 14 December 1982, p. 18; and Weinberger's statement, *MX Missile Basing System and Related Issues*, Hearings before the Committee on Armed Services, United States Senate, 20 April 1983, p. 98.

See also *Strategic Survey 1982–1983*, IISS, London, Spring 1983, p. 36.

81. *Weinberger 1982*, pp. I–17ff. and II–10f.; Caspar W. Weinberger, *Annual Report To The Congress on the FY 1984 Budget, FY 1985 Authorization Request and FY 1984–1988 Defense Programs*, 1 February 1983 (Weinberger 1983), p. 51 and 54–5, where it is stated, for instance: 'To talk of actions that the U.S. Government could not, in good conscience, and in prudence, undertake tends to defeat the goal of deterrence' (p. 55).

Weinberger 1984, p. 38, phrases the requirements of deterrence in extremely demanding terms, for instance: 'Since there can be no winners in a nuclear war, we have no alternative to ensuring the *absolute certainty* of nuclear deterrence' (emphasis added), and 'credible deterrence ... requires that we have the ability, in case deterrence fails, to halt any attack and restore peace on terms favorable to us and our allies. And we must accomplish that while trying to limit the scope, duration, and intensity of conflict'.

See also *Weinberger 1985*, p. 46; and *Weinberger 1986*, p. 75, which states: 'Our nuclear doctrine is designed to ensure that the Soviet Union's leadership also believes that a nuclear war can never be won – *however they define victory*' (emphasis added).

Also, see Weinberger's review of US deterrence policy in US Strategic Doctrine, Hearing before the Committee On Foreign Relations, United States Senate, 14 December 1982, cited in note 80, pp. 17–22; and Secretary Haig, 'Peace and deterrence', address before Georgetown University's Center for Strategic and International Studies on 6 April 1982, *DSB*, May 1982, pp. 31–4.

On the need for an 'Effective capability to attack hard strategic targets promptly', see especially Richard N. Perle, Assistant Secretary of Defense for International Security Policy, *Strategic Programs*, Hearings on Military Posture And H.R. 5968, before the Committee on Armed Services, House of Representatives, 6 October 1981, p. 62; and *Weinberger* 1986, p. 214.

82. *Weinberger 1984*, p. 29, states: 'We must plan for flexibility in our forces and in our options for response, so that we might terminate the conflict on terms favorable to the forces of freedom'. See also Weinberger's statement in hearings on 6 October 1981, cited in note 81; and his statement in hearings on US Strategic Doctrine, 14 December 1982, cited in note 80, p. 19.

83. Announcement by President Reagan: 'Strategic arms program', 2 October 1981, *Doc. 1981*, pp. 461f; at a news conference on 31 March 1982, President Reagan stated that 'on balance, the Soviet Union does have a definite margin of superiority, enough so that there is a risk and there is ... "a window of vulnerability"', *Doc. 1982*, p. 187.

Three years later this rather gloomy view of the deterrence situation was restated by Robert C. McFarlane, the then Assistant to the President for National Security Affairs, when he declared in an address before the Overseas Writers Association on 7 March 1985: 'It is becoming increasingly apparent that the Soviet Union is acquiring a survivable, first-strike capability which will be far less easy to deter', *DSB*, June 1985, p. 57.

Secretary Weinberger and Secretary Haig, *Strategic Weapons Proposals*, Hearings before the Committee on Foreign Relations, United States Senate, 3 and 4 November 1981, pp. 3ff. and 59ff.; *Weinberger 1982*, pp. I, 17–9, II 7f. and III, 57–8.

84. Cf. President Reagan's radio address to the nation, 11 December 1982, *DSB*, February 1983, pp. 5–6.

Weinberger in the hearings on MX, cited in note 80, pp. 5–13; and *Weinberger 1983*, pp. 220–1.

85. Report of the President's Commission on Strategic Forces, 6 April 1983, *Doc. 1983*, pp. 273–300; President Reagan's endorsement of the report can be seen from his remarks on 19 April 1983, *DSB*, June 1983, pp. 17–18.

Caspar Weinberger's comments, see the hearings on MX, cited in noted 80, p. 116; and Weinberger, *Review of Arms Control Implications Of The Report Of The President's Commission On Strategic Forces*, Hearings before the Committee on Foreign Affairs, House of Representatives. 17 May 1983, pp. 9ff.

86. Remarks by President Reagan: Prospects for Arms Control Negotiations, 14 October 1982, *Doc. 1982*, p. 736; see also interview with President Reagan: 'Strategic arms reduction talks', 21 May 1982, *ibid.*, p. 315; 'U.S. program for peace and arms control', speech by President Reagan before the National Press Club in Washington, DC on 18 November 1981, *DSB*, December 1981, p. 11; 'Reducing the danger of nuclear weapons', address by President Reagan before the Los Angeles World Affairs Council on 31 March 1983, cited in note 69.

The term 'truly comparable systems' was used by Richard Burt, the then Director of the Department of State's Bureau of Politico-Military Affairs, in a statement to NATO's Special Consultative Group in Brussels on 20 November 1981, *DSB*, January 1982, p. 31.

Richard Perle, *Department Of Defense Authorization For Appropriations For Fiscal Year 1983*, Hearings before the Committee On Armed Services, United States Senate, 1 March 1982, p. 4369 on 'ultimate superiority'.

See also *Weinberger 1983*, pp. 56–7.

87. Interview with President Reagan: 'Intermediate-range nuclear force negotiations', 26 May 1983, *Doc. 1983*, p. 444.

88. Cf. Caspar Weinberger, *Fiscal Year 1981 Department Of Defense Supplemental Authorization*, Hearing before the Committee on Armed Services, United States Senate, 23 March 1981, p. 6.

Richard Perle declared in the hearings on 22 March (1 March), 1981, cited in note 86, pp. 4925 and 5001, that the underlying logic of the ABM treaty is destabilizing because of the preclusion of strategic defense.

89. 'Peace and national security', address to the nation on 23 March 1983, *DSB*, April 1983, pp. 8–14.

President Reagan's comments a few days later are reproduced in *Doc. 1983*, pp. 262f; the idea has been repeated later by President Reagan, cf. *DSB*, October 1987, p. 2.

90. *The President's Strategic Defense Initiative*, the President of the United States, January 1985, particularly pp. 3ff; *Weinberger 1985*, p. 54; and *Weinberger 1986*, pp. 287–9.

President Reagan has presented SDI in plain terms; for example: 'our Strategic Defense Initiative ... might one day enable us to put in space a shield that missiles could not penetrate, a shield that could protect us from nuclear missiles just as a roof protects a family from rain', cf. speech on 19 June 1986,

DSB, September 1986, p. 22; in an address before the UN General Assembly on 22 September 1986, he argued: 'The threat does not come from defensive systems, which are a shield against attack, but from offensive weapons', *DSB*, November 1986, p. 3.

91. The criteria have been defined by Paul Nitze, Special Advisor to the President and the Secretary of State on arms control matters, cf., for example, Nitze's address before the World Affairs Council in Philadelphia on 20 February 1985, *DSB*, April 1985, p. 28; and 'The objectives of arms control', address by Nitze before the International Institute for Strategic Studies in London on 28 March 1985, *DSB*, May 1985, pp. 57–63, in particular p. 62 where the highly demanding criteria are stated in plain terms.

See also *Soviet Military Power 1986*, The Department of Defense Washington, DC, 1986, p. 150.

Secretary Weinberger has not applied similar criteria, cf. *Weinberger 1987*, pp. 51f., and Caspar W. Weinberger, 'Why Offense Needs Defense ' *Foreign Policy*, No. 68, Fall 1987, pp. 3–18.

92. The President's Strategic Defense Initiative, *op. cit.*, p. 3.

93. *Weinberger 1985*, p. 26; *Weinberger 1986*, p. 39; and Weinberger's article in *Foreign Affairs*, cited in note 78, where he also states: 'progress toward an effective SDI will have to proceed hand in hand with regaining an effective offensive deterrent and, paradoxically enough, with arms reduction as well' (p. 683).

That SDI is a supplement to traditional deterrence through retaliation was also stressed by Secretary Shultz, 'A New International Era: The American Perspective', address before the Pilgrims of Great Britain in London on 10 December 1985, *DSB*, February 1986, p. 25.

See also 'SDI: Setting the record straight', address by Kenneth A. Adelman before the Council on Foreign Affairs in Baltimore on 7 August 1985, *DSB*, October 1985, pp. 42–5.

94. Cf. Weinberger's article in *Foreign Affairs*, cited in note 78, p. 683; *Weinberger 1986*, p. 76; *Soviet Military Power 1987*, The Department of Defense, Washington, D.C., 1987, p. 127; and *Carlucci 1988*, p. 109.

Weinberger 1985, p. 55, states: 'Clearly, Soviet Military planners and scientists are confident that strategic missile defense will be effective'.

In 1986 and 1987, Secretary Weinberger has elaborated 'competitive strategies' that 'capitalize on our advantages and exploit our adversaries' weaknesses' to secure the deterrence, and one such strategy is SDI (together with, for instance, anti-submarine warfare), cf. *Weinberger 1986*, pp. 85–6; *Weinberger 1987*, pp. 65–9 and 213; and *Carlucci 1988*, pp. 115f.

The Soviet strategic defense program is reviewed in 'SDI: the Soviet program', address by Paul Nitze before the Chautauqua Conference on Soviet–American Relations, 28 June 1985, *DSB*, September 1985, pp. 40–2.

95. Alexander Haig's address on 6 April 1982, cited in note 81. Statement of George Shultz in the hearings on MX, cited in note 80, p. 108; Shultz's statement in *Department Of Defense Authorization For Appropriations For Fiscal Year 1986*, Hearings before The Committee On Armed Services, United States Senate, 26 February 1985, pp. 3525f.

Caspar Weinberger's statement, *Department Of Defense Authorization For Appropriations For Fiscal Year 1982*, Hearings before the Committee on Armed Services, United States Senate, 28 January 1981, 12; and Weinberger's statement in hearing on US Strategic Doctrine, 14 December 1982, cited in note 80, p. 16.

Richard Burt phrased the relationship between Soviet strategic nuclear strength and Soviet foreign policy in more cautious terms in *Strategic Programs*, Hearings on Military Posture before the Committee on Armed Services, House of Representatives, 23 February 1982, especially p. 34; a more typical presentation was made by Burt in *Strategic Arms Control And U.S. National Security Policy*, Hearings And Mark-up before the Committee on Foreign Affairs and its Subcommittee on International Security and Scientific Affairs, House of Representatives, 2 April 1982, p. 7.

96. *Weinberger 1984*, p. 56; *Carlucci 1988*, pp. 27–8. *Soviet Military Power 1984*, The Department of Defense, Washington, DC, 1984, pp. 31 and 136; The President's Strategic Defense Initiative, *op. cit.*, p. 1.

President Reagan's remarks at a meeting with members of Congress on 25 March 1985, just before an important vote in Congress, *DSB*, June 1985, p. 60.

97. 'Nuclear arms control and the future of U.S.–Soviet relations', address before the Los Angeles World Affairs Council, 10 September 1982, *DSB*, November 1982, p. 16.

Rostow has presented this thinking in several speeches, cf., for example, 'Prospects for arms control', statement made in Committee I of the UN General Assembly in New York on 21 October 1981, *DSB*, December 1981, p. 70; 'The unnecessary war', address at the Winston Churchill Lecture of the English-speaking Union in London on 30 November 1981, *DSB*, February 1982, pp. 32–7 (p. 34 on 'equal deterrence'); and statement before the Senate Committee on Foreign Relations, 13 May 1982, *Doc. 1982*, p. 302.

98. New conference of 22 May 1981, p. 12, *DSB*, July 1982, p. 12; statement on a National Foreign Policy Conference for US editors and broadcasters at the Department of State on 2 June 1981, *ibid.*, p. 22.

See also 'NATO and the restoration of American leadership', commencement address before the graduating class at Syracuse University, New York, on 9 May 1981, *DSB*, June 1981, p. 12; and Haig interviewed for French television on 22 February 1981, *DSB*, April 1981, pp. 13–16.

99. Cf. particularly the address by Richard Burt in Brussels on 23 September 1981 *Doc. 1981*, pp. 442–51; Burt ended his speech: 'The nuclear debate in Europe today has become a battle for the soul of Europe. The alternatives are clear. The West can reaffirm its faith in collective defense, deterrence, and serious arms control and thus remain free. Or America can turn upon itself, and Europe can rest its hopes for security and its prospects for freedom upon Soviet good will. For 30 years America has rejected isolationism. For 30 years Europe has rejected Soviet patronage. For 30 years the West has instead chosen unity, strength, and freedom. There is no other choice'.

Statement by Eugene Rostow before the Senate Committee on Armed Services, 24 July 1981: 'On a day-to-day basis, the Soviet drumbeat acts on the collective psyche of the United States and its friends and allies. There is great fear abroad, not only of nuclear war but of American inadequacies and, ultimately, of abandonment by the United States.' *Doc. 1981*, p. 289; see also Rostow's statement before the House Committee on Foreign Affairs: Intermediate-Range Nuclear Forces, 20 November 1981, *ibid.*, pp. 600–5.

See also several statements by Vice-President Bush on his trip to Europe early 1983, cf. *DSB*, March 1983, passim.

'Review of U.S. relations with the Soviet Union', address by Lawrence Eagleburger, Under-Secretary for Political Affairs, before the Governing Board of the World Jewish Congress On 1 February 1983, *ibid.*, pp. 81–4; the American interpretation of the supreme significance of INF deployment appeared clearly from these words: 'If NATO, as a result of Soviet political pressure, were to abandon a program that is essential to assure the security of Europe, it would be the beginning of the end of an effective Western alliance. If the Soviets learn that we and our allies lack the will, in the face of missile rattling, to carry out difficult decisions commonly arrived at, then we can look forward to ever more aggressive behavior each time we seek to respond to Soviet provocations (p. 83). See also *Weinberger 1983*, p. 56.

100. Statement by the Department of State: 'U.S. policy on strategic arms limitations, 3 March 1981, *Doc. 1981*, p. 84; see also news conference remarks by ACDA Director Rostow, 29 September 1981, *Doc. 1981*, p. 457; and Defense Secretary Weinberger's statement in hearings on 3 November 1981, cited in note 83, p. 15.

President Reagan's address on 16 January 1984, cited in note 72; the President's statement 'U.S.–Soviet Union expand "Hot Line" agreement', 17 July 1984, *DSB*, September 1984, p. 45, and the White House fact-sheet on a direct communications line between Washington and Moscow, *ibid*. Also 'U.S., Soviet Union to establish nuclear risk reduction centers', White House statement, 5 May 1987, *DSB*, July 1987, pp. 21–2.

101. Address by Secretary of State Haig: 'Arms control Policy', 14 July 1981, *Doc. 1981*, pp. 264–71; Secretary Shultz's address on 18 October 1984, cited in note 76; and ACDA Director Kenneth L. Adelman's address 'Paradox, problems, and promise of arms control' before the Los Angeles World Affairs Council on 17 November 1983, *DSB*, January 1984, pp. 45–9.

102. Among the many speeches and statements stressing this theme: news conference statement and remarks by President Reagan, 13 May 1982, *Doc. 1982*, p. 300; interview with President Reagan: 'Strategic reduction talks', 21 May 1982, *ibid.*; remarks by President Reagan: 'Nuclear war and negotiating from strength', 11 November 1983, *Doc. 1983*, pp. 954–5; and the President's address on 26 February 1986, cited in note 78.

Secretary Haig's testimony, *Nuclear Arms Reduction Proposals*, Hearings before the Committee on Foreign Relations, United States Senate, 30 April 1982, p. 113; Secretary Shultz's statement in the hearings on MX on 20 April 1983, cited in note 80, p. 10; Shultz's statement in the hearings on 26 February 1985, cited in note 95, p. 3527 and 3543f.

Defense Secretary Weinberger has emphasized this reasoning several times, cf. for example: interview in *U.S. News & World Report*: 'Strategic arms limitation treaty', 13 April 1981, *Doc. 1981*, p. 162; Weinberger's statement in a hearing before the Committee on Foreign Affairs, cited in note 85, p. 23; *Weinberger 1987*, p. 219; and *Carlucci 1988*, pp. 20, 50, 107 and 113.

103. *Arms Control Policy, Planning and Negotiating*, Hearings Before The Committee on Armed Services, United States Senate, 1 December 1981, pp. 92–7; Perle presented the same reasoning in *Overview of Nuclear Arms Control and Defense Strategy in NATO*, Hearings Before the Subcommittee on International Security and Scientific Affairs and on Europe and the Middle East of the Committee on Foreign Affairs, House of Representatives, 23 February 1982, pp. 54–67.

104. Cf., for instance, Weinberger's statement in the hearings on *Strategic Programs*, cited in note 81, p. 12.

105. See Defense Secretary Weinberger's statement in *The MX Missile And Associated Basing Decision*, Hearing before the Committee on Armed Services, United States Senate, 8 December 1982, p. 13.

Numerous statements from members of the administration through 1982 evidence this thinking, cf. *Doc. 1982*, pp. 451–2, 821ff., 879–81, 887–91 and 897–9; and *Doc. 83*, p. 566.

See also President Reagan's radio broadcast on 8 January 1983, cited in note 71, p. 5 and 'MX missile', radio address by President Reagan on 9 March 1985, *DSB*, May 1985, p. 12; commenting on negotiations, it is worth noting that President Reagan, in June 1984, dissociated himself from superiority – 'I would prefer that we not ask for superiority', cf. *Doc. 1984*, pp. 468–9.

106. Statements by President Reagan and Paul Nitze, Chairman of the US delegation to the INF negotiations on 23 November 1983, *Doc. 1983*, pp. 999–1001.

107. Department of State Paper: 'Nuclear freeze proposal', April 1982, *Doc. 1982*, pp. 188–92; Letter from President Reagan to Members of the House of Representatives: 'Proposed resolutions on a freeze of nuclear weapons', 23 July 1982, *ibid.*, p. 473; and letter from Reagan to the Chairman of the House Committee on Armed Services: 'Proposed resolutions on a freeze of nuclear weapons', 3 August 1982, *ibid.*, p. 487.

Address by President Reagan: 'Nuclear freeze and administration military policy', 8 March 1983, *Doc. 1983*, pp. 162–3; 'American foreign policy challenges in the 1980's', address by the President before the Center for Strategic and International Studies (CSIS) on 6 April 1984, *DSB*, May 1984, p. 3; and statement by Richard Perle before the House Committee on Foreign Affairs: 'Nuclear arms control and nuclear freeze proposals', 17 February 1983, *Doc 1983*, pp. 127–30.

108. In October 1985 the administration announced a new broad interpretation of the ABM Treaty under which the development and testing of SDI components will be in accordance with the Treaty to a far greater extent than hitherto assumed. However, it was also announced that the administration would pursue the SDI program within the confines of the traditional so-called 'restrictive' interpretation, cf. *DSB*, December 1985, pp. 37–40. See also Paul H. Nitze's address before the International Law Weekend Group on 31 October 1986, *DSB*, January 1987, pp. 39–40; and Nitze's address on 1 April 1987, *DSB*, June 1987, pp. 31–3; and: Abraham D. Sofaer, 'The ABM Treaty: legal analysis in the political cauldron', *The Washington Quarterly*, Vol. 10, No. 4, Autumn 1987, pp. 59–75. (Sofaer was legal advisor to the State Department.)

109. Cf. note 89. See also Paul Nitze's speech on 20 February 1985, cited in note 91; his commencement address before the Johns Hopkins School of Advanced International Studies (SAIS) 'SDI and the ABM Treaty', 30 May 1985, *DSB*, August 1985, pp. 37–9; and Nitze's statement before the Subcommittee on Arms Control, International Security, and Science of the House Foreign Affairs Committee on 22 October 1985, *DSB*, December 1985, pp. 37–8.

Soviet Military Power 1985, The Department of Defense, Washington, DC, 1985, p. 137; and the President's Strategic Defense Initiative, *op. cit.*, p. 5.

110. Cf. Vice-President Bush in a speech on 23 May 1987, *DSB*, August 1987, pp. 27–8.

111. The first report was submitted on 23 January 1984, cf. 'Report on Soviet non-compliance with arms control agreements', President Reagan's message to the Congress, *DSB*, March 1984, pp. 8–11; the second report on 1 February 1985, cf. *Soviet Treaty Violations*, Hearings before the Committee on Armed Services, United States Senate, 20 February and 7 May 1985 and *DSB*, April 1985, pp. 29–34; a third report on 23 December 1985, *DSB*, February 1986, pp. 65–72; a fourth report on 10 March 1987, *DSB*, June 1987, pp. 37–42; a fifth report on 2 December 1987, *DSB*, March 1988, pp. 51–7.

112. Cf. *DSB*, August 1986, pp. 36–8; Richard Perle expressed this issue as

whether Congress 'will side with the Soviets' or 'stand with the administration'; cf. *U.S. Nuclear Forces And Arms Control Policy*, Hearings before the Defense Policy Panel of the Committee on Armed Services, House of Representatives, 20 May 1986, p. 65.

113. See especially Secretary Shultz's statement at a question-and-answer session with the American Society of Newspaper Editors on 11 May 1981, *DSB*, July 1984, p. 41.

This theme on negotiation with the Soviets has been elaborated by Edward L. Rowny, US Chief Negotiator at START; cf. 'START in a Historical Perspective', address before the Kiwanis Club in Atlanta on 10 April 1984, *DSB*, June 1984, pp. 44–7; 'Nuclear arms control and the NATO Alliance', address before the Royal United Services Institute in London on 21 June 1984, *DSB*, August 1984, pp. 38–44; and Rowny's address on 20 March 1987, *DSB*, June 1987, pp. 33–6. See also 'Arms control: the first round in Geneva', Address by Paul Nitze before the National Press Club on 1 May 1985, *DSB*, July 1985, pp. 44–7.

That the Reagan administration's approach to arms control negotiations differs from its predecessors has been underscored by Caspar Weinberger, particularly in his article in *Foreign Affairs*, cited in note 78, pp. 692–4.

114. 'U.S. offers new START initiatives', remarks by the President on 4 October 1983, *DSB*, November 1983, pp. 29–30.

Secretary Shultz's address on 14 May 1984, cited in note 76, p. 32.

115. *DSB*, November 1987, pp. 34 7.

116. Cf. the President's remarks on 3 March 1987, *DSB*, May 1987, pp. 16–17.

117. *DSB*, February 1988, passim, especially p. 18.

118. *DSB*, March 1988, pp. 31–40 (p. 33); see also *Carlucci 1988*, p. 113.

119. *Soviet Military Power 1983*, The Department of Defense, Washington, DC, 1983, p. 13; and *Soviet Military Power 1984*, *op. cit.*, p. 19.

Eugene Rostow has elaborated this thinking, cf. his speech on 21 October 1981, cited in note 97; in his address 'The unnecessary war' in London on 30 November 1981, also cited in note 97, Rostow portrayed the Soviet goal in vivid terms: 'The highest objective of Soviet strategy is to separate Western Europe from the United States. If Western Europe could be brought within the Soviet domain, the geopolitical theorists of the Soviet Union believe, Japan, China, and many other nations would draw the necessary conclusions, and the United States would be left impotent. The enormous Soviet effort in the field of intermediate-range missiles is intelligible only in the perspective of this Soviet doctrine. In that perspective, it is all too intelligible. The objective, as always, is to decouple the United States from Europe. The scenario would follow these lines: the subliminal radiations of the Soviet intermediate-range nuclear arsenal would cause panic in Europe while the growing Soviet long-range arsenal would paralyze any possibility of an American strategic response. Presto and checkmate. The Japanese, Chinese, and many others would follow suit' (p. 36).

120. News conference remarks by President Reagan: Nuclear war and Strategic Arms, 1 October 1981, *Doc. 1981*, p. 460; remarks by President Reagan: 'MX missile and nuclear policy', 16 October 1981, *ibid.*, p. 471; see also President Reagan's speech to the European Parliament, Strasbourg, 8 May 1985, *DSB*, July 1985, pp. 18–22, particularly p. 20.

Secretary Weinberger's statement to *Los Angeles Times*, 25 August 1982, cited in note 80, pp. 563–5; Weinberger's statement in a hearing on US Strategic Doctrine on 14 December 1982, cited in 80, pp. 7 and 12; newspaper article by Weinberger in *Washington Post*, 22 November 1983, *Doc. 1983*, pp. 992–3 (a comment on the film 'The Day After' which, Weinberger noted, did not try to take us into the 'minds of the Soviet leaders. ... in fact we cannot know if those leaders share our vision of nuclear disaster.')

See also *Weinberger 1984*, p. 27; *Weinberger 1985*, p. 45; *Weinberger 1986*, p. 60; and 'Soviet military power 1987', *op. cit.*, p. 15; also, Secretary Shultz in an address on 17 November 1986, *DSB*, January 1987, pp. 31–5, especially p. 32.

On the Soviet command, control and communcations system, see especially Richard Perle in hearings on 2 April 1982, cited in note 95, p. 31; concerning the Soviet desire to have superiority at all levels, see Perle in hearings on 1 March 1982, cited in note 86, p. 4370.

121. Cf. Eugene Rostow in his speech on 10 September 1982, cited in note 97, p. 18.
122. See, in particular, 'Relationship of foreign and defense policies', statement by Secretary Haig before the Senate Armed Services Committee on 30 July 1981, *DSB*, September 1981, p. 16f.
123. Cf. especially Edward Rowny's address on 10 April 1984, cited in note 113.
124. 'A foundation for enduring peace', address by President Reagan to the UN General Assembly on 24 October 1985, *DSB*, December 1985, p. 5; 'Arms control: objectives and prospects', address by Secretary Shultz before the Council on Foreign Affairs in Austin, Texas, on 28 March 1985, *DSB*, May 1985, p. 26.
125. 'Arms control and the future of East–West relations', address by President Reagan at Eureka College, Illinois, on 9 May 1982, *DSB*, June 1982, p. 36; news conference statement and remarks by President Reagan, 13 May 1982, *Doc. 1982*, p. 299; and the President's address on 22 November 1982, cited in note 71, p. 2.

President Reagan on 'U.S.–U.S.S.R. negotiations on nuclear and space arms', 8 March 1985, *DSB*, May 1985, p. 55. 'U.S. response to Soviet arms proposals', President's statement, 24 February 1986, *DSB*, April 1986, p. 64.
126. *Carlucci 1988*, pp. 51 and 24–5; *Soviet Military Power: An Assessment of The Threat 1988*, Department of Defense, Washington, DC, 1988, pp. 10 and 96.
127. *DSB*, April 1988, p. 12.
128. 'Soviet military power: an assessment of the threat 1988', *op. cit.*, p. 96.
129. *Carlucci 1988*, p. 23.

CHAPTER 5   THE PROCESS OF PERCEPTION: THE DOMESTIC SETTING

1. Robert Jervis, Essay-review. 'Political decision-making: recent contributions', *Political Psychology*, Summer 1980. p. 90; Karl Popper, *Unended Quest. An Intellectual-Autobiography*, Glasgow 1977, pp. 51–2; and Henry Kissinger, 'Domestic structure and foreign policy', Richard G. Head and Erwin J. Rokke (eds), *American Defense Policy*, third edition, Baltimore and London, 1973, p. 20 (reprint from *Dædalus*, no. 2, 1966).
2. Herbert A. Simon, *Models of Man. Social and Rational*, New York, 1957, pp. 162f. and 196f.
3. Robert Jervis, *Perception and Misperception in International Relations*, Princeton, 1976, pp. 154, 175 and 187; Ernest Nagel, *The Structure of Science. Problems in the Logic of Scientific Explanation*, London, 1971, pp. 30–3.
4. Katarina Brodin, 'Belief systems, doctrines, and foreign policy', *Cooperation*

and Conflict, VII, 1972, p. 106.

See also Ernest R. May, 'The nature of foreign policy: the calculated versus the axiomatic', *Dædalus*, Vol. 91, No. 4, Fall 1962, pp. 653–67, especially pp. 666–7; Richard C. Snyder, H.W. Bruck and Burton Sapin (eds), *Foreign Policy Decision Making. An Approach to the Study of International Politics*, New York, 1963, p. 144, on 'in order to' and 'because of' motives; and Jervis, 1980, *op. cit.*, p. 98, on motivated and unmotivated distortions of reality.

5. Eugene J. Meehan, *The Theory and Method of Political Analysis*, Homewood, Illinois, 1965, pp. 98 and 116–25; Nagel, *op. cit.*, pp. 20–6, and Björn Söderfeldt, *Statsvetenskapliga metoder* (Methods in Political Science), Stockholm, 1972, pp. 126ff.

6. That problem is considered from different angles in many parts of the literature, for instance: Karl W. Deutsch, *The Nerves of Government*, New York and London, 1966, pp. 145ff; Karl W. Deutsch and Richard L. Merritt, 'Effects of Events on National and International Images', Herbert C. Kelman (ed.), *International Behavior. A Social Psychological Analysis*, New York, 1965, pp. 130–87; Robert Jervis, 'Hypotheses on misperception', James N. Rosenau (ed.), *International Politics and Foreign Policy*, New York, 1969, pp. 239–54 (first published in *World Politics*, Vol. XX, 1968, pp. 454–79), and Jervis, 1976, *op. cit.*, chapter 11 on 'Cognitive dissonance and international relations'.

The most extensive studies of the theory of cognitive dissonance are: Leon Festinger, *A Theory of Cognitive Dissonance*, Stanford University Press, 1957; and Leon Festinger (ed.), *Conflict, Decision, and Dissonance*, Stanford University Press, 1964.

On 'unperceived environmental factors', see also Hyam Gold, 'Foreign policy decision-making and the environment. The claims of Snyder, Brecher, and the Sprouts', *International Studies Quarterly*, Vol. 22, No. 4, December 1978, pp. 582f.

7. John D. Steinbruner, *The Cybernetic Theory of Decision*, Princeton University Press, 1974, pp. 125–8; and William A. Scott, 'Psychological and social correlates of international images', Kelman (ed.), *op. cit.*, pp. 70–103, especially p. 97.

8. Cf. Thomas C. Schelling, *The Strategy of Conflict*, Oxford University Press, 1960; Knut Midgaard, *Strategisk Tenkning* (Strategic Thinking), Oslo, 1967; and Anatol Rapport, *Strategy and Conscience*, New York, 1969.

9. Cf. Göran Rystad, *Prisoners Of The Past? The Munich Syndrome And Makers Of American Foreign Policy In The Cold War Era*, Lund, 1982; see also Ernest R. May, *'Lessons' Of The Past. The Use and Misuse of History in American Foreign Policy*, London, 1973.

10. See especially Gabriel A. Almond, *The American People and Foreign Policy*, New York, 1967, pp. 29ff.; Michael H. Armacost, *The Foreign Relations of the United States*, Belmont, California, 1969, pp. 14–16; Michael Banks, 'The foreign policy of the United States', F.S. Northedge (ed.), *The Foreign Policies of the Powers*, London, 1969, p. 41; Cecil V. Crabb, Jr, *Policy-Makers and Critics. Conflicting Theories of American Foreign Policy*, New York, 1976, pp. 34–6.

Stanley Hoffmann, *Gulliver's Troubles, or the Setting of American Foreign Policy*, New York, 1968, pp. 87ff.; Knud Krakau, 'American foreign relations: a national style?', *Diplomatic History*, Vol. 8, No. 3, Summer 1984, pp. 253–72; Charles O. Lerche, Jr, *Foreign Policy of the American People*, Englewood Cliffs, N.J., 1961, pp. 139–58. Geir Lundestad, 'Uniqueness and pendulum swings in US foreign policy', *International Affairs*, Vol. 62, No. 3, Summer 1986, p. 419; May, *op. cit.*; Arthur Schlesinger, Jr, 'Foreign policy and the American character', *Foreign Affairs*, Vol. 62, No. 1, Fall 1983, pp. 1–16; and Edmund Stillman and William Pfaff, *Power And Impotence. The Failure of America's Foreign Policy*, London, 1966, passim.

11. Cf. Daniel Bell, 'The end of American exceptionalism', Nathan Glazer and Irving Kristol (eds), *The American Commonwealth – 1976–*, New York, 1976, pp. 198–203; Edward McNall Burns, *The American Idea of Mission. Concepts of National Purpose And Destiny*, New Jersey, 1957, pp. 5, 16, 32, and 348ff.; Crabb, *op. cit.*.

Felix Gilbert, *To The Farewell Address. Ideas of Early American Foreign Policy*, Princeton, 1961, passim; Samuel P. Huntington, *American Politics: The Promise of Disharmony*, Cambridge, Mass. and London, 1981, pp. 23–30. Adrienne Koch, *Power, Morals, and the Founding Fathers. Essays in the Interpretation of the American Enlightenment*, Cornell University Press, 1961, pp. 122ff.; Reinhold Niebuhr and Alan Heimert, *A Nation So Conceived. Reflections on the History of America from Its early Visions to Its Present Power*, London, 1963, pp. 123ff.

12. Almond, *op. cit.*, p. 60; Roger H. Brown, 'Politics and ideology: The American world mission', Gene M. Lyons (ed.), *America: Purpose and Power*, Chicago, 1965, pp. 19f.; Henry Steele Commager, *Living Ideas In America*, New York, 1951, pp. 650–2; Henry Steele Commager, *The American Mind. An Interpretation of American Thought and Character Since the 1880's*, New York, 1970 (first edition 1950), passim; statement of Henry Steele Commager, *Changing American Attitudes Toward Foreign Policy*, Hearing Before the Committee on Foreign Relations, United States Senate, 20 February 1967, pp. 2ff.

Harold J. Laski, *The American Democracy. A Commentary And An Interpretation*, New York, 1948, pp. 559–63; Max Lerner, *America as a Civilization, Volume Two. Culture and Personality*, New York, 1957, pp. 919f. Frederick Merk, *Manifest Destiny And Mission In American History. A Reinterpretation*, New York, 1970.

Robert H. Puckett, *America Faces the World: Isolationist Ideology in American Foreign Policy*, New York, 1972, pp. 7 and 18; Anatol Rapoport, 'Changing conceptions of war in the United States', Ken Booth and Moorehead Wright (eds), *American Thinking About Peace and War*, New York, 1978, pp. 63f.; and W.W. Rostow, *The United States in The World Arena. An Essay In Recent History*, New York and Evanston, 1960, pp. 480–1.

13. David L. Larson, 'Objectivity, propaganda, and the Puritan ethic', David L. Larson (ed.), *The Puritan Ethic in United States Foreign Policy*, New York, 1966, p. 6f.

14. Cf. Margaret Mead, *And Keep Your Powder Dry. An Anthropologist looks at the American Character*, London, 1967 (first published 1942), pp. 160–1; Burns, *op. cit.*, pp. 11 and 259f., and Merle Curti, *The Roots of American Loyality*, New York, 1946, pp. 53 and 65f.

15. Louis J. Halle, *The Cold War As History*, London, 1970, pp. 20f.; Richard Hofstadter, *The Paranoid Style in American Politics and Other Essays*, New York, 1966, pp. xi and 3–40; Lerner, *op. cit., Volume One. The Basic Frame*, p. 13, and Stillman and Pfaff, *op. cit.*, p. 51.

16. Armacost, *op. cit.*, pp. 66ff.; Michael Donelan, *The Ideas of American Foreign Policy*, London, 1963, p. 51; I.M. Drestler, 'Congress', Joseph S. Nye, Jr (ed.), *The Making of America's Soviet Policy*, New Haven and London, 1984, p. 55; Hoffmann, *op. cit.*, pp. 112–13 and 197; William Hyland, 'The Soviet Union in the American perspective: perception and realities, America's security in the 1980s. Part II', *Adelphi Papers*, No. 174, IISS, London, Spring 1982, p. 52.

17. Seweryn Bialer, 'Soviet–American conflict: from the past to the future', Seweryn Bialer, Lee Hamilton, Jerry Hough and John Steinbruner, *U.S.–Soviet Relations: Perspectives for the Future*, Center for National Policy, Washington, DC, September 1984, p. 20; Howard Bliss and M. Glen Johnson, *Beyond the Water's Edge: America's Foreign Policies*, Philadelphia, 1975, pp. 113f.; Hoffmann, *op. cit.*, pp. 190f., and Robert H. Johnson, 'Periods of peril', *Foreign Affairs*, Vol. 61, No. 4, Spring 1983, p. 967.

18. Almond, *op. cit.*, pp. 43f.; Bliss and Johnson, *op. cit.*, p. 196: D.W. Brogan, 'The illusion of American omnipotence', *Harper's Magazine*, December 1952, pp. 21–38, and D.W. Brogan, *American Aspects*, London, 1964, pp. 100–11.

    Dexter Perkins, *The American Approach To Foreign Policy*, rev. edition, Cambridge, 1962, p. 154, finds some evidence that the rhythm in the American public mood may have a connection with the movements of the business cycle; see also Frank L. Klingberg, 'The historical alternation of moods in American foreign policy', *World Politics*, Vol. XLVI, No. 2, January 1952, pp. 239–73, and two later works by Klingberg: 'Cyclical trends in American foreign policy moods and their policy implications', Charles W. Kegley Jr and Patrick J. McGowan (eds), *Challenges To America. United States Foreign Policy in the 1980s*, Vol. 4. Sage International Yearbook of Foreign Policy Studies, Beverly Hills and London, 1979, pp. 37–55; *Cyclical Trends in American Foreign Policy Moods. The Unfolding of America's World Role*, New York, 1983, pp. 7–37.

19. Rapoport, 1971, *op. cit.*, pp. 48ff. and Rapoport, Booth and Wright (eds), *op. cit.*, pp. 59–82.

20. David J. Finlay, Ole R. Holsti and Richard R. Fagen, *Enemies in Politics*, Chicago, 1967, pp. 6ff., Hoffmann, *op. cit.*, pp. 180f., and Barbara Tuchman, 'The American people and military power in an historical perspective, America's security in the 1980s. Part I', *Adelphi Papers*, No. 173, IISS, London, Spring 1982, pp. 5–13.

21. Banks, *op. cit.*, pp. 47f.; Hyland, *op. cit.*, p. 53, and Frank Tannenbaum, *The American Tradition in Foreign Policy*, University of Oklahoma Press, 1955, pp. 48f.

22. Armacost, *op. cit.*, pp. 48–50, and Stanley Hoffmann, 'Restraints and choices in American foreign policy', *Dædalus*, Vol. 91, No. 4, Fall 1962, pp. 668–704.

23. Geoffrey Gorer, *The American People. A Study In National Character*, New York, 1948, pp. 220ff., and Charles D. Tarlton, 'The styles of American international thought: Mahan, Bryan, and Lippmann', *World Politics*, Vol. XVII, No. 4, July 1965, pp. 594–602 on William Jennings Bryan.

24. Armacost, *op. cit.*, pp. 47–8, and Kenneth W. Thompson, *Political Realism And The Crisis of World Politics. An American Approach to Foreign Policy*, Princeton University Press, 1960, pp. 211ff.

25. Cf. Tarlton, *op. cit.*

26. Cf. Jeff Smith, 'Reagan, Star Wars, and American culture', *Bulletin of the Atomic Scientists*, January–February 1987, pp. 19–25.

27. Cf. John F. Lehman, *The Executive, Congress, and Foreign Policy. Studies of the Nixon Administration*, New York, 1976, p. 29.

28. Cf. Richard E. Neustadt, *Presidential Power. The Politics of Leadership*, New York and London, 1960, especially pp. 33ff. on 'The power to persuade'.

    See also Richard Haass, 'Congressional power: implications for American security policy', *Adelphi Papers*, No. 153, IISS, London, 1979, p. 33.

29. Cecil V. Crabb and Pat M. Holt, *Invitation to Struggle: Congress, the President and Foreign Policy*, Washington, DC, 1980, pp. 8ff.; Haass, *op. cit.*, p. 3f: and: Goran Rystad, 'From the "imperial presidency" to "neo-congressional government"? Congress and American Foreign Policy in the 1970s', Rystad

(ed.), *Congress and American American Foreign Policy*, Lund Studies in International History 13, Lund, 1981, pp. 11f.

The American Constitution is reprinted in William Ebenstein, C. Herman Pritchett, Henry A. Turner and Dean Mann, *American Democracy in World Perspective*, New York, 1976, pp. 461–91.

30. During the period 1940–64, the number of Executive agreements and treaties was, respectively, 4358 and 244; cf. Barry B. Hughes, *The Domestic Context of American Foreign Policy*, San Francisco, 1978, p. 107; during 1970–82, the numbers were, respectively, 4026 and 228, cf. John Spanier and Eric M. Uslaner, *American Foreign Policy and the Democratic Dilemmas*, fourth edition, New York, 1985, p. 118.

See also Edward J. Laurance, 'The changing role of Congress in defense policy-making', *Journal of Conflict Resolution*, Vol. 20, No. 2, June 1976, pp. 213–53; John F. Murphy, 'Knowledge is power: foreign policy and information interchange among Congress, the Executive branch, and the Public', *Tulane Law Review*, Vol. 49, No. 3, March 1975, pp. 505–54, especially p. 510; and Rystad, *op. cit.*, pp. 11–12. Francis D. Wormuth and Edwin B. Firmage with Francis P. Butler, contributing author, *To Chain The Dog Of War. The War Power of Congress in History and Law*, Dallas, Texas, 1986, pp. 267f.

31. Anne Hessing Cahn, *Congress, Military Affairs and (a Bit of) Information*, Beverly Hills and London, 1974, passim; Thomas M. Franck and Edward Weisband, *Foreign Policy By Congress*, New York, 1979, pp. 227ff.; Alton Frye, 'The Congressional resource problem', Alan Platt and Lawrence D. Weiler (eds), *Congress and Arms Control*, Westview Press/Boulder, Colorado, 1978, pp. 29f.; and Francis O. Wilcox, *Congress, The Executive, And Foreign Policy*, New York, 1971, pp. 74f.

In addition see Werner J. Feld and John K. Wildgren, *Congress And National Defense. The Politics of the Unthinkable*, New York, 1985, pp. 31f. Stanley J. Heginbotham, 'Foreign policy information for Congress: patterns of fragmentation and advocacy', *The Washington Quarterly*, Vol. 10, No. 3, Summer 1987, pp. 149–62; and John Spanier and Joseph Nogee (eds), *Congress, the Presidency and American Foreign Policy*, New York, 1981, p. xxvii.

32. Slightly varying definitions of these concepts are applied in the literature; see especially: H. Schuyler Foster, *Activism Replaces Isolationism: U.S. Public Attitudes 1940–1975*, Washington, DC, 1983, pp. 1f.; Hughes, *op. cit.*, pp. 23f.; James A. Nathan and James K. Oliver, *Foreign Policy Making and the American Political System*, Boston, 1983, pp. 157f; and James N. Rosenau, *Public Opinion and Foreign Policy. An Operational Formulation*, New York, 1968 (first published 1961), pp. 35f.

33. Lloyd A. Free and Hadley Cantril, *The Political Beliefs Of Americans*, New Brunswick, 1967, pp. 59ff.; Charles W. Kegley and Eugene R. Wittkopf, *American Foreign Policy. Pattern and Process*, New York, 1979, pp. 203f; and William Schneider, 'Public opinion', Joseph S. Nye (ed.), *op. cit.*, pp. 14 and 30. An analysis which concludes that the wider public *have* responded in a coherent and consistent way is Eugene R. Wittkopf, 'Elites and masses: another look at attitudes toward America's world role', *International Studies Quarterly*, Vol. 31, No. 2, June 1987, pp. 131–59, especially p. 154.

34. Cf. Hoffmann, *op. cit.*, pp. 239–40; Nathan and Oliver, *op. cit.*, p. 13; Joseph S. Nye, 'Can America manage its Soviet policy?', Nye (ed.), *op. cit.*, p. 337; Donelan, *op. cit.*, pp. 79f. See also John P. Robinson and Robert Meadow, *Polls Apart*, Washington, DC, 1982, pp. 27 and 30; and Kenneth W. Thompson, *op. cit.*

35. Cf. Jerome B. Wiesner, 'Arms control: current prospects and problems', *Bulletin of the Atomic Scientists*, May 1970, p. 6. Desmond Ball, *Politics and Force Levels. The Strategic Missile of the Kennedy Administration*, Los Angeles and London, 1980, pp. 126, 217–23 and 246f; see also Arthur M. Schlesinger, Jr, *A Thousand Days. John F. Kennedy in The White House*, New York, 1965, pp. 461–2.

36. Desmond Ball, *op. cit.*, pp. 183f.

    To illustrate the extent of the consensus on the superiority idea: even Senator George McGovern, who also at the time belonged to the most military-skeptical group in Congress, believed in the necessity of 'American strategic superiority', cf. *ibid.* Congressman Melvin Laird, later to become Secretary of Defense in the Nixon administration, advocated in a book published in 1962 that the United States must 'reserve to ourselves the initiative to strike first', cf. *ibid.*, p. 185. When Laird became Defense Secretary and was questioned about this view, he said that it been stated at a time of confrontation that had now passed, cf. Lawrence Freedman, *The Evolution of Nuclear Strategy*, New York, 1981, p. 432.

    See also William W. Kaufmann, *The McNamara Strategy*, New York, Evanston and London, 1964, pp. 204–50.

37. Hazel Gaudet Erskine, 'The polls: atomic weapons and nuclear energy', *Public Opinion Quarterly*, Vol. XXVII, No. 2, Summer 1963, p. 185; Louis Driesberg and Ross Klein, 'Changes in public support for U.S. military spending', *Journal of Conflict Resolution*, Vol. 24, No. 1, March 1980, p. 81; Eugene J. Rosi, 'Mass and attentive opinion on nuclear weapons tests and fallout, 1954–63', *Public Opinion Quarterly*, Vol. XXIX, No. 2, Summer 1965, p. 294; Theodore C. Sorensen, *Kennedy*, London, 1965, pp. 617–24.

38. Freedman, *op. cit.*, pp. 239–44; Alton Frye, *A Responsible Congress: The Politics of National Security*, New York, 1975, pp. 6–11.

39. Bernard J. Firestone, *The Quest for Nuclear Stability. John F. Kennedy and the Soviet Union*, London, 1982, pp. 121–38; Foster, *op. cit.*, pp. 254–6; Harold Karan Jacobson and Eric Stein, *Diplomats, Scientists, and Politicians. The United States and the Nuclear Test Ban Negotiations*, Ann Arbor, 1966, pp. 458–66; Michael Mandelbaum, *The Nuclear Question: The United States and Nuclear Weapons, 1946–1976*, Cambridge University Press, 1979, pp. 179–89; Rosi, *op. cit.*, passim; Schlesinger, *op. cit.*, pp. 830–4; Glenn T. Seaborg, *Kennedy. Krushchev and the Test Ban*, Los Angeles, 1981, pp. 263–82; Sorensen, *op. cit.*, pp. 736–40.

    See also *Nuclear Test Ban Treaty*. Hearings before the Committee On Foreign Relations. United States Senate, 12 August 1963.

40. Cf., for instance, Frye, *op. cit.*, p. 11; Fred Kaplan, *The Wizards of Armageddon*, New York, 1983, p. 319; and Michael MccGwire, 'The dilemmas and the delusions of deterrence', Gwyn Prins (ed.), *The Nuclear Crisis Reader*, New York, 1984, p. 77.

41. Frye, *op. cit.*, pp. 15ff.; and Morton H. Halperin, *Bureaucratic Politics and Foreign Policy*, The Brookings Institution, Washington, DC, 1974, passim; John Newhouse, *Cold Dawn. The Story of SALT*, New York, 1973, pp. 83ff.

42. Thomas W. Graham and Bernard M. Kramer, 'The polls: ABM and Star Wars: attitudes toward nuclear defense, 1945–1985', *Public Opinion Quarterly*, Vol. 50, 1986, p. 126; Elizabeth Young, *A Farewell to Arms Control*, Penguin Books, 1972, p. 196.

43. Frye, *op. cit.*, pp. 20ff; Benson D. Adams, *Ballistic Missile Defense*, New York, 1971, pp. 130ff., 159–160 and 178f.; Robert A. Bernstein and William W. Anthony, 'The ABM issue in the Senate, 1968–1970: the importance of

ideology', *The American Political Science Review*, Vol. LXVIII, No. 3, September 1974, pp. 1198–1206; and James R. Kurth, 'Aerospace production lines and American defense spending', Steven Rosen (ed.), *Testing the Theory of the Military-Industrial Complex*, Toronto and London, 1973, pp. 149–51.

44. Cf. *Strategic And Foreign Policy Implications Of ABM Systems*. Hearings before the Subcommittee on International Organization and Disarmament Affairs of the Committee On Foreign Relations. United States Senate. Parts I–III, March–July 1969.

    See also Abram Chayes and Jerome B. Wiesner (eds), *ABM. An Evaluation of the Decision to Deploy an Antiballistic Missile System*, New York, 1969; and Adams, *op. cit.*, pp. 202f.

45. Lawrence Kaagan, 'Public opinion and the defense effort: trends and lessons. The United States', in 'Defence and consensus: the domestic aspects of Western security. Part I', *Adelphi Papers*, No. 182, IISS, London, Summer 1983, p. 15.

    Foster, *op. cit.*, pp. 305–6; Frye, *op. cit.*, pp. 28ff.; and Kreisberg and Klein, *op. cit.*

46. William Schneider, 'Peace and strength: American public opinion on national security', Gregory Flynn and Hans Rattinger (eds), *The Public and Atlantic Defense*, London and Canberra, 1985, pp. 321f.

47. Frye, *op. cit.*, pp. 34f.; and Jerome H. Kahan, *Security in the Nuclear Age. Developing U.S. Strategic Arms Policy*, The Brookings Institution, Washington, DC, 1975, pp. 151–3.

48. Frye, *op. cit.*, pp. 47–66; see also Ted Greenwood, *Making the MIRV: A Study of Defense Decision Making*, Cambridge, Mass., 1975, pp. 4, 8, 15, 65, 73–9, 100 and 115; Ronald L. Tammen, *MIRV and the Arms Race. An Interpretation of Defense Strategy*, New York, 1973. pp. 77, 87 and 115f.

49. Cf. Greenwood, *op. cit.*, pp. 116–39; Frye, *op. cit.*, pp. 53ff. It is worth noting that Frye served as legislative and administrative assistant to Senator Brooke from 1968 to 1971. See also *ABM, MIRV, SALT And The Nuclear Arms Race*, Hearings before the Subcommittee on Arms Control, International Law and Organization of the Committee on Foreign Relations. United States Senate, March–June 1970.

50. Henry Kissinger, *White House Years*, Boston, 1979, p. 217f.

51. Frye, *op. cit.*, pp. 77–8.

52. *Ibid.*, p. 63.

53. *Ibid.*, pp. 82–3; and Kahan, *op. cit.*, pp. 161 and 191–2.

54. Frye, *op. cit.*, pp. 83–90; Newhouse, *op. cit.*, pp. 37 and 187–88; Alan Platt, 'Congress and arms control: a historical perspective, 1969–1976', Alan Platt and Lawrence D. Weiler (eds), *op. cit.*, pp. 6–11; Thomas W. Wolfe, *The SALT Experience*, Cambridge, Mass., 1979, p. 45.

55. Frye, *op. cit.*, p. 84; Raymond L. Garthoff, *Détente and Confrontation. American–Soviet Relations From Nixon to Reagan*, The Brookings Institution, Washington, DC, 1985, chapter 5, passim; Kahan, *op. cit.*, pp. 175–77; Alan Platt, *The U.S. Senate and Strategic Arms Policy, 1969–1977*, Westview Press, Boulder, Colorado, 1978, pp. 9–36; and Gerard Smith, *Doubletalk. The Story of SALT I*, New York, 1985, pp. 29–31, 204 and 469.

56. Richard Nixon, *The Memoirs of Richard Nixon*, London, 1978, p. 615; Foster, *op. cit.*, p. 334.

57. Platt (cf. note 55), *op. cit.*, pp. 26f.

    The critical sentence in the Jackson amendment read: 'a future treaty that ... would not limit the United States to levels of intercontinental strategic forces inferior to the limits provided for the Soviet Union'; cf. Mason Willrich and John B. Rhinelander (eds), *SALT. The Moscow Agreements and Beyond*, New

York and London, 1974, p. 315.

58. Platt (cf. note 55), *op. cit.*, pp. 29–30; and Duncan L. Clarke, *Politics of Arms Control. The Role and Effectiveness of the U.S. Arms Control and Disarmament Agency*, New York and London, 1979, pp. 50f.
59. Platt (cf. note 55), *op. cit.*, pp. 71–96.
60. The most important Congressional hearings were: *U.S.–U.S.S.R. Strategic Policies*. Hearing before the Subcommittee on Arms Control, International Law and Organization of The Committee on Foreign Relations. United States Senate, 4 March 1974, (Top secret hearing; sanitized and made public on 4 April 1974); *Nuclear Weapons And Foreign Policy*. Hearings before the Subcommittee on US Security Agreements and Commitments Abroad and the Subcommittee on Arms Control, International Law and Organization of the Committee On Foreign Relations. United States Senate, 7, 14 March, and 4 April 1974; *Briefing on Counterforce Attacks*, Hearing before the Subcommittee on Arms Control, International Law and Organization of the Committee on Foreign Relations. United States Senate (secret hearing held on 11 September 1974; sanitized and made public on 10 January 1975).

   Among the most active Senators then querying counterforce were Mondale and Muskie who later became prominent members of the Carter administration.
61. Schneider, *op. cit.*, pp. 325 and 335; Kaagan, *op. cit.*
62. William Schneider, 'Conservatism, not interventionism: trends in foreign policy opinion, 1974–1982', Kenneth A. Oye, Robert J. Lieber and Donald Rotchild (eds), *Eagle Defiant. United States Foreign Policy in the 1980s*, Boston and Toronto, 1983, pp. 60f. See also Schneider, *op. cit.*
63. Among the most noticed were articles by Paul Nitze, especially: 'Deterring our deterrent', *Foreign Policy*, No. 17, Winter 1974–75, pp. 136–56 (Nitze had resigned from the administration in June 1974).

   In particular, articles and pamphlets by Albert Wohlstetter and Edward Luttwak seem to have influenced opinion leaders. See also the overview in William C. Green, *Soviet Nuclear Weapons Policy. A Research and Bibliographic Guide*, Boulder, Colorado and London, 1987, pp. 14–23.
64. Michael Mandelbaum and William Schneider, 'The new internationalisms. Public opinion and American foreign policy', Kenneth A. Oye, Donald Rotchild and Robert J. Lieber (eds), *Eagle Entangled. U.S. Foreign Policy in a Complex World*, New York and London, 1979, pp. 34–88.

   See also Ole R. Holsti and James N. Rosenau, *American Leadership in World Affairs. Vietnam and the breakdown of consensus*, Boston, 1984, passim.
65. Lawrence Freedman, *U.S. Intelligence And The Soviet Strategic Threat*, London, 1977, pp. 194–8; and Garthoff, *op. cit.*, pp. 551–2.
66. Foster, *op. cit.*, pp. 365–6; Wolfe, *op. cit.*, pp. 178–81.
67. Stephen J. Flanagan, 'The domestic politics of SALT II: implications for foreign policy process', Spanier and Nogee (eds), *op. cit.*, pp. 44–76, particularly pp. 52–3. Platt, *op. cit.*, pp. 110–17; Wolfe, *op. cit.*, pp. 46–7.
68. *Strategic Survey 1978*, IISS, London, 1979, p. 35; Strobe Talbott, *Endgame. The Inside Story of SALT II*, New York, 1979, pp. 215–16.

   Daniel Patrick Moynihan, 'Reflections (SALT)', *The New Yorker*, 19 November 1979, is a good illustration of a prominent Democratic Senator's reflections on the Soviet–American nuclear relationship in the late 1970s.
69. Talbott, *op. cit.*, pp. 55–6; Clarke, *op. cit.*, pp. 182–5; and Stanley J. Heginbotham, 'Constraining SALT II: the role of the Senate', Michael Barnhart, *Congress and United States Foreign Policy. Controlling the Use of Force in the Nuclear Age*, New York, 1987, pp. 98–121. Also *Warnke*

Nomination. Hearings before the Committee on Foreign Relations. United States Senate, 8 and 9 February 1977; *Consideration of Mr. Paul C. Warnke To Be Director Of The U.S. Arms Control And Disarmament Agency And Ambassador.* Hearings together with individual views. Committee on Armed Services. United States Senate, 22, 23 and 28 February 1977. The most prominent witness against Warnke was Paul Nitze, cf., respectively, pp. 135–75 and 161ff.

70. Robinson and Meadow, *op. cit.*, pp. 42–50; Schneider, Flynn and Rattinger (eds), *op. cit.*, pp. 341–3; Tom W. Smith, 'The polls: American attitudes toward the Soviet Union and communism', *Public Opinion Quarterly*, Vol. 47, 1983, pp. 287–8.

71. Alan Platt, 'The politics of arms control and the strategic balance', Barry M. Blechman (ed.), *Rethinking The U.S. Strategic Posture*, Cambridge, Mass., 1982, p. 157.

72. *Strategic Survey 1980–1981*, IISS, London, 1981, pp. 41f; Daniel Yankelovich and Larry Kaagan, 'Assertive America', *Foreign Affairs*, 'America and the World 1980', Vol. 59, No. 3, 1981, pp. 696–713; and John E. Rielly, 'The American mood: a foreign policy of self-interest', *Foreign Policy*, No. 34, Spring 1979, pp. 74–86.

73. *Strategic Survey 1979*, IISS, London, 1980, p. 33; *World Armaments and Disarmament. SIPRI Yearbook 1986*, Stockholm International Peace Research Institute, Oxford, 1986, p. 22. John. E. Rielly, 'American opinion: continuity, not Reaganism', *Foreign Policy*, No. 50, Spring 1983, pp. 86–104; Rielly mentions (p. 95) that (other) surveys indicate that the support for increased defense spending reached its highest point in January 1981.

    See also Connie De Boer, 'The polls: our commitment to World War III', *Public Opinion Quarterly*, Vol. 45, 1981, pp. 133; Bruce Russett and Donald R. Deluca, '"Don't tread on me": public opinion and foreign policy in the eighties', *Political Science Quarterly*, Vol. 96, No. 3, Fall 1981, p. 383 and 'Strategic survey 1980–1981', *op. cit.*, p. 42.

74. Cf. Seweryn Bialer, 'Lessons of history: Soviet–American relations in the postwar era', Arnold L. Horelick (ed.), *U.S.–Soviet Relations. The Next Phase*, Ithaca and London, 1986, p. 101.

75. Schneider, in Oye, Lieber and Rothcild (eds), *op. cit.*, p. 37.

76. *Strategic Survey 1982–1983*, IISS, London, 1983, p. 37; 'World armaments and disarmament' *SIPRI Yearbook 1986, op. cit.*, p. 22; and John E. Rielly (ed.), *American Public Opinion And U.S. Foreign Policy 1983*, The Chicago Council on Foreign Relations, 1983, passim.

77. *Strategic Survey 1983–1984*, IISS, London, 1984, pp. 46–7; and: *Congress and Foreign Policy 1983*, Committee on Foreign Affairs, US House Of Representatives, Washington, DC, 1984, pp. 86f.

78. 'Strategic survey 1982–1983', *op. cit.*, p. 37; Rielly, *op. cit.* (cf. note 76), pp. 6 and 31–2; Schneider, in Flynn and Rattinger (eds), *op. cit.*, pp. 323 and 347–52.

79. 'Congress and foreign policy 1983', *op. cit.*, p. 70; and the references in note 78.

80. Schneider, in Flynn and Rattinger (eds), *op. cit.*, pp. 344–6; 'World armaments and disarmament', *SIPRI Yearbook 1986, op. cit.*, pp. 22–6; and Daniel Yankelovich and John Double, 'The public mood: nuclear weapons and the U.S.S.R.', *Foreign Affairs*, Vol. 63, No. 1, Fall 1984, pp. 33–46.

81. *Strategic Survey 1984–1985*, IISS, London, 1985, pp. 32–3; William D. Anderson and Sterling J. Kernek, 'How "realistic" is Reagan's diplomacy?', *Political Science Quarterly*, Vol. 100, No. 3, Fall 1985, p. 390.

82. Cf. especially Graham and Kramer, *op. cit.*; 'World armaments and disarmament', *SIPRI Yearbook 1986, op. cit.*, pp. 22–6; and Andrew Kohut,

'What Americans want', *Foreign Policy*, No. 70, Spring 1988, pp. 159f.
83. William J. Durch, 'The future of the ABM Treaty', *Adelphi Papers*, 223, IISS, London, Summer 1987, pp. 26f.; Sam Nunn, 'The ABM re-interpretation issue', *The Washington Quarterly*, Vol. 10, No. 4, Autumn 1987, pp. 45–57. Also 'The debate over the ABM Treaty', *Strategic Survey 1986–1987*, IISS, London, 1987, pp. 44–51; *Strategic Survey 1987–1988*, IISS, London, 1988, pp. 46–7; Michael Krepon, 'Nunn's modest SDI', *Bulletin of the Atomic Scientists*, April 1988, p. 5; Stephen Daggettt and Robert D. English, 'Assessing Soviet strategic defense', *Foreign Policy*, No. 70, Spring 1988, pp. 129–49.

See also the exchange of arguments in *Review of ABM Treaty Interpretations Dispute And SDI*, Hearing before the Subcommittee on Arms Control, International Security and Science of the Committee on Foreign Affairs, House of Representatives, 26 February 1987; and *The ABM Treaty And The Constitution*, Joint Hearings before the Committee on Foreign Relations and the Committee on the Judiciary, United States Senate, 11 March 1987.
84. Cf. Graham T. Allison, *Essence of Decision. Explaining the Cuban Missile Crisis*, Boston, 1971; and Halperin, *op. cit.* A pertinent critique is Desmond Ball, 'The Blind men and the elephant: a critique of bureaucratic politics theory', *Australian Outlook*, 28 April 1974, pp. 71–92.
85. Cf. Ken Booth, *Strategy and Ethnocentrism*, New York, 1979.
86. *Ibid.*, p. 47; and Colin S. Gray, 'National style in strategy: the American example', *International Security*, Vol. 6, No. 2, Fall 1981, pp. 21–47.
87. Miroslav Nincic, 'The United States, the Soviet Union, and the politics of opposites', *World Politics*, Vol. XL, No. 4, July 1988, pp. 452–75.

CHAPTER 6   THE OBJECT OF PERCEPTION. THE SOVIET UNION AS A SUPERPOWER

1. Kenneth E. Boulding, 'The learning and reality-testing process in the international system', *Journal of International Affairs*, Vol. XXI, No. 1, 1967, especially p. 3; Thomas G. Hart, *The Cognitive World of Swedish Security Elites*, Stockholm, 1976, pp. 10 and 107; Richard Nisbett and Lee Ross, *Human Inference: strategies and short-comings of social judgment*, New Jersey, 1980, p. 3, distinguishes between the 'intuitive' and the 'formal' scientist.
2. George W. Breslauer, *Five Images Of The Soviet Future: Critical Review & Synthesis*, Berkeley, California, 1978, p. 8; William Welch, *American Images of Soviet Foreign Policy. An Inquiry into Recent Appraisals from the Academic Community*, New Haven and London, 1970, pp. 183f.
3. Cf. Bjarne Nørretranders, *Sovjetologiens metodeproblemer* (Methodproblems in Sovietology), Copenhagen, 1978, pp. 17–25.
   See also Jack Snyder, 'Richness, rigor, and relevance in the study of Soviet foreign policy', *International Security*, Vol. 9, No. 3, Winter 1984–85, pp. 89ff.
4. Milton Leitenberg, 'The numbers game or "who's on first?"', *Bulletin Of The Atomic Scientists*, June 1982, pp. 27–32.
5. Chapters 6 draws on but extends Erik Beukel, *Sovjetunionen og Atomvåben. Indre og ydre forudsætninger for sovjetisk atomvåbenpolitik* (The Soviet Union and Nuclear Arms. Domestic and Foreign Conditions of Soviet Nuclear Arms Policy), Dansk Udenrigspolitisk Institut. Samfundsvidenskabeligt Forlag, 1982.
6. Cf., for example, William H. Baugh, *The Politics of Nuclear Balance.*

Ambiguity And Continuity In Strategic Policies, New York and London, 1984, pp. 124–5.

The Military Balance 1976–1977, IISS, London, 1976, pp. 106–8.

7. *The Military Balance 1973–1974*, p. 71; *1976–1977*, *op. cit.*, p. 75; *1983–1984*, p. 120–21; and *1988–1989*, p. 230.

    The numbers for 1960–1 are from Richard K. Herrmann, *Perceptions and Behavior in Soviet Foreign Policy*, University of Pittsburgh Press, 1985, p. 59.

    The numbers given in other sources vary slightly from these.

8. *Ibid.*; *The Military Balance 1982–83*, IISS, London, 1982, p. 140. These numbers also vary slightly from those given in other sources.

9. *What About The Russians and Nuclear War?*, Ground Zero, New York, 1983, p. 233; and *The Military Balance 1985–1986*, IISS, London, 1985, p. 181.

    EMT of a specific weapon is expressed as two-thirds power of its explosive yield ($Y^{2/3}$). For yields above 1 MT, a lower scaling is used ($Y^{1/2}$), cf. 'The military balance 1976–1977', *op. cit.*, p. 106.

10. *Ibid.*, p. 107.

11. *Ibid.*

12. 'The military balance 1983–1984', *op. cit.*, 1983, pp. 118–19; and 'The military balance 1986–1987', *op. cit.*, p. 204.

13. *Strategic Survey 1980–1981*, IISS, London, 1981, p. 14.

14. *The Military Balance 1986–1987*, IISS, London, 1986, pp. 200 and 204. Here it has to be noted that the United States in 1986 began deploying the *Peacekeeper* missile with ten independently targetable vehicles with a CEP of 100 m and a throw-weight of 7000 lb, *ibid.*, p. 200.

15. 'The military balance 1976–1977', *op. cit.*, p. 106.

16. Robert P. Berman and John C. Baker, *Soviet Strategic Forces. Requirements and Responses*, The Brookings Institution, Washington, DC, 1982, p. 136; and 'The military balance 1986–1987', *op. cit.*, pp. 204–6.

    The numbers published by the Soviet Union in connection with the December 1987 agreement diverge somewhat from these. The total number of land-based missiles was almost the same (690 compared to 683), but the Soviet Union had fewer intermediate-range and more medium-range missiles than expected, cf. *International Herald Tribune*, 11 December 1987.

17. *Ibid.*; and 'The military balance 1985–1986', *op. cit.*, pp. 162–4.

18. 'The military balance 1986–1987' *op. cit.*, p. 205.

19. *Strategic Survey 1984–1985*, IISS, London, 1985, pp. 19–20.

20. Berman and Baker, *op. cit.*, pp. 147–50; Lawrence Freedman, *U.S. Intelligence And The Soviet Strategic Threat*, London, 1977, pp. 86–96; Johan J. Holst, 'Missile defense, the Soviet Union, and the arms race', Johan J. Holst and William Schneider, Jr (eds), *Why ABM? Policy Issues in the Missile Defense Controversy*, New York, 1969, pp. 150–1; Nikolaj Petersen, *Afskrækkelse og Forsvar. Antiraketforsvarets Problematik* (Deterrence and Defense. The Missile Defense Problem,) Dansk Udenrigspolitisk Instituts Skrifter 1, 1969, pp. 54–9.

    Sayre Stevens, 'The Soviet BMD program', Ashton B. Carter and David N. Schwartz (eds), *Ballistic Missile Defense*, The Brookings Institution, Washington, DC, 1984, pp. 189–97; Ronald L. Tammen, *MIRV and the Arms Race. An Interpretation of Defense Strategy*, New York, 1973, pp. 100–5; and Thomas W. Wolfe, *Soviet Power And Europe. 1945–1970*, Baltimore and London, 1970, pp. 437–41.

21. *World Armaments and Disarmament. SIPRI Yearbook 1986*, Oxford 1986, pp. 55–6.

22. Berman and Baker, *op. cit.*, pp. 144–6.

23. *Strategic Survey 1976*, IISS, London, 1977, pp. 31–4; and Lawrence S. Hagen, *Civil Defence: The Case For Reconsideration*, National Securilty Series, No. 7/77, Centre for International Relations, Queens University, Kingston, Ontario, 1977, pp. 21–31.

24. Christen Jönsson, *Soviet Bargaining Behavior. The Nuclear Test Ban Case*, New York, 1979, pp. 35–8.

25. Joseph G. Whelan, *Soviet Diplomacy and Negotiating Behavior: Emerging New Context For U.S. Diplomacy*, Committee on Foreign Affairs, Congressional Research Service, Washington, DC, 1979, pp. 374f.

26. Jönsson, *op. cit.*, p. 37.

27. Raymond L. Garthoff, 'BMD and East–West relations', Carter and Schwartz (eds), *op. cit.*, pp. 297–8; Jerome H. Kahan, *Security in the Nuclear Age. Developing U.S. Strategic Arms Policy*, The Brookings Institution, Washington, DC, 1975, pp. 119f; Whelan, *op. cit.*, p. 444; Thomas W. Wolfe, *The SALT Experience*, Cambridge, Mass., 1979, pp. 1–2.

28. Gerard Smith, *Doubletalk. The Story of SALT I*, New York, 1985, pp. 83f.

29. Garthoff, *op. cit.*, p. 302.

30. Cf., for example, Keith Payne and Dan L. Stroude, 'Arms control: the Soviet approach and its implications', *Soviet Union/Union Soviétique*, Vol. 10, Parts 2–3, 1983, p. 242; Jeffrey Richelson, 'Ballistic missile defense and Soviet strategy', Roman Kolkowicz and Ellen Propper Michiewicz (eds), *The Soviet Calculus of Nuclear War*, Lexington, Mass., 1984, pp. 72–3: and Stevens, *op. cit.*, pp. 203–4.

31. Samuel B. Payne Jr, *The Soviet Union and SALT*, Cambridge, Mass., and London, 1980, especially pp. 71f.

32. Smith, *op. cit.*, pp. 86–7.

33. Reported by Henry Kissinger, *White House Years*, Boston, 1979, p. 1152, and *Years of Upheaval*, Boston, 1982, p. 277.

34. Mason Willrich and John B. Rhinelander (eds), *SALT. The Moscow Agreements And Beyond*, New York and London, 1974, p. 310.

    See also Raymond L. Garthoff, 'SALT and the Soviet military', *Problems of Communism*, Vol. XXIV, January–February 1975, pp. 25f.

    On the broader Soviet goal with SALT I, see for instance Coit D. Blacker, 'The Kremlin and détente: Soviet conceptions, hopes, and expectations', Alexander L. George (ed.), *Managing U.S.–Soviet Rivalry: Problems of Crisis Prevention*, Boulder, Colorado, 1979, pp. 119–37.

35. Reprinted in *International Affairs* (the Soviet periodical), No. 5, 1977, pp. 3–11.

36. *Strategic Survey 1982–1983*, IISS, London, 1983, pp. 24f.

37. *Strateguic Survey 1983–1984*, IISS, London, 1984, pp. 31–3.

38. *Strateguc Survey 1985–1986*, IISS, London, 1986, p. 56. For the next paragraph. *Strategic Survey 1986–1987*, IISS, London, 1987, pp. 54ff.

39. *Ibid.*, pp. 53ff. and pp. 52ff., respectively. See also Survival, September–October 1987, pp. 455–8; *Strategic Survival 1987–1988*, IISS, London, 1988, p. 46; Stephen Meyer, 'Soviet views on SDI', *Survival*, November–December 1985, pp. 274–92; Karen Puschel, 'Can Moscow live with DSI?', *Survival*, January–February 1989, pp. 34–51; and David B. Rivkin, 'What does Moscow think?', *Foreign Policy*, No. 59, Summer 1985, pp. 85–105.

    Another aspect of the Soviet policy in the mid-1980s has been its unilateral moratorium on nuclear tests and its call for a comprehensive test ban. The Soviet moratorium began in August 1985 and ended in February 1987 with a new Soviet test, cf. *Strategic Survey 1986–1987, op. cit.*, p. 72.

40. *Strategic Survey 1982–1983, op. cit.*, pp. 21–4; Strobe Talbott, *Deadly*

Gambits. The Reagan Administration and the Stalemate in Nuclear Arms Control, New York, 1985, pp. 116–51.

41. *Strategic Survey 1983–1984, op. cit.*, pp. 30–1.
42. *Strategic Survey 1985–1986, op. cit.*, pp. 50ff.; *Strategic Survey 1986–87, op. cit.*, pp. 52ff; General Secretary Gorbachev's statement of INF, 28 February 1987, *Pravda* and *Izvestia*, 1 March, *CDSP*, 1 April 1987, p. 12. See also David B. Rivkin, 'The Soviet approach to nuclear arms control: Continuity and change', *Survival*, November–December 1987, pp. 483–510, especially pp. 501f.
43. A good introduction is Julian Lider, *The Political and Military Laws of War. An Analysis of Marxist-Leninist Concepts*, Saxon House, Aldershot, 1979.
44. Cf., for example, *Dictionary of Basic Military Terms. A Soviet View*, Moscow, 1965, pp. 37 and 48 (published under the auspices of the United States Air Force and translated by the DGIS Multilingual Bureau, Secretary of State Department, Ottawa, Canada); and A. A. Grechko, *The Armed Forces of The Soviet Union*, Progress Publishers, Moscow, 1977, passim, especially pp. 250– 86. *Marxism-Leninism On War And Army*, Progress Publishers, Moscow, 1972, pp. 13ff. This book has been published several times in Russian since the early 1960s and is written by several Soviet (14 are mentioned on its back) philosophers, historians and teachers at military educational establishments; it was nominated for a Frunze Prize in 1966 and is listed in *Belshaya Encyclopedia* as a basic reference in military doctrine, cf. William F. Scott, *Soviet Sources of Military Doctrine and Strategy*, New York, 1975, pp. 30–1.
   See also Harriet Fast Scott (ed.), *V.D. Sokolovskiy. Soviet Military Strategy*, London, 1975, especially pp. 38f. Sokolovskiy's book was published in three editions (1962, 1963 and 1968) which are reproduced, compared and commented in this volume. In 1962, it was the first work of its kind since 1926 (cf. *ibid.*, p. vxiii) and for several years it was considered an authoritative presentation of Soviet military doctrine; many of its ideas seem, by successive steps, to have been abandoned (cf. below) and in 1985, it was authoritatively repudiated, cf. James M. McConnell, 'The irrelevance today of Sokolovskiy's book *Military Strategy'*, *Defense Analysis*, Vol. 1, No. 4, pp. 243–54, especially the last pages.
45. Grechko, *op. cit.*; 'Marxism-Leninism on war and army', *op. cit.*, pp. 22, 34– 47 and 324f. *The Philosophical Heritage of V.I. Lenin and Problems of Contemporary War*, Moscow, 1972, pp. 100f.; the book has been written by a 'collective' of Soviet authors, mentioned on p. ix, of whom two also contributed to 'Marxism-Leninism on War and Army'; the edition used here has been published in Washington, DC. See also N.A. Lomov (ed.), *Scientific-Technical Progress and the Revolution in Military Affairs*, Moscow 1973, translated and published under the auspices of the United States Air Force, pp. 5, 40, 193, 210f., 261f. and 273f, in particular. And Harriet Fast Scott and William F. Scott, *The Armed Forces of the USSR*, Westview Press, Boulder, Colorado, 1982, pp. 47–9.
46. *Dictionary of Basic Military Terms, op. cit.*, p. 48; Grechko, *op. cit.*, p. 276.
47. Cf., for example, 'Marxism-Leninism on war and army', *op. cit.*, p. 87f.
48. Sokolovskiy, *op. cit.*, pp. 208 and 211.
49. 'Marxism-Leninism on war and army', *op. cit.*, pp. 46, 283, 327 and 392. See also Raymond L. Garthoff, *Détente and Confrontation, American–Soviet Relations From Nixon to Reagan*, The Brookings Institution, Washington, DC, 1985, p. 780; and Alfred L. Monks, *Soviet Military Doctrine: 1960 to the Present*, New York, 1984, particularly pp. 298f. on the 1980s.
50. 'Marxism-Leninism on war and army', *op. cit.*, pp. 283 and 393; Lomov (ed.),

op. cit., p. 147. Also Robbin F. Laird and Dale R. Herspring, *The Soviet Union and Strategic Arms*, Boulder and London, 1984, pp. 69f.

51. Michael MccGwire, *Military Objectives in Soviet Foreign Policy*. The Brookings Institution, Washington, DC, 1987, pp. 28ff., 274, 335ff. and 381–405; a close comparison of the second and the third edition of Sokolovskiy shows that some assertions emphasizing the need to preempt were deleted in 1968, cf. *ibid.*, p. 388. A useful review of MccGwire's book is Christoph Bluth, 'The evolution of Soviet military doctrine', Survival, March–April 1988, pp. 149–61.

52. Cf., for example, Makhmut Gareyev, 'The revised Soviet military doctrine', *Bulletin of the Atomic Scientists*, December 1988, pp. 30–4. (Gareyev is Deputy Chief of the General Staff of the Soviet armed forces).

     Among Western writings, see in particular, Raymond L. Garthoff, 'New thinking in Soviet military doctrine', *The Washington Quarterly*, Vol. 11, No. 3, Summer 1988, pp. 131–58; Leon Goure, 'A "new" Soviet military doctrine: reality or mirage?', *Strategic Review*, Summer 1988, pp. 25–32; and Edward L. Warner III, 'New thinking and old realities in Soviet defence policy', *Survival*, January–February 1989, pp. 13–33.

53. *Dictionary of Basic Military Terms, op. cit.*, pp. 38–9, 137, 143 and 215; *The Officer's Handbook. A Soviet View*, Moscow, 1971, pp. 64–6, especially p. 64 (this book has been translated and published in the same way as *Dictionary Of Basic Military Terms*, cf. note 44).

     See also David Holloway, *The Soviet Union and the Arms Race*, New Haven and London, 1983, pp. 29f. and Edward L. Warner III, *The Military in Contemporary Soviet Politics. An Institutional Analysis*, New York, 1977, pp. 118f.

54. Cf. Erik Beukel, 'Soviet views on strategic nuclear weapons: orthodoxy and modernism', *Cooperation and Conflict*, Vol. XIV, No. 4, 1979, pp. 223–37.

     A similar approach to analyzing Soviet views has often been applied by Western observers, see especially, Lawrence T. Caldwell, 'Soviet attitudes to SALT', *Adelphi Papers*, No.75, IISS, London, 1971, pp. 2–4; John Lenczowski, *Soviet Perceptions of U.S. Foreign Policy. A Study of Ideology, Power, and Consensus*, Ithaca and London, 1982, pp. 232–60; and Samuel B. Payne, Jr, *op. cit.*, pp. 29ff.

55. J.M. Mackintosh, *Strategy and Tactics Of Soviet Foreign Policy*, London, 1962, pp. 95–6.

     A few weeks later, Malenkov reversed his position and publicly endorsed the traditionalist view that a nuclear war would inflict enormous damage to both sides, but that only capitalism would be annihilated, *ibid.* Party Secretary Krushchev opposed Malenkov's view and he resigned as Premier in February 1955.

     While Malenkov hinted at his ideas in only a few phrases, Mikoyan spelled out the corresponding thinking more elaborately. However, these paragraphs in Mikoyan's speech, which was delivered at Erevan, Armenia, were not published in the Moscow press and appeared only in the local Erevan party newspaper; cf. H.S. Dinerstein, *War and the Soviet Union. Nuclear Weapons And The Revolution In Soviet Military And Political Thinking*, Westport, Conn., 1962, pp. 71–2.

     In addition, see Raymond L. Garthoff, 'The death of Stalin and the birth of mutual deterrence', *Survey*, Vol. 25, No. 2 (111), pp. 10–16.

56. N.S. Khrushchev, *On Peaceful Coexistence*, Foreign Languages Publishing House, Moscow, 1961, particularly pp. 145–52. See also Benjamin S. Lambeth. *The Evolution of Soviet Party-Military Relations Since Khrushchev,*

The Second International Congress of Professors World Peace Academy, Geneva, August 1985, pp. 3f.; Mackintosh, *op. cit.*, pp. 277–8; Warner, *op. cit.*, pp. 139–40; and Thomas W. Wolfe, *Soviet Strategy At The Crossroads*, Cambridge, Mass., 1964, p. 31.

57. Holst, Holst and Schneider (eds), *op. cit.*, p. 150; N.S. Khrushchev, *Communism – Peace and Happiness for the Peoples*, Foreign Languages Publishing House, Moscow, 1963, p. 319; see also Malinovskiry's article in *Kommunist*, May 1962, reprinted in *Survival*, September–October 1962, pp. 229–32, especially p. 231. Also Wolfe, *op. cit.* (cited in note 56), pp. 32f.

58. Cf. Merle Fainsod, 'Some reflections on Soviet–American relations', *The American Political Science Review*, Vol. LXII, No. 4, December 1968, p. 1101; Jönsson, *op. cit.*, p. 198; Holloway, *op. cit.*, p. 62.

59. Lambeth, *op. cit.*, p. 8.

60. Malinovskiy's speech is reprinted in *Survival*, July 1966, pp. 232–5; see especially p. 233.

61. John Van Oudenaren, 'Deterrence, war-fighting and Soviet military doctrine', *Adelphi Papers*, 210, IISS, London, 1986, p. 22; Thomas A. Wolfe, 'Military power and Soviet policy', William E. Griffith (ed.), *The Soviet Empire: Expansion & Détente. Critical Choices for Americans*, Lexington, Mass., 1976, p. 198, note 26.

Holloway, *op. cit.*, p. 45; it appears that Kosygin's statement in London – which was widely reported in the Western press and since has been cited frequently to indicate the Soviet attitude – was, in fact, wrongly translated from Russian into English; moreover, the incorrect translation was only partially revised when Pravda reproduced Kosygin's statement, cf. Garthoff, Carter and Schwartz (eds), *op. cit.*, pp. 295–6.

62. *Ibid.*, p. 299.

63. The following is based on Erik Beukel, 'Analysing the views of Soviet leaders on nuclear weapons', *Cooperation and Conflict*, Vol. XV, No. 2, 1980, pp. 71–84.

64. L.I. Brezhnev, *Our Course: Peace and Socialism*, Novostii Press Agency Publishing House, Moscow 1978, pp. 9–22, especially pp. 17–19.

65. Garthoff, *op. cit.* (cited in note 49), pp. 45–6 and 753–4.

66. *International Affairs*, No. 5, 1977, pp. 3–11.

67. One evidence of this is that Grechko's book, cited in note 44, and which was published in the mid-1970s did not mention SALT; he wrote: 'An agreement on averting a nuclear war was concluded between the USSR and the USA' (p. 276). That was all in a book of 342 pages.

Grechko's traditionalist views are also shown in a book he published in 1971 'On guard for peace and the building of communism', reprinted in excerpts in *Selected Soviet Military Writings 1970–1975*, translated and published under the auspices of the United States Air Force, Washington, DC, 1976, pp. 165–89, especially p. 167.

See also, for instance, Michael J. Deane, *Political Control of the Soviet Armed Forces*, New York and London, 1977, pp. 224–5; and Wolfe, *op. cit.* (cited in note 27), pp. 21–2 about Grechko's public speeches when SALT I was entered.

68. Cf., for example, *International Affairs*, No. 1, 1980, pp. 3–10, a reprint of Ustinov's article in *Pravda*, 25 October 1979.

69. See Brezhnev's report to the 26th Party Congress in February 1981, excerpts in *Survival*, May–June 1981, pp. 134–7, particularly p. 135; see also Brezhnev's report in *The Current Digest Of The Soviet Press* (CDSP), 25 March 1981, p. 11 (Brezhnev's statement on 'dangerous madness' is not

included in the excerpt in *Survival*). William G. Hyland, 'The USSR and nuclear war', Barry M. Blocman (ed.), *Rethinking the U.S. Strategic Posture*, Cambridge, Mass., p. 58.

Other Soviet leaders have also expressed the idea that the 'approximate balance of armed forces, including nuclear forces ... has objectively served the cause of ... security and stability'; cf. Andropov's statement, reprinted in *Pravda* and *Izvestia*, 25 November 1983, *CDSP*, 21 December 1983, p. 3.

70. On Chernenko's speech in April 1981, see Thomas N. Bjorkman and Thomas J. Zamostny, 'Soviet politics and strategy toward the West: three cases,' *World Politics*, Vol. XXXVI, No. 2, January 1984, 206; and David R. Jones, 'Nuclear war and Soviet policy', *International Perspectives*, Novermber–December 1982, p. 19.

D. Ustinov, 'To avert the threat of nuclear war', *International Affairs*, No. 9, 1982, pp. 12–22; Marshal Ustinov, *The Existing Parity Must Not Be Destroyed*, Novosti Press Agency Publishing House, Moscow, 1982, pamphlet reprinting Ustinov's replies to questions, *Pravda*, 7 December 1982; see also Ustinov's address, 7 November 1981, *CDSP*, 9 December 1981, pp. 1–5; concerning Ustinov's pamphlet in May 1982, see Isuyoshi Hasegawa, 'Soviets on nuclear war fighting', *Problems of Communism*, July–August 1986, p. 74.

Concerning the Soviet no-first-use statement, it should be noted that when Soviet sources censure NATO's refusal to assume the no-first-use commitment, they seem to use the two terms 'first-use of nuclear weapons' and 'nuclear first-strike' as if they were synonyms, cf., for example, *How to Avert the Threat to Europe*, Progress Publishers, Moscow, 1983, pp. 14–15; and 'Space-strike arms and international security', extract from the English language version of the Report of the Committee of Soviet Scientists published in Moscow, October 1985, in Steven W. Guerrier and Wayne C. Thompson (eds), *Perspectives on Strategic Defense*, Boulder, Colorado and London, 1987, pp. 297–321 (especially p. 308).

71. The quotation is from Ustinov's statement, *Pravda*, 7 December 1982 (cited in note 70); see also Ustinov's article in *Pravda*, 24 July 1981, reprinted in *Survival*, November–December 1981, pp. 274–7; and Brezhnev's interview with *Der Spiegel* in November 1981, excerpts in *Survival*, January–February 1982, pp. 32–7.

72. Cf. Brezhnev's speech on 16 March 1982, *Survival*, July–August 1982, pp. 184–5. See also Berman and Baker, *op. cit.*, p. 34.

73. *Pravda*, 31 July 1983, *CDSP*, 31 August 1983, p. 11; speech by Ustinov, 10 September 1983, *Pravda*, 11 September 1983, *CDSP*, 5 October 1983, p. 9.

Andropov: speech on 21 December 1982, Yuri Andropov, *Our Aim is to Preserve Peace*, A Collection of Speeches from November 1982 to April 1983, Novosti Press Agency Publishing House, Moscow, 1983, for instance p. 15; *Pravda* interview, 27 August 1983, reprinted in excerpts in *Survival*, November–December 1983, pp. 281–2; statement on 28 September 1983, *Pravda* and *Izvestia*, 29 September, *CDSP*, 26 October, pp. 1–4; answers to questions by *Pravda*, 27 October 1983, excerpts in *Survival*, January–February 1984, pp. 35–6; statement, *Pravda* and *Izvestia*, 25 November 1983, *CDSP*, 21 December 1983, pp. 3–5. See also Andrei Gromyko, *On the International Situation and the Foreign Policy of the Soviet Union*, Report at the Session of the USSR Supreme Soviet, 16 June 1983, Novosti Press Agency Publishing House, Moscow, 1983, especially pp. 12ff. Also, Vladimir E. Shlapentokh, 'Moscow's war propaganda and Soviet public opinion', *Problems of Communism*, September–October 1984, pp. 88–94.

74. *CDSP*, 26 March 1986, pp. 27ff. It should be noted, that Gorbachev had first

used the formulation 'reasonable sufficiency' in a speech in Paris, 2 October 1985, cf. Garthoff (cited in note 52), *op. cit.*, p. 138. Gorbachev has expressed distinct modernist views on several other occasions since then, cf., for instance: speech to Moscow Peace Forum, *Pravda*, 17 February 1987, *CDSP*, 18 March 1987, pp. 11–12; a notable article in *Pravda*, 17 September, 1987, *CDSP*, 21 October 1987, pp. 16–18, See also Foreign Minister Shevardnadze, *International Affairs*, 10 October 1988, pp. 3–34.

Two useful American reviews of the 'new political thinking' are: Graham T. Allison, Jr, 'Testing Gorbachev', *Foreign Affairs*, Vol. 67, No. 1, Fall 1988, pp. 18–32; and Stephen M. Meyer, 'The sources and prospects of Gorbachev's new political thinking on security', *International Security*, Fall 1988, Vol. 13, No. 2, pp. 124–63. Also Mikhail Gorbachev, Perestroika and the New Thinking, Harper & Row, 1987, especially chapter 7.

75. One case occurred when SALT I had been concluded in 1972, cf. Warner, *op. cit.*, p. 131. More conspicuous cases have occurred during recent years; cf. below.

76. Jerry F. Hough, *The Struggle for the Third World. Soviet Debates and American Options*, The Brookings Institution, Washington, DC, 1986, pp. 13f.; and my article, cited in note 54, pp. 231–33.

77. Jönsson, *op. cit.*, p. 199; Warner, *op. cit.*, pp. 140f. James McConnell, *Soviet and American Strategic Doctrine: One More Time*, Professional Paper 271/January 1980, Center for Naval Analysis, Virginia, pp. 23–4; and David Holloway, 'Technology, management and the Soviet Military establishment', *Adelphi Papers*, No. 76, IISS, London, April 1971, pp. 7–8.

78. Raymond L. Garthoff, 'Mutual deterrence and strategic arms limitation in Soviet policy', *International Security*, Vol. 3, No. 1, Summer 1978, p. 115.

79. N. Talenskiy, 'The late war: some reflections', *International Affairs*, No. 5, May 1965, p. 15; see also N. Talenskiy, 22 June: 'Lessons of history', *International Affairs*, No. 6, June 1966, especially pp. 46 and 48; and N. Talenskiy, 'The "absolute weapon" and the problem of security', *International Affairs*, No. 4, April 1962, pp. 22–7. In 1964, Talenskiy wrote that 'the creation of an effective anti-missile system enables the state to make its defenses dependent chiefly on its own possibilities, and not only on mutual deterrence, that is, on the goodwill of the other side'; cf. 'Anti-missile systems and disarmament', *International Affairs*, No. 10. October 1964, p. 18.

80. Two evident examples are Lt-Col. E. Rybkin (a so-called political officer, cf. p. 251) in an article in autumn 1965, cf. *Survival*, January 1966, p. 12–16; V.D. Sokolovskiy and M. Cherednichenko in an article in April 1966, cf. *Survival*, August 1966, pp. 266–70. Also Hough, *op. cit.*, pp. 208ff.; Lambeth, *op. cit.*, pp. 9ff.; and Warner, *op. cit.*, p. 88.

One interesting indicator of the traditionalist surge was a work by Maj. Gen. Bochkarev, first published in 1963, which had included the words: 'Thermonuclear war ... will create a real threat to the very existence of mankind.' In the second edition of the work, published 1965–66, this sentence, together with another modernist-marked, was excised; cf. James McConnell, 'Shifts in Soviet views on the proper focus of military developments', *World Politics*, Vol. XXVII, No. 3, April 1985, p. 324.

81. Warner, *op. cit.*, p. 89.

82. Lawrence T. Caldwell, 'Soviet attitudes to SALT', *Adelphi Papers*, No. 75 IISS, London, February 1971, p. 19; and Roman Kolkowicz, and others, *The Soviet Union and Arms Control: A Superpower Dilemma*, Baltimore and London, 1970, pp. 15–17.

83. *Ibid.*; Samuel B. Payne, Jr, 'The Soviet debate on strategic arms limitation:

1968–72', *Soviet Studies*, Vol. XXXVII, January 1975, No. 1, pp. 27–44. Thomas W. Wolfe, *Soviet Power and Europe, 1945–1970*, Baltimore and London, 1970, pp. 439–40.

An unusually distinct type of traditionalism was expressed by the former Chief of the Strategic Missile Forces, Marshal N.I. Krylov: 'The imperialist ideologists are trying to lull the vigilance of the world's people by having recourse to propaganda devices to the effect that there will be no victors in a future nuclear war. These false affirmations contradict the objective laws of history .... Victory in war, if the imperialists succeed in starting it, will be on the side of world socialism and all progressive mankind', *Sovetskaia Rossiia*, 30 August 1969, cf. Leon Gouré, Foy D. Kohler and Mose L. Harvey, *The Role of Nuclear Forces In Current Soviet Strategy*, Center for Advanced International Studies, University of Miami, 1975, p. 61.

84. A general source on the 1970s is my article, cited in Note 54.

85. Cf. Caldwell, *op. cit.*, p. 11; William D. Jackson, 'Soviet images of the U.S. as nuclear adversary, 1969–1979', *World Politics*, Vol. XXXIII, No. 4, July 1981, pp. 619–24.

86. Garthoff, *op. cit.* (cited in note 34), p. 25; Payne, *op. cit.*, p. 64; and Warner, *op. cit.*, pp. 244f.

One distinct traditionalist case appeared in Colonel M.P. Skirdo, *The People, the Army, the Commander*, Moscow, 1970 (published and translated as the first-mentioned book in note 44); on p. 91, one reads: 'The fact is that employment of mass destruction weapons can suddenly and swiftly alter the correlation of all other forces and capabilities possessed by the adversaries prior to the outbreak of hostilities. This constitutes a qualitatively new aspect in the prospect of fighting for victory in the war of today'.

87. Bjorkman and Zamostny, *op. cit.*, p. 199; Garthoff, *op. cit.* (cited in note 78), p. 116.

88. Bjorkman and Zamostny, *op. cit.*, pp. 201–2; Gouré, Kohler and Harvey, *op. cit.*, p. 60; and Warner, *op. cit.*, pp. 251ff. The 1973–74 wave of traditionalism is said to have been opened by (cf. *Ibid.*, p. 252) General-Major A.S. Milovodov with the article 'A philosophical analysis of military thought', *Krasnaya Zvezda*, 17 May 1973, reprinted in *Selected Soviet Military Writings 1970–1975, op. cit.*, pp. 69–75.

89. Benjamin S. Lambeth, *Selective Nuclear Operations And Soviet Strategy*. P–5506, RAND, Calif., September 1975, pp. 12–14; and William F. Scott and Harriet Fast Scott, 'Soviet perceptions of US military strategies and forces', Graham D. Vernon (ed.), *Soviet Perceptions Of War And Peace*, National Defense University, Washington, DC, 1981, pp. 106–8.

90. Bjorkman and Zamostny, *op. cit.*, pp. 203–4; Garthoff, *op. cit.* (cited in note 78), pp. 142–3; Jackson, *op. cit.*, pp. 631–2; and Anne T. Sloan, 'Soviet positions on strategic arms control and arms policy: a perspective outside the military establishment', Kolkowicz and Mickiewicz (eds), *op. cit.*, p. 124.

91. A notable example was an address in a Moscow broadcast of 19 June 1979, by Aleksandr Bovin; cf. *Survival*, September–October 1979, pp. 213–16.

92. Ogarkov wrote about the Soviet Union and the fraternal socialist countries having 'objective possibilities of attaining victory' if 'nuclear war is forced on the Soviet Union'; cf. Holloway, *op. cit.*, p. 54. See also Bjorkman and Zamostny, *op. cit.*, p. 205; and Jackson, *op. cit.*, pp. 635–8.

93. Cf., for example, N.N. Azovtsev, *V.I. Lenin and Soviet Military Science*, Moscow, 1981 (in Russian), excerpts in Harriet Fast Scott and William F. Scott, *The Soviet Art Of War. Doctrine, Strategy, and Tactics*, Boulder, Colorado, 1982, pp. 257–63. See also a book reviewed in *Soviet Military*

Reviews, No. 2, February 1985, pp. 54–5; and Major-General Nikolai Tabunov, 'The Essence of war and its role in history', *Soviet Military Review*, No. 10, October 1987, p. 11.

94. Holloway, *op. cit.*, p. 53; Hasegawa, *op. cit.*, pp. 73–4; George G. Weickhardt, 'Ustinov versus Ogarkov', *Problems of Communism*, January–February 1985, p. 79.

   Other leading military officers have included similar modernist-like references to the threat of nuclear war, cf. 'Stephen Shenfield, Soviet thinking about the unthinkable,' *Bulletin of the Atomic Scientists*, February 1985, p. 25.

95. *Krasnaya Zvezda*, 9 May 1984, excerpts in *Survival*, July–August 1984, pp. 187–8; in an article in the same newspaper on 23 September 1983, Ogarkov directly referred to McNamara as he mentioned 'unacceptable damages'; cf. Sidney D. Drell, Philip J. Farley and David Holloway, 'Preserving the ABM Treaty: A critique of the Reagan Strategic Defense Initiative', *International Security*, Vol. 9, No. 2, Fall 1984, p. 61. And Mary C. FitzGerald, 'The Soviet military on the Strategic Defense Initiative', *Soviet Armed Forces Review Annual*, Vol. 10, *1985–1986*, pp. 218–19; and Mary C. FitzGerald, 'Marshal Ogarkov and the new revolution in Soviet military affairs', *Defense Analysis*, Vol. 3, No. 1, 1987, pp. 3–19, in particular pp. 4–6.

96. Cf. The review in Lothar Jung, 'Hält Moskau einen Atomkrig für gewinnbar?', *Osteuropa*, March 1986, pp. 220–2; Dale R. Herspring, 'Marshal Akhromeyev and the future of the Soviet armed forces', *Survival*, November–December 1986, pp. 524–35. See also Marshal Akhromeyev's press conference on 4 June 1986, commenting on the new American policy on the SALT II agreement (cf. p. 119), *Moscow News*, No. 24, 22–29 June 1986.

97. Vojtech Mastny (ed.), *Soviet–East European Survey, 1986–1987. Selected Research and Analysis from Radio Free Europe/Radio Liberty*, Boulder, Colorado and London, 1988, p. 124.

98. An unusually large number of Soviet pamphlets were published during the early 1980s, for example, *How to Avert the Threat to Europe*, The Soviet Committee For European Security And Cooperation. Scientific Research Council On Peace And Disarmament, Progress Publishers, Moscow, 1983.

   On Soviet scholars who warned that military factors should not be exaggerated, see Hough, *op. cit.*, pp. 215 and 221–2.

99. For example, Alexander Yakovlev, 'Peace American style and modern realities', *Peace and Disarmament*, Academic Studies, Progress Publishers, Moscow, 1984 (Yakovlev has been Director of the Institute for World Economy and International Relations since 1983); cf. Chapter 7, note 26.

100. Cf. Stephen Shenfield, *The Nuclear Predicament. Explorations In Soviet Ideology*, Chatham House Papers, 37, London, 1987, passim; see also the article by three Soviet scholars A.S. Ginsburg, G.S. Golitsyn and A.A. Valitsev, 'Global consequences of a nuclear war: a review of recent Soviet studies', *World Armaments and Disarmament. SIPRI Yearbook 1985*, London, 1985, pp. 107–25.

101. David Holloway, 'Gorbachev's new thinking', *Foreign Affairs*, Vol. 68, No. 1, 1989, p. 74; Meyer, *op. cit.*, (note 74); Warner, *op. cit.* (note 52).

102. David Holloway, 'The Strategic Defense Initiative and the Soviet Union', *Dædalus*, Summer 1985, pp. 266–7; F. Stephen Larrabee, *Foreign Affairs*, Vol. 66, No. 5, Summer 1988, p. 1015; Puschel, *op. cit.* (note 39), p. 46.

103. Vitaly Zhurkin, Sergei Karaganov, Andrei Kortunov (all three on staff of SShA, cf. below, p. 251f.), 'Reasonable sufficiency – on how to break the vicious circle', *New Times*, No. 40, 12 October 1987, pp. 13–15, called for *glasnost* in the military sphere. Alexander Bovin, *Moscow News*, No. 10,

8 March 1987, questioned, after having endorsed the new Soviet INF policy announced in late February 1987, the deployment of these Soviet medium-range missiles. In the following issue, *Moscow News*, No. 11, 15 March 1987, Yuri Lebedev, a Soviet officer, answered Bovin's unprecedented public question.

104. The most notable case is Georgi Arbatov, see, for instance, *Pravda*, 10 June 1988, *CDSP*, 6 July 1988, p. 19. Arbatov is one of the most prominent Soviet *Amerikanisti* (he is Director of SShA, cf. p. 252 below) and has at any time defended current Soviet policy.

105. See, for example, Ken Booth, *The Military Instrument In Soviet Foreign Policy 1917–1972*, London, 1973, pp. 5–6.

106. Hannes Adomeit, 'Soviet risk-taking and crisis behaviour: from confrontation to coexistence?', *Adelphi Papers*, No. 101, IISS, London, Autumn 1973, pp. 2f.; and Hannes Adomeit, *Soviet Risk-taking and Crisis Behavior. A theoretical and empirical analysis*, London, 1982, pp. 9–10.

107. It has to be stressed that as the aim only is to provide parts of the basis for the analysis in Chapter 7, I shall merely present a short outline of patterns of Soviet risk-taking and use of armed forces since the early 1960s.

108. Stephen S. Kaplan (ed.), *Diplomacy of Power. Soviet Armed Forces as a Political Instrument*, The Brookings Institution, Washington, DC, 1981, pp. 127–9.

109. James L. Richardson, *Germany And The Atlantic Alliance. The Interaction of Strategy And Politics*, Cambridge, Mass., 1966, pp. 301f.

110. Graham T. Allison, *Essence Of Decision. Explaining the Cuban Missile Crisis*, Boston, 1971, pp. 40f.; Kaplan (ed.), *op. cit.*, pp. 129–31; and Arnold L. Horelick, 'The Cuban missile crisis: an analysis of Soviet calculations and behavior', *World Politics*, Vol. XVI, No. 3, April 1964, pp. 363–89, especially pp. 375–77.

111. Kaplan (ed.), *op. cit.*, pp. 167ff.; Christer Jönsson, *Superpower. Comparing American and Soviet Foreign Policy*, London, 1984, pp. 164f.; and Bradford Dismukes, 'Soviet Employment of Naval Power For Political Purposes, 1967–75', Michael MccGwire and John McDonnell (eds), *Soviet Naval Influence. Domestic and Foreign Dimensions*, New York, 1977, pp. 484 and 496–98.

112. Bradford Dismukes, 'Large-scale intervention ashore: Soviet air defense forces in Egypt', Bradford Dismukes and James McConnell, *Soviet Naval Diplomacy*, New York, 1979, pp. 221f.; Alex P. Schmid, *Soviet Military Interventions Since 1945*, New Jersey, 1985, p. 95.

113. *Ibid.*, pp. 96f; Stephen T. Hosmer and Thomas W. Wolfe, *Soviet Policy and Practice toward Third World Conflicts*, Mass., 1983, pp. 50ff.; Jönsson, *op. cit.*, pp. 181f.; Bruce D. Porter, *The USSR In Third World Conflicts. Soviet arms and diplomacy in local wars 1945–1980*, London, 1984, pp. 113ff.; and Robert S. Litwak and, S. Neil MacFarlane, 'Soviet activism, in the Third World,' *Survival*, January–February 1987, pp. 221–39.

114. Cf. Dismukes and McConnell (eds), *op. cit.*, pp. 28, 42f. and 88f.: and Porter, *op. cit.*, pp. 40–6.

115. Robert G. Weinland, 'The state and future of the Soviet Navy in the North Atlantic', Christoph Bertram and Johan J. Holst (eds), *New Strategic Factors In The North Atlantic*, Oslo, 1977, pp. 55–73; Dismukes, MccGwire and McDonnell (eds) , *op. cit.*, pp. 493–5, and Dismukes and McConnell (eds), *op. cit.*, pp. 49 and 103.

116. Cf. the establishment of the Soviet naval presence outside West Africa at the invitation of Guinea which had been giving shelter to rebels from Portuguese Guinea and, in late 1970, invaded from the sea by a Portuguese force, *ibid.*,

p. 260.

117. *Ibid.*, pp. 192ff. and 240–79; and Avigdor Haselkorn, 'The "external function" of Soviet armed forces', *Naval War College Review*, Vol. XXXIII, No. 1/Sequence 277, January–February 1980, pp. 35–45.

118. Michael MccGwire, 'The evolution of Soviet naval policy', Michael MccGwire, Ken Booth and John McDonnell (eds.), *Soviet Naval Policy. Objectives and Constraints*, New York, 1975, pp. 505–46.

119. Neil Macfarlane, 'Intervention and regional security', *Adelphi Papers*, 196, IISS, London, Spring 1985, pp. 10 and 24–6; Hosmer and Wolfe, *op. cit.*, pp. 84–8; Colin Legum, 'Angola and the Horn of Africa', Kplan (ed.), *op. cit.*, pp. 573–605; and Porter, *op. cit.*, pp. 147–81.

120. *Ibid.*, pp. 182–215; Hosmer and Wolfe, *op. cit.*, pp. 88–94; Legum, Kaplan (ed.), *op. cit.*, pp. 605–37; and Macfarlane, *op. cit.*, pp. 10 and 26–7.

121. Joseph J. Collijns, *The Soviet Invasion of Afghanistan. A Study in the Use of Force in Soviet Foreign Policy*, Mass., 1986, especially pp. 133f. and 165f.; Mark Heller, 'The Soviet invasion of Afghanistan', *The Washington Quarterly*, Vol. 3, No. 3, Summer 1980, pp. 36–59; Hosmer and Wolfe, *op. cit.*, pp. 155ff.; and R.J. Vincent, 'Military power and political influence: the Soviet Union and Western Europe', *Adelphi Papers*, No. 119, IISS, London, 1975, p. 29.

122. Macfarlane, *op. cit.*, p. 28.

CHAPTER 7   COMPARING IMAGES AND OPERATIONAL ENVIRONMENTS

1. Alan Ryan, *The Philosophy of the Social Sciences*, London, 1970, p. 25; and Philip A.G. Sabin, 'Shadow or substance? Perceptions and symbolism in nuclear force planning', *Adelphi Papers*, No. 222, IISS, London, Summer 1987, p. 37.

2. Harold and Margaret Sprout, 'Environmental factors in the study of international politics', *The Journal of Conflict Resolution*, Vol. I, No. 4, 1957, pp. 313 and 324; and Harold and Margaret Sprout, *The Ecological Perspective on Human Affairs*, Princeton, 1965, pp. 83ff.

3. Herbert A. Simon, *Models of Man*, New York, 1957, pp. 198f. and 241f.; and Kenneth E. Boulding, 'The learning and reality-testing process in the international system', *Journal of International Affairs*, Vol. XXI, No. 1, 1967, pp. 1–15.

4. *The Structure of Scientific Revolutions*, Chicago, 1962.

5. William A. Scott, 'Psychological and social correlates of international images', Herbert C. Kelman (ed.), *International Behavior. A Social-Psychological Analysis*, New York, 1965, p. 72. It should be noted that Scott's definitions differ slightly from mine.

6. The most recent and thorough work on the problem, Sabin, *op. cit.*, applies this term.

7. Jerome H. Kahan and Anne K. Long, 'The Cuban missile crisis: a study of its stratetgic context', *Political Science Quarterly*, Vol. LXXXVII, No. 4, December 1972, pp. 564–90; Sabin, *op. cit.*, p. 33; Marc Trachtenberg, 'The influence of nuclear weapons in the Cuban missile crisis', *International Security*, Vol. 10, No. 1, Summer 1985, pp. 137–63, especially pp. 155–6 and 161–3; Walter Slocombe, 'The political implications of strategic parity', *Adelphi*

Papers, No. 77, IISS, London, May 1971, pp. 29–32; Graham T. Allison, *Essence Of Decision. Explaining the Cuban Missile Crisis*, Boston, 1971, pp. 52–6 and 62–6; and Richard K. Betts, *Nuclear Blackmail and Nuclear Balance*, The Brookings Institution, Washington, DC, 1987, pp. 109–23.

8.   Hannes Adomeit, 'Soviet risk-taking and crisis behavior: from confrontation to coexistence', *Adelphi Papers*, No. 101, IISS, London, Autumn 1973, pp. 24–5.

9.   Hannes Adomeit, *Soviet Risk-Taking and Crisis Behavior: A theoretical and empirical analysis*, London, 1982, p. 339.

10. Cf., for example, Jerome H. Kahan, *Security in the Nuclear Age. Developing U.S. Strategic Arms Policy*, The Brookings Institution, Washington, DC, 1975. pp. 237f; Benjamin S. Lambeth, 'The political potential of Soviet equivalence', *International Security*, Vol. 4, No. 2, Fall 1979, pp. 22–39; Benjamin S. Lambeth, 'Uncertainties for the Soviet war planner', *International Security*, Vol. 7, No. 3, Winter 1982/83, pp. 139–66; Sabin, *op. cit.*, p. 33; Karl F. Spielmann, *The Political Utility Of Strategic Superiority. A Preliminary Investigation Into the Soviet View*, Institute for Defense Analysis, Virginia, May 1979, pp. 21f., 51f., particularly pp. 57–8; Rajan Menon, 'Military power, interventions, and Soviet policy in the Third World', Roger E. Kanet (ed.), *Soviet Foreign Policy In The 1980s*, New York, 1982, p. 267; Neil Macfarlane, 'Intervention and regional security', *Adelphi Papers*, 196, IISS, London, Spring 1985, pp. 57–8; and Bruce D. Porter, *The USSR In Third World Conflicts. Soviet arms and diplomacy in local wars 1945–1980*, London, 1984, pp. 58–9 and 240–5.

11. About the methodical problems, see Herbert Goldhamer, 'Perceptions of the US–USSR balance: problems of analysis and research', Donald C. Daniel (ed.), *International Perceptions Of The Superpower Balance*, New York, 1978, pp. 3–20.

12. *Ibid.*, pp. 17–8.

13. An interesting case of this line of reasoning is Colin S. Gray, *The Soviet–American Arms Race*, New York, 1976, p. 136; another reasoning, but reaching the same conclusion, is Steven Kull, 'Nuclear nonsense', *Foreign Policy*, No. 58, Spring 1985, pp. 28–52.

14. The reviewed conditions of the American political process may have some further consequences which contribute to the making of a highly troublesome international environment for a successful pursuing of this policy. The problem is that when the United States' allies in Europe on different occasions express their concern about the state of the strategic nuclear balance, such worries often have US governments' pronouncements and the American debate about the 'deteriorating' balance as their primary source. Particularly in connection with the American budgetary process these worries frequently assume a simple and cocksure form. Hence, the result is that domestically prompted declarations in the United States easily become self-fulfilling prophesies also through their repercussions among America's allies.
     However, as it is obvious that the political ideologies and traditions among West European NATO countries in many ways diverge from the American, these American concerns may as well come to have an adverse effect in Europe in that many European reactions to US government declarations dramatizing the Soviet nuclear threat instead may be to increase the opposition to a need for Western counter-arms. That is, the American concerns may also appear self-denying prophesies.
     Two useful reviews of these processes (the first from *before* NATO's December 1979 double-track decision) are: Herbert Goldhamer, 'The US–Soviet strategic balance as seen from London and Paris', *Survival*, September–

October 1977, pp. 202–7; Bruce Russett and Donald R. Deluca, 'Theater nuclear forces: public opinion in Western Europe', *Political Science Quarterly*, Vol. 98, No. 2, Summer 1983, pp. 179–96. See also Lawrence Freedman, *The Evolution of Nuclear Strategy*, New York, 1981, p. 392.

15. Raymond L. Garthoff, 'SALT and the Soviet military', *Problems of Communism*, January–February 1975, pp. 30–1; Raymond L. Garthoff, *Détente and Confrontation. American Soviet Relations From Nixon To Reagan*, The Brookings Institution, Washington, DC, 1985, p. 183.

16. Robert J. Einhorn, 'Negotiating from strength. Leverage in U.S.–Soviet arms control negotiations', *The Washington Papers/113*, The Center for Strategic and International Studies (CSIS), Washington, DC, 1985, pp. 6–8, 38 and 104–5.

17. David Holloway, 'The Strategic Defense Initiative and the Soviet Union', *Dædalus*, Summer 1985, pp. 257–78.

18. Albert Carnesale and Richard N. Haass, 'Lessons learned from superpower arms control', *The Washington Quarterly*, Vol. 10, No. 3, Summer 1987, pp. 29f.; and Albert Carnesale and Richard N. Haass (eds), *Superpower Arms Control. Setting the Record Straight*, Cambridge, Mass., 1987, pp. 330f. Also Russell J. Leng, 'Reagan and the Russians: crisis bargaining beliefs and the historical record', *The American Political Science Review*, Vol. 78, No. 2, 1984, pp. 338–55.

19. William Potter, in Roman Kolkowicz and Neil Joeck (eds), *Arms Control and International Security*, Boulder, Colorado and London, 1984, p. 58.

20. Jack L. Snyder, *The Soviet Strategic Culture; Implications for Limited Nuclear Operations*, R–2154–AF, Rand, Calif., September 1977, p. 8.

21. Cf. in particular, Raymond L. Garthoff, 'Mutual deterrence and strategic arms limitation in Soviet policy', *International Security*, Vol. 3, No. 1, Summer 1978, pp. 112–47; and Richard Pipes, 'Why the Soviet Union thinks it could fight and win a nuclear war', *Commentary*, July 1977, pp. 21–34. See also the exchange between the two scholars in *Strategic Review*, December 1982, pp. 52–63.

22. Peter H. Vigor, 'The semantics of deterrence and defense', Michael MccGwire, Ken Booth and John McDonnell (eds), *Soviet Naval Policy. Objectives and Constraints*, New York, 1975, pp. 471–8.

23. Cf. Benjamin S. Lambeth, 'On thresholds in Soviet military thought', *The Washington Quarterly*, Vol. 7, No. 2, Spring 1984, pp. 71f.

24. Glenn H. Snyder, *Deterrence and Defense. Toward A Theory Of National Security*, Princeton, 1961, pp. 14–16; Michael MccGwire, 'Soviet military doctrine: contingency planning and the reality of world war', *Survival*, May–June 1980, p. 108; Gerald Segal, 'Strategy and "ethnic chic"', *International Affairs*, Winter 1983/84, pp. 22–4.

25. Snyder, *op. cit.* p. 10; for the following, see especially Dan L. Strode and Rebecca V. Strode, 'Diplomacy and defense in Soviet national security policy', *International Security*, Vol. 8, No. 2, Fall 1983, pp. 107f.

26. Harriet Fast Scott (ed.), *V.D. Sokolovskiy. Soviet Military Strategy*, London, 1975, pp. xxiii–xxiv.

Oded Eran, *Mezhdunarodniki – An Assessment of Professional Expertise in the Making of Soviet Foreign Policy*, Tel Aviv, 1979, passim; and Carl G. Jacobsen, 'Soviet think tanks', *Soviet Armed Forces Review Annual*, Vol. 1, 1977, pp. 140–52; Jerry F. Hough, *Soviet Leadership in Transition*, The Brookings Institution, Washington, DC, 1980, pp. 118–30; on recent developments of the institutes, see Edward L. Warner III, 'New thinking and old realities in Soviet defence policy', *Survival*, January–February 1989, pp. 18–20.

The two most prominent institutes are *Institut Mirovoy Ekonomiki i Mezhdunarodnykh Otnosheny/IMEMO* (institute for World Economy and International Relations) and *Institut Soyedinennykh Shtatov Ameriki i Kanady/ SShA* (Institute for the Study of the United States and Canada). IMEMO was first set up before World War II and re-established under its current name in 1956; it is the largest internationally-oriented institute with a research staff, in the mid-1970s, of about 600 and publishes the monthly journal *Mirovaya Ekonomika i Mezhdunarodnoye Otnosheniye* (World Economy and International Relations). In 1987, IMEMO commenced publishing *Disarmament and Security. 1986 Yearbook*, Novosti Press Agency Publishing House, Moscow, presented as the 'annual analytical review' of disarmament and security (p. 5). SShA was founded in 1968 and received its present name in 1974; it has a staff of about 150 and has since 1970 published the periodical *SShA: Ekonomika, Politika, Ideolgoiia* (USA: Economics, Politics, and Ideology) where several of the most distinct modernist writings have been presented.

27. Cf. Morton Schwartz, *Soviet Perceptions of the United States*, London, 1978; and Jacobsen, *op. cit.*, pp. 140–2.

28. Timothy J. Colton, *Commisars, Commanders, and Civilian Authority. The Structure of Soviet Military Politics*, Cambridge, Mass., and London, 1979, pp. 68f.; Michael J. Deane, *Political Control of the Soviet Armed Forces*, London, 1977, especially pp. 281–3; Ellen Jones, *Red Army And Society. A Sociology of the Soviet Military*, Boston, 1985, pp. 114f., 128–9 and 141–2; and Edward L. Warner III, *The Military in Contemporary Soviet Politics. An Institutional Analysis*, New York, 1977, pp. 49, 73–4 and 98–103.

John J. Dziak, 'The institutional foundations of Soviet military doctrine', Graham D. Vernon (ed.), *Soviet Perceptions of War and Peace*, Washington, DC, 1981, pp. 3–16. William F. Scott, *Soviet Sources of Military Doctrine and Strategy*, New York, 1975, pp. 6 and 10; and Warner, *op. cit.*, pp. 72–3.

MNP publishes the newspaper *Red Star (Krasnaya zvezda)* whose editor is a member of the executive bureau of the MPA; the leading military periodical for the discussion of political matters, *Communist of the Armed Forces (Kommunist Vooruzhennykh Sil) (KVS)*, is published by MPA's most prestigious school, the *Lenin Military-Political Academy*, a kind of 'think tank' for MPA. MPA is also responsible for controlling the content and ideological direction of the literature publishd by the Military Publishing House, Moscow, and all publications of the Ministry of Defense.

29. David Holloway, *The Soviet Union and the Arms Race*, New Haven and London, 1983, pp. 164–5.

30. Cf., for instance, Snyder, *op. cit.*, passim.

31. Raymond L. Garthoff, 'On estimating and imputing intentions', *International Security*, Vol. 2, No. 3, Winter 1978, pp. 22–32, especially p. 26; see also Jonathan Samuel Lockwook, *The Soviet View of U.S. Strategic Doctrine. Implications for Decision Making*, New Brunswick and London, 1983, particularly p. 23; Joseph D. Douglass, Jr and Amoretta W. Hoeber, *Soviet Strategy for Nuclear War*, Stanford, Calif., 1979, pp. 2–6; and Spielmann, *op. cit.* (cited in note 10), pp. 81–104. Also Daniel Frei. *Perceived Images. U.S. and Soviet Assumptions and Perceptions in Disarmament*, New Jersey, 1986, pp. 25f. and 249f.

32. Cf. Pipes, *op. cit.*, pp. 30 and 22. See also Spielmann, *op. cit.* (cited in note 10), pp. 88–94.

33. Garthoff, *op. cit.* (cited in note 31); Michael Howard, 'Social change and the defense of the West', *The Washington Quarterly*, Vol. 2, No. 4, Autumn 1979, p.

24; Daniel S. Papp, 'Soviet perceptions of the strategic balance, *Air University Review*, Vol. 32, January–February 1982, pp. 2–17; George H. Quester, 'On the identification of real and pretended Communist military doctrine', *Journal of Conflict Resolution*, Vol. X, 1966, pp. 172–9; and Karl F. Spielmann, *Analyzing Soviet Strategic Arms Decisions*, Westview Press, Boulder, Colorado, 1978, pp. 5f.

34. Among a vast literature, see especially Patrick M. Morgan, *Deterrence. A Conceptual Analysis*, London, 1977, pp. 17ff.; and Snyder, *op. cit.*, pp. 17f; also R.B. Byers, 'Deterrence under attack: crisis and dilemma', Byers (ed.), *Deterrence in the 1980s. Crisis and Dilemma*, New York, 1985, pp. 9–36, in particular pp. 10–14 on 'Conceptual problems and difficulties'.

35. See especially Philip K. Lawrence, 'Nuclear strategy and political theory: a critical assessment', *Review of International Studies*, Vol. 11, No. 2, 1985, pp. 106f.

36. Stanley Sienkiewicz, 'Observations on the impact of uncertainty in strategic analysis', *World Politics*, Vol. XXXII, No. 1, October 1979, pp. 96f.

37. Richard K. Betts, 'Elusive equivalence: the political and military meaning of the nuclear balance', Samuel P. Huntington (ed.), *The Strategic Imperative: New Policies for American Security*, Cambridge, Mass., 1982, p. 105; Aaron L. Friedberg, 'The evolution of U.S. strategic doctrine, 1945–1980, *ibid.*, 91; Robert Jervis, *The Illogic of American Nuclear Strategy*, Ithaca and London, 1984, passim; Richard Ned Lebow, 'Misconceptions in American strategic assessment', *Political Science Quarterly*, Vol. 97, No. 2, Summer 1982, pp. 187ff.; Roman Kolkowicz (ed.), *The Logic of Nuclear Terror*, Boston, 1987, passim; Bruce M. Russett, 'Ethical dilemmas of nuclear deterrence', *International Security*, Vol. 8, No. 4, Spring 1984, pp. 36–54, in particular p. 51; and Robert W. Tucker, *The Nuclear Debate. Deterrence And The Lapse Of Faith*, New York and London, 1985.

38. At this point it must be noticed that such a development can alleviate the deterrence problem *politically*, of course.

39. Joesph S. Nye, Jr, *Nuclear Ethics*, New York and London, 1986, pp. 106–7; and McGeorge Bundy, 'The bishops and the bomb', *The New York Review of Books*, Vol. XXX, No. 10, 16 June 1983, pp. 3f. on 'existential deterrence'. Janice Gross Stein, 'Deterrence in the 1980s: a political and contextual analysis', Byers (ed.), *op. cit.*, pp. 37ff.; and Leon V. Sigal, 'Stable deterrence or nuclear war-fighting: all unclear on the nuclear front', *ibid.*, pp. 96ff.

40. Robert Jervis, 'Deterrence and perception', *International Security*, Vol. 7, No. 3, Winter 1982/83, pp. 17–19; Richard Ned Lebow, 'Windows of opportunity: do states jump through them?', *International Security*, Vol. 9, No. 1, Summer 1984, pp. 147–86, in particular the last pages. John D. Steinbruner and Thomas M. Garwin, 'Strategic vulnerability: the balance between prudence and paranoia', *International Security*, Vol. 1, No. 1, Summer 1976, pp. 138f; and Tucker, *op. cit.*, p. 120.

41. Robert W. Tucker, *The Nuclear Debate. Deterrence and the Lapse of Faith*, New York and London, 1985, in particular p. 110. See also Charles L. Glaser, 'Why even good defenses may be bad', *International Security*, Vol. 9, No. 2, Fall 1984, pp. 92–123.

42. Jan F. Triska and David D. Finley, 'Soviet–American relations: A multiple symmetry model', *Journal of Conflict Resolution*, Vol. 9, No. 1, March 1965, pp. 37f.; see also Richard Pipes, 'Dealing with the Russians: the wages of forgetfulness', Arnold L. Horelick (ed.), *U.S.–Soviet Relations. The Next Phase*, Ithaca and London, 1986, pp. 281–7; and Amoretta M. Hoeber and Joseph D. Douglas, Jr, 'Soviet approach to global nuclear conflict', Peter

Duignan and Alvin Rabushka (eds), *The United States in the 1980s*, Hoover Institution, Stanford University, 1980, p. 462.

43. Cf. Jervis, *op. cit.* (cited in note 37) pp. 104–7 and 122.

44. Morgan, *op. cit.*, and Snyder, *op. cit.*

45. Sabin, *op. cit.*, p. 29; see also Ken Booth, *Strategy and Ethnocentrism*, New York, 1979, passim.

46. Sabin, *op. cit.*, pp. 29–30.

47. See the reasoning applied by Edward L. Rowny, 'Negotiating with the Soviets', *The Washington Quarterly*, Vol. 3, No. 1, Winter 1980, p. 65.

48. Desmond Ball, 'Can nuclear war be controlled?', *Adelphi Papers*, No. 169, IISS, London, Autumn 1981, especially, p. 30; Theodore Draper, 'How not to think about nuclear war', *The New York Review of Books*, 15 July 1982, pp. 35–43; Benjamin S. Lambeth, 'Selective nuclear operations and Soviet strategy', Johan J. Holst and Uwe Nerlich (eds), *Beyond Nuclear Deterrence. New Aims. New Arms*, New York, 1977, pp. 79–104. Joseph S. Nye Jr, op. cit., pp. 117f.; and Leon Wieseltier, 'When deterrence fails', *Foreign Affairs*, Vol. 63, No. 4. Spring 1985, pp. 827–47, particularly, p. 844.

49. On the convergence issue in this context, see Thomas W. Wolfe, 'The convergence issue and Soviet strategic policy', *Rand. 25th Anniversary Volume*, Rand, Calif., 1973, pp. 137–50. Also Leon Wieseltier, 'The great nuclear debate', *The New Republic*, 10 and 17 January 1983, pp. 20–1 on the Sovietization of American nuclear doctrine.

50. Karen Dawisha, *Eastern Europe, Gorbachev and Reform. The Great Challenge*, Cambridge, 1988, pp. 7–8; Fen Osler Hampson, 'Escalation in Europe', Graham T. Allison, Albert Carnesale and Joseph S. Nye Jr (eds), *Hawks, Doves & Owls*, New York and London, 1985, pp. 80–114; and Francis Fukuyama, 'Escalation in the Middle East and Persian Gulf', *ibid.*, pp. 115–47.

51. Cf. Alexander L. George, *Presidential Decisionmaking in Foreign Policy: the Effective Use of Information and Advice*, Westview Press, Boulder, Colorado, 1980, pp. 26f.

52. See in particular, Daniel Heradsveit, *The Arab–Israeli Conflict. Psychological Obstacles to Peace*, Oslo, 1979.

53. Cf. Christer Jönsson, 'A cognitive approach to international negotiation', *European Journal of Political Research*, Vol. 11, No. 2, June 1983, p. 148.

54. Miles Hewstone, 'Attribution theory and common-sense explanations: an introductory overview, Hewstone (ed.), *Attribution Theory. Social and Functional Extensions*, Oxford, 1983, p. 10; Arie W. Kruglanski, Mark W. Baldwin and Shelagh M.J. Towson, 'The lay-epistemic process in attribution-making', *ibid.*, pp. 90–4; Arie W. Kruglanski and Icek Ajzen, 'Bias and error in human judgment', *European Journal of Social Psychology*, Vol. 13, 1983, pp. 1–44, especially pp. 18–20, 22–3 and 35f.

55. Cf. Robert Jervis, 'Hypotheses on misperception', James N. Rosenau (ed.), *International Politics and Foreign Policy*, New York, 1969, p. 252.

56. Robert Legvold, 'War, weapons, and Soviet foreign policy', Seweryn Bialer and Michael Mandelbaum (eds), *Gorbachev's Russia and American Foreign Policy*, Boulder, Colorado and London, 1988, p. 124.

57. Cf., for example, Ronald Hingley, *The Russian Mind*, New York, 1977, especially pp. 29–33, Tibor Szamuely, *The Russian Tradition*, London, 1974, pp. 17f.; see also the short overview in Michael Nacht, *The Age of Vulnerability. Threats to the Nuclear Stalemate*, The Brookings Institution, Washington, DC, 1985, pp. 20–1.

58. Cyril E. Black, 'Russian interpretations of world history', James N. Rosenau, Vincent Davis and Maurice A. East (eds), *The Analysis of International Politics*,

New York and London, 1972, pp. 371–87, especially p. 385; Kristian Gerner, 'Kazan and Mauchu: cultural roots of Soviet foreign relations', *Cooperation and Conflict*, Vol. XV, No. 2, June 1980, pp. 57–70; John M. Joyce, 'The old Russian legacy', *Foreign Policy*, No. 55, Summer 1984, pp. 132–53; Malcolm Mackintosh, 'The Russian attitude to defence and disarmament', *International Affairs*, Vol. 59, No. 3, Summer 1985, pp. 385–94; and Stephen M. Meyer, 'Soviet national security decision-making: what do we know and what do we understand?', Jiri Valenta and William Potter (eds), *Soviet Decisionmaking for National Security*, London, 1984, pp. 276–8 (on the paranoia model).

59. Freeman Dyson, *Weapons and Hope*, New York, 1985, pp. 181–97; David Holloway, 'Military power and political purpose in Soviet policy', *Dædalus*, special issue on US Defense Policy in the 1980s, Fall 1980, pp. 25f.; and Dennis Ross, 'Rethinking Soviet strategic policy: inputs and implications', *The Journal of Strategic Studies*, Vol. 1, No. 1, May 1978, pp. 4f.

60. *The Fundamentals of Marxist-Leninist Philosophy*, Progress Publishers, Moscow, 1982, passim, for instance pp. 308–10 and 425–30; also *Problems of War and Peace. A Critical Analysis of Bourgeois Theories*, Progress Publishers, Moscow, 1972, pp. 57ff. Among Western reviews: V. Kubálková and A.A. Cruickshank, *Marxism-Leninism and Theory of International Relations*, London, 1980, pp. 191ff.; R. Judson Mitchell, *Ideology of a Superpower. Contemporary Soviet Doctrine On International Relations*, Stanford, Calif., 1982; and Pål Kolstφ, Krig og fred i sovjetisk ideologi (War and peace in Soviet ideology), *Internasjonal Politikk*, No. 4, 1985, pp. 77–104.

61. Vernon V. Aspaturian, 'Soviet global power and the correlation of forces', *Problems of Communism*, May–June 1980, pp. 1–18; Julian Lider, 'The correlation of world forces: the Soviet concept', *Journal of Peace Research*, Vol. XVII, No. 2, 1980; and Michael J. Deane, 'Soviet perceptions of the military factor in the "correlation of world forces"', Donald C. Daniel (ed.), *op. cit.* (note 11), pp. 72–94.

62. For slightly different distinctions, see Hannes Adomeit, *op. cit.*, (note 8), pp. 19–20; David Dinsmore Comey, 'Marxist-Leninist ideology and Soviet policy', *Studies in Soviet Thought*, Vol. 2, No. 4, 1962, p. 315; Daniel Frei, *Perceived Images. U.S. and Soviet Assumptions and Perceptions in Disarmament*, New Jersey, 1986, pp. 189–91; and Jan F. Triska and David D. Finley, *Soviet Foreign Policy*, New York and London, 1968, pp. 109f. Also Paul Dibb, *The Soviet Union. The Incomplete Superpower*, London, 1986, pp. 12–16.

63. Alexander Dallin, 'Some lessons of the past', Mark Garrison and Abbott Gleason (eds), *Shared Destiny. Fifty Years of Soviet–American Relations*, Boston, 1985, pp. 67–8.

64. Cf., for example, the interesting interventions by Soviet participants in John Somerville (ed.), *Soviet Marxism and Nuclear War. An International Debate*, From the Proceedings of the Special Colloquium of the XVth World Congress of Philosophy held in Varna, Bulgaria, in 1973, London, 1981.

   See also Stanley Sienkiewicz, 'Soviet nuclear doctrine and the prospects for strategic arms control', Derek Leedaert (ed.), *Soviet Military Thinking*, London, 1981, p. 78; Fritz W. Ermath, 'Contrasts in American and Soviet strategic thought', *International Security*, Vol. 3, No. 2, Fall 1978, pp. 143–4; Keith B. Payne, *Nuclear Deterrence in U.S.–Soviet Relations*, Westview Press, Boulder, Col., 1982, p. 141; and Stephen Shenfield, *The Nuclear Predicament. Explorations In Soviet Ideology*, Chatham House Papers 37, London, 1987, p. 18.

65. Johan Jφrgen Holst, 'Soviet international conduct and the prospects of arms control', *Cooperation and Conflict*, 1965, No. 1, pp. 53–64; also Elizabeth and

Wayland Young, 'Marxism-Leninism and arms control', *Arms Control*, Vol. 1, No. 1, 1980, pp. 3–29.

66. A useful review of these theories is Colin S. Gray, *The Soviet–American Arms Race*, Lexington, Mass., 1976, pp. 1–127.

67. Holloway, *op. cit.*, pp. 178–9; Johan Jørgen Holst, *Comparative U.S. and Soviet Deployments, Doctrines, and Arms Limitation*, An Occasional Paper of the Center for Policy Study. The University of Chicago, 1971, particularly, p. 19; Meyer, *op. cit.*, pp. 257ff; and Warner, *op. cit.*, pp. 171–2. One study actually found that there was no interaction between Soviet and American expenditures on nuclear weapons, Jacek Kugler, and A.F.K. Organski with Daniel Fox, 'Deterrence and the arms race: the impotence of power', *International Security*, Vol. 4, No. 4, Spring 1980, pp. 105–38, especially pp. 122–3; see also Albert Wohlstetter, 'Is there a strategic arms race?', *Foreign Policy*, No. 15, Summer 1974, pp. 3–20, and 'Rivals but no "race"', *Foreign Policy*, No. 16, Fall 1974, pp. 48–81.

68. Robert P. Berman and John C. Baker, *Soviet Strategic Forces. Requirements and Responses*, The Brookings Institution, Washington, DC, 1982, p. 148.

69. John Erickson, 'The Soviet view of deterrence: a general survey', *Survival*, November–December 1982, p. 249; David Holloway, 'Strategic concepts and Soviet policy', *Survival*, November 1971, pp. 367–8; Paul Stockton, 'Strategic stability between the super-powers', *Adelphi Papers*, No. 213, IISS, London, Winter 1986, pp. 22 and 83.

70. Kjell Goldmann, *Tension and Détente in Bipolar Europe*, Stockholm, 1974, pp. 23f.

71. Kjell Goldmann and Johan Lagerkranz, 'Neither tension nor détente: East–West relations in Europe, 1971–1975', *Cooperation and Conflict*, XII, 1977, pp. 251–64. The description of the late 1970s and early 1980s as a period of 'rising East–West tension' is based on my own overall impression.

72. Goldmann, *op. cit.*, p. 200.

73. Norman Moss, 'McNamara's ABM policy: a failure of communications', *The Reporter*, 23 February 1967, p. 346. At this point it is interesting to note that it has been an important part of the Soviet essentialist trend that this learning process should work in the *opposite* direction: America should, for its own sake, 'learn' from the Soviets and imitate their doctrine.

74. Jervis, *op. cit.* (cited in note 55), pp. 251–3, advances two hypotheses: 'when people spend a great deal of time drawing up a plan or making a decision, they tend to think that the message about it they wish to convey will be clear to the receiver', and 'when actors have intentions that they do not try to conceal from others, they tend to assume that others accurately perceive these intentions'.

CHAPTER 8   CONCLUSIONS

1. Cf. J.H. Hexter, *On Historians. Reappraisals of some of the makers of modern history*, London, 1979, pp. 241f.; John Lewis Gaddis, *Strategies of Containment. A Critical Appraisal of Postwar American National Security Policy*, Oxford, 1982, pp. vii–viii.

2. Charles Kiselyak, 'Round the prickly pear: SALT and survival', *Orbis*, Vol. 22, No. 4, Winter 1979, p. 816.

3. Cf., for example, Marshall Brement, *Organizing Ourselves To Deal With The Soviets*, P-6123, Rand, Calif., June 1978, p. 11; Stanley Hoffmann, 'Détente',

Joseph S. Nye Jr (ed.), *The Making Of America's Soviet Policy*, New Haven and London, 1984, p. 262. See also Dorothy Atkinson, 'Understanding the Soviets: the development of U.S. expertise on the USSR', *The Washington Quarterly*, Vol. 10, No. 3, Summer 1987, particularly p. 198; and Steven J. Rosen and Walter S. Jones, *The Logic Of International Relations*, third edition, Cambridge, Mass., 1980, pp. 197–9.

4. Concluding that the American defeat in Vietnam is one part of the explanation for the Soviet essentialist trend in the 1970s, it can also be observed that the actual American engagement in Vietnam in the 1960s may have strengthened the nulear essentialist trend. By downgrading the role of nuclear arms, members of the Johnson administration may have reasoned, it would be easier to maintain the necessary domestic political support for its Vietnam policy, and this perspective may be further related to the weight attached to conventional arms during those years, cf. p. 52 above.

On the other hand, many strong supporters of the American engagement in Vietnam advocated a Soviet essentialist-like nuclear policy in the 1960s while several opponents of American policy in Vietnam strongly supported a kind of nuclear essentialism. One must therefore not overdo this explanation for the Johnson presidency's nuclear essentialist-like policy but considered in the overall context of American politics, that explanation has to be noted.

5. Joseph S. Nye Jr, 'Nuclear learning and U.S.–Soviet security regimes', *International Organization*, Vol. 41, No. 3, Summer 1987, pp. 371–402.

6. Albert Carnesale *et al.*, *Living With Nuclear Weapons*, Harvard Study Group, Toronto, 1983, pp. 42–3, is a useful and short introduction to the communication problems.

7. Samuel P. Huntington, *American Politics: The Promise of Disharmony*, Cambridge, Mass. and London, 1981, p. 53. Also André Fontaine, 'Beyond Wilson and Rambo', *Foreign Policy*, No. 65, Winter 1986–87, pp. 33–8; and George F. Kennan, *The Nuclear Delusion. Soviet–American Relations in the Atomic Age*, New York, 1982, p. 51 (reprint of an article from 1976).

8. Robert Jervis, *Perception and Misperception in International Politics*, Princeton, 1976, pp. 128ff.; Jervis, 'Hypotheses on misperception', James N. Rosenau (ed.), *International Politics and Foreign Policy*, New York, 1969, p. 244. Also Leon Festinger, *A Theory of Cognitive Dissonance*, Stanford University Press, 1957.

9. Cf. the two publications by Jervis, cited in note 8, pp. 319f. and 251–2, respectively. Raymond A. Bauer, 'Problems of perception and the relations between the United States and the Soviet Union', *The Journal of Conflict Resolution*, Vol. V, 1961, pp. 225f.

10. A useful and classical introduction to this subject is Karl Deutsch, 'On political theory and political action', *The American Political Science Review*, Vol. LXV, No. 1, March 1971, pp. 11–27.

11. Cf. the debate on modernization of NATO's nuclear weapons in Europe. Compare, for instance, Hans Binnendijk, 'NATO's nuclear modernization', *Survival*, March–April 1988, pp. 137–55; and Lawrence Freedman, 'NATO myths', *Foreign Policy*, No. 45, Winter 1981/82, pp. 48–68.

12. See especially Wolfgang K.H. Panofsky and Samuel F. Wells, *Perceptions: Relations Between the United States and the Soviet Union*, Committee On Foreign Relations. United States Senate, Washington, DC, 1979, pp. 360 and 367; and Stephen F. Cohen, *Sovieticus. American Perceptions and Soviet Realities*, New York, 1985, pp. 19f. on 'Sovietophobia: our other Soviet problem'. See also Michael Mandelbaum on 'strategic mercantilism' in *The*

Nuclear Revolution. International Politics Before And After Hiroshima, Cambridge, 1981, pp. 123 ff.

13. Stanley Hoffmann, 'Janus and Minerva', *Essays in the Theory and Practice of International Politics*, Boulder, Colorado and London, 1987, p. 425.

14. Nye, *op. cit.*, pp. 382f.

15. Earl C. Ravenal, 'Perceptions of American power', Franklin D. Margiotta (ed.), *Evolving Strategic Realities: Implications for U.S. Policymakers*, Washington, DC, 1980, pp. 160–1, see also Johan Jørgen Holst in conversation with George R. Urban, *NUPI notat*, No. 257, Oslo, December 1982, for example p. 11.

16. Ralph K. White, *Fearful Warriors. A Psychological Profile of U.S.–Soviet Relations*, New York and London, 1984, p. 8; Charles William Maynes, 'Old errors in the new cold war', *Foreign Policy*, No. 46, Spring 1982, pp. 100f.

17. Michael Howard, 'The Gorbachev challenge and the defence of the West', *Survival*, November–December 1988, pp. 483–92.

18. Charles Gati, *Foreign Affairs*, Vol. 68, No. 1, 1989, pp. 99–119; Robert Legvold, 'The revolution in Soviet foreign policy', ibid., pp. 82–98; and Richard H. Ullman, 'Ending the cold war', *Foreign Policy*, No. 72, Fall 1988, pp. 135–6.

19. Cf. Seweryn Bialer, '"New thinking" and Soviet foreign policy', *Survival*, July–August 1988, pp. 291–309; and Thomas M. Cynkin, 'Glasnost, perestroika and Eastern Europe', *ibid.*, pp. 310–31.

Bibliography

PRIMARY SOURCES

a. **The Department of State Bulletin**, January 1961–September 1988. Published by the Department of State, until 1978 weekly, thereafter monthly.

b. **Documents on Disarmament**, 1961–84, published annually by the Arms Control and Disarmament Agency.

c. **Documents On American Foreign Relations**, 1961–70, published yearly by the Council on Foreign Relations, New York, from 1971 to 1978 as *American Foreign Relations. A Documentary Record.*

d. **Annual Statements or Reports by Secretaries of Defense**

Statement to the House Armed Servies Committee by Secretary Robert S. McNamara, 18 February 1965, *Survival*, May–June 1965, pp. 98–107.

Statement before the Senate Subcommittee on Department of Defence Appropriations, 23 February 1966, *Survival*, May 1966, pp. 138–42.

Statement Of Secretary of Defense Robert S. McNamara Before The House Armed Services Committee On the Fiscal Year 1968–72 Defense Program And 1968 Defense Budget, 23 January 1967.

Statement by Secretary of Defense Robert S. McNamara on The Fiscal Year 1969–73 Defense Program And 1969 Defense Budget, 30 April 1968.

Statement Of Secretary of Defense Melvin R. Laird Before The House Armed Services Committee On The FY 1972–1976 Defense Program And The 1972 Defense Budget, 9 March 1971.

Statement Of Secretary Of Defense Melvin R. Laird Before The Senate Armed Services Committee On The FY 1973 Defense Budget and FY 1973–1977 Program, 15 February 1972.

Final Report To The Congress Of Secretary Of Defense Melvin R. Laird Before The House Armed Services Committee, 8 January 1973.

Statement of Secretary Of Defense Elliot L. Richardson Before The House Armed Services Committee On The FY 1974 Defense Budget And FY 1974–1978 Program, 10 April 1973.

Report Of The Secretary Of Defense James R. Schlesinger To The Congress On The FY 1975 Defense Budget And FY 1975–1979

Defense Program, 4 March 1974.

Report Of Secretary Of Defense James R. Schlesinger To The Congress On The FY 1976 and Transition Budgets, FY 1977 Authorization Request And FY 1976–1980 Defense Programs, 5 February 1975.

Secretary of Defense Donald H. Rumsfeld, *Annual Defense Department Report. FY 1977*, 27 January 1976.

Report Of Secretary Of Defense Donald R. Rumsfeld To The Congress On The FY 1978 Budget, FY 1979 Authorization Request And FY 1978–1982 Defense Programs, 17 January 1977.

Harold Brown, *Department of Defense. Annual Report. Fiscal Year 1979*, 2 February 1978.

Harold Brown, *Department of Defense. Annual Report. Fiscal Year 1980*, 25 January 1979.

Harold Brown, *Department of Defense. Annual Report. Fiscal Year 1981*, 29 January 1980.

Report of Secretary of Defense Harold Brown To The Congress On The FY 1982 Budget, FY 1983 Authorization Request And FY 1982–1986 Defense Programs, 19 January 1981.

Caspar W. Weinberger, *Annual Report To The Congress On The FY 1983 Budget, FY 1984 Authorization Request And FY 1983–1987 Defense Programs*, 8 February 1982.

Caspar W. Weinberger, *Annual Report To The Congress on the FY 1984 Budget, FY 1985 Authorization Request and FY 1984–1988 Defense Programs*, 1 February 1983.

Report of the Secretary of Defense Caspar W. Weinberger to the Congress on the FY 1985 Budget, FY 1986 Authorization Request and FY 1985–89 Defense Programs, 1 February 1984.

Report of the Secretary of Defense Caspar W. Weinberger to the Congress on the FY 1986 Budget FY 1987 Authorization Request and FY 1986–90 Defense Programs, 4 February 1985.

Caspar W. Weinberger, *Annual Report to the Congress. Fiscal Year 1987*, 5 February 1986.

Report of the Secretary of Defense Caspar W. Weinberger to the Congress on the FY 1988/FY 1989 Budget and FY 1988–92 Defense Programs, 12 January 1987.

Report of the Secretary of Defense Frank C. Carlucci to the Congress on the Amended FY 1988/FY 1989 Biennial Budget, 18 February 1988.

e. **Congressional Hearings** (the date adduced for each hearing may represent one, principally the first, among more)

Military Posture Briefings, Hearings Before The Committee On Armed Services. House of Representatives, 23 February 1961.

Military Procurement Authorization Fiscal Year 1962, Hearings Before the Committee On Armed Services. United States Senate, 4 April 1961.

Hearings Before The Subcommittee Of The Committee On Appropriations. House of Representatives, 7 April 1961.

Military Procurement Authorization Fiscal Year 1963, Hearings Before the Committee on Armed Services. United

States Senate. 19 January 1962.

Hearings on Military Posture And H.R. 9751. Committee On Armed Services. House Of Representatives, 24 January 1962.

Department of Defense Appropriations For 1963. Hearings Before A Subcommittee Of the Committee on Appropriations. House of Representatives, 29 January 1962.

Military Procurement Authorization Fiscal Year 1964, Hearings Before The Committee On Armed Services. United States Senate, 19 February 1963.

Nuclear Test Ban Treaty. Hearings Before The Committee On Foreign Relations. United States Senate, 12 August 1963.

Military Procurement Authorizations, Fiscal Year 1966, Hearings Before The Committee On Armed Services And The Subcommittee On Department Of Defense Of The Committee On Appropriations. United States Senate, 24 February 1965.

Hearings On Military Posture and H.R. 13456, Before The Committee On Armed Services. House Of Representatives, 8 March 1966.

Changing American Attitudes Toward Foreign Policy, Hearing Before The Committee On Foreign Relations, United States Senate, 20 February 1967.

Hearings On Military Posture, Before The Committee On Armed Services. House of Representatives, 2 March 1967.

Authorization for Military Procurement, Research And Development, Fiscal Year 1969, And Reserve Strength, Hearings Before The Committee On Armed Services. United States Senate, 2 February 1968.

Nonproliferation Treaty, Hearings Before The Committee on Foreign Relations. United States Senate, 10 July 1968.

Strategic And Foreign Policy Implications Of ABM Systems. Hearings Before the Subcommittee On International Organization And Disarmament Affairs Of the Committee On Foreign Relations. United States Senate. Parts I–III, March–July 1969.

Authorization For Military Procurement, Research And Development, Fiscal Year 1971, And Reserve Strength, Hearings Before the Committee On Armed Services, United States Senate, 20 February 1970.

Hearings On Military Posture, Committee On Armed Services, House of Representatives, 27 February 1970.

ABM, MIRV, SALT And The Nuclear Arms Race, Hearings Before The Subcommittee On Arms Control, International Law And Organization Of The Committee On Foreign Relations. United States Senate, March–June 1970.

Military Implications Of The Treaty On The Limitations Of Anti-Ballistic Missile Systems And The Interim Agreement On Limitation Of Strategic Offensive Arms, Hearing Before The Committee On Armed Services. United States Senate, 6 June 1972.

Strategic Arms Limitation Agreements, Hearings Before The Committee On Foreign Relations. United States Senate, 19 June 1972.

Nuclear Weapons And Foreign Policy, Hearings Before the Subcommittee On US Security Agreements And Commitments Abroad And The Subcommittee On Arms Control, International Law And Organization Of The Committee On Foreign Relations, United States Senate, 7 March 1974.

U.S.–U.S.S.R. Strategic Policies, Hearing Before The Subcommittee On Arms Control, International Law And Organization Of The Committee On Foreign Relations, United States Senate, 4 March 1974, top secret hearing, sanitized and made public on 4 April.

Briefing On Counterforce Attacks, Hearing Before The Subcommittee On Arms Control, International Law And Organization Of The Committee On Foreign Relations, United States Senate, Secret Hearing Held On 11 September 1974: Sanitized and Made Public on 10 January 1975.

Soviet Compliance With Certain Provision Of The 1972 SALT I Agreements, Hearings Before The Subcommittee On Arms Control Of The Committee On Armed Services, United States Senate, 6 March 1975.

The Vladivostok Accord: Implications To U.S. Security, Arms Control, And World Peace, Hearings Before The Subcommittee On International Security And Scientific Affairs Of The Committee On International Relations. House Of Representatives, 24, 25 June and 8 July 1975.

Warnke Nomination. Hearings Before The Committee On Foreign Relations. United States Senate, 8 and 9 February 1977.

Consideration of Mr. Paul C. Warnke To Be Director Of The U.S. Arms Control And Disarmament Agency And Ambassador. Hearings Together With Individual Views. Committee On Armed Services. United States Senate, 22, 23 and 28 February 1977.

Hearings on H.R. 8390 and Review Of The State of U.S. Strategic Forces, Committee On Armed Services, House Of Representatives, 1977.

Perceptions: Relations Between the United States and the Soviet Union, Committee On Foreign Relations. United States Senate, Washington, DC, 1979.

Nuclear War Strategy, Hearing Before the Committee On Foreign Relations, United States Senate, 16 September 1980. Top secret hearings; sanitized and printed on 18 February 1981.

Department Of Defense Authorization For Appropriations For Fiscal Year 1982, Hearings Before The Committee On Armed Services, United States Senate, 28 January 1981.

Fiscal Year 1981 Department Of Defense Supplemental Authorization, Hearing Before The Committee on Armed Services, United States Senate, 23 March 1981.

Strategic Programs, Hearings on Military Posture And H.R. 5968, Before The Committee On Armed Services, House of Representatives, 6 October 1981.

Strategic Weapons Proposals, Hearings Before The Committee On Foreign Relations, United States Senate, 3 and 4 November 1981.

Arms Control Policy, Planning and Negotiating, Hearings Before The

Committee On Armed Services, United States Senate, 1 December 1981.

Overview Of Nuclear Arms Control And Defense Strategy in NATO, Hearings Before the Subcommittee On International Security And Scientific Affairs And On Europe And The Middle East of The Committee On Foreign Affairs, House of Representatives, 23 February 1982.

Strategic Programs, Hearings on Military Posture Before The Committee On Armed Services, House of Representatives, 23 February 1982.

Department Of Defense Authorization For Appropriations For Fiscal Year 1983, Hearings Before The Committee On Armed Services, United States Senate, 1 March 1982.

United States And Soviet Civil Defense Programs, Hearings Before the Subcommittee On Arms Control, Oceans, International Operations And Environment Of The Committee On Foreign Relations. United States Senate, 16 and 31 March 1982.

Strategic Arms Control And U.S. National Security Policy, Hearings And Markup Before The Committee On Foreign Affairs And Its Subcommittee On International Security And Scientific Affairs, House of Representatives, 2 April 1982.

Nuclear Arms Reduction Proposals, Hearings Before The Committee On Foreign Relations, United States Senate, 30 April 1982.

The MX Missile And Associated Basing Decision, Hearing Before The Committee On Armed Services, United States Senate, 8 December 1982.

U.S. Strategic Doctrine, Hearing Before the Committee On Foreign Relations, United States Senate, 14 December 1982.

MX Missile Basing System And Related Issues, Hearings Before The Committee On Armed Services, United States Senate, 20 April 1983.

Review of Arms Control Implications Of The Report Of The President's Commission On Strategic Forces, Hearings Before the Committee On Foreign Affairs, House of Representatives, 17 May 1983.

United States–Soviet Relations, Hearings Before The Committee On Foreign Relations. United States Senate, Parts 1 and 2, June 1983.

The Role Of Arms Control In U.S. Defense Policy, Hearings Before The Committee On Foreign Affairs. House Of Representatives, 20 June 1984.

Soviet Treaty Violations, Hearings Before The Committee On Armed Services, United States Senate, 20 February and 7 May 1985.

Department Of Defense Authorization for Appropriations For Fiscal Year 1986, Hearings before The Committee On Armed Services, United States Senate, 26 February 1985.

The MX Missile And The Strategic Defense Initiative–Their Implications On Arms Control Negotiations, Hearings Before The Defense Policy Panel Of The Committee On Armed Services. House Of Representatives, 27 February 1985.

Review of Arms Control and Disarmament Activities, Hearings before the Special Panel on Arms Control And Disarmament of the

Procurement And Military Nuclear System Subcommittee of the Committee On Armed Services, House of Representatives, 10 September 1985.

U.S. Nuclear Forces And Arms Control Policy, Hearings Before The Defense Policy Panel Of The Committee On Armed Services. House Of Representatives, 20 May 1986.

Continued Compliance With The SALT Agreements, Markup Before The Committee On Foreign Affairs. House Of Representatives, 12 June 1986.

Review Of ABM Treaty Interpretation Dispute And SDI, Hearing Before The Subcommittee On Arms Control, International Security And Science Of The Committee On Foreign Affairs. House Of Representatives, 26 February 1987.

The ABM Treaty And The Constitution, Joint Hearings Before The Committee On Foreign Relations And The Committee On The Judiciary. United States Senate, 11 March 1987.

f. Articles, pamphlets and interviews

U.S. News & World Report, 12 April 1965; interview with Defense Secretary McNamara.

Robert S. McNamara, The Limitations of Military Power, *Survival*, July 1966, pp. 210–16.

The Meaning Of Detente, Department of State, June 1974.

Lester A. Sobel (ed.), *Kissinger & Detente*, New York, 1975; extract from Kissinger's speech on 12 May 1975.

Robert J. Pranger and Roger P. Labrie (eds), *Nuclear Strategy And National Security. Points of View*, American Enterprise Institute for Public Policy Research, Washington, DC, 1975, pp. 167–88; extracts from: James R. Schlesinger, 'The theater nuclear force posture in Europe'. A report to the United States Congress, April 1975.

Survival, March–April 1974, pp. 86–90; Defense Secretary Schlesinger's two press conferences in January 1974.

Survival, May–June 1977, pp. 121–4; statement by Defense Secretary Harold Brown to Congress on 22 February 1977.

Survival, May–June 1977, pp. 129–31; President Carter's press conference on 30 March 1977.

Survival, July–August 1978; speech by Paul Warnke on 3 April 1978.

Soviet Military Power, The Department of Defense, Washington, DC, September 1981, March 1983, April 1984, April 1985, March 1986, March 1987 and April 1988.

Security and Arms Control: The Search for a More Stable Peace, Department of State, rev. September 1984.

The President's Strategic Defense Initiative, the President of the United States, January 1985.

Soviet Strategic Defense Programs, Department of Defense and Department of State, October 1985.

Caspar W. Weinberger, U.S. Defense Strategy, *Foreign Affairs*, Vol. 64, No. 4, Spring 1986, pp. 675–97.

Abraham D. Sofaer, 'The ABM Treaty: legal analysis in the political cauldron', *The Washington Quarterly*, Vol. 10, No. 4, Autumn 1987, pp. 59–75.

Caspar W. Weinberger, 'Why offense needs defense', *Foreign Policy*, No. 68, Fall 1987, pp. 3–18.

International Herald Tribune, 9 and 11–13 December 1987; statements by President Reagan.

SECONDARY SOURCES

a. Books

Adams, Benson D., *Ballistic Missile Defense*, New York, 1971.

Adomeit, Hannes, *Soviet-Taking and Crisis Behavior. A theoretical and empirical analysis*, London, 1982.

Allison, Graham T., *Essence of Decision. Explaining the Cuban Missile Crisis*, Boston, 1971.

Allison, Graham T., Carnsesale, Albert and Nye, Joseph S. (eds), *Hawks, Doves & Owls*, New York and London, 1985.

Almond, Gabriel A., *The American People and Foreign Policy*, seventh printing, New York 1967.

Anschel, Eugene (ed.), *American Appraisals Of Soviet Russia, 1917–1977*, The Scarecrow Press, Inc. Metuchen, N.J. & London, 1978.

Arkin, William M., *Research Guide to Current Military and Strategic Affairs*, Institute for Policy Studies, Washington, DC, 1981.

Armacost, Michael H., *The Foreign Relations of the United States*, Belmont, Calif., 1969.

Arms Control. Readings From Scientic American, San Francisco, 1973.

Aspaturian, Vernon V. (ed.), *Process and Power in Soviet Foreign Policy*, Boston, 1971.

Axelrod, Robert (ed.), *Structure of Decision. The Cognitive Maps of Political Elites*, Princeton University Press, Princeton, N.J., 1976.

Ball, Desmond, *Politics and Force Levels. The Strategic Missile Program of the Kennedy Administration*, Los Angeles and London, 1980.

Barnet, Richard J., *The Giants. Russia and America*, New York, 1977.

Barnhart, Michael (ed.), *Congress and United States Foreign Policy. Controlling the Use of Force in the Nuclear Age*, New York, 1987.

Baugh, William H., *The Politics of Nuclear Balance. Ambiguity And Continuity in Strategic Policies*, New York & London, 1984.

Baylis, John and Segal, Gerald (eds), *Soviet Strategy*, London, 1981.

Beloff, Max, *Foreign Policy and the Democratic Process*, Johns Hopkins Paperbacks edition, Baltimore, 1965.

Berkowitz, Leonard (ed.), *Advances In Experimental Social Psychology*, Vol. 10, New York, 1977.

Berman, Robert T. and Baker, John C., *Soviet Strategic Forces. Requirements and Responses*, The Brookings Institution, Washington, DC, 1982.

Bertram, Christoph and Holst, Johan J. (eds), *New Strategic Factors In*

The North Atlantic, Oslo, 1977.

Betts, Richard K., *Nuclear Blackmail and Nuclear Balance*, The Brookings Institution, Washington, DC, 1987.

Beukel, Erik, *Sovjetunionen og Atomvåben. Indre og ydre forudsætninger for sovjetisk atomvåbenpolitik* (The Soviet Union and Nuclear Arms. Domestic and Foreign Conditions of Soviet Nuclear Arms Policy), Dansk Udenrigspolitisk Institut. Samfundsvidenskabeligt Forlag, 1982.

Bialer, Seweryn, *The Soviet Paradox. External Expansion. Internal Decline*, New York, 1986.

Bialer, Seweryn, Hamilton, Lee, Hough, Jerry and Steinbruner, John, *U.S.–Soviet Relations: Perspectives for the Future*, Center for National Policy, Washington, DC, September 1984.

Bialer, Seweryn and Mandelbaum, Michael, *Gorbachev's Russia and American Foreign Policy*, Boulder and London, 1988.

Blair, Bruce G., *Strategic Command And Control. Redefining The Nuclear Threat*, The Brookings Institution, Washington, DC, 1985.

Blechman, Barry M. (ed.), *Rethinking The U.S. Strategic Posture*, Cambridge, Mass., 1982.

Bliss, Howard and Johnson, W. Glen, *Beyond The Water's Edge: America's Foreign Policies*, Philadelphia, 1975.

Bonham, Matthew G. and Shapiro, Michael J. (eds), *Thought and Action in Foreign Policy*, Proceedings of the London Conference on Cognitive Process Models of Foreign Policy, March 1973, Basel and Stuttgart, 1977.

Booth, Ken, *The Military Instrument In Soviet Foreign Policy*, London, 1973.

Booth, Ken, *Strategy and Ethnocentrism*, New York, 1979.

Booth, Ken and Wright, Moorehead (eds), *American Thinking About Peace and War*, New York, 1978.

Border, William Liscum, *There Will Be No Time*, New York, 1946,

Bottome, Edgar M., *The Missile Gap: A Study Of The Formulation of Military And Political Policy*, New Jersey, 1971.

Boulding, Kenneth E., *The Image. Knowledge in Life and Society*, the University of Michigan Press, 1966 (first edition, 1956).

Brecher, Michael, *The Foreign Policy System of Israel. Setting, Images, Process*, London, 1972.

Breslauer, George W., *Five Images Of The Soviet Future: Critical Review & Synthesis*, Institute of International Studies, University of California, Berkeley, 1978.

Brodie, Bernard (ed.), *The Absolute Weapon: Atomic Power and World Order*, New York, 1946.

Brogan, D.W., *American Aspects*, London, 1964.

Bruun, H.H., *Science, Values and Politics in Max Weber's Methodology*, Copenhagen, 1972.

Burgess, Philip M., *Elite Images and Foreign Policy Outcomes. A Study of Norway*, The Ohio State University Press, 1967.

Burns, Edward McNall, *The American Idea of Mission. Concepts of National Purpose and Destiny*, Rutgers University Press, 1957.

Byers, R.B. (ed.), *Deterrence in the 1980s. Crisis and Dilemma*, New York, 1985.

Byrnes, Robert F. (ed.), *After Brezhnev. Sources of Soviet Conduct in the 1980s*, CSIS, Washington, DC, 1983.

Cahn, Anne Hessing, *Congress, Military Affairs and (a Bit of) Information*, Beverly Hills and London, 1974.

Caldwell, Dan, *American–Soviet Relations. From 1947 to the Nixon–Kissinger Grand Design*, London, 1981.

Carnesale, Albert and Haass, Richard N. (eds), *Superpower Arms Control. Setting the Record Straight*, Cambridge, Mass., 1987.

Carnesale, Albert *et al., Living with Nuclear Weapons*, Harvard Study Group, Toronto, 1983.

Carter, Ashton B. and Schwartz, David N. (eds), *Ballistic Missile Defense*, The Brookings Institution, Washington DC, 1984.

Catudal, Honoré M., *Nuclear Deterrence. Does it Deter?*, London, 1985.

Charlesworth, James C., *Contemporary Political Analysis*, New York, 1967.

Chayes, Abram and Wiesner, Jerome B. (eds), *ABM. An Evaluation of the Decision to Deploy an Antiballistic Missile System*, New York, 1969.

Cimbala, Stephen J., *Rethinking Nuclear Strategy*, Delaware, 1988.

Clarke, Duncan L., *Politics of Arms Control. The Role and Effectiveness of the U.S. Arms Control and Disarmament Agency*, New York and London, 1979.

Cline, Ray S., *World Power Trends and U.S. Foreign Policy for the 1980's*, Westview Press, Boulder, Colorado, 1980 (revision of *World Power Assessment. A Calculus of Strategic Drift*, The Center for Strategic and International Studies (CSIS), Georgetown University, Washington, DC, 1975).

Cohen, Stephen F., *Sovieticus. American Perceptions and Soviet Realities*, New York, 1985.

Collins, Joseph J., *The Soviet Invasion of Afghanistan. A Study in the Use of Force in Soviet Foreign Policy*, Mass. and Toronto, 1986.

Colton, Timothy J., *Commissars, Commanders, and Civilian Authority. The Structure of Soviet Military Politics*, Cambridge, Mass., 1979.

Commager, Henry Steele, *Living Ideas In America*, New York, 1951.

Commager, Henry Steele, *The American Mind. An Interpretation of American Thought and Character Since the 1880's*, New York, 1970 (1st edition 1950).

Crabb, Cecil V. Jr, *Policy-Makers and Critics. Conflicting Theories of American Foreign Policy*, New York, 1976.

Crabb, Cecil V. and Holt, Pat M., *Invitation to Struggle: Congress, the President and Foreign Policy*, Washington, DC, 1980.

Curtin, Merle, *The Roots of American Loyalty*, New York, 1946.

Dahl, Robert, *Controlling Nuclear Weapons. Democracy Versus Guardianship*, Syracuse University Press, 1985.

Dallek, Robert, *The American Style of Foreign Policy. Cultural and Foreign Affairs*, New York, 1983.

Daniel, Donald C. (ed.), *International Perceptions Of The Superpower Military Balance*, New York, 1978.

David, Charles-Philippe, *Debating Counterforce. A Conventional Approach in a Nuclear Age*, Boulder, Colorado and London, 1987.

Dawisha, Karen, *Eastern Europe, Gorbachev and Reform. The Great Challenge*, Cambridge, 1988.

Deane, Michael J., *Political Control of the Soviet Armed Forces*, New York and London, 1977.

Deane, Michael J., *The Role of Strategic Defense in Soviet Strategy*, Miami, 1980.

Deutsch, Karl W., *The Nerves of Government*, New York and London, 1966.

Dibb, Paul, *The Soviet Union. The Incomplete Superpower*, London, 1986.

Dinerstein, H.S., *War and the Soviet Union. Nuclear Weapons And Revolution In Soviet Military And Political Thinking*, Westport, Conn., 1962.

Dismukes, Bradford and McConnell, James, (eds), *Soviet Naval Diplomacy*, New York, 1979.

Donclan, Michael, *The Ideas of American Foreign Policy*, London, 1963.

Douglass, Joseph D. and Hoeber, Amoretta M., *Soviet Strategy for Nuclear War*, Hoover Institution Press, Stanford, Calif., 1979.

Downs, Roger M. and Stea, David (eds), *Image and Environment. Cognitive Mapping and Spatial Behavior*, Chicago, 1973.

Duignan, Peter and Rabushka, Alvin (eds), *The United States in the 1980s*, Hoover Institution, Stanford University, 1980.

Dyson, Freeman, *Weapons And Hope*, New York, 1985.

Dziak, John J., *Soviet Perceptions of Military Power: the Interaction of Theory and Practise*, National Strategy Information Center, Inc., New York, 1981.

Ebenstein, William, Pritchett, C. Herman, Turner, Henry A. and Mann, Dean, *American Democracy in World Perspective*, New York, 1967.

Edelman, Murray, *Political Language. Words That Succeed and Politics That Fail*, New York, 1977.

Eide, Asbjørn, and Thee, Marek (eds), *Contemporary Militarism*, New York, 1980.

Eran, Oded, *Mezhdunarodniki – an assessment of professional expertise in the making of Soviet foreign policy*, Tel Aviv, 1979.

Etzold, Thomas H. and Gaddis, John Lewis (eds), *Containment: Documents on American Policy and Strategy, 1945–1950*, New York, 1978.

Falkowski, Lawrence S. (ed.), *Psychological Models in International Politics*, Westview Press, Boulder, Colorado, 1979.

Fallows, James, *National Defense*, New York, 1982.

Farrell, John C. and Smith, Asa P. (eds), *Image and Reality in World Politics*, New York and London, 1968 (first published in *Journal of International Affairs*, Vol. XXI, No. 1, 1967).

Feld, Werner J. and Wildgren, John K., *Congress And National*

Defense. The Politics of the Unthinkable, New York, 1985.

Festinger, Leon, *A Theory of Cognitive Dissonance*, Stanford University Press, 1957.

Festinger, Leon (ed.), *Conflict, Decision, and Dissonance*, Stanford University Press, 1964.

Filene, Peter G. (ed.), *American Views of Soviet Russia 1917–1965*, Homewood, Illinois, 1968.

Finlay, David J., Holsti, Ole R. and Fagen, Richard R., *Enemies in Politics*, Chicago, 1967.

Firestone, Bernard J., *The Quest for Nuclear Stability. John F. Kennedy and the Soviet Union*, London, 1982.

Flynn, Gregory and Rattinger, Hans (eds), *The Public and Atlantic Defense*, London & Canberra, 1985.

Foster, H. Schuyler, *Activism Replaces Isolationism: U.S. Public Attitudes 1940–1975*, Washington, DC 1983.

Franck, Thomas M. and Weisband, Edward, *Word Politics. Verbal Strategy Among the Superpowers*, New York, 1971.

Franck, Thomas M. and Weisband, Edward, *Foreign Policy by Congress*, New York, 1979.

Frederikson, Gunnar, *Det Politiska Språket* (The Political Language), Uddevala, 1969 (first published in 1962).

Free, Lloyd A. and Cantrill, Hadley, *The Political Beliefs of Americans. A Study of Public Opinion*, Rutgers University Press, 1967.

Freedman, Lawrence, *U.S. Intelligence And The Soviet Strategy Threat*, London, 1977.

Freedman, Lawrence, *The Evolution of Nuclear Strategy*, New York, 1981.

Freedman, Lawrence, *The Price of Peace. Living with the Nuclear Dilemma*, London, 1986.

Frei, Daniel, *Perceived Images. U.S. and Soviet Assumptions and Perceptions in Disarmament*, New Jersey, 1986.

Friedrich, Carl J., *Man and His Government. An Empirical Theory of Politics*, New York, 1963.

Frye, Alton, *A Responsible Congress: The Politics of National Security*, New York, 1975.

Gaddis, John Lewis, *Russia, the Soviet Union, and the United States. An Interpretative History*, New York, 1978.

Gaddis, John Lewis, *Strategies of Containment. A Critical Appraisal of Postwar American National Security Policy*. Oxford, 1982.

Gallagher, Matthew P. and Spielmann, Karl F. Jr, *Soviet Decision-Making for Defense. A Critique of U.S. Perspectives on the Arms Race*, New York, 1972.

Garner, William V., *Soviet Threat Perceptions of NATO's Eurostrategic Missiles*, The Atlantic Institute for International Affairs, Paris, 1983.

Garrison, Mark and Gleason, Abbott (eds), *Shared Destiny. Fifty Years of Soviet–American Relations*, Boston, 1985.

Garthoff, Raymond L., *Détente And Confrontation. American–Soviet Relations From Nixon To Reagan*, The Brookings Institution, Washington, DC, 1985.

Gati, Charles (ed.), *Caging The Bear: Containment And The Cold War*, Indianapolis and New York, 1974.

George, Alexander L., *Presidential Decision-Making in Foreign Policy: the Effective Use of Information and Advice*, Westview Press, Boulder, Colorado, 1980.

George, Alexander L. (ed.), *Managing U.S.–Soviet Rivalry: Problems of Crisis Prevention*, Boulder, Colorado, 1979.

Gilbert, Felix, *To The Farewell Address. Ideas of Early American Foreign Policy*, Princeton, 1961.

Glazer, Nathan and Kristol, Irving (eds), *The American Commonwealth – 1976–*, New York, 1976.

Goldmann, Kjell, *International Norms And War Between States*, Stockholm, 1971.

Goldmann, Kjell, *Tension and Détente in Bipolar Europe*, Stockholm, 1974.

Gompert, David C., Mandelbaum, Michael, Garwin, Richard L. and Burton, John J., *Nuclear Weapons and World Politics: Alternatives for the Future*, New York, 1971.

Gorer, Geoffrey, *The American People. A Study In National Character*, New York, 1948.

Gouré, Leon, Hyland, William G., Gray, Colin S., *The Emerging Strategic Environment: Implications for Ballistic Missile Defense*, Institute For Foreign Policy Analysis, Inc., Cambridge, Mass., and Washington, DC, December 1979.

Gouré, Leon, Kohler, Foy D. and Harvey, Mose L., *The Role of Nuclear Forces in Current Soviet Strategy*, Center for Advanced International Studies, University of Miami, 1975.

Gray, Colin S., *The Soviet–American Arms Race*, Lexington, Mass., 1976.

Gray, Colin S., *The Geopolitics of the Nuclear Era: Heartland, Rimlands, and the Technological Revolution*, National Strategy Information Center, Inc., New York, 1977.

Gray, Colin S., *Strategic Studies. A Critical Assessment*, London, 1982.

Gray, Colin S., *Nuclear Strategy and National Style*, Lanham, Md., 1986.

Green, William C., *Soviet Nuclear Weapons Policy. A Research and Bibliographic Guide*, Boulder and London, 1987.

Greenwood, Ted, *Making the MIRV: A Study of Defense Decision Making*, Cambridge, Mass., 1975.

Griffith, William E. (ed.), *The Soviet Empire: Expansion & Détente. Critical Choices for Americans*, Lexington, Mass., 1976.

Guerrier, Steven W. and Thompson, Wayne C. (eds), *Perspectives on Strategic Defense*, Boulder and London, 1987.

Halle, Louis J., *The Cold War As History*, London, 1970.

Halperin, Morton H., *Bureaucratic Politics and Foreign Policy*, The Brookings Institution, Washington, DC, 1974.

Hardin, Russell, Mearsheimer, John J., Dworkin, Gerald and Goodin, Robert E., *Nuclear Deterrence. Ethics And Strategy*, Chicago and London, 1985.

Hart, Thomas G., *The Cognitive World of Swedish Security Elites*, Stockholm, 1976.

Hasselkorn, Avigdor, *The Evolution of Soviet Security Strategy 1965–1975*, National Strategy Information Center, Inc., New York, 1975.

Head, Richard G. and Rokke, Ervin J. (eds), *American Defense Policy*, third edition, Baltimore and London, 1973.

Heckrotte, Warren and Smith, George C., *Arms Control in Transition. Proceedings of the Livermore Arms Control Conference*, Westview Press, Boulder, Colorado, 1983.

Heradsveit, Daniel, *The Arab–Israeli Conflict. Psychological Obstacles to Peace*, Oslo, 1979.

Herrman, Richard K., *Perception and Behavior in Soviet Foreign Policy*, University of Pittsburgh Press, 1985.

Herspring, Dale R. and Volgyes, Ivan (eds), *Civil–Military Relations in Communist Systems*, Westview Press, Boulder, Colorado, 1978.

Hewstone, Miles (ed.), *Attribution Theory. Social and Functional Extensions*, Oxford, 1983.

Hexter, J.H., *On Historians. Reappraisals of some of the makers of modern history*, London, 1979.

Hiebsch, Hans (ed.), *Social Psychology*, New York, 1982.

Hingley, Ronald, *The Russian Mind*, New York, 1977.

Hoffmann, Stanley, *Gulliver's Troubles. Or the Setting of American Foreign Policy*, New York, 1968.

Hoffmann, Stanley, *Janus and Minerva. Essays in the Theory and Practice of International Politics*, Boulder, Colorado and London, 1987.

Hofstadter, Richard, *The Paranoid Style in American Politics and Other Essays*, New York, 1966.

Holloway, David, *The Soviet Union and the Arms Race*, New Haven and London, 1983.

Holst, Johan J. and Nehrlich, Uwe (eds), *Beyond Nuclear Deterrence. New Aims, New Arms*, New York, 1977.

Holst, Johan J. and Schneider, William (eds), *Why ABM? Issues in the Missile Defense Controversy*, New York, 1969.

Holsti, Ole R. and Rosenau, James N., *American Leadership in World Affairs. Vietnam and the breakdown of consensus*, Boston, 1984.

Horelick, Arnold L. (ed.), *U.S.–Soviet Relations. The Next Phase*, Ithaca and London, 1986.

Horelick, Arnold L. and Rush, Myron, *Strategic Power and Soviet Foreign Policy*, London, 1965.

Horton III, Frank B., Rogerson, Anthony C. and Warner III, Edward L. (eds), *Comparative Defense Policy*, Baltimore and London, 1974.

Hosmer, Stephen T. and Wolfe, Thomas W., *Soviet Policy and Practice toward Third World Conflicts*, Toronto, 1983.

Hough, Jerry F., *Soviet Leadership in Transition*, The Brookings Institution, Washington, D.C., 1980.

Hough, Jerry F., *The Struggle for the Third World. Soviet Debates and American Options*, The Brookings Institution, Washington, D.C., 1986.

Howard, Michael, *War And The Liberal Conscience*, Rutgers University Press, 1978; the George Macaulay Trevelyan Lectures in the University of Cambridge, 1977.

Hughes, Barry B., *The Domestic Context of American Foreign Policy*, San Francisco, 1978.

Huntington, Samuel P., *The Common Defense. Strategic Programs in National Politics*, New York and London, 1961.

Huntington, Samuel P., *American Politics: The Promise of Disharmony*, Cambridge, Mass. and London, 1981.

Huntington, Samuel P. (ed.), *The Strategic Imperative: New Policies for American Security*, Cambridge, Mass., 1982.

Jacobsen, Carl G., *Soviet Strategic Initiatives. Challenge and Response*, New York, 1979.

Jacobson, Harold Karan and Stein, Eric, *Diplomats, Scientists, and Politicians. The United States and the Nuclear Test Ban Negotiations*, Ann Arbor, 1966.

Jervis, Robert, *The Logic of Images in International Relations*, Princeton University Press, 1970.

Jervis, Robert, *Perception and Misperception in International Politics*, Princeton, 1976.

Jervis, Robert, *The Illogic of American Nuclear Strategy*, Ithaca and London, 1984.

Jervis, Robert, Lebow, Richard Ned and Stein, Janice Gross (eds), *Psychology and Deterrence*, Baltimore and London, 1985.

Jones, Ellen, *Red Army And Society. A Sociology of the Soviet Military*, Boston, 1985.

Jönsson, Christer, *Soviet Bargaining Behavior. The Nuclear Test Ban Case*, New York, 1979.

Jönsson, Christer (ed.), *Cognitive Dynamics and International Politics*, London, 1982.

Jönsson, Christer, *Superpower. Comparing American and Soviet Foreign Policy*, London, 1984.

Kahan, Jerome H., *Security in the Nuclear Age. Developing U.S. Strategic Arms Policy*, The Brookings Institution, Washington, DC, 1975.

Kanet, Roger E. (ed.), *Soviet Foreign Policy In The 1980s*, New York, 1982.

Kaplan, Fred, *The Wizards of Armageddon*, New York, 1983.

Kaplan, Stephen S. (ed.), *Diplomacy of Power. Soviet Armed Forces as a Political Instrument*, The Brookings Institution, Washington, DC, 1981.

Kaufmann, William W., *The McNamara Strategy*, New York, Evanston and London, 1964.

Keeble, Curtis (ed.), *The Soviet State. The Domestic Roots of Soviet Foreign Policy*, London, 1985.

Kegley, Charles W. and McGowan, Patrick J. (eds), *Challenges To America. United States Foreign Policy in the 1980s*, Vol. 4, Sage International Yearbook of Foreign Policy Studies, Beverly Hills and London, 1979.

Kegley, Charles W. and Wittkopf, Eugene R., *American Foreign Policy. Pattern and Process*, New York, 1979.

Kelman, Herbert C. (ed.), *International Behavior. A Social-Psychological Analysis*, New York, 1965.

Kennan, George F., *The Nuclear Delusion. Soviet–American Relations In The Atomic Age*, New York, 1982.

Kincade, William H. and Porto, Jeffrey D. (eds), *Negotiating Security. An Arms Control Reader*, The Carnegie Endowment for International Peace, 1979 (essays from *Arms Control Today*).

Kintner, William R. (ed.), *Safeguard: Why the ABM Makes Sense*, New York, 1969.

Kintner, William R. and Pfaltzgraff, Robert L. Jr, (eds), *SALT. Implications for Arms Control in the 1970's*, Pittsburgh, 1973.

Kissinger, Henry, *White House Years*, Boston, 1979.

Kissinger, Henry, *Years of Upheaval*, Boston, 1982.

Klingberg, Frank L., *Cyclical Trends In American Foreign Policy Moods. The Unfolding of America's World Role*, New York, 1983.

Knorr, Klaus and Verba, Sidney (eds), *The International System. Theoretical Essays*, Princeton, 1961.

Koch, Adrienne, *Power, Morals, and the Founding Fathers. Esssays in the Interpretation of the American Enlightment*, Cornell University Press, 1961.

Kolkowicz, Roman (ed.), *The Logic of Nuclear Terror*, Boston, 1987.

Kolkowicz, Roman and Joeck, Neil (eds), *Arms Control and International Security*, Boulder and London, 1984.

Kolkowicz, Roman and Mickiewicz, Ellen Propper (eds), *The Soviet Calculus of Nuclear War*, Lexington, Mass., 1986.

Kolkowicz, Roman *et al., The Soviet Union and Arms Control: A Superpower Dilemma*, Baltimore and London, 1970.

Krepon, Michael, *Strategic Stalemate: Nuclear Weapons and Arms Control in American Politics*, London, 1984.

Kubálková, V. and Cruickshank, A.A., *Marxism-Leninism and the Theory of International Relations*, London, 1980.

Kuhn, Thomas S., *The Structure of Scientific Revolutions*, Chicago, 1962.

Laird, Robbin F., *The Soviet Union, the West and the Nuclear Arms Race*, Worcester, 1986.

Laird, Robbin F. and Herspring, Dale R., *The Soviet Union and Strategic Arms*, Boulder and London, 1984.

Larson, David L. (ed.), *The Puritan Ethic In United States Foreign Policy*, New York, 1966.

Larson, Joyce E. and Bodie, William C., *The Intelligent Layperson's Guide to The Nuclear Freeze and Peace Debate*, National Strategy Information Center, Inc., New York, 1983.

Laski, Jarold J., *The American Democracy. A Commentary And An Interpretation*, New York, 1948.

Lau, Richard R. and Sears, David O. (eds), *Political Cognition. The 19th Annual Carnegie Symposium on Cognition*, held at the Carnegie-Mellon University, Pittsburgh, Pa., 18–20 May,

1984, New Jersey, 1986.

Lee, William T. and Staar, Richard F., *Soviet Military Policy. Since World War II*, Stanford, Calif., 1986.

Leebaert, Derek (ed.), *Soviet Military Thinking*, London, 1981.

Legault, Albert and Lindsey, George, *The Dynamics of the Nuclear Balance*, rev. edition, Ithaca and London, 1976.

Lehman, John F., *The Executive, Congress, and Foreign Policy. Studies of the Nixon Administration*, New York, 1976.

Lenczowski, John, *Soviet Perceptions of U.S. Foreign Policy. A Study of Ideology, Power, and Consensus*, Ithaca and London, 1982.

Lerche, Charles O. Jr, *Foreign Policy of the American People*, Englewood Cliffs, N.J., 1961.

Lerner, Max, *America as a Civilization. Volume One. The Basic Frame*, and *Volume Two. Culture and Personality*, New York, 1957.

Levine, Robert A., *The Arms Debate*, Cambridge, Mass., 1963.

Lider, Julian, *The Political and Military Laws of War. An Analysis of Marxist-Leninist Concepts*, Saxon House, 1979.

Little, Richard and Smith, Steve (eds), *Belief Systems and International Relations*, Oxford, 1988.

Litwak, Robert, *Détente And The Nixon Doctrine. American Foreign Policy and the Pursuit of Stability, 1969-1976*, Cambridge, 1984.

Lockwood, Jonathan Samuel, *The Soviet View of U.S. Strategic Doctrine. Implications for Decision Making*, New Brunswick and London, 1983.

Luttwak, Edward N., *The Grand Strategy of The Soviet Union*, With appendices by Block, Herbert and Carus, W. Seth, New York, 1983.

Lyons, Gene M. (ed.), *America: Purpose And Power*, Chicago, 1965.

Mackintosh, J.M., *Strategy and Tactics of Soviet Foreign Policy*, London, 1962.

Macridis, Roy C. (ed.), *Foreign Policy In World Politics*, fourth edition, New Jersey, 1972.

Mandelbaum, Michael, *The Nuclear Question: The United States and Nuclear Weapons, 1946-1976*, Cambridge University Press, 1979.

Mandelbaum, Michael, *The Nuclear Revolution. International Politics Before And After Hiroshima*, Cambridge, 1981.

Mann, Thomas E. and Ornstein, Norman J. (eds), *The New Congress*, The American Enterprise Institute for Public Policy Research, Washington, DC, 1981.

Margiotta, Franklin D. (ed.), *Evolving Strategic Realities: Implications for U.S. Policymakers*, Washington, DC, 1980.

Marshall, Charles Burton, *The Exercise of Sovereignty: Papers on Foreign Policy*, Baltimore, 1965.

Martin, Laurence (ed.), *Strategic Thought in the Nuclear Age*, Baltimore, 1979.

Mastny, Vojtech (ed.), *Soviet-East European Survey, 1986-1987. Selected Research and Analysis from Radio Free Europe/Radio Liberty*, Boulder, Colorado and London, 1988.

May, Ernest R., *'Lessons' of The Past. The Use and Misuse of History in American Foreign Policy*, London, 1973.

MccGwire, Michael, *Military Objectives In Soviet Foreign Policy*, The Brookings Institution, Washington, DC, 1987.

MccGwire, Michael, Booth, Ken and McDonnell, John (eds), *Soviet Naval Policy. Objectives and Constraints*, New York, 1975.

MccGwire, Michael and McDonnell, John (eds), *Soviet Naval Influence. Domestic and Foreign Dimensions*, New York, 1977.

Mead, Margaret, *And Keep Your Powder Dry. An Anthropologist Looks at the American Character*, London, 1967.

Meehan, Eugene J., *The Theory and Method of Political Analysis*, Homewood, Illinois, 1965.

Merk, Frederick, *Manifest Destiny And Mission In American History. A Reinterpretation*, New York, 1970.

Midgaard, Knud, *Strategisk Tenkning* (Strategic Thinking), Oslo, 1967.

Mitchell, R. Judson, *Ideology of A Superpower. Contemporary Soviet Doctrine On International Relations*, Stanford, Calif., 1982.

Monks, Alfred L., *Soviet Military Doctrine: 1960 to the Present*, New York, 1984.

Morgan, Patrick M., *Deterrence. A Conceptual Analysis*, London, 1977.

Moss, Norman, *Men Who Play God. The Story of the Hydrogen Bomb*, Penguin Books, 1972.

Moulton, Harland B., *From Superiority to Parity. The United States and the Strategic Arms Race, 1961–1971*, London, 1973.

Nacht, Michael, *The Age of Vulnerability. Threats to the Nuclear Stalemate*, The Brookings Institution, Washington, DC, 1985.

Næss, Arn, *Empirisk Semantik* (Empirical Semantic), Oslo, 1970.

Nagel, Ernest, *The Structure of Science. Problems in the Logic of Scientific Explanation*, London, 1971.

Nathan, James A. and Oliver, James K., *Foreign Policy Making and the American Political System*, Boston, 1983.

Neidle, Alan F. (ed.), *Nuclear Negotiations: Reassessing Arms Control Goals in U.S.–Soviet Relations*, The University of Texas at Austin, 1982.

Neustadt, Richard E., *Presidential Power. The Politics of Leadership*, New York and London, 1960.

Newhouse, John, *Cold Dawn. The Story of SALT*, New York, 1973.

Niebuhr, Reinhold and Heimert, Alan, *A Nation So Conceived. Reflections on the History of America from Its Early Vision to Its Present Power*, London, 1963.

Nisbett, Richard and Ross, Lee, *Human Inference: strategies and shortcomings of social judgment*, New Jersey, 1980.

Nixon, Richard, *The Memoirs of Richard Nixon*, London, 1978.

Nørretranders, Bjarne, *Sovjetologiens metodeproblemer* (Method-problems in Sovietology), Copenhagen, 1978.

Northedge, F.S. (ed.), *The Foreign Policies of the Powers*, London, 1969.

Nye, Joseph S. Jr, *Nuclear Ethics*, New York and London, 1986.

Nye, Joseph S. Jr (ed.), *The Making of America's Soviet Policy*, New Haven and London, 1984.

O'Neill, Robert and Horner, D.M., *New Directions In Strategic Thinking*, London, 1981.

Osgood, C.E., *An Alternative to War and Surrender*, Urbana, 1962.

Osgood, Robert E. (ed.), *Containment, Soviet Behavior, And Grand Strategy*, Policy Papers in International Affairs, Number 16, Institute of International Studies, University of California, Berkeley, 1981.

Oye, Kenneth A., Rotchild, Donald, Lieber, Robert J. (eds.), *Eagle Entangled. U.S. Foreign Policy in a Complex World*, New York and London, 1979.

Oye, Kenneth A., Lieber, Robert J. and Rotchild, Donald (eds.), *Eagle Defiant. United States Foreign Policy in the 1980s*, Boston and Toronto, 1983.

Payne, Keith B., *Nuclear Deterrence in U.S.–Soviet Relations*, Westview Press, Boulder, Colorado, 1982.

Payne, Samuel B. Jr, *The Soviet Union and SALT*, Cambridge, Mass. and London, 1980.

Perkins, Dexter, *The American Approach To Foreign Policy*, rev. edition, Cambridge, 1962.

Petersen, Nikolaj, *Afskraekkelse og Forsvar. Antiraketforsvarets Problematik* (Deterrence and Defense. The Missile Defense Problem), Dansk udenrigspolitisk Instituts Skrifter 1, 1969.

Pipes, Richard, *U.S.–Soviet Relations In The Era Of Détente*, Westview Press, Boulder, Colorado, 1981; reprints of articles.

Platt, Alan, *The U.S. Senate and Strategic Arms Policy. 1969–1977*, Westview Press, Boulder, Colorado, 1978.

Platt, Alan and Weiler, Lawrence D. (eds), *Congress and Arms Control*, Westview Press, Boulder, Colorado, 1978.

Popper, Karl, *Unended Quest. An Intellectual–Autobiography*, Glasgow, 1977.

Porter, Bruce D., *The USSR In Third World Conflicts. Soviet arms and diplomacy in local wars 1945–1980*, Cambridge, 1980.

Prados, John, *The Soviet Estimate. U.S. Intelligence Analysis & Russian Military Strength*, New York, 1982.

Prins, Gwyn (ed.), *The Nuclear Crisis Reader*, New York, 1984.

Pruitt, Dean G. and Snyder, Richard C. (eds), *Theory & Research On The Causes Of War*, Englewood Cliffs, N.J., 1969.

Puckett, Robert H., *America Faces the World: Isolationist Ideology in American Foreign Policy*, New York, 1972.

Pursell, Carroll W. Jr (ed.), *The Military-Industrial Complex*, New York, 1972.

Quester, George H., *Nulcear Diplomacy. The First Twenty-Five Years*, New York, 1970.

Quester, George H., *The Future of Nuclear Deterrence*, Lexington, Mass. and Toronto, 1986.

Rand. 25th Anniversary Volume, Rand, Calif., 1973.

Rapoport, Anatol, *Strategy and Conscience*, New York, 1969.

Rapoport, Anatol, *The Big Two. Soviet–American Perceptions of Foreign Policy*, New York, 1971.

Richardson, James L., *Germany And The Atlantic Alliance. The Interaction Of Strategy And Politics*, Cambridge, Mass., 1966.

Rielly, John E. (ed.), *American Public Opinion And U.S. Foreign Policy 1983*, The Chicago Council on Foreign Relations, 1983.

Rivera, Joseph de, *The Psychological Dimension of Foreign Policy*, Columbus, Ohio, 1968.

Robinson, John P. and Meadow, Robert, *Polls Apart*, Washington, DC, 1982.

Rosen, Steven (ed.), *Testing the Theory of the Military-Industrial Complex*, Toronto, 1973.

Rosen, Steven J. and Jones, Walter S., *The Logic Of International Relations*, third editon, Cambridge, Mass., 1980.

Rosenau, James N., *Public Opinion And Foreign Policy. An Operational Formulation*, New York, 1968 (first published 1961).

Rosenau, James N. (ed.), *International Politics and Foreign Policy*, New York, 1969.

Rosenau, James N., Davis, Vincent and East, Maurice A. (eds), *The Analysis of International Politics*, New York and London, 1972.

Rostow, W.W., *The United States In The World Arena. An Essay In Recent History*, New York and Evanston, 1960.

Ryan, Alan, *The Philosophy of the Social Sciences*, London, 1970.

Rystad, Göran, *Prisoners Of The Past? The Munich Syndrome And Makers Of American Foreign Policy In The Cold War Era*, Lund, 1982.

Rystad, Göran (ed.), *Congress and American Foreign Policy*, Lund Studies in International History 13, Lund, 1981.

Schelling, Thomas C., *The Strategy of Conflict*, Oxford University Press, 1960.

Schilling, Warner R., Hammond, Paul Y. and Snyder, Glenn H., *Strategy. Politics, and Defense Budgets*, New York and London, 1962.

Schlesinger, Arthur M. Jr, *A Thousand Days. John F. Kennedy in The White House*, New York, 1965.

Schmid, Alex P., *Soviet Military Interventions Since 1945*, New Brunswick and Oxford, 1985.

Schwartz, David N., *NATO's Nuclear Dilemma*, The Brookings Institution, Washington, DC, 1983.

Schwartz, Morton, *Soviet Perceptions of the United States*, London, 1978.

Scott, Harriet Fast and Scott, William F., *The Armed Forces Of The USSR*, Westview Press, Boulder, Colorado, 1982.

Scott, Harriet Fast and Scott, William F., *The Soviet Art Of War. Doctrine, Strategy, and Tactics*, Boulder, Colorado, 1982.

Scott, William F., *Soviet Sources of Military Doctrine and Strategy*, New York, 1975.

Scoville, Herbert, Jr, *MX. Prescription for Disaster*, Cambridge, Mass., and London, 1981.

Seaborg, Glenn T., *Kennedy. Krushchev and the Test Ban*, Los Angeles, 1981.

Shapiro, Michael J. (ed.), *Language and Politics*, Oxford, 1984.

Shenfield, Stephen, *The Nuclear Predicament. Explorations In Soviet Ideology*, Chatham House Papers 37, London, 1987.

Simon, Herbert A., *Models of Man. Social and Rational*, New York, 1957.

Sloss, Leon and Davis, M. Scott (eds), *A Game For High Stakes. Lessons Learned in Negotiating with the Soviet Union*, Cambridge, Mass., 1986.

Smith, Gerald, *Doubletalk. The Story of SALT I*, New York, 1985.

Smith, Myron J., *The Soviet Air and Strategic Rocket Forces 1939–1980. A Guide to Sources in English*, Santa Monica, Calif., 1981.

Smoke, Richard, *National Security And The Nuclear Dilemma. An Introduction to the American Experience*, New York, 1984.

Snyder, Glenn H., *Deterrence and Defense. Toward A Theory of National Security*, Princeton, 1961.

Snyder, Richard C., Bruck, H.W. and Sapin, Burton (eds), *Foreign Policy Decision-Making. An Approach to the Study of International Politics*, New York, 1963.

Söderfeldt, Björn, *Statsvetenskapliga metoder* (Methods in Political Science), Stockholm, 1972.

Somerville, John (ed.), *Soviet Marxism And Nuclear War. An International Debate*, From the Proceedings of the Special Colloquium of the XVth World Congress of Philopsophy, Varna, Bulgaria, 1973, London, 1981.

Sorensen, Theodore C., *Kennedy*, London, 1965.

Spanier, John and Nogee, Joseph (eds), *Congress, the Presidency and American Forerign Policy*, New York, 1981.

Spanier, John and Uslaner, Eric M., *American Foreign Policy and the Democratic Dilemma*, fourth edition, New York, 1985.

Speed, Roger, *Strategic Deterrence in the 1980s*, Stanford, Calif., 1979.

Spielmann, Karl F., *Analyzing Soviet Strategic Arms Decisions*, Westview Press, Boulder, Colorado, 1978.

Sprout, Harold and Margaret, *The Ecological Perspective on Human Affairs*, Princeton, 1965.

Sprout, Harold and Margaret, *Toward A Politics of the Planet Earth*, New York, 1971.

Stein, Jonathan B., *From H Bomb to Star Wars*, Lexington, Mass., 1984.

Steinbruner, John D., *The Cybernetic Theory of Decision*, Princeton, 1974.

Stern, Paula, *Water's Edge. Domestic Politics and the Making of American Foreign Policy*, Westport, Conn., 1979.

Stillman, Edmund and Pfaff, William, *Power And Impotence. The Failure of America's Foreign Policy*, London, 1966.

Strategic Survey, published yearly, IISS, London.

Sylvan, Donald A. and Chan, Steve (eds), *Foreign Policy Making. Perception, Cognition, and Artificial Intelligence*, New York, 1984.

Szamuely, Tibor, *The Russian Tradition*, London, 1974.

Talbott, Strobe, *Endgame. The Inside Story of SALT II*, New York, 1979.

Talbott, Strobe, *The Russians And Reagan*, New York, 1984.

Talbott, Strobe, *Deadly Gambits. The Reagan Administration and the Stalemate in Nulcear Arms Control*, New York, 1985.

Tammen, Ronald L., *MIRV and the Arms Race. In Interpretation of Defense Strategy*, New York, 1973.

Tannenbaum, Frank, *The American Tradition in Foreign Policy*, University of Oklahoma Press, 1955.

The Military Balance, published yearly, IISS, London.

Thompson, Kenneth W., *Political Realism And The Crisis of World Politics. An American Approach to Foreign Policy*, Princeton University Press, 1960.

Tocqueville, Alexis de, *Democracy in America*, Vols. 1 and 2, New York edition, 1945.

Triska, Jan F. and Finley, David D., *Soviet Foreign Policy*, New York, 1968.

Tucker, Robert W., *The Nuclear Debate. Deterrence And The Lapse of Faith*, New York and London, 1985.

Ulam, Adam B., *Dangerous Relations. The Soviet Union in World Politics, 1970–1982*, New York and Oxford, 1983.

Ungar, Sanford J., *Estrangement. America And The World*, New York, 1985.

United States/Soviet Military Balance. A Frame of Reference for Congress, A Study by The Library of Congress. Congressional Research Service, January 1976, US Government Printing Office, Washington: 1976.

Valenta, Jiri and Potter, William (eds), *Soviet Decisionmaking for National Security*, London, 1984.

Van Cleave, William R. and Scott Thompson, W., *Strategic Options for the Early Eighties. What can Be Done?*, National Strategy Information Center, Inc., New York, 1979.

Vernon, Graham D. (ed.), *Soviet Perceptions of War And Peace*, National Defense University, Washington, DC, 1981.

Vigor, P.H., *The Soviet View of War, Peace and Neutrality*, London and Boston, 1975.

Vigor, P.H., *The Soviet View of Disarmament*, New York, 1986.

Warner III, Edward L., *The Military in Contemporary Soviet Politics. An Institutional Analysis*, New York, 1977.

Weber, Max, *Gesammelte Aufsätze zur Wissenschaftslehre*, Johannes Winckelmann (ed.), Tübingen, 1968.

Weisband, Edward, *The Ideology of American Foreign Policy: A Paradigm of Lockian Liberalism*, Sage Publications, Beverly Hills and London, 1973.

Welch, William, *American Images of Soviet Foreign Policy. An Inquiry into Recent Appraisals from the Academic Community*, New Haven and London, 1970.

What About The Russians – and Nuclear War?, Ground Zero, New York, 1983.

Whelan, Joseph G., *Soviet Diplomacy and Negotiating Behavior: Emerging New Context For U.S. Diplomacy*, Committee On Foreign Affairs, Congressional Research Service, Washington, DC, 1979.

Whetten, Lawrence L., *The Future of Soviet Military Power*, London, 1976.

White, Ralph K., *Fearful Warriors. A Psychological Profile of U.S. – Soviet Relations*, New York and London, 1984.

Wilcox, Francis O., *Congress, The Executive, And Foreign Policy*, New York, 1971.

Williams, Robert C. and Cantelon, Philip L. (eds), *The American Atom. A Documentary History of Nuclear Policies from the Discovery of Fission to the Present. 1939–1984*, Philadelphia, 1984.

Willrich, Mason and Rhinelander, John B. (eds), *SALT. The Moscow Agreements And Beyond*, New York and London, 1974.

Wolfe, Alan, *The Rise and Fall of the 'Soviet Threat:Domestic Sources. of the Cold War Consensus*, Institute for Policy Studies, Washington, DC, 1979.

Wolfe, Thomas W., *Soviet Strategy At The Crossroads*, Cambridge, Mass., 1964.

Wolfe, Thomas W., *Soviet Power And Europe, 1945–1970*, Baltimore and London, 1970.

Wolfe, Thomas W., *The SALT Experience*, Cambridge, Mass., 1979.

Woolsey, R. James (ed.), *Nuclear Arms. Ethics, Strategy, Politics*, San Francisco, 1984.

World Armaments and Disarmament. SIPRI Yearbook 1985, Stockholm International Peace Research Institute, London, 1985.

World Armaments and Disarmament. SIPRI Yearbook 1985, Stockholm International Peace Research Institute, Oxford, 1986.

Wormuth, Francis D. and Firmage, Edwin B. with Butler, Francis P., Contributing Author, *To Chain The Dog Of War. The War Power of Congress in History and Law*, Texas, 1986.

Yergin, Daniel. *Shattered Peace. The Origins of the Cold War and the National Security State*, Pelican Books, 1980.

York, Herbert, *The Advisors. Oppenheimer, Teller & The Superbomb*, San Francisco, 1976.

Young, Elizabeth, *A Farewell to Arms Control*, Penguin Books, 1972.

b. Articles and papers

Adomeit, Hannes, 'Soviet risk-taking and crisis behaviour: from confrontation to coexistence?', *Adelphi Papers*, No. 101, IISS, London, Autumn, 1973.

Alexander, Arthur J., 'Decision-making in Soviet weapons procurement', *Adelphi Papers*, Nos. 184 and 185, IISS, London, Winter 1978/9.

Allison, Graham T., 'Testing Gorbachev', *Foreign Affairs*, Vol. 67, No. 1, Fall 1988, pp. 18–32.

'America's security in the 1980's', *Adelphi Papers*, Nos. 173 and 174, IISS, London, Spring 1982.

Anderson, William D., and Kernek, Sterling J., 'How "realistic" is Reagan's diplomacy?', *Political Science Quarterly*, Vol. 100, No.3, Fall 1985, pp. 389–409.

Aspaturian, Vernon V., 'Soviet Global power and the correlation of forces', *Problems of Communism*, May–June 1980, pp. 1–18.

Atkinson, Dorothy, 'Understanding the Soviets: the development of U.S. expertise on the USSR', *The Washington Quarterly*, Vol. 10, No. 3, Summer 1987, pp. 183–201.

Axelrod, Robert and Zimmerman, William, 'The Soviet press on Soviet foreign policy, a usually reliable source', *British Journal of Political Science*, No. 11, 1981, pp. 183–200.

Bailey, Sydney D., 'Paradoxes and predicaments of nuclear weapons', *The World Today*, Vol. 37, No. 1, January 1981, pp. 1–7.

Ball, Desmond, 'The blind men and the elephant: a critique of bureaucratic politics theory', *Australian Outlook*, No. 28, April 1974, pp. 71–92.

Ball, Desmond, 'Can nuclear war be controlled', *Adelphi Papers*, No. 169, IISS, London, Autumn, 1981.

Ball, Desmond, 'U.S. strategic forces: how would they be used?', *International Security*, Vol. 7, No. 3, Winter 1982/1983, pp. 31–60.

Ball, Desmond, 'Targeting for strategic deterrence', *Adelphi Papers*, No. 185, IISS, London, Summer 1983.

Barnett, Roger W., 'Trans-SALT: Soviet strategic doctrine', *Orbis*, Vol. XIX, No. 2, Summer 1975, pp. 533–61.

Bauer, Raymond A., 'Problems of perception and the relations between the United States and the Soviet Union', *The Journal of Conflict Resolution*, Vol. V, 1961, pp. 223–9.

Beres, Louis René, 'Tilting toward Thanatos: America's "countervailing" nuclear strategy', *World Politics*, Vol. XXXIV, No. 1, October 1981, pp. 25–46.

Berkowitz, Bruce D., 'Intelligence in the organizational context: coordination and error in national estimates', *Orbis*, Vol. 29, No. 3, Fall 1985, pp. 571–96.

Bernstein, Robert A. and Anthony, William W., 'The ABM issue in the Senate, 1968–1970: the importance of ideology', *The American Political Science Review*, Vol. LXVIII, No. 3, September 1974, pp. 1198–206.

Betts, Richard, 'Nuclear peace: mythology and futurology', *The Journal of Strategic Studies*, Vol. 2, No. 1, 1979, pp. 83–101.

Beukel, Erik, 'Soviet views on strategic nuclear weapons: orthodoxy and modernism', *Cooperation and Conflict*, Vol. XIV, No. 4, 1979, pp. 223–37.

Beukel, Erik, *Lighed på strategiske atomvåben* (Strategic Nuclear Parity), FOV, 1979, 1981 and 1985.

Beukel, Erik, 'Konvergens mellem supermagternes doktriner for Interkontinentale kernevåben?' (Convergence between the superpowers' doctrines for strategic nuclear weapons?), *Militaert Tidsskrift*, April 1979, pp. 149–79.

Beukel, Erik, 'Analysing the views of Soviet leaders on nuclear weapons', *Cooperation and Conflict*, Vol. XV, No. 2, 1980, pp. 71–84.

Beukel, Erik, 'The Reagan administration, the Soviet Union and nuclear arms: hopes and fears', *Cooperation and Conflict*, Vol. XIX, No. 1, March 1984, pp. 15–38.

Bialer, Seweryn, ' "New Thinking" and Soviet foreign policy', *Survival*, July–August 1988, pp. 291–309.

Billington, James H., 'Realism and vision in American foreign policy', *Foreign Affairs*, America and the World 1986, Vol. 65, No. 3, pp. 630–52.

Binnendijk, Hans, 'NATO's nuclear modernization', *Survival*, March–April 1989, pp. 137–55.

Bjorkman, Thomas N. and Zamostny, Thomas J., 'Soviet politics and strategy toward the West: three cases', *World Politics*, Vol. XXXVI, No. 2, January 1984, pp. 189–214.

Blechman, Barry M. and Powell, Robert, 'What in the name of God is strategic superiority?', *Political Science Quarterly*. Vol. 97, No. 4, Winter 1982–83, pp. 589–602.

Bluth, Christoph, 'The evolution of Soviet military doctrine', *Survival*, March–April 1988, pp. 149–61.

Boer, Connie De, 'The polls: our commitment to World War III', *Public Opinion Quarterly*, Vol. 45, 1981, pp. 126–34.

Boulding, Kenneth E., 'The learning and reality-testing process in the international system', *Journal of International Affairs*, Vol. XXI, No. 1, 1967, pp. 1–15.

Brecher, Michael, Steinberg, Blema and Stein, Janice, 'A framework for research on foreign policy behavior', *Journal of Conflict Resolution*, No. 13, March 1982, pp. 75–101.

Brement, Marshall, *Organizing Ourselves To Deal With The Soviets*, P-6123, Rand, Calif., June 1978.

Brennan, D.G., 'The case for missile defense', *Foreign Affairs*, Vol. 47, No. 3, April 1969, pp. 433–48.

Brodie, Bernard, 'The development of nuclear strategy', *International Security*, Vol. 2, No. 4, Spring 1978, pp. 65–83.

Brodin, Katarina, 'Belief systems, doctrines, and foreign policy', *Cooperation and Conflict*, No. VII, 1972, pp. 97–112.

Brogan, D.W., 'The illusion of American omnipotence', *Harper's Magazine*, December 1952, pp. 21–38.

Brower, Michael, 'Nuclear strategy of the Kennedy administration', *Bulletin of the Atomic Scientists*, October 1962, pp. 34–41.

Brown, Thomas, A., 'Number mysticism, rationality and the strategic balance', *Orbis*, Vol. 21, No. 3, Fall 1977, pp. 479–96.

Brown, Thomas A., 'U.S. and Soviet strategic force levels: problems of assessment and measurement', *Annals of the American Academy of Political and Social Science*, No. 457, September 1981, pp. 18–27.

Bundy, McGeorge, 'The presidency and the peace', *Foreign Affairs*, Vol. 42, No. 3, April 1964, pp. 353–65.

Bundy, McGeorge, 'To cap the volcano', *Foreign Affairs*, Vol. 48, No. 1, October 1969, pp. 1–20.

Bundy, McGeorge, 'The bishops and the bomb', *The New York Review of Books*, Vol. XXX, No. 10, 16 June 1983.

Bundy, William P., 'Who lost Patagonia?, Foreign policy in the 1980 campaign', *Foreign Affairs*, Vol. 58, No. 1, Fall 1979, pp.1–27.

Burks, R.V., 'The arcane art of Kremlinology, faults in the stars, faults in ourselves', *Encounter*, Vol. LX, No. 3, March 1983, pp. 20–30.

Caldwell, Lawrence T., 'Soviet attitudes to SALT', *Adelphi Papers*, No. 75, IISS, London, 1971.

Carnesale, Albert and Haass, Richard N., 'Lessons learned from superpower arms control', *The Washington Quarterly*, Vol. 10, No. 3, Summer 1987, pp. 29–45.

Carrington, Lord, 'The 1983 Alastair Buchan Memorial Lecture', *Survival*, July–August 1983, pp. 146–53.

Cleveland, Harland, 'U.S. foreign policy: illusions of powerlessness and realities of power', *The Atlantic Community*, Vol. 20, No. 2, Summer 1982, pp. 143–52.

Cobb, Tyrus W., 'National security perspectives of Soviet "think tanks"', *Problems of Communism*, November–December 1981, pp. 51–9.

Comey, David Dinsmore, 'Marxist-Leninist ideology and Soviet policy, *Studies in Soviet Thought*, Vol. 2, No. 4, 1962, pp. 301–20.

Committee on The Present Danger, Washington, DC; several pamphlets since November 1976.

Congress and Foreign Policy 1983, Committee On Foreign Affairs, US House of Representatives, Washington, DC, 1984.

Cynkin, Thomas M., 'Glasnost, perestroika and Eastern Europe', *Survival*, July–August 1988, pp. 310–31.

Daggett, Stephen and English, Robert D., 'Assessing Soviet strategic defense', *Foreign Policy*, No. 70, Spring 1988, pp. 129–49.

'Defence and Consensus: The domestic aspects of Western security', Part I–III, *Adelphi Papers*, Nos. 182, 183, and 184, IISS, London, Summer 1983.

Deibel, Terry L., 'Why Reagan is strong', *Foreign Policy*, No. 62. Spring 1986, pp. 108–25.

Deutsch, Karl, 'On political theory and political action', *The American Political Science Review*, Vol. LXV, No. 1, March 1971, pp. 11–27.

Douglass, Joseph D. Jr, *The Soviet Theater Nuclear Offensive*, Studies In Communist Affairs, Vol. 1, Washington, DC, 1977.

Draper, Theodore, 'How not to think about nuclear war', *The New York Review of Books*, 15, July 1982, pp. 35–43.

Drell, Sidney D., Farley, Philip J. and Holloway, David, 'Preserving the ABM treaty: a critique of the Reagan Strategic Defense Initiative', *International Security*, Vol. 9, No. 2, Fall 1984, pp. 51–91.

Dulles, John Foster, 'Policy for security and peace', *Foreign Affairs*, Vol. 32, No. 3, April 1954, pp. 353–64.

Dulles, John Foster, 'Challenge and response in US policy', *Foreign Affairs*, Vol. 36, No. 1, October 1957, pp. 25–43.

Dunn, Keith, A., '"Mysteries" about the Soviet Union', *Orbis*, Vol. 26, No. 2, Summer 1979, pp. 361–79.

Durch, William J., 'The future of the ABM treaty', *Adelphi Papers*, No. 223, IISS, London, Summer 1987.

Edeen, Alf, The strategy debate in the Soviet Union', *Cooperation and Conflict*, 1965, No. 2, pp. 1–15.

Einhorn, Robert J., 'Negotiating from strength. Leverage in U.S.–Soviet arms control negotiations', *The Washington Papers/113*, The Center for Strategic and International Studies (CSIS), Washington, DC, 1985.

Erickson, John, 'The Soviet view of deterrence: a general survey', *Survival*, November–December 1982, pp. 242–51.

Ermath, Fritz W., 'Contrasts in Amerian and Soviet strategic thought', *International Security*, Vol. 3, No. 2, Fall 1978, pp. 138–55.

Erskine, Hazel Gaudet, 'The polls: atomic weapons and nuclear energy', *Public Opinion Quarterly*, Vol. XXVII, No. 2, Summer 1963, pp. 155–90.

Fainsod, Merle, 'Some reflections on Soviet–American relations', *The American Political Science Review*, Vol. LXII, No. 4, December 1968, pp. 1093–103.

Fascell, Dante, 'Concepts and communication in American foreign policy', *Harvard International Review*, Vol. IV, No. 6, March–April 1982, pp. 15–29.

Finan, J.S., 'Nuclear deterrence in trouble', *International Perspectives*, May June 1983, pp. 8 10.

FitzGerald, Mary C., 'The Soviet military on the strategic defense initiative', *Soviet Armed Forces Review Annual*, Vol. 10, 1985–86, pp. 213–30.

FitzGerald, Mary C., 'The strategic revolution behind Soviet arms control', *Arms Control Today*, June 1987, pp. 16–19.

FitzGerald, Mary C., 'Marshal Ogarkov and the new revolution in Soviet military affairs', *Defense Analysis*, Vol. 3, No. 1, 1987, pp. 3–19.

Fontaine, André, 'Beyond Wilson and Rambo', *Foreign Policy*, No. 65, Winter 1986–87, pp. 33–8.

Freedman, Lawrence, 'NATO myths', *Foreign Policy*, No. 45, Winter 1981–82, pp. 48–68.

Frye, Alton, 'Congressional politics and policy analysis: bridging the gap', *Policy Analysis*, 2 Spring 1976, pp. 265–81.

Gaddis, John Lewis, 'NSC 68 and the problem of ends and means', *International Security*, Vol. 4, No. 4, Spring 1980, pp. 164–70.

Garthoff, Douglas F., 'The Soviet military and arms control', *Survival*, November–December 1977, pp. 242–50.

Garthoff, Raymond L., 'SALT and the Soviet military', *Problems of Communism*, Vol. XXIV, January–February 1975, pp. 21–37.

Garthoff, Raymond L., 'Negotiating with the Russians: some lessons from SALT', *International Security*, Vol. 1, No. 4, Spring 1977, pp. 3–24.

Garthoff, Raymond L., 'Negotiating SALT', *The Wilson Quarterly*, 1977:1 Autumn, pp. 76–85.

Garthoff, Raymond L., 'On estimating and imputing intentions',

International Security, Vol. 2, No. 3, Winter 1978, pp. 22–32.

Garthoff, Raymond L., 'SALT I: an evaluation', *World Politics*, Vol. XXXI, No. 1, October 1978, pp. 1–25.

Garthoff, Raymond L., 'The death of Stalin and the birth of mutual deterrence', *Survey*, Vol. 25, No. 2 (111), pp. 10–16.

Garthoff, Raymond L., 'Mutual deterrence and strategic arms limitation in Soviet policy', *International Security*, Vol. 3, No. 1, Summer 1978, pp. 112–47.

Garthoff, Raymond L., 'Soviet view on the interrelation of diplomacy and military strategy', *Political Science Quarterly*, Vol. 94, No. 3, Fall 1979, pp. 391–405.

Garthoff, Raymond L., 'A rebuttal by Ambassador Garthoff', *Strategic Review*, Fall 1982, pp. 58–63 (cf. Richard Pipes' article in the same issue).

Garthoff, Raymond L., *Perspectives on the Strategic Balance*, A Staff Paper, The Brookings Institution, Washington, DC, 1983.

Garthoff, Raymond L., *Intelligence Assessment and Policy-making: A Decision Point in the Kennedy Administration*, A Staff Paper, The Brookings Institution, Washington, DC, 1984.

Garthoff, Raymond L., 'Refocusing the SDI debate', *Bulletin of the Atomic Scientists*, September 1987, pp. 44–50.

Garthoff, Raymond L., 'New thinking in Soviet military doctrine', *The Washington Quarterly*, Vol. 11, No. 3, Summer 1988, p. 131.

Gati, Charles, 'Eastern Europe on its own', *Foreign Affairs*, Vol. 68. No. 1, 1989, pp. 99–119.

Gelman, Harry, *The Politburo's Management of its America Problem*, R–2707–NA, Calif., April 1981.

Gerner, Kristian, 'Kazan and Manchu: cultural roots of Soviet foreign relations', *Cooperation and Conflict*, Vol. XV, No. 2, June 1980, pp. 57–70.

Glagolev, Igor, 'The Soviet decision-making process in arms-control negotiations', *Orbis*, Vol. 21, No. 4, Winter 1978, pp. 767–76.

Glaser, Charles L., 'Why even good defenses may be bad', *International Security*, Vol. 9, No. 2, Fall 1984, pp. 92–123.

Gold, Hyam, 'Foreign policy decision-making and the environment. The claims of Snyder, Brecher, and the Sprouts', *International Studies Quarterly*, Vol. 22, No. 4, December 1978, pp. 569–86.

Goldhamer, Herbert, 'The US–Soviet strategic balance as seen from London and Paris', *Survival*, September–October 1977, pp. 202–7.

Goldberg, Andrew C., 'The present turbulence in Soviet military doctrine', *The Washington Quarterly*, Vol. 11, No. 3, Summer 1988, pp. 159–70.

Goldmann, Kjell and Lagerkranz, Johan, 'Neither tension nor détente: East–West relations in Europe, 1971–1975', *Cooperation and Conflict*, XII, 1977, pp. 251–64.

Gouré, Leon, 'The U.S. "countervailing strategy" in Soviet perception', *Strategic Review*, Fall 1981, pp. 51–64.

Gouré, Leon, '"Nuclear winter" in Soviet mirrors', *Strategic Review*, Summer 1985, pp. 22–38.

Gouré, Leon, 'A "new" Soviet military doctrine: reality or mirage', *Strategic Review*, Summer 1988, pp. 25–33.

Gouré, Leon and McCormick, Gordon, H., 'Soviet strategic defense: the neglected dimension of the U.S.–Soviet strategic balance', *Orbis*, Vol. 24, No. 1, Spring 1980, pp. 103–27.

Graham, Thomas W. and Kramer, Bernard M., 'The polls: ABM and Star Wars: attitudes toward nuclear defense, 1945–1985, *Public Opinion Quarterly*, Vol. 50, 1986, pp. 125–34.

Gray, Colin S., 'What RAND hath wrought', *Foreign Policy*, No. 4, Fall 1971, pp. 111–29.

Gray, Colin S., 'The arms race is about politics', *Foreign Policy*, No. 9, Winter 1972–73, pp. 117–29.

Gray, Colin S., 'The urge to compete: rationales for arms racing', *World Politics*, Vol. XXVI, No. 2, January 1974, pp. 207–33.

Gray, Colin S., 'Foreign policy and the strategic balance', *Orbis*, Vol. XVIII, No. 3, Fall 1974, pp. 706–27.

Gray, Colin S., 'Rethinking nuclear strategy', *Orbis*, Vol. XVII, No. 4, Winter 1974, pp. 1145–60.

Gray, Colin S., 'Nuclear strategy: a case for a theory of victory', *International Security*, Vol. 4, No. 1, Summer 1979, pp. 54–87.

Gray, Colin S., 'Targeting problems for central war', *Naval War College Review*, Vol, XXXIII, No. 1, January–February 1980, pp. 3–21.

Gray, Colin S., 'The most dangerous decade: historic mission, legitimacy, and dynamics of the Soviet empire in the 1980s', *Orbis*, Vol. 25, No. 1, Spring 1981, pp. 13–28.

Gray, Colin S., 'National style in strategy: the American example', *International Security*, Vol. 6, No. 2, Fall 1981, pp. 21–47.

Gray, Colin S., '"Dangerous to your health": the debate over nuclear strategy and war', *Orbis*, Vol. 26, No. 2, Summer 1982, pp. 327–49.

Gray, Colin S., 'Nuclear strategy: a regrettable necessity', *SAIS Review*, Winter–Spring 1983, Vol. 3, No. 1, pp. 13–28.

Gray, Colin S., 'War fighting for deterrence', *The Journal of Strategic Studies*, Vol. 7, No. 1, March 1984, pp. 5–28.

Gray, Colin S. and Barlow, Jeffrey G., 'Inexcusable restraint: the decline of American military power in the 1970s', *International Security*, Vol. 10, No. 2, Fall 1985, pp. 27–69.

Gray, Colin S. and Payne, Keith, 'Victory is possible', *Foreign Policy*, No. 39, Summer 1980, pp. 14–27.

Greenwood, Ted and Nacht, Michael L., 'The new nuclear debate: sense or nonsense', *Foreign Affairs*, Vol. 52, No. 4, July 1974, pp. 761–80.

Gromoll, Robert H., 'SDI and the dynamics of strategic uncertainty', *Political Science Quarterly*, Vol. 102, No. 3, Fall 1987, pp. 481–500.

Guertner, Gary L., 'What is "proof"?', *Foreign Policy*, No. 59, Summer 1985, pp. 73–84.

Haass, Richard, 'Congressional power: implications for American security policy', *Adelphi Papers*, No. 153, IISS, London, Summer 1979.

Hagelin, Björn, 'Swords into daggers. The origins of the SS–20 missiles', *Bulletin of Peace Proposals*, Vol. 15, No. 4, 1984, pp. 341–53.

Hagen, Lawrence S., *Civil Defence: The Case For Reconsideration*, National Security Series, No. 7/77, Centre for International Relations, Queens University, Kingston, Ontario, 1977.

Halperin, Morton H., 'The Gaither Committee and the policy process', *World Politics*, xiii: 3 April 1961, pp. 360–84.

Hanson, Donald W., 'Is Soviet strategic doctrine superior?', *International Security*, Vol. 7, No. 3, Winter 1982/83, pp. 61–83.

Harris, William R., 'Arms control treaties: how do they restrain Soviet strategic defense programs?', *Orbis*, Vol. 20, No. 4, Winter 1986, pp. 701–8.

Harrison, Michael M., 'Reagan's world', *Foreign Policy*, No. 43, Summer 1981, pp. 3–16.

Hart, Doulas M., 'The hermeneutics of Soviet military doctrine', *The Washington Quarterly*, Vol. 7, No. 2, Spring 1984, pp. 77–88.

Hasegawa, Tsuyoshi, 'Soviets on nuclear war fighting', *Problems of Communism*, July–August 1986, pp. 68–79.

Haselkorn, Avigdor, 'The "external function" of Soviet armed forces', *Naval War College Review*, Vol. XXXIII, No. 1/Sequence 277, January–February 1980, pp. 35–45.

Heginbotham, Stanley J., 'Foreign policy information for Congress: patterns of fragmentation and advocacy', *The Washington Quarterly*, Vol. 10, No. 3, Summer 1987, pp. 149–62.

Heller, Mark, 'The Soviet invasion of Afghanistan', *The Washington Quarterly*, Vol. 3, No. 3, Summer 1980, pp. 36–59.

Herspring, Dale R., 'Marshal Akhromeyev and the future of the Soviet armed forces', *Survival*, November–December 1986, pp. 524–35.

Hoeber, Francis P. and Amoretta M., 'The Soviet view of deterrence: who whom?, *Survey*, Vol. 25, No. 2 (111), Spring 1980, pp. 17–24.

Hoffmann, Stanley, 'Restraints and choices in American foreign policy', *Dædalus*, Vol. 91, No. 4, Fall 1962, pp. 668–704.

Hoffmann, Stanley, 'Muscle and brains', *Foreign Policy*, No. 37, Winter 1979–80, pp. 3–27.

Holloway, David, 'Technology, management and the Soviet military establishment', *Adelphi Papers*, No. 76, IISS, London, April 1971.

Holloway, David, 'Military power and political purpose in Soviet policy', *Dædalus*, Fall 1980, pp. 13–30; special issue on US defense policy in the 1980s.

Holloway, David, 'The Strategic Defense Initiative and the Soviet Union', *Dædalus*, Summer 1985, pp. 257–78.

Holloway, David, 'Gorbachev's new thinking', *Foreign Affairs*, Vol. 68, No. 1, 1989, pp. 66–81.

Holst, Johan Jørgen, 'Soviet international conduct and the prospects of arms control', *Cooperation and Conflict*, 1965, No. 1, pp. 53–64.

Holst, Johan Jørgen, *Comparative U.S. and Soviet Deployments, Doctrines, and Arms Limitation*, An Occasional Paper of the Center for Policy Study. The University of Chicago, 1971.

Holst, Johan Jørgen, in conversation with George R. Urban, *NUPI notat*, No. 257, Oslo. December 1982.

Holsti, Ole R. and Rosenau, James N., 'Vietnam, consensus, and the belief system of American leaders', *World Politics*, Vol. XXXII, No. 1, October 1979, pp. 1–56.

Holsti, Ole R. and Rosenau, James N., 'Consensus lost. Consensus regained?: Foreign policy beliefs of American leaders, 1976–1980', *International Studies Quarterly*, 30, 1986, pp. 375–409.

Holsti, Ole R. and Rosenau, James N., 'The foreign policy beliefs of American leaders: some further thoughts on theory and method', *International Studies Quarterly*, Vol. 30, 1986, pp. 473–84.

Horelick, Arnold L., 'The Cuban missile crisis: an analysis of Soviet calculations and behavior', *World Politics*, Vol. XVI, No. 3, April 1984, pp. 363–89.

Howard, Michael, 'Social change and the defense of the West', *The Washington Quarterly*, Vol. 2, No. 4, Autumn 1979, pp. 18–31.

Howard, Michael, 'On fighting a nuclear war', *International Security*, Vol. 5, No. 4, Spring 1981, pp. 3–17.

Howard, Michael, 'The Gorbachev challenge and the defence of the West', *Survival*, November–December 1988, pp. 483–92.

Hughes, Thomas L., 'On the causes of our discontents', *Foreign Affairs*, Vol. 47. No. 4, July 1969, pp. 653–67.

Hughes, Thomas L., 'The crack-up', *Foreign Policy*, No. 40, Fall 1980, pp. 33–60.

Iklé, Fred C., 'Can nuclear deterrence last out the century', *Foreign Affairs*, Vol. LI, No. 2, January 1973, pp. 267–85.

International Herald Tribune; various articles from 1987.

Jackson, William D., 'The Soviets and strategic arms', *Political Science Quarterly*, Vol. 94, No. 2, Summer 1979, pp. 243–61.

Jackson, William D., 'Soviet images of the U.S. as nuclear adversary, 1969–1979', *World Politics*, Vol. XXXIII, No. 4, July 1981, pp. 614–38.

Jacobsen, Carl G., 'Soviet think tanks', *Soviet Armed Forces Review Annual*, Vol. 1, 1977, pp. 140–52.

Jacobsen, Carl G., 'Ballistic missile defense. The evolution of Soviet concepts, research and development', *Soviet Armed Forces Review Annual*, Vol. 1, 1977, pp. 164–75.

Jastrow, Robert, 'Why strategic superiority matters', *Commentary*, Vol. 75, No. 3, March 1983, pp. 27–31.

Jervis, Robert, 'Hypotheses on misperception', *World Politics*, Vol. XX, 1968, pp. 454–79.

Jervis, Robert, 'Why nuclear superiority doesn't matter', *Political Science Quarterly*, Vol. 94, No. 4, Winter 1979–80, pp. 617–33.

Jervis, Robert, 'Political decision-making: recent contributions', *Political Psychology*, Summer 1980, pp. 86–101.

Jervis, Robert, 'Deterrence and perception', *International Security*, Vol. 7, No. 3, Winter 1982/1983, pp. 3–30.

Jervis, Robert, 'The nuclear revolution and the common defense', *Political Science Quarterly*, Vol. 101. No. 5, 1986, pp. 698–703.

Johnson, Robert H., 'Periods of peril', *Foreign Affairs*, Vol. 61, No. 4,

Spring 1983, pp. 950–70.

Jones, David R., 'Nuclear war and Soviet policy', *International Perspectives*, November–December 1982, pp. 17–20.

Jones, T.K. and Thompson, W. Scott, 'Central war and civil defense', *Orbis*, Vol. 22, No. 3, Fall 1979, pp. 681–712.

Jones, William M., *Modeling Soviet Behavior and Deterrence: A Procedure for Evaluating Military Forces*, R1065–PR, Rand, Cal., June 1974.

Jönsson, Christer, 'A cognitive approach to international negotiations', *European Journal of Political Research*, Vol. 11, No. 2, June 1983, pp. 139–50.

Journal of Social Issues, Vol. 39, No. 1, Spring 1983; special issue on 'Images of nuclear war'.

Joyce, John M., 'The old Russian legacy', *Foreign Policy*, No. 55, Summer 1984, pp. 132–53.

Jung, Lothar, 'Hält Moskau einen Atomkrieg für gewinnbar?', *Osteuropa*, March 1986, pp. 209–22.

Jung, Lothar, 'Die sowjetische militärdoktrin hat sich gewandelt', *Osteuropa*, December 1986, pp. 1038–40.

Kahan, Jerome H. and Long, Anne K., 'The Cuban missile crisis: a study of its strategic context', *Political Science Quarterly*, Vol. LXXXVII, No. 4, December 1972, pp. 564–90.

Kamoff-Nicolsky, George, *Soviet Military Doctrine And Strategy: The Evolution of Nuclear Doctrine*, ORAE Extramural Paper No. 46, Ottawa, March 1988.

Kaplowitz, Noel, 'Psychopolitical dimensions of international relations: the reciprocal effects of conflict strategies', *International Studies Quarterly*, Vol. 28, No. 4, December 1984, pp. 373–406.

Kelley, Harold H., 'The process of causal attribution', *The American Psychologist*, February 1973, pp. 107–28.

Kelley, Harold H. and Michela, John L., 'Attribution theory and research', *Annual Review of Psychology*, No. 31, pp. 457–501.

Kennan, George F., 'Scholarship, politics and East–West relationship', *Bulletin of the Atomic Scientists*, May 1981, pp. 4–7.

Kennedy, Robert, 'The strategic balance in transition: interpreting changes in US/USSR weapons levels', *Soviet Armed Forces Review Annual*, Vol. 4, 1980, pp. 352–72.

Kiselyak, Charles, 'Round the prickly pear: SALT and survival', *Orbis*, Vol. 22, No. 4, Winter 1979, pp. 815–44.

Kissinger, Henry, 'NATO: The next thirty years', *Survival*, November–December 1979, pp. 264–8; speech in Brussels on 1 September 1979.

Kissinger, Henry, 'Issues before the Atlantic alliance', *The Washington Quarterly*, Vol. 7, No. 3, Summer 1984, pp. 132–44.

Klingberg, Frank L., 'The historical alternation of moods in American foreign policy', *World Politics*, Vol. XLVI, No. 2, January 1952, pp. 239–73.

Knudsen, Baard B., 'The paramount importance of cultural *sources: American foreign policy and comparative foreign policy research reconsidered'*, *Cooperation and Conflict*, Vol. XXII,

No. 2, 1987,   pp. 81–113.

Kohut, Andrew, 'What Americans want', *Foreign Policy*, No. 70, Spring 1988, pp. 150–65.

Kolkowicz, Roman, 'Strategic parity and beyond', *World Politics*, Vol. XXIII, No. 3, April 1971, pp. 431–51.

Kolkowicz, Roman 'Strategic elites and politics of superpower', *Journal of International Affairs*, vol. 26, No. 1, 1972, pp. 40–59.

Kolkowicz, Roman, 'U.S. and Soviet approaches to military strategy: theory vs. experience', *Orbis*, Vol. 25, No. 2, Summer 1981, pp. 307–29.

Kolstφ, Pål, 'Krig og fred i sovjetisk ideologi' (War and peace in Soviet ideology), *Internasjonal Politikk* No. 4, 1985 pp. 77–104.

Kolt, George, 'The Soviet civil defense program', *Strategic Review*, Spring 1977, pp. 52–62.

Krakau, Knud, 'American foreign relations: a national style?', *Diplomatic History*, Vol. 8, No. 3, Summer 1984, pp. 253–72.

Krepon, Michael, 'Nunn's modest SDI', *Bulletin of the Atomic Scientists*, April 1988, p. 5.

Kricsberg, Louis and Klein, Ross, 'Changes in public support for U.S. military spending', *Journal of Conflict Resolution*, Vol. 24, No. 1, March 1980, pp. 79–111.

Kruglanski, Arie W. and Ajzen, Icek, 'Bias and error in human judgment', *European Journal of Social Psychology*, Vol. 13, 1983, pp. 1–44.

Kugler, Jacek, Organski, A.F.K. with Fox, Daniel, 'Deterrence and the arms race: the impotence of power', *International Security*, Vol. 4, No. 4, Spring 1980, pp. 105–38.

Kull, Steven, 'Nuclear nonsense', *Foreign Policy*, No. 58, Spring 1985, pp. 28–52.

Kupperman, Robert H., Behr, Robert M, and Jones, Thomas P. Jr, 'The deterrence continuum', *Orbis*, Vol. XVIII, No. 3, Fall 1974, pp. 728–49.

Laird, Robbin F. (ed.), *Soviet Foreign Policy*, Proceedings of The Academy of Political Science, Vol. 36, No. 4, New York, 1987.

Lambeth, Benjamin S., *Selective Nuclear Operations And Soviet Strategy*, P–5506, Rand, Calif., September 1975.

Lambeth, Benjamin S., *Selective Nuclear Options in American and Soviet Strategic Policy*, R–2034–DDRE, A report prepared for Director of Defense Research And Engineering, Rand, Calif., December 1976.

Lambeth, Benjamin S., *How To Think About Soviet Military Doctrine*, P–5939, Rand, Calif., February 1978.

Lambeth, Benjamin S., 'The political potential of Soviet equivalence', *International Security*, Vol. 4, No. 2, Fall 1979, pp. 22–39.

Lambeth, Benjamin S., 'Uncertainties for the Soviet war planner', *International Security*, Vol. 7, No. 3, Winter 1982/83, pp. 139–66.

Lambeth, Benjamin S., 'On thresholds in Soviet military thought', *The Washington Quarterly*, Vol. 7, No. 2, Spring 1984, pp. 69–76.

Lambeth, Benjamin S., *The Evolution of Soviet Party–Military Relations Since Khrushchev*, paper, The Second International

Congress of Professors World Peace Academy, Geneva, August 1985.

Lambeth, Benjamin and Lewis, Kevin, 'The Kremlin and SDI', *Foreign Affairs*, Vol. 66, No. 4, Spring 1988, pp. 755–70.

Laqueur, Walter, 'What we know about the Soviet Union', *Commentary*, Vol. 75, No. 2, February 1983, pp. 13–21.

Larrabee, F. Stephen, 'Gorbachev and the Soviet military', *Foreign Affairs*, Vol. 66, No. 5, Summer 1988, pp. 1002–26.

Laurance Edward J., 'The changing role of Congress in defense policy-making', *Journal of Conflict Resolution*, Vol. 20, No. 2, June 1976, pp. 213–53.

Lawrence, Philip K., 'Nuclear strategy and political theory: a critical assessment', *Review of International Studies*, Vol. 11, No. 2, 1985, pp. 105–21.

Lebow, Richard Ned, 'Soviet incentives for brinkmanship', *Bulletin of The Atomic Scientists*, May 1981, pp. 14–21.

Lebow, Richard Ned, 'Misconceptions in American strategic assessment', *Political Science Quarterly*, Vol. 97. No. 2, Summer 1982, pp. 187–206.

Lebow, Richard Ned, 'Windows of opportunity: do states jump through them?, *International Security*, Vol. 9, No. 1, Summer 1984, pp. 147–86.

Legvold, Robert, 'Strategic "doctrine" and SALT: Soviet and American views', *Survival*, January–February 1979, pp. 8–13.

Legvold, Robert, 'The revolution in Soviet foreign policy', *Foreign Affairs*, Vol. 68, No. 1, 1989, pp. 82–98.

Leitenberg, Milton, 'The numbers game or "who's on first?"' *Bulletin of the Atomic Scientists*, June 1982, pp. 27–32.

Leng, Russell J., 'Reagan and the Russians: crisis bargaining beliefs and the historical record', *The American Political Science Review*, Vol. 78, No. 2, 1984, pp. 338–55.

Levy, Jack S., 'Misperception and the causes of war: theoretical linkages and analytical problems', *World Politics*, Vol. XXXVI, No. 1, October 1983, pp. 76–99.

Lewis, Kevin N., 'The US–Soviet strategic balance in the 1980s: Missing the trees for the leaves', *Survival*, May–June 1982, pp. 108–16.

Licklider, Roy, 'The missile gap controversy', *Political Science Quarterly*, Vol. LXXXV, No. 4, December 1970, pp. 600–15.

Lider, Julian, 'The correlation of world forces: the Soviet concept', *Journal of Peace Research*, Vol. XVII, No. 2, 1980, pp. 151–71.

Litwak, Robert S. and MacFarlane, S. Neil, 'Soviet activism in the Third World', *Survival*, January–February 1987, pp. 21–39.

Lundestad, Geir, 'Uniqueness and pendulum swings in US foreign policy', *International affairs*, Vol. 62, No. 3, Summer 1986, pp. 405–21.

Luttwak, Edward N., 'Strategic power: military capabilities and political utility', *The Washington Papers*, 38, Center for Strategic and International Studies (CSIS), Georgetown University,

Washington, DC, 1976.

Luttwak, Edward N., 'Perceptions of military force and US defence policy', *Survival*, January–February 1977, pp. 2–8.

MacFarlane, Neil, 'Intervention and regional security', *Adelphi Papers*, No. 196, IISS, London, Spring 1985.

Mackintosh, Malcolm, 'The Russian attitude to defense and disarmament', *International Affairs*, Vol. 61, No. 3, Summer 1985, pp. 385–94.

Makins, Christopher K., 'TNF modernization and "countervailing Strategy"', *Survival*, July–August 1981, pp. 157–64.

Margolis, Howard and Ruina, Jack, 'SALT II: shadow and substance', *Technology Review*, October 1979, pp. 31–41.

Marsh, Rosalind, J., 'Soviet fiction and the nuclear debate', *Soviet Studies*, Vol. XXXVIII, No. 2, April 1986, pp. 248–70.

Martin, Lawrence, 'Changes in American strategic doctrine – an initial interpretation', *Survival*, July–August 1974, pp. 158–64.

Marvik, Dwaine, 'Elite politics: values and institutions', *American Behavioral Scientist*, Vol. 21, No. 1, September–October 1977, pp. 111–34.

May, Ernest R., 'The nature of foreign policy: the calculated versus the axiomatic', *Dædalus*, Vol. 91, No. 4, Fall 1962, pp. 653–67.

May, Michael M., 'The U.S.–Soviet approach to nuclear weapons', *International Security*, Vol. 9, No. 4, Spring 1985, pp. 140–53.

Maynes, Charles William, 'Old errors in the new cold war', *Foreign Policy*, No. 46, Spring 1982, pp. 86–104.

MccGwire, Michael, 'Soviet military doctrine: contingency planning and the reality of world war', *Survival*, May–June 1980, pp. 107–13.

MccGwire, Michael, 'Deterrence: the problem – not the solution', *International Affairs*, Vol. 62, No. 1, Winter 1985–86, pp. 55–70.

McConnell, James, *Soviet and American Strategic Doctrine: One More Time*, Professional Paper 271, January 1980, Center for Naval Analysis, Virginia.

McConnell, James M., 'Shifts in Soviet views on the proper focus of military developments', *World Politics*, Vol. XXXVII, No. 3, April 1985, pp. 317–43.

McConnell, James M., 'The Irrelevance Today of Sokolovskiy's Book *Military Strategy*', *Defense Analysis*, Vol. 1, No. 4, pp. 243–54.

McNamara, Robert S., 'The military role of nuclear weapons: perceptions and misperceptions', *Foreign Affairs*, Vol. 62, No. 1, Fall 1983, pp. 59–80.

Mertes, Alois, 'Der Atomkrieg in der Militärdoktrin der USSR', *Aussenpolitik*, 2nd quarter 1985, pp. 107–16.

Meyer, Stephen M., 'The sources and prospects of Gorbachev's new political thinking on security', *International Security*, Vol. 13, No. 2, Fall 1988, pp. 124–63.

Meyer, Stephen M., 'Soviet theatre nuclear forces: Part I: Development of doctrine and objectives, and Part II: Capabilities and implications', *Adelphi Papers*, Nos. 187 and 188, IISS, London, Winter 1983/84.

Meyer, Stephen M., 'Soviet views on SDI', *Survival*, November–December 1985, pp. 274–92.

Miller, Steven E., 'Politics over promise: domestic impediments to arms control', *International Security*, Vol. 8, No. 4, Spring 1984, pp. 67–90.

Miller, Steven E., 'The viability of nuclear arms control. US domestic and bilateral factors', *Bulletin of Peace Proposals*, Vol. 16, No. 3, 1985, pp. 263–76.

Mills, Richard M., 'One theory in search of reality: the development of United States studies in the Soviet Union', *Political Science Quarterly*, Vol. LXXXVII, No. 1 March 1972, pp. 63–79.

Miner, Deborah Nutter and Rutan, Alan H., 'What role for limited BMD?, *Survival*, March–April 1987, pp. 118–36.

Moss, Norman, 'McNamara's ABM policy: a failure of communication', *The Reporter*, 23 February 1967, pp. 34–7.

Moynihan, Daniel Patrick, 'Reflections (SALT)', *The New Yorker*, 19 November 1979, pp. 104–80.

Muravchik, Joshua, 'The Senate and national security: a new mood', *The Washington Papers*, 80, CSIS, Georgetown University, Washington, DC, 1980.

Murphy, John F., 'Knowledge is power: foreign policy and information interchange among Congress, the Executive branch, and the public', *Tulane Law Review*, Vol. 49, No. 3, March 1975, pp. 505–54.

Myers, Kenneth A. and Simes, Dimitri K., *Soviet Decision Making, Strategic Policy and SALT*, CSIS, Georgetown University, Washington, DC, 1974.

Nacht, Michael, 'The delicate balance of error', *Foreign Policy*, No. 19, Summer 1975, pp. 163–77.

Nincic, Miroslav, 'The United States, the Soviet Union, and the politics of opposites', *World Politics*, Vol. XL, No. 4, July 1988, pp. 452–75.

Nitze, Paul, 'Deterring our deterrent', *Foreign Policy*, No. 17, Winter 1974–75, pp. 136–56.

Nitze, Paul, 'The development of NSC 68', *International Security*, Vol. 4, No. 4, Spring 1980, pp. 170–6.

Nitze, Paul, 'No longer a choice', *Bulletin of the Atomic Scientists*, September 1980, pp. 6–8.

Nitze, Paul, 'Strategy in the decade of the 1980s,' *Foreign Affairs*, Vol. 59, No. 1, Fall 1980, pp. 82–101.

Nunn, Sam, 'The ABM re-interpretation issue', *The Washington Quarterly*, Vol. 10, No. 4, Autumn 1987, pp. 45–57.

Nye, Joseph S. Jr, 'Nuclear learning and U.S.–Soviet security regimes', *International Organization*, Vol. 41, No. 3, Summer 1987, pp. 371–402.

Oudenaren, John Van, *U.S. Leadership – Perceptions of the Soviet Problem Since 1945*, R–2843–NA, Rand, California, March 1982.

Oudenaren, John Van, 'Deterrence, war-fighting and Soviet military doctrine', *Adelphi Papers*, 210, IISS, London, 1986.

Panofsky, Wolfgang, K.H., 'The mutual-hostage relationship between American and Russia', *Foreign Affairs*, Vol. 52, No. 1,

October 1973, pp. 109–18.

Papp, Daniel S., 'Nuclear weapons and the Soviet world-view', *Soviet Armed Forces Review Annual*, Vol. 4, 1980, pp. 337–51.

Papp, Daniel S., 'Toward an estimate of the Soviet world-view', *Naval War College Review*, Vol. XXXII, No. 6, November–December 1979, pp. 60–77.

Papp, Daniel S., 'Soviet perceptions of the strategic balance', *Air University Review*, Vol. 32, January–February 1982, pp. 2–17.

Parrott, Bruce, 'The Soviet debate on missile defense', *Bulletin of the Atomic Scientists*, April 1987, pp. 9–12.

Payne, Keith B., 'The Soviet Union and strategic defense: the failure of arms control', *Orbis*, Vol. 29, No. 4, Winter 1986, pp. 673–89.

Payne, Keith and Stroude, Dan L., 'Arms control: the Soviet approach and its implications', *Soviet Union/Union Soviétique*, Vol. 10, Parts 2–3, 1983, pp. 218–43.

Payne, Samuel B. Jr, 'The Soviet debate on strategic arms limitation: 1968–72, *Soviet Studies*, Vol. XXVII, January 1975, No. 1, pp. 27–44.

Petersen, Philip A. amd Trulock III, Notra, 'A "new" Soviet military doctrine: origins and implications', *Strategic Review*, Summer 1988, pp. 9–23.

Pilat, Joseph, 'Star peace: Soviet space arms control strategy and objectives', *The Washington Quartely*, Vol. 10, No. 1, Winter 1987, pp. 137–52.

Pipes, Richard, 'Why the Soviet Union thinks it could fight and win a nuclear war', *Commentary*, July 1977, pp. 21–34.

Pipes, Richard, 'Militarism and the Soviet state', *Dædalus*, Fall 1980, pp. 1–12.

Pipes, Richard, 'Soviet strategic doctrine: another view', *Strategic Review*, Fall 1982, pp. 52–8 (a comment to Raymond L. Garthoff's article in *International Security*, 1978).

Porro, Jeffrey D., 'The policy war: Brodie vs. Kahn', *Bulletin of the Atomic Scientists*, June–July 1982, pp. 16–19.

Powell, Robert, 'The theoretical foundations of strategic nuclear deterrence, *Political Science Quarterly*, Vol. 100, No. 1, Spring 1985, pp. 75–96.

'Prospects of Soviet power in the 1980s: Part I and II', *Adelphi Papers*, Nos. 151 and 152, IISS, London, Summer 1979.

Puschel, Karen, 'Can Moscow live with SDI?', *Survival*, January–February 1989, pp. 34–51.

Quester, George H., 'On the identification of real and pretended Communist military doctrine', *Journal of Conflict Resolution*, Vol. X, 1966, pp. 172–9.

Ra'anan, Uri, 'Soviet decision-making and international relations', *Problems of Communism*, November–December 1980, pp. 41–7.

Richelson, Jeffrey, 'Soviet responses to MX', *Political Science Quarterly*, Vol. 96, No. 3, Fall 1981, pp. 401–10.

Rielly, John E., 'The American mood: a foreign policy of self-interest', *Foreign Policy*, No. 34, Spring 1979, pp. 74–86.

Rielly, John E., 'American opinion: continuity, not Reaganism',

Foreign Policy, No. 50, Spring 1983, pp. 86–104.

Rielly, John E., 'America's state of mind', *Foreign Policy*, No. 66, Spring 1987, pp. 39–56.

Rivkin, David B., 'What does Moscow think?', *Foreign Policy*, No. 59, Summer 1985, pp. 85–105.

Rivkin, David B., 'The Soviet approach to nuclear arms control, *Survival*, November–December 1987, pp. 483–510.

Rosenau, James N. and Holsti, Ole R., 'U.S. leadership in a shrinking world: the breakdown of consensus and the emergence of conflicting belief systems, *World Politics*, Vol. XXXV, No. 3, April 1983, pp. 368–92.

Rosenberg, David Alan, 'Reality and responsibility: power and process in making of the United States nuclear strategy 1945–68', *The Journal of Strategic Studies*, Vol. 9, No. 1, March 1986, pp. 35–52.

Rosi, Eugene J., 'Mass and attentive opinion on nuclear weapons tests and fallout, 1954–63', *Public Opinion Quarterly*, Vol. XXIX, No. 2, Summer 1965, 280–97.

Ross, Dennis, 'Rethinking Soviet strategic policy: inputs and implications', *The Journal of Strategic Studies*, Vol. 1, No. 1, May 1978, pp. 3–30.

Rowny, Edward L., 'Negotiating with the Soviets', *The Washington Quarterly*, Vol. 3, No. 1, Winter 1980, pp. 58–66.

Russett, Bruce M., 'Ethical dilemmas of nuclear deterrence', *International Security*, Vol. 8, No. 4, Spring 1984, pp. 36–54.

Russett, Bruce and Deluca, Donald R., ' "Don't tread on me": public opinion and foreign policy in the eighties', *Political Science Quarterly*, Vol. 96, No. 3, Fall 1981, pp. 381–99.

Russett, Bruce and Deluca, Donald R., 'Theater nuclear forces: public opinion in Western Europe', *Political Science Quarterly*, Vol. 98, No. 2, Summer 1983, pp. 179–96.

Sabin, Philip A.G., 'Shadow or substance? Perceptions and symbolism in nuclear force planning', *Adelphi Papers*, 222, IISS, London, Summer 1987.

Schlesinger, Arthur, Jr, 'Foreign policy and the American character', *Foreign Affairs*, Vol. 62, No. 1, Fall 1983, pp. 1–16.

Schlesinger, James R., 'Rhetoric and realities in the Star Wars debate', *International Security*, Vol. 10, No. 1, Summer 1985, pp. 3–12.

Scott, William F., 'Soviet military doctrine and strategy: realities and misunderstandings', *Strategic Review*, No. 3, Summer 1975, pp. 57–66.

Scoville, Herbert, Jr, 'Flexible MADness', *Foreign Policy*, No. 14, Spring 1974, pp. 164–77.

Segal, Gerald, 'Strategy and "ethnic chic" ', *International Affairs*, Winter 1983/84, pp. 15–30.

Segal, Gerald, 'Sino-Soviet relations after Mao', *Adelphi Papers*, No. 202, IISS, London, Autumn, 1985.

Shapiro, Michael J., 'Interpretation and political understanding', *NUPI notat*, No. 186, July 1980, Norsk Utenrikspolitisk Institut, Oslo.

Shapiro, Michael J. and Bonham, G. Matthew, 'Cognitive process and foreign policy decision-making', *International Studies Quarterly*,

Vol. 17, No. 2, June 1973, pp. 147–74.

Shenfeld, Stephen, 'Soviet thinking about the unthinkable', *Bulletin of the Atomic Scientists*, February 1985, pp. 23–5.

Sherr, Alan B., 'Sound legal reasoning or policy expedient? The "new interpretation" of the ABM treaty', *International Security*, Vol. 11, No. 3, Winter 1986–87, pp. 71–93.

Shlapentokh, Vladimir E., 'Moscow's war propaganda and Soviet public opinion', *Problems of Communism*, September–October 1984, pp. 88–94.

Sienkiewicz, Stanley, 'SALT and Soviet nuclear doctrine', *International Security*, Vol. 2, No. 4, Spring 1978, pp. 84–100.

Sienkiewicz, Stanley, 'Observations on the impact of uncertainty in strategic analysis', *World Politics*, Vol. XXXII, No. 1, October 1979, pp. 90–110.

Sigal, Leon V., 'Rethinking the unthinkable', *Foreign Policy*, No. 34, Spring 1979, pp. 35–51.

Simes, Dimitri K., 'Detente and conflict, Soviet foreign policy 1972–1977', *The Washington Papers*, 44, CSIS, Georgetown University, Washington, DC, 1977.

Simes, Dimitri K., 'Deterrence and coercion in Soviet policy', *International Security*, Vol. 5, No. 3, Winter 1980/81, pp. 80–103.

Simes, Dimitri K., 'Are the Soviets interested in arms control', *The Washington Quarterly*, Vol. 8, No. 2, Spring 1985, pp. 147–57.

Simes, Dimitri K., 'Gorbachev: a new foreign policy?', *Foreign Affairs*, America And The World 1986, Vol. 65, No. 3, 1987, pp. 477–500.

Slocombe, Walter, 'The political implications of strategic parity', *Adelphi Papers*, No. 77, IISS, London, May 1971.

Slocombe, Walter, 'The countervailing strategy', *International Security*, Vol. 5, No. 4, Spring 1981, pp. 18–27.

Sloss, Leon and Millot, Marc Dean, 'U.S. nuclear strategy in evolution', *Strategic Review*, Winter 1984, pp. 19–28.

Smith, Jeff, 'Reagan, Star Wars, and American culture', *Bulletin of the Atomic Scientists*, January–February 1987, pp. 19–25.

Smith, Tom W., 'The polls: American attitudes toward the Soviet Union and communism', *Public Opinion Quarterly*, Vol. 47, 1983, 277–92.

Snyder, Jack, 'Richness, rigor, and relevance in the study of Soviet foreign policy', *International Security*, Vol. 9, No. 3, Winter 1984–85, pp. 89–108.

Snyder, Jack L., *The Soviet Strategic Culture: Implications for Limited Nuclear Operations*, R–2154–AF, Rand, Calif., September 1977.

Sofaer, Abraham D., 'The ABM treaty; legal analysis in the political cauldron', *The Washington Quarterly*, Vol. 10, No. 4, Autumn 1987, pp. 59–775.

Sonnenfeldt, Helmut and Hyland, William G., 'Soviet perspectives on security', *Adelphi Papers*, No. 150, IISS, London, 1979.

Sonnenfeldt, Helmut, *Soviet Style In International Politics*, The Washington Institute for Values in Public Policy, Washington, DC, 1985.

Spielmann, Karl F., *The Political Utility Of Strategic Superiority. A Preliminary Investigation Into the Soviet View*, Institute for Defense Analysis, Virginia, May 1979.

Sprout, Harold and Margaret, 'Environmental factors in the study of international politics', *The Journal of Conflict Resolution*, Vol. I, No. 4, 1957, pp. 309–28.

Sprout, Harold and Margaret, *An Ecological Paradigm for the Study of International Politics*, Research Monograph No. 30, Center of International Studies, Princeton University, March 1968.

Stein, Arthur A., 'When misperception matters', *World Politics*, Vol. XXXIV, No. 4, July 1982, pp. 505–26.

Steinbruner, John, 'Beyond rational deterrence: the struggle for new conceptions', *World Politics*, Vol. XXXVIII, No. 2, January 1976, pp. 223–45.

Steinbruner, John D. and Garwin, Thomas M., 'Strategic vulnerability: the balance between prudence and paranoia', *International Security*, Vol. 1, No. 1, Summer 1976, pp. 138–81.

Stevens, Sayre, 'The Soviet factor in SDI', *Orbis*, Vol. 29, No. 4, Winter 1986, pp. 689–700.

Stockton, Paul, 'Strategic stability between the superpowers', *Adelphi Papers*, No. 213, IISS, London, Winter 1986.

Strode, Dan L. and Rebecca, 'Diplomacy and defense in Soviet national security policy', *International Security*, Vol. 8, No. 2, pp. 91–116.

Stubbs, Eric, 'Soviet strategic defense technology', *Bulletin of the Atomic Scientists*, April 1987, pp. 14–19.

Tarlton, Charles D., 'The styles of American international thought: Mahan, Bryan, and Lippmann', *World Politics*, Vol. XVII, No. 4, July 1965, pp. 584–614.

Tetlock, Philip E., 'Cognitive style and political ideology', *Journal of Personality and Social Psychology*, Vol. 45, No. 1, 1983, pp. 118–26.

Tetlock, Philip E., 'Policymakers' images of international conflict', *Journal of Social Issues*, Vol. 39, No. 1, Spring 1983, pp. 67–86.

Tonelson, Alan, 'Nitze's world', *Foreign Policy*, No. 35, Summer 1979, pp. 74–90.

Trachtenberg, Marc 'The influence of nuclear weapons in the Cuban missile crisis', *International Security*, Vol. 10, No. 1, Summer 1985, pp. 137–63.

Triska, Jan F. and Finley, David D., 'Soviet–American relations: a multiple symmetry model', *Journal of Conflict Resolution*, Vol. 9, No. 1, March 1965, pp. 37–53.

Ullman, Richard H., 'Ending the cold war', *Foreign Policy*, No. 72, Fall 1988, pp. 130–51.

Vertzberger, Yaacov Y.I., 'Foreign policy decision-makers as practical-intuitive historians: applied history and its shortcomings', *International Studies Quarterly*, 1986, No. 30, pp. 223–47.

Vincent, R.J., 'Military power and political influence: the Soviet Union and Western Europe', *Adelphi Papers*, No. 119, IISS, London, Autumn 1975.

Walker, Paul F., 'Soviet military doctrine in the 1970's', *Problems of*

Communism, July–August 1979, pp. 55–60 (book review).

Warner III, Edward L., 'New thinking and old realities in Soviet defence policy', *Survival*, January–February 1989, pp. 13–33.

Weickhardt, George G., 'Ustinov versus Ogarkov', *Problems of Communism*, January–February 1985, pp. 77–82 (book review).

Wells, Samuel F., 'Sounding the tocsin, NSC–68 and the Soviet threat', *International Security*, Vol. 4, No. 2, Fall 1979, pp. 116–58.

Wieseltier, Leon, 'The great nuclear debate', *The New Republic*, 10 and 17 January 1983.

Wieseltier, Leon, 'When deterrence fails', *Foreign Affairs*, Vol. 63, No. 4, Spring 1985, pp. 827–47.

Wiesner, Jerome B., 'Arms control: current prospects and problems', *Bulletin of the Atomic Scientists*, May 1970, pp. 6–8 and 38.

Windsor, Philip, 'America's moral confusion', *Foreign Policy*, No. 13, Winter 1973–74, pp. 139–53.

Wittkopf, Eugene R., 'Elites and masses: another look at attitudes toward America's world role', *International Studies Quarterly*, Vol. 31, No. 2, June 1987, pp. 131–59.

Wohlstetter, 'Is there a strategic arms race?', *Foreign Policy*, No. 15, Summer 1974, pp. 3–20; continued in 'Rivals but no "race"', *Foreign Policy*, No. 16, Fall 1974, pp. 48–81.

Yankelovich, Daniel and Double, John, 'The public mood: nuclear weapons and the U.S.S.R.', *Foreign Affairs*, Vol. 63, No. 1, Fall 1984, pp. 33–46.

Yankelovich, Daniel and Kaagan, Larry, 'Assertive America', *Foreign Affairs*, America And The World 1980, Vol. 59, No. 3, 1981, pp. 696–713.

Yost, David S., 'France's deterrent posture and security in Europe. Part I: capabilities and doctrine', *Adelphi Papers*, No. 194, IISS, London, Winter 1984/85.

Young, Elizabeth and Wayland, 'Marxism-Leninism and arms control', *Arms Control*, Vol. 1, No. 1, 1980, pp. 3–29.

c. **Soviet sources**

Andropov, Yuri, *Our Aim Is To Preserve Peace*, a collection of speeches from November 1982 to April 1983, Novosti Press Agency Publishing House, Moscow, 1983.

Brezhnev, L.I., *Our Course: Peace and Socialism*, Novosti Press Agency Publishing House, 1978; Brezhnev's speeches have been published in a number of volumes with a similar title.

Dictionary Of Basic Military Terms. A Soviet View, Moscow, 1965 (published under the auspices of the United States Air Force and translated by the DGIS Multilingual Bureau, Secretary of State Department, Ottawa, Canada).

Gareyev, Makhmut, 'The revised Soviet military doctrine', *Bulletin of the Atomic Scientists*, December 1988, pp. 30–4.

Gorbachev, Mikhail, *Perestroika And The New Thinking*, Harper & Row, 1987.

Grechko, A.A., *The Armed Forces of The Soviet Union*, Progress Publishers, Moscow, 1977.

Gromyko, Andrei, *International Affairs*, No. 5, May 1977, pp. 3–11; Gromyko's press conference of 31 March, 1977.

Gromyko, Andrei, *Only for Peace*, Pergamon Press, Oxford, 1979 (collection of speeches).

Gromyko, Andrei, *Lenin and the Soviet Peace Policy*, Progress Publishers, Moscow, 1980 (collection of speeches).

Gromyko, Andrei, *On the International Situation and the Foreign Policy of the Soviet Union*, Report at the Session of the USSR Supreme Soviet, 16 June 1983, Novosti Press Agency Publishing House, Moscow, 1983.

How to Avert the Threat to Europe, The Soviet Committee For European Security And Cooperation. Scientific Research Council On Peace And Disarmament, Progress Publishers, Moscow, 1983.

Krushchev, N.S., *On Peaceful Coexistence*, Foreign Languages Publishing House, Moscow, 1961.

Krushchev, N.S., *Communism – Peace and Happiness for The Peoples*, Foreign Languages Publishing House, Moscow, 1963.

Lomov, N.A. (ed.), *Scientific–Technical Progress and The Revolution in Military Affairs*, 1973; translated and published under the auspices of the United States Air Force.

Luzin, Nikolai, *Nuclear Strategy and Common Sense*, Progress Publishers, Moscow, 1981.

Marxism-Leninism On War And Army, Progress Publishers, Moscow, 1972. Published several times in Russian and written by 14 Soviet philosophers, historians and teachers at military educational institutes.

Milshtein, Mikhail and Semeiko, Leo S., 'Problems of the inadmissibility of nuclear conflict', *International Studies Quarterly*, Vol. 20, No. 1, March 1976 (reprint from SShA: Ekonomika, Politika, Ideologiia, No. 11, 1974).

Moscow News, various issues from the 1980s.

New Times, various issues from the 1980s.

Peace and Disarmament, Academic Studies, Progress Publishers, Moscow, 1984.

Problems of War and Peace. A Critical Analysis of Bourgeois Theories, Progress Publishers, Moscow, 1982.

Selected Soviet Military Writings 1970–1975, translated and published under the auspices of the United States Air Force, Washington, DC, 1976.

Shevardnadze, Eduard, *International Affairs*, No. 10, October 1988, pp. 3–34.

Skirdo, M.P., *The People, the Army, the Commander*, Moscow, 1970; translated and published as *Dictionary ....,op.cit.*

Sokolovskiy, V.D.,*Soviet Military Strategy*, London, 1975. Published in Russian in three editions, 1962, 1963 and 1968, which are reprinted and commented in this edition by Harriet Fast Scott (ed).

Soviet Military Review, various issues from the 1970s and 1980s.

Survival, translations of Soviet speeches and articles, eventually excerpts.

Talenskiy, N., 'The "absolute weapon" and the problem of security', *International Affairs*, No. 4, April 1962, pp. 22–7.

Talenskiy, N., 'Anti-missile systems and disarmament', *International Affairs*, No. 10, October 1964, pp. 15–19.

Talenskiy, N., 'The late war: some reflections', *International Affairs*, No.5, May 1965, pp. 12–18.

Talenskiy, N., 'June 22: lessons of history', *International Affairs*, No. 6, June 1966, pp. 45–9.

The Current Digest of The Soviet Press, translations of speeches and articles from the Soviet press.

The Fundamentals of Marxist-Leninist Philosophy, Progress Publishers, Moscow, 1982.

The Officer's Handbook. A Soviet View, Moscow, 1971; translated and published as *Dictionary..., op.cit.*

The Philosophical Heritage of V.I. Lenin and Problems of Contemporary War, Moscow, 1972.

The Threat to Europe, Moscow, 1981.

Trofimenko, Henry, 'The "theology" of strategy', *Orbis*, Vol. 21, No. 3, Fall 1977, pp. 497–515.

Trofimenko, Henry, 'SALT II: a fair bargain', *Bulletin of the Atomic Scientists*, June 1979, pp. 30–4.

Trofimenko, Henry, Counterforce: illusion of a panacea', *International Security*, Vol. 5, No. 4, Spring 1981, pp. 28–48.

Ustinov, D., 'Military detente-imperative of the time', *International Affairs*, No. 1, January 1980, pp. 3–10 (reprint from Pravda, 25 October, 1979).

Ustinov, D., 'To avert the threat of nuclear war', *International Affairs*, No. 9, 1982, pp. 12–22.

Ustinov, D., *The Existing Parity Must Not Be Destroyed*, Novosti Press Agency Publishing House, Moscow, 1982; reprint of Ustinov's replies to questions, *Pravda*, 7 December 1982.

Whence the Threat to Peace, the Soviet Ministry of Defense, Moscow, 1982.

Name index

Subject index